THE MIDNIGHT SUN

Praise for Alan Alford's previous book
PYRAMID OF SECRETS

'A beautifully researched, thoughtful, and thought-provoking study... stands well against the very best work produced by the acknowledged experts.'
Fortean Times magazine

'In Pyramid of Secrets, Alan Alford makes the case that the Great Pyramid was a giant stone symbol and memorial to the creation myth, and a repository for the meteoritic seed of the creator-god. This is a fascinating hypothesis that is worthy of serious consideration.'
Robert Schoch, author of 'Voices of the Rocks' and 'Voyages of the Pyramid Builders'

'I found your arguments compelling... I buy your argument that kings were to be returned to the earth... Similarly, I accept your emphasis on creation... All in all, I congratulate you warmly... I think that you have moved the argument about the nature of the Pyramid and its significance to Egypt on to an entirely new level.'
Michael Rice, author of 'Egypt's Making', 'Egypt's Legacy', 'The Power of the Bull', and 'Who's Who in Ancient Egypt'

'Well done for moving things in a new and worthwhile direction.'
Ian Lawton, co-author of 'Giza The Truth'

'This work by Alan Alford is brilliant. Not only is his research superb, but his insights are unsurpassable. Archaeologists think that the Great Pyramid is 'a tomb and nothing but a tomb' and a symbol of the sun, but Mr Alford has stolen first prize. His work clearly shows that it was the product of a complex and sophisticated culture based on creation.'
Crichton Miller, author of 'The Golden Thread of Time'

'Without doubt, the best book ever written on the Great Pyramid.'
John Reid, author of 'Egyptian Sonics'

'A courageous and original interpretation of all the available evidence.'
David Elkington, author of 'In the Name of the Gods'

'This fascinating book is an inexhaustible mine of information, concisely and objectively presented for the serious pyramid scholar and for those with a more casual interest. It deserves a place on every thinking person's book shelf.'
Chris Bingham-Hunter

Also by Alan F. Alford

WHEN THE GODS CAME DOWN (2000)

THE ATLANTIS SECRET (2001)

PYRAMID OF SECRETS (2003)

THE MIDNIGHT SUN

The Death and Rebirth of God in Ancient Egypt

Alan F. Alford

Eridu Books
http://www.eridu.co.uk

Copyright 2004 by Alan F. Alford

First Published in Great Britain in 2004 by Eridu Books

The right of Alan F. Alford to be identified as the Author of this Work has been asserted by him in accordance with the Copyright, Designs and Patents Act 1988.

All rights reserved. No part of this publication may be reproduced, stored in a retrieval system, or transmitted, in any form or by any means without the prior written permission of both the publisher and the copyright owner, nor be otherwise circulated in any form of binding or cover other than that in which it is published and without a similar condition being imposed on the subsequent purchaser.

Hieroglyphic fonts by MacScribe.

Pages 372-73 (Illustration credits) constitutes an extension of this copyright page.

A CIP catalogue record for this book is available from the British Library.

ISBN 0 9527994 3 X

Printed and bound in Great Britain by Bookcraft Limited.

Eridu Books
P.O. Box 107
Walsall
WS9 9YR
England
http://www.eridu.co.uk

To Sumu,
for ever and eternity.

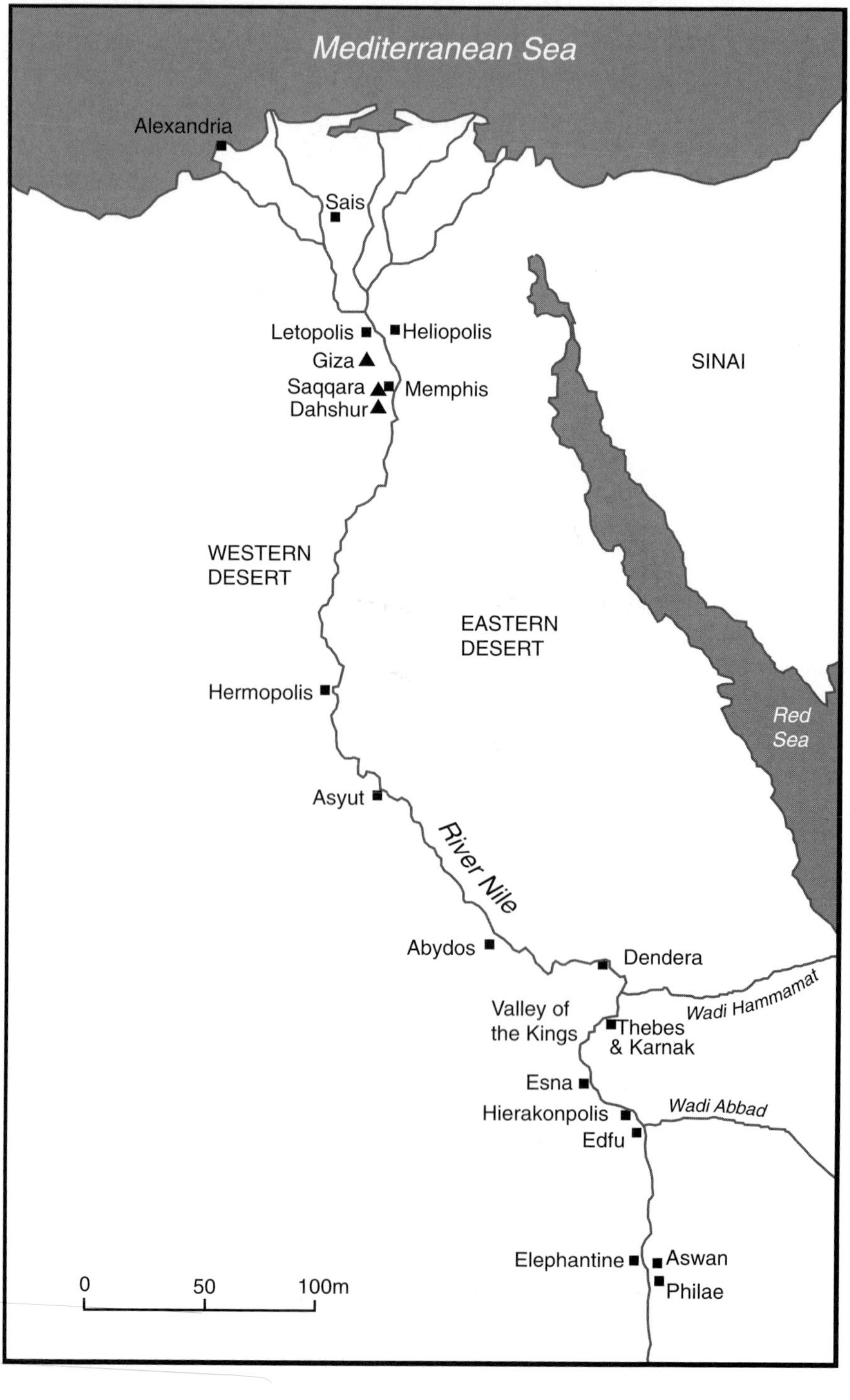
Mediterranean Sea
Alexandria
Sais
Letopolis
Heliopolis
Giza
Saqqara
Memphis
Dahshur
SINAI
WESTERN
DESERT
EASTERN
DESERT
Hermopolis
Red
Sea
Asyut
River Nile
Abydos
Dendera
Valley of
the Kings
Thebes
& Karnak
Wadi Hammamat
Esna
Hierakonpolis
Wadi Abbad
Edfu
Elephantine
Aswan
Philae
0
50
100m

CONTENTS

PREFACE		I
CHAPTER 1:	COSMIC TIME	1
CHAPTER 2:	THE COSMOS	7
CHAPTER 3:	THE CREATION	34
CHAPTER 4:	POWER IN THE EARTH	66
CHAPTER 5:	GOD AND THE GODS	95
CHAPTER 6:	RAISING THE SKY	114
CHAPTER 7:	KING OF CREATION	142
CHAPTER 8:	OPENING THE MOUTH	181
CHAPTER 9:	THE DAY OF THE STORM	199
CHAPTER 10:	SPLITTING THE IRON	209
CHAPTER 11:	THE BULL OF THE SKY	228
CHAPTER 12:	THE FIERY EYE	253
CHAPTER 13:	HORUS AND SETH	282
CHAPTER 14:	THE ONE AND THE OTHER	309
CHAPTER 15:	PYRAMIDS AND TEMPLES	326

CHAPTER 16: **THE TOMB OF KHUFU**	349
ACKNOWLEDGEMENTS	372
NOTES	374
BIBLIOGRAPHY	421
INDEX	424

PREFACE

Beneath the Giza plateau lies a secret tomb, cunningly contrived, that has remained undisturbed for nearly five thousand years. In the darkness and stillness of an eternal night-time, the mummy of an Egyptian king lies in splendid isolation, adorned with gold and gemstones, and surrounded by his burial treasure. If our eyes could penetrate the primeval darkness, we might well imagine the king smiling at the thought that he had cheated the tomb raiders of his own day, as well as the archaeologists of modern times. But perhaps he will not be smiling for much longer.

I am convinced that I have pinpointed the precise location of the tomb of the greatest of the pyramid builders, Khufu – the legendary king who built the Great Pyramid of Giza. If I am right, we may soon witness one of the greatest archaeological discoveries in history – far surpassing that of the tomb of Tutankhamun in 1922. It would be the first ever discovery of a pyramid builder's intact tomb, and would open a unique window on the mysteries of the pyramids, from a time 1,200 years before the birth of Tutankhamun.

Before we can make this discovery, however, we have to pass a test – a test of confidence in the hypothesis. We have to grasp the significance and purpose of the pyramids and of the roles played by the mummies for whom they were built. In short, we have to be initiated into the secrets of the pyramid builders' religion.

Egypt's great age of pyramid building began *circa* 2600 BC when an unknown genius mastered the seemingly impossible feat of assembling a pyramid with smooth sides and an apex – a 'true pyramid' as it is called today. Until that momentous breakthrough, the Egyptians had built step pyramids, whose multiple stages gave the semblance of a stairway to the heavens.

The first king to take advantage of the new design was Sneferu, the founder of the 4th dynasty, who had two huge pyramids built at Dahshur, each with a height of 345 feet. One of these pyramids was presumably

II THE MIDNIGHT SUN

his tomb and the other a cenotaph, though no-one can say for certain which was which.

Sneferu was followed by his son Khufu, who is credited with building the Great Pyramid of Giza. It is the largest true pyramid in Egypt with a height of 481 feet and a volume of 91 million cubic feet. Its complicated system of internal passageways culminates in an elegant granite chamber which contains a broken and empty sarcophagus. It is here that Khufu's body was supposedly interred – a theory that this author does not share, for reasons that will shortly be explained.

The Giza plateau is home to two further pyramids, those of Khafre and Menkaure. The former stands as high as the Great Pyramid, but a steeper angle causes it to have a lesser volume of 78 million cubic feet, while the latter is much smaller, with a height of just 213 feet. Both these pyramids were found to contain empty sarcophagi.

Together, the three pyramids of Giza contain a staggering 178 million cubic feet of stone, and weigh an estimated 12 million tons. They are testimony to a profound belief in the afterlife. But what exactly do these pyramids signify?

It is a remarkable fact that Egyptologists cannot agree on the precise meaning of the pyramid. Various theories have been proposed: that the pyramid symbolised the sun's rays sloping down through the clouds, that it symbolised the newly emerged earth of the creation myth, or that it symbolised a star. But none of these theories has proved satisfactory in itself since all appear to have some validity. This confusion has persisted despite the fact that detailed inscriptions – the so-called Pyramid Texts – are contained on the internal walls of eight pyramids of the late-5th and 6th dynasties – enough magic spells to fill a 300-page book.

The real problem lies deeper – in modern conceptions of the ancient Egyptian religion. Their religion was nothing like ours, on the surface at least. They worshipped One God under many different names. They also worshipped 'him' as a Goddess, or as a 'he-she', i.e. a God and Goddess merged in a single being. And they worshipped God as a collectivity of gods – a multitude of beings that had issued from him and were united in him. Moreover, unlike the Supreme Being of modern religions, the God of the Egyptians was both transcendent and immanent in his creation. He was not only invisible, but also visible – in the sun, the moon, the stars, indeed in all of nature.

Early Egyptologists struggled to comprehend the Egyptian religion. To them, it seemed like a mishmash of beliefs, most of which belonged to a semi-savage past. In order to make sense of it, they focused on the most prominent cult – that of the sun – which some regarded as the world's first monotheism. A consensus then developed that Egyptian religion was a sun cult – a conclusion that has coloured all subsequent studies of this mighty civilisation.

According to Egyptology, the sun cult came to prominence during the 4th dynasty – the exact time when the first true pyramids were conceived and built. The giant pyramids of Dahshur and Giza are thus believed to be solar symbols and monuments to the sun-god.

But this view of Egyptian religion hardly does justice to the incredible achievements of the 4th dynasty kings. Was Sneferu inspired to erect 7.5 million tons of stone by an epiphany of the sun's rays falling through the clouds in the shape of a pyramid? Did his successors at Giza erect 12 million tons of stone because of their awe of the sun? Surely there has to be more to it than that.

I believe that there was indeed more to it than that.

The hypothesis presented in this book is that Egyptian religion was not a cult of the sun but a 'cult of creation', i.e. a cult whose primary aim was to celebrate and re-enact perpetually the myth of the creation of the cosmos.

According to this myth, the original cosmos had fallen into a state of darkness and chaos, and would have died had it not been revivified by a supernatural power that may best be described as 'the magic of creation'. As a result, the old cosmos had been reborn as a new cosmos of light, in which the sun, moon, and stars orbited the earth.

The aim of the Egyptians was to prevent this cosmos from reverting to its former state of chaos. Or, to put it another way, their abiding task was to ensure that the cosmos would endure for ever.

To do this, the king was initiated into the magic of creation and tasked with re-creating the magic spells which had brought the earth, sun, moon, and stars into being.

Creation had involved death and rebirth, and the Egyptians saw this as a template for the continuance of life. On earth, they imagined the river Nile to die and be reborn every year, while in the sky they imagined the sun and stars to die and be reborn every day, and the moon to die and be reborn every month.

The king's magic was aimed at making every rebirth a re-enactment of the original rebirth of the cosmos. When the Nile came forth in its annual flood, it was born anew as it had been in the beginning, and when the sun rose from the eastern horizon, it was born anew as it had been on the day of creation. The entire cosmos was thus made to endure by rejuvenating itself.

The king's role did not end with his death, but instead continued in the

IV   THE MIDNIGHT SUN

afterlife. And it is here that we find the key to the meaning and purpose of the pyramids.

The king did not die as an ordinary human being. He died as a god, just as he had once lived as a god. And this guaranteed that he would be reborn as a god.

A central element of my hypothesis – which will undoubtedly prove controversial – is that the god in question was the creator-god, and that his death and rebirth personified the death and rebirth of the cosmos. By dying in the image of this god, Osiris, the king re-enacted the myth of creation. His mummified body became one with the primeval earth and waters in the netherworld, while his soul went forth to become the sun, moon, and stars in the sky.

The death of the king was thus the life of the cosmos.

Once he became a part of the cosmos, the reborn king was tasked with rejuvenating it, to ensure that it – and he – would endure for ever. To this end, he became the director of the stars in their orbits or the rower of the sun-god in the barque which encircled the earth. Every day, like the sun and the stars, he was reborn and rejuvenated. It was thus said of the king 'his afterlife is for ever and eternity'.

The pyramid was designed to resurrect the king in accordance with the creation myth. But its role did not end with the funeral, for this was not the rebirth of a man but a god, whose continued rebirth was necessary for the sake of the cosmos. The magic of creation was thus repeated at the pyramid every day, to ensure that the king would circulate in the cosmos for ever.

In order to carry this off, the king's body had to be mummified so that it would endure for eternity, and buried in the earth beneath the pyramid so that it became one with Osiris. The mummy then became the locus of the soul's rebirth each night. Having traversed the sky with the sun and the stars, the soul would pass into the earth through mysterious doors and unite with its body in the tomb. It would then be recharged by the magic of creation, and would go forth at dawn to bring a new and rejuvenated light to the world.

The endurance of the mummy was therefore pivotal to the continued survival of the soul – and to the survival of the cosmos.

The pyramid was built to protect the mummy and it too was created to last for eternity. A spell in the Pyramid Texts beseeches the creator-god to 'set your protection over this king, over this pyramid of his... prevent anything evil from happening against it for ever'. Much of the pyramid's power seems to have derived from its smooth, flowing shape, which was probably intended to symbolise the cosmos in its moment of coming-into-being.

This brings us back to the Great Pyramid and to an anomaly that can no longer be ignored. Since the earliest days of Egyptology it has been assumed that Khufu was laid to rest in the granite chamber which houses the broken sarcophagus. However, this chamber is located at a height of 140 feet in the pyramid's superstructure – in contravention of the custom, and indeed the fundamental rule, that the mummy should be buried in the earth. According to Egyptologists, Khufu broke with convention in order to thwart the tomb raiders, who would never have conceived of searching for an elevated tomb chamber. This is permissible under the theory that Egyptian religion was a sun cult and the pyramid a monument to the sun-god.

However, if Egyptian religion was a cult of creation and the pyramid a monument to the creation, as I believe it was, then it is inconceivable that Khufu would have had himself buried anywhere but in the earth – below the Great Pyramid – in accordance with the axiom 'the body to earth, the spirit to the sky'.

This approach requires us to abandon all previous notions of the Great Pyramid's passages and chambers, and explore the possibilities of a sub-pyramid burial. When we do so, a pattern emerges which is suggestive of a burial in the most remote recess of the monument – a small cave which has been almost totally neglected by archaeologists.

Figure 1.
THE GREAT PYRAMID, VERTICAL SECTION, LOOKING WEST.
1 = SUPPOSED TOMB (ROBBED). 2 = REAL TOMB (INTACT).

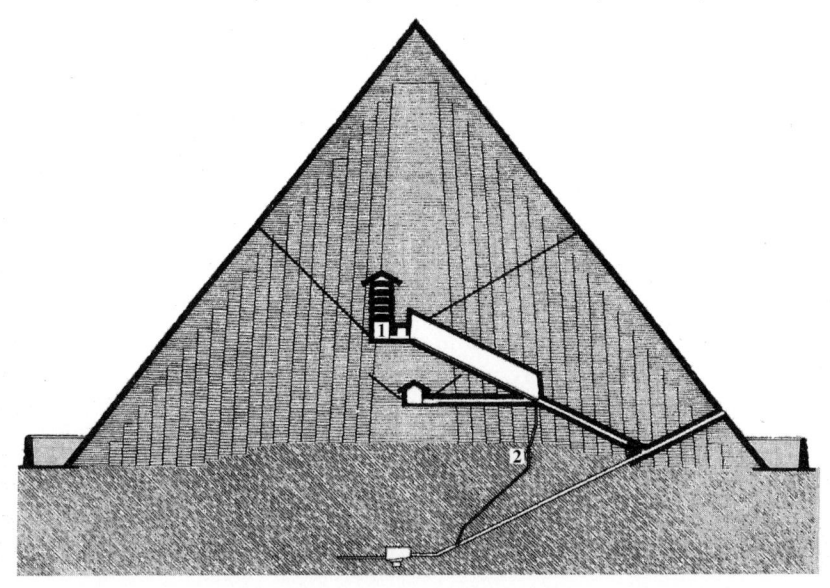

VI   THE MIDNIGHT SUN

Today, this cave stands empty and there are indications that something was dug up and removed by tomb raiders in antiquity. But this may be exactly what Khufu wanted us to think. For when we cast our eye around this cave, we find a number of perplexing anomalies, which suggest the presence of further, hidden caves nearby. It is in these caves, I believe, that Khufu has lain in peace for more than four thousand years, sealed behind a 'door' whose position I have pinpointed.

This all hinges on the cult of creation hypothesis, which is the primary focus of this book. In one sense, this theory is not so controversial: the importance of the creation myth is well known to scholars. In another sense, however, it is controversial. The problem is that the creation myth is a muddle. It does not exist as a coherent narrative but as a collection of fragments, drawn from several different traditions which appear in some respects to be inconsistent. Scholars have thus developed a jaundiced view of the creation myth, and do not consider it worthy as the basis for a religion.

I have therefore devoted much of this book to a reconstruction of the creation myth – joining together the known fragments, discovering new fragments, elucidating the key principles, ironing out the inconsistencies, and filling in the gaps – to the extent that it can plausibly bear the burden of the cult of creation that I wish to place upon it. The resulting picture is a surprisingly sophisticated 'physics of creation'.

But there is more to this book than reassembling a creation myth and discovering a hidden tomb. It is also about reuniting us with our religious heritage and opening our eyes to some simple but profound truths. There is much for us to learn from the religious philosophy of the Egyptians, and if this book helps to bring this perennial wisdom to a wider audience then – archaeological discoveries notwithstanding – the effort involved in writing it will have been absolutely worthwhile.

Important Reading Note

In writing this book, I have tried to strike a balance between satisfying the requirements of the academic specialists – at whom the argument is primarily directed – and keeping things accessible for the general reader. The latter may find the detailed arguments to be beyond his immediate needs, in which case he may pick up the gist of the hypothesis from this preface, and chapters one, fifteen and sixteen, together with the key point summaries for the chapters in between. If he feels a little more ambitious, he could also read chapter seven, which provides a detailed interpretation of the rituals and spells performed at the pyramids. Then, if he wishes to mix it with the specialists, he can go for the whole deal.

CHAPTER ONE

COSMIC TIME

Great is *maat*, enduring and effective. It has not been disturbed since the time of Osiris.
(The Maxims of Ptahhotep)

At the centre of the Egyptian cosmos was the earth, conceived as a kind of sausage of land immersed to its waist in a dish of water (see figure 2). Around the earth, it was believed, a pressurized bubble of air supported the sky which took the form of an ocean of water. On the inner surface of this oceanic garment, orbs of light – the sun, moon, stars, and planets – navigated to and fro like boats on predestined courses. But beyond these heavenly shipping lanes, the star-spangled sky became an unfathomable abyss of darkness, whose limits remained untouched even by the light of the sun.[1]

How this cosmos came into being is the ultimate mystery of ancient Egypt – and the subject of this book.

Figure 2. THE EGYPTIAN COSMOS.

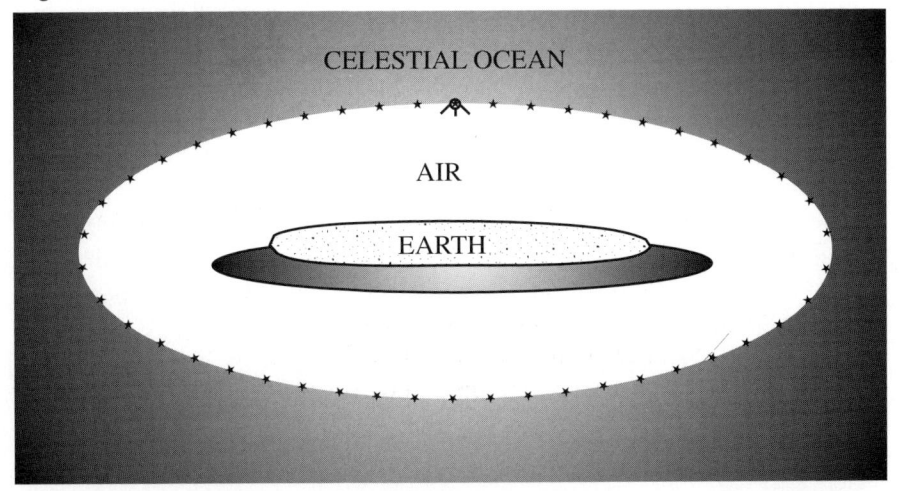

The Order of the Cosmos (Maat)

The ancient Egyptian cosmos was a perpetual motion machine, designed to function for 'millions upon millions of years'. The system possessed not so much longevity as immortality – an idea enshrined in the divine principle *djet*, which is translated 'eternal duration'.[2]

Eternal duration (*djet*) was dependent upon the ordered motion of the cosmos. The sun, moon, and stars were required to orbit according to preordained cycles, while on earth (the land of Egypt) the river Nile had to flood in its due time and the soil bear produce in its due season. These recurrent cycles enshrined the divine principle *neheh*, which is translated 'eternal repetition'.[3]

Eternal repetition (*neheh*) was not understood in the modern sense of repeating the *previous* event or cycle but in the ancient sense of repeating the *original* event or cycle which had been initiated by the creator-god at the beginning of time. Every sunrise was thus the original sunrise; every new moon was the original new moon; every new star was the original birth of that star; every Nile flood was the original flood that covered the earth; every emergence of land was the original emergence of the earth from the waters; and every coronation of a king was the coronation of the original king. In short, every day was the first day, as was yesterday and as was tomorrow.

The 'eternal endurance' of the cosmos was thus brought about by the 'eternal repetition' of a design that had been established at the time of the creation. This primeval age was known as *zep tepi*, which is translated 'the first time' or 'the first occasion'.[4] It witnessed the establishment of *maat*, 'the cosmic order'.[5]

Maat was the system of laws that governed the cosmos. It was not just the celestial order, nor just the earthly order, nor just the divine order, nor just the human order, but *the complete cosmic order* in the sense that all manifestations of spirit and matter were harmonically interdependent for their continued existence. Such was the importance of this concept that if we had to describe the Egyptian religion in a single word, then that word would be '*maat*'.

The eternal repetition (*neheh*) of the events of the first time (*zep tepi*) thus guaranteed the continuance of cosmic order (*maat*) and, in turn, the eternal endurance (*djet*) of the cosmos. The cosmos was thus a perpetual motion machine with an ever-unchanging order, conceived as a virtuous circle of time – see figure 3.

But the wheels of this cosmic time machine did not turn of their own accord. Crucially, the creator-god had set up a system that depended on

Figure 3.
THE VIRTUOUS CIRCLE OF TIME.

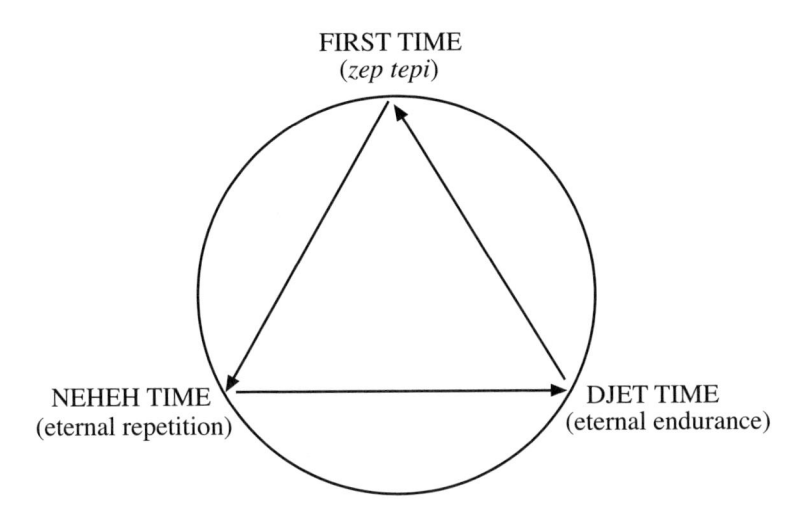

```
                FIRST TIME
                 (zep tepi)


NEHEH TIME                    DJET TIME
(eternal repetition)          (eternal endurance)
```

the inputs of gods and men. He had populated the cosmos with sentient beings – gods in the sky, in the earth, and in the atmosphere, and human beings on the earth – and tasked them with maintaining the right order of the cosmos. If all these beings obeyed the codes of proper behaviour (the laws of *maat*), the cosmos could be made to sustain itself, allowing the creator to rest in a state of quiet, eternal contemplation.

To this end, the creator had established hierarchical structures for the running of the cosmos. In the realm of the gods, he had appointed Re, the sun-god, as ruler; and in the realm of man, he had appointed pharaoh, the king of Egypt, as ruler. These two delegates were to oversee the eternal repetition of the first time – the one in the skies and the netherworld, the other on the earth.[6] In this way, the original cosmic order (*maat*) would be maintained and the cosmos would endure for eternity. Together, the sun-god and the pharaoh would be partners in turning the virtuous circle of time (figure 3).

Arrayed against the sun-god and the pharaoh were the forces of chaos, personified by Seth or the monstrous serpent Apep, and conceptualised as *isfet*, a state of 'chaos' or 'lack', which was the antithesis of *maat*.[7] At any unguarded moment, these forces might attack the barque of the sun-god or cause disturbance in the land of Egypt. Such a threat had existed at the first time (*zep tepi*), when the chaos-gods had opposed the creation of the cosmos. The creator had triumphed then, but the forces of chaos had remained ever present at the edges of the created universe, and hence the battle had to be waged again and again in an eternal repetition of the

4 THE MIDNIGHT SUN

original event.[8]

In the case of the sun-god, it was believed that his rebirth during the night was opposed by the serpent Apep who obstructed the course of his barque. Each morning, when the sun rose anew on the eastern horizon, it signified the triumph of the creator-god who had defeated the forces of darkness – as at the first time. The moment of sunrise was thus described as a repetition of creation:

> Re comes into being like his original coming-into-being in the world on the first occasion.[9]

> The earth becomes bright; Re shines over his land; he has triumphed over his enemies.[10]

In the case of the pharaoh, his appearance on the throne corresponded to the sunrise on the horizon: it was proof that the forces of chaos had been overcome and that *maat* would continue to prevail in Egypt, just as it had at the time of creation. Crowned as a living god – an embodiment of the creator himself – he possessed the vital powers of *heka* 'primeval magic', *hu*, 'creative utterance', and *sia*, 'divine insight', which he tapped each day to repeat authoritatively the acts of creation.[11] As an embodiment of Horus – the original and eternal conqueror of Seth – the king was well equipped 'to realise *maat* and to annihilate *isfet*'.[12]

Remarkably, the pharaoh's sphere of influence overlapped with that of the sun-god. By building palaces and temples as representations of the cosmos in the process of creation (see chapter fifteen), the Egyptians brought not only the sun but the moon and the stars too into a mystical bond with their place of origin, and enabled the king – as delegate of the creator-god – to become the prime mover of the cosmos. Each day he, or the chief priest in his name, performed magic rituals which repeated the original acts of the creator in order to set the celestial bodies turning in their orbits around the earth.[13] During the temple ceremonies, the king or the priest presented the god's cult statue with offerings and an image of *maat* (figure 4), both acts signifying that order had prevailed over chaos, as it had done at the first time.[14]

This is an astonishing vision indeed – a cosmic time machine that was remade anew every day, not by the turnings of its own component parts, nor by the triumph of its gods over its gremlins, but by the actions of 'a human in the role of a god'.[15] For the clear implication is that the gods of the sky, the earth, and the atmosphere were incapable of sustaining the cosmos by their own means, but rather depended on the pharaoh and his cult to guarantee the eternal repetitions (*neheh*) and the eternal duration (*djet*) of the universe. Or, to put it another way, it was believed that if

Figure 4.
THE PHARAOH PRESENTS THE SYMBOL OF MAAT.

Egypt's support for the gods were withdrawn, the entire cosmos, far from being immortal, would revert to an abyss of undifferentiated darkness and chaos.[16]

More astonishing still is the idea that the pharaoh, even in death, was tasked with vanquishing chaos and bringing order to the cosmos. In the Pyramid Texts (the earliest set of religious writings in ancient Egypt), the king in the afterlife is portrayed as pacifying the rival gods Horus and Seth, and bringing peace to the earth and the sky. In the inscriptions of Pepi II, the king's spirit is said to circulate through the skies with the result that: 'The sky is at peace, the earth is in joy, for they have heard that Pepi will set *maat* in the place of *isfet*.'[17] But this job was entrusted not only to Pepi but to all his predecessors who had died in this world and been reborn in the next. The spirits of these deceased kings, it would seem, had coalesced into a unity of a higher order which regulated the cosmos from the sky and the 'other world' even while the present king was ruling it from the land of Egypt.

The role of the deceased king as regulator of the cosmos merged to a significant degree with the role of the sun-god, who was resurrected from death in the middle hour of the night (the motif of 'the midnight sun') and reborn subsequently from the eastern horizon. For this reason, many kings had their tombs illustrated with scenes from 'the night journey of the sun' in the belief that they too would conquer death and go forth into the sky. In this regard, both the king and the sun-god were dependent on the great god Osiris, who had 'died' and come back to life during the first time (*zep tepi*). In the king's case, his body was mummified in order to create an identity with Osiris, while in the sun-god's case, his soul was said to engage with Osiris's body in a mystical union. All parties then benefited from the 'fact' that the body of Osiris had come back to life in the netherworld and sent out its soul into the wider universe.

Of course, once the deceased king had 'become Osiris', via the magic of the funerary rituals, he was then able to assume his seat as a spirit in the barque of the sun-god, to revisit the body of Osiris every night, and to be born as a spirit every day. In this way, the king and the sun-god were engaged in an eternal repetition (*neheh*) of death and rebirth, which had the desired effect of constantly rejuvenating the cosmos and ensuring that it would last for ever (*djet*).[18]

Such was the importance of these ideas that the Egyptians developed a sophisticated cosmology of netherworld and sky in order to describe and portray the transformations of the king and the sun-god. In chapter two, we shall take a detailed look at these realms in order to gain insight into how the cosmos was created.

Chapter One Summary

- Cosmic order (*maat*) was established by the creator-god at the time of creation, and maintained by eternal repetitions of the events of creation.

- The sun-god and the pharaoh were appointed by the creator-god to perform the eternal repetitions (*neheh*) of creation, and thereby ensure the eternal endurance (*djet*) of the cosmos.

- Upon coronation, the king became an incarnation of the creator-god and was therefore able to draw upon the magic of creation in order to rejuvenate the cosmos.

- Upon death, the king became a spirit in the barque of the sun-god and began to circulate through the cosmos. In company with the sun-god he was reborn anew every day, with the result that the cosmos itself was rejuvenated for ever and eternity.

CHAPTER TWO

THE COSMOS

The decoding of this civilisation requires of us some of that intimate knowledge claimed for the king, of how the world and in particular the heavens move – of a very different solar system.
(Stephen Quirke, *The Cult of Ra*, 2001)

In order to investigate the origins of the Egyptian cosmos, we must first consider the cosmos itself. How was it structured? Of what was it made? How was it kept in a state of perpetual motion?

An overview of the cosmos is presented in figure 5, which shows the main realms of which it was formed. These comprise not only the visible realms of the earth and the sky, separated by the atmosphere, but also the invisible realms of the primeval ocean (*nun*), the netherworld (*duat*), the eastern and western horizons (*akheti*), and the lower sky that rested on a lower atmosphere.

One is immediately struck by two points.

First, the Egyptian cosmos is geocentric; it has the earth at its centre. If modern authorities sometimes give the opposite impression – that the sun was at the centre, this is because the sun was the principal driver of the cosmic time machine. There is no intent to suggest that the cosmos went around the sun. On the contrary, the texts are emphatic on the point that the sun – and the other celestial bodies – went around the earth.

This geocentrism may prove a stumbling block for some readers, since Nicolaus Copernicus and the age of modern science have long consigned it to the dustbin of history. Nevertheless, it is an indisputable fact that the Egyptians, in common with other ancient peoples, believed implicitly in geocentrism and predicated their religion upon it. Anyone seeking to understand Egyptian religion therefore has no choice but to suspend their disbelief and embrace this ancient world-view – at least for the duration

8   THE MIDNIGHT SUN

Figure 5.
THE EGYPTIAN COSMOS.

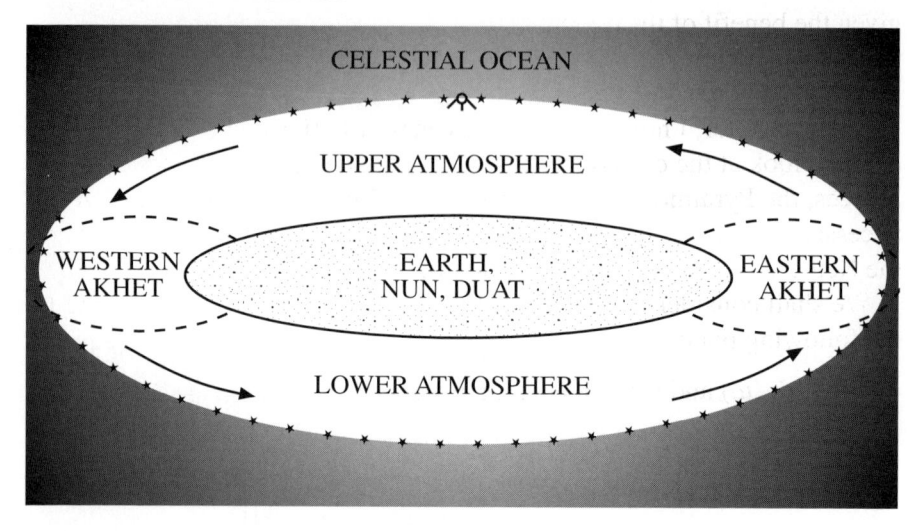

```
                    CELESTIAL OCEAN

                   UPPER ATMOSPHERE

    WESTERN              EARTH,              EASTERN
    AKHET               NUN, DUAT             AKHET

                   LOWER ATMOSPHERE
```

of this study.

The second key point is that the cosmos is designed in such a way that the sun, moon, stars, and transfigured kings were able to circuit the earth in two different but complementary ways:

1   By traversing the underbelly of the upper sky **and then continuing to traverse the underbelly of the lower sky**.

2   By traversing the underbelly of the upper sky **and then passing through the western *akhet*, into the *duat* (the depths of the earth), into the eastern *akhet*, and back onto the underbelly of the sky**.

The first of these two circuits receives only a brief treatment in the texts. Remarkably, it is the second, journey-through-the-earth circuit which is the centre of attention. It is this second circuit that accounts for the motif of the midnight sun – the sun shining at midnight in the depths of the netherworld.

This cosmology will strike the reader as passing strange, and he may well be tempted to dismiss the Egyptians as naive and incompetent fools. How, in the name of Amun, could the sun, moon, and stars pass through the centre of the earth?

In defence of the Egyptians, it should be stressed that there were two routes through the cosmos, and it is possible that the real sun followed the natural circuit on the underbelly of the lower sky, while a phantom or double of the sun followed the circuit through the netherworld (likewise

THE COSMOS 9

with the moon and the stars). It is not the purpose of this book to resolve this issue, which may in any case be insoluble. The Egyptians should be given the benefit of the doubt.

The question nevertheless remains: why was it necessary to have such a strange and convoluted system?

In this chapter, I hope to provide an answer to this question by taking a detailed look at the cosmic realms as they are described in Egypt's oldest sources, the Pyramid Texts dating from *c.* 2350 BC (supplemented, where necessary, by the Coffin Texts dating from *c.* 2000 BC and the Books of the Netherworld dating from *c.* 1500 BC).

We shall consider the realms of the cosmos individually, according to the following plan:

- the earth (*ta*) and the primeval ocean (*nun*)
- the netherworld (*duat*)
- the horizons (*akhet*, or plural *akheti*)
- the field of reeds (*sekhet iaru*)
- the field of offerings (*sekhet hetep*)
- the sky (*pet, qebhu, nun, Nwt, mehet weret, sekhet hetep*)
- the celestial bodies and the milky way

The Earth and the Primeval Ocean

We begin at the centre of the cosmos by examining the Egyptian concept of the earth and the primeval ocean.

The earth was called *ta*, written hieroglyphically as an elliptical island ⟝. In keeping with this idea, it was surrounded by an ocean of water, the *nun*, and was occasionally described as an 'island' (*iw*).

As is the case with virtually all parts of the Egyptian cosmos, the earth was personified by a god. Usually, this god was Geb, who represented the earth in opposition to the sky. His realm was described as a mound (*iat*), which contained an unspecified number of subsidiary mounds, 'the mounds of Horus' and 'the mounds of Seth'.[1]

The earth was also identified with Ta-tenen, a god who personified the idea of 'the risen land', i.e. 'the land risen from the primeval water'.[2] In addition, there was a god Aker, who could personify the earth but who specialised in guarding the gates to the netherworld.[3]

Peculiarly, the earth was conceived as a duality, comprising a southern part and a northern part (possibly signifying an upper part and a lower part).[4] This duality is seen also in the topography and political structure of Egypt, whose most common name was *tawi*, 'the Two Lands', i.e. the dual regions, or 'kingdoms', of the south and the north.[5] According to the Greeks, the Two Lands signified 'the whole inhabited earth', and it is not difficult to find support for this view in the Egyptian texts.[6] Other names for Egypt, such as *ta meri* 'beloved land' and *kemet* 'black land', might also have signified the entire earth, while the elongated shape of the Nile valley might well explain the elliptical island hieroglyph that was used to portray the earth (*ta*).

The earth was believed to have an interior, underground realm, which could be reached by the soul of the deceased via the tomb. This region, which was of huge importance in the quest for the afterlife, was known by a variety of names, the most prominent of which were: *duat*, usually translated 'netherworld'; *ament* (or *amentet*), literally 'hidden place' but often rendered 'land of the west' or simply 'the West'; *netjer-khert*, 'the divine under-place'; and *ta-djesert*, 'the sacred land'.

This chthonian realm was occupied by gods. The Pyramid Texts refer to 'the gods (*netjeru*) who are in the earth',[7] 'the ennead which is in the earth',[8] 'those who are in the middle of the earth',[9] 'those whose seats are hidden',[10] 'those who are in the tombs',[11] 'the Westerners' (*amentiu*),[12] and 'the earth-gods' (*akeru*).[13] Some of these gods aimed to seize the soul of the deceased king,[14] but others would open the doors of the earth for him and lift him into the sky.[15] In the latter case, the earth-gods were often twinned with 'the gods in the sky'.

The gods in the earth were commanded by a sole god, who is named in the Pyramid Texts as 'He whose Seats are Hidden' and 'the Foremost of the Westerners' (Khenti-amentiu).[16] The latter is identified several times with Anubis,[17] but also with Osiris who is said to dwell 'in the middle of this earth'.[18] The aim of the deceased king was to become this god, and to give commands to the gods of the earth.

In theory, the earth had a lower surface which should have enjoyed the rays of the sun when it traversed the lower sky during the night. But this lower surface is nowhere described, and it was perhaps imagined to be immersed in the primeval waters (*nun*) which kept it in a permanent state of darkness.

The primeval ocean *nun* (the word is actually written *nw* or *nnw*) is often translated 'abyss', but literally meant 'water', with the particular connotation 'primeval water'.[19] The name evoked the myth of creation in which the waters were portrayed as the first principle and source of all things.[20] The god Nun, who personified these waters, was thus called 'the Old One, the primeval one of the Two Lands' and 'the Old One, who developed at the first time' (*kheper m zep tepi*).[21] Out of this primeval water had emerged the first land (*ta*), which had remained immersed in and surrounded by it.[22]

That this ocean was joined physically to the earth is clear from the belief that its waters were the source of the Nile, and indeed all springs, wells, rivers, and seas.[23] It is also evident from the idea, recorded in the Pyramid Texts and Coffin Texts, that the sky had been separated 'from the earth and the *nun*'.[24] Thus the earth and the *nun* formed an integral duality at the centre of the cosmos.

Interestingly, the *nun* that encircled the earth had a counterpart in the sky – a second *nun*, or primeval ocean, which was particularly associated with the outermost region of darkness. In the upper sky, this ocean was called *nw* or *nnw* (as with the terrestrial *nun*), but in the lower sky it was given the feminine form *nwt* or *nnwt* (and later *nnt*). We will return to this celestial abyss in our later section on the sky.

The chthonian *nun*, like the netherworld, could be accessed by man only via the tomb. The first act of the king's soul, having separated from his body, was 'to go down into the water... to go down into the earth'.[25] In so doing, it returned to its place of birth in primeval times and became one with the soul of the primeval god.[26]

The Pyramid Texts present a picture of *nun* which is wholly consistent with the first time of creation. Its chief characteristics are darkness and flood.[27] It contains gates,[28] a portal,[29] a cavern,[30] and a great lake.[31] And it is occupied by primeval gods: a tribunal of magistrates;[32] Osiris in his name 'Dweller in Nun';[33] 'the two lords of *nun*', who release the king from his knotted bonds;[34] and unnamed gods, 'those who are in the *nun*', who give life to the king (having been assembled by him) and row him across the waters in a ferryboat.[35]

The Netherworld (Duat)

The realm of the *duat* (actually written *dwat* or *dat*) was perceived to encompass the nether regions of the earth (as shown in figure 5), and on this basis is usually translated 'netherworld'. The importance of this chthonian realm was such that, together with sky and earth, it formed the totality of the cosmos. Thus the creator-god Khnum, for example, was acclaimed as 'the maker of the sky, the earth, and the *duat*' (*pet, ta, dwat*).[36]

As noted earlier, the *duat* was connected to the sky at the eastern and western horizons, enabling the sun, moon, and stars to orbit through the depths of the earth. According to some texts, this connection was made via the two *akheti*.[37] However, other texts suggest that the *duat* extended directly to a border with the sky. As a result, the stars could disappear from the sky into the *duat*, and at the same time set in life in the *akhet*.[38] The two realms could thus overlap, but were not identical since the *duat* was a netherworld while the *akhet* was an interstitial realm between the earth and the sky.

Whilst its primary identity was the netherworld, the *duat* could also be pictured as the birthplace of the stars at the border of the sky, or even as a name of the sky itself. The first of these ideas appears in Utterance 610 of the Pyramid Texts, where the king receives a ladder 'to the *duat*, to the place where Sah is'.[39] The use of the ladder indicates a higher realm than the netherworld, perhaps the eastern horizon, where the star-god Sah is born. The second idea appears in four spells. In Utterance 437, the *duat* is said to grasp the king's hand at the place where Sah is, as if to identify the *duat* with the sky;[40] the sign for *duat* is here determined by a sky-sign.[41] In Utterance 271, the king is lifted to the *duat* by Horus and Seth in parallel with ascending on the ladder of Re; again, this would suggest that the *duat* is the sky.[42] In Utterance 568, the king ascends to the sky 'to the *duat*-lakes', as if these lakes were in the sky.[43] And in Utterance 504, the sky is said to be 'pregnant of wine' when Nut 'gives birth by means of her daughter the *duat*', as if the *duat* were an alter ego of Nut the sky-goddess.[44]

These, it must be emphasised, are exceptional references – a hangover perhaps from an earlier age.[45] As a general rule, the *duat* is to be equated with the netherworld, or as a New Kingdom text puts it, every place that is neither sky nor earth:

> As for every place void of sky and void of earth, that is the entire *duat*.[46]

This statement suggests a distinction between the risen earth (*ta*) and the netherworld on which it rests. The *duat* would be separate from the sky and the earth in the sense of predating their existence, in the same way as the primeval ocean *nun* was said to exist 'before the sky came into being, before the earth came into being'.[47] A passage in the Coffin Texts seems to confirm this supposition, stating that the *duat* was fashioned during the time of chaos, before Horus had prevailed over Seth.[48]

Consistent with this idea, the *duat* was a place of birth and rebirth for the gods and the king. In the Pyramid Texts, Nut gives birth through the *duat* (or in a variant of the spell causes the *duat* to give birth),[49] the *duat* gives birth to Osiris and the king (they are said to have 'emerged from the *duat*'),[50] and Horus of the Duat seemingly gives birth to a sky-god of the same name.⁵¹ The latter myth is echoed in the Book of Gates where Horus the son of Isis refers to Osiris as 'the great one who begot me in the *duat*'.⁵²

It is possible that the *duat* was conceived specifically as the birthplace of the stars. Nut, who gave birth through the *duat*, was the mother of the stars;⁵³ Osiris, 'the Lord of the Duat', was identified with the stellar-god Sah;⁵⁴ Horus of the Duat was connected to the morning star (Venus) and placed at the head of the imperishable stars;⁵⁵ the *duat*-gods (*datiu*) had their name determined by three stars;⁵⁶ the *duat* was described as giving birth to Sah and other stars;⁵⁷ and, as noted earlier, an upper *duat* existed at 'the place where Sah is'.

This theory is strengthened by the fact that the name *duat* (which was spelled out 'alphabetically') was determined by the hieroglyph of a star enclosed by a circle or ellipse ⊕.⁵⁸ According to scholars, the word is derived from the root *dwa*, meaning 'morning',⁵⁹ and a literal translation would thus be 'place of the morning twilight', or even 'birthplace of the stars'.⁶⁰

All of this would suggest that the *duat*, like the *nun*, was the place of creation, and that the king in entering it was returning to the first time in order to establish his identity with the primeval god.

The texts present a picture of the *duat* which is wholly consistent with the time of creation, and indeed remarkably similar to the portrayal of the *nun* which we examined earlier.

The *duat* is a watery place. It is traversed by boat,⁶¹ and it contains a 'lake of the *duat*' (*sh dati*) where the king's spirit is said to be purified.⁶² In addition, the word *duat* is twice determined in the Pyramid Texts by the hieroglyph of a lake.⁶³

The *duat* is a dark place. In the Pyramid Texts, it is identified with *ament*, 'the hidden land', which may imply a state of darkness.⁶⁴ In later writings, notably the Books of the Netherworld, darkness is a prominent feature. In these books, the sun-god journeys from the western horizon to the eastern horizon by traversing 'the thick darkness' of the *duat*, which is equated to the realm of *amentet*.⁶⁵

Occasionally, the *duat* is said to contain 'green fields'.⁶⁶ This seems an unlikely attribute, unless it relates to the higher realm of the *duat* which bordered on the sky.

Significantly, the *duat* is occupied by primeval gods. Its ruler is Osiris, the 'Lord of the Duat' (*neb dat*);⁶⁷ his corpse is identified with Horus of the Duat, and in later texts is located in a secret chamber in its uttermost depths; his spirit, however, is able to 'navigate the *duat*' as if sailing a boat.⁶⁸ Other denizens of the *duat*, according to the Pyramid Texts, are:

Horus;[69] the Eye of Horus;[70] an obscure god named Wr-skat;[71] and a group of unnamed gods who attend the king.[72] To these, the Coffin Texts make the notable addition of Anubis, who is credited with knowing the secrets of the *duat* and its portals,[73] and Shu who is 'in front of his green fields in the *duat*'.[74]

There are hints in the Pyramid Texts of a mass annihilation of gods in the *duat*.[75] This idea is developed in the Coffin Texts, where the place of slaughter is *amentet* and the island of fire,[76] and in the Books of the Netherworld, where the massacre is located specifically in the *duat*.[77] In the latter books, the inimical gods are dismembered and cast into pits of fire.

In the Books of the Netherworld, the *duat* is personified by a god or goddess, namely Osiris or Nut.[78] It is in this context that Re the sun-god travels through the *duat* during the night, in order to be rejuvenated and reborn in the morning. In the one instance, Re is reborn from a mystical union with his 'body' or 'corpse', i.e. Osiris (this is the moment of 'the midnight sun'). In the other instance, he is reborn by passing through the womb of his mother, i.e. Nut. These two themes are skilfully merged in the texts, the Osiris body being reduced to a tomb chamber in the middle section of the *duat* within the body of Nut.

An important theme of Re's passage through the *duat* is the constant threat posed by inimical gods, who launch repeated attacks on his barque or disc of light. Every night, the sun-god must defeat these gods, led by the giant serpent Apep, in order to reach the *akhet* and be reborn in the sky the next morning.

The king entered the *duat* at the precise moment his mummified body was sealed for eternity in the earth. The name of the tomb chamber, 'the house of the *duat*' (*per duat*), suggests an identity of the tomb with the *duat* in its primary form as the netherworld.[79] The Pyramid Texts confirm that the king became a spirit in the *duat*,[80] and that he proceeded to exit the *duat* via a gate which corresponded to 'the doors of Geb' (the earth-god).[81] He is then described as 'this spirit which emerged from the *duat*, Osiris-the-king who emerged from Geb'.[82] The Coffin Texts add that the king 'opened up paths' in the *duat*,[83] and breached its door by 'breaking it' or 'splitting it open'.[84]

By exiting the *duat*, the king's spirit gained access to the sky (*pet*), in some cases directly but in most cases via the *akhet*.[85]

Akhet – the Radiant Place

A third cosmic realm reserved for gods and departed kings was the *akhet*.

Situated just below the rim of the eastern horizon, the *akhet* was entered from the *duat* and gave access by way of its east side to the sky (*pet*). A second *akhet* was positioned at the western horizon, on the opposite side of the sky, but the eastern *akhet* is the main focus of the Egyptian texts, and it is to this realm that the following comments are primarily directed.

Often translated misleadingly 'horizon', the *akhet* was far more than a cosmic border zone. In the earliest texts, the word is written with an oval determinative, similar to that used for the earth (*ta*), signifying the idea of an 'island',[86] while the word's phonetic root *akh* conveys the basic meaning of 'light', 'brightness', or 'radiance'.[87] Egyptologists have thus offered alternative translations of *akhet* such as 'light land', 'the radiant place', or 'the place of becoming *akh*',[88] while for the Egyptians it was equivalent to *ta-netjer*, 'god's land'.[89] It may therefore be seen that the *akhet* was a cosmic realm, to which the translation 'horizon' fails to do justice.

The exact location of the *akhet* is a problem for Egyptology.

On the one hand, the texts give the impression that the *akhet* was part of the sky. In the Pyramid Texts, it is reached by using 'the reed-floats of the sky';[90] its entrance is described as a 'sky-door';[91] its gods are said to dwell 'in the limits of the sky';[92] there is a reference to 'the *akhet* of the sky' (*akhet nt pet*);[93] and on one occasion the word *akhet* is determined by the 'sky' hieroglyph.[94] Moreover, it is suggested that possession of the *akhet* is equivalent to possession of the sky.[95]

On the other hand, the texts portray the *akhet* as a realm separate from the sky. In the Pyramid Texts, it is the place of 'the door of the sky', i.e. the door to the sky,[96] and its own gate provides access to the sky.[97] The Coffin Texts support this view by referring to 'the sky, the earth, and the *akhet*' as if they were three separate realms.[98]

This conundrum is solved by placing the *akhet* between the *duat* and the sky, as shown in figure 5. The *akhet* here is a separate realm from the sky, but it is intimately connected with it, indeed its sole purpose is to provide access to the sky. For this reason, the *akhet* has sky associations, and possession of it presupposes possession of the sky. It may also be viewed as belonging to the sky in the sense of an antechamber that leads to it. The reader should also observe that the *akhet* has borders on its west side with the *duat* and on its east side with the sky. The latter is the east side (*gs iabt*) and limits (*djru*) of the *akhet*, but at the same time the east side and limits of the sky.[99] Hence the gods of the *akhet* may be said to dwell in the limits of the sky.

It almost goes without saying that the *akhet* was not a completed part of the created cosmos (like the earth or the sky) but an imaginary realm, which was designed for the purpose of the rebirth of gods and kings who came forth from the *duat* en route to the sky.

In the Pyramid Texts, the *akhet* is described as 'the place where the gods were born',[100] the precise place of birth being 'the east side of the sky',[101] which was synonymous with 'the east side of the *akhet*'.[102] The king claims to have been conceived and born there, in company with the gods, as Horus the *akhet*-dweller (alias Horus of the Akhet);[103] it is said to be the place where the gods fashioned him.[104] In the Coffin Texts, the *akhet* is on one occasion described as 'the inner compartment of Nut who bore the gods',[105] as if to portray it as a cosmic womb. It is also reported that the creator-god Atum and the sun-god Re appeared for the first time when they emerged from the *akhet*.[106]

The texts present a picture of the *akhet* which is wholly consistent with the time of creation, and in some respects similar to the *nun* and the *duat* which we examined earlier.

The *akhet* is a watery place. In the Pyramid Texts, it is said to have banks,[107] and it is determined on one occasion by the sign of a body of water.[108] The sun-god, the stars, and the king are said to bathe in it, and the gods of the *akhet* are said to row in it.[109] According to one spell, the Lakes of Shu are to be found there, while another describes the spirits sitting on the shores of Lake Shsh in the *akhet*.[110] On the far shores of the *akhet* is the place of the great flood (*mehet weret*) which is bound for the sky.[111] It is here that the king finds a 'place of contentment, green with fields' which is stocked with green plants.[112] The paradisiacal vision is thus complete.

Other notable features of the *akhet* in the Pyramid Texts are its paths and its two conclaves.

The paths or ways (*wawt*) are mentioned briefly in a passage where the king is conducted on the ways of the *akhet* by Nut.[113]

The two conclaves or shrines (*itrti*) are the place of assembly of the gods.[114] The king is said to sit in front of these shrines on his throne, or to stand up in them.[115] In the latter case, they are said to be located 'upon the void (*shu*) of the sky'. It is probable that 'the two shrines of the *akhet*' are synonymous with 'the two shrines of the sky'.[116]

As with the *nun* and the *duat*, the *akhet* is a dwelling place of primeval gods.

In the Pyramid Texts, there is reference to a sun-god called Lord of the Akhet.[117] This was possibly Re, for the *akhet* is described as 'the place where Re is',[118] and in the Coffin Texts Re is identified by the epithet 'Lord of the Akhet' and, more evocatively, 'Lord of the Akhet on the day of eternity'.[119]

On the other hand, the original Lord of the Akhet may have been the sun-god Horakhti, 'Horus of the Two Horizons'. In the Pyramid Texts, he is cited frequently as the god of the eastern *akhet*, in parallel with Re, and he is specifically associated with the idea of having power in the two *akheti*.[120]

The *akhet* is also home to a group of homogeneous gods, variously described as 'those in the *akhet*', 'those of the *akhet*', 'the *akhet*-gods', or 'the two enneads'.[121] The Coffin Texts describe this divine group as 'the old ones, who belong to Re'.[122]

Surprisingly, Osiris too is associated with the *akhet*, though not as a god who dwells in it. In the Pyramid Texts, he is given the name 'Akhet from which Re emerges', as if to suggest that he is a personification of the entire realm.[123] This is interesting, since Osiris is normally portrayed as the corpse of Re, entombed in the netherworld (which in a later period of history he also personified). The implication of this is that Osiris can be viewed dualistically – as a corpse and chthonian realm (the *duat*), but also as a spirit (*akh*) and radiant realm (the *akhet*). We will discuss this idea further in later chapters.

In the Pyramid Texts, Re and Horakhti reach the *akhet* by traversing the field of reeds using reed-floats, although Re may also make use of his barque (on the field of reeds, see the next section).[124] In the later Books of the Netherworld, the reed-floats are dropped in favour of the barque, the field of reeds is absorbed into the *duat*, and Re subsumes the powers of Horakhti. Re then reaches the *akhet* by traversing the *duat* in his barque, in which he is rowed by the gods.

The king could reach the *akhet* by various means: the reed-floats of Re and Horakhti, the barque of Re, a ferryboat, or the wing of Thoth.[125] With the exception of the barque of Re whose route is unclear, these journeys entailed a crossing of the field of reeds. More fundamentally, however, the king's soul entered the *akhet* by traversing the *duat* in which his body was buried.[126] At this point, the king became 'an *akh* in the *akhet*', and was crowned 'Lord of the Akhet'.[127] He then emerged into the sky as a radiant spirit (*akh*), in company with the sun, the moon, and the stars.

The Field of Reeds

An important realm of the Egyptian cosmos was the field of reeds, *sekhet iaru*, which was probably synonymous with the field of offerings (*sekhet hetep*). As we shall see, both these realms refer in certain contexts to the sky, as does the winding waterway (*mr nkha*) which was a prominent feature of the two fields. These celestial fields will be discussed in due

18   THE MIDNIGHT SUN

course, but for now we will focus on the primary or lower field, whose existence predated that of the sky.

According to the Pyramid Texts, the field of reeds was neither sky, nor earth, but the remainder of the cosmos. The deceased king is told: 'The sky is given to you, the earth is given to you, the field of reeds is given to you'.[128] The field of reeds is thus accorded the same cosmic status as the *nun*, the *duat*, and the *akhet*, which each likewise appeared in a triad with sky and earth (see earlier).

Where was the field of reeds situated?

According to a group of spells in the Pyramid Texts, the field of reeds lay beyond the 'jackal lake' or 'lake of the *duat*', which suggests that it was situated beyond, or to the east of, the *duat*.[129] This idea receives a more explicit treatment in the Coffin Texts and Book of the Dead where the door of the *duat* is said to lead into the field of reeds.[130] Significantly, this was the door through which the creator-god Atum had gone to reach the *akhet* at the beginning of time.[131] The field of reeds is thus placed in a creational setting.

Less consistent is the idea that the field of reeds preceded the *akhet*. Although, as we have seen, the Pyramid Texts portray Re, Horakhti, and the king sailing across the field of reeds to the *akhet* as if they were two adjoining realms, other spells in later texts give the impression that they were one and the same realm. In Spell 335 of the Coffin Texts (and Spell 17 of the Book of the Dead), the field of reeds is made identical to 'the land of the *akhet*-dwellers';[132] in Spell 159, the *akhet*-dwellers are said to

Figure 6.
THE EGYPTIAN COSMOS, SHOWING THE LOCATION OF THE FIELD OF REEDS.

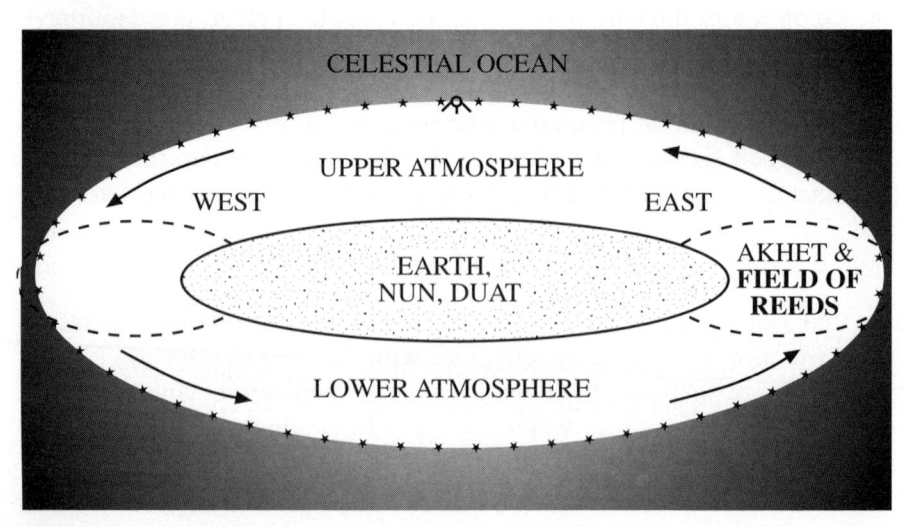

reap the crops in the field of reeds;[133] and in Spell 397, it is suggested that the field of reeds corresponds to 'the east side of the sky'.[134]

The Pyramid Texts seem to bear out this identity. In Utterance 268, the king is said to ferry across to the fields of reeds whereupon 'those who are in the *akhet* row him';[135] in several spells the reborn king ascends to the sky directly from the field of reeds (emulating the gods Atum, Re, Shu, and Horus);[136] and in other spells, as already mentioned, the field of reeds is specified as the third cosmic realm alongside the sky and the earth.

The field of offerings also seems to have an identity with the *akhet*. In Utterance 465 of the Pyramid Texts, the gods of the *akhet* take the king's hand and place him in the field of offerings, whereupon he ascends to the sky.[137] And in two other spells the king is lifted into the sky directly from this field.[138]

In the light of this evidence, it is tempting to believe that the *akhet*, the field of reeds, and the field of offerings represent parallel descriptions of the same cosmic realm, which was located between the netherworld and the doors of the sky in the east (see figure 6).

The texts present a fairly detailed picture of the field of reeds and the field of offerings.

As with the *nun*, *duat*, and *akhet*, the field of reeds is a watery place. According to the Pyramid Texts, its most prominent feature is a winding waterway (*mr nkha*), which is made to flood by the opening of a 'nurse canal' (*mr mn*). This flood fills the field of reeds with water, and enables it to be crossed by means of a ferryboat or reed-floats. In some spells, the expression 'field of reeds' is replaced by 'lake of reeds', in recognition perhaps of this flooding of the realm.[139] This lake is a place of bathing for Re, Shu, Horus, and the king.[140] The field is also said to contain a pool and a lotus-flower.[141]

The field of offerings is likewise a watery place. It too is filled with water by the flood of the winding waterway.[142]

Apart from its flooded waterway, the main feature of the field of reeds is its green fields.[143] These fields, unspecified in number, yield not only the reeds from which the reed-floats are presumably made,[144] but also the bountiful crops on which the gods and the king live.[145] These crops, along with their produce, are called 'offerings'; hence the overlap between the field of reeds and the field of offerings.

The field of offerings is said to contain food, abundance, grain, flour, and herbs which are pure and pleasant.[146] By virtue of the fact that it lies on the banks of the great flood (*mehet weret*) it is also able to produce bread and beer for the gods and the king.[147]

This paradisiacal picture is elaborated in the Coffin Texts, where the field of reeds yields crops of miraculous size. The deceased declares:

> I know that field of reeds which belongs to Re, whose enclosure wall is of iron; the height of its barley is four cubits, its ear is one cubit, its stalk is three cubits, its emmer is seven cubits, its ear is two cubits, its stalk is five cubits.[148]

In later times, this field of reeds came to be seen as the dwelling place of the blessed dead – a fact that has prompted some modern commentators to compare it to the Elysian fields.[149] However, the original Egyptian idea was not that the deceased make his permanent abode in the field of reeds, but rather that he reap and consume its produce, thus gaining the energy to ascend to the sky, where he would feed once again on the produce of the celestial fields (see next section) and then return to the netherworld in the west – a process that he would repeat ad infinitum.

An important feature of the field of reeds is an island that stands proud of its floodwaters. In Utterance 516 of the Pyramid Texts, the king asks the ferryman of the field to take him at once to 'the landing-place of that field which the gods made',[150] while in Utterance 517 the king tells the ferryman: 'I am deemed righteous in this island of earth (*iw ta*) to which I have swum and arrived, which is between the thighs of Nut.'[151]

This island is found also in the field of offerings. In Utterance 519, the king declares: 'I have gone to the great island in the midst of the field of

Figure 7.
THE FIELD OF OFFERINGS.
A scene from the Book of the Dead (Papyrus of Ani).

offerings on which the swallow-gods alight'.[152] Here, the swallow-gods are called 'the imperishable stars' in anticipation of their ascent from the island into the sky.[153]

In the Coffin Texts, the island of the field of reeds is described as 'the island of the just', 'the island of the *akhet*-dwellers', and 'the mound of the two sycamores of the flood-land'.[154] The latter description refers to the 'sycamore trees of turquoise', which are located in the east side of the sky. It is from between these two great trees that Re goes forth.[155]

The significance of this island, by whichever name it is called, may lie in the creation myth whereby the primeval mound (the earth) emerged from the floodwaters of *nun*. If so, the field of reeds would itself recall the creation, and its abundant produce would represent archetypal food and drink of the first time. In support of this theory, the field of reeds is on one occasion paralleled with 'the field of Kheprer' – a reference to the creator-god in the form of the scarab beetle.[156]

In keeping with this idea, the field of reeds is inhabited by primeval gods. In the Pyramid Texts, 'two great gods' are said to preside over the field; one passage names them as Shu and Tefnut (the twin children of Atum).[157] It is also the place of Re and Horus (who bathe in its lake), 'he who is tall of plumes',[158] the two enneads,[159] the followers of Horus,[160] and a divine ferryman.[161]

It is a similar story with the field of offerings. It too is the home of Shu and Tefnut ('the two great gods'),[162] the two enneads,[163] and a ferryman.[164] In addition, it contains inimical gods who have been decapitated and thus deprived of an afterlife.[165]

By the time of the Coffin Texts, the sun-god Re had become chief god of the field of reeds. The field is thus said to belong to Re; it is called 'the city of Re'; men reap its produce in the presence of Re; and Re goes forth to the sky from between its two sycamores.[166]

Later, in the Book of the Dead, Osiris acquired pre-eminence in the field of reeds, in keeping perhaps with his earlier role as the *akhet*.[167]

As foreshadowed earlier, the king entered the field of reeds from the *duat* and traversed its floodwaters using reed-floats, a ferryboat, or the wing of Thoth. While in it, his main tasks were to provision food and drink, to bathe in its lake (having already bathed earlier in the lake of the *duat*), and to reach his island or throne.[168] Preparations were made here for his ascent to the sky. In one group of spells, the king is bathed by the followers of Horus who recite magic spells for his ascent on the right path; he then goes to the sky aboard the barque of Re.[169] In another group of spells, the king is enthroned as Netjer-dwau, 'the morning star'.[170] In the latter spells (and perhaps also the former), the king then ascends to

22   THE MIDNIGHT SUN

the sky via the *akhet*. However, as discussed earlier, the king may bypass the *akhet* and reach the sky directly from the field of reeds or field of offerings.

The Sky

In common with other ancient peoples, the Egyptians believed that the sky was made of water and extended beyond the two horizons to form a celestial ocean that completely surrounded the earth. In Egypt, this ocean was conceived as a duality: an upper sky began at the eastern horizon and arched above the earth as far as the western horizon; there, a lower sky began and ran, like a mirror image, all the way around to the eastern horizon. At all times, the upper sky-ocean was separated from the earth by the atmosphere, personified by Shu, while the lower sky-ocean, as far as can be determined from the texts, was separated from the netherworld by a lower atmosphere, personified by Tefnut.[171] The upper atmosphere acted as a support for the sky and thus could be depicted more concretely as two pillars (*iunu*) or four sceptres (*djmu*).[172]

The sky-ocean was reached through doors that were located in its east side, at the eastern *akhet*, and was exited by doors that were placed in its west side, at the western *akhet*. The latter are described as 'the doors of iron' or 'doors of *Ba-ka*'.[173]

The sky was crossed by means of secret paths or ways that had been cleared on its inner surface, or underbelly. It was here that the sun, moon, and stars navigated like boats on a route which was sometimes described as 'the winding waterway' (*mr nkha*). Beyond, or above, its surface, the sky was an unfathomable ocean of darkness.

The most common name for the upper sky was *pt* (pronounced *pet*), a term synonymous with *hrt*, meaning 'that which is far above'.[174] Often translated misleadingly 'heaven' (with all the modern connotations that such a word bears),[175] the term *pet* in fact described the celestial ocean, and accordingly its primary feature was water. In the Pyramid Texts, it possesses 'waters of life';[176] it has two banks (*idbwi*);[177] it is entered by way of 'looking waters' (*ptru* or *ptrti*);[178] it is traversed on its underside by the winding waterway;[179] and it is 'navigated' in a nautical sense by means of a boat or reed-floats.[180]

The hieroglyph for *pt* took the form of a flat bar with two downward protrusions – a representation of the upper sky supported on two pillars ⌐⌐. However, this sign was also used to determine the word for 'lower sky' (*nwt* or *nnwt*), and when written twice it determined the words for 'skies' (*pwt*) and 'two skies' (*pti*), i.e. the upper sky and lower sky.[181]

Another term used frequently for the sky was *qbhw* (pronounced *qebhu*). Often translated 'firmament', it literally meant 'fresh water' and might best be rendered 'sky-water'.[182] *Qebhu* is determined by the *pt*-sign on several occasions, and like *pet* seems to have been a general term for the upper sky.[183] The term occurs most often in the recitation: 'The doors of the sky are opened, the doors of *qebhu* are thrown open', which might better be rendered: 'The doors of the sky are opened, the sluicegates of the sky-water are thrown open.'[184] On one occasion the king is told 'you shall bathe in the fresh water of the stars' (*qebhu sbau*).[185]

A third term for the sky was *nw* or *nnw* (pronounced *nu* or *nnu*, but simplified to *nun*).[186] Often translated 'abyss' or 'celestial waters', *nun* literally meant 'water', with the particular connotation 'primeval water'. Originally joined as one with the primeval waters of the earth, it had been parted from them when 'the sky (*pet*) was separated from the earth and the *nun*'.[187] In its manifestation as sky-ocean, the *nun* was associated particularly with the night-sky and its hidden depths.[188] In the Book of Nut, this region is described vividly as follows:

> How the upper side of this sky [Nut] exists is in uniform darkness, the southern, northern, western and eastern limits of which are unknown, these having been fixed in the *nun*, in inertness (*nnwt*). There is no light there... (a place) whose south, north, west and east land is unknown by the gods or *akhu*, there being no brightness there.[189]

In addition to its manifestation as the upper sky, *nun* also appeared in the lower sky, where it took the feminine form *nwt* or *nnwt* (and later *nnt*).[190] This lower *nun* was determined sometimes by the hieroglyph of a body of water, and at other times by an inverted *pet*-sign, as if to suggest that it was a mirror image of the upper sky.[191] In one spell of the Pyramid Texts the king is told: 'You demand that you ascend to the upper sky (*pet* with sky-sign), and you shall ascend... You demand that you descend to the lower sky (*nwt* with inverted sky sign), and you shall descend.'[192]

Another name for the sky was *sekhet hetep*, 'the field of offerings'.[193] This term is used for the entire sky on at least five occasions in the Pyramid Texts.[194] In Utterance 496, it is paralleled with the 'great flood' (*mehet weret*), which is a term for the sky-ocean; it is here described as 'that field of offerings of Re'.[195] In Utterance 684, the gods are guided to the fair paths of the sky and to those of the field of offerings, as if they were one and the same realm.[196] In Utterance 519, it is described as the 'great field' of the star-gods, where the king will eat and drink the food and drink of the gods.[197] In Utterance 512, the king is told to traverse the sky and make his abode in the field of offerings among the gods who have gone to their doubles (*kau*), i.e. the star-gods.[198] And in Utterance 419, the king is told to traverse the sky to the field of reeds and dwell 'in the field of offerings among the imperishable stars, the followers of Osiris'.[199] (In these last two examples, the king 'traverses the sky' in the sense of crossing the threshold of the sky as it comes into being – see detailed discussion in chapter ten.)

The field of the sky was also given other names, such as *sekhet ankh*, 'the field of life', and *sha Hp*, 'the meadow of Apis'. The former appears in Utterance 515, where the king joins Re at the *akhet* and states: 'I am bound for the field of life, the resting place of Re in the fresh water (*qebhu*)'.[200] The latter appears in Utterance 254, where the king crosses the street of stars (*msqt shdu*) and causes destruction in the meadow of Apis.[201]

This field of the sky was the counterpart of the imaginary, unseen field which lay beneath the eastern horizon. The latter, like the sky, was called 'the field of offerings' (*sekhet hetep*), but was better known as 'the field of reeds' (*sekhet iaru*). Did the field of reeds also have a counterpart in the sky?

That the field of reeds lay in the sky (as well as beneath the horizon) is a matter beyond dispute. In one spell of the Pyramid Texts (which exists in four variants), Horus, Horakhti, Osiris, and the king ascend through 'the doors of the sky' and 'the doors of the *qebhu*' to bathe in the field of reeds.[202] In Utterance 461, the king passes through 'the doors of the sky' and travels by boat to the field of reeds, in order to cultivate barley and reap emmer therein.[203] And in Utterance 419, the king traverses the sky to the field of reeds (again in the sense of crossing the threshold of the sky as it comes into being).[204]

What exactly did this upper field of reeds signify? A probable answer lies in the crucial statement that the gods and the king go forth to bathe in the field of reeds *at dawn*.[205] Since dawn implies the unfolding of the day sky, this contradicts any notion that this field might be equivalent to the upper field of offerings, namely the night sky. And yet the field of reeds of the sky was closely connected to the field of offerings of the sky – in the Book of the Dead it is said to be 'in it'.[206] We may conclude from this that the upper field of reeds signified a region of the night sky, probably the dawn sky in which the stars still remained visible. This would explain why the morning star – the brightest body of the dawn sky – is said to be prepared in the lower field of reeds.[207]

As with the imaginary field beneath the horizon, the field of the sky contained an unspecified number of subsidiary fields, which are referred to in the Pyramid Texts as 'the fields of *khakha*' and the 'fields of Re which are in Iasu'.[208]

The lower sky was also described as a field. In Utterance 548, the king navigates the barque of Re 'to the field of the two lower skies at this south (or underside) of the field of reeds'.[209] The intention here seems to be that the lower sky is a field that lies in front of the dawn region of the upper sky, the field of reeds. Quite why the lower sky should comprise two skies is unclear, although it might refer to the two alternative circuits of the lower cosmos outlined at the start of this chapter. In other words, it is possible that the netherworld (*duat*) was conceived as an inner sky or middle sky.[210]

The fact that the upper sky and the lower sky were both portrayed as a field would explain several references in the Pyramid Texts to 'the two fields of offerings'.[211] One of these fields would be the upper sky and the other the lower sky, although the texts are not clear on this point.

The sky was also conceived as a mansion (*hwt*). Two spells refer to 'the mansion of Horus which is in the *qebhu*', while one spell mentions 'the mansion of Horus which is in the sky (*pet*)'.[212] In connection with the former, there is a 'Lady of the Mansion' who is probably to be identified as Hathor, whose name *Hwt-Hr* meant literally 'Mansion of Horus' or 'Mansion of the Falcon'. This *hwt* is hardly to be imagined as a structure 'in' the sky. It is rather a term for the entire sky; hence the reference in another spell to 'the great mansion' which has two pillars.[213] In a similar vein, the king is said to have a house (*pr*) in the sky.[214]

As with most parts of the Egyptian cosmos, the sky was personified by a deity. Often this was Nun, the god of the primeval waters (*nun*); less often it was Mehet-weret, the cow-goddess whose name meant literally 'the great flood';[215] but most often it was the goddess Nut.

Nut was synonymous with the sky. In the majority of cases her name is determined by the sky-sign (*pt*), and in several spells her name appears as a textual variant for *pet*.[216] She also possesses the name '*pet*', as well as the name '*hrt*', meaning 'that which is far above'.[217] Like the sky, Nut has doors (*awi*) and paths or ways (*wawt*).[218]

As we would expect, Nut was a watery body. In the Pyramid Texts, she is said to contain 'a great flood';[219] the winding waterway is in her north side;[220] there is a 'sea' under her belly;[221] and she is 'traversed' in a nautical sense.[222]

In Utterance 548 of the Pyramid Texts, Nut is referred to as 'the long-horned one, with pendulous breast' – a description evocative of a cow.[223] In later periods, she is indeed depicted as a cow, standing upon the earth, supported by Shu and his air-gods, the Infinite Ones (see figure 8).

More often, Nut was depicted as a woman bent over the earth, with her

Figure 8.
NUT AS A COW, SUPPORTED BY SHU AND THE INFINITE ONES.

feet touching one horizon and her hands the other, supported by Shu whose upraised hands are placed under her vulva and breast (figure 9). This image does not appear until the New Kingdom, but it is anticipated by the Pyramid Texts, which refer to Nut as encircling the earth, holding all things in her embrace.[224]

In both these guises – cow and woman – Nut was depicted with her belly, or body, covered in stars. Again, this is anticipated by the Pyramid Texts, for in Utterance 434 it is stated that Nut took to herself every god who possessed a barque in order that they remain with her in the form of stars.[225] In this spell, Nut is given the epithet *Nwt kha ba.s*, literally 'Nut of a thousand souls' but often translated 'starry sky'.[226] This emphasis on the stars might well indicate that Nut's primary identity as upper sky was that of night sky, rather than day sky.

It is not inconsistent with this idea that Nut also personified the lower sky, which was envisioned as a place of darkness (the so-called 'night-barque'). In this guise, her mouth was placed at the western horizon and her vulva at the eastern horizon, with her inverted body arching beneath the earth. Nut was thus believed to swallow and give birth to stars every night (and certain stars every year), and swallow and give birth to the sun every day. This idea becomes prominent in the New Kingdom period, but again the Pyramid Texts seem to anticipate it. In respect of the stars, Nut is said to give birth to Sah and the king at the due season,[227] while in respect of the sun, she is said to bear Re and the king every day.[228]

Figure 9.
NUT AS A GODDESS, SUPPORTED BY SHU.

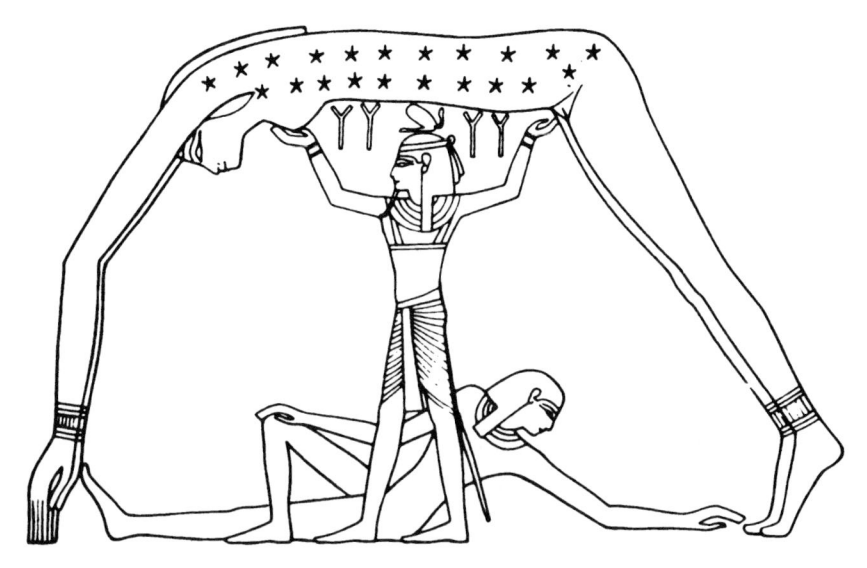

Appropriately enough, Nut's name (*Nwt*) bears a close resemblance to that of the lower sky (*nwt* or *nnwt*), which was also portrayed as a mother who gave birth.[229] This would suggest that Nut's original identity lay in the nether regions of the cosmos, as a kind of womb from which the sun and the stars emerged.

The Celestial Bodies

We turn finally to the celestial bodies which orbited the earth, namely the sun, the moon, and the stars. These bodies were believed to travel on the underbelly of the sky-ocean (*cht pet*, or *cht Nwt*) through paths or ways that were known only to the gods.[230] Each was believed to be a living being – a soul (*ba*) or radiant spirit (*akh*).

The sun was the most important celestial body. In the Pyramid Texts, it is personified by Re and Horakhti, one of whom was probably the Lord of the Akhet. It is also referred to as the Eye of Re.[231] A notable theme in these texts is the daily rebirth of the sun: Re is said to be borne by Nut (the lower sky) every day, while the Eye of Re is said to spend the night (in the netherworld) and be conceived and born every day.[232] It was by means of this continual rebirth that the sun-god was able to orbit the two skies for ever (*neheh*) and thus ensure the eternal endurance (*djet*) of the cosmos. For this reason, the texts focus on the sun-god's night journey in the field of reeds and the sailing of his barque from the *akhet* in the east side of the sky.

The moon is mentioned less frequently in the texts, but was a powerful symbol of the Eye of Horus (the Great Goddess). The phases of the moon were believed to commemorate the death and rebirth of this Eye, which had been stolen by Seth, the god of chaos and darkness, but rescued by Horus, the god of order and light.[233] The empty moon thus symbolised the triumph of chaos, while the full moon symbolised reconciliation and the restoration of order (*maat*). This symbolism would have been felt even more strongly at the time of lunar eclipses.

According to the myth as recounted in the Pyramid Texts, the Eye of Horus was saved by Thoth, who drove off Seth, protected the Eye, and took it to the sky on his wing (in the Coffin Texts he is also credited with healing the Eye).[234] On account of this heroic act, Thoth was envisaged as the god of the moon. In Utterance 210, he is said to traverse the sky as the companion of Re the sun-god.[235] This mythological association with the moon may explain why Thoth became the god of writing, measuring, and time-keeping.[236]

In later times, the moon was personified by Khons, whose name meant 'wanderer'.[237]

Together, the sun and the moon were regarded as the twin 'eyes' of the sky-god, the right eye and left eye respectively. This identification is implicit in the Pyramid Texts, where possession of the two intact eyes is a prominent theme, but it receives its most explicit treatment in later writings, such as a hymn which says of Horus: 'when he opens his eyes he fills the world with light, but when he shuts them darkness comes into being'.[238]

The stars were referred to by various names, the most common in the Pyramid Texts being *akhmu-sku*, 'the imperishable ones', and *akhmu-wrdu*, 'the untiring ones', both names being determined by the sign of a star (*sba*) ✶ .

The night sky in its entirety was also known by various names: *shdu pet*, 'the starry sky'; *qebhu sbau*, 'the fresh water of the stars'; and *pdjt*, 'the celestial expanse' (the latter also appears in the plural form *pdjwt*).[239]

The stars were described as gods (*netjeru*). In the Pyramid Texts, they are called 'those gods',[240] 'those excellent and wise gods',[241] 'those who are in the sky',[242] 'the gods who are in the sky',[243] 'those who are in the fresh water' (*qebhu*),[244] 'the gods who are on the great flood' (*mehet weret*),[245] and 'those who are in the celestial expanses'.[246]

Other names for these star-gods were 'the followers of Re',[247] 'the followers of Osiris',[248] 'the beings of light' (*hnmmt*),[249] and 'the ennead' or 'two enneads' (*psdjt* or *psdjwt-snu*).[250]

The star-gods were also placed in the lower sky. Here they were called 'those who are in the lower sky', 'the gods of the lower sky... who do not die', and 'the gods of the lower sky, the imperishable stars'.[251]

Some of these star-gods dwelt in the northern circumpolar sky and thus remained visible every night, while the others – the vast majority – followed the course of the sun and thus constantly circumnavigated the eastern and western horizons. We will consider these two groups of stars in turn.

The northern stars were called 'those northern gods', 'those in the north of the sky', and 'the spirits in the north of the sky'.[252] These star-gods formed two constellations of similar shape, each comprising seven stars, which were interpreted as two adzes or two forelegs (or thighs) of a bull (today we know these constellations as Ursa Minor and the Plough or Big Dipper, i.e. the rump and tail of Ursa Major). In Utterance 302 of the Pyramid Texts, these two groups are named *mskhtiu akhmu-sku*, i.e. '*mskhtiu* the imperishable stars' and equated (so it would seem) with the two enneads.[253] The name *mskhtiu* is determined by the hieroglyph of an adze and one of the words for adze was *mskhtiu*, hence it is probable that *mskhtiu* meant 'the adze', or perhaps originally 'the two adzes'.[254] The connection to the limbs of the bull is reflected in Utterance 274, where the great ones in the north of the sky use the forelegs of the oldest ones in making the cauldron of the gods.[255]

There is some interesting mythology behind the northern stars, though it is difficult to unravel. According to one myth, Horus and Seth fought each other with two adzes in Hermopolis.[256] It is possible that the adzes of *mskhtiu* commemorated this battle. In support of this idea, Utterance 21 refers to 'the adze of Wepwawet' and 'the adze of Seth', the former god being closely related to Horus.[257] In addition, in Utterance 61, Horus is said to have torn off the foreleg of Seth, which might well have been spiritualized in the northern stars, although there is no textual evidence that this act was reciprocated.[258] A final clue is the tradition which placed the four sons of Horus in the northern stars. The Book of the Dead states that these gods 'are behind *mskhtiu* in the northern sky' and it names them as the first four of the seven spirits who protect Osiris (seven is the number of stars in each adze).[259] The Pyramid Texts are less explicit on this point, but they do describe the four sons of Horus as 'these four gods who lean on their staffs and watch over Upper Egypt' – an apt reference indeed to the circumpolar stars.[260] As for the four stars in question, they would be those that formed the head of the adze, or the fleshy part of the leg, i.e. the thigh.[261]

We turn now to the second group of stars – the myriad which followed

30   THE MIDNIGHT SUN

the course of the sun. These star-gods were conceived as the crew of a great boat, known variously as 'the barque of Re' or 'the barque of the two enneads'. In the upper sky, they rowed the barque from east to west in their names of *akhmu-sku*, 'the imperishable stars', and *akhmu-wrdu*, 'the untiring stars'.[262] In the lower sky, they rowed the barque from west to east in their name *netjeru-nwtiu akhmu-sku* 'the gods of the lower sky, the imperishable stars'.[263] (In the Books of the Netherworld, they also tow the barque through the *duat*.) Together these gods formed an entourage around Re, encircling the two skies both in front of and behind him.[264] By rowing simultaneously, they caused the sun-god to travel through the two skies.[265]

It is often asserted by Egyptologists that the 'imperishable stars' were the northern circumpolar stars, which were imperishable by virtue of the fact that they never set, i.e. never disappeared beneath the horizon. But this is plain wrong. The literal meaning of *akhmu-sku* was 'not knowing destruction'; thus in the Pyramid Texts when the king is given the name 'imperishable star' he is told: 'you will never perish nor be destroyed'.[266] Nowhere in the texts do we find any suggestion that this meant 'to not set in the horizon'. On the contrary, those stars that did set in the horizon were always reborn, and never destroyed. The northern stars were indeed imperishable, but in the sense that they had been created as spirits – who were immortal by definition. Consistent with this, the northern stars did not have a monopoly on imperishability. Contrary to the pronouncements of scholars, the Egyptian texts apply the term *akhmu-sku* to the ordinary multitude of stars.[267] These stars were imperishable not only because they were spirits but also – ironically enough – because they were constantly setting in the west in order to re-enact their births from the *duat* and the *akhet* – a guarantee of eternal life according to the principles of *neheh* and *djet*. This would explain the references in the Pyramid Texts to the stars of the lower sky: 'the gods of the lower sky... who do not die', and 'the gods of the lower sky, the imperishable stars'.

Death and rebirth was an important characteristic of this multitude of star-gods, and there is no better example of this than the triad Sopdet, Sah, and Netjer-dwau.

Sopdet was the Egyptian name for Sirius, the brightest star in the night sky (it is often rendered in its Greek form Sothis). In dynastic times, the heliacal rising of this star prefigured the annual flooding of the Nile, and on this account it was designated 'the great provider' and 'the pure of thrones'.[268] Sopdet was associated particularly with the goddess Isis, and its seventy-day period beneath the horizon was held to represent the time during which Isis sought for her partner Osiris and resuscitated his slain body.[269] Such was the importance of the Sopdet-Nile conjunction that a deceased king was mummified in a process that lasted exactly seventy days.[270]

In the Pyramid Texts, Sopdet is mentioned alongside a star-god named Sah.[271] He is called 'father of the gods' and 'the far-strider' (an allusion to his striding across the sky).[272] He is said to traverse the sky from the east to the west, and to have a season in the sky and a season in the earth (an allusion to his period of invisibility).[273] Sah is identified several times with Osiris,[274] but he is also identified implicitly with Horus in that this god is consistently cited as the partner of Sopdet when he emerges into the sky from the *duat* and the *akhet*.[275]

The consensus in Egyptology is that Sah represented the constellation Orion. That this was so is proven by the so-called 'star-clocks' of the early-Middle Kingdom, which show Sah rising heliacally *before* Sopdet (Sirius) and portray him as a human-like figure (Orion has the shape of a striding man).[276] Sah (Osiris) was thus imagined to be reborn from the *duat*, having spent seventy days beneath the horizon being revivified by Sopdet (Isis).

But this identification of Sah might not have held true at the time of the Pyramid Texts. In fact, close study of these texts points to a number of problems with the Orion hypothesis. Firstly, it seems to be suggested in Utterance 216 that Sah rises *after* Sopdet (in that it disappears into the *duat* before Sopdet).[277] Secondly, it is stated in Utterance 422 that Sopdet acts as a guide for Sah and the king.[278] Thirdly, Sah (as the 'brother of Sopdet') is described in Utterance 266 as 'this star which illumines the sky', i.e. a single star not a constellation.[279] And fourthly, the term 'far-strider', which is taken to be a description of Orion, is in fact applied to any god who crosses the sky (in two spells, it is actually used of the sun-god Horakhti).[280] It is therefore possible, as some scholars have proposed, that Sah was originally the star Canopus – the second brightest star in the sky and thus a fitting companion for Sopdet/Sirius.[281] The allegory of Sopdet (Isis) following Sah (Osiris) into the *duat* for seventy days would arguably make better sense under this hypothesis.

This would, of course, imply a switch in the Sah-Osiris identity from Canopus to Orion at some time between the Old Kingdom and the early-Middle Kingdom. Such a change is not so hard to imagine, and may have resulted from the overlap between Osiris and Horus, especially if Horus was originally (in one of his many incarnations) the god of Orion.[282]

The third star-god in the triad with Sopdet and Sah was Netjer-dwau, 'the god of the dawn-light', or 'morning star'.[283] The Pyramid Texts refer to him as the offspring of Sopdet and Sah.[284] In Utterance 366, this triad is equated to that of Isis, Osiris, and their son Horus:

> (O Osiris)... Your sister Isis comes to you, rejoicing for love of you. You have placed her on your phallus and your seed issues into her, she being ready as Sopdet, and Horus-Spdu has come forth from you as 'Horus who is in Sopdet'.[285]

Consistent with this, the star-god Netjer-dwau is named in one spell as Horus of the Duat (Horus was said to have been conceived by Isis and fathered by Osiris in the *duat*).[286]

Netjer-dwau has been identified by scholars with the planet Venus – the third brightest celestial body after the sun and the moon – which in its phase as morning star rises in the eastern sky just before dawn.[287] That the Egyptians were interested in its role as morning star but not evening star is consistent with their general focus on rebirth in the eastern sky, for which a prior death in the western sky was taken as read. In conjunction with the heliacal risings of Sirius and Orion (or perhaps originally Sirius and Canopus), the first appearance of Venus as morning star signified the birth of the divine child, or the dawn of the soul.

The only other part of the night sky to receive significant attention in the Pyramid Texts is the milky way. According to scholars, it is referred to by two different names: *mr nkha*, 'the winding waterway', and *msqt shdu*, 'the beaten path of stars'. We will consider both these expressions in turn.

The winding waterway (*mr nkha*) has already been encountered in its lower form as a river that flooded the field of reeds beneath the horizon. But this waterway was also a feature of the upper sky – specifically the night sky. This is proven by several spells, in particular Utterance 624 where the king asks to be lifted up to the winding waterway in order to be set among the imperishable stars,[288] and Utterance 684 where the king is said to be 'on the underbelly of the sky as (or with) the beautiful star upon the bends of the winding waterway'.[289] What was the nature of this waterway? In addition to its bends, it also has banks, and a state of flood may be implied by the fact that the barques of Re and the two enneads sail in it.[290] Its route is not clearly described; however, it seems to have its origins in the east side of the sky and to traverse the entire night sky from the east to the west.[291] Hence its identification by scholars as the milky way.[292] (This would imply that the winding waterway in the field of reeds beneath the horizon was also the milky way, imagined prior to its rising into the sky.)

This vision of the winding waterway – with its bends and its banks – is most evocative of the river Nile, and suggests that the Egyptians saw in the sky a celestial duplicate of their terrestrial river (in keeping with the idea of the sky as a great field). In the Coffin Texts, this idea is indeed developed explicitly in a group of spells which sings the praises of Hapi, the spirit of the Nile. In Spells 317-321, Hapi compares himself to the creator-god and boasts of his fertilizing powers both in the earth and in the sky. In the latter respect, he makes the following claims: 'my shape is in the sky', 'the entire earth is under my shadow', and 'my soul crawls over the sky throughout the Two Lands', thus confirming that his river spanned the sky from horizon to horizon.[293] Although these spells do not mention the winding waterway, the term used for Hapi's bends (*kabu*) is the same as that used in respect of the *mr nkha* in Utterance 684 of the Pyramid Texts (see above).[294] All things considered, therefore, there can be little doubt that these two celestial waterways were one and the same river, modelled on the Nile of Egypt, and that this river extended across the entire sky at night – just like the milky way.[295]

The second feature of the sky to have been identified with the milky way is the *msqt shdu*, which is translated 'the beaten path of stars' or 'the street of stars'.[296] The Pyramid Texts provide little information about this place; it is mentioned in only three spells, two of which are essentially a duplicate. From these we can gather that the *msqt shdu* was traversed by boat, that it was a means of reaching the uppermost height of the sky, and that it was guarded by 'the great ones of the castle of the mace'.[297] We can also tell from the determinatives that it was a place of land – perhaps a marsh or a series of islands.[298] Some further information is provided by the Coffin Texts, notably that the *msqt shdu* was reached by opening the gates of the *duat*.[299] In conclusion, although the clues are sparse, there are reasonable grounds for supposing, as scholars have done, that 'the beaten path of stars' was another name for the milky way.[300]

Chapter Two Summary

- The Egyptian cosmos was geocentric.

- Although the celestial bodies orbited the earth by circumnavigating the upper and lower skies, they could also pass through the netherworld of the earth. It is this latter route which is emphasised in the texts. It is the route of rebirth for the sun-god, the gods, and the king.

- The hidden realms of the cosmos are characterised by floodwaters and green fields, and the sky is conceived in similar fashion. The scenery is evocative of the time of creation.

CHAPTER THREE

THE CREATION

**It was primeval magic which came into being by itself...
The gods rejoiced at the sight of it.**
(Coffin Texts, Spell 648)

How did the cosmos originate? In ancient Egypt, there was no dogma, no single holy book, no single centre of religious wisdom such as Jerusalem or Mecca. Instead, many cult centres developed their own versions of events, which they credited to the local or regional creator-god. We have thus inherited a panoply of creation myths in which the unique event is described in diverse and distinct images and attributed to various gods such as Atum, Re, Ptah, Khnum, and Amun, to name but a few.

In an ideal world, such diversity of tradition would be a boon for the scholar of creation mythology, who might hope for a penetrating insight into the mythopoeic mind. But unfortunately for the modern scholar, the ancient authors of these diverse traditions seem to have been united in a general belief that the myth of creation should never be written down in a continuous narrative form. Instead, they referred to the events of creation in the context of hymns and prayers, funerary and temple liturgies, and spells for the deceased, and committed to writing only the minimum of information that was required for each purpose. We are thus faced with the task of reconstructing the creation myth from fragmentary extracts and fleeting allusions, which seem to constitute but some of the *disiecta membra* of the original corpora. And, as if this were not obstacle enough, we must contend also with the problems of obscure idiom and metaphor, and language translation uncertainties.

Faced with these formidable difficulties, Egyptology in its early days developed a jaundiced view of the creation myths. Unable to determine a coherent overall picture, scholars placed emphasis on what they regarded as inconsistencies in the records, and dismissed the myths as a collection of primitive, meaningless and unimportant stories – not worthy of serious study. The multiplicity of myths, far from stimulating the interest of the academic world, resulted in fact in the devaluation of their currency, both individually and collectively. In the words of James H. Breasted, writing in 1912, the Egyptian creation myths were nothing but 'simple folk tales of the origins of the world'.[1]

Certain inconsistencies cannot be denied. In some myths, the Great God acts alone; he brings himself into being, no other god or goddess being present. In other myths, God acts with a female partner or a group of gods; the Great Goddess revivifies him; the gods push together to bring him into being. Or in yet other myths, the Goddess acts alone – the virgin mother of all creation. In addition, the mechanism of creation can differ. The Great God may create the universe by ejaculation from his phallus, by sneezing or spitting from his nose and mouth, by moulding or crafting with his hands, by conceiving a plan in his heart or mind, or by uttering creative words from his mouth. The Egyptian scribes seem to have rejoiced in the uncertainty of how it all happened. But to the scholar of modern times, this uncertainty is a curse. Despite two hundred years of intense debate, Egyptology has yet to resolve the most basic question of whether Egyptian religion was a monotheism or a polytheism.[2]

In the second half of the 20th century, Egyptology began to revise its opinion of the creation myths. In an influential study, published in 1948, Henri Frankfort argued that the Egyptian philosophy of religion differed from the modern philosophy in that it was permissible, indeed desirable, to render the divine by way of multiple perspectives. The variations in religious texts, in words and images, thus amounted to a 'meaningful inconsistency'.[3] Frankfort's theory has since found broad support among Egyptologists, and prompted a fundamental re-evaluation of the creation myths. In 1988, James P. Allen, one of the leading specialists in this field, wrote:

> Fifty years ago it was fashionable to view documents like the 'Memphite Theology' and the Leiden papyrus as relics of competing theological systems... Such an analysis not only runs counter to the persistent syncretism of Egyptian thought: it also falters on a careful reading of the texts themselves. Egyptian cosmology presents a fairly uniform picture of the universe throughout Egyptian history. It should not be surprising, then, that Egyptian cosmogony was equally consistent... Far from being competing systems of thought, the Egyptian creation accounts are facets of a persistently uniform understanding of what the universe is and how it came to be. The texts translated here, and others like them, are more remarkable for their

ultimate compatibility than for their differences. Like differently coloured bits of glass, viewed whole they fit together into a single startling mosaic of ancient Egyptian thought.[4]

Egyptologists now recognise three consistent themes at the heart of the creation myths. These are:

1 All things originated from a primeval ocean (*nun*), which apparently contained the building blocks of primeval matter (*pautt*). This abyss was initially in a state of darkness, chaos, and flood.

2 A primeval mound (*iat*) or island (*iw*) was knit together and raised from the *nun*, thereby forming the earth (*ta*). This process involved a mysterious receding of the waters.

3 The sky (*pet*) was separated from the earth (*ta*). This paved the way for the creation of the stars, the sun, and the moon.

The identification of these three central themes provides the opportunity to define a singular creation myth and to find a rational explanation for the evolutionary process by which the abyss was transformed to become the differentiated cosmos. J.P. Allen is one of the few Egyptologists who has attempted to do this by postulating the creation of a bubble-like void within the waters.[5] However, his interpretation of the creation myth stops short of explaining how the celestial bodies appeared in the sky, and thus offers only a partial solution. Generally in Egyptology, there is a lack of study on this question, most scholars taking the view that there is nothing further of value to be teased out from the texts.

Why this negative and defeatist attitude? One reason is the persistence of the old view that the creation myths are primitive and unimportant stories. But the primary reason is that Egyptology has always understood Egyptian religion to be a sun cult, and in keeping with this view it has given the creation myths a solar interpretation. It was the sun-god who stirred in the primeval ocean; the sun-god who raised himself onto the primeval mound; and the sun-god who created himself, the sun, and the other celestial orbs. Granted, this cosmic drama sounds like superstitious nonsense, but why should it make sense when it was conceived by crude and primitive minds? Dazzled thus by the sun, scholars have had no incentive to seek a more rational basis for the creation myth. They have had better things to do with their time.

This is surely a mistake of gargantuan proportions. The creator-god in Egypt was not always the sun-god. In fact, in the majority of cases he was *not* the sun-god at all. Rather, he was the god of creation, whose task was to *create* the cosmos – in contrast to the sun-god whose task was to *maintain* the cosmos. The roles of the creator-god and the sun-god must therefore be distinguished. Granted, the creator-god had created the sun and manifested himself in it, thereby causing the sun-god to come into being as an image of himself; in this sense, it might be said that the sun-god was the creator-god. However, when the Egyptians claimed that the sun-god was the creator, they did not mean to imply that the sun was the first cause or the centre of the cosmos. In taking such claims literally, based on their assumption that the religion was a sun cult, Egyptologists have perverted the meaning of the creation myths, and relegated them to the status of trivial tales.

The moment has now come to put aside the solar bias that has afflicted Egyptology for the past two centuries and to reconsider the significance of the creation in ancient Egypt. Evidently, the concept of creation was important: both the sun and the pharaoh re-enacted the first time in order to power the time machine of the cosmos (see chapter one). Yet the myth of creation itself has remained far too vague and fragmentary in our eyes to justify the importance that was attached to it. Why is this? Was there a fault line at the heart of the Egyptian theocracy, between its cosmology and its cosmogony? Or do the creation myths contain hidden depths of meaning which modern scholars have failed to apprehend? If we were to re-evaluate the creation and the creator-god from a non-solar perspective, would we perceive the fault line, or would we perceive the hidden depths of meaning?

To begin our investigation, we must first ascertain the basic facts, as they are known to Egyptology, but without the solar veneer that is often laid incautiously on the texts. In this chapter, we will consider all of the Egyptian creation myths, which we may classify according to the name of the creator as follows: Atum; Shu; Neber-djer; Re; Horus the son of Isis; Ptah; Khnum; Amun; Horus and the Shebtiu; the Primeval Ones; the Ogdoad; and the Goddess. For some of these myths the information provided will be brief and formulaic, while for others it will be lengthy and distinctive. There will be few surprises here for the specialist reader, except that I have chosen to include Horus the son of Isis as a creation myth (it is normally classified as a kingship myth) for reasons which will become clear in due course. The reader's attention is also drawn to the fact that the myths derive from literature of various periods, separated in some cases by two thousand years. Nevertheless, one must be careful in asserting chronological primacy for any particular myth, for it might well be the case that the various cult centres possessed beliefs of comparable antiquity and that the beliefs of a particular cult centre came to the fore only when the centre itself rose to prominence in the political-religious history of the Nile valley.

Atum, the All

Atum was the creator-god at Heliopolis (ancient name Iunu, 'City of the Pillar'), one of the most important religious centres from the beginning to the end of Egyptian civilisation.[6] His name confronts us with an enigma, for it meant both 'to not be' and 'to complete'.[7] A possible interpretation of this is that Atum personified the entire creative transformation. His other epithets included 'Lord of All' (*neb-tm*), and 'Lord to the Limits of the Sky', abbreviated to 'Lord to the Limit' (*neb-r-djr*).[8]

The creation by Atum is first recorded in the Pyramid Texts. In Utterance 527, it is stated:

> Atum is the one who came into being, who masturbated in Heliopolis. He took his phallus in his grasp that he might create orgasm by means of it, and so were born the twins Shu and Tefnut.[9]

This brief passage is amplified by Utterance 600:

> O Atum-Kheprer, you became the high hill (*qay qaa*); you rose up as the *benben* stone (*bnbn*) in the mansion of the *benu*-bird (*hwt benu*) in Heliopolis. You sneezed out Shu, you spat out Tefnut, and you set your arms about them as the embrace of *ka*, that your *ka* might be in them.[10]

These passages inform us that Atum's primary manifestations were the high hill, the *benben* stone, and the twins Shu and Tefnut. Immediately, we are introduced to several important themes.

The rising of the high hill (*qay qaa*) and the *benben* represents the emergence of land from the abyss. The exact significance of the high hill is debatable (see chapter eleven), but the *benben* is known to have been the principal cult object of Heliopolis (the city of Atum and the sun-god Re), where it took the form of a conical stone raised upon a pillar in the main temple courtyard. There is a probable connection here to the city's Egyptian name Iunu, which meant literally 'Pillar City'. It is also likely, in view of the first passage above, that the *benben* pillar represented the phallus of Atum.[11]

The ejection of Shu and Tefnut is open to interpretation. According to Egyptologists, Shu personified air and Tefnut moisture.[12] This works for Shu, whose main function was to support the sky, but it is less persuasive for Tefnut, whose role was ill defined.[13] An alternative reading is that Shu personified the sun and Tefnut the moon, hence the claim that they were 'twins'. This solar-and-lunar identity is attested in other texts, and is certainly a possibility here.[14] In any event, Shu and Tefnut symbolised the totality of existence and it was in this sense that Atum gave them his *ka* – the 'vital spirit' of the cosmos. The *ka* is a fundamental idea in Egyptian religion and myth, and the second passage above is a crucial authority for tracing its origin to the time of creation.

Another important theme is self-development, or self-creation. In the first passage above, Atum is called 'the one who came into being' in the sense that he developed *from himself*. The verb here is *khpr*, written with the sign of the scarab beetle 🪲 , which supposedly created itself from a ball of dung. This self-developing beetle (*khprr*) provided the image for the creator-god Kheprer (or in later writing Khepri), by whose name Atum is invoked in the second passage.[15] Their close relationship is also attested in Utterance 587, where Kheprer is specifically said to come into being from himself:

> Hail to you, Atum! Hail to you, Kheprer, self-developing (*khpr-djs.f*)! May you be high (*qay*) in this your name of 'Height' (*qaa*). May you come into being in this your name of 'Kheprer'.[16]

To come into being (*khpr*) therefore meant to develop from oneself – to change or evolve – or in Atum's case to become high.[17] The implication of this, as Jan Assmann has observed, is that the cosmos emanated from Atum – that Atum turned himself into the cosmos.[18]

According to the Pyramid Texts, the place where Atum transformed himself was Heliopolis (Iunu), or at least the primeval equivalent of that city. However, the Coffin Texts, while repeating this idea,[19] at the same time present a different slant on the myth. Here, the creator is seen as a spirit stirring in the primeval waters of *nun*, coming into being 'out of the flood (*hhu*), out of the waters (*nu*), out of the darkness (*kku*), out of the chaos (*tnmu*)'.[20] Spell 80 contains a speech by Atum which provides an unusual degree of detail on the creation. He declares:

> I sent out my Eye when I was at one with Nun in inertness, when I could find no place on which to stand or sit, when Heliopolis had not yet been founded that I might dwell in it, when my lotus had not yet been knit together, before I had made Nut that she might be above me, so that Geb could marry her, before the first company (of gods) had been born, before the primeval ennead had come into being that they might be with me. Thus said Atum to Nun: "I am floating, very weary, and the progenitors are inert. It is Geb who lives and lifts up my heart, enlivens my heart, when he gathers together these very weary limbs of mine."[21]

40   THE MIDNIGHT SUN

There are several interesting themes in this passage. Firstly, it introduces us to the Eye, a form of the Great Goddess. Her presence alongside Atum in the *nun* is a puzzle, since Atum is supposed to have come into being in splendid isolation. How, then, could Atum have an Eye that he sent out of the abyss? The significance of the Eye and its travels will be discussed in chapter twelve.

Secondly, there is reference here to the knitting together of the lotus for Atum. This, as we shall see, is an allusion to the breaking of light and life on the surface of the primeval ocean.

Thirdly, the last line of the above passage refers to the 'weary limbs' of Atum. Since it is Geb, the earth-god, who gathers together these limbs, the allusion is almost certainly to the formation of the primeval mound (see discussion in chapter four).

In order to evolve from 'not-being' to 'complete', Atum had to emerge from the watery abyss and manifest himself in the sky above the earth. In this development, he manifested himself as Re (supposedly the sun-god). An intriguing insight into this evolutionary process is presented in Spell 335 of the Coffin Texts (which exists in several variants) and Spell 17 of the Book of the Dead. Unusually, these spells are provided with 'glosses' which provide an explanation of the more obscure passages. The text is too long to be quoted in full, but the opening lines are as follows.

> The word came into being. All was mine when I [Atum] existed alone. [Variant: I was Atum when I was alone in the *nun*.]
>
> I was Re in his first appearances when he emerged from the *akhet*. [Variant: I was Re in his glorious appearances when he began to rule what he had made.]
> *What does it mean? It means Re when he began to rule what he had made, when he began to appear as king, before the Supports of Shu had come into being, when he was upon the hill which is in Hermopolis, when the Children of Impotence had been given to him as the Hermopolitans...*
>
> I am the great god, the self-creating.
> *Who is the great god, the self-creating? He is the water of the nun. Otherwise said, he is Re.*
>
> (I am the one) who created his names, Lord of the Ennead, who is not opposed among the gods.
> *Who is he? He is Atum who is in his sun-disc. [Variant: He is Re, who created his names and his limbs; it means the coming into being of those gods who are in his following.]*[22]

To modern eyes, the explanations provided in these glosses (italicised) may seem just as opaque as the original text. A few words of additional commentary are required.

A key idea is that Atum became Re. The creator was Atum when he was alone in the *nun*; he then became Re when he emerged from the *akhet* (into the sky). In a later part of the text, not quoted above, Atum is said to have proceeded from the *nun* and the *duat* to the field of reeds and the *akhet* in the east side of the sky.[23] The creator's identity as Atum is thus retained right up to the point where he emerges into the sky as Re.

The first gloss makes an interesting reference to the primeval mound, here the hill (*qaa*) in Hermopolis. The subjugation of the Hermopolitans, the Children of Impotence, on this hill reflects a hugely important theme in Egyptian religion, namely the constant need to defeat the forces of chaos. The text suggests that these dark powers, usually personified by Seth or Apep, first appeared at the time of creation, but were thwarted in their attempts to obstruct the developing order. The name of the rebels, the Children of Impotence, indicates the futility of their battle against an all-powerful creator.

The second gloss is interesting for the identity it draws between Atum, Re, and Nun the god of the primeval waters. Because the god develops himself from the waters, he *is* the waters. In Atum's case, this identity extends to the waters of the sky: Spell 78 of the Coffin Texts identifies him with the sky-ocean, while Spell 437 suggests that he ascended from the *nun* to the celestial ocean.[24]

Finally, the third gloss introduces us to the gods (*netjeru*), otherwise known as the ennead (*psdjt*). These beings are made to correspond to the creator-god's limbs.

Shu, the Sneeze of Life

In the Pyramid Texts, Shu appears as the emanation of Atum, along with Tefnut. But in the Coffin Texts there is a series of spells – the so-called 'Shu texts' – in which Shu himself claims to be the creator-god, even while acknowledging that Atum created him.[25] He is thus said to be 'the father of the gods',[26] 'the begetter of the gods',[27] 'the one who bore repeated millions',[28] and on one occasion 'the begetter of Atum'.[29] The Shu texts, written from Shu's perspective, offer a unique insight into the myth of the creation by Atum, and thus warrant a separate treatment. A selection of passages is quoted and discussed below.

In Spell 75, we learn that Shu was a soul, mysterious of form, who came forth from the body of Atum. The passage reads:

> I am the soul of Shu, the self-created god, I have come into being from the body of the self-created god. I am the soul of Shu, the god mysterious of form. I have been knit together from the body of the self-created god...[30]

Picking up on themes in the Pyramid Texts, this body of Atum, the self-created god, is pictured as having a mouth, a nose, a phallus, and a hand, each of which is used to effect the emission of Shu and Tefnut. Here, there is open disagreement on the method of procreation. In Spell 75, it is emphasised that Shu was exhaled from Atum's nose, *not* born in his mouth or conceived in his fist. In Spell 76, to the contrary, it is held that Shu was born in a sneeze of the mouth, *not* created in a womb or an egg. In Spell 77, we find another strange combination: Shu is spat out from the mouth after Atum's masturbatory climax. And then in Spell 80, it is asserted, with no hint of awkwardness, that Shu was 'the one who Atum sneezed, who emerged from his mouth, as he used his hand'![31] These variant traditions echo similar inconsistencies in the Pyramid Texts, as the panel opposite demonstrates.

The Shu texts provide information on the creation of the sky, adding to the Pyramid Texts which state only that Shu placed himself under Nut and lifted her.[32] Shu is here portrayed explicitly as air or wind. In Spell 75, he declares: "My garment is the wind of life, which came forth about me from the mouth of Atum",[33] while in Spell 76, he emerges from the mouth 'hooded in the air of the phoenix's throat'.[34] But the most explicit account comes in Spell 80, where Shu states more fully:

> My garment is the air of life, which emerged for it behind me, from the mouth of Atum, and opens the winds on my path. I am the one who made the sky light after the darkness. My skin is the pressure of the wind, which emerged behind me from the mouth of Atum.[35]

Here, one must envision Shu's air forcefully separating the sky from the earth and the *nun*, creating a void between them which is the atmosphere of Shu. The end result is proclaimed in Spells 76 and 78:

> I lifted up my daughter Nut from upon myself, that I might give her to my father Atum in his realm, and I have set Geb under my feet...
> I have set myself between them, but the ennead cannot see me.[36]

> I am the soul of Shu, for whom Nut was placed above and Geb under his feet, and I am between them.[37]

Shu was thus portrayed as a standing god, who towered above the earth-god Geb and supported the sky-goddess Nut upon his upraised arms (see

The Origin of Shu and Tefnut

Atum is the one who came into being, who masturbated in Heliopolis. He took his phallus in his grasp that he might create orgasm by means of it, and so were born the twins Shu and Tefnut.
(Pyramid Texts, Utterance 527)

O Atum-Kheprer, you became the high hill; you rose up as the *benben* stone... You sneezed out Shu, you spat out Tefnut...
(Pyramid Texts, Utterance 600)

He [Atum] created me [Shu] in his heart, he made me by his power, he exhaled me from his nose... He did not give me birth with his mouth, he did not conceive me with his fist, (rather) he exhaled me from his nose...
(Coffin Texts, Spell 75)

I indeed am Shu whom Atum created on the day that he came into being. I was not built up in the womb, I was not knit together in the egg, I was not conceived in a conception, (rather) my father Atum sneezed me in a sneeze of his mouth, together with my sister Tefnut.
(Coffin Texts, Spell 76)

I am this soul of Shu which is the first one of the fiery blast which Atum kindled with his own hand. He created orgasm and semen fell from his mouth. He spat me out as Shu together with Tefnut.
(Coffin Texts, Spell 77)

It is I [Shu] who am eternal repetition, who bore repeated millions, the one who Atum sneezed, who emerged from his mouth, as he used his hand...
(Coffin Texts, Spell 80)

figure 9 in chapter two). As the cited passages indicate, Shu's form was that of an invisible soul; hence he is elsewhere called 'the god mysterious of form'.[38]

Interestingly, the Shu texts connect the lifting of the sky to a knitting together of the earth and a gathering together of a great flood. Both Spell 76 and Spell 79 refer to these events:

> This god [Geb] knits together the Two Lands for my father Atum, and gathers together for him the great flood.[39]

Shu was (still) in his realm, Shu was (still) in the *nun*, when the earth-gods had not yet been knit together, when the great flood of Atum had not yet come into being so that he might come to rest upon it.[40]

These passages seem to suggest that the primeval mound was formed at the same time as the great flood (*mehet weret*), the latter referring to the sky-ocean which would be lifted up by Shu. In Spell 80, Shu indeed appears as 'the soul at the head of the great flood, who ascends to the sky as he wishes'.[41] The impression is given that Shu lifted up the flood and gave it to Atum as the celestial ocean (just as he lifted up Nut and gave her to Atum in Spell 76).[42] Atum then retired on these waters, or became at one with the waters themselves.[43]

One final point of note in the Shu texts is the creation of the eight *hh*-gods, 'the Infinite Ones', whose role was to assist Shu in supporting the sky.[44] These gods are said to have been fashioned by Shu in the chaos and darkness of *nun*, where he knit them together from 'the efflux which was in his flesh' (perhaps the air),[45] although a variant text suggests that their names were created by Atum.[46] According to Spell 76, the *hh*-gods assembled a ladder for Atum, enabling him to ascend from the abyss to the sky,[47] and this ladder was used also by Shu, who left the gods behind him to support the sky as his delegates.[48] Meanwhile, the eight gods were raised up by Nun or Shu to become the four supports of the sky, two at each of its four pillars or 'limbs'.[49] They were thus said to 'encircle the sky with their arms' and 'hold together the sky and the land of Geb'.[50]

Neber-djer, Lord to the Limit

The creator-god Neber-djer was probably an alter ego of Atum, who is described in the Coffin Texts as *neb-r-djr n pet*, 'Lord to the Limit of the Sky'.[51] 'Neber-djer' is thought to be an abbreviation of this name, and thus whilst it literally meant 'Lord to the Limit', it may also be translated 'Lord of All' or 'Lord of the Universe'.[52]

The myth of the creation by Neber-djer is preserved in the Bremner-Rhind Papyrus, which was composed in the Ptolemaic Period (*c.* 310 BC), though the original may date to the New Kingdom.[53] While drawing on the Old Kingdom myth of Atum masturbating and ejaculating Shu and Tefnut, and the Middle Kingdom myth of Atum sending out his Eye in search of them,[54] it brings these ideas together in a more informative (if occasionally mystifying) narrative. The account is rendered as a speech of Neber-djer, who is made to say:

I am the one who came into being as Khepri. When I came into being, being (itself) came into being. All beings came into being after I came into being. Many were the beings which came forth from my mouth, before the sky came into being, before the earth came into being, before the offspring of the earth, the snakes, were created in that place. I knit (myself) together in them, out of the *nun*, out of inertness, having not found a place in which I might stand. I became effective in my heart. I made a plan with my face. I made every form when I was alone, before I sneezed out Shu, before I spat out Tefnut, before (any) other came into being to act with me. I made a plan in my own heart, and there came into being a multitude of beings... I am indeed the one who masturbated with my fist, copulated with my shadow, and spewed (seed) from my mouth. I sneezed out Shu, I spat out Tefnut.[55]

There are several noteworthy aspects of this passage.

Firstly, there is a particular emphasis on the verb *khpr*, meaning 'to come into being', and its related noun *khpru*, meaning 'state of being' or 'development'. A typical line thus reads *khpr.i khpr khpru*: 'my coming-into-being was the coming-into-being of being'. As discussed earlier, this signified a process of change and evolution of form – an idea personified by the beetle-god Khepri (or Kheprer).

Secondly, the author of this text has adapted the Atum, Shu and Tefnut myth to lend greater importance to creation via the mouth. Like Atum, Neber-djer masturbates his phallus, but here the semen mysteriously ends up being spat from the mouth. At the same time, Neber-djer creates Shu and Tefnut from his mouth in the usual way (in Shu's case by a sneeze of the mouth). It is assumed by scholars that this is an illogical combination of two separate myths. But, be that as it may, the author is consistent in insisting that creation came from the mouth.

Thirdly, the serpents who are knit together in Neber-djer in the *nun* echo the 'primeval ennead' and 'progenitors' of Atum in Spell 80, as well as the gods, the ennead, the followers of Re, who correspond to the creator's limbs in Spell 335. The meaning is not clear here, but it may anticipate the emergence of the 'place to stand', namely the primeval mound.

Neber-djer's speech goes on to describe the mysterious appearance of the Eye, at which point the text becomes difficult to understand. Shu and Tefnut are said to bring the Eye to their father, in contradiction to Spell 76 of the Coffin Texts where the Eye is sent out in search of them.[56] The Eye then sheds tears upon the limbs of Neber-djer, causing mankind to come forth, along with plants and creeping things.[57] In addition, there is a strange incident involving a jealous eye which burns in anger at a second eye, both of which appear in the creator-god's face.[58] This would appear to describe the birth of the sun and the moon, since the eyes (*irti*) were a widely-used metaphor for the twin celestial bodies.

Re, the Sun-god

Re's usual identity was the sun-god, whose primary task was to repeat the creation by emerging from the primeval ocean (*nun*) and rising from the horizon (*akhet*) each day. However, many texts praise Re as the creator-god, and from the Middle Kingdom onwards he often plays a part in the myths of creation. In these myths, Re is sometimes portrayed as a second generation god, for example the transfigured form of Atum (see earlier) or a soul created by ancestors in the abyss.[59] But occasionally he appears as the first generation creator-god.

One of the earliest proclamations of Re as creator appears in Spell 648 of the Coffin Texts. Here Re is called 'the self-created' (*khpr-djs.f*) and 'Lord of the Akhet on the day of eternity'.[60] Having gathered together the fluid of his egg (*swht*), he rises into the sky, accompanied by the ennead-gods:

> He [Re] rises as a flood (*nun*), his entourage is serpents, his ennead is behind him... his millions of spirits are within his mouth. It was primeval magic (*heka*) which came into being by itself... (he is) the one who created the mountains and knit the *qebhu* together.[61]

This text also states that the sky (*pet*) was pregnant with Re and that Nut (the sky-goddess) gave birth to him. As strange as it might appear to the modern mind, the Egyptians had no difficulty with the idea of Nut giving birth to Re, even though he was the self-created god.

In New Kingdom times, numerous hymns began to appear, praising Re as a solar creator-god. These hymns are largely formulaic, and need not be considered at length. A typical example reads as follows:

> Hail to you Re at (your) rising, and to you Atum at (your) setting. You rise every day, you shine brightly every day, while you appear in glory, king of the gods. You are lord of the sky and lord of the earth, who has created the creatures above and those below. Sole god who came into being on the first occasion, who made the land and created human beings, who made the *nun* and created the Nile, who created the waters and imparted life to what is in them, who raised up the mountains and bestowed existence upon men and herds... Divine youth, heir to eternity, who engendered himself and gave birth to himself, unique one with many forms.[62]

More interesting for our purposes are the solar creation narratives which were written during the 18th and 19th dynasties. In one of these, entitled the Book of the Heavenly Cow, Re is depicted as an ageing creator-god who decides to depart from the world of men. To this end, he lifts up Nut in the form of a cow and unites with her by stretching himself out upon her back. At the same time, he creates a great field of stars on the belly of the goddess. When Nut trembles because of the height, Re creates the Infinite Ones to act as her supports and places them under the command of Shu. Thus the creation is completed. The following extract captures the essence of the myth:

> His Majesty [Re] said: "Let a great field (*sekhet*) be provided (*hetep*)." That is how the field of offerings (*sekhet hetep*) came into being. (And Re said:) "I will gather reeds (*iaru*) therein." That is how the field of reeds (*sekhet iaru*) came into being. (And Re said:) "I will make to dwell in it things like stars of all sorts." That is how the twilight-stars (*ikhkhu*) came into being. Then the goddess Nut trembled because of the height, and the Majesty of Re said: "I decree that there be millions (of gods) to bear her up." And that is how the Infinite Ones came into being.[63]

The above passage contains a unique account of the origin of the celestial fields, and confirms that the field of offerings – the dwelling place of the stars – was a name for the entire sky.

In another solar creation narrative, entitled by scholars *Isis and Re*, Re is laid low by the bite of a serpent which has been placed on his path by Isis. His heart and limbs stricken by pain, he calls out for the gods, his children, to come to his aid. But their words of magic cannot save him. Only Isis can remove the poison, on condition that Re reveals to her his secret name. Re tries to avoid the issue by reciting a formulaic summary of his achievements as creator.[64] But he is eventually forced to allow Isis to search through his body to steal his secret name. What then transpires is analogous to the creation. Re lives by releasing the Eye from his mouth; his heart comes forth; and he gives up his two eyes (the sun and the moon).[65]

Horus the Son of Isis

The story of Horus the son of Isis was a national myth which provided the archetype for the kingship of Egypt – the king as the living image of Horus ruling upon the throne of Isis. Although the story is not usually regarded as a creation myth per se, it is treated so here on the basis that it explains the genesis of the great falcon-god Horus, who was born blind but filled the universe with light when he opened his two eyes.[66] These eyes were the sun and the moon.

The backdrop to the birth of Horus is the 'death' of his father, the god Osiris. The latter is portrayed as a slain, unconscious body which has fallen apart or drowned in its own floodwaters. There is a close parallel here to the other creation myths in that Osiris lies in a state of darkness, chaos, and flood.

The goddess Isis then acts as saviour. She finds Osiris, reassembles his body, revivifies him, and brings him out of the water. At the same time, she unites with his body and, by miraculous means, conceives a son and heir, namely Horus. The Pyramid Texts contain two brief references to this event:

> Isis comes to you [Osiris] rejoicing through love of you, your seed issues into her...[67]

> Your sister Isis comes to you [Osiris], rejoicing for love of you. You have placed her on your phallus and your seed issues into her...[68]

A hymn from the New Kingdom develops the story, explaining how Isis as a bird revivified Osiris with the breath of life from her wings; having conceived Horus, she then gave birth to him and nursed him in a secret place:

> Isis (is) the powerful one, the protector of her brother, who searched for him tirelessly, who traversed the earth in her grief, and did not rest until she had found him. She cast a shadow with her feathers, created a wind with her wings, and uttered the cry of the mourning-woman for

Figure 10.
ISIS IN THE FORM OF A KITE BEGETS HORUS FROM THE REVIVIFIED BODY OF OSIRIS.

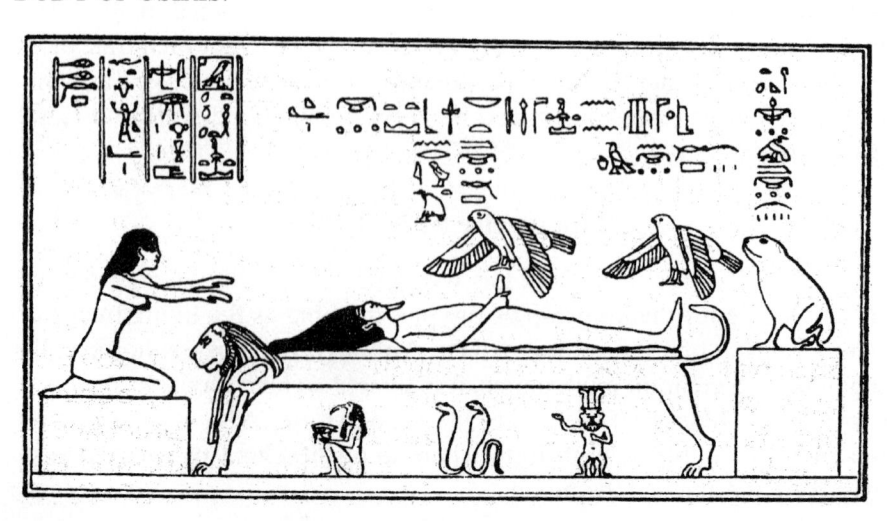

her brother. She made joy of life enter the limbs of the weary of heart. She drew his seed into her body, and (thus) created an heir. She suckled the child in solitude, in an unknown place, and, when his arm had grown strong, led him into the hall of Geb.[69]

The assembled gods then found Horus worthy of inheriting the kingship of Osiris, whereupon he received the white crown and took possession of the entire sky and earth.

The ascent of Horus to the sky is described in Spell 148 of the Coffin Texts, where he emerges as a falcon from the womb of Isis:

See Horus, you gods! I am Horus the Falcon who is on the battlements of the mansion of Him whose Name is Hidden. My flight aloft has reached the *akhet*, I have overpassed the gods of the sky. I have made my position more prominent than that of the Primeval Ones... I have used the roads of eternity to the dawn. I go up in my flight, and there is no god who can do what I have done... I am Horus, born of Isis, whose protection was made within the egg... I am Horus, more distant of place than men or gods. I am Horus the son of Isis.[70]

The womb of Isis is here portrayed as an egg (*swht*). At the beginning of the spell, it is stated that the womb, or egg, was fertilized by the seed of Osiris, which appeared with the flash of a thunderbolt.[71]

As noted earlier, the defining moment of the creation by Horus was the opening of his eyes – the sun and the moon – which filled the world with light. In order to take possession of his two eyes, the god needed to have ownership of the Sole Eye, which necessitated a battle against Seth, the personification of chaos.

According to the Pyramid Texts, Seth had stolen the Eye, either from Horus or his father Osiris. In order to effect the creation, this wrong had to be righted. Horus therefore seized back the Eye, tore off the testicles and foreleg of Seth, and forced him to become a subordinate to Osiris in the netherworld.[72] Order was thus made to prevail over chaos.

Figure 11.
IMAGES OF HORUS THE FALCON.

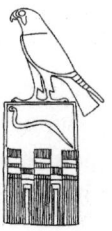

Ptah, the Cosmic Craftsman

Ptah was the creator-god at Memphis (ancient name Mn-nfr, 'Enduring and Beautiful'),[73] the capital city of Egypt for most of the pharaonic era. Although the earliest texts provide little information about him, he was renowned from the Middle Kingdom onwards as a craftsman-god, patron of the trades of sculpture, masonry and construction.[74] The meaning of his name is uncertain, although in later times it was connected to the verb *pth*, 'to create' or 'to open'.[75] A common epithet of Ptah was 'the One who is to the South of his Wall', a reference perhaps to the mythical wall 'which separated the sky from the body of the god'.[76]

Ptah's role as creator-god is known from a number of texts, of which the most informative date to the New Kingdom. These include the Great Harris Papyrus (20th dynasty), Berlin Papyrus 3048 (22nd dynasty), and the Shabaka Stone (25th dynasty).

In the Great Harris Papyrus, Ptah is praised as follows:

> Hail to you, O great and old one, Ta-tenen, father of the gods, the great god from the first primeval time, who fashioned mankind and made the gods, who developed developments in primeval times,
> O first one after whom developed everything that appeared, the one who made the sky as something that his heart created, who raised it by the act of Shu supporting it, who founded the earth by fashioning (it) himself, who surrounded it with the *nun* and the sea, who made the *duat* and sanctified the dead, who caused Re to travel that he might resuscitate them as lord of eternal repetition (*neheh*) and eternal duration (*djet*).[77]

In this passage, Ptah is identified with another Memphite creator-god Ta-tenen, whose name meant 'the risen land', i.e. 'the land risen from the primeval water'.[78] The implication is that Ptah emerged from the *nun* in the form of Ta-tenen before causing the sky to be raised above the earth. Shu is here seen in his usual role of supporting the sky, while Re is seen in his usual role of the sun-god repeating creation in his travels around the skies and passage through the *duat*.

Ta-tenen also features prominently in the Berlin Papyrus 3048, or, as it is often referred to, the Berlin Hymn to Ptah. This text provides further information on the creation of the earth:

> You knit together the earth, you assembled your own limbs, you embraced your own members, and found yourself alone, the one who made his seat, the one who fashioned the Two Lands... When you stood up on the land in its inertness, it drew together thereafter, you

Figure 12.
PTAH, SHOWN MUMMIFORM (AS USUAL) WITH HIS SYMBOL THE DJED-PILLAR.

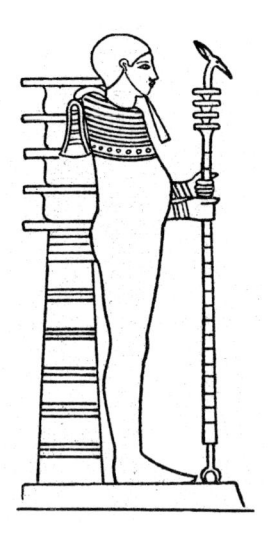

> being in your form of Ta-tenen, in your appearance of 'the Unifier of the Two Lands'.[79]

In this papyrus, as in the Great Harris Papyrus, Ptah brings things into existence by 'building', 'fashioning', and 'smelting', in keeping with his reputation as a craftsman-god.[80] However, in our third text, the Shabaka Stone, otherwise known as *The Theology of Memphis*, Ptah creates the world by means of his heart and his tongue. His heart conceives the plan, and his tongue, in co-ordination with his lips and teeth, announces it.[81] Unfortunately, the text does not reveal the details of this plan, but it does offer an insight into the origin of the gods, whom Ptah is said to bear in his name of Ta-tenen, 'the risen land':

> Ptah is the one who made everything and brought the gods into being. He is indeed Ta-tenen, who gave birth to the gods, from whom everything came forth... So the gods entered into their bodies – of every kind of wood, of every kind of stone, of every kind of clay, or anything that might grow upon him, in which they had taken form. So all the gods, as well as their *kau*, gathered to him, content and associated with the Lord of the Two Lands.[82]

This is an important passage which suggests that the gods were born from the primeval mound, after it had emerged from the *nun*.

Khnum, the Potter-god

Khnum was the creator-god at Elephantine (ancient name Abu, 'Elephant City'),[83] an island at the first Nile cataract which marked the southern border of Egypt. His name, written Chnmu, may have derived from the verb *chnm*, meaning 'to join' or 'to protect'.[84]

According to Egyptian belief, Elephantine was the place where the Nile had originated to fertilize the Two Lands, having flooded forth from the *nun* via two underground caverns.[85] As the god of this island, Khnum was intimately linked to the source of the Nile. In one text, he claims to be an alter ego of both Nun and the Nile-god:

> I am the self-created god, Nun, the Great One, who came into being at the beginning, and I am Hapi [the Nile-god], who rises at my desire.[86]

On account of his associations with the water and the earth, as well as the minerals of the Aswan region, Khnum was renowned as a potter-god and craftsman-god. As early as the Pyramid Texts, he is named as the builder of a cosmic boat and a ladder for reaching the sky,[87] while in later times he became the god who moulded living creatures on his potter's wheel and fashioned the world out of clay and stone.[88] But he also represented the spirit immanent in all creation, and hence assumed the head of a flat-horned ram – a powerful fertility symbol (figure 13).

Figure 13.
KHNUM, CREATING LIFE ON HIS POTTER'S WHEEL.

Unfortunately, we do not possess a narrative account of the creation by Khnum. However, New Kingdom texts do contain summaries of the god's titles and epithets which, despite their formulaic nature, provide some insight into the usual themes of creation. These include:

> Fashioner of men, maker of the gods, the father who was in the beginning.

> Maker of the things which are, shaper of the things which shall be... the father of fathers and the mother of mothers.

> Father of the fathers of the gods and goddesses, lord of things that he creates from himself, maker of the sky, the earth, and the *duat*, and the water and the mountains.

> The one who raises the sky upon its four pillars and supports it there for ever.[89]

Amun, the Hidden God

Amun was the creator-god at Thebes (ancient name Waset, 'City of the *Was*-sceptre'),[90] one of Egypt's most important religious centres during the Middle Kingdom and New Kingdom. His name meant 'the hidden one' or 'the one who conceals himself'.[91]

In the Pyramid Texts, Amun receives only brief mention, once in an obscure pairing with Amaunet (his female partner) and once as the god of a throne on which the king sits – a possible allusion to the primeval mound.[92] In later periods, however, numerous hymns expand on Amun's role as creator-god, reflecting Thebes' newly-acquired status as capital of Upper Egypt. Among these, there is one particularly detailed text known as the Papyrus Leiden, or 'Great Hymn to Amun', which brings many of Egypt's creator-gods together under the umbrella of Amun. This hymn is too lengthy to be reproduced in full, but four passages are significant for the light they shed on the creation myth.

In the eightieth chapter, we read:

> Your body was hidden among the old ones; you concealed yourself as Amun at the head of the gods. You developed yourself into Ta-tenen, in order to cause the Primeval Ones to be born from your original primeval state. Your beauty was raised aloft as *ka-mut.ef* ('bull of the mother') and you distanced yourself in the sky, as the one established in the sun... You began development with nothing, without the world being empty of you on the first occasion. All gods developed after you.[93]

There are a number of interesting ideas here. Firstly, it is suggested that the gods, the Primeval Ones, were born from the primeval mound Ta-tenen (compare the Ptah Ta-tenen myth). Secondly, the lifting of the *ka-mut.ef* is an allusion to a sacred stone (see chapter eleven). Thirdly, the god appears to develop from the mound into the sun which orbits it. And fourthly, the penultimate line indicates that the cosmos pre-existed in an unshaped form, personified by Amun himself. This creation was not *ex nihilo*.

Turning to the ninetieth chapter, we read:

> You emerged first, you began from the beginning, O Amun, whose identity is hidden from the gods... The one who appeared in the sun out of the primeval waters, that he might rejuvenate himself. The one who sneezed as Atum from his mouth and gave birth to Shu and Tefnut combined in manifestation... Light was his development on the first occasion, when all that exists was in stillness for awe of him. He honked by voice, as the Great Honker, at the District, creating for himself while he was alone. He began speaking in the midst of silence, opening every eye and causing them to look. He began crying out while the world was in stillness, his yell in circulation while he had no companion, in order that he give birth to what exists and cause it to live...[94]

Here it is stated that the sun was born from the primeval waters; the same line intimates that the sun's role was to ensure the constant rejuvenation of itself (by circulating through the skies and the *duat*, see earlier). The next line is borrowed from the Atum myth and illustrates how creational themes were fluid and non-exclusive (note again the oddity of the sneeze from the mouth). There follows a reference to the creation of light; this is not the light of the sun, but the light of the creator-soul which emerges from the darkness of the *nun*. Finally, it is suggested that the breaking of light was accompanied by the breaking of sound. The Great Honker is probably a reference to Geb, who in the form of a goose laid the egg of the universe.[95] The District (*swau*) where he honked is thought to be an allusion to the primeval mound.[96]

In the hundredth chapter, we are given further insights into the origin of Amun:

> The one who came into being on the first occasion, Amun, who developed in the beginning, whose nature is unknown. No god came into being prior to him; there was no other god with him who might tell of his form; there was no mother for whom his name was made, no father who begot him and said: "This is I". The one who smelted his

own egg, a power mysterious of birth, the creator of his (own) beauty, the divine god who came into being by himself, all the gods developed after he developed himself.[97]

Here, it is emphasised that Amun was self-created. He originated from an egg, but this egg was not fertilized by a father or laid by a mother; it was smelted by Amun himself. This passage picks up on an earlier reference to the egg (not cited here) in which Amun is called 'the one who knit his semen together with his body to create his egg in isolation, the *kheperu kheperu*, bearer of birth'.[98]

Our final selection comes from the two-hundredth chapter:

Re himself is united with his body; he is the Great One who is in Heliopolis. He is also called Ta-tenen, the Amun who emerged from the primeval waters that he might guide mankind. Another of his developments is the Hermopolitans; he is the Primeval One (*pauti*) who begot the Primeval Ones (*pautiu*) and caused Re to be born. He completed himself in Atum, a single body with him; he is Neber-djer, who brought being into being.[99]

Here, Amun is associated with an array of other important creator-gods; his body is Osiris (with whom Re unites in Heliopolis);[100] another of his forms is Ta-tenen, the primeval mound; another is Atum, the completed cosmos; another is Neber-djer, the uttermost limits of the cosmos; and another is the Primeval One. Interestingly, Re is referred to as a second generation god – one born of the Primeval One. The Hermopolitans are mythical beings, in this context probably the eight creator-deities known as the Ogdoad (see later).[101]

Horus and the Shebtiu

Earlier, we encountered Horus the son of Isis – the falcon who broke out of the womb, or egg, and soared up into the sky to become the great god whose eyes were the sun and the moon. But elsewhere in Egypt, Horus was an independent creator-god of great antiquity, who had no ostensible connection to the myth of Isis and Osiris. One of the most important of these many Horus-cults, or falcon-cults, existed at Edfu (ancient name Wetjeset-Hor, 'the Place where Horus is Raised Up').[102]

The temple of Horus at Edfu, constructed during the Ptolemaic period, contains a series of inscriptions, the so-called Building Texts, in which is found one of the best preserved and most detailed creation accounts in Egypt. Although the texts are admittedly difficult to interpret, owing to the apparent combination of several parallel traditions involving a wide range of gods, it is nevertheless possible to reconstruct a central myth in which the cosmos is created by the Falcon (Horus) in conjunction with a group of deities named the Shebtiu. These inscriptions, despite their comparatively recent origin (*c.* 250 BC), almost certainly draw on much older material.

The myth begins with the primeval waters (here called *hbbt*), in which there is a region called *waret*, signifying a stagnant pool of reeds.[103] All is in darkness. Suddenly, the waters of *waret* are filled with a radiant light, and the reeds float to its surface.[104] At the same time, the god Heter-her (an image of Horus) appears hovering over the primeval waters.[105] Also, two divine beings, Wa and Aa, leaders of the Shebtiu-gods, emerge from the *waret*, perceive the floating raft of reeds, and make their home upon it.[106]

The next event is shrouded in mystery, but signifies the resurrection of the creator-god. One of the floating reeds is split in two, and the upper half is planted in the primeval water, possibly in a field of reeds that still remains submerged beneath the surface.[107] This reed is called 'the pole that uplifts the god' (*nbi wtjs ntjr*),[108] and it becomes a perch (*djeba*) for the Falcon, who henceforth becomes known as 'Lord of Djeba'.[109] The *djeba*-perch is said to be situated in a place called Wetjeset-Netjer, 'the Place where the God is Raised Up'.[110] A variant tradition in the Edfu texts states that the Falcon was uplifted on the willow tree which grew radiant.[111]

At this time, the flood still covered the fields of reeds, and firm ground had yet to appear.[112] But the Shebtiu then performed a magic rite *su akht ta*, 'investing with power the earth-substances',[113] and upon utterance of their magic spells the waters receded and the earth – in the form of '*pay-lands*' – began to emerge.[114] This process culminated, so it would seem, in the creation of the Great Primeval Mound (*khay-wr*), which was also called 'the Great Place' and 'the Territory of the Circuit'.[115]

Unfortunately, the Edfu texts contain few references to the creation of the sky and the celestial bodies; their focus is rather on the creation of the earth. However, the mention of the Great Primeval Mound, which is 'the Territory of the Circuit', might well imply that the stars, sun, and moon were created to orbit the earth, and in addition there are suggestive lines such as 'the Shebtiu sailed' (having completed their creative tasks) and 'the Falcon united with the sky'.[116] In any event, it is a commonplace in Egyptian mythology that Horus as a falcon flew up to become the sky-god whose two eyes were the sun and the moon.

The Primeval Ones and the Great Lotus

The temple of Horus at Edfu contains a second creation myth, which is rarely reported in the popular Egyptological literature. It features in the ritual scenes of 'Offering the Lotus' and draws to a significant extent on the traditions of Hermopolis (see later).[117] Such is the detail of this myth that it is possible to compile a sequence of diagrams (these are presented here for the first time), which show the initial stages of the development of life and matter in the primeval ocean and the subsequent emergence of the primeval island.

As usual, the creation myth begins with the primeval ocean (*nun*) in a state of darkness. Suddenly, there appear on the scene a group of gods, the Primeval Ones (*pautiu*), who fertilize an inner part of the *nun* called *bnnt*. The text addresses these gods thus:

> You placed your seed into the *bnnt* which you fertilized with your phallus (*wba iwau*), which you have plunged into *nun*, being united as one.[118]

This mysterious *bnnt* is said to exist as a discrete place 'in the *nun*' and we may envisage it as a womb or unfertilized ovum. As a result of its fertilization by the Primeval Ones, the *bnnt* develops into an egg (*swht*); the Primeval Ones are thus said to be 'the ones who were first to beget and to create the egg'.[119]

The Edfu texts go on to refer to 'the island of the egg' (*iw swht*), an image perhaps suggested by the egg floating in the waters of *nun* like an island.[120] The Primeval Ones make their home in this island of the egg, and proceed to create therein their own physical forms or embodiments (*djt*), although these forms have yet to realise their final shape.[121]

Eventually, the island of the egg, inhabited by the Primeval Ones, rises within the *nun*, breaches its surface, and hatches, whereupon a domain of light is born. The genesis of the light is the pivotal moment in this myth, and is to be understood as the prelude for the origin of the stars, the sun, and the moon.

At its hatching the island of the egg acquires a new name – the isle of flames (*iw nsrsr*) – signifying the birth of the light.[122] This island contains a pool (*sh*) from which the creator-god emerges in the form of the Great Lotus (*nkhb wr*). The Great Lotus is said to be 'the ruler of the Primeval Ones, the First Primeval One (*pauti tpi*), who came into being before the Primeval Ones'.[123]

The texts explain that the Great Lotus is brought forth from the pool by the *djt*-forms of the Primeval Ones. In a scene of Offering the Lotus, the Primeval Ones are told:

58   THE MIDNIGHT SUN

> Take for yourselves that god who resides in his pool (*sh*). He was led from your embodiment (*djt*), the Great Lotus (*nkhb wr*) who issued from the pool in the isle of flames (*iw nsrsr*), the district of the beginning (*spt hat*), which initiated light ever since the first occasion in the high hill (*qay qaa*), at the beginning of coming-into-being.[124]

And similarly, in another scene of Offering the Lotus:

> Receive for yourself that god who resides in his pool, who initiated the light at the first occasion, the Great Lotus who emerged from the pool in the isle of flames, the district of the beginning.[125]

In these inscriptions, the Great Lotus is praised as the creator of the light – the light of the stars, the sun, and the moon. However, the Primeval Ones too were revered as the creators of the light, since it was they who had brought forth the Great Lotus. The Edfu texts thus refer to these gods as:

> The lords of the light, the makers of the radiance and sunlight, who were first to illumine and to give the light.[126]

> The creators of the light... who illumined this land when they came forth unitedly, who created the light by the work of their hands.[127]

The texts suggest that this 'coming forth' involved the spiritualization of the *djt*-forms of the Primeval Ones in the mounds of the lands (*iawt n tawi*).[128] The Primeval Ones were thus said to have 'created themselves' and 'issued from themselves'.[129]

The Edfu texts also incorporate the tradition that Re was the god of the light. In one text, it is said that Re 'came into being in the great pool (*sh-wr*) and was led forth from *nun* within the lotus', while another informs us that Re came forth as a child from the egg which opened within the lotus.[130] (These ideas are not incompatible if we visualise the egg opening directly beneath the lotus.) Significantly, the texts treat Re as a second generation god – a stripling, heir, or child. Moreover, they describe how Re burnt everything in the environs of the egg when his *two flaming eyes* were born from the isle of flames.[131] This would seem to imply that Re's light was not just that of the sun but also that of the moon – the two eyes of the creator-god.

Finally, we should note the contradictory nature of the Primeval Ones. On the one hand, they are portrayed as an exclusively male group – 'the males without female among them'.[132] But on the other hand, they are portrayed as males and females – 'the fathers who fertilized, the mothers who gave birth', 'the bulls who impregnated, the cows who conceived',

THE CREATION 59

Figure 14. THE EVOLUTION OF THE ISLAND OF CREATION.

STAGE 1: AN UNFERTILIZED OVUM IN THE NUN.

STAGE 2: THE FERTILIZED OVUM BECOMES AN EGG.

STAGE 3: THE EGG FLOATS TO THE SURFACE OF THE NUN.

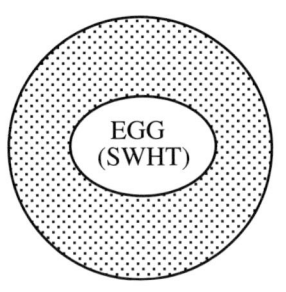

STAGE 4: THE EGG HATCHES AND A LOTUS EMERGES.

STAGE 5: THE SUN-GOD EMERGES FROM THE LOTUS.

and 'the gods who created sexual pleasure, the goddesses who bore forth the egg that fertilized them'.[133] It is this latter idea, as we shall now see, that underlies the myth of the Ogdoad.

The Ogdoad

The Ogdoad was a company of eight creator-gods at Hermopolis (ancient name Khmnu, 'City of the Eight'), one of the oldest religious centres in Egypt.[134] The eight gods comprised four male-and-female couples, who each personified aspects of primeval chaos: Nun and Nunet (the waters), Heh and Hehet (the flood),[135] Kek and Keket (the darkness), and Amun and Amaunet (invisible wind).[136] The male-gods were frog-headed and the females serpent-headed.[137]

The myth of the Ogdoad begins, as is usual, with a primeval ocean in a state of darkness and flood. Suddenly, there appears a mysterious wind which stirs the waters into motion and creates a vortex of energy.[138] The Ogdoad, until now in a state of division and lassitude, push themselves together into a single force, and form a mound of land, presumably from the mud in the depths of the abyss.[139] This land then rises from the waters in the form of a hill (*qay*) onto which the Ogdoad steps and creates light (*shu*).[140] The Ogdoad are thus called 'the fathers and mothers who made the light', 'the men and women who created the light', or 'the waters that made the light'.[141]

The Ogdoad are also said to be 'the fathers and the mothers who gave birth to Re', who here probably signifies the light of creation rather than sunlight or the sun disc.[142] All known versions of the Hermopolis myth climax with the birth of Re, who is said to emerge from the egg, or from the lotus which is in the pool of the isle of flames in Hermopolis.[143] Here, there is an overlap with the myth of the Great Lotus (*nkhb wr*), who emerged from the pool by means of the embodiment of the Primeval Ones and 'initiated the light at the first occasion' (see earlier). The Edfu texts confirm this connection: in two instances the inscription refers to the Primeval Ones but the deities represented are the Ogdoad.[144] In both cases, then, the creator-god comes forth from the abyss as a result of a group of gods coming together into a unity.

Creation by the Goddess

For the most part, the creator-god in Egypt is portrayed as a masculine power who acts alone. However, some myths place an emphasis on a feminine power working alongside the god. Earlier, we encountered the mysterious Eye which Atum sent out from the abyss; we observed how the goddess Isis appeared as prime mover in her role of revivifying Osiris and giving birth to Horus; and in the myth of the Ogdoad we noted that four of the eight primeval powers were conceived as female. And yet a number of Egyptian myths go further in confirming the importance of a feminine power behind the creation. In this section, we will consider briefly the myths of two creator-goddesses, Hathor and Neit.

Hathor was popular throughout Egypt, but her primary cult centre was at Dendera (ancient name Iunet, 'City of the Pillar').[145] In this town she was worshipped from archaic times in the form of a cow – the ultimate symbol of fertility and motherhood.[146] Hathor's name meant 'Mansion of Horus', which is assumed by scholars to refer to the surface of the sky on which the falcon-god flew.[147] In keeping with this identification, her epithets included 'Lady of the Sky', 'the Golden One', and 'Lady of the Stars'.[148]

Although a detailed narrative of Hathor's creation myth is lacking, we do possess some interesting fragments. The earliest allusions appear in the Coffin Texts, which refer to her ascent to the sky:

Hathor rises within the *akhet*... her entourage is about her.[149]

Weaving the dress for Hathor. The mountain is broken asunder, the stone is split, the caverns of Hathor are broken open; she ascends in turquoise...[150]

In addition, the Edfu texts record the sacred marriage rite of Hathor and Horus, the goddess being praised therein as 'she who brought the gods

Figure 15.
HATHOR AS A STAR-SPANGLED COW.

into the world', 'the one who fashioned mankind', 'she who formed the animals', 'the one who created every offering and brought greenery into being'.[151] According to this myth, Hathor conceived a son for Horus of Edfu, and returned to Dendera where she gave birth to him in his name Hor-sma-tawi, 'Horus who Unites the Two Lands'.[152]

This myth of the divine child was central to Hathor's role as a creator-goddess. In another myth, which became the subject of a mystery play at Dendera,[153] her son appears as Ihy, 'the sistrum-player', who according to the Coffin Texts had emerged from her egg (or womb) and ascended to the sky:

> Look, I have come as Lord of the Entourage... I am the sistrum-player, the son of Hathor. I am indeed the great seed. I have passed between her thighs in this my name 'Jackal of the Light'. I have broken out of the egg, I have flowed on its *sfs*, I have glided on its blood, I am the Lord of Blood, I am a raging bull... I am the child of my mother, I am a youth, the son of Hathor, I am the inert one who was in the *nun*.[154]

Once again, we find a close association between the *nun* and a cosmic egg.

Hathor's name may also testify to her role as mother-goddess. In one Egyptian text it is explained: '(the child is) inside her body; inside her a mansion (*hwt*) of Horus is being prepared, hence her name is Hathor (i.e. 'Mansion of Horus').[155] Hathor would thus appear to be an alter ego of Isis, from whose egg-like womb the falcon-god was born.[156] It is possible that her hieroglyphic name – a falcon inside an enclosure – signified not only the realm of Horus in the sky but more fundamentally the place in which Horus was conceived. The latter idea is also consistent with her identity as Lady of Amentet, referring to the hidden netherworld that lay beyond the western horizon.[157]

In keeping with her identity as 'mother of the god', Hathor was also the goddess behind the great cycle of rebirth in the natural world. As the historian E.O. James has put it: 'she was the great mother of the world, the personification of creative power in nature, and the mother of every god and goddess in heaven and on earth, all of whom were regarded as her forms though they might be worshipped under a variety of names'.[158]

Turning to Neit, this creator-goddess was based at the city of Sais (ancient name Sau, possibly 'Guardian City').[159] It has been suggested that her name signified primeval waters, although it might also be read as 'the Terrifying One' in keeping with her image as an arrow-bearing war-goddess.[160]

As early as the 4th dynasty, Neit was the goddess of the lower sky, who conceived and gave birth to the sun-god every day, in re-enactment of creation.[161] In keeping with this role, she is described in New Kingdom texts as 'the god's mother who bore Re',[162] and 'the eldest one, mother of the gods, who shone in the primeval time'.[163]

In the late period, Neit received the formulaic title 'father of fathers' and 'mother of mothers'.[164] It was said that 'she came into being when nothing else existed and created that which exists after she came into being'.[165] It was she who had 'fashioned the seed of gods and men'.[166] At this time, Neit was worshipped as 'the one god' – a virgin mother who had acted alone.[167]

But the most complete narrative of Neit's creation is preserved in the temple of Khnum at Esna, dating to the Roman period. Here, we learn that Neit emerged from the primeval waters and brought the primeval mound into being by pronouncing its name. Having rested on the mound (on which the temple would later be built), she created the light and the gods, and prophesied the birth of a child, the sun-god. The creation was perfected when this newborn sun rose from the *akhet* and appeared in the world.[168]

An Overview of Creation

What is to be made of the Egyptian creation myths? If the reader finds them bewildering, he may take consolation from the fact that the experts find them bewildering too. Even so, a number of constant themes can be recognised, and these form a framework for deciphering the less clear aspects.

All of the myths agree that in the beginning the cosmos consisted of a primeval ocean, *nun*, which apparently contained material in the form of mud or reeds. These elements were initially inert, but were brought into motion by the creator-god who stirred as a soul in the waters.

According to some myths, the creator-god was alone, but according to others he was accompanied by a goddess or a company of gods. In the former version, the creator created himself, whereas in the latter versions he was brought into being by the goddess or the gods (these gods are thus said to be 'the fathers and the mothers'). This is one of the most puzzling 'inconsistencies' in the corpus of creation texts.

The first physical change of creation was the emergence of an island or mound from the primeval waters. This land may have coagulated in the depths of *nun* prior to its emergence. It is portrayed as an egg and an isle of flames, and is personified by the creator-god Ta-tenen, 'the risen land'. In the Edfu myth, this land first took shape as a reed marsh, but it is seemingly understood that it eventually dried out to form the solid land of the earth, 'the Two Lands'.[169]

What happened next is pivotal, but is only vaguely described in the texts. According to one myth, the primeval mound split open, like an egg or a womb. This marked the birth of Re, the birth of the gods, and the creation of light. In some ill-defined way, these events led to the creation of the sky and the celestial bodies.

The creation of the sky (the celestial ocean) is explained by the myth of Shu. Expelled from Atum's body by means of a penile ejaculation or sneeze, Shu was said to have separated the sky from the earth, apparently by the pressure of his air. Thus was created the atmosphere. However, the role of his partner Tefnut is not well defined, and nor is it clear how the sun, moon, and stars developed in the sky. The texts do contain some allusions to these crucial events, but these have never been deciphered by Egyptologists, and must be reserved for consideration in later chapters.

The role of Re in the creation of the sky is crucial. To Egyptologists, he is the sun-god and the self-created creator-god. However, although Re does appear as creator in some myths, a prominent theme of this chapter, which ought to give scholars pause for thought, is that Re mostly features in a secondary context. He does not usually 'create', but rather 'appears', and his appearance usually coincides with the creation of light. By light, I do not mean sunlight, since strictly speaking the sun at this stage had not yet been created. Rather, I mean primeval light – the light of creation. The classic exposition of this idea occurs in Spell 17 of the Book of the Dead, where the creator-god declares: "I was Atum when I was alone in the primeval ocean; I was Re in his glorious appearances when he began to rule what he had made."[170] For the same reason, we may presume, it is rare to find Re pre-existent in the *nun*; when he does appear there, at the beginning of all things, he tends to be in the form of the beetle Khepri, the self-created creator who originally may have had no connection with the sun cult.[171]

The path forks at this point. Traditional Egyptology maintains that the Egyptian religion was a sun cult, and that the sun-god Re was the creator of the universe. Although it acknowledges the creation to be an important concept, it finds the creation myths to be of no further value, regarding them as an incoherent and unfathomable mishmash of ideas. There is no way, in its view, that these tangled myths can support the full weight of Egyptian religion.

I beg to differ from this orthodoxy.

It is my intention in this book to demonstrate that the supreme god of Egypt was the creator-god, whose role is to be distinguished from that of the sun-god.

The creator-god, I will argue, personifies the ineffable power behind the creation of the universe as well as the process of creation itself. His identity is therefore to be found in the myth of creation, which contrary to the beliefs of traditional Egyptology actually represents a coherent theory of the origins of the universe.

The logic of this ancient cosmogony has eluded modern scholars for two reasons: firstly, because of the Egyptians' reluctance to write about it in scientific fashion; and secondly, because of the gulf that has developed between ancient and modern modes of thought.

My aim is to rationalise the physics and philosophy of the creation myth, and thereby restore it to its rightful place at the heart of Egyptian religion.

As for the sun-god, it is not my intention to question his importance in Egypt, but rather to demonstrate that his role and mythology best make sense in the context of a 'cult of creation', that is to say a cult whose aim was to perpetuate the cosmic order (*maat*) by constantly re-enacting the events of creation.

Chapter Three Summary

- The time has come to put aside the solar bias that has afflicted Egyptology for the past two centuries and to reconsider the significance of the creation in ancient Egypt.

- The roles of the creator-god and sun-god must be distinguished. The former created the cosmos. The latter was assigned by the former to maintain it.

- There were many different creator-gods in Egypt and several different versions of the creation myth.

- Despite certain inconsistencies – which will be resolved in subsequent chapters – the creation myths share a number of central themes: the origin of all things from a primeval ocean (*nun*); the emergence from that ocean of an island (*iw*) or mound (*iat*) which became the earth (*ta*); and the separation of the sky (*pet*) from the earth and the primeval waters.

- Re, the supposed sun-god, is usually cited in the creation myths as the god of light – the emerged form of the creator-god.

CHAPTER FOUR

POWER IN THE EARTH

The beetle was believed to create itself in the earth and was therefore a fitting symbol for a self-created god.
(Henri Frankfort, *Ancient Egyptian Religion*, 1948)

Egyptology believes that the sun was not only the centre of the Egyptian cosmos but also its source. In its interpretation of the creation myth, it was the sun-god who stirred in the darkness of the primeval ocean; the sun-god who created the primeval mound; the sun-god who fought and annihilated the forces of chaos; and the sun-god who separated the sky from the earth and rose up to become ruler of the cosmos. According to Stephen Quirke, writing in *The Cult of Ra*, all the disparate sources from three thousand years of Egyptian religious history 'provide substantially consistent evidence for a single, coherent picture of creation as an act of the sun'.[1]

How does this orthodoxy square with our review of the creation myths in chapter three? Yes, there was a myth in which the sun-god Re created the universe. However, as a general rule Re appeared in the guise of a second generation god: he was the son of Atum; the son of the Primeval One; the son of Nut; and he was brought into being by the Primeval Ones or the Ogdoad. Other texts reinforce this impression: in the Coffin Texts, Re is said to be the offspring of frog-goddesses;[2] in a solar hymn, he is the son of Ta-tenen and Nunet;[3] and in the inscriptions at Medamud, he is created by ancestor-gods at the site of the primeval mound.[4]

Moreover, in the earliest texts there is a conspicuous lack of a creation by Re. The Pyramid Texts instead place emphasis on a creation by Atum or the beetle-god Kheprer.

As for the later sources, they often attribute the creation to a god who is not ostensibly a sun-god, such as Ptah, Khnum, or Amun.

How, then, can Egyptologists possibly maintain that creation was an act of the sun? The explanation lies in the power of preconception. For two hundred years, it has been believed that Egyptian religion was a sun cult; therefore, it is reasoned, the sun-god *must* have been the creator. To this end, *assumptions* have been made, which through constant repetition have attained the status of facts. In particular, that Heliopolis was a city of the sun; that Atum was a solar creator-god; and Kheprer likewise.[5] In this way, scholars have convinced themselves that the creation really was an act of the sun-god.

I wish to question this consensus.

Take, for example, the assumption that Heliopolis was a city of the sun. This is an important issue, since this city was the religious capital of Egypt and the cult centre of Atum and Re. If it was the home of a solar cult, then this would indeed argue strongly for a solar religion and a solar creation. But the facts simply do not support the stance that Egyptology has taken. Yes, the name 'Heliopolis' translates as 'City of the Sun', but it does so in Greek! Many scholars take this name at face value – even those who have a background in classical studies – because it fits their preconception that Atum and Re were sun-gods. However, the Egyptian name of Heliopolis was Iunu, written with a pillar hieroglyph , which literally meant 'Pillar City'.[6] Of course, there is no reason to suppose that the pillar was an inherently solar symbol. Generally in the myths, pillars are associated with the lifting up of the creator-god and the raising of the sky. In the case of Heliopolis, if this city was named after the pillar of the *benben* stone, as seems likely, then it would indeed have been an icon of creation – an image perhaps of the phallus of Atum (see chapter three).[7] Heliopolis would therefore be the centre of a 'cult of creation'.

This is not to deny that a sun cult was practised at Heliopolis. Rather, it is to suggest that the sun was worshipped there for its role in repeating the creation, with the aim of ensuring the immortality of the cosmos (see chapter one). This would also explain the evidence for a stellar cult, and possibly a lunar cult too, at Heliopolis.[8] This is not an entirely new idea to Egyptology. In 1959, R.T. Rundle Clark wrote:

> The temple which enclosed the *benben* stone was the centre of calendrical rites as well as the scene of the rising of the High God. It was the place where the mysteries of creation were ceremonially repeated.[9]

Unfortunately, Clark's theory of Egyptian myth was shipwrecked by the prevailing winds of solar orthodoxy.

Equally untenable is the assumption that Atum and Kheprer were solar creator-gods. Granted, they featured in the mythology of the sun – as the setting sun and rising sun respectively. But the rationale for this myth lay in the sun's re-enactment of creation. For the myth to work properly, the sun-god had to be identified with a creator-god in the western horizon, and a creator-god in the east. When the sun-god claimed "I am Khepri in the morning, Re at midday, Atum in the evening",[10] he was asserting his *origin from* the creator in the form of Atum 'the non-being' and Khepri 'the becoming one'. Atum and Khepri were not solar creator-gods; they were creator-gods pure and simple, who for understandable reasons were co-opted into the cult of the sun.

What, then, is the alternative to this heliocentric view of the creation myth? If the sun was not at the centre of creation, then what was?

According to the Egyptians, 'the earth and the *nun*' were at the centre of creation. It was from the earth and the primeval waters that the sky was separated.[11] This idea is exemplified by the creator-god Kheprer (in later writing Khepri), whose image and name were inspired by the scarab beetle (*khprr*) . This insect was born from the earth – from a ball of dung which had been buried in the sand – but also from the waters – its appearance coincided with the rise of the Nile.[12]

Egyptology indeed acknowledges that some creation myths portray the creator as a chthonian power and the earth as first cause. Supposedly, these myths are the exception, not the rule. But I intend to show that the opposite is true: that the rule was for creation from the primeval earth, or to be more precise from the earth and the *nun*. The creation myth is thus found to be geocentric, not heliocentric.

The idea of a geocentric creation may strike the Egyptologist as odd, since it implies the creation of the outer cosmos (the atmosphere, the sky, and the bodies in the sky) from a terrestrial centre. This is contrary to the orthodox view, as expressed by J.P. Allen for example, which envisages an infinite cosmos, unchanging in size. If the reader will indulge me, I would like to defer this controversy to chapter six, where the relative merits of the geocentric theory and Allen's theory can be compared and contrasted.

For now, I wish to focus on facts rather than theories. In this chapter, I aim to demonstrate that chthonian creation was not the exception but the rule in ancient Egypt.

Ptah and Ta-tenen

One of Egypt's most important cities, rivalling Heliopolis, was Memphis, the legendary place of the 'unification of the Two Lands'.[13] It was here that the gods ordained kingship for man; here that the sages brought the plans of the gods to fruition by constructing the first temples, palaces, and pyramids of stone; here that the priests brought gods and man into an eternal harmony for the benefit of the cosmos. While Heliopolis was the centre of Egypt's sexual energy, Memphis was the centre of its thought and emotions. It was the veritable heart of the Two Lands.

Memphis was the home of Ptah, the craftsman-god, the moulder of the cosmos, gods and men. But it was also the cult centre of Ta-tenen, 'the land risen from the primeval water', and of Sokar, a hawk-god who was associated with iron (*bja*), the netherworld, and the sky.[14] The cults of Ta-tenen and Sokar at Memphis are particularly ancient, and it is likely that Ptah co-opted them into his cult, thus becoming Ptah Ta-tenen and Ptah-Sokar (by Middle Kingdom times, the latter god was expanded into the form Ptah-Sokar-Osiris).

It is universally accepted in Egyptology that the creation by Ptah is a chthonian myth. This is certainly the intention in the Shabaka Stone (*The Theology of Memphis*), where Ptah in the form of Ta-tenen gives birth to the gods and all things. It is also the case in several other texts, notably the Great Harris Papyrus, Berlin Papyrus 3048, and Berlin Papyrus 13603. The common theme in all these texts is that Ptah gave birth to the cosmos in his identity of Ta-tenen, the primeval mound; it is said that he used his heart to create the sky.[15] But there is no suggestion that Ptah himself was anything but an earth-god, and in one text he is indeed called 'the *agrty* earth-god'.[16]

Supposedly, the creation by Ptah Ta-tenen represented an aberration in the normal solar scheme of things. Henri Frankfort thus wrote about *The Theology of Memphis*: 'We have seen that the most novel feature of this theology consists in its claim that the earth, and not the sun, was the first cause.'[17] But was it really such a novelty? Or was it a more fundamental idea?

The Earth-god at Edfu

The belief that the earth was the first cause and the creator an earth-god is found also in the Building Texts of the temple of Horus at Edfu. These texts, translated and published for the first time by Eve Reymond in 1969,[18] record the history and significance of the Egyptian temple in unprecedented detail.[19] But they also offer a unique insight into the mythical origins of the temple, whose original form was held to be the handiwork of the earth-god. In examining Reymond's findings, it is important for us to bear in mind that the Egyptian temple was conceived to be a simulacrum of the cosmos (see chapter fifteen).[20] In building the temple, therefore, the earth-god was at the same time constructing the universe.

Reymond's study is divided into two parts. In the first part, she deals with those inscriptions which relate to the mythical origin of the Edfu temples. In the second part, she deals with those inscriptions which relate to the primeval world of the gods.

The temple material comprises two different traditions. One relates to the origins of the temples and sacred domains of the Falcon. The other relates to the origins of the temples of the sun-god Re. For convenience, these may be designated 'the Falcon texts' and 'the Sun-god texts'.

The Falcon texts refer to the construction of temples, but concentrate in the main on the origin of earlier, primitive structures, namely a shelter (*nht*) and a perch (*djba*) for the Falcon. These inscriptions emphasise the mythical origins of the Falcon's domains, explaining that when the first land emerged from the primeval ocean it became the 'foundation ground' on which the shelter, perch, and temples were built.

The Sun-god texts focus on the construction of temples, and seemingly provide the dimensions of actual buildings (though they are not known to archaeology).[21] These inscriptions provide less useful information on the mythical origins of the temple (they tend to focus on the sun-god's battle against an enemy snake).[22]

The two sets of texts cover much common ground; they refer to many of the same deities and similar themes. However, while the Falcon texts seem to cite pure myth, the Sun-god texts seem to cite historical rituals in which the temple was founded in re-enactment of myth.

The Falcon texts are the source of the creation myth of Horus and the Shebtiu (see chapter three). The texts begin with the events preceding the emergence of land from the primeval ocean (*hbbt*). In the beginning, primeval matter and water are mingled together in an abyss of darkness and chaos. The primeval matter is reed, and it seems to come together to form a reed marsh, or swamp, called *waret*. This submerged proto-earth is described as an island (*iw*) and a 'foundation ground' (*sntjt*), which will in due course emerge from the waters of *waret/hbbt* to form the risen earth, the primeval mound or island of creation.[23] The texts concentrate on this process of land formation and on the ensuing construction of the shelter, perch, and temples for the Falcon (these are seemingly built out of reeds).[24] They provide hardly any information on the creation of the sky, and so do not state explicitly that the sky was created *from* the earth and the *waret/hbbt*. However, this process may have been implied by the popular belief that the sky had been separated from the earth. Moreover, as mentioned earlier, it may be that the building of the temple on the land symbolised the creation of the greater cosmos.

According to Reymond, the creator in the Edfu texts is consistently an earth-god. His identity is primarily Ta-tenen, the Memphite god of the primeval mound. But he also appears in other guises, namely Ir-ta, 'the earth-maker' (also called Ir-akht, 'the maker of substances'),[25] Mesenti,[26] and Pn the falcon-god (*pn* means 'this one'; he is in effect unnamed).[27] It is also likely that the First Primeval One (*pauti tpi*), alias the Great Lotus (*nkhb wr*), was an earth-god.

The most striking thing to emerge from the Edfu texts is that the earth-god had a soul, which rose up from the netherworld and orchestrated the building of the primeval temple.[28] This divine soul receives a variety of names: 'the Soul' (*ba*); 'the Spirit' (*ka*); 'the Flying Soul' (*ba-hatty*); and 'the Lord of the Wing' (*ndm-ndb*). According to Reymond, these soul-gods were associated particularly with the Pn-god, and represented his inanimate form, or spiritual likeness.[29]

Significantly, Reymond observed that the Pn-god had seemingly died and been buried in the *duat n ba,* 'the netherworld of the soul' – a realm which lay directly under the island of creation.[30] While his material form had remained buried in the netherworld, his soul, or spirit, had flown up into the realm of light, and made its resting place upon the *djed*-pillar of reed.[31]

Reymond thus concluded that the creator-god's soul (*ba* or *ka*) was the offspring of a deceased earth-god.[32]

The second striking thing to emerge from the Edfu texts is that the primeval temple was regarded as the offspring of the earth. The soul of the earth-god had supposedly emerged from the netherworld to become embodied in the temple.[33] Accordingly, the temple was called 'the son of the earth',[34] and the earth-god Ta-tenen was called 'the ancestor' of the temple.[35]

There is a plausible connection here to the temple of Ptah at Memphis. Its name *Hwt-Ka-Pth*, 'the Mansion of the Ka of Ptah', implies that the spirit (*ka*) of Ptah either filled the temple or was embodied in it.[36] This is the very idea which is preserved in the Edfu records. Since Ptah too was a chthonian power, we may hypothesise that he was the ancestor of this temple, that his spirit rose up from the earth to create it, and that it too was 'the son of the earth'.

What is the significance of the Edfu Building Texts? According to Reymond, the temple foundation myth may have been aetiological, i.e. designed to explain the origin of the foundation ground on which the temples would be built.[37] However, it must surely be relevant that in the late period, and quite probably throughout Egyptian history, the temple was understood to be a simulacrum of the cosmos. It therefore seems likely that the Edfu texts preserve a bona fide creation myth, the soul of the earth-god being responsible for the creation of the greater cosmos upon the foundation ground of the primeval earth which emerged from the waters. And Reymond indeed acknowledges this possibility on page 275 of her epic work by suggesting that the Edfu traditions expanded on the Memphite doctrine of the creation by Ptah and Ta-tenen.[38]

In summary, Reymond's study lends weight to the idea of a chthonian creation and places a serious question mark over the orthodox theory of a solar creation. But its significance in this respect has been overlooked by Egyptology, partly because of the complexity of its subject matter, and partly because of its being designated a work on temple history rather than a work on creational mythology.

The Creation by Atum and Geb

In defence of the solar orthodoxy, it might be argued that the Edfu texts draw on Memphite traditions, and that the primacy of the earth remains the exception to the rule. However, as we shall now see, a similar idea germinated at Heliopolis in the mythologies of Atum and Geb.

As discussed in chapter three, Atum created everything by emanation from himself, and this would have included the earth. Utterance 222 of the Pyramid Texts describes the primeval land as 'this earth which issued from Atum, this spittle which issued from Kheprer'.[39]

Did Atum create the cosmos *from* the earth? This depends totally on how we define the god's original identity. In this regard, an important clue is the tradition that Atum created the cosmos either while alone in the *nun* or while alone in Heliopolis. Since Heliopolis was a microcosm of the primeval mound (as were all major Egyptian cities), it is possible to interpret this myth as a statement of Atum's creation from the earth. In other words, Atum was *in* Heliopolis in the sense that he was *in* the primeval mound.[40]

A possible corroboration of this theory is found in the Coffin Texts, where it is seemingly suggested that Atum came forth from the earth. In Spell 306 it is stated:

> Hail to you Atum, you who made the sky and created what exists, who came forth from the earth, who created seed, Lord of All, who fashioned the gods.[41]

This passage is admittedly not decisive in that Atum's manifestation as seed coming forth from the earth might be interpreted as an expression of his immanence in the latter phase of creation (the appearance of grass, plants and trees upon the earth). However, the text does say that Atum 'came forth from the earth', and his 'seed' might well be interpreted as the cosmic seed which came forth from his phallus or mouth.

It should be noted that in the Coffin Texts Atum also came forth from the primeval waters and the *akhet*.[42] On the significance of the *akhet*, the reader is referred to the discussion in chapter six.

It may be significant that Atum was often associated with the earth-god Geb. The Pyramid Texts attest to an intriguing relationship between the two gods: when Atum gives Geb his heritage, he joins the assembled ennead to him, himself included;[43] the gods are urged to assemble for Geb just as they once assembled for Atum in Heliopolis;[44] the deceased king is revivified by Geb and Atum together;[45] he sits on the throne of Horus and says: "I have succeeded to Geb, I have succeeded to Atum.";[46] when Atum gives the sky and earth to the king, it is Geb who speaks about it;[47] when Geb assembles the gods for the king, he first confers with Atum;[48] and when Atum assembles the cities for the king, they are 'the cities of Geb', and it is Geb who speaks about it.[49]

The Coffin Texts also attest to the importance of this relationship. In Spell 76, Geb knits together the earth for Atum, and gathers together for him the great flood,[50] while in Spell 80 Geb lifts up Atum's heart and gathers together his weary limbs (apparently an allusion to the creation of the primeval mound).[51]

The exact relationship between Atum and Geb is unclear. According to the theologians of Heliopolis, Geb was the son of Shu and Tefnut, and thus the grandson of Atum.[52] He has come to be regarded as something of a junior deity. However, a closer examination of the texts reveals that Geb was a very important god indeed, and possibly a creator-god in his own right.[53]

The importance of Geb is first attested in the Pyramid Texts. In Utterance 592, he is invoked as 'the sole great god' and 'the *ka* of all the gods' – typical titles of the creator-god.[54] The heritage of Atum is given to him and the ennead (including Atum) are assembled and joined to him.[55] He stands on the earth, governing the ennead, in his name 'Sharp Mouth', the chiefest of the gods.[56] He is also given the impressive title 'Bull of the Sky (*Nwt*)'.[57]

Elsewhere in the Pyramid Texts, Geb raises the Eye of Horus to the sky by the power of his spirits,[58] and it is said of Geb: 'The Eye has issued from your head as the Upper Egyptian crown Great of Magic; the Eye has issued from your head as the Lower Egyptian crown Great of Magic'.[59] The significance of these statements lies in the fact that the Eye played a pivotal role in the creation, causing the birth of the two eyes, the

Figure 16.
GEB AS THE DARK EARTH. SHU SUPPORTS NUT.

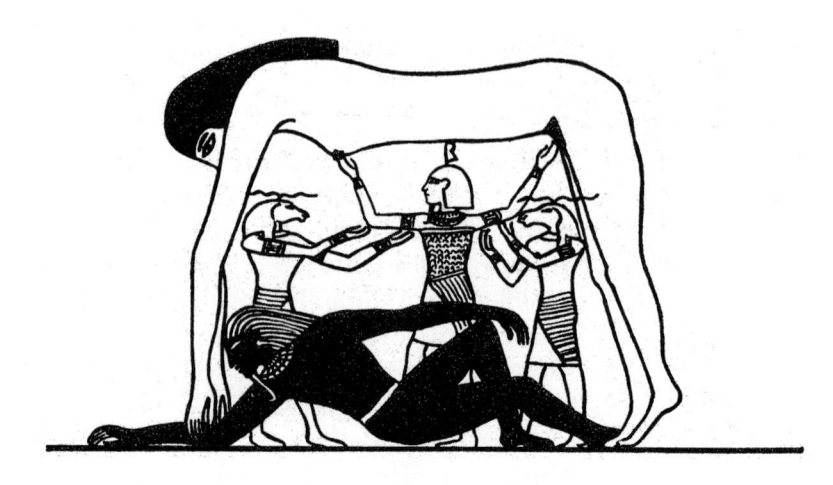

sun and the moon. Geb, the earth-god, would thus be the source of these celestial bodies. In a similar vein, four gods are said to have issued from Geb's head, and an unnamed goddess is said to have ascended from it.[60] (This echoes the idea that Ta-tenen, the primeval mound, was the source of the gods.)

According to Egyptian myth, the gods had ascended to the sky at the time 'when the sky was separated from the earth'. This again brings us to Geb, for he personified the earth from which the sky, the goddess Nut, had been uplifted. This lifting was normally done by Shu, but in one passage of the Pyramid Texts, Geb is portrayed 'with one arm to the sky, and the other to the earth', as if he were the power who raised the sky.[61] Either way, the myth seems to suggest that the earth was the place from which the sky was created (see further discussion in chapter six).

Geb also plays a central role in the myth of Osiris. According to the Pyramid Texts, Geb searches for and finds Osiris, who has been thrown down on his side by Seth;[62] he rescues Osiris from the water and puts his bones in order (or else brings Isis and Nephthys, or Horus, or Thoth to reassemble the god's body);[63] he protects Osiris, while smiting Seth and his followers;[64] he gives judgement against Seth and awards the heritage of the Two Lands to Horus;[65] he resurrects Osiris as a spirit, his firstborn son;[66] and he causes this spirit to come forth from himself (the earth and the *duat*).[67] The entire saga of Osiris's death and resurrection, which is of a creational significance as we shall see, is thus placed unambiguously in the realm of the earth-god.

In later times, Geb was depicted as a goose, 'the Great Honker', who laid the egg from which the sun emerged (further evidence for the earth as the place of origin of the sun).[68] He also became known as 'father of the gods'.[69]

All of this tends to suggest that Geb was a creator-god, in which case the earth which he personified would be the centre of creation.

This in turn strengthens the argument made earlier that the creator-god Atum was a chthonian power.

We are therefore led to the conclusion that the idea of creation from the earth was by no means a dissenting, minority point of view, restricted to Memphis and Edfu, but a broad philosophy that was also shared by the sages of Heliopolis.

The Primeval Island – a World Destroyed and Reborn

We will shortly consider a fourth example of the chthonian creation myth in Egypt. But first, it is necessary to introduce a degree of interpretation, the importance of which cannot be overstated. For this, we must return to the Edfu texts, and in particular those records that deal with the creation of the temples and sacred domains of the Falcon.

As we have already seen, the first temple to the Falcon was built upon a 'foundation ground' (*sntjt*) which had emerged from the waters during primeval times. This proto-earth, we are told, originally developed in the form of a submerged reed island, which was known by the curious name of 'the island of trampling' (*iw titi*).

Eve Reymond, who translated and published the Edfu texts in 1969, was for the most part cautious in her interpretation of the inscriptions. However, in one respect she did cross the line of academic restraint. In her opinion, the submerged island of trampling signified a former world that had been destroyed, and the myth of creating the earth amounted to the resurrection of this world. Summarising her impressions, she wrote:

> It may be surmised that the first era known by our principal sources was a period which started from what existed in the past. The general tone of the beginning of the first record seems to convey the view that an ancient world, after having been constituted, was destroyed, and as a dead world it came to be the basis of a new period of creation which at first was the re-creation and resurrection of what once had existed in the past.[70]

If Reymond is correct in this surmise, then the Edfu texts may offer us a plausible rationale for the chthonian creation myth. But more than that, if her speculation were to find wider support outside the Edfu texts, then it might even provide the basis for a new theory of Egyptian religion, in which the central myth of the sun's death and rebirth is subsumed by that of an earth-god who died but was revivified.

So, what is the evidence for Reymond's theory?

Firstly, there is the name of the submerged world, *iw titi*, 'the island of trampling', which alludes to some kind of battle.[71] The subsidiary names of this island, *iw aha*, 'island of combat', and *iw hetep*, 'island of peace', reinforce this impression.[72] Reymond was uncertain about the nature of this primeval battle, but it almost certainly allegorizes a cosmic struggle between the forces of order and chaos, in which the latter were initially victorious.[73]

Secondly, there is the fact that the island of creation, once emerged, rested directly upon the *duat n ba*, 'the netherworld of the soul'.[74] Now this name is suggestive of death and resurrection (Osiris is indeed said to be pre-eminent there),[75] and it ties in with the theme of the soul of the earth-god rising up as the Flying Soul (*ba-hatty*) 'to unite with the sky of the One whose Command is Unknown'.[76] Reymond thus suggested that the island of trampling had been transformed by the battle into the *duat n ba*, whereupon it became a tomb for the earth-god and his company, the *djajsu* ('sages').[77] Although she never quite spelled it out, the general thrust of her argument is that the death and resurrection of the earth-god, the ruler of the former world, echoed the fate of the reed island itself.[78]

Thirdly, the founding act in the creation of the world was the planting of a reed which was given the semblance of a relic from a former world. This act occurred immediately after the submerged island of reeds had floated to the surface of the *waret*. The Shebtiu-gods cut off the top of a reed and planted it in the reed island, whereupon it became a *djeba*-perch or *djed*-pillar for the Falcon.[79] This reed perch or pillar was called 'the reed that uplifts the god' (*nbi wtjs ntjr*), and was equated with the relic (*akht*) of the Pn-god (who also resided upon the pillar).[80] Interestingly, the reed was said to 'restore' (*twa*) the place of the *djed*-pillar, while the wider region of reeds was said to 'restore' the ancestor-gods.[81] Reymond thus concluded that: 'the reed was the sole relic of the former domain of the Pn-god and his fellows... the relic of the early domain was the only means through which the dead world might have been brought to its former state.'[82]

Fourthly, the general tone of the Falcon texts is suggestive of a process of decay and restoration. In addition to the names of the cosmic realms (*waret*, *iw titi*, *duat n ba*)[83] and the frequent allusions to the souls, spirits, and relics of deceased gods, there are also obscure references to archaic temple enclosures which were apparently destroyed. One such reference is to *hwt-isdn*, 'the Mansion of Isden', in which Ir-ta, 'the earth-maker', resided; it is reported that the earth-god 'entered into what was in decay', but no other information is provided.[84] A second such reference alludes to the destruction of a shelter for the relics (*djt-wtt*) of the creator-god.[85]

It is evident from the above that Reymond had good cause to interpret the Edfu myth of the primeval island as the rebirth of a terrestrial world that had once been destroyed. Nevertheless, the significance of this myth remained unclear to her, and her primary concern was to explore the Egyptian temple and its mythical origins, not to rationalise the meaning of the myths; and for this reason her interpretation of the reed island was allowed to wilt on the vine. It is understandable, in these circumstances, that Egyptologists have overlooked Reymond's comments on the myths, since she is not recognised as an authority on that particular subject. A major factor here, of course, is that a heliocentric orthodoxy has no place for a terrestrial rebirth myth. In fairness, however, the Edfu account is problematic on its own terms, since it focuses excessively on the creation of the earth and almost totally ignores the creation of the sky (although the building of the temple might well be read as a cipher for the creation of the greater cosmos). It is as if we are dealing with only half a creation myth.

Nevertheless, Reymond's speculation fits neatly with the argument in this chapter that the creation myth was geocentric and the creator-god a chthonian power. And, as we shall now see, it dovetails quite remarkably with one of Egypt's most important and enduring myths: the death and resurrection of Osiris.

The Death of Osiris

The myth of Osiris stood at the heart of Egyptian religion, providing the source of vitality both to the pharaoh and the sun-god. In the case of the pharaoh, the myth enabled the king to be crowned as Horus, the son of Osiris (while at the same time enabling his predecessor to be transfigured as Osiris), while in the case of the sun-god, the myth enabled his light to be reborn from the netherworld (*duat*) each day. The myth of Osiris thus facilitated the eternal rebirth of the king and the eternal rebirth of the sun-god, both of whom were tasked with the eternal repetition (*neheh*) of creation in order to guarantee the eternal endurance (*djet*) of the cosmos. Osiris was the key to this cosmic order (*maat*) for the simple reason that he personified the triumph of life over death.

But what exactly did the death and resurrection of Osiris signify? In order to take a view on this crucial question, we must establish the basic facts as they are recorded in the earliest Egyptian texts. We will look first at that part of the myth dealing with Osiris's death, and then at that part dealing with his resurrection.

The earliest authority on the Osiris myth is the Pyramid Texts. There, the god is said to have suffered his bodily death in three different ways: by dismemberment, drowning, and being cast down onto his side. These are not incompatible when viewed as a cosmic allegory, as we shall soon see.

By far the most prominent myth is that of Osiris's dismemberment, this being attested by the fact that his body had to be assembled in order to revivify him.[86] The cause of this decadent state is left unexplained: no god is held responsible for it, and there is no suggestion that it resulted from violence.[87] It might therefore be the case, as Henri Frankfort has opined, that dismemberment was a natural outcome of bodily death and decay.[88] On the other hand, a violent act may be implicit, consistent with the fact that Osiris was thrown down by Seth (see later) and with the fact that Seth and his followers were mutilated.[89] Indeed, the Coffin Texts confirm that Osiris was 'pulled apart' by an unnamed foe, whom we may presume to be Seth.[90]

A second important myth suggests death by drowning: three spells in the Pyramid Texts refer to 'the place where Osiris drowned', while one spell recalls 'that day of Geb fishing him complete out of the water'.[91] Significantly perhaps, the drowning incident is mentioned in connection with the assembly of the god's body. One spell mentions the drowning and then turns immediately to the myth of assembling the body,[92] while another connects Geb's fishing episode to 'that day for the putting of bones in order'.[93] Furthermore, three of the spells refer to what may be a parallel idea: the assembly of the gods and the mustering of the children of Horus at the place where Osiris drowned.[94]

Details of the drowning incident are scanty. The Pyramid Texts refer on several occasions to the water and the flood which flowed out from Osiris,[95] and on one occasion this is said to be 'the efflux which issued from the putrefaction of Osiris'.[96] To this picture, the Coffin Texts add some further details. According to one spell, the efflux of Osiris filled the pools and streams,[97] while according to another 'the efflux of Osiris flooded out when he was buried'.[98] In the first of these, a connection is made again to the assembly of the god's body by Isis and Nephthys, who are said to have built a dam in his side.[99]

Finally, on the subject of Osiris's drowning, *The Theology of Memphis* contains a particularly interesting passage which suggests that the god drowned in his own water and was then brought to land:

Osiris drowned in his water while Isis and Nephthys watched. They

Figure 17.
THE BODY OF OSIRIS IS RESTORED BY ANUBIS AND HEKET UNDER THE DIRECTION OF THOTH. ISIS AND NEPHTHYS KNEEL AT THEIR MASTER'S BEDSIDE.

saw him and they were distressed at him. Horus commanded Isis and Nephthys repeatedly that they lay hold of Osiris and prevent his drowning. They turned their heads in time, and so brought him [Osiris] to land.[100]

Turning to the third myth of Osiris's death, it is stated several times in the Pyramid Texts that he had 'fallen upon his side',[101] and it is alleged in some passages that he was 'thrown down' or 'laid low' by Seth, or else felled by an unnamed foe.[102] One passage states that Osiris was floored by a throw-stick.[103] Seth's involvement might not be original to this myth, but a borrowing from a separate myth in which Seth was the protagonist of Horus (see chapter thirteen).

The crucial fact of Osiris's death is that it is not a final annihilation but a temporary condition and a gateway to a new form of existence. Osiris conquers death and rises like a phoenix from the ashes. It is not death as we humans know it, but a state of inertness, passivity, tiredness, or sleep, from which the god recovers or awakens.

In order for Osiris to recover, his body or body-parts must be found and revivified. This task sometimes falls to his son Horus,[104] or his father Geb,[105] or his mother Nut,[106] but more often it falls to his two sisters Isis and Nephthys, who are described as 'the two spirits, the ladies of this land'.[107] Important motifs in the revivification process are: the finding of the body; the wailing lament; the rejoicing with love; the gathering together and assembly of the god's limbs or flesh; the laying hold of the body; the provision of the heart for the body; the raising of the body or its head; the turning of the body from its left side to its right side; the cleansing of the body to remove evil spirits; the mystical union with the revivified body; and the opening of its mouth and eyes.[108]

The aim and climax of all these divine activities is to make a spirit of Osiris, i.e. to cause him to come forth from his body in the intangible form of a soul or spirit. Osiris is thus regenerated, either in his own name of Osiris (the son of Geb and Nut) or in the name of his son Horus, and this spirit emerges from the *duat* to take possession of the *akhet* and the sky.

What is the meaning of this myth? Why did it play such a central role in Egyptian religion? For two hundred years, Egyptologists have debated this subject without coming to any definite conclusion. Several eminent scholars have been persuaded by ancient Greek and Roman writers that Osiris was originally a human being, who brought civilisation to Egypt, and was deified posthumously in honour of his achievements; according to this theory, his death and rebirth signified his miraculous passage into heaven.[109] Other scholars, however, are of the opinion that Osiris was a nature-spirit, who personified the Nile inundation and the fertility of the land; under this theory, his death and rebirth signified the ebb and flow inherent in the cycle of the seasons.[110] But to other scholars, Osiris was a celestial god, whose death and rebirth were seen in the movements of the heavens; according to some, he was a sun-god whose death and rebirth occurred every day, once a year, and at the time of eclipses;[111] according to others, he was a moon-god, whose death and rebirth occurred every month, and at the time of eclipses;[112] and according to others still, he was a star-god, whose death and rebirth was witnessed in the disappearance and reappearance of certain stars.[113]

In keeping with these diverse views, Osiris's dismemberment has been explained in numerous ways: as an allegory for the waning moon, whose orb appears to be reduced, limb by limb, during the last fourteen days of its monthly cycle;[114] as an allegory for the stars that appear scattered across the sky at the setting of the sun;[115] and as a product of the many cult centres that laid claim to his body or body-parts.[116]

As for the drowning of Osiris in his flood, this is held to be symbolic of the Nile in its annual flood.

All these theories appear plausible, with the exception of the deified king theory which is contradicted by numerous statements in the earliest texts.[117] And yet they seem to be inconsistent with one another – unless, of course, they are parts of a bigger picture which scholars have hitherto missed.

Could the geocentric creation myth provide that bigger picture?

From a geocentric perspective, it is immediately significant that Osiris was an earth-god who generated a spirit, and it is doubly significant that

Figure 18.
OSIRIS RESURRECTED IN THE ARMS OF ISIS AND NEPHTHYS.

that spirit went forth to the sky. The fact that Osiris was a fertility-god, a sun-god, a moon-god, and a star-god would be entirely consistent with a creation from the earth.

Did Osiris personify the primeval earth and its death and rebirth at the beginning of time? Was he, in fact, a creator-god?

The evidence from the Egyptian texts indeed adds up to a persuasive and compelling case.

The myth begins with Osiris being interred in the earth. He is said to be in darkness, inert, in a state of dismemberment, which could well be an allegory for the initial state of chaos which is found in all Egyptian creation myths. It should be noted that the supposed places of Osiris's death, namely Memphis, Nedyt, Ghsty, and Andjet, are probably each to be understood as the mythical, original city, representing the primeval world (just as Atum created while 'in Heliopolis').[118] This would explain why Osiris's corpse was found by Isis 'in the middle of the earth',[119] and why the god was restored and spiritualized by the earth-gods Geb and Anubis.[120]

Osiris was also equated with primeval water. The Pyramid Texts state that his corpse was found on the river bank at Nedyt, and that his waters went forth as a result of his putrefaction.[121] The Coffin Texts add that the efflux of Osiris flooded out when he was buried,[122] while the Shabaka

Stone explains that he drowned in his own waters (see earlier). There is a clear parallel here with the primeval ocean, from which all things were created. Osiris would appear to be the source of this ocean – the origin of the chaos of the primeval flood.

Osiris is thus seen to be in a state of chaos both in the earth and in the water. This is the opening of the creation myth to a tee.

The revivified Osiris then becomes the source of water to the world. In the Pyramid Texts, Isis and Nephthys restore Osiris to health, whereupon he receives the names 'Wall of the Bitter Lakes', 'Sea', 'Ocean', and 'Surrounder of the Islanders'.[123] Both the Pyramid Texts and Coffin Texts assert that the floodwaters of Osiris filled the canals and waterways of the Two Lands.[124]

In the midst of this great flood, Osiris becomes land. According to the Shabaka Stone, Isis and Nephthys lay hold of Osiris, who is drowning in his water, and 'bring him to land' (see earlier).[125] This is almost certainly an allegory for the primeval mound emerging from the waters of *nun*. In support of this interpretation, Isis and Nephthys are the assemblers of Osiris's limbs, and the mound is said to be formed by the assembly of the creator-god's limbs (see later in this chapter).

Osiris may thus be identified with the earth and the *nun* in their initial state of chaos, with the world flood that came from the *nun*, and with the primeval mound that emerged from the *nun*.

But there is more.

According to the Pyramid Texts, Osiris was spiritualized by the earth-god Geb.[126] This is a classic trait of the creator-god, who emerges as a spirit from the earth and the *nun*.

But Osiris was more than just a spirit who emerged from the earth. He was the entire realm of spirit which emerged from the netherworld. This is made clear in several spells in the Pyramid Texts where Osiris receives the name 'Akhet from which Re goes forth'.[127] Osiris thus personifies the cosmic realm in which the creator-god became *akh* and ascended to the sky. In later texts, he is also made to personify the entire netherworld, the *duat*, from which the *akhet* came forth.[128]

But Osiris too goes to the sky like a creator-god. In the Pyramid Texts, he ascends to the sky alone, or in the company of Horus his son, whom he makes into 'a great god in the sky-water'.[129] He also becomes the star-god Sah,[130] and his limbs become the imperishable stars.[131] And to round things off, the eyes go up from his head to appear in the form of the day-barque and the night-barque – the sun and the moon.[132]

At the same time, Osiris seems to raise the sky and separate it from the earth. The evidence for this comes from Utterance 577 of the Pyramid

Texts, where the god is told: 'You support the sky with your right side, possessing life... You support the earth with your left side, possessing dominion'.[133] Now the Pyramid Texts often refer to Osiris turning from his left side onto his right side,[134] and we know from other sources that this signified the god returning to life (he died on his left side and was reborn on his right side).[135] Therefore, it would seem that in turning onto his right side, Osiris was made to support the sky and separate it from the earth (which he supported with his left side). This is especially evocative of the creation by Shu, who as god of the atmosphere separated the sky from the earth.

In summary, the points of contact between the myth of Osiris and the myth of creation are compelling. In every important respect, Osiris has the traits of the creator-god. In particular, his dismembered and drowned body is a perfect allegory for the primeval world (the earth and the *nun*) in its original state of division, chaos and want. If there is a difference between Osiris and the other creator-gods, it lies solely in the fact that his condition of inertness and lassitude is explained by the myth of an assault by Seth (the other gods are rarely subjected to such violent action). Osiris is thus unique by virtue of the fact that he has 'died' and come back to life.

If this interpretation of Osiris is so obvious – as it certainly appears to be – the question naturally arises of how Egyptology has managed to miss it.

One reason is the treatment of the myth in late antiquity, in particular by the Greek commentators Diodorus and Plutarch. These writers, overly influenced by the Euhemerist theory of myth, fostered the completely absurd notion that Osiris had been a human king who brought civilisation to Egypt. Early Egyptologists generally found this idea credible, in some cases because of the myth's similarities to the historicised Christian story of Jesus Christ, who died for the world and came back to life.[136] Even today, many scholars fall into the trap of quoting Plutarch's corrupt form of the Osiris myth rather than going to the trouble of synthesising the original Egyptian sources.

A second reason is that the death of the god is an unusual motif in Egyptian myth. Apart from the Edfu tradition, which is of late date, there is only the Osiris myth, and scholars have been understandably reluctant to reinterpret Egyptian religion from such a narrow base, even more so because Osiris was not widely worshipped prior to the 5th dynasty. This remains a concern, despite the evident importance of the Osiris myth to the kingship and the cult of the sun.

In response to this problem, it must be emphasised that Osiris accreted the cults of other gods, in particular Andjeti, Khenti-amentiu, Horus, and Sokar.[137] It is possible that several dying-and-rising god cults once held sway in Egypt, only to be swallowed up by the Osiris cult by the time of the Pyramid Texts.[138] Owing to the similarity in these cults, Osiris would have become a magnet for them all.

But the most decisive factor in the orthodox interpretation of the Osiris myth has been the absolute and unshakeable belief that Egyptian religion was a sun cult. To the Egyptologist, the supreme god must be solar, and all non-solar gods must be subordinate to the sun. Osiris cannot therefore be accorded a prominent position in the Egyptian pantheon, since he was primarily an earth-god. To this end, scholars have emphasised Osiris's identity as a chthonian god and played down his celestial aspect. Osiris, it is maintained, had no rightful place in the sky; he appeared in the firmament only because the theologians of Heliopolis felt compelled by political pressures to put him there.[139] His myth had thus been corrupted and could not be taken literally.[140] Osiris was strictly a nature-god, who personified the annual rebirth of the earth.

This theory, by its own admission, goes against the grain of what the Egyptians actually said. Even in the earliest texts, Osiris appears happily embedded in the earth and the sky, with a fully-developed myth of his ascent from the one realm to the other. There is no hard evidence for the idea that the Osiris myth was celestialized. This is but mere speculation, contrived to rationalise a heliocentric preconception.

It is all a matter of perspective. From a heliocentric point of view, the sun-god appears supreme and Osiris subordinate. But from a geocentric point of view, Osiris appears supreme and the sun-god subordinate. If we change perspective, all the attributes of Osiris – terrestrial and celestial – make perfect sense, and we may dispense with the idea that his myth was corrupted to political ends. Osiris becomes a chthonian creator-god; and there is no need to invent an unnecessary hypothesis.

The crux, of course, is the death of Osiris – a feature which is lacking in other creator-gods. From a heliocentric perspective, it is a peripheral issue; its importance is assigned to the mortality of the pharaoh and his desire for an afterlife; by becoming Osiris, the king is reborn with the Nile and the crops. But from a geocentric perspective, the death of Osiris becomes a central and profound issue. It signifies the destruction of an old cosmos and its rebirth as a new cosmos. It puts Osiris at the heart of the creation myth. Indeed, it makes him the creator-god *par excellence*.

This brings us back to the Edfu myth of the reed island. As deciphered by Reymond, it describes the death and rebirth of a terrestrial world, and the parallel death and resurrection of an ancestral god of that world, the

Pn-god. Although the myth is vague concerning the creation of the sky, it bears obvious points of contact with the myth of the death and rebirth of Osiris, as Reymond herself observed.[141] Might Osiris personify the idea of the primeval world destroyed and reborn? Reymond failed to ask this basic question, since the principal focus of her study was the Egyptian temple and its mythical origins. It was not within her remit to challenge the orthodox theories of the Osiris myth or the creation myth.

Nevertheless, the time for that challenge has now surely come.

Reassembling the World

I have suggested that Osiris's dismemberment symbolised the initial state of chaos in the world, and that the reassembly of his limbs signified the reversal of that state. But there is evidence to suggest that this allegory was taken further – that the limbs of Osiris signified disintegrated earth elements submerged in the primeval ocean, and that the reassembly of these limbs signified the reassembly of the earth, which then emerged as the primeval mound. Interestingly, this evidence is found not only in the myths of Osiris but also in the myths of creator-gods such as Atum and Ptah.

The earliest expression of this idea occurs in the Pyramid Texts, in the spells concerning the resurrection of Osiris. Besides the usual references to the reassembly of the god (the interpretation of which is the point at issue), there is one passage in which he is literally 'built' by the goddess Nephthys:

> Nephthys has collected all your limbs for you in this her name of 'Seshat, Lady of Builders'.[142]

Now Seshat was an important character in the building of temples; she figures prominently, for example, in the building of the temples of the Falcon and the sun-god at Edfu, particularly in the laying out of the foundations.[143] It may thus be argued that, even as early as the Pyramid Texts, the Egyptians regarded the reassembly of Osiris as analogous to the building of a temple's foundations. And since the temple, as a model of the cosmos, stood upon the primeval mound, it could be further argued that Osiris *was* the primeval mound on which the temple would be built, in which case the assembly of his limbs would allegorize the assembly of that mound.[144]

For a more explicit reference to this idea, we must go forward in time to the Coffin Texts. In Spell 76, in the context of the creation of the sky above the earth, Shu states: "Geb knits together the Two Lands for my father Atum."[145] This statement is then expanded in Spell 80, where Atum proclaims:

> I was at one with Nun in inertness, when I could find no place on which to stand or sit, when Heliopolis had not yet been founded that I might dwell in it, when my lotus had not yet been knit together, before I had made Nut that she might be above me... I am floating, very weary, and the progenitors are inert. It is Geb who lives and lifts up my heart, enlivens my heart, when he gathers together these very weary limbs of mine.[146]

In this passage, Geb comes into being when he gathers together the limbs and lifts up the heart of Atum. Since Geb personifies the primeval earth, there can be little doubt that his assembly of Atum's limbs corresponds to the creation of the primeval mound, especially since the creation of the mound is alluded to three times in the preceding lines (the place to stand or sit, Heliopolis, and the lotus). The parallel to the myth of Osiris is striking, and tends to suggest that the reassembly of his body likewise allegorized the creation of the primeval mound, either in its submerged or risen form.

A second example of the same theme is found in the Berlin Hymn to Ptah (22nd dynasty). In the following passage, we read how Ptah in his identity of Ta-tenen, 'the risen land', assembled the limbs of his body in order to form the primeval earth:

> [O Ptah Ta-tenen] You built up your limbs and fashioned your own body before the sky came into being, before the earth came into being, before the [primeval] waters came forth. You knit together the earth, you assembled your own limbs, you embraced your own members, and found yourself alone, the one who made his seat, the one who fashioned the Two Lands.[147]

Here, the identity between the creator-god's limbs and the primeval earth is made explicit. In the first line, Ptah builds the proto-earth while still in the *nun*; in the second line, he fashions the emerged earth, the primeval mound, which is described idiomatically as the god's 'seat' and 'the Two Lands'. Again, the parallel to the Osiris myth is striking.

There is more. The Berlin Hymn to Ptah continues:

> When you stood up on the land in its inertness, it drew together thereafter, you being in your form of Ta-tenen, in your appearance of 'the Unifier of the Two Lands'.[148]

In this line, it is stated clearly that the land which became the primeval mound (Ta-tenen) began in a state of inertness, but recovered when the creator-god stood upon it.

A similar idea appears in a text of the Ptolemaic period, which refers to the city of Thebes as a microcosm of the primeval mound:

> When the earth was in the depths of the primeval waters, he [Amun] waded upon it [Thebes]. It dispelled his weakness entirely when he rested on it. It was the 'place of life' that became the primeval mound, which rose up in the beginning.[149]

Here, we see another good example of the proto-earth pre-existing while submerged in the primeval waters. This time, it is Amun, not the mound, who recovers from weakness, and yet the manner in which he does so – by resting on the mound – demands comparison with the Ptah text, cited above, in which the mound itself, personified by the god, recovers from a state of inertness.

Both of these sources offer parallels to the myth of Osiris, whose death is portrayed as a condition of inertness or tiredness,[150] and they prompt the thought that the reassembly of his limbs might allegorize the knitting together of the land elements which formed the primeval mound.

In support of this possibility, there is a suggestive passage in the Book of the Dead, where Osiris is roused from his primeval sleep by the magic of Thoth:

> O Lord of the Sacred Land. He [Thoth] made the light shine on your inert body, for you he illumined the dark ways, for you he dispelled the weakness in your limbs by means of the power in his mouth.[151]

There is a remarkable parallel here to the myth cited earlier in which Geb gathered together the 'very weary limbs' of Atum in order to create the primeval mound.

All things considered, while the case cannot be proven (as few things can ever be in Egyptology), a persuasive case can be made that Osiris personified the death and rebirth of a primeval terrestrial world, and that the dismemberment of his body signified the disintegration of the earth, which was later reassembled to form the primeval mound.

The Midnight Sun

If Osiris was a creator-god, who personified the death and rebirth of the terrestrial world, then his relationship with the sun-god Re requires to be reconsidered.

As mentioned earlier, Osiris was the energy source for the sun-god's rebirth – the veritable fountainhead of his immortality. By his repeated unions with Osiris during the night, Re acquired the power to orbit the earth perpetually and perform the eternal repetitions (*neheh*) of creation which ensured the eternal endurance (*djet*) of the cosmos. The sun-god Re thus enshrined the principle of *neheh* time, while the chthonian god Osiris enshrined the principle of *djet* time.[152] Or, as the Egyptians put it: 'As for *neheh*, it is day; as for *djet*, it is night.' and 'As for yesterday, it is Osiris; as for tomorrow, it is Re.'[153] Each new day was thus understood as a repetition of the first day of creation.

This special relationship between Osiris and Re is evident as early as the Pyramid Texts. In several spells, Osiris is called 'Akhet from which Re goes forth',[154] while in another spell the two gods share the epithet 'Horus at the head of the spirits', but with Osiris being placed statically 'in the sea' and Re placed dynamically 'crossing the sea'.[155] In another highly unusual passage, Re is pictured inside the earth 'in his fetters', as if he is synonymous with the body of Osiris.[156]

The Coffin Texts develop these ideas further. One spell describes how Re descended from the sky to weep for his corpse in Heliopolis,[157] while another spell states that the soul of Osiris entered Djedu, encountered the soul of Re there, and embraced it, at which point they became 'the twin souls'.[158] And in a similar vein, the Book of the Dead identifies the great god of the netherworld as Osiris, but at the same time as 'Re, the soul of Re, who copulated with himself.'[159]

But it is in the Books of the Netherworld that the union of Osiris and Re is most fully expressed. In these books, painted on the walls of royal tombs during the New Kingdom period, the sun-god's journey through

Figure 19.
THE SOULS OF RE AND OSIRIS UNITE IN DJEDU.

the netherworld and encounter with Osiris is portrayed in the form of illustrations, accompanied by text. There are several different versions of the myth, each constituting a book in the overall genre. The modern titles are: the Book of the Hidden Chamber (Am Duat), the Book of Gates, the Enigmatic Book of the Netherworld, the Book of Caverns, and the Book of the Earth.[160] A detailed study of these books is beyond the scope of this book, but the broad themes may be summarised as follows.

In the first instance, Re is seen descending from the sky and entering the western horizon (*akhet*). From there, he passes through 'the doors of the earth' and enters the netherworld, referred to as *duat* or *amentet*. This realm, which is divided into twelve regions (or hours), or in one case six caverns, comprises land and water, enveloped in thick darkness. In some of the books, Re travels in his solar barque, which is towed along by the gods, while in others he travels in the form of the sun disc. The god himself is depicted as a ram-headed *ba*-soul, but also as 'flesh' (*awf*).[161]

Figure 20.
RE IN HIS SOLAR BARQUE PASSES THROUGH THE NETHERWORLD.
A scene from the Book Am Duat.

As Re passes through the netherworld, his light awakens a land of the dead, populated by a bewildering variety of gods. For some of these gods he ordains offerings and eternal life; for others he ordains punishment and eternal death; the latter gods are dismembered, burned in pits of fire, or scalded in lakes of boiling water.[162]

Re's declared aim is to unite with his body, which is represented by the corpse of Osiris. This encounter takes place in the middle hour of the night in the uttermost depths of the netherworld, where Osiris lies inert in his sarcophagus. There, the *ba*-soul of the sun-god unites with the corpse of the earth-god, and revivifies it, causing both gods to resurrect in their soul forms. This process is described as the greatest of mysteries.

90   THE MIDNIGHT SUN

Figure 21.
THE UNION OF RE AND OSIRIS.
A scene from the Enigmatic Book of the Netherworld.

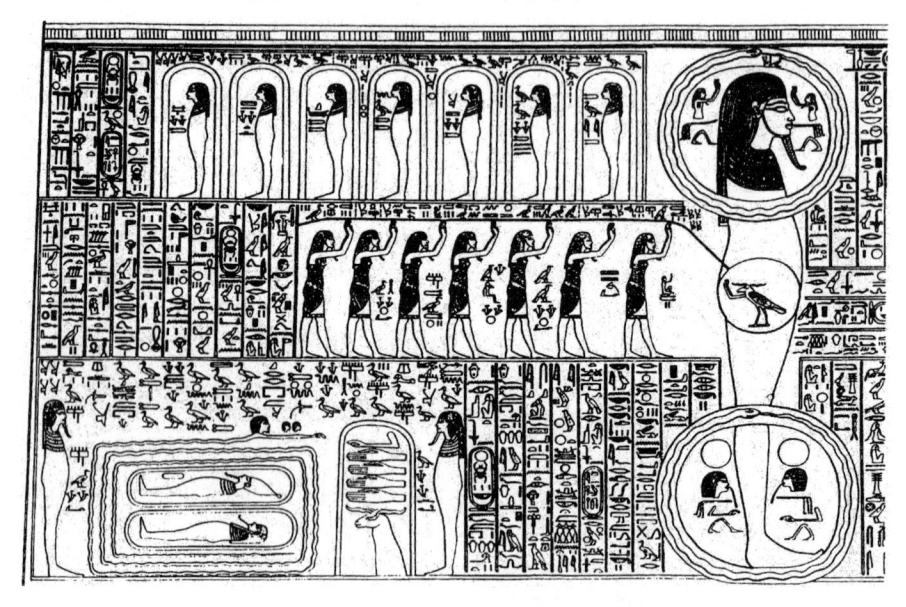

Following this rebirth, Re proceeds through the remaining divisions of the *duat*, and eventually departs for the eastern *akhet*, whence he will go to the sky. In these stages, Re is repeatedly opposed by the giant serpent Apep, whose attacks on the solar barque are thwarted by the gods who accompany the sun-god through the circuit of the *duat* and the sky.

What is to be made of this remarkable myth?

Egyptology has for many years regarded the Books of the Netherworld with scepticism and disdain. In its view, Re is a god of the sky and Osiris a god of the earth, and the idea that Re might visit Osiris in the middle of the earth is a grotesque anomaly.[163] The explanation for this anomaly is supposed to be found in the historical rivalry between the cults of Re and Osiris, and the consequent 'Osirianization' of the myth of the death and rebirth of the sun-god (in his orbit around the earth).[164] The kings and priests of the New Kingdom supposedly decided to adapt and corrupt an original solar myth to a funerary end, to bring the sun-god's powers of daily rebirth into the tombs of the kings.[165] The leading specialists in Egyptology have therefore dismissed the Books of the Netherworld as priestly fantasies, which provide no useful insights into Egyptian religion and myth.[166] The books have been deemed interesting only as a historical source for the Greek mysteries, specifically the cult of Isis and the motif of 'the midnight sun' (see the panel opposite).[167]

The Mystery of the Midnight Sun

I entered the boundary of death, and as I stepped across Proserpina's threshold, I was carried by all the elements and returned.
At midnight, I caught sight of the sun, dazzling in radiant light, I approached the lower and upper gods and prayed to them face to face.
(Lucius Apuleius, *Metamorphoses*, 2nd century AD)

The Egyptian associations present in this description have often been emphasised. We are dealing here with a *katabasis*, i.e. a ritual descent into the underworld, which, in this case, is visually and architectonically actualized by a descent into a crypt decorated with cosmographic representations. In the precise same way, the royal tombs of the New Kingdom are decorated with representations of the underworld, thereby equating the entombment of the king to a *descensus ad inferos*. The wall-paintings of these tombs are cosmographies: they describe the path of the sun-god, sailing in his barque through the hourly regions of the underworld and of the sky. The mystical character of these 'books', in the sense of a codification of an esoteric and secret knowledge, is clearly expressed in these representations, as are the clues that the origins of this literature are to be found not in funerary religion, but in the solar cult... In the cosmographic 'books' of the royal tombs, both *dei inferi* and *dei superi* are found together. The *dei inferi* are the inhabitants of the underworld, to whom the sun-god, accompanied by his divine retainers, descends nightly in his barque. The deceased king sails along in the solar barque and prays to the gods *'de proxumo'*. The conception that a human being, once dead, meets the gods face to face, after having only worshiped them in their symbolic representations during his earthly existence, is an oft repeated motif in Egyptian funerary liturgies... To look upon the sun, when it sets and is worshiped by the gods, is the professed goal of the funerary spells. In the initiation of Lucius, the voyage through the underworld stands for a symbolic death, followed on the next morning by his resurrection as the sun-god: adorned with a palm wreath *ad instar solis*, he appears to the cheering crowd, just as the justified deceased at the judgement of the dead... No one doubts that the initiation rites of the Isis-mysteries, as Apuleius ventures to describe them, are deeply rooted in the uniquely elaborated rituals and conceptions of Egyptian funerary religion.
(J. Assmann, 'Death and Initiation in the Funerary Religion of Ancient Egypt', 1989)

In recent years, a number of Egyptologists have taken a more positive view of the relationship between Re and Osiris. In 1948, Henri Frankfort argued that there never was a conflict between the two gods; rather they were united by their parallel roles in a religion that was founded on the principle of 'the perennial cyclic rhythms of nature... the recurring movement that was part of the established and unchanging order of the world'.[168] And in keeping with this idea, Jan Assmann proposed in 1984 that Re and Osiris together expressed the totality of cosmic time, Re representing the principle of *neheh*, 'eternal recurrence', and Osiris the principle of *djet*, 'eternal duration'.[169] The union of these two gods thus signified the renewal of cosmic time, which by its constant repetition ensured the immortality of time (or as Assmann put it 'the continuity of reality'). In Assmann's opinion, this concept of time had derived from a solar cycle in which Khepri ('the becoming one') had represented *neheh*, and Atum ('the completed one') *djet*.[170]

Egyptology has thus moved to a position where Re's passage from the sky into the netherworld (via the western *akhet*) and then back to the sky (via the eastern *akhet*) is deemed logical within the Egyptian framework of cyclical time.

But might there have been a more fundamental reason for Re's visit to the centre of the earth – a reason related to *the origin of neheh* time and *djet* time?

As noted in chapter one, the role of the sun-god Re was to re-enact the events of the first occasion (*zep tepi*). In the Book of Nut, for example, Re's disc is shown emerging at daybreak from the body of Nut (the *duat*) and the text states:

> He becomes effective [*akh*] again through his father Osiris, in the Abydene district, on the first occasion of his primeval state. He comes into being and goes away to the sky... He comes into being like his original coming-into-being in the world on the first occasion.[171]

This principle of the repetition of creation is made explicit in numerous religious texts, and several eminent Egyptologists have drawn attention to it – at least up to a point. It is well understood that Re's appearance each day repeated his original birth from the waters of *nun* and the womb of Nut.[172] And it is vaguely appreciated that Re's defeat of his enemies, both in the horizon and in the sky, repeated his original cosmic triumph over the forces of chaos.[173] By the same principle, then, it is conceivable that Re's passage through the *duat* and his rebirth through the medium of the corpse of Osiris also re-enacted the creation.

To Egyptologists, such a suggestion is anathema, because the creation myth is held to be heliocentric and Osiris is not recognised as a creator-god. It is difficult under this view to perceive Re's journey through the earth as a re-enactment of creation. And yet scholars have observed that the Books of the Netherworld contain numerous creator-gods, scenes of creation, and allusions to creation, not just in the final hour of emergence in the east but throughout the entire *duat*.[174] We see Atum, Khepri, Nun, Nut, Shu, Tefnut, in addition to the earth-gods Ta-tenen, Geb, Aker, and Sokar (remarkably, all these gods appear in the form of corpses, usually interred in sarcophagi).[175] We see the thick darkness of the time of chaos, along with the primeval waters which give life to Re.[176] We see Sia and Heka accompanying Re in his barque.[177] We see the barque being towed by star-gods, who fend off the forces of chaos.[178] And everywhere we see the destruction of those who oppose the birth of Re.

All of this creational imagery begins to make sense once we view the creation myth as geocentric rather than heliocentric. Re would then enter the earth in order to revisit the place of creation, and his barque would pass through the chthonian realm in order to re-enact its original journey from the darkness into the light. Re's union with his corpse in the form of Osiris, and his rebirth therefrom, would re-enact the creator-soul going forth from its body – the primeval earth sending forth its *ka*. Consistent with this, a strong case can be made that Osiris personified the death and rebirth of the cosmos, his mummified corpse signifying the reassembled parts of a dismembered former world (see earlier). The union of Re and Osiris in the depths of the night would therefore symbolise a very great mystery indeed – the creation of the cosmos from the remnants of the destroyed world. The midnight sun motif would symbolise not only the rebirth of the sun in its daily course, but more fundamentally the birth of the cosmos, for which the rising sun was the primary symbol.

By illustrating these mysteries on the walls of the tomb (synonymous with the *duat*), the Egyptians ensured that the deceased king's soul would participate in Re's rebirth from the body of Osiris (the king's mummy was held to be Osiris) and thereafter take its seat in Re's barque in which it would traverse the sky and revisit its body in the earth each day. Under the creational interpretation, this would mean that the deceased king was reborn as the image of the creator-god; that is to say he became one with the primeval earth, participated in its recovery from its former state of lassitude, and emerged from the earth as a soul, thereupon to dwell in the starry sky. His soul would then be able to return to the depths of the earth each day and renew its fertility by repeating the miracle of creation.

We see here the concept of *neheh* and *djet* – eternal repetition ensuring eternal endurance. Re's revolutions around the earth repeated the events of creation (the sun's setting and rising re-enacted the original death and rebirth of the world), and thus he guaranteed immortal life for the earth, personified by the mummy of Osiris.

This brings us back to Assmann's theory that Re and Osiris together represented the totality of cosmic time. He is undoubtedly correct. But the truth may be even more fundamental, for under the creational view Re and Osiris were complementary aspects of a single terrestrial creator-god, the former representing his emerged soul, the latter representing his revivified body. The mystical union of these two great gods would thus have signified not only the totality of cosmic time but also *the origin* of cosmic time – the principle known to the Egyptians as *zep tepi*, 'the first occasion'.[179]

Chapter Four Summary

- The Egyptian creation myth was geocentric, not heliocentric.
- Creation from the earth was the rule, not the exception, witness the chthonian creator-gods Atum, Kheprer, Geb, and Ptah Ta-tenen.
- The Edfu texts describe how the creator-god emerged as a soul from the earth and became embodied in the first temple. This temple was a model of the cosmos.
- According to the Edfu texts, the earth and the temple were re-created from the remnants of a destroyed world. The creator-god and the gods were likewise restored from their decadent forms.
- Osiris, a god of the earth and primeval waters, was the creator-god *par excellence*. The myth of his death and rebirth is a perfect allegory for the death and rebirth of a terrestrial world.
- The myth of the dismemberment of Osiris is an allegory for the initial state of chaos in the cosmos, but may also allude to the physical division of the earth in the primeval waters.
- In the myths of creation by Atum and Ptah Ta-tenen, the assembly of the god's limbs is explicitly compared to the assembly of the primeval mound. These myths echo that of the dismemberment and reassembly of Osiris.
- Re's union with Osiris in the depths of the earth signified a repetition of creation. The midnight sun was a symbol of the great mystery of the death and rebirth of the primeval cosmos.

CHAPTER FIVE

GOD AND THE GODS

Ho all you gods! Come all together, come into assembly, just as you (once) came together and assembled for Atum in Heliopolis.
(Pyramid Texts, Utterance 599)

The Egyptians did not believe in a creation *ex nihilo*. On the contrary, the religious texts state clearly that the cosmos was created from pre-existent materials, namely primeval water, matter, and air. Creation involved the transformation of these materials from a state of chaos into a state of order. It involved the construction of a new cosmos from the remains of an old cosmos.

That old cosmos was described as the body, or corpse, of the creator-god. In this sense, it may be stated that the creator-god *personified* the old cosmos. A prime example of this personification principle is the god Nun who personified the primeval waters of *nun*. Another prime example is Osiris, whose corpse personified the old cosmos in its initial state of chaos, inertness, and want. For the creation to proceed, the body of the creator had to be awakened from its sleep of death.

The power that stirred the inert body was the soul – an irresistible life-force which the Egyptians called *ba*. The soul of the creator-god gained consciousness in the *nun*, and then emerged from the waters to direct the creation of the new cosmos. One of the clearest expositions of this idea occurs in Spell 307 of the Coffin Texts:

> I am Re who issued from the *nun* in this my name of 'Khepri'. My soul is divine... I am Hu [creative utterance] who will never perish in this my name of 'Soul' (*ba*)... I am the eldest of the Primeval Ones, the soul of them of the Temple of Eternity... The great soul has come upon . . . the limits of the sky... I am the soul who created the celestial waters, who made my seat in the realm of the dead.[1]

As the soul *transforms*, so the body *is transformed*. In order to create the new cosmos, the creator-god has to reshape the materials of his own self, namely his primeval waters, matter, and air. He is thus described in the texts as *khpr-djs.f* (*kheper-djesef*), meaning 'self-developing' or 'self-creating'.[2] Atum, Re, Ptah, and Amun all assumed this title, but the principle was exemplified by Kheprer, the scarab beetle, who symbolised the miracle of genesis from water and earth. His name embodied the verb *kheper*, meaning 'to come into being' or 'to develop', and anticipated the *kheperu* – 'developments', 'evolutions', or 'emanations' – which would unfold in his creation of the new cosmos.

Many texts attest to this principle of the creator producing the cosmos from himself.

Atum, for example, is said to have developed himself by rising high in Heliopolis and ejecting Shu and Tefnut from his mouth or phallus. The One God thus became three, and his *ka* (vital spirit) became manifest in the wider cosmos.[3] The risen earth is called 'this land which issued from Atum, this spittle which issued from Kheprer'.[4]

Neber-djer is said to have gathered together the limbs of his body, whereupon he 'developed into this earth'.[5] He also claims that:

> I fashioned myself out of the primeval matter. I made myself out of the primeval matter of primeval times. My name is Ausars, the primeval matter (*pautt*) of the Primeval Ones (*pautiu*).[6]

Another example is Ptah Ta-tenen. He is said to have formed the risen earth by knitting together his own flesh and limbs.[7] He was thus called 'the maker of himself' ('your own Khnum').[8] He transformed himself by standing up and placing his feet on the earth and his head in the sky, and thereafter 'supported himself' in the form of his own great work.[9]

Shu, in his role as creator, is said to have created the atmosphere from 'the efflux of his own flesh'. His offspring were the eight air-gods, 'the Infinite Ones', who stood on the earth and supported the sky.[10]

As a final example, it is said of Amun that 'when he came into being nothing existed except himself'.[11] The god then developed himself into a new form:

> You developed yourself into Ta-tenen ('the risen earth')... Your beauty was raised aloft as *ka-mut.ef* ('bull of the mother'), and you distanced yourself in the sky, as the one established in the sun...[12]

As suggested earlier, the creator was a soul (*ba*) whose task was to bring new life and order to its body, the cosmos. In the beginning, this body comprised water, matter, and air in a mixture which was motionless and shrouded in darkness. The soul, by virtue of its appearance, then added the mysterious phenomena of wind and light, and used all these elements in the transformation of its body. The matter was solidified to form dry land; the waters were divided into a lower *nun* and an upper *nun*; the air was separated to become the atmosphere that supported the sky; and the light was separated to create the sun, the moon, and the stars.

In all this, the creator-soul was the prime mover, the divine spark so to speak. Although the mystery of beginning is personified by the body and soul of the god, it is the soul in particular that represents the true essence of the creator. On account of this fact, the Great God of ancient Egypt can take on a transcendent quality, not unlike the Supreme Being of the Judaeo-Christian and Islamic traditions. At times, he may appear to be independent of his creation,[13] while he may also be portrayed as a power who can neither be seen nor comprehended.[14] But this does not detract from the fact that the creator developed the cosmos from himself and became immanent in his creation. As if to prove the point, Amun was described as both transcendent and immanent.[15]

Seen thus, the creation myth seems to support a monotheistic view of Egyptian religion. Since there was only one cosmos, there could only be One God (and for this reason we will henceforth refer to him as God with a capital 'G'). But even if we were to regard Egypt's most prominent deities as parallel or specialised forms of this One God (thus accounting for the vast proportion of their number), there would still remain the question of the *netjeru*-gods, i.e. the plurality of gods that were known collectively as the ennead. Their role is confusing, to say the least, for while it is often stated that God created the gods, it is also maintained that they, the gods, created him![16] But such confusion aside, the existence of these gods lends an air of polytheism to Egyptian religion, and presents a formidable objection to the proponents of monotheism.

This author has no axe to grind as regards monotheism or polytheism in Egyptian religion. However, a rational explanation for the relationship between God and the gods does emerge from our preceding discussion of the body and soul of God, in particular from the notion that the corpse of the creator represented the old cosmos in a state of chaos, inertness, and want. In the remainder of this chapter, these ideas will be explored in more detail, with the aim of finally solving this two-hundred-year-old crux. Our study will focus initially on the texts for the information they provide on the relevant issues (the body and soul of God, the bodies and souls of the gods, and the assembly of the gods), but it will culminate in a possible interpretation of this data from a geocentric perspective.

The Death and Rebirth of God

The body of God is an ubiquitous theme in Egyptian religious texts, but an under-reported phenomenon in Egyptological books. Let us consider, briefly, what we know about this motif.

In the Pyramid Texts, the body of Osiris is the central theme of the spells. The god's body is portrayed in a state of dismemberment and decay, and at the same time submerged in the waters that have leaked from it (see chapter four). In Utterance 532, the putrefying body of Osiris is paralleled with the body of Horus (Horus of the Duat, not Horus the son of Isis), as if the two bodies were identical,[17] while in Utterance 362 the body is seemingly named Atum (the king refers to 'my father Atum in darkness').[18]

In the Coffin Texts, the body of Osiris is again the prominent theme, but there are also references to the body of Atum, the body of Shu, the body of Re, the body of Horus, and the body of Thoth.

The body of Atum is mentioned several times. In one spell, Nun refers to 'my father, Lord of the Evening, the body who is in Heliopolis';[19] in another, there is mention of 'Atum on his day of burial';[20] and in another, the body of Atum produces a falcon-spirit from its flesh.[21]

The body of Shu is mentioned several times. One spell refers to 'Shu who is in the coffin';[22] another refers to a place called 'the shambles of Shu';[23] another suggests that the soul of Shu came into being from his own body;[24] and another states that the air-gods came into being from the body of Shu.[25]

The body of Re is mentioned once. He is said to descend from the sky to weep for his corpse in Heliopolis.[26]

Figure 22.
THE MUMMY OF HORUS, PROTECTED BY NEPHTHYS.

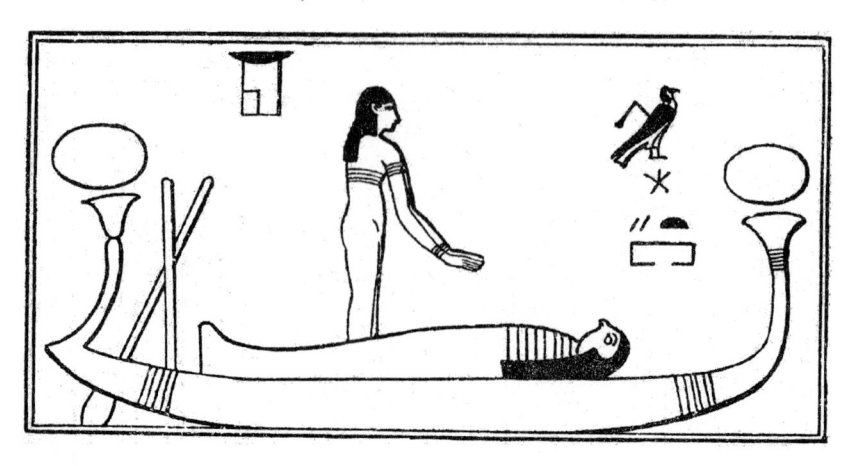

GOD AND THE GODS 99

The body of Horus is mentioned once, in a spell which is similar to Utterance 532 of the Pyramid Texts.[27]

The body of Thoth is mentioned once, and is identified with Osiris, whose corpse rests in the isle of fire.[28]

Moving on to later texts, the Great Hymn to Amun refers several times to the body of Amun. The great soul of Amun is said to have created his own egg by mixing his semen with his body;[29] afterwards, his body 'was hidden among the old ones';[30] the hymn proclaims that: 'His soul (*ba*) is in the sky, his body (*djt*) is in the land of the west (*ament*)'.[31]

In the Books of the Netherworld, the body of Osiris is the central icon. Here, the main theme is the union of the sun-god Re with the corpse of Osiris in the uttermost depths of the *duat* (see discussion of the midnight sun in chapter four). The tomb of the god is described as a great secret and mystery.[32] But the netherworld is also shown to contain the corpses of other creator-gods. In the Am Duat and the Book of Caverns, there are sarcophagi containing the corpses of Atum and Khepri, in addition to Re and Osiris, buried in mounds of sand (see figure 23).[33] And in the Book of the Earth, there are remarkable scenes in which the corpses of Geb, Ta-tenen, Shu, Tefnut, Khepri, Nun, Isis, and Nephthys all apparently come to life in the underworld.[34] Interestingly, in this book, the entire realm of the dead is portrayed as 'the corpse of Shetit'.[35]

Figure 23.
THE CREATOR-GOD IN THE FORMS OF ATUM, KHEPRER, RE AND OSIRIS, BURIED IN MOUNDS OF SAND IN SARCOPHAGI.
A scene from the seventh division of the Book Am Duat.

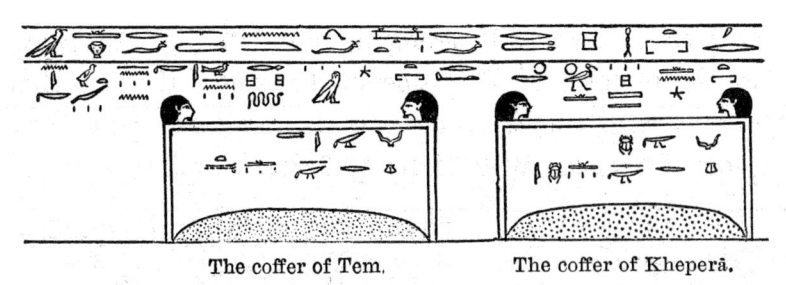

In the late-18th and 19th dynasties, two myths appeared in which the sun-god Re experienced a traumatic crisis in his body. The first of these myths is recorded in the Book of the Heavenly Cow and is known to scholars as *The Destruction of Mankind*, while the second is recorded in the Turin Papyrus number 1993 and has been entitled *Isis and Re*.[36]

The story of *The Destruction of Mankind* is set in the first time, when the sky has yet to be separated from the earth.[37] Re, the ruler of the *nun*, has become old and decrepit, and the beings who have issued from his Eye are mounting complaints against him, saying: "His Majesty has grown old; his bones have become like silver; his limbs have turned into gold; and his hair is like real lapis-lazuli."[38] Re then orders his Eye, Hathor, to destroy the rebels, but, that task having been accomplished, he begins to feel poorly. He exclaims: "I am laid low by the pain of the fire of sickness; whence comes to me this pain?... My limbs are weak, as at the first time."[39] Re then escapes his bodily fate by creating the sky and ascending to it.

In *Isis and Re*, Re is portrayed as the sun-god who sails in his barque through the sky and the netherworld, accompanied by his followers, the star-gods. Re has become old and saliva is dribbling from his mouth to the earth. Isis creates from this spittle a poisonous serpent which she sets on Re's path in order to lay him low; her plan is to acquire his secret name and thereby live, i.e. ascend to the sky. The serpent, as planned, bites Re, who cries out with pain and falls into the throes of death: 'His jaws shook, his lips trembled, and the poison took possession of all his flesh.'[40] As 'the living fire' flows out from Re's body, he calls to his followers, saying: "I have been laid low by some deadly thing... I have never before felt any pain like this... Behold, is it fire? Behold, is it water? My heart is full of burning fire, my limbs are shivering, and my members have darting pains in them."[41] Isis now interrogates Re and is allowed to search his body for his secret name. Upon discovering it, she drives out the poison from Re's body and permits him to live.

In these last two myths, the body of God is technically not a corpse; it is rather a body in crisis that is saved from approaching death. But such a distinction would have been lost on the Egyptian. For him, death was but a threshold from one state of existence to another. When God died, it was a foregone conclusion that he would come back to life again. His corpse possessed 'the living word'. It presupposed new life. No Egyptian would ever have claimed that Osiris died, for that would have signified the end of all things, which was patently not the case. God had not really 'died' in the modern sense of the word. He had conquered death and come back to life, and thereby ensured the rebirth of the cosmos. Death meant life, and life meant death: this was the great paradox of Egyptian religion.

Upon mummification of the body, the God's soul came into being and emerged from the mummy as an independent metaphysical entity. This soul was called *ba*, but it was otherwise said that the God had 'gone to his *ka*', i.e. become a spiritual double of his body.[42] This transformation of the God provided the archetype for the translation of the pharaohs to the afterlife.

Such was the great mystery of this event that the texts always referred to it in cryptic terms. The clearest exposition of the relationship of body to soul is probably found in Spell 75 of the Coffin Texts, where Shu as a soul claims to have originated from the creator-god's body:

> I am the soul (*ba*) of Shu, the self-created god, I have come into being from the body of the self-created god.[43]

Here, it is not clear whether the body belonged to Shu, or to his father Atum. Either scenario is possible, since both Atum and Shu could appear in the role of creator. And as creator, the god possessed a dual identity – the body and the soul.

On account of this dual identity, the creator-god can be visualised in a spell or myth at one moment in his bodily form and at another moment in his soul form. Thus Atum, for example, may appear in one passage as the body in the earth, but in another as the soul in the sky. For the modern reader, the continuing use of the name Atum does not signify any change in his form; but for an Egyptian reader, it would have been obvious from the context whether Atum was a body or a soul; there was absolutely no need for the scribe to spell it out.

Osiris is another fine example of this duality of form. For two hundred years Egyptology has puzzled over the fact that this earth-god can be also in the sky.[44] The straightforward explanation is that he was a creator-god, who sent out his soul from his body (or 'went to his *ka*', as the Egyptians put it). So, while Osiris as a body remained in the earth, Osiris as a soul freely circulated in the sky. Incidentally, this principle also explains why the earth-god Geb was sometimes pictured in the sky.[45]

The relationship of the body and the soul was commonly pictured as that of father and son. The body of the God was 'the father'; the soul of the God was 'the son'. The creator-god thus spanned two generations, of the old world and the new. In the Coffin Texts, the creator-god Nun is called 'the god (*netjer*), the father of the god (*netjer*)'.[46] The deceased king, having become one with the creator's body, is called 'Osiris, the father of Horus', and on one occasion 'Re, the father of Re'.[47] Having been reborn as the creator-soul, he then becomes Horus, or 'a great one, the son of a great one'.[48]

Different creator-gods were often merged, in the sense that the body of one begot the soul of another. The classic example here is the myth of Osiris as a living corpse begetting Horus as a son and heir. While Osiris remained in the earth, Horus in the form of a falcon soared into the sky where he produced light from his two eyes, the sun and the moon. Horus and Osiris then became locked in a mutual embrace on which the eternal vitality of the cosmos depended. But this was not a story of two gods. It was a story of the One God, expressed as a duality, rising and embracing himself. What we see here is a merger of two creator dualities, Osiris becoming specialised as the body and Horus becoming specialised as the soul. (In different historical circumstances, Horus might have become the father of Osiris, i.e. Horus the body and Osiris the soul.)

Figure 24.
HORUS RESURRECTS THE MUMMY OF OSIRIS.
The relationship of the son and the father was that of the soul and the body.

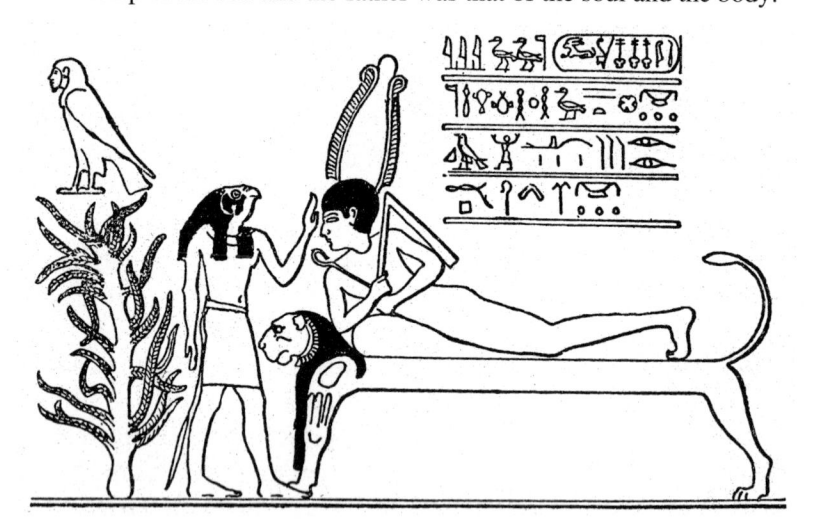

By the same principle, Nun, as the body of primeval water, could be father to the soul of Atum, or Re, as well as to the soul of himself. Atum as a body could be father to the soul of Shu, or Re, as well as to the soul of himself. Osiris as a body could be father to the soul of Re, as well as to the soul of Horus or himself. In a similar vein, Geb as a body could be father to the soul of Osiris and the soul of Horus,[49] and Ta-tenen as a body could be father to the soul of Re.[50] All of these permutations were allowed because each creator-god personified the same fundamental idea – the same duality of body and soul. It might seem confusing to us, but it all made sense if you were an Egyptian.

The Mystery of the Gods

The above discussion will please those who believe that the Egyptians were monotheists, since it suggests that there was but One God (*netjer*), whose many names signified one and the same creator-god. However, monotheism encounters a further obstacle – the existence of the gods (*netjeru*).

What do we know about these gods?

The *netjeru*-gods were a group of homogeneous beings whose primary attribute was membership of that group. Collectively, they were known as the ennead (*psdjt*), a term which meant 'nine' but implied 'a plural of plurals', i.e. a countless multitude.[51] Only in rare circumstances were the gods of this ennead assigned individual names or characters; even then the idea was to represent a totality of beings.[52]

The ennead-gods belonged to primeval times. Hence they were called by names such as *pautiu*, 'Primeval Ones', *wru*, 'Senior Ones', and *iawt*, 'Old Ones'. Its members were usually portrayed as souls or spirits, but there was also a class of dead gods, or ancestors (*tpiu*), who had expired at the time of the creation.

The gods stood in a close relationship with the God. The creator had made the gods by various means, such as speech, thought, birth, or an act of masturbation;[53] he was 'the *ka* of all the gods'; they were said to be his children.[54] On the other hand, it was claimed that the gods had created the God; they had joined together and brought him out of the *nun*; thus they were praised as his 'fathers and mothers'. This is one of the great puzzles of the creation in Egypt.

This close relationship was established for all eternity. The living gods were portrayed as a company united in the presence of God, and as an entourage who followed him (in his incarnation as the sun) in his circuit of the skies and the *duat*. God and the gods were often invoked together. In the temples, the creator did not live alone, but in the company of his ennead.[55]

The gods populated all realms of the Egyptian cosmos. They dwelt in the *nun*, the *duat*, the *akhet*, the field of reeds, the field of offerings, and the skies (see chapter two). An important dichotomy was 'the gods of the earth' and 'the gods of the sky'. In the Pyramid Texts, these two groups come together to form a ladder for the ascent of the king's soul from the earth to the sky.[56] Another important dichotomy was the dead gods and the living gods. The former lay entombed in the depths of the earth (they were thus called 'those whose seats are hidden'),[57] whereas the latter in the forms of souls or spirits inhabited the upper parts of the earth, the *akhet*, and the sky.

What was the origin of the gods? According to one tradition, God had created the gods from himself; he was thus their 'father', and they were his 'children'. Another tradition, however, suggested that the gods had originated from the God and the Goddess. Utterance 301 of the Pyramid Texts refers to 'Shu and Tefnut, who made the gods, who begot the gods, and established the gods'.[58]

But the genesis of the gods was also explained cosmographically.

According to one tradition, the gods were conceived in the *nun*. In the Pyramid Texts, Nun and Nunet are called 'the wellspring' of the gods.[59] In the Coffin Texts, Atum states that the ennead, as yet unborn, were already with him when he was alone in the *nun*,[60] while another spell reveals that Neber-djer was 'in the flood in the *nun* with the inert ones when he was weary'.[61] The latter myth is confirmed by the Bremner-Rhind Papyrus in which Neber-djer explains that a multitude of beings came forth from his mouth and: "I knit (myself) together in them, out of the *nun*, out of inertness."[62] Similarly in the Shu texts, Shu claims to have begotten the gods 'in chaos, in the *nun*, in darkness and in gloom'.[63] And, consistent with all of this evidence, it is stated in the Book of the Dead that the father of the gods was Nun, the personification of the primeval waters.[64]

According to a second tradition, the gods originated from the earth. In *The Theology of Memphis*, it is alleged that the gods came forth from Ta-tenen, the personification of the primeval land in its appearance from the *nun*.[65] Consistent with this, Ta-tenen is elsewhere called 'father of the gods, maker of the gods',[66] whilst according to the Papyrus Leiden the creator-god Amun 'took the form of Ta-tenen in order to give birth to the Primeval Ones'.[67] In respect of these latter gods, the Edfu Building Texts indeed describe them as 'the progeny of Ta-tenen', praising them *inter alia* as 'the Spirits (*kau*), the Senior Ones (*wru*), who came into being at the beginning, who illuminated this land when they came forth unitedly, who created the light'.[68] It may also be significant that the earth-god Geb was called 'father of the gods' and '*ka* of the gods'.[69]

But in apparent contradiction to the above claims, the Pyramid Texts record that the gods were born on the east side of the sky at the *akhet*.[70] The significance of this idea, vis-a-vis the myths of origin from the *nun* and the earth, will be examined in chapter six.

Whatever the place of origin of the gods, there is no ambiguity as to what happened next. The gods went up to the sky. This momentous event is recorded in Utterance 519 of the Pyramid Texts as the day 'when the sky was separated from the earth, when the gods went up to the sky'.[71] It

GOD AND THE GODS 105

is also recalled in the shout of the deceased king: "To the sky! To the sky among the gods who shall ascend! I am bound for the sky among the gods who shall ascend!"[72] The gods thereupon became stars in the belly of the sky-goddess Nut, as recorded in Utterance 434:

> O distant one above the earth, you [Nut] are at the head of Shu... He has loved you and has set himself underneath you and all things. You have taken to yourself every god who possesses his barque, that you may instruct them among Nut-of-a-thousand-souls (*Nwt kha ba.s*), lest they – the stars – depart from you.[73]

These star-gods, infinite in number, were portrayed as followers (*shmsu*) of the sun-god and mariners in the great sky-barque that revolved around the earth. But together they formed part of a single cosmic unity, the new body of God: hence of Amun it was said: 'The ennead is combined in your body: your image is every god, joined in your person.'[74]

Such is the mythology of the gods. What is to be made of it? As far as Egyptology is concerned, the *netjeru*-gods are an enigma. It has never been satisfactorily explained, for example, why there was a dichotomy of gods of the earth and gods of the sky, nor why some gods were dead and other gods living.[75] The impression is often given by modern writers that the Egyptians lacked a logical framework for these ideas.

But was this really the case?

Earlier, I presented a rationale for the Egyptian concept of God, based on the twin principles of personification and body-soul duality. The body of God, I argued, personified an old cosmos in a state of chaos, inertness, and want, while the soul of God represented the divine spark, which had been temporarily extinguished. The latter had rekindled itself, separated from its body, and transformed it into a new cosmos, comprising earth, sky, sun, moon and stars. The creator-soul was thus self-creating (*khpr-djs.f*) in the sense that it had revivified itself and reordered its own body.

The gods too possessed body-soul duality. Their bodies were the dead gods, the ancestors, who lay entombed in the earth having fulfilled their role in creation. Their souls were the living gods, who had ascended from the earth to the sky to become stars in the belly of Nut.

This transformation is attested in the Pyramid Texts. Several passages confirm that the gods had 'gone to their *kau*', i.e. become living spirits, either in the *akhet* or in the field of offerings in the sky.[76] This implies an evolution from the body.

The nature of the gods' transformation is made more explicit in a late myth in which Re assumes the role of creator. One day, so the story goes, Re summoned all the gods and goddesses to an assembly, whereupon he took them into his belly by swallowing them. The deities then went into battle, with the result that every last one of them was killed. Re then spat out the gods in the forms of birds and fishes.[77] This tale is undoubtedly an allegory of God's creation of the gods, the birds and fishes symbolising the gods' ascent to, and crossing of, the sky. Significantly, the gods are here resurrected from dead bodies.

A more solemn version of the same story appears in the Edfu Building Texts. In these inscriptions, much importance is attached to the ancestor-gods, who expired in the process of creation but were later 'restored' (*twa*) to life.[78] In one of the Edfu traditions, these olden gods are called *pautiu*, 'the Primeval Ones'. Significantly, these gods are described as if they were both first generation *and* second generation gods. On the one hand, they are 'the fathers of the fathers' and 'the mother of the mothers' who created the egg, gave birth to Re and the Great Lotus, and begot themselves.[79] On the other hand, they are the ghosts and the spirits who issued from themselves.[80]

The Edfu texts explain that the Primeval Ones originated in the island of the egg as formless bodily matter (*djt*), but were spiritualized when the egg surfaced and hatched. An interesting passage invokes the Primeval Ones as follows:

> The fathers of the fathers who came into being at the beginning, the mother of the mothers who were born since the primeval time (*djr-a*), whose bodily forms (*djt*) were divinized in the mounds of the lands (*iawt n tawi*).[81]

This statement suggests that the bodies of the ancestor-gods gave rise to souls or spirits in the mounds of the primeval mound.[82] Consistent with this, a related passage describes how the Primeval Ones were buried after fulfilling their creative tasks, and how their offspring came to their tombs to perform the funerary rites.[83]

A separate passage in the Edfu texts provides further information, this time pertaining to 'the nine ancestor-gods' who had been buried beneath a sacred orchard close to Edfu. Once these gods had completed their role in creation, Re had ordered that 'their bodies be mummified on the very spot on which they had been active'.[84] Thus it came to pass that:

> The great sacred necropolis of Edfu gives shelter to the bodies of the gods of the caverns.[85]

As for the souls of the gods, we are told that:

> Their souls have flown up to the sky where they dwell among the stars.[86]

The text refers to these gods as 'the ennead of the children of Atum' and 'the living gods come forth of Re'.[87]

It should be evident from the above sources that the *netjeru*-gods, like the God, spanned two generations, their bodies having generated souls or spirits, which had ascended from the earth and the *nun* to the sky. Such an interpretation may appear contentious to Egyptologists, but it would explain a category of statements about the gods which has hitherto made little or no sense. In the Pyramid Texts, for example, there is a reference to 'the fathers of the gods', while the term 'the children of their fathers' is applied to the gods in one instance and the imperishable stars in another.[88] How are these references to be explained, if not as reflections of body-soul duality? Similarly in the Coffin Texts, there is a reference to 'the elder gods who formerly came into existence with the ancestors'.[89] What was the relationship between these two groups, if not that of souls who were born from bodies?

Figure 25.
THE TWELVE GODS WHO ARE ASLEEP IN THE BODY OF OSIRIS.
A scene from the seventh division of the Book of Gates.

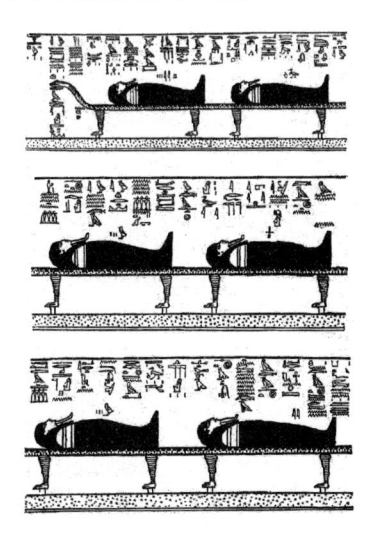

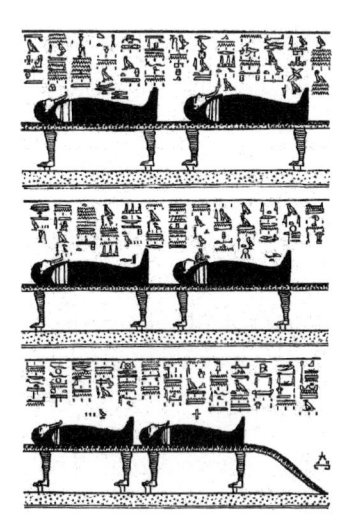

Assembly of the Gods

I have argued above that the transformation of the gods echoes that of the God in that both came into being as living soul from inert bodily matter. In this way, the gods were able to beget and create themselves, and father children; and the God was able to beget and create himself, and beget a son. The question now arises of the relationship between the gods and the God. How was it that they were able to create him, even while he was supposed to create them?

The basic relationship between the gods and the God is defined in the Pyramid Texts. There, it is stated that God created the gods, that he was 'the *ka* of all the gods', that the gods were his children, and that the gods formed his *psdjt*, the 'divine company' or 'ennead'. In Egyptology, these ideas are assumed to be symbolic only, reflecting the belief that God was the unique source of all things. But might they also support a more literal reading?

In the Coffin Texts, it is suggested that God literally created the gods from his body. We find the idea firstly in the Shu texts, which maintain that Shu created the Infinite Ones (the air-gods) either from his own body or the body of Atum:

> O you eight Infinite Ones who are in charge of the divisions of the sky, whom Shu made from the efflux of his body... whose names Atum made when the *nun* was created.[90]

> O you eight Infinite Ones whom Shu conceived, whom Shu fashioned, whom Shu created, whom Shu knit together, whom Shu begot from the efflux which was in his body...[91]

> O you eight Infinite Ones who went forth from Shu, whose names the body of Atum created... in chaos, in the *nun*, in darkness and in gloom.[92]

These Infinite Ones are air-gods. But the same principle applies to sky-gods, as Spell 312 makes clear. Here, a primeval serpent-god (one of a group) describes his birth as a spirit of light from the body of Atum:

> I am one who dwells in the light. I am a spirit who came into being and was created out of the body of the god. I am one of those gods or spirits who dwell in the light whom Atum created from his body, who came into being from the root of his Eye, whom Atum created and whom he spiritualized... I am distinguished above the (other) beings who dwell in the light – the spirits who came into being along with me.[93]

The context of this spiritualization is explained by the excluded middle of this spell. It states that Atum created the serpent-gods 'that they might be with him while he was alone in *nun*', and that they might 'announce him when he came forth from the *akhet*'.

Was there a logical basis for this claim that God created the gods from his body? And, if so, how do we reconcile this idea to the genesis of the gods from their own bodies?

A possible answer is provided by the mythology of Re, whose titles included 'Lord of the Ennead'. In Spell 17 of the Book of the Dead, this title is explained by the gloss: 'It means Re who created his names of his limbs (*hau*); it means the coming into existence of those gods who are in his following.'[94]

What were these 'limbs' of Re? In the myth *Isis and Re*, cited earlier, Re, having been laid low by a serpent in the netherworld, called out to the gods, his followers, who were in the sky, saying: "Come to me, all you gods who came into being from my limbs, who proceeded from me... Let there be brought to me my children, the gods, who possess words of magic."[95] This is a most interesting address, since it seems to suggest that the ennead was created not from his singular, integral body per se, but rather from *the limbs of his divided body*.

An earlier form of this remarkable tradition, dating to the early-18th dynasty, is found in the Am Duat. It occurs in Re's address to the gods of the netherworld, at the beginning of his journey. He says: "Give light to me and be guides to me, O you who came into being from my limbs... You are made of my bodies (*khatu*). I have made you, fashioned you, by means of my soul..."[96] One of the key themes of this book and the later Book of Gates is the uniting of Re with the gods who have issued from his limbs.[97]

The essence of this myth can also be found in the Coffin Texts, but in relation to Shu. A variant of Spell 76, cited earlier, states that Shu created the air-gods from the efflux of his limbs.[98]

What is the meaning of this? Is there a logical basis for supposing that the gods came forth from the limbs of the God, or was it just a figure of speech? In favour of the first possibility, a prominent theme in Egyptian mythology is the dismemberment of the God.

The theme of dismemberment is best known from the myth of Osiris, where a crucial act in the revivification of his body is the reassembly of his body-parts. In chapter four, I argued that Osiris was in fact a creator-god and that his divided limbs signified the initial state of chaos which is fundamental to the creation myth. But Osiris was by no means the only dismembered god in ancient Egypt. In addition, there was a myth of the dismemberment of Horus;[99] a myth of the dismemberment of Seth;[100] a myth of the dismemberment of the Eye (the Great Goddess);[101] and even a hint of the dismemberment of Atum (the Coffin Texts refer to 'the day of putting Atum together').[102] Dismemberment may also be implied by the myth of Ptah Ta-tenen assembling his limbs to form the primeval mound, and by the myth of Geb gathering together the weary limbs of

Atum (see chapter four).

There is a clear rationale here for the myth that God created the gods from his body, from his limbs; the idea seems to be that he spiritualized his limbs and thus brought the gods to life. But there is also a possible rationale here for the opposite myth – that the gods created God. This is seen in the idea that the dismembered God had to be restored to life by *the reassembly of his limbs*. It would follow that the gods, representing the limbs, were able to bring God to life by joining themselves together to form a single body. Logically, this would require conscious thought and action by the gods, suggesting that each god possessed a fragment of the original divine soul.

A good illustration of exactly this process may be seen in the creation myth of the Ogdoad, which we covered in chapter three. These eight gods of the primeval chaos were said to have pushed themselves together into a single force, whereupon they generated the primeval mound and gave birth to Re. On account of this, the Ogdoad were known as 'the fathers and the mothers who gave birth to Re'.

But this creation process may be far more prevalent in the texts than Egyptologists have realised.

An important idea in Egyptian religious literature is the assembly of the gods before the creator-god. In the Pyramid Texts, this occurrence is portrayed as a momentous event, which was enjoyed by both Atum and Geb:

> Ho all you gods! Come all together, come into assembly, just as you (once) came together and assembled for Atum in Heliopolis.[103]

> O Geb... you are the sole great god (*netjer aa*). Atum has given you his heritage, he has given to you the assembled ennead, and Atum himself is with them, whom his eldest children joined to you.[104]

In these passages, the purpose of the assembly of the gods goes unstated. Elsewhere in the Pyramid Texts, however, the assembly is treated in far greater detail. In particular, it is a major theme in the resurrection of the king, whose mummy is identified with Osiris.

The task of assembling the gods before Osiris usually falls to his son Horus: he assembles all the gods for Osiris ('there is none of them who will escape from him');[105] he gives them to Osiris;[106] he causes them to go up to Osiris;[107] he causes the gods to join Osiris and not reject him;[108] he sets Osiris before the gods;[109] and he causes Osiris to enclose all the gods within his embrace.[110]

For the most part, the assembled gods are called *netjeru*, but in several instances they are made synonymous with the *msu Hru*, 'the children of

Figure 26.
THE GODS OF THE ENNEAD ASSEMBLE ON THE STAIRWAY BEFORE THE THRONE OF OSIRIS.
A scene from the sixth division of the Book of Gates.

Horus', and these in turn are often equated with the four sons of Horus – Hapy, Duamutef, Imsety, and Qebhsenuf.[111] The children are referred to as 'those of his body',[112] while the four sons are described as his souls.[113] The father of the four sons is simultaneously Horus and Osiris.[114]

The children of Horus are mustered by Horus at the place where Osiris drowned.[115] They are said to go under Osiris, support him and carry him, and smite his foe.[116] Osiris is urged to unite himself to them, because they have loved him.[117] He becomes mighty though them.[118] On one occasion, the four sons of Horus bring Osiris-the-king his name of 'Imperishable Star'.[119]

Occasionally, Geb assembles the gods or brings Horus for the purpose of assembling the gods. In the former case, the gods are named as 'all the gods of Upper and Lower Egypt'; they raise up Osiris and cause him to be mighty.[120]

In a separate genre of spells, the gods assemble themselves for a god whom we may tentatively identify as either Osiris or Horus. Here, the assembly comprises 'the gods who are in the sky' and 'the gods who are in the earth',[121] and these are identified with 'the gods the Souls of Pe' and 'the gods the Souls of Nekhen'.[122] These gods go under the god, support him with their arms, and make a ladder for his ascent to the sky.[123]

A final example of the assembly myth (in the Pyramid Texts, at least)

Figure 27.
THE FOUR SONS OF HORUS, REPRESENTATIVE OF THE GODS, EMERGE ON A LOTUS FROM THE THRONE OF OSIRIS.

concerns Horus. Upon receiving news of his inheritance (the thrones of Geb), he exclaims: "My limbs which were in concealment are reunited, and I join together those who are in the *nun*... I go forth today in the form of a living spirit... those who are in the *nun* assign life to me."[124] As to the identity of 'those who are in the *nun*', a later version of this spell refers to them as 'the souls of Geb'.[125]

Putting all these clues together, it becomes clear that the purpose of the assembly of the gods, at least as it affected Osiris and Horus, was to revivify the God's body and spiritualize him, i.e. translate his soul from the *nun* to the sky. This, we may suppose, was also the idea behind the assembly of the gods for Atum and Geb.

There is a striking similarity here to the creation myth of the Ogdoad, in which the eight deities united in the *nun* to form the primeval mound and to give birth to Re. It seems inherently probable, therefore, that the assembly of the gods describes the very same scenario, namely a creation myth. (On the subject of Osiris and Horus as creator-gods, specialising as creator-body and creator-soul, many words have already been expended in this and the preceding chapter.)

Furthermore, there is a striking parallel between the assembly of the gods and the assembly of the limbs of the God's body (the two themes are often juxtaposed in the Pyramid Texts). Here, again, creation is the connecting theme, but there is an important distinction in that the gods are portrayed as active souls who *come together*, whereas the limbs are portrayed as passive body-parts which are *put together*. We must recall, however, that in the mythology of Re the gods came into being from the limbs of the creator. The distinction, then, is surely to be understood as a complementary duality of body and soul.

In summary, it would appear that God emanated the gods from himself via a process of disintegration, each of the gods inheriting a fragment of the divine body and a fragment of the divine soul. For a while, all was in chaos and confusion – the limbs in a state of inertness, the soul in a state of disorientation. Then the gods as souls took charge of their bodies, and came together in assembly to form a unity of body and soul. In this way, they created the God and became his 'fathers and mothers'. God, in turn, then rose up as a soul, transformed his own body into a higher unity, and created the gods by spiritualizing them from his limbs, whereupon they became the stars.

Or, otherwise said, God created himself.

Thus we solve a two-hundred-year-old crux of Egyptology.

Chapter Five Summary

- It was an axiom of Egyptian religion that the creator-god was a duality of body and soul. The once dormant body of the creator had acquired and sent forth a soul. The relationship of body and soul was viewed as one of 'father' and 'son'.

- The body of the creator-god personified the old cosmos. The crisis of the creator's body signified the crisis of that old cosmos, which was held to be in a state of darkness, chaos, and division.

- The God's body, comprising water, matter, and air was revivified by his soul, which brought energy and light. The soul transformed the body into the new cosmos and filled it with light. The creator was in this sense self-developing or self-creating (*kheper-djesef*).

- The gods too had body-soul duality. Their bodies lay entombed in the earth while their souls lived for ever as stars.

- God created the gods from the limbs of his body. They created him by assembling the limbs of his body. The myths are not inconsistent when viewed as an allegory for the reconstruction of the cosmos.

CHAPTER SIX

RAISING THE SKY

O Nut, distant one above the earth, you are at the head of Shu... He has loved you and set himself underneath you and all things.
(Pyramid Texts, Utterance 434)

The ancient Egyptian sky was conceived as an ocean of water, separated from the earth by an atmospheric bubble (*shu*). On the surface of this oceanic garment, the stars, the sun, and the moon ploughed their courses like ships sailing in a celestial sea.

How did this sky come into being? And how did the stars, the sun, and the moon come into being within it?

The essential creation myth in this regard is the separation of the sky from the earth, or to be more precise the separation of the sky from the earth and the *nun*.[1] This myth is alluded to several times in the Pyramid Texts: Shu is said to have raised the sky with his arms, and thereafter supported it on his arms;[2] he is said to have set himself beneath Nut, who took into her care every god in his barque;[3] and these gods are said to have ascended to the sky on the day when the sky was separated from the earth.[4]

Egyptologists understand this myth as a separation of the elements that were once confused in the *nun*: light is separated from darkness; land is separated from water; and sky is separated from earth; the differentiated cosmos thus comes into being.[5] Beyond this, however, scholars have not attempted to find a rational basis for the myth of creation by separation; it is widely regarded as one of those 'simple folk tales of the origins of the world'.

In recent years, a consensus has gradually formed around a particular interpretation of the separation myth, which has been developed by James P. Allen. In his view, the myth is best understood as the creation of a void inside a pre-existent, infinite ocean of water. He writes:

> Within the monad [Atum] appeared a space devoid (Shu) of the primeval waters, separating earth (Geb) from the surface of the waters (Nut). As the waters receded, the first mound of land became distinct (Ta-tenen)...[6]

As Allen understands it (based on the Middle Kingdom Shu texts),[7] the void was formed by Shu, representing the pressure of air exhaled from Atum. This blast of air compacted or pushed back the primeval waters in the outer parts of the cosmos and allowed the primeval mound to emerge at the bottom of the void.

The void of air (Shu) took the shape of a dome covering the earth. But according to Allen, the void also comprised a lower part, the *duat*, which was primarily conceived as a netherworld beneath the earth.[8] Together, the earth, the atmosphere, the *duat*, and the surface of the sky formed a kind of bubble, surrounded by the infinite chaos of the primeval waters. As Allen put it to me:

> The ancient Egyptian concept of the cosmos was a 'bubble' of air, light, and matter floating in an infinite ocean.[9]

In Allen's view, the creation of the void is to be understood as an act of the sun-god, who was the ultimate creator of the universe. He argues that Atum was a form of the sun-god, and that his emission of Shu therefore signified the first rising of the sun.[10] He also maintains that Kheprer was a form of the sun-god.[11]

Egyptology thus regards creation as an act of the sun-god, who created himself in the name of Atum-Kheprer, ascended to the sky in the form of Shu (or 'made a void' as Allen translates it),[12] and manifested himself in the form of the sun, Re, the ruler of the cosmic order.

Such is Allen's interpretation of the separation myth, which has gained considerable currency in Egyptology. And yet, as we shall now see, there are some serious problems with it.

Firstly, although the *duat* was a part of the created cosmos, there is no evidence that it belonged to the void (there is no myth of its creation by Shu). In fact, as Allen himself concedes elsewhere in his work, there is evidence for the existence of a lower sky beneath the earth, along with hints that this lower sky was supported by Tefnut (Shu's partner).[13] This would tend to suggest that Allen's 'bubble' was actually a sphere of air which entirely surrounded the earth (see my scheme, outlined in chapters one and two).

Secondly, although Allen's theory explains how the sky was separated from the earth, it is less clear how the sky was separated from the *nun* (as the creation myth requires). Granted, *pet* and *Nwt* signified the surface of the sky, which was distinct from the outermost depths of the *nun*; but it is unclear how this separation came about. How did Shu, as the pressure of air, manage to distinguish the waters of *pet* and *Nwt* from the waters of *nun*? In addition, Allen's theory offers no explanation for the origin of the celestial bodies – the sun, the moon, and the stars.

Thirdly, Allen theorises that the size of the universe was unchanged by the creation – it was infinite before and infinite afterwards. The creation of the void, bounded by the earth at its bottom and the surface of the sky at its top, therefore represented an inward shrinkage from the mass that existed in the beginning. But this jars with the many statements that the creator-god or sky-goddess 'went up' to the sky or 'became high' in the sky. In the Pyramid Texts, Atum is said to have risen up in the form of the high hill and the *benben* stone,[14] while the gods are said to have gone up to the sky.[15] In the Coffin Texts, Shu is said to have lifted up Nut from upon himself, and to have lifted up Atum,[16] while Atum is said to have created Nut so that she might be above him.[17] Re is made to say: "I am raised aloft on my standard above yonder places of the *nun*", while Nun says: "I am one who is raised aloft... I am the lord of those who are on high",[18] and Shu states: "The sky was made for me in order that I become high".[19] Under Allen's theory of creation, these passages are problematic, for according to his scenario the creator, who personified the developing cosmos (indisputably so in Atum's case), ought to have become smaller, not bigger.

Granted, this problem might be reduced by careful retranslation of the texts. Allen, for example, revises the line 'the gods went up to the sky' to 'the gods went to the sky';[20] by dropping the word 'up', he eliminates the problem. But certain things cannot be translated away, such as the high hill of Atum, or the ladder of Atum and Shu.[21] Again and again, the texts inform us that the creator-god flew up to the sky like a bird or a winged beetle, or assumed his throne upon a pillar, perch, tree, or standard that was erected upon the earth and the abyss.

Fourthly, and finally, there are problems concerning the notion of the sun-god as creator. These problems are twofold. First, it is quite incorrect to treat Atum and Kheprer as forms of the sun-god; in the earliest texts, they are creator-gods, with strong chthonian characteristics. Second, the myths of Re contradict the solar creator theory in that he originates from the *nun and the primeval mound*. For example, in one myth Re is said to be born from the lotus *in the pool of the primeval island*, while in others he is said to be *the son of Ta-tenen (the primeval earth)* or the offspring

Figure 28.
THE BARQUE OF OSIRIS AT ABYDOS.
The principle of lifting the god is especially evident in this image.

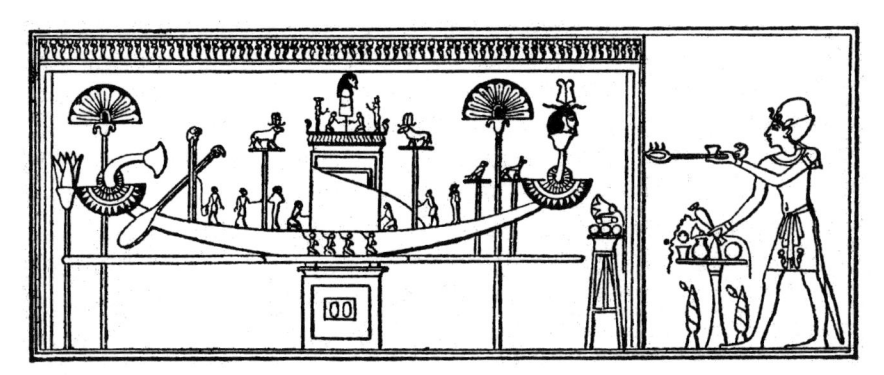

of the *pautiu*-gods, *the Children of Ta-tenen*.[22] If Re was a solar creator, then why would he go from the *nun* to the sky *via the earth*? That he did so tends to suggest that he was not so much a solar creator as a *chthonian creator*.

Is there an alternative to Allen's theory? If we take a geocentric, rather than heliocentric, approach to the creation myth, a different interpretation indeed arises. Under this approach, the original *nun*, containing primeval matter and air, is finite in size, but is caused to expand by the process of creation. Accordingly, the creator's actions are not directed inward in the sense of creating a void of earth, air, and sky within the *nun*, but outward in the sense of creating a purely atmospheric void above the earth, along with a celestial ocean supported upon that void. Primeval waters are thus separated from primeval waters by being elevated, allowing the primeval mound to emerge from the waters below. In this scheme, the sky is quite literally separated from the earth and the *nun* (the materials of the former cosmos) by the outward pressure of Shu's air; this atmosphere does not form a dome, as in Allen's scheme, but is made to surround the earth and the *nun* completely in a true geocentric arrangement (see figure 29). The *duat* is here an imaginary realm, representing the former cosmos in its metamorphosis from death to life; logically enough, it is located beneath the earth at the centre of the new cosmos.

The key attribute of this theory, in contrast to Allen's, is that it adheres strictly to the Egyptian belief that the sky was *raised* from the earth, and that the creator-god and the gods *went up* to the sky. It therefore involves an *expansive* creation process, whereas Allen's model involves what we might call a *reflective* creation process. The latter model describes a *fixed*-separating cosmos, which we might designate by the symbol O-O

Figure 29.
THE GEOCENTRIC COSMOS (ALFORD MODEL).

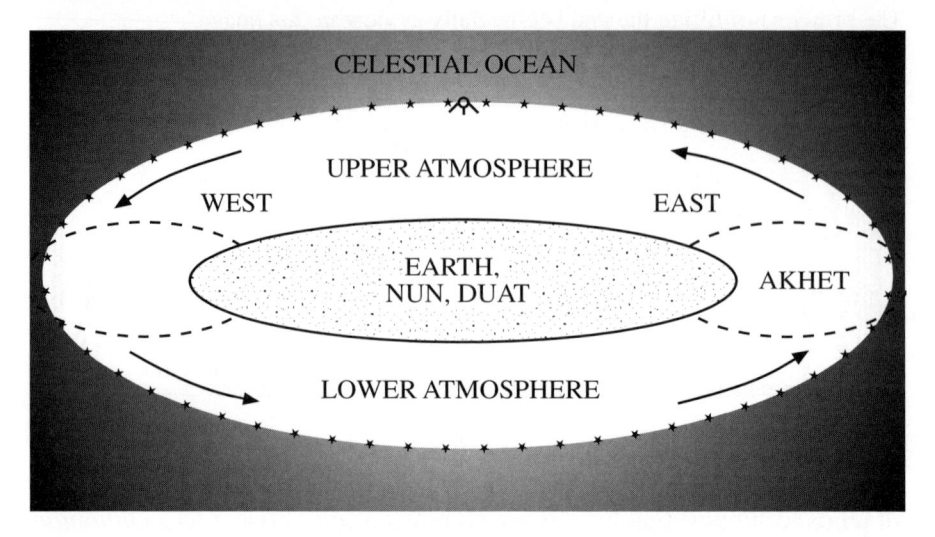

[Diagram: An oval showing CELESTIAL OCEAN around the outer edge with stars, UPPER ATMOSPHERE above, LOWER ATMOSPHERE below, WEST on left, EAST on right, EARTH, NUN, DUAT in the centre, and AKHET on the right inner ring.]

whereas my model describes an *expanding*-separating cosmos, which we might designate by the symbol o-O.[23] These symbols communicate the before-and-after sizes of the evolving cosmos.

A second key attribute of this theory is that it describes a geocentric rather than heliocentric cosmogony. According to the orthodox view, *the sun-god* is the centre and creator of the cosmos; the creation may thus be deemed heliocentric. Under the alternative theory, however, the *creator-god* is the centre and creator of the cosmos, and he is not the sun but the primeval matter, the earth and the *nun*; the creation may thus be deemed geocentric. In this geocentric scheme, everything in the outer cosmos – the atmosphere, the sky, and the celestial bodies – originated in a process of expansion from the inner. The sun, therefore, was not the creator, but a created object.

Do the Egyptian texts support such a theory? Egyptologists will have their doubts, since they have been trained to read the relevant texts from a heliocentric perspective. It is this author's contention, however, that if we reread the texts from a geocentric perspective, we will find repeated and consistent allusions to the origins of the sky and the celestial bodies from the earth.

Our task begins in this chapter with a study of three key problems:

- The origin of the sky-ocean
- The origin of the stars
- The origin of the sun and the moon

The Origin of the Sky-ocean

In Egypt, as elsewhere in the ancient world, the sky was envisaged as a celestial ocean on which the sun, moon, and stars navigated like boats in a procession. As discussed at length in chapter two, this sky-ocean was known by a variety of names:

> *pt*, pronounced *pet*, usually translated as 'sky' (sometimes referred to as *hrt*, 'that which is far above').
>
> *qbhw*, pronounced *qebhu*, usually translated 'firmament', but literally 'fresh water'.
>
> *nw* or *nnw*, pronounced *nun*, usually translated 'celestial waters' or 'abyss', but literally 'primeval waters'.
>
> *Nwt*, pronounced Nut, the sky personified as goddess.
>
> *mht wrt*, pronounced *mehet weret*, literally 'the great flood', the sky personified as the cow-goddess Mehet-weret.

How did this body of water come to be in the sky? While no information has come down to us on the origins of *pet*, *qebhu*, or Mehet-weret, we do possess myths of the origins of *nun* and Nut.

For the origin of the *nun*, we must look to the mythology of Nun, the god who personified the primeval waters. He discloses his origins in a highly revealing speech in the Coffin Texts. But before we consider that account, we must first take a brief look at how Nun was perceived during Middle Kingdom times.

In Spell 335 of the Coffin Texts, Nun is described as a self-created creator-god. This information is provided in a question-and-answer gloss, appended to the pronouncement of Atum:

> I am the great god (*netjer aa*), the self-created (*kheper-djs.f*).
> *Who is the great god, the self-created? He is the water of the nun; he is the god, the father of the god.*[24]

In the equivalent text in the Book of the Dead, this statement is expressed slightly differently:

> I am the great god, the self-created.
> *Who is he? The great god, the self-created, is water; he is Nun, the father of the gods.*[25]

Nun was thus regarded as a form of the creator-god. Indeed, such was his importance that other creator-gods were associated with him in order to bolster their credentials. Amun was thus called 'Nun, the Old One, who evolved first', or more fully 'Nun, the Old One, who came into being at the first time (*khpr m zp tpi*)', or 'Nun, the Old One, the Primeval One of the Two Lands, who created the Primeval Ones'.[26] While Khnum, in a late text, is made to boast: "I am the one who created himself, Nun, the great god, who came into being at the beginning."[27]

As a creator-god, Nun possessed both a body and soul, the body in this case being the primeval waters. His self-creation is to be understood as his awakening as a soul, followed by the transformation which his soul performed on his body (see chapter five). Hence in the Book of the Dead, Nun claims:

> I am Nun... I am the eldest of the primeval gods, this soul of the souls (*ba pu bau*) of the eternal gods; my body is everlasting, my shape is eternity... I am the one who created darkness and who made his seat in the limits of the sky... I am the soul who created the *nun*.[28]

This speech has a precedent in Spell 307 of the Coffin Texts. But it is in Spell 714 of these texts that we find the all-important information on the creation (or better, evolution) of the *nun*. Here, Nun as creator describes how he came into being amidst a flood:

> I am Nun, the Sole One, who has no equal, and I came into being yonder on the great occasion of my flood (*mht*), when it came into being. I am the one who came into being in my form 'Circlet who is in his Egg'. I am the one who originated there, in the primeval waters. Look, the flood is subtracted from me; look, I am the remainder. It was by means of my power that I created my body, and I made myself, as I wished, according to my heart.[29]

The crucial line here is "Look, the flood is subtracted from me; look, I am the remainder." (Allen's translation). Clearly Nun is referring to his act of creation, but what exactly does he mean? Under Allen's theory of creation, the subtraction of waters from Nun makes no sense, since the void which Shu forms is supposed to be enclosed by a continuous and infinite *nun*. How can there be a subtraction or remainder if the waters are left intact as one body?

The flood is also a curious matter. Why should there be a flood in the *nun* if, as Allen suggests, the creation of the void is the significant event? Why would Nun create himself in a flood? In what way might the flood be deemed his 'great occasion'?

All of this would make sense, however, if the creation were viewed as an expansive process. Under this interpretation, the primeval waters of *nun* would indeed be divided – between those that remained at the centre of the cosmos and those that were raised up to form the sky. Moreover, the lifting up of the latter waters by Shu (representing the pressure of air) would indeed amount to a flood. This flood would be 'subtracted' from Nun's original body and would leave behind a 'remainder', adjoined to the earth at the centre of the cosmos. This remaining reservoir of water would then feed the Nile, and the wells and springs of Egypt – an idea which is well attested in the Egyptian texts.[30]

In support of this interpretation, the Coffin Texts inform us that 'Atum issued from the *nun* into the *hnhnit*-water of the sky',[31] while in the Book of the Dead the same god declares: "I ascended from the *nun* (primeval ocean) to the *nun* (celestial waters)."[32]

This theory differs radically from that proposed by Allen. Whereas Allen interprets the original *nun* as celestial waters, the geocentric theory lends primacy to the chthonian waters – those that remain attached to the earth – and makes the celestial waters derivative. This distinction leads to a profoundly different reading of the texts in which Nun personifies the primeval waters.

We turn now to Nut and the myth of her origins. In Utterance 432 of the Pyramid Texts, it is stated:

> O Great One [Nut] who came into being in the sky, you have achieved power... the entire land is under you... you have enclosed the earth and all things in your embrace.[33]

According to this passage, Nut came into being in the sky. However, this was not her place of origin. In Utterance 484, we read:

> Thus says Nut: "I am the Great One (*wrt*) who ascends to the sky . . . in peace."[34]

It would thus appear that Nut ascended to the sky, and thereupon came into being in the sky, or rather *became* the sky.

This picture is consistent with the myth that Shu uplifted the sky (*pet*), as mentioned earlier in this chapter. In several texts, it is specifically said that Shu *lifted Nut* to become the sky. This claim appears first in the Pyramid Texts:

> O distant one above the earth, you [Nut] are at the head of Shu... He has loved you and has set himself underneath you and all things.[35]

It is then repeated, more explicitly, in the Coffin Texts, where Shu says:

> I lifted up my daughter Nut from upon myself, that I might give her to my father Atum in his realm, and I have set Geb under my feet...
> I have set myself between them...[36]

This claim is hard to fathom under Allen's interpretation of the creation myth. Why would the sky-goddess first be low, and then be raised high? Why would Shu be standing upon the earth (Geb)? All of this suggests a geocentric and expansive creation.

It should be recalled at this juncture that Nut, as the sky-goddess, was essentially a body of water (see chapter two). The myth of her separation from Geb would thus allegorize a lifting of waters from the earth into the sky. This is exactly the scenario deduced earlier with regard to Nun, the god of the primeval waters.

Figure 30.
NUN LIFTS UP THE BARQUE OF KHEPRI, CREATING A VOID IN THE PRIMEVAL WATERS. THE SUN DISC EMERGES FROM THE DUAT BUT AT THE SAME TIME IS LIFTED INTO THE ARMS OF NUT. NUT HERSELF IS EMERGING FROM THE DUAT, WHICH IS PERSONIFIED BY THE CIRCULAR BODY OF OSIRIS.
The climactic scene from the Book of Gates.

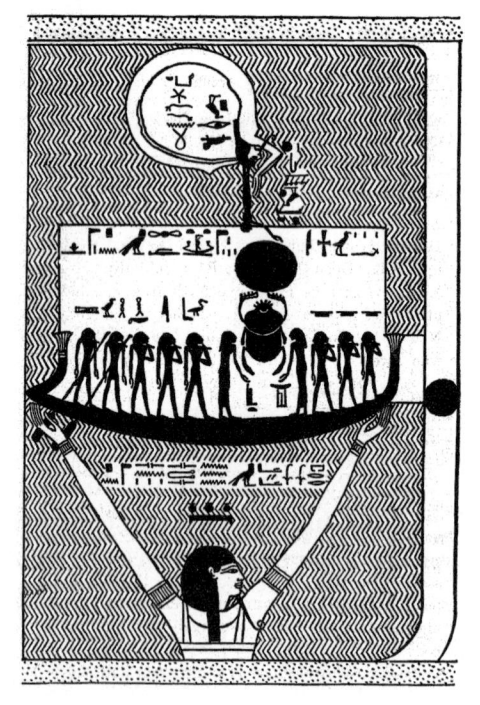

Might Nut's origins lie with the primeval waters that were attached to the earth – the waters which gave birth to the waters of sky?

In this regard, a series of spells in the Pyramid Texts provides food for thought:

O Nut, you are effective (*akh*); power was yours in the womb of your mother Tefnut before you were born.[37]

You are strong of heart; you move about in your mother's womb in your name of 'Nut'.[38]

You are the daughter, mighty in her mother, who appeared as a bee.[39]

To these, we may add a New Kingdom inscription from the sarcophagus of Seti I:

I am Nut of the mighty heart, and I took up my being in the body of my mother Tefnut in my name of Nut; over my mother none have gained the mastery.[40]

These passages may be interpreted as follows: that Tefnut personified the primeval womb of the cosmos; that Nut stirred as a soul or spirit in these waters; and that Nut's soul then emerged from these waters and ascended to the sky. The two goddesses would thus represent a 'mother' cosmos and a 'daughter' cosmos.[41]

But there are other spells in the Pyramid Texts that blur the distinction between Tefnut and Nut, making Nut herself the primeval womb of the cosmos. Nut is on one occasion called 'the great well' (*chnmt wrt*);[42] she gives birth though her daughter the *duat*;[43] she bears four beings whom Atum begot;[44] Re is said to have come forth from Nut;[45] and Osiris is said to have split open her womb.[46]

Nut's role as a mother cosmos is particularly striking in the Book of Nut. Here, the sun-god Re passes through Nut's mouth in the western horizon and is reborn through her vulva in the east. Remarkably, the body of Nut is equated to the *duat*. In Allen's words:

[The text] locates the *duat* within the body of Nut – that is somehow 'inside' the sky. At sunset, the sun 'enters her mouth, inside the *duat*'. This is equivalent to the moment of conception, 'at her second hour of pregnancy'. During the night, the sun 'sails inside her' and 'gives directions in the *duat*'. At dawn 'he parts the thighs of his mother Nut', 'as he opens in his splitting and swims in his redness' of 'after birth', and moves into the day sky, 'apparent and born'.[47]

This passage through the body of Nut is also depicted in the Books of the Netherworld, in which the sun-god makes his night journey through the *duat*. In the Am Duat, at the beginning of Re's journey, the gods of the netherworld say:

O great god, the doors are opened to you, the portals of the secret land of the west are thrown open before you, *the doors of Nut the great are thrown wide open*. Make light in the thick darkness... approach the place where Osiris Khenti-amentiu is.[48] (emphasis added)

Here, Nut is equated with the land of the west, *ament*, which was a name of the *duat*. Twelve hours later, Re emerges from the *duat* in the form of Khepri by 'rising from between the thighs of Nut'.[49] The goddess is thus identified, once again, with the entire netherworld.

Commenting on the Books of the Netherworld, Erik Hornung makes the following observation:

The nocturnal journey [of the sun] leads through an inner region of the cosmos that was regarded not only as the netherworld and the depths of the earth, but also as water (the primeval water, called *nun*), as darkness, *and as the interior of the sky*.[50] (emphasis added)

In the light of our earlier discussion of the midnight sun (chapter four), it is highly probable that Nut's role in conceiving and giving birth to the sun-god each day served the purpose of repeating creation. But far from being a symbolic presence in this drama, it would rather appear that Nut belonged at the heart of it as mother of the cosmos – a veritable creator-goddess who evolved from a single watery body, pregnant with the spirit of life, into the separated waters of the earth and the sky – the mother and the daughter, the mother giving birth to herself – 'the mysterious one'.[51]

This interpretation may be tested by examining Nut's role as mother of the deceased king. As explained in earlier chapters, the Egyptian pharaoh in death was identified with Osiris in the belief that his soul would come forth from his body. Since in myth Osiris was the son of Geb and Nut (in the sense of a soul from a body), the deceased king too, in his soul form, was the son of Geb and Nut. Already, in chapter four, we have explored the relationship of Geb and Osiris in the Pyramid Texts in the context of geocentric creation. But we have yet to consider the relationship of Nut and Osiris. Does Nut's role in revivifying Osiris-the-king and taking him to the sky accord with the model of expansive creation?

In the Pyramid Texts, Nut performs a pivotal role in restoring the dead king Osiris to life. She spreads herself over him, conceals, and protects him;[52] she reassembles his limbs;[53] she brings his heart and places it in his body;[54] she cleanses and purifies him;[55] she embraces and enfolds him;[56] she gives birth to him (on one occasion in *ament*, 'the hidden land');[57] she bears him as 'a great one, the son of a great one' and a spirit (*akh*);[58] she takes his hand, or lays her hands on him, and gives him a road to the *akhet*;[59] she carries him to the sky;[60] she receives him in the sky;[61] she bears him in the sky;[62] she makes him an imperishable star in her body;[63]

and she bears him alive every day like Re, as he circuits with the sun-god from the west to the east.[64]

All of these incidents fit a pattern, the deceased king taking the role of Osiris, who is reassembled, revivified, spiritualized, and translated to the sky. We are thus dealing with a re-enactment of the Osiris myth. But the remarkable thing is the presence of Nut alongside Osiris at each stage of the myth. First, we see Nut in the *duat*, protecting Osiris-the-king and bringing him back to life; next, we see Nut taking the Osiris-king to the *akhet*; and finally, we see Nut taking the Osiris-king to the sky (*pet*), to make him a star in her body (*Nwt*). Nut thus spans all major realms of the evolving cosmos, consistent with the idea that she is developing into the cosmos herself.

The names of Nut in the Pyramid Texts confirm this suspicion. On the one hand, she is given the name 'Sky':

> You [Nut] are made fruitful by Geb in your name of 'Sky' (*pet*).[65]

> Do not let this king be far from you in your name of 'Sky' (*hrt*).[66]

On the other hand, she is given the names 'Tomb', 'Sarcophagus', and 'Mastaba':

> You [Osiris-the-king] have been given to your mother Nut in her name of 'Tomb' (*qrst*), she has embraced you in her name of 'Sarcophagus' (*qrs*), and you have been brought to her in her name of 'Mastaba' (*aa*).[67]

And, to complete the picture, she is given the name 'Ladder':

> He [Osiris-the-king] goes to his mother Nut, he ascends upon her in this her name of 'Ladder' (*maqt*).[68]

These passages are enlightening indeed. Egyptologists have never really been able to explain why the king's tomb and sarcophagus, located in the earth, were identified with Nut, the goddess of the sky.[69] Why would the sky have its resting place inside the earth?[70] Might the explanation be that Nut was not just a sky-goddess, but a creator-goddess, the mother of the cosmos? The third quote above is certainly consistent with this theory; it seems to suggest that Nut raised herself to a great height, like a ladder to the sky.

Such is the mythology of Nut. Although we do not possess an explicit statement that she divided or uplifted the primeval waters to form the sky (as in the myth of Nun), it is highly probable that this was the implicit meaning of her separation from Geb and her ascent to the sky. Consider. Nut's primary identity was water (her sky was a watery realm and her name *Nwt* was probably derived from *nw*, the word for primeval water);[71] one of her names was 'the great well'; she was the mother-womb which gave birth to various gods; she came forth from the womb of Tefnut; she was separated from Geb (earth); she ascended to the sky and came into being in the sky; and she personified the sky-ocean.

It is worth recalling at this juncture the flood of Nun. Nun, as we have seen, came into being on 'the great occasion' of his flood (*mht*), and this flood was subtracted from him, as if it were used to create the celestial ocean. This interpretation of the flood is a problem for Allen's theory of the creation of the void. But it is exactly what we would expect under the geocentric and expansive model of creation. In fact, if this theory has any validity at all, we would expect the flood to have been something of a leitmotif in Egyptian mythology.

We are not to be disappointed.

A recurring theme in the creation myth is the flood in the *nun* at the beginning of time. In the Coffin Texts, Atum is depicted 'in the flood (*hhu*), in the *nun* with the inert ones';[72] he is said to come into being 'out of the flood, out of the *nun*';[73] Shu likewise is placed 'in the flood, in the *nun*',[74] and he and Atum are said to have created the Infinite Ones in that place.[75] In these and other passages, the *nun* and the flood are seen to be synonymous.[76] The flood of the beginning is also mirrored by a flood of the end. In an unusual spell in the Book of the Dead, Atum states that after millions and millions of years the earth will eventually return to the *nun* and the flood (*huhu*) as in its original state.[77]

The flood appears in all realms of the Egyptian cosmos, except for the *duat* (and even then, the *duat* is described as a watery place, traversed by boat).

The field of reeds and the field of offerings are both portrayed in a state of flood. In the Pyramid Texts, it is this flood which carries the king towards the *akhet* at the eastern side of the sky. The emergence of fertile land from these floodwaters may recall the myth of the primeval mound emerging from the *nun*.

The *akhet* is depicted as a watery place with banks and shores. In the Pyramid Texts, one of these banks is said to contain 'the flood of the great flood (*mht wrt*)'.[78] In the Coffin Texts, Neber-djer claims that the flood was one of the four good things that he made 'within the portal of the *akhet*'.[79]

Finally, the surface of the sky is depicted in a state of flood. The *pet*, the *qebhu*, and *Nwt* are all synonymous with *mehet weret*, literally 'the great flood'. In the Pyramid Texts, the gods of the sky are said to live on this great flood,[80] while in the Coffin Texts, Atum goes to rest upon it.[81]

As with Nun and Nut, our challenge is to pin down the dynamics of this flood. Can it be shown to be separated from its source, as in the myth of Nun? Does Shu lift it up with the pressure of his air? Can it be traced from the *nun* into the *akhet*, and thence into the *mehet weret* of the sky?

Several clues indeed point in this direction.

Firstly, the Pyramid Texts (and later derivatives) speak of 'the night of the great flood (*mht wrt*) which issued from the Great One (*wrt*)'.[82] The Great One (feminine) is not identified, and no explanation for the flood is offered, but the context involves the king's soul passing from the isle of fire to the *akhet* and beyond.

Again in the Pyramid Texts, Re is given the name 'Great Flood which issued from the Great One' (this is an unusual epithet for a sun-god, and suggests a wider creational remit).[83] The 'great one' here may be Osiris, who was often called 'the great one' and whose body was the source of a flood (see chapter four).[84]

These references are vague, but they demonstrate at the very least that the flood was a mythical event of huge importance, and that the waters originated from a great goddess or god.

A second clue is found in the Coffin Texts, in the account of creation by Atum and Shu. In Spell 79, there is mention of a time when the *nun* existed, but the great flood (*mht wrt*) did not exist; the great flood was then created so that Atum could rest upon it (this means that Atum went to rest upon the surface of the sky).[85] But according to Spell 76, there was a crucial moment when Geb, the earth-god, gathered together the great flood (*mht wrt*) for Atum.[86] The impression is thus given that the flood was somehow lifted from the earth to the sky.

Did Shu lift the flood? A passage in the Pyramid Texts does describe a lifting of waters by Shu, but the context is ambiguous and might refer to the terrestrial upsurge of rivers, seas, and springs.[87] The Coffin Texts are more forthcoming, thankfully. Although it is not stated explicitly that Shu lifted the great flood, it is said that his soul (*ba*) was 'at the head of the great flood',[88] and that his face (*hr*) was 'that of the great flood'.[89] Both these lines might imply that Shu had lifted the flood. Furthermore, one spell describes how Shu in his role of father of the gods 'appeared in glory with the river (*itru*) around him in the flame of the light'.[90] If this is a celestial river, as the context suggests, then it might well describe the flood in its ascent to the sky.

A third clue pertains to the flood in the *akhet*. In the Coffin Texts, the deceased states in one spell: "I hear the noise of the flood at the eastern gate of the sky",[91] and in another: "the gates of the *akhet* are opened to me, my floodwater (*mht*) is that of the great flood (*mht wrt*)."[92] Both these lines suggest strongly that the flood issued forth from the *akhet* to form the *mehet weret* of the sky. This idea is also suggested by the myth of Neheb-kau, 'the bestower of doubles (*kau*)', who swallowed the flood (*hhu*) and issued from the *akhet*, whereupon he became the *ouroboros*-serpent of the skies.[93] The significance of the *akhet* in the creation myth is itself a moot point, to which we shall return in the next section of this chapter.

All of this evidence supports the hypothesis that the flood originated from a former, finite cosmos (the earth and the *nun*) and was separated from this terrestrial world to become the waters of the sky (*mht wrt*, alias *pet*, *qebhu*, *nun*, and *Nwt*). It all fits the model of a geocentric, expansive creation.

So much for the origin of the sky-ocean. Let us turn our attention now to the origin of the stars.

The Origin of the Stars

The origin of the stars is not straightforward. There is no single text that declares 'the stars originated in the following manner...', at least not in a language that modern readers can understand. It is plausible, however, that a theory of stellar genesis did exist, the knowledge of which was taken for granted. In order to determine this theory, we must go back to basics and examine some fundamental relationships, particularly that of the stars and the gods (the ennead) and that of the star-gods and the souls and spirits that dwelt in the sky.

To begin, we must establish the basic facts.

The Egyptian word for star was *sba*, written with the sign of a five-pointed star ✶.[94] The night sky was thus called *qebhu sbau*, often rendered 'the starry firmament', but literally 'the fresh water of the stars'.[95]

Less often a star was termed *shd*. This word is more usually found in the plural form *shdu*, 'stars', or in the expressions *shdu pet*, 'the starry sky', and *msqt shdu*, 'the beaten path of stars'.[96]

Another word for star was *nkhkh*. The *nkhkhu*-stars possibly conveyed the meaning 'the aged ones'.[97]

Some stars were given special names. Those that have been identified are Sopdet (Sothis in Greek), which was the star Sirius, and Netjer-dwau, the so-called 'morning star', which was the planet Venus.[98] Those stars that have not yet been identified include *sba-wati*, 'the unique star' (or 'lone star'),[99] *sba-wr*, 'the great star',[100] and *iad*-star (untranslatable).[101]

Two small groups of stars are mentioned in the texts. The first of these is *mskhtiu*, which has been identified with the constellations Ursa Minor and the Plough respectively, but perhaps originally signified the northern circumpolar stars in their entirety.[102] The second is Sah, which in later times signified the constellation Orion, but in earlier times may have signified the star Canopus.[103]

The texts also lend names to the stars en masse, namely *akhmu-sku*, 'the imperishable stars', and *akhmu-wrdu*, 'the untiring stars'. These names reflected the indestructible and inexhaustible nature of the stars, which for ever reappeared and circulated in the sky. It is not the case, as Egyptologists maintain, that the imperishables were the circumpolar stars that never dipped beneath the horizon. These stars were *akhmu-sku* in the sense of a subgroup, and their identity was usually indicated by the context of the spell, or else by qualifying their name with the tag 'those northern gods', 'those in the north of the sky', or 'the spirits in the north of the sky'.[104]

The stars were often referred to as 'gods' (*netjeru*). The imperishable stars were called 'those gods',[105] 'those excellent and wise gods',[106] 'the swallow-gods',[107] 'those northern gods' (et cetera, see above), and 'the gods of the lower sky'.[108] The untiring stars were called 'the gods who are in the sky'.[109] The deceased king was said to become 'a star in the sky among the gods'.[110]

These gods (the stars) formed an entourage around Re, both in front of and behind the sun-god. Together, they formed his great barque, which comprised the day-barque (*mndjt*) for travelling in the region of light and the night-barque (*msktt*) for travelling in the region of darkness.[111] The gods are said to row the day-barque across the sky until it sinks into the west and becomes the night-barque.

The gods as a group were defined by the term *psdjt*, literally meaning 'nine', but actually signifying a plural of plurals, or an indeterminate number. The word *psdjt* is often translated 'company' or 'corporation', but more usually 'ennead', which is the term we will employ here. In Egyptian literature, *psdjt* is used as a synonym, or variant, for the term *netjeru*, 'the gods'.[112] Thus in the account of creation by Ptah Ta-tenen it is stated: 'all the gods were formed and the ennead was completed'.[113]

The ennead (*psdjt*) comprised gods of the earth and the *nun*, as well as gods of the *duat* and gods of the *akhet*. However, the term was often used to refer specifically to the star-gods. Hence the expression *psdjt n pet*, 'the ennead of the sky',[114] and the linguistic connection to *psdj*, the verb 'to shine'.[115] As we might expect, the sun-god was acclaimed as 'Lord of the Ennead'.[116]

The term ennead thus signified the infinite multitude of the star-gods.

And yet, in a manner typical of Egyptian dualistic thought, this singular concept could also be described as *psdjwt-snu*, 'the two enneads', which was apparently conceived as a 'great ennead' presiding over a 'lesser ennead'.[117] These two enneads could appear in the *nun*, in the *duat*, in the field of reeds, in the field of offerings, and in the *akhet*.[118] But our present concern is with the sky. Here, the two enneads had a dual identity; on the one hand, they were identified with the stars of the great barque,[119] but on the other hand, they were placed in the northern circumpolar sky, where they were envisaged as twin adzes (and possibly twin forelegs).[120]

The star-gods were often identified as spirits (*akhu*). The imperishable stars were called 'the spirits',[121] and the king was urged to stand up at the head of these indestructible stars, and govern them 'as a spirit at the head of the spirits'.[122] The term 'spirits' was used both for the regular stars and the circumpolar stars.

The star-gods were also described as souls (*bau*). The gods of the sky were identified with 'the souls of Heliopolis',[123] or with the duality 'the souls of Pe and the souls of Nekhen'.[124] In the Pyramid Texts, the king is urged: 'O king, be a soul like the souls of Heliopolis! Be a soul like the souls of Nekhen! Be a soul like the souls of Pe! Be a soul like a living star at the head of its brethren!'[125] The terms for soul (*ba*) and spirit (*akh*) appear in many instances to be synonymous;[126] to be 'a soul at the head of the living' was equivalent to being 'a spirit at the head of the spirits'.[127]

A clear statement of the identity between the stars, the gods, and the souls appears in Utterance 434 of the Pyramid Texts, where Nut, the sky-goddess, is said to possess 'a thousand' star-souls – symbolic for a great multitude:

> You [Nut] have taken to yourself every god who possesses his barque, that you may instruct (*sba*) them among Nut-of-a-thousand-souls (*Nwt kha ba.s*), lest they – the stars (*sbau*) – depart from you.[128]

What was the origin of the stars? As noted earlier, there is no Egyptian text that states 'the stars originated in the following manner...'. However, there is a myth of the origin of the gods (*netjeru*), many of whom became stars in the belly of Nut, as the above quote testifies. Although there is no exact identity between the stars and the gods, for the reasons set out in chapter five, there is a significant overlap, with the stars being referred to as gods, souls, spirits, and the ennead, and the gods being referred to as stars, souls, spirits, and the ennead. With care, therefore, we can learn the origin of the stars by reading across from the origin of the gods.

Let us begin with the sky-gods. In the Pyramid Texts, it is stated that the gods 'ascended to the sky' during primeval time, 'when the sky was

Figure 31.
NUT, THE STARRY SKY.

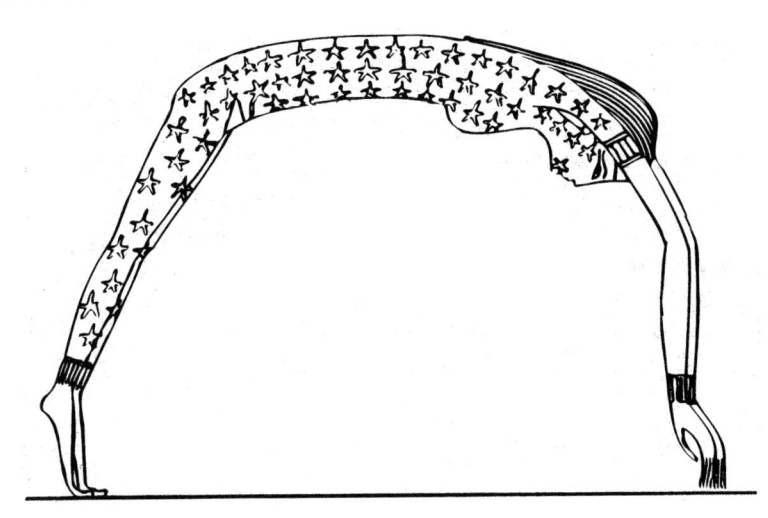

separated from the earth'.[129] The gods were then reborn *in the form of stars* upon the belly of Nut. The origin of the gods *as gods*, however, must predate this birth, for they ascended to the sky. This logically raises the question: "ascended from where?".

What was the origin of the gods? As discussed in the previous chapter, the basic myth was that the gods were the children of the creator-god (or of Shu and Tefnut), who conceived them in the primeval ocean, the *nun*. It is thus implied that some of the gods went up from the *nun* to the sky at the time when the sky was separated from the earth.

But how are we to understand this ascent from the *nun*?

A second tradition may shed some light on this question. It claims that the gods originated from the primeval earth. This idea is attested in four different ways.

Firstly, it is claimed that Ta-tenen, the personification of the primeval earth in its appearance from *nun*, was 'father of the gods, maker of the gods'.[130] In the *Theology of Memphis*, it is written:

> It happened that Ptah was called 'the one who made all and brought the gods into being'. He is indeed Ta-tenen, who gave birth to the gods, from whom everything came forth...[131]

In a similar vein, in the Papyrus Leiden, it is disclosed that Amun 'took the form of Ta-tenen in order to give birth to the Primeval Ones'.[132]

Secondly, the Edfu Building Texts confirm that the Primeval Ones indeed came forth from the earth. The inscriptions state that the bodily forms of these gods were divinized in the mounds of the lands (*iawt n tawi*).[133]

Thirdly, there is a myth of the gods coming forth from the earth-god Geb. In the Pyramid Texts and Coffin Texts, it is claimed that gods 'went forth from the head of Geb', as if ascending to the sky.[134] Consistent with this, Geb was called 'father of the gods' and '*ka* of the gods'.[135]

Fourthly, it is stated in the Pyramid Texts that the mouths of the gods were split open by 'the adze of iron, the adze of Wepwawet, the iron which issued from Seth'.[136] This splitting of the mouth signified the rebirth or spiritualization of the gods, and was usually performed on the earth (or *in* the earth, mythically speaking).[137] Although the iron adze was made in the image of the circumpolar stars (*mskhtiu*), this indicates not the origin of the iron but its destiny (see discussion in chapters eight and ten on the significance and origin of the iron).

Fifthly, in the Books of the Netherworld, Re's barque comprising the star-gods is depicted inside the earth as a 'barque of the earth', as if the earth were its place of origin. In the Book of Gates, it is stated:

Figure 32.
ABOVE, STAR-GODS TOW RE'S BARQUE IN THE NETHERWORLD.
BELOW, THE BULL-HEADED 'BARQUE OF THE EARTH'.
Scenes from the third division of the Book of Gates.

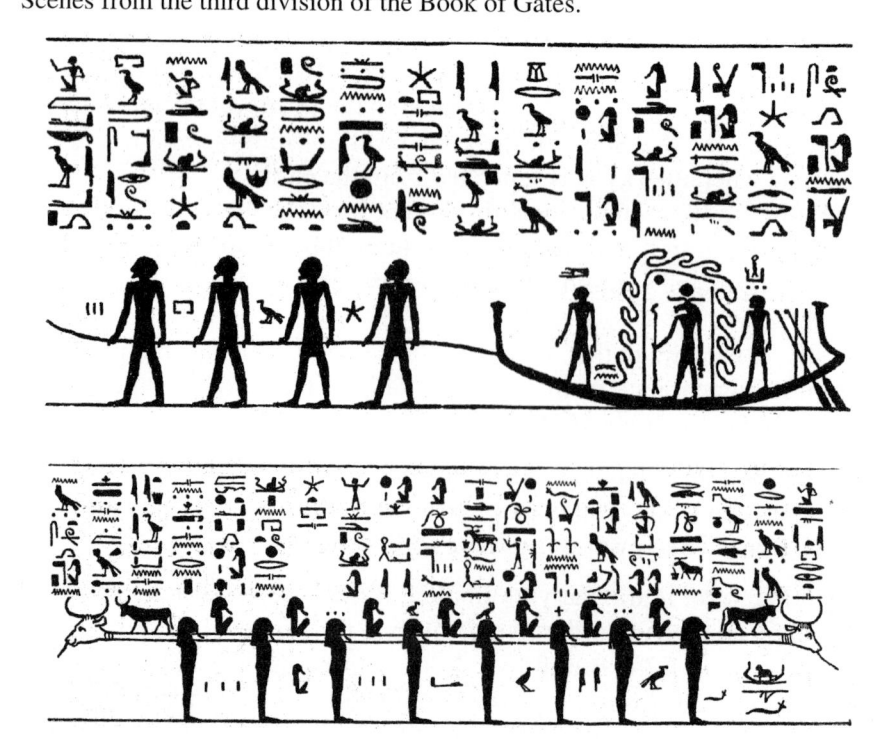

This great god [Re] is towed along by the gods of the *duat*, and advances to the barque of the earth, which is the barque of the gods. Re greets them: "Hail, you gods who bear up this barque of the earth and who lift up the barque of the *duat*... Holy is the one who is in the barque of the earth."[138]

In keeping with this, the interior of the earth (the *duat*) is depicted as the home of the dead gods, the place of the gods' rebirth, and possibly also the birthplace of the stars. As discussed in chapter four, the journey of the sun-god Re through the *duat* may be interpreted as a re-enactment of creation, in which case we would be witnessing here the original birth of the gods.

All of this presents a fairly consistent picture of the origin of the gods from the primeval earth, which may be reconciled with the first tradition of origin from the *nun* by recalling that the earth joined itself together in the primeval waters and emerged therefrom. God would thus have given birth to the gods in the sense that he personified the primeval water and matter from which the gods came forth.

There was, however, a third tradition of the origin of the gods, which seems, at first glance, to contradict the idea of a chthonian genesis.

In the Pyramid Texts, in three spells, the deceased king is urged to go to 'the east side of the sky, to the place where the gods were born', while in one spell he is urged to go to 'the *akhet*, to the place where the gods were born'.[139] In the three spells, the east side of the sky is paralleled with the *akhet*, giving the impression that the *akhet* was the precise location of the gods' birth.

But what exactly was the *akhet*? Although it lay on the east side of the sky, as if it formed part of the sky, it was actually a self-contained realm which gave access to the sky for souls and spirits travelling from the earth, the *duat*, or the lower sky. On the face of it, the tradition that the gods were born here, in this interstitial realm, agrees neither with the tradition of their birth in the sky as stars, nor with the tradition of their birth from the earth/*duat*/*nun* as gods.

Or does it?

To explain how these various traditions might be reconciled requires a digression on the nature and role of the *akhet*, and a reassessment of its significance from a geocentric perspective. In the following pages, I shall argue that the *akhet* was in fact a spiritualized equivalent of the earth and the *duat*.

As noted in chapter two, *akhet* meant literally 'the place of becoming *akh*' (i.e. being spiritualized), and presupposed an ascent as a spirit to the sky. Although Egyptologists usually refer to the *akhet* in a solar context

– as the place where the sun-god became *akh* every day – its primary significance lay in the creation, since it was a fundamental premise of the creation myth that the creator-god and the gods were spiritualized from their bodily forms. It is no coincidence that the creator-god Atum passed through the *akhet* on his way to the sky.[140]

The texts feature two of these *akhet*-realms, one placed in the eastern side of the sky and one placed in the western side. It is a curious fact that the sun-god Re had to pass through both these *akheti* in his orbit of the two skies, rather than sail uninterrupted through a continuous ocean of water. It is even more curious that Re's night-barque departed from some kind of structure called 'the platform of the *jzkn*' in the western *akhet*,[141] and that his day-barque departed from land in the eastern *akhet*.[142] Why would there be land in a region of the sky?

Another curious fact is that the mounds of Horus and the mounds of Seth are placed in the east side of the sky, and yet at the same time they belonged to the earth-god Geb (in the Pyramid Texts, Geb claims: 'the mounds of my mound are the mounds of Horus and the mounds of Seth').[143] Why do these earth-mounds appear in the *akhet* – supposedly in the circuit of the sky?

Yet another telling clue comes from the myth of Osiris and Re in the Pyramid Texts. Osiris personified the primeval earth, and yet in several resurrection spells he is depicted in the embrace of his son Horus and is given the name 'Akhet from which Re goes forth'.[144] That this represents a spiritualized form of Osiris is made clear by one such spell in which Osiris is urged to 'be a spirit (*akh*) in your name of 'Akhet from which Re goes forth''.[145] And yet elsewhere in the Pyramid Texts, Osiris is said to be a spirit which emerged from the *duat* and the earth:

> The god [Osiris] wakes; the god stands up because of this spirit [*akh*] which came forth from the *duat*, Osiris-the-king who came forth from Geb.[146]

Putting all these clues together, it would appear that Osiris in his name 'Akhet' personified a realm of spirit which had emerged directly from the earth and the *duat* (which he also personified).

Might the *akhet* be primarily a terrestrial phenomenon? As mentioned in chapter two, the *akhet* was indeed a remarkably earth-like place, with its waters, its green fields, and its green plants that grew on its banks. In addition, in the earliest texts, the word *akhet* is determined by an oval-shaped hieroglyph ⬭ which meant 'island' – the same sign as was used to write the word 'earth' (*ta*) ⬭.[147] The *akhet* therefore fits the picture of a realm that emerged directly from the earth or *duat* – a living realm born from the remnants of a destroyed world.[148]

All of this makes sense from a geocentric perspective. What we appear to have before us is a series of snapshots of a dead terrestrial world in the process of being revivified. The *nun* and the *duat* represent the old world, which is inert but pregnant with the possibilities of new life; the field of reeds represents the revived world, its fertile land beginning to emerge from the floodwaters; and the *akhet* represents the creation of the new cosmos, the rising earth and floodwaters giving birth to the expanded realms of the atmosphere of Shu, the sky of Nut, and the light of Re and his company, the gods.

There would be no inconsistency, therefore, in the claims that the gods were born (a) from the *nun*; (b) from the primeval earth; and (c) from the *akhet*.

As for the *akhet* being placed 'in the east side of the sky', this makes sense according to the geocentric theory. As explained earlier, the *akhet* was not part of the sky proper, but a realm which gave access to the sky. It was in fact neither earth nor sky, but *that place in primeval time where the earth became sky*. By placing it beneath the horizon, as if it formed a continuity with the lower sky and the upper sky, the Egyptians created a cosmos in which the sun-god and the gods in his barque could repeat their rebirth from the earth every day. The *akhet* thus existed only notionally in the sky; it was not a real region of the cosmos, but a picture of the entire cosmos – a snapshot of the world in its metamorphosis of the first time.[149]

The existence of the western *akhet* may be explained in the same way. By placing the *akhet* beneath both horizons, the Egyptians in effect made the entire lower sky equivalent to the *akhet*. The *akhet* thus enclosed the *duat* in the sense that a living world (*akhet*) had come forth from a dead world (*duat*). Or, to be more precise, the *akhet* represented the terrestrial world being spiritualized after first having overcome death. Thus when the sun and stars entered the western *akhet*, passed through the *duat*, and then emerged from the eastern *akhet*, they repeated their original births from the earth.

Now that we have identified the place of origin of the gods, the stars, we may take a brief look at the dynamics of their ascent into the sky.

The key to the gods' ascent, it would seem, was the great flood. In the Pyramid Texts, the gods are said to be 'on the great flood', and the great flood is said to lead them in their name *hnmmt*.[150] In one spell, the gods row Horus on the procession of the great flood, whereupon the doors of the sky and the *qebhu* (fresh water) are thrown open and the god ascends to the sky.[151] As we observed earlier, the floodwaters were released from the gates of the *akhet* in the east side of the sky (the place of the gods' birth), and thus became the waters of the sky-ocean.

Although it is not stated explicitly that the gods went to the sky 'upon the flood', a number of texts do seem to imply that this was the case. The clearest is Spell 648 of the Coffin Texts, which describes the original birth of Re and the gods:

> The sky was pregnant on the day when Nut bore him [Re]... the Lord of the Akhet on the day of eternity. He rises as a flood (*nun*), his entourage is serpents, his ennead is behind him... his millions of spirits are within his mouth.[152]

Consistent with this, it was believed that the gods had sailed or rowed to the sky – an idea sometimes rendered by the vague statement 'the gods sailed'.[153] From the time of the Pyramid Texts, the gods were depicted as reaching the sky by rowing the barque of the sun-god from its departure point in the *akhet*. Although it is not said explicitly that the gods rowed Re or his barque 'upon the flood', the existence of a waterway is clearly implied, and a flood is indicated by the triple facts that the flood was in the *akhet*, that the *akhet* contained gates which led to the sky, and that the sky bore the name *mehet weret*, 'great flood'.

According to the Pyramid Texts, the gods had built the barque of the sun-god. In Utterance 519, it is stated that Horus of the Duat ascended to the sky in front of his 'boat of 770 cubits which the gods of Pe bound together... which the eastern gods built'.[154] This at the time when the sky had been separated from the earth, when the gods had ascended to the sky. That the gods built this boat but also took their seats in it suggests that it was a metaphor for the assembly of the gods themselves; and this idea is indeed confirmed by later texts, in which the constituent pieces of the boat are equated with various gods.[155] There is a clear parallel here to the gathering together of the limbs of the creator-god, representing the assembly of the primeval earth (see chapter four).

As we might expect, the barque had its origins in the primeval earth and *nun*. A passage in the Pyramid Texts locates the self-creating beetle Kheprer 'in the bow of the barque which is in *nun*',[156] while the Book of Gates portrays the netherworld as 'the barque of the earth', which is synonymous with 'the barque of the gods'.[157] Of particular interest are the *hnu*-barque and the *hnhnu*-barque; the former was used to lift up the god Sokar,[158] while the latter was said to 'open the mouth of the earth' and lift up Atum to the two barques of Khepri (probably the day-barque and the night-barque).[159] This opening of the earth echoes an earlier text which claims that an egg was broken when Nut was born.[160] Since Nut emerged from the womb of Tefnut, and since this birth involved a breaking of waters, the intention here may well be that the *hnhnu*-barque sailed forth upon a flood.

So much for the stars and their origin. We turn now to the myths of the origin of the sun and the moon.

The Origin of the Sun and the Moon

How did the sun and moon come into being? Did they too ascend into the sky from the earth and the *nun*?

The natural place to begin is with the gods who personified the sun and the moon, namely Re and Thoth (we may also consider Khons, the moon-god in the Theban tradition). How did the sun-god and moon-god originate?

In the case of Re, there are numerous origin myths, which require to be disentangled.

According to the majority of sources, Re was born from the primeval ocean (*nun*).[161] His father was thus Nun, the personification of the waters. Some texts expand on this idea, claiming that the sun-god was born from the lotus which emerged from *nun*, or from the egg which was laid in *nun*.[162] Certain texts envisage a role for the gods in this process. In one tradition, the frog-goddesses bore Re,[163] while in another Re was brought out of the lotus in *nun* by the Primeval Ones (*pautiu*).[164]

The earliest sources, the Pyramid Texts, are surprisingly vague about the origins of Re. However, in one spell it is stated that Re 'came forth from Nut'.[165] This is probably a reference to Nut in her role as mother of the cosmos, rather than sky-goddess (see earlier). In view of Nut's close association with primeval water, it is consistent with the myth of Re's origin from *nun*.

A third tradition makes Ta-tenen the father of Re.[166] This suggests that the sun-god came forth from the primeval mound. Consistent with this, the Hermopolitan tradition relates that Re was born from the lotus in the pool in the isle of flames, and suggests that the gods who brought him out of the pool were the Children of Ta-tenen.[167] Similarly, the Medamud inscriptions claim that the ancestor-gods (*tpiu*) created Re at the place of the primeval mound.[168]

Having been born from the *nun* and/or the primeval mound, Re went up to the sky. This myth is made explicit in the Coffin Texts but finds its clearest exposition in the Book of the Heavenly Cow, where the sun-god is lifted up to the sky upon the back of Nut in the form of a cow.[169]

The ascent of Re to the sky would explain a further set of myths which locate his birth in the sky. In the Coffin Texts, it is stated that 'the sky was pregnant on the day when Nut bore him'.[170] Similarly, other sources claim that the sun was born as a golden calf from the womb of the sky-goddess Mehet-weret,[171] or as the son of the sky-goddess when she was raped by her son Min.[172] The traditions that Re's mother was Neit or Mut probably belong to this same genre of myths.[173]

This double birth myth – first in the *nun* and second in the sky above – echoes the origin myths of Nut and the gods (see earlier) and the creator-god (see chapter five). Under Allen's theory of the creation myth, the sun-god is born only once, in the *nun*, but under the geocentric theory the god is born firstly in (and from) the original, inert cosmos and secondly in the expanded, revivified cosmos. Two distinct births are thus involved, although they might represent one continuous, dynamic process.

Turning to the moon-god Thoth, the myths of his origin are sparse. In one passage of the Coffin Texts, he is called 'that star which was borne by the land of the west', which indicates a birth from the netherworld.[174] According to later myths, he emerged from the head of Seth,[175] or from the heart of the creator in a moment of bitterness.[176]

Thoth had a close connection with Re. In the Pyramid Texts, Re is said to 'go forth as Thoth',[177] while in a late myth Re appoints Thoth to act as his deputy.[178] This connection is also seen in regard to the Theban moon-god Khons. An inscription at Karnak describes his origin thus:

> Mut, the resplendent serpent, wound herself around her father Re and gave birth to him as Khons.[179]

All of these myths present an interesting picture, but it is insufficiently clear for our purposes. The problem is that the term 'Re' is ambiguous; it may refer either to the sun-disc or to the sun-god; and more seriously, it may represent the sun-god or the creator-god.[180] Therefore, when Re is described as being born from the *nun*, it might not necessarily refer to the origin of the sun; rather, it may be a restatement of the basic fact that the creator-soul emerged from the abyss.

Similarly with Thoth, the myths of his origin may refer nor to the birth of the moon, but to the birth of the moon-god, or the creator-god (Thoth was occasionally proclaimed as the creator of the cosmos).[181]

We are therefore back at 'square one' as regards the origins of the sun and the moon.

Fortunately, there is another way forward.

Numerous Egyptian myths refer to the sun and the moon as the 'eyes' (*irti*) of the creator-god or sky-god. The idea probably has its origins in the Letopolite myth of Khenti-irti, 'The Foremost One of the Eyes',[182] who had allegedly been born blind, but had had his eyes restored by his son Horus.[183] Over time, this god Khenti-irti became synonymous with Horus of Letopolis, and the myth of his two eyes was assimilated into the characters of other Horus-gods up and down the land.

It was thus said of Horus the falcon-god and sky-god: 'When he opens his eyes he fills the world with light, but when he shuts them darkness comes into being.'[184]

Such was the importance of this tradition that virtually every creator-god in Egypt was made to acquire the eyes to demonstrate his rulership of the cosmos. Thus Ptah Ta-tenen was praised: 'You illuminate the sky with your two eyes... You destroy the night and scatter the darkness by your two eyes... When you go to rest, darkness comes, and when you open your two eyes, beams of light come forth'.[185] Similarly, Sobek-Re was invoked as 'the great god whose eyes emit the twin discs of light, whose right eye shines by day and whose left eye shines at night, whose two large eyes light up the darkness'.[186] As this last verse shows, the sun was regarded as the god's right eye and the moon as his left eye.[187]

As a result of this identification of the sun and the moon with the two eyes (*irti*) – a fact that is well known to Egyptologists – we can continue our quest for their origins without any problem of ambiguity, and with the added bonus that the genesis of the eyes will solve the solar and lunar mysteries in one fell swoop.

So, what was the origin of the eyes?

In Utterance 670, the eyes are caused to appear 'in the head' of Osiris by Isis and Nephthys:

> Isis has poured out a libation for you, Nephthys has cleansed you –
> your two great and mighty sisters who gathered your flesh together,
> who raised up your limbs, and who caused your eyes to appear in your head, namely the night-barque and the day-barque.[188]

Here, the night-barque is the moon and the day-barque is the sun, and the eyes appear (*kha*) in the sense of rising up.[189] The head of Osiris probably refers to the mummy on whose face the two eyes were painted, although it might be a metaphor for the entire cosmos.

Utterance 443 is a little more helpful. It states that the eyes 'went forth from the head' of Nut:

> O Nut, the eyes have gone forth from your head. You have carried off Horus and his Great of Magic, you have carried off Seth and his Great of Magic.[190]

Here, the eyes go forth (*prr*) from Nut's head in the sense of 'going up' or 'separating' from it.[191]

The expression 'Great of Magic', used in the above passage, refers to the eyes, which are on one occasion identified with the crowns of Upper and Lower Egypt.[192] These two crowns 'Great of Magic' (*weret hekau*) are said to have been created by a singular Eye which, like the eyes, went forth from the head. In Utterance 592, it is the head of Geb, the earth-god and 'sole great god', from which the Eye goes forth:

> The Eye has gone forth from your head (Geb) as the Upper Egyptian crown Great of Magic; the Eye has gone forth from your head (Geb) as the Lower Egyptian crown Great of Magic.[193]

What is the meaning of this myth? An implicit idea in the Egyptian texts is that the going forth of the Sole Eye created the two eyes, the sun and the moon, enabling the creator-god to 'see'. Hence it could be claimed, on the one hand, that *the Eye* went forth from the head, and, on the other hand, that *the eyes* went forth from the head. In going up or separating from the head, the Eye *became* the two eyes.

How exactly this transpired will be the subject of discussion in a later chapter. For now, our primary concern is the origin of the eyes, which requires that we identify the head.

If the eyes appeared *in* the head, then it would work as a metaphor for the entire cosmos. However, since the eyes go *up from* the head, it must be a metaphor for the earth and the *nun*, or for the primeval mound that emerged from the *nun*. The going forth of the eyes from the head of Nut (Utterance 443) argues for the former identification, in keeping with her role as mother cosmos (see earlier discussion). However, the going forth of the Eye from the head of Geb argues for the latter identification, in keeping with his role as the risen earth. Other texts favour this second hypothesis. Amun, for example, is said to have raised up his head from *nun* when nothing else existed,[194] while Nut's head is supposed to have been 'cracked open' in an argument with Geb.[195] One way or another, it is suggested that the eyes – the sun and the moon – had a geocentric origin.

In support of this interpretation, the Pyramid Texts and Coffin Texts contain several striking references to the Eye and the eyes originating from the earth.

In Utterance 587, the Eye of Horus is called 'City' and 'Settlements', and all the produce of the earth is lifted up from it;[196] in Utterance 610, the deceased king is told: 'Your eyes are opened by the earth... He who presides over Letopolis raises you';[197] in Spell 316, the deceased takes the identity of the Eye of Horus and declares: "I am a primeval one of the earth";[198] in Spell 608, the Eye of Horus is said to have 'issued from the earth';[199] and in Spell 820, the deceased identifies himself with the blind Horus and claims to have been born by Nut 'within the secret places of the house of Geb'.[200]

In keeping with this idea, the myth *Isis and Re* describes how the Eye and the eyes came forth from the body of Re.[201] Significantly, Re's body is said to be hidden from the gods and in the throes of death when Isis, by means of her great magic, causes the Eye to emerge from his mouth. The two eyes then appear and the great god lives.

In further support of the geocentric theory, the Eye and the eyes are said to be lifted up to the sky, either by Horus, Shu, or Thoth.

In Spell 316 of the Coffin Texts, it is Horus who lifts the Eye. The deceased claims an identity with Horus and says: "I am Horus who lifted up his Eye, which appeared besouled, high and mighty."[202]

In Spells 76 and 746 of the Coffin Texts, it is Shu who lifts the Eye. Shu, the raiser of the sky, states: "It was through me that the Eye gave light to the darkness', while Atum explains: "I came into being on the Supports of Shu and the flames of my Eye are about me."[203]

Finally, Thoth 'lifts up the two eyes' of the creator in an 18th dynasty hymn to Amun-Re.[204]

We are now in a position to tackle the physics behind the creation of the sky-ocean, the stars, the sun, and the moon. But before we may do so, we must first grasp an essential principle, namely the king's role in re-enacting the creation. It is to this task that chapter seven is dedicated.

Chapter Six Summary

- Contrary to the consensus view, creation was an expansive process, centred on the earth and its chthonian waters.

- The sky was created by the separation of upper waters from lower waters. The waters of the sky were lifted by Shu – hence the myth of the great flood. The lower waters remained attached to the earth.

- Nut was a mother cosmos who evolved from the primeval waters into the sky.

- The stars were the gods who ascended to the sky. The gods were born from the earth and the primeval ocean (*nun*), but also from the *akhet*. The *akhet* was a spiritualized realm which had emerged from the earth and the *nun*. The stars thus had a chthonian origin.

- The sun and the moon were the eyes of the creator-god. They too went forth to the sky from the earth and the *nun*.

CHAPTER SEVEN

KING OF CREATION

O king, mighty in waking, great in sleeping... Raise yourself, for you have not died.
(Pyramid Texts, Utterance 462)

Kingship in ancient Egypt was as old as the world. According to the earliest tradition, the first king had been Osiris.[1] His death (allegedly at the hands of Seth) had triggered a period of chaos in which Horus and Seth fought each other for his heritage. After a long struggle, Horus had triumphed. Rule of the Two Lands was granted to him, and the dual crowns of Upper Egypt and Lower Egypt were placed upon his head.

Later, Horus had departed to his throne in the sky and delegated his throne on the earth to the pharaoh (*per-aa*).[2] According to belief, this first king had been Menes. A semi-mythical figure, Menes was credited with founding the city of Memphis by dyking the Nile and reclaiming the land. He was also said to have unified the Two Lands, i.e. the southern kingdom of the Nile valley and the northern kingdom of the Delta. In this way, Menes became the first man to wear the dual crowns of Upper and Lower Egypt.[3]

Upon wearing the dual crowns, Menes became more than a man. Like all Egyptian kings, he became a god – the 'likeness' (*snn* or *mit*), 'image' (*tit*), and 'embodiment' (*hm*) of the god (*netjer*).[4] In particular, the king became an incarnation of Horus. He sat on the throne of Horus; he wore the crowns of Horus; he spoke with the authority of Horus; he repeated the triumph of Horus over Seth; to all intents and purposes, he *was* the god Horus.

In theory, the kingship of Egypt was unique and eternal. In a treatise on the sun cult, from the New Kingdom period, it is stated that Re had ordained *a single king* to rule for ever and eternity:

Re has placed the king on the earth of the living for ever (*neheh*) and eternity (*djet*), in order to judge men, to satisfy the gods, to realise order (*maat*) and to annihilate chaos (*isfet*).[5]

The king's mortality jarred with this ideal, but was accommodated by the ingenious trick of causing the dead king to become one with the deceased god Osiris. A successor could then be appointed as a replacement Horus, following the mythical model of Horus, the son of Osiris and Isis.

The Horus-Menes thus died and became Osiris-Menes, whereupon he gave rise to his successor Horus-Aha.

Horus-Aha then died and became Osiris-Aha, whereupon he gave rise to his successor Horus-Djer.

And so on and so forth.

In this way, Egyptian history may be viewed as a succession of Osiris-Horus constellations, stretching across a period of nearly four thousand years.[6] But this would not have been how the Egyptians saw it. For them, there was only one Osiris and one Horus, who together formed a single god of body and soul. Each king, in the fullness of time, became that god – that one, unique god. They were not dead kings, as we tend to imagine them, but living kings who had gone forth from their collective body to the sky. They were facets of one singular, collective, cosmic identity.

This cult of the god-king allows profound insights to be gained into Egyptian religion – of a kind not on offer in the other great civilisations of antiquity. More than this, it provides a huge resource for our study of the creation myth, that is *if* it be accepted that Osiris and Horus were creator-gods.

My aim is to utilize this resource in developing our understanding of the creation myth, and to this end the onus is on me to demonstrate that the kingship of Egypt followed a creational template, at least from the time of the Pyramid Texts onwards. In this chapter, I shall build on my earlier argument that Osiris was the creator-god *par excellence* (chapter four), and show how fundamental the creation myth was in the role of the pharaoh – both as Horus-king in this world and as Osiris-king in the next world.

The King's Identities – A Riddle Resolved

To begin, I must clarify the confusion that exists concerning the divine identity of the Horus-king.

From the earliest times, the pharaoh was Horus son of Isis.[7] His name was written in a *serekh*, surmounted by the falcon of Horus; we may call this 'the Horus name'. But during the 4th dynasty, the king acquired the additional title *sa Re*, which Egyptologists translate 'son of Re'; this title was normally used in conjunction with the cartouche that enclosed the king's birth name.[8] Thereafter, the Horus name and the *sa Re* title were used as regular elements in the king's fivefold titulary.

Figure 33.
THE HORUS NAME (LEFT) AND THE SA RE NAME (RIGHT).

Egyptologists see some consistency here in that the king in both cases was 'the son' of the Great God. However, a difficulty arises in the fact that the Horus name points to the king's father being Osiris, whereas the *sa Re* title points to the king's father being Re. This is a real problem for scholars, since Osiris is understood to be a chthonian god, whereas Re is understood to be a sun-god, the antithesis of Osiris. How, then, can the king be the son of Osiris, and yet simultaneously the son of Re?

One way around this problem has been to view Horus as a senior god, the sky-god, who was originally independent of Osiris. However, while there is merit in this approach, it has generated a further problem for Egyptologists, who cannot explain why the king's role would have been downgraded from senior god (Horus) to 'son' of the god (*sa Re*).[9]

An alternative approach has been to argue that the name Horus and the title 'son of Re' signified different aspects of the king's divinity, perhaps one relating to his rule and one to his birth.[10]

Nevertheless, the consensus among scholars is that the Egyptians were themselves confused on this issue, and that there was a real inconsistency in their philosophy of kingship.[11]

For further evidence of this confusion, Egyptologists point to the fact that the king was not only 'son of Re', but also Re himself. This identity is first suggested by the throne names of several Old Kingdom pharaohs, which utilized the hieroglyph that signified the name Re.[12] It is attested more decisively in the texts of later periods. Amenemhet III is said to be 'Re... who is seen in his rays';[13] Amenhotep II is told 'you are Re'; Ramesses II is called 'the likeness of Re, illuminating this world like the sun disc (*aten*)', and he declares himself to be 'Re, Lord of the Sky, who is upon earth'; and Merenptah is called 'the sun disc of mankind, who drives out the darkness from Egypt'.[14]

KING OF CREATION

Egyptologists are puzzled by these statements. How could the king be Re, while also assuming the title 'son of Re'?

The picture is clouded further by inscriptions which identify the king as Atum. In one text, Senusert I is given the title *neb-r-djr*, 'Lord of All', an epithet of Atum;[15] in another, Amenemhet II is said to have driven out chaos from the Two Lands by 'appearing as Atum himself';[16] and in others, Ramesses II is described as 'the likeness of Atum', and Atum is said to live by speaking through his mouth.[17]

The reigning king thus had three identities: Horus, Re, and Atum, in addition to being the 'son of Re'.

At the risk of complicating matters, it must be stated that certain texts combined or expanded these multiple identities.

In a 12th dynasty inscription, the king is identified with no less than five deities: he is Sia, the god of insight, who is in men's hearts; he is Re, the sun-god, by whose beams men see; he is Khnum, the creator-god, who fashions mankind in the womb; he is Bastet, the cat-goddess, who protects the Two Lands; and he is Sekhmet, the lion-goddess, who punishes transgressors.[18]

In a similar vein, Ramesses II is identified with the gods Re, Atum, and Khnum.[19] And, rather interestingly, he claims to be Re and Horus simultaneously:

> I shine as Re for the people, being upon the great throne of Atum as Horus the son of Isis.[20]

Here, the king appears as both the god and 'the son' of the god (Horus was the son of Isis and Osiris).

The king's sonship was indeed a prominent idea in Egypt. In addition to being Horus, the son of Osiris, and the son of Re (*sa Re*), the king was also called 'son of Ta-tenen' and 'son of Hathor',[21] while the names of the 18th dynasty kings suggest that he could also be viewed as the son of Thoth.[22]

How could the king be simultaneously the god and the son of the god? How could he be both Re and the son of Re? Clearly, this idea did not bother the Egyptians, but it does pose a serious problem for scholars.[23]

From all this confusion, there emerges a glimmer of light. If we put to one side, for the moment, the issue of the god and the son of the god, we find a familiar set of themes, namely the creator-god, his creation of the cosmos, and the need for the king to repeat the creation. The king is thus described in one text as 'the father and the mother of all men, alone by himself without an equal',[24] while in the New Year rituals it is said of the king 'He has created the earth from which he emerged, he has come into being on its first occasion, when it came into being.'[25] In keeping with this idea, the king appears as Atum to drive out chaos from the lands; he appears as Re to bring light to the world; and he fashions like Khnum to create each new generation of men in the womb.

Egyptologists are aware of this theme. They readily concede that the king incarnated the creator-god, and repeated the god's creative thoughts, words, and deeds.[26] But – and it is an enormous but – they view this theme from a heliocentric perspective. According to their theory, the Egyptian religion was a sun cult, and Re the sun-god was the creator of the cosmos. The king was therefore an incarnation of the sun-god, and by the same token an image of the creator. In order to maintain this view, emphasis is placed on the king's identities of Re and 'son of Re' (*sa Re*), and his other identities are solarized (notably Atum, Horus, and Sia), or else understood to be accretions from creation myths that were secondary to the solar creation myth (hence Khnum). In short, the king is presented primarily as a sun-king, who by virtue of that fact was also a creator-king.

But still the problems remain. How can the king be the god, and yet at the same time the son of the god? And how can he be the son of Osiris, but also the 'son of Re'?

Were the Egyptians really confused about the king's divine identity, as scholars have suggested, or might these 'inconsistencies' have a rational explanation?

I believe that all the problems can be solved if the creator-god, rather than sun-god, is placed centre stage. As explained in chapter five, the creator-god personified the creation of the cosmos, but more than this he represented the death and rebirth of a primeval world. In order to render this idea in myth, the Egyptians developed the concept of the body-soul duality of the creator-god. His body, in the first instance, represented the corpse of the old cosmos – a confused mass of water and earth in a state of darkness and inertness – while his soul, in the first instance, signified the revivification of this corpse – the appearance of light and life amidst the chaos and gloom. The going forth of the soul from the abyss then signified the creation of the greater cosmos – the atmosphere, the sky, and the celestial bodies, which were made to surround the earth and the well of the primeval waters. The entirety of this cosmos formed the new body of the creator.

This duality of body and soul was pictured as a relationship of 'father' and 'son'. The body of the old cosmos was the father, while the soul that went forth from it to create the new cosmos was the son.

The classic rendering of this father and son relationship was Osiris and

Horus. Osiris personified the slain corpse of the old cosmos, while Horus personified the soul that had generated itself from the corpse and flown into the heights of the sky (hence the image of Horus as a falcon). Osiris was thus the father, or creator-body, while Horus was the son, or creator-soul. Together, these two gods formed a single cosmic entity – the god who had created himself.

The same principle is seen in other combinations of gods. Nun could be pictured as the body and father of Atum; Atum could be pictured as the body and father of Re (or Shu); Ta-tenen too could be pictured as the body and father of Re; and Geb could be pictured as the body and father of Osiris (or Horus).

More fundamentally, the creator-god was the father of himself. Atum the body was the father of Atum the soul. Osiris the body was the father of Osiris the soul. And, in later times at least, Re the body was the father of Re the soul. In these instances, the particular nature of a god, i.e. body or soul, was not always specified, but could be understood easily enough from the context of the myth.

Herein lies the key to the king's identity as both the god and the son of the god. The king embodies the living god, but this god is none other than the son of himself – the son who revivified his father, who brought himself into being as a soul. The living god and the son of the god are therefore one and the same being. When the king of Egypt is identified with the living god, as the human embodiment of that god, he is always 'the son' in a cosmic sense. This idea is at times implicit, and at other times explicit; there is no contradiction at all between the king being the god in one text and the son of the god in another.

One problem now remains. How can the king be the son of Osiris, but also the 'son of Re' (*sa Re*)? Is there, or is there not, a conflict between these two divine identities?

Let us first consider the king's oldest identity, that of Horus, the son of Isis. What did it mean to be the embodiment of Horus? From the earliest times, Horus was worshipped as a sky-god – a giant falcon, whose two eyes were the sun and the moon. Consistent with this identity, he was one of Egypt's oldest sun-gods in his name Horakhti, 'Horus of the Two Horizons'.[27] And he could also be pictured as a creator-god, as we saw in chapter three. But the Horus of the kingship myth is Horus the son of Isis and Osiris – the soul which came forth from the revivified body of the cosmos. As this Horus, the king was the *ka* of Osiris, the son and image of the creator-god *par excellence*.

So, how does this dovetail with the king's other identity as the son of Re? To Egyptologists, the title *sa Re* meant 'son of Re', i.e. 'son of the sun' or 'son of the sun-god'. This title is interpreted quite literally, on the grounds that an Egyptian myth describes Re physically impregnating the mother of the future king. But is this the correct interpretation? In fact, the myth in question occurs in two sources, dating to around 1600 BC and 1450 BC respectively,[28] and it seems to derive from a Middle Kingdom creation myth in which Re is credited with impregnating the womb of Isis (a mother cosmos, like Nut).[29] During the Old Kingdom, when the title *sa Re* was first used, there is no suggestion that *sa* meant 'son' in a genetic, human sense. On the contrary, in the classical Egyptian religion as I understand it (as a 'cult of creation'), the expression 'son of the sun' had no inherent meaning.[30] However, *sa Re* would make sense if Re were taken as a name of the creator. Then, the translation 'son of Re' would mean 'soul of Re', in the sense of the soul that had emerged from the body of Re.

A possible problem with this theory is that Re's body is not mentioned in the Old Kingdom texts. It is first alluded to in the Middle Kingdom Coffin Texts, and is not made explicit until the New Kingdom Books of the Netherworld.[31] We can not therefore be certain that *sa Re* referred to the soul of Re's body.

It nevertheless remains a strong possibility. In the Pyramid Texts, the reborn king is called 'son of Re', which might well imply the belief in a body,[32] and on one occasion he is said to be 'the son of the body' of Re-Atum (though this body may belong primarily to Atum).[33] Furthermore, one spell refers to 'Re in his fetters' in the earth, which is suggestive of a body,[34] while three spells refer to a uraeus, viper, and falcon respectively coming forth from Re, which would normally imply a body.[35]

A second way to support this theory is to make a subtle modification of the accepted translation of *sa Re*, changing it from '*son of* Re' to '*the son* Re'. (This is permissible since the title is in fact written 'son Re', the preposition 'of' being added by Egyptologists to bring out the sense of the term.) The Pyramid Texts indeed portray Re as a second generation god – the offspring of Osiris in his name of Akhet, and 'the Great Flood which issued from the Great One' – and it is possible that the authors of these texts understood Re to be the visible, expanded form of Atum, or his 'son' in cosmic terms.[36]

Either way, whether *sa Re* meant '*son of* Re' or '*the son* Re', it is clear that it signified the creator-soul of Re made manifest in the king. There is no inconsistency, therefore, between the king's identities as *sa Re* and Horus. In both cases, the king embodied the soul that had emerged from the old cosmos and created the new. It was a cosmic sonship.

In summary, the Egyptians were not at all confused about the cosmic nature of their king. From the first dynasty to the last, the king was the incarnation of the creator-god, the embodiment of the creator-soul, the delegate of the creator upon earth.

Osiris and Horus – a Kingship of Creation

The notion of the creator-king is not controversial. It is an accepted fact in Egyptology that the king incarnated the creator-god, and repeated the god's creative thoughts, words, and deeds. The problem, however, is that Egyptologists have laboured under the misapprehension that the creator-god was the sun-god and the king a sun-king – an incarnation of the solar creator. As a result, the full import of the king's role as delegate of the creator has never been apprehended.

The moment has now come to review what is known about kingship in Egypt, from a creational rather than a solar perspective.

The proper starting point is the deceased king, for as mentioned earlier the kingship was a duality of Osiris and Horus – the dying father with the son in his arms.

It is known that the death of the king caused the Two Lands to return to their former state of darkness and chaos, symbolically speaking. Loud wailing filled the land; there was self-flagellation, fasting and abstinence; and the people smeared mud on their heads and faces as if to signify their return to the subterranean slime. It was as if the light of the world had been extinguished.

In order that light and life be restored to Egypt, the corpse of the king had to be revivified and made to engender a son and heir. To this end, the royal body was made into an image of Osiris. It was mummified, brought to life by various rituals, and then buried in a tomb chamber beneath the earth.

It now becomes apparent that these revivification rituals were steeped in creational imagery. The mummification of the king's body symbolised the reassembly of Osiris's limbs, which in turn signified the rebuilding of the primeval cosmos. The coffin, or sarcophagus, in which the body was sealed, was identified with Nut, the mother cosmos who would evolve into the sky. And the tomb chamber, *per duat*, represented 'the house of the netherworld', the place where the creator and the gods (his limbs) were reborn.[37] The burial of the mummy in the earth is also evocative of the creation. It signified the king's 'union with the earth' – his becoming at one with the body of the primeval cosmos.[38]

If these funerary rituals were not performed properly, Osiris would not engender his son and heir Horus, and the dead king would not engender the new king of Egypt. This would have been a political disaster, but at a symbolic level it would have been a cosmic disaster. The horror of death, as it is expressed in the Egyptian texts, does not reflect merely the fear of personal death, but also the fear of the end of the world – a universal state of total non-being.

The revivification of the dead king paved the way for the accession and coronation of the new king.[39] Significantly, the texts reveal that the new king acceded to the throne at the same time as the old king ascended to the sky. The accession of Thutmose III, for example, is described as follows:

> Having ascended into the sky, he became united with the gods, and his son, being arisen in his place as king of the Two Lands, ruled upon the throne of his begetter...[40]

Later, when Thutmose died, he ascended to the sky at the same time as his successor Amenhotep II acceded to his throne:

> King Thutmose went up to the sky; he was united with the sun disc (while) the body of the god joined him who had made him. When the next morning dawned, the sun disc shone forth, the sky became bright, and king Amenhotep was installed on the throne of his father.[41]

In the rituals of accession and coronation, the myth of creation is again a prominent motif. In the accession ceremonies, the death and resurrection of Osiris were re-enacted, as was the struggle of Horus and Seth,[42] while in the coronation ceremonies, held at Memphis, the creation of the world was re-enacted. In the latter, the designate king re-enacted 'the Union of the Two Lands' and 'the Circuit of the White Walls';[43] he stepped onto the dais and sat on the throne (both symbols of the primeval mound) and was crowned by the dual crowns, denoting the sun and the moon; he was also presented with sceptres and regalia which were charged with the magic of creation. When the king rose from the throne, he repeated the rising of the creator-god (or sun-god) on the first day of creation.[44] To complete the re-enactment, four arrows were despatched to the cardinal points, to fix the boundaries of the newly-expanded cosmos.[45] The world was thus created anew.

Upon coronation, the king became the embodiment of the creator-god, his likeness, and his image. His primary identity was Horus, the son of Isis and Osiris, but he was often described more simply as *netjer*, 'the god', or *netjer nefer*, 'the good god'.[46] The essence of his divinity was the creator-god's soul (*ba*) or spirit (*ka*) which was enshrined in his body and limbs. The king was thus equated with the sole living god (*netjer*) and all the living gods (*netjeru*).

As the creator-god's delegate on earth, the king's role was to maintain the balance of cosmic order (*maat*) by subjugating the forces of chaos (*isfet*). Significantly, this task involved renewing a state of order that had been established at the time of creation. Amenhotep III thus expressed his desire 'to make the country flourish as in primeval times by means of the designs of *maat*',[47] while Tutankhamun was praised for 'driving out chaos (*isfet*) from the Two Lands that order (*maat*) might be established in its place as at the first time (*zep tepi*)'.[48]

The king was uniquely qualified to maintain the state of *maat*. As the image of Horus, he was the master over Seth. Indeed, it would seem that he incarnated both these gods, in order that the former might subjugate the latter.[49] Moreover, as the image of the creator-god, he possessed the all-important powers of *hu*, 'creative utterance', *sia*, 'divine insight', and *heka*, 'primeval magic'. Every day, he would use his secret knowledge to bring the powers of creation into the world anew. He filled his heart with *sia*, placed *hu* in his mouth, and spoke the magic words which the creator himself had pronounced.[50] Chaos was thus driven back and order brought to the Two Lands. As a result of the king's work, the Nile would always flood in its due season, the land would always be fertile, and the people would enjoy the abundant blessings of life.

The king was also tasked with regulating the cosmos, and was initiated into its workings, in particular the circuit of the sun. As one text informs us: 'There is nothing which he does not know. He is Thoth in everything. There is no subject which he has not comprehended.'[51] Using this divine wisdom, the king built temples in the image of the cosmos (see chapter fifteen) and designed procedures by which he, or his delegate the high priest, could rejuvenate the powers of the celestial bodies.

When the king built the temple and performed the rituals that brought it to life, he created an image of himself. Like the king, the temple was the 'son of the earth' and the embodiment of the creator's *ka* (see chapter four). When the king entered the temple, his presence filled it; he became at one with it – at one with the entire cosmos and the gods who populated it.

At the heart of the temple, in its innermost sanctum, stood a statue of the creator-god, hidden inside its shrine. This was the focal point of the temple cult. Each morning, the king or his delegate the priest would approach the shrine, open its doors, and cause the god to appear. He would kiss the ground, intone hymns of adoration, circumambulate the shrine, and present a symbol of *maat*. Next, he would remove the god's statue, and set it on a bed of pure, freshly-strewn sand. He would then purify the god, dress him, and present him with offerings representing all the produce of the earth. At the end of the day, the god would be returned to the shrine, to the accompaniment of further hymns of adoration.[52]

Significantly, this daily ritual re-enacted the creation. The opening of the doors of the shrine signified the opening of the gates of the sky;[53] the raising of the *maat*-symbol reaffirmed the triumph of order over chaos; and the presentation of offerings symbolised the recapturing of the Eye from Seth and the destruction of the forces of chaos (*maat* again).[54] The idea of this ritual re-enactment was to rejuvenate the powers of creation and thus guarantee the regular functioning of the cosmos. It was the king who made this possible.

Figure 34.
KING RAMESSES II MAKES THE MAAT OFFERING TO PTAH.

As explained earlier, kingship was a duality of Osiris and Horus. The living king embodied the soul, or spirit, that had emerged from the body of Osiris, and his existence thus depended on the vitality of his father's body in the tomb. It was therefore essential that the king perform various rituals to rejuvenate and immortalise the mummy. These rituals were first conducted at the time of burial, but were continued thereafter on a daily, half-monthly, monthly, and annual basis. To this end, the tomb would often be equipped with a mortuary temple in which the *ka*-statue of the king became the focal point of the cult. The rituals performed included the opening of the mouth, cleansing and dressing, and the provision of offerings, i.e. all the produce of the earth.[55] As at the temple, the offerings symbolised the all-consuming power of the creator-god and his mastery over the forces of chaos.

Interestingly, the king performed these rituals not only at the tomb of his genetic father, but also at the tombs of each and every king who had ruled the Two Lands. This was necessary because each of these departed kings was Osiris, the father of Horus, and thus father of the living king, mythically speaking. In rendering service to these fathers, the king was not so much worshipping a myriad of human ancestors as harnessing the energies of a single cosmic god whose resurrection from death had given life to the world.

By harnessing these Osirian energies, the king consolidated his tenure upon earth for, as we have seen, his powers depended on the vitality of the body in the tomb. But there was more to it than this.

As explained in chapter one, the king was assisted in his regulation of the cosmos by his predecessors, who had passed into the next world by becoming spirits in the sky – stars in the barque of the sun-god. It was the task of these transfigured kings to assist the sun-god in directing the cycles of the cosmos. Following Re's example, they traversed the skies, the *duat*, and the *akhet* in a dying-and-rising process which repeated the death and rebirth of the former cosmos. Fittingly, these star-kings were a multitude but conceptually a unity.

The servicing of the ancestors' tombs by the king generated a virtuous circle of creative energy. By rejuvenating the bodies of the ancestors, the king enabled their spirits to make the circuit of the cosmos. These spirits were then able to pass through the *duat* and rejuvenate their own bodies (or body, Osiris), which in turn transmitted vital energy to the living king (Horus). He was then able to draw on this power to service the tombs of the ancestors. And so it continued, ad infinitum.

Kingship thus comprised an indivisible duality. Without Osiris, Horus was ineffective. Without Horus, Osiris was ineffective. The king of this world and the kings of the 'other world' worked together in harmony for the good of the cosmos.

In summary, we have a situation in which the king on the earth and his ancestors in the 'other world' maintained the cosmic order by a joint re-enactment of creation. By supporting each other, across the threshold of death, the Horus-king and the Osiris-kings ensured that the repetitions of creation – of the death and rebirth of the world – could be performed in perpetuity, with the end result that the cosmos could be made to endure for eternity.

The principles involved here – *zep tepi*, *creatio continua*, and *neheh* and *djet* – are not controversial. They underpin the orthodox view of a solar creation and solar rule of the cosmos. What *is* controversial is the idea that the king was a creator-king in the sense that Osiris and Horus were creator-gods. This idea, I believe, provides a unique explanation for the relationship between the living king, Horus, and his deceased father Osiris, and paves the way for a dramatic leap in our understanding of the kingship. But I would now like to redirect our study away from the world of the living, toward the world of the dead, for it is here, I believe, that we will find the all-important clues in our quest to understand the myth of creation. My proposition is that the deceased king, in his identity as Osiris, re-enacted the creation myth, all the way from the rebirth in the earth to the creation of the sky and the celestial bodies.

In order to develop this controversial theory – the importance of which cannot be overstated – we must now get to grips with the primary source of evidence for it, namely the Pyramid Texts.

The Pyramid Texts

During the late-5th and 6th dynasties, from *circa* 2350 to 2180 BC, eight pyramids at Saqqara had their interior chambers and corridors inscribed with hieroglyphics.[56] These inscriptions – the oldest known surviving corpus of religious writings in the world – have come to be known as the Pyramid Texts.

The content of the Pyramid Texts is rich and varied. According to the pyramid expert Mark Lehner, the seven hundred and fifty-nine utterances may be grouped into five main categories: dramatic texts; mythological allusions; litanies (in verse); glorification spells; and archaic magical spells.[57] More simply, the Pyramid Texts have been defined as 'a series of invocations and magical formulae connected to the funerary ritual'.[58] This definition captures the point that many of the spells echo, or even directly repeat, the words that were spoken in the various rituals, from the death of the king, to the mummification of his body, to the burial of his mummy, to the ongoing services at the tomb.[59] Seen in this way, the Pyramid Texts provide a fascinating insight into the oral traditions of the first eight hundred years of Egyptian kingship.

What was the aim of the Pyramid Texts? In brief, the magical spells and ritual actions were intended to revivify the corpse of the deceased king, and despatch his soul to the 'other world' in the form of a spirit (*akh*).[60] But more than that, they were intended to fuel the king's spirit in its circuit of the cosmos, so that it could perpetually revisit the tomb and rejuvenate its body. In this way, the body, the soul, and the spirit would exist for ever in harmony with the cosmos.

Herein lies the raison d'etre for the Pyramid Texts. By immortalising the spells in stone, in sacred hieroglyphs which carried the same magical power as the words spoken by the priests, the king was insuring himself against any calamity that might prevent the performance of the ongoing rituals at the tomb.[61] In the absence of this precaution, if for any reason the rituals had failed, the circulation of the king's spirit in the cosmos would have ceased, the body in the tomb would have returned to a state of inertness, and the cosmos would have collapsed into a state of chaos. We must presume that such a calamity was perceived as a real threat *c.* 2350 BC (for the first time during the pyramid age).

All of this sounds straightforward enough. However, upon delving into the Pyramid Texts, the modern reader soon finds himself caught up in a dense jungle of weird and convoluted religious and mythological ideas that constitutes a formidable barrier to progress. Writing in 1912, James Henry Breasted summarised his impressions as follows:

> These archaic texts... form together almost a *terra incognita*. As one endeavours to penetrate it, his feeling is like that of entering a vast primeval forest, a twilight jungle filled with strange forms and elusive shadows peopling a wilderness through which there is no path... An archaic orthography veils and obscures words... They vaguely disclose to us a vanished world of thought and speech... Combined with these words, too, there is a deal of difficult construction, much enhanced by the obscure, dark, and elusive nature of the content of these archaic documents; abounding in allusions to incidents in lost myths, to customs and usages long since ended, they are built up out of a fabric of life, thought, and experience largely unfamiliar or entirely unknown to us.[62]

Faced with these difficulties, a degree of caution was surely warranted in the interpretation of the Pyramid Texts. Nevertheless, early Egyptologists were adamant that the texts comprised a mishmash of primitive and often inconsistent ideas concerning the afterlife.

Breasted spoke for many when he offered the following interpretation of the Pyramid Texts:

> The men in whose hands the Pyramid Texts grew up took the greatest delight in elaborating and reiterating in ever new and different pictures the blessedness enjoyed by the king... in the sun-god's realm. Their imagination flits from figure to figure, and picture to picture, and, allowed to run like some wild tropical plant without control or

> guidance, weaves a complex fabric of a thousand hues which refuse to merge into one harmonious or coherent whole. At one moment the king is enthroned in oriental splendour as he was on earth, at another he wanders in the field of reeds in search of food; here he appears in the bow of the solar barque, yonder he is one of the imperishable stars acting as the servant of Re. There is no endeavour to harmonise these inconsistent representations...[63]

This view was supported by Sir Ernest Alfred Wallis Budge. Toward the end of a prolific writing career, he expressed his thoughts thus:

> Beliefs, legends and myths formulated by the Egyptians at many stages of their development are thrown together and have become a confused mass... The priests found great difficulty in arranging their different views and trying to harmonise them; they failed to do so, and therefore we find many contradictions in the Pyramid Texts... and it is now impossible to correct the mistakes they made and to disentangle the confusions which they caused.[64]

What were these supposed contradictions? Firstly, Egyptologists found it impossible to reconcile the beliefs that Re, the sun-god, and Osiris, the god of the netherworld, could both be supreme rulers in the realms of the 'other world'. As far as they were concerned, Egyptian religion at the time of the pyramid age was a sun cult, and the netherworld and the sky were two separate realms which did not belong together. The importance of Re and Osiris in the Pyramid Texts could only be explained by the assumption that the solar spells had been corrupted, for political reasons, by the Osirian mythology.[65]

Secondly, Egyptologists found it impossible to reconcile the beliefs in a solar and stellar afterlife. How could it make sense that in one spell the deceased king would join the sun-god (or even become the sun-god), but in another he would become a star in the north of the sky? Surely this was a contradiction. It was therefore decided that the Pyramid Texts were solar in origin but preserved the remnants of an archaic stellar cult which the Egyptians had been loathe to abandon.[66]

Egyptologists thus came to the view that the Pyramid Texts were too corrupt to qualify as a religion per se. Moreover, they were a tangled web which no man could ever hope to unravel. As a result of this thoroughly depressing analysis, the texts were allowed to drift to the periphery of Egyptology, where none but the specialist might study them. The result was that scholars lost interest in what the Pyramid Texts had to say about Egyptian religion and used them primarily as a philological resource.[67]

In 1948, Henri Frankfort penned a devastating critique of Breasted and his mentor Adolf Erman, accusing Breasted of biblical bias and Erman of a patronising and overly rational approach to Egyptian religion.[68] He also observed, rather tellingly, that interpretation of the Pyramid Texts had lagged since Breasted.[69] Frankfort failed to rationalise the texts in their entirety, but he provided some interesting insights and did a great deal to counter the theory of contradictions in the texts, particularly concerning the relationships of Re and Osiris, and the sky and the netherworld.[70]

Following Frankfort's influential intervention, the Pyramid Texts have been viewed in a positive light, and a new generation of Egyptologists has begun to call for a reappraisal of the texts, particularly as regards their religious meaning.[71] Nevertheless, the field remains specialised, and no specialist has yet succeeded in generating any profound new insights, let alone a new vision of the Pyramid Texts. The call for a new prophet has gone unanswered.

Today, the Pyramid Texts remain poorly understood and many of the old prejudices, fostered by Budge and Breasted, are still in evidence. The basic interpretation is unchanged: the texts are viewed as the product of a solar cult, interwoven with ideas about the netherworld and the stars, and scarred by the remnants of earlier, primitive beliefs such as animism and fetishism.[72]

This orthodoxy has occasionally been challenged from the fringes of academia. In 1992, the Egyptologist Jane Sellers argued that the Pyramid Texts conveyed beliefs about solar eclipses and the precession of the equinoxes,[73] while in 1994 the unaffiliated scholar Robert Bauval drew upon her work to argue that the texts were primarily a cult of the stars.[74] The main problem with these studies is that they both make selective use of the source material to support their particular astronomical theory, just as Egyptologists have done with their solar theory. In addition, they both reflect a modern, new-age predilection towards cosmology, as opposed to cosmogony.

This, in a nutshell, is the story of the Pyramid Texts since they were discovered in the pyramids at Saqqara in 1880-81.

The Pyramid Texts Decoded

We will now take a fresh look at the Pyramid Texts in the light of the theory of the 'cult of creation'. It is my belief that, when viewed from the creational perspective, all the supposedly disparate elements in the texts – the sun, the moon, the stars, and the netherworld – come together in a united whole. The texts, I will argue, describe a ritualistic re-enactment of a geocentric creation, in which the king takes the role of the chthonian creator-god Osiris.

Before we see how this re-enactment worked in the various spells, it is first necessary to explain some key principles and develop an overview of what is happening in the texts.

The first key principle is personification. Although the king and his spirit (*ka*) are depicted in anthropomorphic form, he actually personifies a cosmic idea. The king's cosmic origin is evident from five spells which proclaim 'There is no human father of yours who could beget you, there is no human mother of yours who could bear you.'[75] It is also clear from his statements 'I was conceived in the night, I was born in the night... I was conceived in the *nun*, I was born in the *nun*',[76] and 'I was born in the *nun* before the sky existed, before the earth existed, before that which was to be made firm existed'.[77] To be born in the *nun* was, of course, the preserve of the creator-god.

According to the five aforementioned spells, the king's mother was 'the Great Wild Cow who dwells in Nekheb', while a similar spell adds that his father was 'the Great Wild Bull'.[78] Alternatively, Utterance 571 declares that the king's father was Atum, who fashioned the king before sky and earth existed.[79]

The primary myth of the Pyramid Texts, however, identifies the king with Osiris, the son of Geb and Nut, i.e. the offspring of the earth and the mother cosmos.

The second key principle is that the deceased king re-enacts the dying-and-rising transformation of Osiris. It is not disputed that this is the main theme of the Pyramid Texts,[80] and the spells are often quite explicit about the fact that this myth is being re-enacted.[81] What *is* controversial is my argument that Osiris was the creator-god *par excellence*, who personified the death and rebirth of the cosmos.

It follows that the aim of the Pyramid Texts was to turn the deceased king into an image of the creator-god and cause his soul to go forth from his body, just as the creator-soul had gone forth from the primeval earth and the *nun* on the day of creation. This development then brought the king into an identity with the created cosmos, both in its individual parts and in the aggregate. He became the celestial ocean, the sun, the moon, and the stars.

However, the Pyramid Texts did not stop there. Crucially, the spells were designed to despatch the king's spirit on an eternal circuit of the cosmos, in order that he perpetually re-enact the death and rebirth of creation in the form of the sun, the moon, or a star. As explained earlier, the purpose of this eternal repetition (*neheh*) was to ensure the eternal duration (*djet*) of the cosmos.

If the Pyramid Texts had been designed solely to send the king into the sky as a one-off ritual, then the spells would focus on five elements of the cosmos: the earth, the *nun*, the atmosphere, the sky, and the celestial bodies. A collection of such spells would not be too difficult to decipher. However, because the spells were designed to do more than this one-off ritual – because they were intended to facilitate an eternal repetition of the creation – much emphasis is placed on invisible, otherworldly realms such as the *duat*, the *akhet*, the field of reeds (*sekhet iaru*), and the field of offerings (*sekhet hetep*). This makes the Pyramid Texts complicated to read, at least for a person unfamiliar with the big picture.

In order to understand the significance of the invisible cosmic realms in the Pyramid Texts, it is useful to view the creation from a geocentric perspective. According to the geocentric theory, as expounded in earlier chapters, creation began with a proto-cosmos, the earth and the *nun*, in a state of darkness and chaos – perhaps the remnants of an old cosmos that had collapsed. This proto-cosmos was visualised as an egg, which split open and gave birth to the new, expanded cosmos. The earth was at the centre of this cosmos for the simple reason that the cosmos derived from it.

Geocentric creation would explain why the invisible cosmic realms – the *duat*, the *akhet*, the field of reeds, and the field of offerings – were all portrayed as earth-like places, characterised chiefly by waters and green fields. As observed in chapter six, these realms seem to represent a series of snapshot pictures of a dead terrestrial world in the process of being revivified. But it is quite likely that they were once independent, parallel images of the evolving proto-cosmos. Hence the fact that the king could ascend to the sky directly from the *duat* or the field of reeds, as well as via the *akhet* (see chapter two).

The king's circuit through the *duat*, the *akhet*, and the field of reeds may therefore be understood as a perpetual re-enactment of a geocentric creation (the death and rebirth of the world), modelled on the circuit of the sun, moon, and stars, which were likewise engaged in a perpetual re-enactment of creation. By crossing to the east side of the sky and joining the barque of the sun-god at the *akhet*, the king was not simply becoming the sun or a star, or re-enacting a sunrise or star-rise. Rather, he was re-enacting the *creation of* the sun and the stars – the first sunrise and first star-rise – just as those celestial bodies were *themselves* re-enacting their own origin.

In the Pyramid Texts, then, the king has two options to reach the sky – either by a direct ascent from the earth (followed by the circuit of the cosmos) or by a shortcut to the focal point of the cosmic circuit, namely the *akhet* in the east side of the sky. A close study of the texts indicates that the ascent spells indeed fall into these two types. The direct ascent typically involves rising upon air, whereas the shortcut ascent usually involves sailing upon water (see later illustrations).

A further complicating factor in the Pyramid Texts is the duplication of the terrestrial realms in the sky. The field of reeds could designate the dawn sky as well as the region beneath the horizon, while the field of offerings could designate the entire sky as well as the region beneath the horizon. In addition, the Nile of Egypt had a celestial counterpart in the form of 'the winding waterway' – a name for the milky way – which traversed both the upper and lower skies. Again, geocentrism explains this. Since creation proceeded from the earth and the *nun*, it makes sense that fields and a river should be located in the sky.

So much for the cosmic realms, but what about the divine being that passed through them? As noted earlier, the king personifies Osiris; his body is the god's body, and his soul is the god's soul. But nothing is ever simple in the Pyramid Texts. While Osiris may be regarded as the default character, the king *in his soul form* may appear under other names, all of which designate the risen creator-god. The king is Atum;[82] he is Shu;[83] he is Geb;[84] he is Re;[85] he is Horus;[86] he is Min;[87] he is Thoth;[88] he is Wepwawet;[89] he is Wepiu;[90] he is Montju;[91] he is Nefertem;[92] he is Sokar of Rostau;[93] he is Babi, Lord of the Night Sky;[94] he is Zuntju;[95] he is the Great Wild Bull;[96] he is Neheb-kau;[97] he is the Eye of Horus;[98] he is the Eye of Re;[99] he is the lone star;[100] he is any god he wishes to be;[101] and he may even be a hybrid of different gods.[102]

In addition, the king is the son of various gods. As Osiris, he is the son of Geb and Nut; this is his primary identity. But he also appears as the son of Atum,[103] the son of Re,[104] the son of Re-Atum,[105] the son of Shu,[106] and as Sobek, the son of Neit.[107] He appears as the son because he is the soul which came forth from the body of the creator-god.[108]

The king may also appear as one of the gods (*netjeru*). He is one of the four sons of Horus;[109] he is one of the four regional spirits whom Geb made;[110] he is 'one of the great company which was born in Heliopolis';[111] and he also becomes one of the gods by becoming a star.

All these identities may at first sight seem confusing. But what matters here is not the name but the principle. The king does not pass through the cosmos in human form, despite the impression that is often given in the texts. Rather, he travels as an image of the creator-god, who personifies the principle of the self-creating cosmos. All confusion then disappears if Osiris is recognised as the creator *par excellence*. By his identification with the body of Osiris, the deceased king may send forth his soul in any name he wishes. The Pyramid Texts are thus a kind of play in which the genesis of the cosmos is re-enacted. While the performance of the play varies, with different actors and settings, the characters and script always remain the same.

This is a strange concept for the modern mind to comprehend. But we must try to visualise the king in his cosmic form passing from his tomb into the field of reeds, crossing to the *akhet*, and ascending into the sky. We must then visualise his cosmic form traversing the sky to the western horizon, passing through the *akhet* into the *duat*, and uniting there with his primeval body, which represents the earth and the *nun*. Finally, we must visualise the king's cosmic form emerging from the *duat* to embark on a new circuit of the cosmos.

The Egyptians had a word for this cosmic form of the king, namely *ka*, written with the sign of open arms ⊔ . It is translated by Egyptologists 'vital spirit' or 'double', depending on the context in which it appears.[112] The Pyramid Texts refer repeatedly to the *ka*, and cannot be understood unless the full significance of this term is apprehended.

The texts make it clear that the *ka* originated at the time of creation. In Utterance 600, Atum is said to have imparted his *ka* to Shu and Tefnut when he sneezed and spat them into being. Here, *ka* is translated 'vital spirit'.[113]

The Pyramid Texts also inform us that Osiris and the gods had once gone to their *ka*.[114] It is implied that this involved an ascent to the sky, to the realm of the spirits, and it may be surmised that this event signified their coming-into-being at the creation of the world.

The king too is said to have gone to his *ka*. In this case, the ascent to the sky is made explicit,[115] and it is suggested that the king went to his *ka* in emulation of Osiris and the gods.[116]

The *ka* of the king is a major theme of the Pyramid Texts. The king is said to be *ka*, but also to have a *ka*; both forms are imperishable by virtue of being *ka*.[117] The king descends into the field of his *ka*;[118] he sleeps with his *ka* and spends the day with it;[119] he lives with his *ka*;[120] the *ka* sits down and eats with the king for ever and eternity;[121] the *ka* stands at his side;[122] the *ka* is vindicated;[123] the *ka* is pure and mighty;[124] the *ka* is cleansed in the lake of the *duat*;[125] the *ka* lives in the *akhet* for ever and eternity;[126] and the *ka* ascends to the sky.[127] It is as if there are two living beings in the other world – the king and his *ka*.

In all these references, *ka* is best translated 'double'. The idea stems from the king's identity as the creator-god – a duality of body and soul. In repeating the transformation of the god, the king's soul issues from its body, like a son in the image of its father, and is thus conceived as its

162   THE MIDNIGHT SUN

'double'. And likewise, vice versa, the body is conceived as the 'double' of the soul.

The word *ka* is used in both senses, sometimes referring to the king's body in the *duat*, and sometimes to the king's soul, or spirit, in the circuit of the cosmos. The particular usage may be determined by the context of the spell, and would have been more obvious to the Egyptians than to us. In the vast majority of cases, however, it is the king's spirit-double that is referred to.[128]

In summary, the *ka* concept captures precisely the idea of the king's cosmic form travelling through the *duat*, the *akhet*, the field of reeds, and the sky, entering the earth to revisit and reinvigorate its source, and then embarking once again on the eternal cosmic circuit. It is a picture of the spirit of the primeval cosmos flowing rhythmically through the realms of the present cosmos, and infusing it with the energy of life in an eternal repetition of the creative moment.

Most of the conceptual issues have now been dealt with. It is time to see how all this works in practice.

Figure 35.
THE ARMS OF KA RAISE THE SUN DISC ABOVE THE EMBLEMS OF ANKH (LIFE) AND DJED (ENDURANCE).

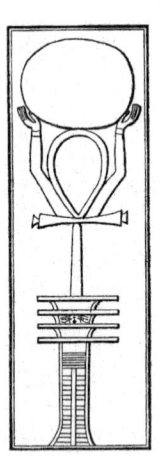

Osiris-the-King

There is no single spell in the Pyramid Texts that captures the essence of the entire corpus. Instead, there are many diverse spells, which focus on one or more aspects of the creation myth re-enactment. It follows that to reconstruct the overall vision one has no choice but to select spells from the corpus and pull them together in an order which follows the creation myth. The following reconstruction is therefore biased and subjective – inevitably so. Nevertheless, while falling short of any kind of proof, the exercise will at the very least allow us to test the plausibility of the idea under consideration, namely that the supposedly diverse elements in the texts – chthonian, solar, lunar, and stellar – all belong together in the context of the creation myth and its re-enactment.

The natural starting point is the death of the king, which is pictured in mythical terms as the death of Osiris. The myth of Osiris's death receives various treatments in the texts (see chapter four), but a consistent idea is the presence of evil which causes the body to decompose. This attack is halted when Isis and Nephthys discover the body lying on its side and raise cries of lamentation. We might imagine the following spell to have been recited at the side of the king's deceased body, at the earliest stage in the funerary rituals:

> Isis comes, Nephthys comes, one from the west, one from the east, one as a screecher, one as a kite. They have found Osiris, his brother Seth having laid him low in Nedyt, when Osiris said "Get away from me", when his name became 'Sokar'. They prevent you from rotting in accordance with this your name of 'Anubis'; they prevent your putrefaction from dripping to the ground... they prevent the smell of your corpse from becoming foul...[129]

The king's recovery was by no means automatic or guaranteed. Rather, it was brought about by the magic rituals of the priests, which invoked the original revivification of Osiris. Foremost among these rituals was the mummification of the body. As with the king's death, this is described in mythical terms – as the reassembly of the limbs of Osiris, whose body had fallen into a state of dismemberment.

The reassembly of Osiris-the-king is the central event of the Pyramid Texts. It is usually performed by the king himself (this corresponds to the idea of the self-created creator) or by his son Horus (i.e. his soul, ditto), but it may also be credited to his sister Isis, his mother Nut, or his father Geb. The following spell might well have been recited by the priest or designate king at the beginning of the mummification ritual:

> Stand up for me, O my father, stand up for me, O Osiris-the-king, for I indeed am your son, I am Horus. I have come for you that I may cleanse you and purify you, that I may bring you to life and collect your bones for you, that I may gather together your soft parts for you and collect your dismembered parts for you.[130]

This reassembly of Osiris's body was also envisioned as the assembly of the gods. Numerous spells describe the gods being brought together for Osiris, usually by his son Horus (see chapter five). It is implicit here that the assembly of the gods corresponds to the assembly of the limbs of the god. But this is made explicit in Utterance 562:

> Your body is this king, O god. So also, your bodies are the king, O gods.[131]

According to my hypothesis, the reassembly of Osiris's limbs signified the reassembly of the elements of the old cosmos, and the bandaging of the king's corpse signified the same. The mummy is therefore to be seen as a symbolic representation of the primeval world – an assemblage of earth and waters.

After the mummy has been prepared, it is subjected to further magic rituals which restore it to life. Of these, four warrant special mention: the presentation of waters; the presentation of offerings; the presentation of the Eye and the eyes; and the splitting open of the mouth and the eyes. For three, and possibly all four, of these rituals, Osiris is urged to turn himself from his left side (associated with death) onto his right side (associated with life).[132] At this point, we should envisage the mummy being turned, to correspond with the myth.

The presentation of waters to Osiris-the-king features prominently in the Pyramid Texts. A frequent refrain, addressed to the mummy, is: 'You have your water, you have your flood',[133] to which is sometimes added the line 'You have your efflux which issued from Osiris'[134] or 'You have your milk which is in the breast of your mother Isis'.[135] The ritual itself is described in Utterance 33, in which we must envisage the priest reciting the words as he brings jars of pure water to the king's mummy:

> O king, take this cold water of yours, for you have coolness with Horus in your name of 'Him who Issued from Cold Water'. Take the efflux which issued from you. Horus has caused the gods to assemble for you at the place where you have gone. Horus has caused the children of Horus to muster for you at the place where you drowned... O Osiris-the-king... Nut has caused you to be a god... you being young in your name of 'Fresh Water'.[136]

The meaning of the ritual is here made clear. The waters signify the flood which leaked out from Osiris's body – the flood in which he drowned, but from which he then issued forth in his name of Horus. By presenting these primeval waters to Osiris-the-king, the priest not only purifies him and 'refreshes the heart of the great god',[137] but also provides him with a fundamental element for the creation of the cosmos. Using these waters, the king will form the seas, rivers, and springs of the world, and the great ocean of the sky.

A second important ritual is the presentation of offerings. The typical formula for these offerings is 'a thousand of bread, a thousand of beer, a thousand of ointment, a thousand of alabaster, a thousand of clothing, a thousand of cattle'.[138] All these and more are symbolised by the Eye of Horus, which is said to bear all the produce of the earth.[139]

Offerings derive from the world of man but are transubstantiated by the ritual into their archetypal forms. The presentation of these immortal substances to Osiris-the-king endows him with a soul:

> Raise yourself O king, receive your water, gather together your bones... raise yourself to this bread of yours that does not grow mouldy and your beer that does not grow sour, that you may have a soul thereby, that you may be effective thereby, that you may be powerful thereby.[140]

The significance of the offerings lies in the myth of the Eye. At the time of Osiris's death, Seth, the god of chaos, had snatched the Eye; but Horus had seized it back and returned it to Osiris. The presentation of offerings, symbolised by the Eye, therefore signifies the subjugation of Seth and the forces of chaos.[141] The creation can thus proceed unhindered.

Beyond this, offerings symbolised the essential energy of the primeval earth. This is implied by the ritual text of Utterance 49:

> O Osiris-the-king, take the ferment which issued from you – beer, a *hnt*-bowl of black *mnu*-stone.[142]

Here, it is suggested that the beer (or rather its ingredients) issued from the body of Osiris – the personification of the primeval earth and waters. The offering is therefore returning to the god what is rightfully his at the beginning of time.

Offerings of bread, ointment, alabaster, clothing, and cattle would also follow this same principle.

The idea was to present the mummy with all the produce of the earth, that it might gain full control over the primeval elements of creation.

The third important ritual is the presentation of the Eye and the eyes. The ritual itself is described in Utterance 80, where the priest approaches the mummy with a bag of black eye-paint:

> O Horus who is this Osiris-the-king, take the uninjured Eye of Horus. I paint it on your face for you, for Horus painted his uninjured Eye. O king, I attach your eyes to your face for you intact, so that you may see with them – black eye-paint, one bag.[143]

This ritual re-enacts one of the most pivotal myths in Egyptian religion. Seth had stolen the Eye from Osiris and tried to destroy it; but Horus had recovered it and returned it uninjured to Osiris. The Eye – symbol of the Great Goddess – had then ensured the resurrection of Osiris.

As noted earlier, the Eye symbolised offerings – all the produce of the earth. By returning the Eye to Osiris, Horus gave him the power to come into being and create the cosmos. The Eye is thus said to fill or complete Osiris-the-king,[144] to purify him,[145] to strengthen and protect him,[146] and to provide him with a soul.[147]

More than that, the presentation of the Eye causes the king to see with his two eyes, which when opened disperse the darkness by means of the light.[148] These two eyes, which the king receives from Horus or Geb,[149] are usually painted on the face of the mummy (see above), but in one spell they are put on the feet 'that they may guide this king to the *qebhu*, to Horus, to the sky, to the great god'.[150] Significantly, the eyes represent the sun and the moon. Thus the ritual prepares the king for the creation of the sky.

The fourth important ritual is the splitting open of the mouth and the eyes. The actual rituals are described in Utterances 20 and 21. We must here visualise the priest approaching the mummy and striking its mouth and eyes with the adze:

> O king, I come in search of you, for I am Horus. I strike your mouth for you... I split open your mouth for you...[151]
>
> I split open your mouth for you. I split open your eyes for you. O king, I open your mouth for you with the adze of Wepwawet... with the adze of iron which split open the mouths of the gods. O Horus, open the mouth of this king![152]

The splitting open of the mouth is performed by Horus, or sometimes by the four sons of Horus. This ritual restores the king to life, causing him to breathe and speak (metaphorically speaking) in the afterlife. Utterance 21 informs us that this ritual re-enacted the opening of the mouths of Osiris and the gods in primeval times. We will discuss the full significance of this act, from a geocentric perspective, in the next chapter.

The splitting open of the eyes is also performed by Horus. This ritual enables the king to see in the afterlife, by means of the light of the sun and the moon. It is often effected by the splitting open of the Sole Eye, which is given the names 'Opener of Roads' and 'She who Opens up the Ways of the God'.[153]

All these magic rituals – the presentation of waters, the presentation of offerings, the presentation of the Eye and the eyes, and the splitting open of the Eye and the eyes – are interwoven with a shared symbolism, which revolves around the Eye. The Eye is synonymous with the cold water which refreshes the heart;[154] it is synonymous with the offerings; it brings forth the two eyes; and it can itself split open the mouth.[155] Moreover, the ointment which went forth from the Eye is able to raise up the king's bones, reassemble his limbs, and gather together his flesh.[156] The full significance of the Eye, from a geocentric perspective, will be discussed in chapter twelve.

After these rituals have been completed, the king's mummy is stood up to signify the ascent of its *ka* into the sky.[157] This ritual is alluded to in many spells where the king is urged to stand up:

> O Osiris-the-king, it is caused that you be restored and that your mouth be split open, so stand up![158]

> O king, awake! Raise yourself! Stand up, that you may be pure and that your *ka* may be pure, that your *ba* may be pure, that your power may be pure.[159]

> O king, stand up for Horus, that he may make you a spirit and guide you when you ascend to the sky.[160]

> Stand upon it, this earth which issued from Atum, this spittle which issued from Kheprer; come into being upon it, be exalted upon it, so that your father may see you, so that Re may see you.[161]

Figure 36.
THE OPENING OF THE MOUTH RITUAL.
A scene from the tomb of Tutankhamun.

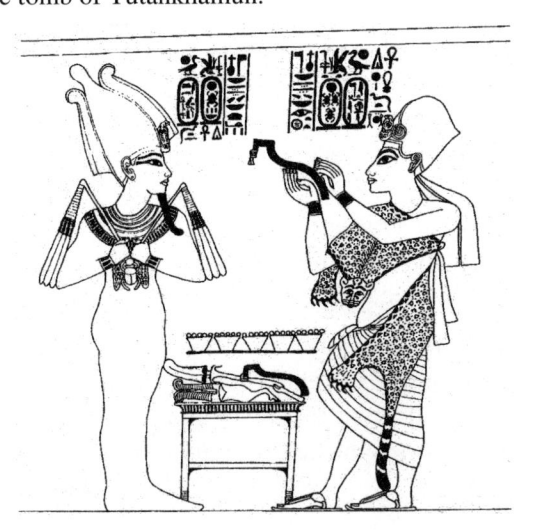

In Utterance 254, the erect king is described as 'the eye-painted pillar, the bull of the sky', 'the Pillar of Kenzet', and 'the Pillar of the Stars'.[162] These names evoke the lifting of the sky and the creation of the sun, the moon, and the stars. The vast majority of spells in the Pyramid Texts belong to this stage of the ritual. They are directed towards the king's erect mummy, and urge it to send out its spirit, or soul, into all parts of the greater cosmos.

Ascending from the Earth to the Sky

How does the reborn king rise up into the sky? As mentioned earlier, he has the choice of a direct ascent from the earth or a shortcut ascent from the *akhet* in the east side of the sky. The direct route is characterised by the traversing of air, whereas the shortcut route is characterised by the crossing of water and fields using a boat. In both types of spell, we see a re-enactment of geocentric creation in that the king passes *from the earth* into the sky. Scholars have long assumed that this ascent reflects the fact that the king was buried in the earth. However, I believe there was much more to it, in that the ascent re-enacted the expansion of the former cosmos into the new.

It is significant in this regard that the king assumes an identity both with the primeval mound and the *akhet*. In Utterance 484, he claims: 'I am the primeval hill (*khay*) of land in the midst of the sea... Shu presses down the earth under my feet',[163] while in several spells he receives the Osirian name 'Akhet from which Re goes forth'.[164] It is clear from these facts that the king is more than a human soul departing from a tomb that is located in the earth for practical reasons. Rather, he is a cosmic being emerging from a tomb that is a microcosm of the primeval cosmos. His rebirth is the rebirth of that cosmos. His revivified body is the primeval hill and his transfigured spirit is the *akhet*.

The following illustrations will allow the reader to judge for himself the validity of this principle. We will here look at the direct ascent from the earth, the ascent via the east being considered in a later section on the king's orbit of the cosmic circuit.

The direct ascent begins in the earth and involves traversing the air to reach the sky. In Utterance 511, the king declares:

> Geb laughs, Nut shouts for joy before me when I ascend to the sky. The sky thunders for me, the earth quakes for me, the hailstorm is unleashed for me, and I roar like Seth. Those who are in charge of the divisions of the sky open the celestial doors for me, and I stand on the air (*shu*)...[165]

Similarly in Utterance 331, the king traverses the space which separates the sky from the earth:

> I ascend to the sky upon the *shedshed* which is in the space which separates.[166]

The same idea is seen in the king's ascent upon Shu, the god of the air. For example:

> I have gone up on Shu, I have climbed on the wing of Kheprer.[167]

Here, the ascent upon the air is visualised as the flight of the self-creating beetle. But elsewhere, the king flies up to the sky in the form of a bird or a locust. For example:

> I have soared to the sky as a heron, I have kissed the sky as a falcon, I have reached the sky as a locust.[168]

> The king has gone up as a swallow, he has alighted as a falcon.[169]

> The king soars as a divine falcon, the king flies skywards like a heron, the king flies up as a goose, the king's wings are those of a divine falcon, the king's wing-feathers are those of a divine falcon.[170]

A further variant of this idea is the king's ascent in a great storm. For example:

> The king is Osiris in a dust devil... The king is bound for the sky on the wind, on the wind![171]

> The hailstones of the sky have taken me, and they raise me up to Re.[172]

By contrast, the king could ascend in a more tranquil manner, by means of a rain-cloud, or the smoke of the incense.[173]

The king could also ascend to the sky on the light of creation, which filled the rising air. In Utterance 508, the king states:

> I ascend to my place, O Re. I have laid down for myself this light of yours as a stairway under my feet on which I will ascend to that mother of mine.[174]

The stairway is elsewhere combined with the idea of traversing the air like a bird. For example:

> A stairway to the sky is set up for me that I may ascend on it to the sky, and I ascend on the smoke of the great censing. I fly up as a bird and alight as a beetle...[175]

The king could also ascend to the sky upon a ladder – made of wood or rope.[176] In three instances, this ladder is used for an ascent from the east side of the sky.[177] But it is unlikely to have belonged there, for elsewhere it was used for a direct ascent from the earth. This is particularly evident in Utterance 333:

> I have cleansed myself upon the earth-hill (*kha n ta*) whereon Re cleansed himself. I place the stairway, I set up the ladder, and those who are in the land of the west (*ament*) grasp my hand.[178]

The ladder, like the stairway, was a means of ascending through the air.

A direct ascent is also implied by several spells where the gods form a ladder for the king, usually in parallel with an assembly of the districts or the mounds of the earth. For example:

> The gods who are (to be) in the sky are brought to you, the gods who are (to be) in the earth assemble for you. They place their hands under you, they make a ladder for you that you may ascend on it to the sky... Atum has assembled the districts for you, he has given the cities of Geb to you... the mounds, the mounds of Horus, the mounds of Seth, and the field of reeds.[179]

The allusion here is to the assembly of the primeval mound (see chapter thirteen). Interestingly, two spells in this genre compare the sky itself to a ladder, as if to recall the coming-into-being of the sky as it was separated from the earth and the *nun*:

> There come to you the gods the souls of Pe and the gods the souls of Nekhen – the gods who are (to be) in the sky and the gods who are (to be) in the earth. They make supports for you upon their arms; may you ascend to the sky and mount up on it in this its name of 'Ladder'.[180]

> The king ascends to the sky among the stars, among the imperishable stars. His power is on him, his terror about him, his magic at his feet, and he goes thereby to his mother Nut, he ascends upon her in this her name of 'Ladder'.[181]

The King Becomes All Parts of the Cosmos

As discussed earlier, the rituals performed on the king's mummy caused its spirit to go forth into the wider cosmos. For this reason, the king was presented with his waters which signified the flood which had flowed out from the body of Osiris. In line with the myth of creation, the king then used these floodwaters to irrigate the newly risen earth and to bring the celestial ocean into being.

The first of these creative tasks is recalled in Utterance 271, where the king states:

> I have irrigated the earth which emerged from the lake.[182]

The second task is suggested by Utterance 685, where the king's rebirth coincides with the separation of the waters of the earth and the sky:

> The waters of life which are (to be) in the sky come, the waters of life which are (to be) in the earth come, the sky is aflame for you, the earth quakes at you before the god's birth... this king comes into being.[183]

This spell goes on to equate the king with Shu, the god who uplifted the waters of the sky. The king is told: 'You shall support the sky with your hand, you shall lay down the earth with your foot.'[184] It is thus suggested that the king will use the pressure of the air (*shu*) to raise his floodwaters and create the sky-ocean.

This process is described most clearly in the Coffin Texts, which place the flood at the east gate of the sky and state that the floodwaters of the deceased become the *qebhu* (the 'sky-water') upon the opening of the gates of the *akhet*.[185] But the result at least is made clear in the Pyramid Texts, which place the king's waters in the sky. The king declares:

> My water is in the sky, my fledgelings are on earth, my heart is drowned (?).[186]

> My water is wine like that of Re, and I go round the sky like Re...[187]

Having created the celestial ocean as a living medium, the king – or to be more precise his *ka* – manifests himself in all parts of it as a great being of light, assuming the forms of the stars, the sun, and the moon. This, of course, follows the pattern of the creator-god who created these celestial bodies, and provides us with persuasive evidence for the re-enactment of creation hypothesis.

We shall begin with the spells in which the king becomes the sun and the moon (jointly or separately), and then consider the spells in which he becomes the stars or a specific star.

In Utterance 210, the king is seemingly identified with the sun and the moon simultaneously in that he travels round the sky in the manner of Re and Thoth, the sun-god and the moon-god respectively:

> O you two companions who cross the sky, who are Re and Thoth, take me with you... that I may sail in that in which you sail... I go round the sky like Re, I traverse the sky like Thoth.[188]

This is an unusual spell. Normally, the king becomes either the sun or the moon.

The king is identified solely with Re, the sun, in at least nine spells. In six of these, he takes the role of Re in command of the gods in the day-barque. For example:

> Go aboard this barque of Re to which the gods desire to draw near... in which Re rows to the *akhet*, that you may go aboard it as Re; sit on this throne of Re that you may give orders to the gods, because you are Re who came forth from Nut who bears Re daily, and you are born daily like Re.[189]

In two of the other spells, the king is identified with the Eye of Re in its solar manifestation. For example:

> O Re... I am you and you are me... I am that eye of yours which is on the horns of Hathor. I spend the night and am conceived and born every day.[190]

The king becomes solely the moon in just one spell, where the Eye of Re manifests itself as the moon:

> May the sky make the light strong for you; may you rise up to the sky as the Eye of Re; may you stand at that left eye of Horus.[191]

Turning to the stars, the king may become all of them, or more often just one of them.

The king becomes all the stars in two spells. Firstly, in Utterance 684, the king emulates Osiris in becoming the imperishable stars:

> This king ascended when you ascended, O Osiris; his word and his *ka* are bound for the sky. The king's bones are iron and the king's limbs are the imperishable stars.[192]

Secondly, in Utterance 723, the afterlife of the king is equated to the life of the stars:

> O king, raise yourself upon your iron bones and golden limbs... The warmth which is on your mouth is the breath which issued from the nostrils of Seth... The sky will be deprived of its stars if the warmth which is on your mouth be lacking. May your flesh be born to life, and may your life be more than the life of the stars.[193]

These spells reflect the myth that the gods were assembled in the king's body (see earlier). The gods are spiritualized from his limbs to become the stars in the sky (see chapter six).

In keeping with this idea, the king inherits all the stars. In Utterance 576, Nut is urged to 'bring the sky to the king and hang up the stars for him',[194] while in Utterance 510 the king declares: 'I take possession of the sky, its pillars, and its stars.'[195]

It is in this context perhaps – of the king becoming *all* the stars – that the king becomes *a single star* among the stars. For example:

> I stand up as this star on the belly of the sky.[196]

> I am a star to whom the gods bow, at which the two enneads tremble.[197]

> I am a star which illumines the sky.[198]

> The king is a star in the sky among the gods.[199]

> The king ascends to the sky among the stars, among the imperishable stars.[200]

> Lift yourself to the sky in company with the stars which are in the sky.[201]

> You belong to the stars which surround Re, which are before the morning star.[202]

> O king, you belong to the *nkhkhu*-stars which shine in the train of the morning star.[203]

There are more than a dozen such references in the Pyramid Texts.[204] In addition, there are a dozen or so spells in which the king is portrayed as a star-god rowing Re across the sky in his barque:

> I take my oar for myself, I occupy my seat, I sit in the bow of the barque of the two enneads. I row Re to the west... I am a *nkhkh*-star, the companion of a *nkhkh*-star, I become a *nkhkh*-star.[205]

> Be pure, occupy your seat in the barque of Re, row over the sky and mount up to the far-above ones. Row with the imperishable stars, navigate with the untiring stars.[206]

In these spells, the king is a star that crosses the sky from the east to the west in the circuit of the sun. These stars are imperishable on account of their unfailing ability to reappear in the sky. But the king could also become an imperishable star in the northern circumpolar sky, among the stars which never set. For example:

> I am back to back with those gods in the north of the sky – the imperishable stars.[207]

> May you go to those northern gods, the imperishable stars.[208]

174 THE MIDNIGHT SUN

You shall set me to be a magistrate among the spirits, the imperishable stars, in the north of the sky.[209]

Several other spells may also imply the king's translation to this group of stars.[210]

The king could also become a named star. Here, the spells focus on a triad of stars whose movements at the eastern horizon recalled the myth of the God, the Goddess, and the divine child. The star-gods in question are Sah, 'the father of the gods', who was identified with Osiris,[211] Sopdet (the Greek Sothis), who was identified with Isis,[212] and Netjer-dwau, 'the god of the dawn-light', who was identified with Horus the son of Isis.[213] Sah was the constellation Orion, but perhaps originally the star Canopus; Sopdet was the star Sirius; and Netjer-dwau was the planet Venus, the so-called 'morning star'.

We see here a classic example of allegorical astronomy. Each year, Sah would set below the horizon and fail to reappear for approximately seventy days; this signified the death of Osiris.[214] Sopdet (Sirius) would then disappear in search of Sah, and would likewise spend about seventy days out of sight, notionally in the *duat*.[215] Then, miraculously, Sopdet would reappear at the horizon, followed by Sah-Canopus (or preceded by Sah-Orion); this signified the rebirth of Osiris.[216] The next appearance of Venus in the east, as the morning star, would then signify the birth of the son Horus, who signified the soul of Osiris.[217] In this way, the stars re-enacted perpetually the great mystery of creation.

As we might expect, the king as a male figure was identified with the

Figure 37.
SAH (OSIRIS) TRAVERSES THE NIGHT SKY, FOLLOWED BY SOPDET (ISIS) AND THREE STARS.
From the ceiling of the tomb of Seti I.

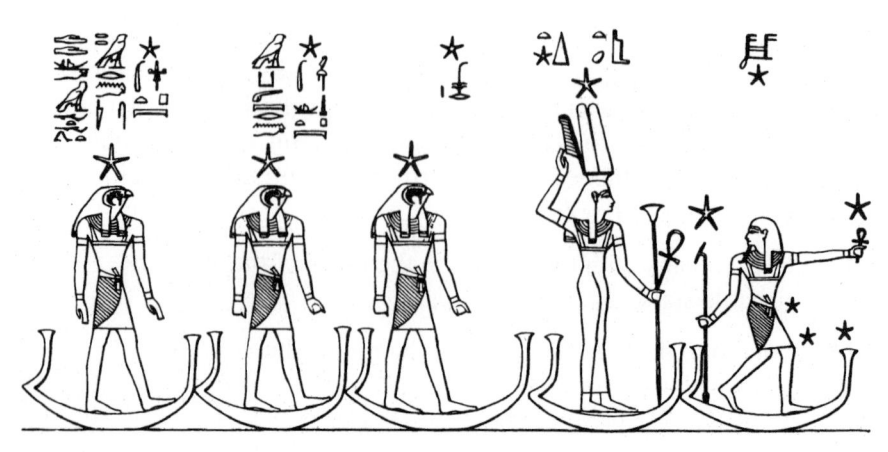

two male gods in this triad – the father Sah and the son Netjer-dwau. In the former case, he became Osiris in his spiritualized, stellar form. In the latter case, he became Horus the son of Isis, i.e. the soul of Osiris.

The king's identity as Sah is not stated explicitly. Rather, it is implied by the statement that the king ascends to the sky as the brother of Sopdet and the father of Netjer-dwau (Sopdet is his sister and the morning star is his offspring).[218] This suggests strongly that he becomes Sah. In addition, the king is probably Sah in Utterance 412, where he is said to 'reach the sky as Sah',[219] and in Utterance 690, where the sky 'gives birth' to him 'like Sah'.[220]

The king becomes Netjer-dwau, the god of the morning star, in six spells. In two instances, Re sets the king as the morning star in the midst of the field of reeds,[221] while in four instances, the king ascends to the sky in the shape of the morning star.[222] For example:

> Re sets you as the morning star (*netjer-dwau*) in the midst of the field of reeds. The door of the sky at the *akhet* opens to you, the gods are glad at meeting you as the star which crosses the sea on the belly of the sky...[223]

> The sky weeps for you, the earth quakes at you... your feet stamp, your arms wave, and you ascend to the sky as a star, as the morning star.[224]

In addition, several spells may *imply* that the king becomes the morning star. In Utterance 216, the king is a star which disappears into the *duat* in parallel with Sah and Sopdet.[225] In Utterance 442, the king is a star which ascends and descends with Sah as a third to Sopdet.[226] In Utterance 699, the king is a star which traverses the sky beside its father Sah.[227] And in Utterance 466, the king is a 'great star' (masculine) which accompanies Sah:

> O king, you are this great star (*sba-wr*), the companion of Sah, who traverses the sky with Sah, who navigates the *duat* with Osiris. You ascend from the east of the sky, being renewed at your due season and rejuvenated at your due time. The sky has borne you with Sah...[228]

On no occasion do the Pyramid Texts state that the king becomes Sopdet (Sirius/Isis). Perhaps the king's masculinity prevents this identification (hence also the fact that he never becomes Nut). However, the Egyptians often described their creator-god as a 'he-she' (see chapter fourteen), and it is possible that the deceased king also possessed this dual sexuality. In Utterance 412, for example, the king is told 'you shall reach the sky as Sah, your soul shall be as effective as Sopdet'.[229] This might suggest that the feminine power was immanent in the king's soul. Furthermore, it is possible that the king's rebirth as the son of Sopdet implied the coming-into-being of Sopdet herself. Hence in Utterance 302, the king declares: 'The sky is cleared, Sopdet lives, because I am a living one, the son of Sopdet.'[230]

The King's Eternal Circuit of the Cosmos

Having reached the sky, the king began to circulate in the eternal cosmic circuit. To this end, he was given possession of all the cosmic realms and power over the beings therein. "The sky is yours, the earth is yours", says Atum.[231] "The field of reeds, the mounds of Horus, the mounds of Seth – all are yours", says Geb.[232] "The king, my son, is my beloved" declares Nut, "I have given him the two *akheti* that he may have power in them as Horakhti... I have given him the *duat* that he may rule it as Horus of the Duat."[233] "I bring to you the gods of the sky, I assemble for you the gods of the earth... and all are yours", proclaims Geb.[234]

Thus the king was able to circulate unhindered through the cosmos for eternity.

There is no one spell that describes the king's circuit of the cosmos in a continuous narrative, but there are enough fragments to allow the idea to be reconstructed. The king traverses the upper sky from east to west;[235] he descends into the land of the west (*ament*) or into the lower sky;[236] he joins the night-barque;[237] he becomes a star in the lower sky or the *duat*;[238] he traverses the *duat*;[239] he ferries over the winding waterway to the *akhet* in the east side of the sky;[240] he crosses to the *akhet* on the reed-floats of the sky or on the wing of Thoth;[241] he travels in the west like Kheprer and shines in the east like Re;[242] he is borne alive by Nut every day like Re;[243] he travels around the two skies (*peti*);[244] and his stars are ever setting and rising: 'My limbs are the imperishable stars... the sky will not be devoid of me and this earth will not be devoid of me for ever.'[245]

It is here that we encounter the second type of ascent spell. Instead of reaching the sky vertically from the tomb and then heading westwards to embark on the cosmic circuit, the king could make a shortcut by joining Re and the gods in their circuit of the lower sky or netherworld, and then heading eastwards to the doors of the sky at the *akhet*.

This journey involved passing over a flooded field, known variously as the field of reeds (*sekhet iaru*) or field of offerings (*sekhet hetep*). The following spells are typical:

> The nurse-canal is opened, the winding waterway is flooded, the fields of reeds are filled, that I may be ferried over to the east side of the sky, to the place where the gods were born. [Variant: to the place where the

gods fashioned me.] [246]

The *pat*-land is opened up, the *pat*-land is filled with water, the field of reeds is flooded, the field of offerings is flooded... These four youths who stand on the east side of the sky bind together for me the two reed-floats on which I go to the *akhet*, to Re.[247]

This journey is accomplished using the reed-floats of the sky (*zkhnu n pet*) and leads directly to the king's ascent as a star (often Sah), either on a reed-float or in the barque of Re.[248]

In a variant tradition, the king pauses in the field of reeds and bathes in its lake, or pool, alongside Re.[249] According to one version of events, the king is washed and dried by the followers of Horus, who recite magic spells for his ascent on the right path;[250] he then goes aboard the barque of Re and sails into the sky from the *akhet*. But according to a second tradition, the king is bathed by Horus and Thoth, who rub his flesh and feet;[251] he is then lifted up into the sky by Nut and Shu:

Re has bathed in the field of reeds... This king has bathed in the field of reeds. This king's hand is in Re's hand. O Nut, take his hand! O Shu, lift him up![252]

This ascent takes place from the field of reeds, and bypasses the *akhet*. It is therefore an exception to the normal rule.

The field of offerings, likewise, can offer a direct route to the east side of the sky. In Utterance 509, for example, the king states:

I ascend to the sky among the imperishable stars, my sister is Sopdet, my guide is Netjer-dwau, and they grasp my hand at the field of offerings.[253]

The fact that the king could bypass the *akhet* suggests that it, the field of reeds, and the field of offerings were originally parallel renderings of the reborn world in the east. The realms are indeed remarkably similar, being characterised by waters, green fields and plants (see chapter two).

In this indirect ascent via the east, the landscape is unmistakeably that of the creation.

Firstly, there is the flood on which the king crosses the field of reeds and the *akhet* en route to the sky. This flood recalls that of the creation, when the waters of *nun* came forth in a flood and were separated (in part) from the earth to form the sky-ocean.

Secondly, there is the field of reeds in whose lake the king bathes with Re. It is described as a place of 'coming to land',[254] and is said to contain an 'island of earth' (*iw ta*) located 'between the thighs of Nut'.[255] As a place of fertile earth amidst floodwaters, it is undoubtedly an image of the primeval mound, or island of creation. It is indeed the birthplace of the morning star.

Thirdly, there is the *akhet*, where the king joins Re for his ascent to the sky. It too is a lush paradise of land amidst floodwaters, but it is here that the gods and the king become *akh*, i.e. spirits or beings of light who are destined for the starry sky. The *akhet* is thus unmistakeably a creational realm – the spiritualized equivalent of the *duat*.

The landscape of the east, with its reeds and floodwaters, is especially evocative of the Edfu creation myth. According to this myth, which was summarised in chapter three, the first manifestation of creation was a reed island that formed on the surface of the primeval waters. It, like the field of reeds, was partially submerged. Moreover, its reeds were utilized as building materials, which seems also to have been the case with the field of reeds which is mentioned in conjunction with the reed-floats of the sky. It must therefore be considered likely that the field of reeds has its origins in a creation myth.[256]

It may also be no coincidence that the field of reeds contained both a pool and a lotus, which were central features in the Hermopolis creation myth.[257]

The king thus reached the *akhet*, and embarked on his first circuit of the cosmos.

As discussed earlier, the purpose of circuiting the cosmos was to keep it in motion and ensure its perpetual rejuvenation, and to this end it was essential that the gods and the king had abundant supplies of drink and food to sustain their activities. The texts confirm that these provisions originated in the flood, the field of reeds, the field of offerings, and the *akhet*, and consisted of archetypal water, crops, and plants. But the texts also place these provisions in the sky, which appropriately enough was called the field of offerings – a mirror image of the field below. This was the great field of the sun-god Re, who by means of his magic, delegated by the creator-god, caused the three seasons of flood, spring, and harvest to occur in the space of a single day.[258]

In order to circulate in the cosmos, then, the king had to satiate himself on the produce of the celestial field. The following spells exemplify this vitally important theme:

> The doors of the sky are opened for you, the doors of the *qebhu* are thrown open for you, that you may travel by boat to the field of reeds, that you may cultivate barley, that you may reap emmer, and prepare your sustenance therefrom like Horus the son of Atum.[259]

> O Re and Thoth, take me with you, that I may eat of what you eat, that
> I may drink of what you drink, that I may live on what you live on...
> My booth is in the field of reeds, my drink supply is in the field of
> offerings, my food-offerings are among you, you gods.[260]

> You shall take me with you to your great field which you have laid
> down with the help of the gods, and what you eat at night when they
> are bright is the fullness of the god of food. I will eat of what you eat,
> I will drink of what you drink... You shall set me to be a magistrate
> among the spirits the imperishable stars in the north of the sky, who
> rule over offerings and protect the reaped corn.[261]

It is no great surprise to find that this celestial paradise was modelled on the world of mankind. The divine population included labourers, bakers, butchers, and brewers, who turned the resources into bread, meat, beer, and wine – the food and drink of the gods.

Interestingly, the king is said to possess five meals, of which three are in the sky and two in the earth.[262] Regarding the latter, the king is said to eat with his *ka*, and the *ka* is on one occasion urged to bring food that the king and his double might eat it together.[263] This would seem to imply that the spirit acquired an excess of food in the sky, which it brought into the netherworld to share with its body. The king's mummy was therefore nourished by two types of offerings – the material offerings from the human world, which were brought to the tomb by his living son Horus, and the immaterial offerings from the divine world, which were brought to the tomb by the ethereal *ka*. The former produce was transubstantiated by the priests into its archetypal form, while the latter represented the genuine article, fresh from the world of the gods.

Following this mystical feast in the tomb, the revitalised mummy sent forth its *ka* once again – eastwards to the green fields and the land of the *akhet* where it was able to gorge once more on the pure drink and food.[264] The entire process then began anew. The king's *ka* traversed the field of the sky, satiated itself with another three meals, and then returned to the *duat* and the tomb.

The king was therefore master of *neheh* and *djet* – 'eternal repetition' and 'eternal endurance'. As Utterance 274 explains:

> The king's afterlife is *neheh*, his limit is *djet*... The king is this one
> who rises and rises, who endures and endures... His pyramid [*st-ib*,
> literally 'the seat of his heart'] is among the living in this land for ever
> and eternity.[265]

As long as the pyramid endured, and its inscriptions endured, and the mummy in the tomb underneath it endured, the cosmos around it would endure and the world would never end. The spells thus provided for the protection of the pyramid:

> O Atum, set your arms about the king, about this construction, about this pyramid (of his) as the arms of a *ka*, that the king's *ka* may be in it, enduring for ever. O Atum, set your protection over this king, over this pyramid of his, over this construction of his, prevent anything evil from happening against it for ever...[266]

Chapter Seven Summary

- The king was the embodiment of the creator-god. His coronation was a re-enactment of the first time, when the god Horus had inherited the kingship of Osiris. The king's primary task was to re-enact the events of creation in order to rejuvenate the cosmos.

- The king was the 'son' of the creator-god in the sense of the soul that came forth from the creator-god's body. The body – the king's father – personified the revivified corpse of the former cosmos.

- Kingship thus comprised a duality of the Horus-king (the son) and the Osiris-king (the father).

- When the Horus-king died, he became Osiris. The mummification of his corpse re-enacted the myth of the death and rebirth of Osiris, i.e. the death and rebirth of the former cosmos.

- The aim of the Pyramid Texts was to turn the deceased king into an image of the creator-god and cause his soul to go forth from his body, just as the creator-soul had gone forth from the primeval cosmos on the day of creation. The king thus became all parts of the cosmos – the sky-ocean, the sun, the moon, and the stars.

- In addition, the Pyramid Texts were designed to despatch the king's spirit on an eternal circuit of the cosmos. By circumnavigating the *duat*, the *akhet*, the field of reeds, and the sky, the king re-enacted the death and rebirth of the former terrestrial world and ensured that the present cosmos would endure for ever.

- All the supposed inconsistencies in the Pyramid Texts evaporate when they are viewed from a creational perspective.

CHAPTER EIGHT

OPENING THE MOUTH

O Osiris-the-king, I have come in search of you... I am your beloved son. I have split open your mouth for you.
(Pyramid Texts, Utterance 20)

There is a gap in the creation myths between the rising of the primeval mound and the appearance of the sun, moon, and stars in the sky. But we can use the principle of the deceased king re-enacting the creation to plug this gap. As a first step, we will examine the opening of the mouth ritual and consider its significance under the geocentric creation hypothesis.

The splitting open of the mouth (*wpt-r*) was one of the most important religious rituals in ancient Egypt. In the divine temple, it was performed upon the statue of the god, with the aim of bringing it to life each day, while in the tomb and the mortuary temple it was performed upon the mummy and the *ka*-statue respectively, with the aim of making the soul, or spirit, of the deceased go forth into the afterlife. Our interest here lies in the latter ritual.

The Pyramid Texts contain the earliest and most informative records of the opening of the mouth ritual. Here, the deceased king is identified with Osiris, whose body must be assembled and restored to life. In three instances, Osiris is said to open his own mouth.[1] But it is usually opened by his son Horus, or the four sons of Horus.[2] Horus is called a 'loving-son priest' of his father.[3]

Osiris-the-king's mouth was split open by various means, of which the most prominent were the adze and the Eye of Horus.[4]

The adze was a special tool, whose distinctive form was modelled on the pattern of the northern circumpolar stars – either Ursa Minor or the Plough in Ursa Major.[5] It features in several passages:

O king, I open your mouth for you with the adze of Wepwawet, I split open your mouth for you with the adze of iron... with the iron which issued from Seth, with the adze of iron which split open the mouths of the gods.[6]

Raise yourself, O king, raise yourself (upon your right side) for the great adze.[7]

O king, Horus has split open your mouth for you, he has split open your eyes with the God's Castle adze, with the Great of Magic adze.[8]

The other chief means of splitting open the mouth was the Eye of Horus. It symbolised offerings and the subjugation of Seth (see discussion in the previous chapter). A typical passage reads:

O king, take the Eye of Horus which was wrested from Seth and saved for you. Your mouth is split open with it – beer, a *hnt*-bowl of white *mnu*-stone.[9]

The presentation of the Eye of Horus endowed the king's mummy with a soul, as did the opening of the mouth. But why the connection between the Eye and the adze?

The explanation lies in the northern circumpolar stars and the myth of the battle of Horus and Seth.

From the earliest times, the Egyptians worshipped God in the form of a bull whose dismembered body-parts had been spiritualized in the sky (see chapter eleven). In particular, it was believed that the northern stars

Figure 38.
HUNEFER HAS HIS MOUTH SPLIT OPEN BY MAGICAL ADZES.
A scene from the Book of the Dead (Papyrus of Hunefer).

formed the pattern of two forelegs or two thighs, which were held to be the limbs of Seth.[10] These stars are known today as Ursa Minor and the Plough in Ursa Major, but the Egyptian name was *mskhtiu*, determined by the sign of a bull's foreleg.[11]

These northern stars provided the magical symbolism for the opening of the mouth ceremony. Firstly, the adze was made in the image of one of Seth's forelegs (either Ursa Minor or the Plough in Ursa Major) and given the stellar name *mskhtiu*, determined by the sign of an adze.[12] And secondly, the key offering in the ritual was the bull's foreleg (*khpsh*), which was the principal form of the Eye of Horus. Hence in Utterance 20, the priest says:

> O Osiris-the-king, I split open your mouth for you with the *khpkh* of the Eye of Horus – one foreleg (*khpsh*).[13]

There is much interwoven symbolism here, relating to the myth of Horus and Seth. Firstly, the foreleg offering that splits open the king's mouth is elsewhere identified as 'the foreleg of Seth which Horus has torn off'.[14] Secondly, the adze that splits open the king's mouth is made of 'the iron which issued from Seth'.[15] And thirdly, the Eye that splits open the king's mouth signifies the subjugation of Seth (because he failed in his attempt to control it).

Figure 39.
THE SEVEN STARS OF THE PLOUGH, PICTURED AS AN ADZE (LEFT) AND A BULL'S FORELEG (RIGHT).

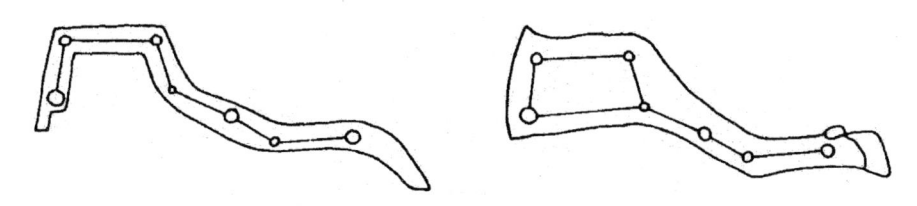

What is the meaning of this? The Pyramid Texts state clearly that the opening of the king's mouth re-enacted an event in the primeval world of the gods, namely the moment when Horus, the loving son, split open the mouth of his father Osiris,[16] and also the moment when the mouths of the gods (*netjeru*) were opened.[17] But what is the significance of the northern stars? What is the significance of the iron? (How did it issue from Seth?) And what significance, if any, lies in the opening of the mouth? Might there be some logical connection between all these themes?

On the question of the northern circumpolar stars, the general view is that they symbolised eternal life, on account of the fact that they always remained visible, never dropping below the horizon. To make the adze in this shape created a magical symbolism which helped ensure the rebirth of the king.

On the question of the iron, the general view is that it attests to a sky cult, or more specifically (in view of the northern sky connection) a star cult.[18] This is plausible, since the Egyptian texts suggest that the iron of which the adze was made was meteoritic iron – the so-called 'iron of the sky' (*bja n pet*). The striking of the mummy's mouth, which is attested in several spells, might well re-enact a meteorite impact.[19]

Finally, on the question of the opening of the mouth, the general view is that it signified nothing more than the deceased being able to breathe and speak in the realms of the afterlife.

The entire ceremony is thus regarded as an attempt to translate the deceased to the afterlife via archaic, magical associations with the world of the gods.

But might there be more to it?

In the previous chapter, I argued that the funerary rituals and spells in the Pyramid Texts were intended to re-enact the myth of creation. To this end, the king's corpse was turned into an image of Osiris – the creator-god *par excellence* – and his soul was induced to separate from his body and enter into the greater cosmos, just as the soul of the creator had done when it created that cosmos. The splitting open of the king's mouth was the crucial ritual that sent his soul on its way, enabling him to breathe and speak in the afterlife. It spiritualized the king, allowing his *ka* to go forth.[20] But this was no human afterlife, no personal affair. Rather, it was the afterlife of the creator-god, who personified the development of the cosmos. The mouth which was split open was therefore a cosmic orifice, whose breath and speech were aimed at the creation of a new cosmos from the remnants of an old cosmos.

If, as I have argued in earlier chapters, the body of the creator-god represented the old cosmos – the primeval earth and the primeval waters – then the splitting open of the mouth could be interpreted literally as the splitting open of this cosmos – an image not inconsistent with the myths of the creator-god being born from an egg or the womb of his mother (the vulva might correspond to the mouth). And it would follow that the myths of the creator-god creating via the mouth – by spitting, speaking, coughing, or sneezing – might also support a literal interpretation.

There are some difficulties with this approach. Firstly, the myth of the gods having their mouths opened jars with this picture, since there should only be one mouth. We would have to regard this idea as a metaphorical extrapolation from the basic myth of the God having his mouth opened, in keeping with the principle of the God being formed by the assembly of the gods (see chapter five). Secondly, the ritual of the king's eyes being split open also suggests that the splitting may be metaphorical rather than literal. But here again, this may be an extrapolation of a literal myth in which the Sole Eye – symbol of the primeval world – was split open in order to give birth to the two eyes – the sun and the moon (see chapter twelve).

Bearing these concerns in mind, we shall now consider the case for a literal, geocentric interpretation of the opening of the mouth, with all that that entails for our understanding of the creation myth.

Opening the Mouth of the Earth

That the primeval earth was conceived as having a mouth is made plain in the Egyptian texts, which refer on several occasions to 'the mouth of the earth' and 'the mouth of Geb'.[21] Sometimes, these passages describe the king going down into the earth[22] – perhaps an allusion to his burial in the tomb – but more often they describe him ascending from the earth into the sky.

In the Pyramid Texts, we read:

> The mouth of the earth is split open for this king, Geb has spoken to him... There is opened for him the eastern door of the sky...[23]

> O king, the mouth of the earth is split open for you, Geb speaks to you... The eastern door of the sky is opened for you...[24]

Similarly in the Coffin Texts, we read:

> O king, the earth opens its mouth for you, Geb throws open his jaws on your account... may you go to the great stairway, may you come to the great city...[25]

> I am Atum who went forth as the great one of the *hnhnu*-barque... The *hnhnu*-barque raises me up to the two barques of Khepri, it opens for me the mouth of the earth.[26]

In this last passage, the *hnhnu*-barque probably represents the barque of the earth while the two barques of Khepri represent the day-barque and the night-barque. The deceased is thus depicted re-enacting the creation of the upper and lower skies from a terrestrial centre.

On one occasion in the Pyramid Texts, the king himself is said to split open the earth. In Utterance 254, a god of the *duat* exclaims:

> Be afraid and tremble, you violent ones who are on the storm-cloud of

the sky! He [the king] split open the earth by means of what he knew on the day when he wished to come thence [from the earth].[27]

This cataclysmic splitting of the earth is echoed in Utterance 685, where two mountains are split apart at the rebirth of the king:

The waters of life which are (to be) in the sky come, the waters of life which are (to be) in the earth come, the sky is aflame for you, the earth quakes at you before the god's birth; the two mountains are split apart, the god comes into being... the two mountains are split apart, this king comes into being.[28]

Consistent with this idea, the earth is hacked up when the king ascends to the sky in an earthquake. In Utterance 719, we read:

The sky thunders, the earth quakes... O king, Geb has given you up and Nut has accepted you. Ascend to the sky, for the doors of the sky are opened for you, the earth is hacked up for you...[29]

This hacking up of the earth may refer to a ritual act. It is mentioned five times in the Pyramid Texts, always in connection with an offering for the king.[30]

As the earth is split open, so also are the realms of the netherworld – the *duat* and the land of the west (*ament* or *amentet*). According to the Coffin Texts, the deceased is 'the one who splits open the *duat*', 'the one who splits open the darkness', and 'the one who splits open the land of the west'.[31]

What is the meaning of this?

According to Egyptologists, the idea that the king split open the earth derives from the simple fact that he was buried in the earth. To enter the afterlife, the king had to come forth from the tomb, which involved him opening the doors of the tomb, or splitting open the earth metaphorically speaking.[32] There is no connection in the minds of scholars between the king opening the mouth of the earth and the priest opening the mouth of the mummy, other than the fact that the latter acted as a trigger ritual for the former.

From a geocentric perspective, however, the king's burial in the earth assumes a profound symbolic importance, since the earth represents the centre point of creation. By becoming an image of Osiris, the king is not only becoming a god of the earth (a god of death and rebirth), but also, more fundamentally, the creator-god who personified the primeval earth and *nun*. It would therefore follow that the mouth of the earth and the mouth of the mummy were one, and that the opening of the one was the opening of the other.

The best illustration of this identity appears in Spell 816 of the Coffin Texts, in which the deceased splits open the land of the west (*ament*) as a result of having his mouth split open by the iron of the adze:

> Ho, iron which split open the land of the west! This is the iron which is on my mouth, which Sokar spiritualized in Heliopolis, which makes the water of my mouth to rise. The iron is washed, and it is sharp and strong. This is the iron which Sokar raised on high in the name of 'Great One in it in Heliopolis', the iron which raises me up, which lifts me up so that I may split open the land of the west in which I dwell.[33]

There are two lines in this passage which give pause for thought: firstly, the statement that the iron split open the netherworld (first line above); and secondly, the statement that the iron was raised on high by Sokar in Heliopolis (fourth line).

From an orthodox perspective, the significance of these statements lies in the adze, which was made of iron. This iron tool opened the mouth of the deceased and raised him up out of the earth and the tomb. Therefore, in a metaphorical sense, it may be said that the iron itself split open the netherworld. As for the raising of the iron, this might be explained by the priest raising the adze to the lips of the mummy.

Now, let us interpret this passage from a geocentric perspective. As we have seen, the earth had a mouth, and the opening of this mouth enabled the king to ascend to the sky. If this cosmic mouth was the mouth of Osiris, the opening of which was re-enacted in the opening of the mouth ritual (which is plausible, since Osiris was an earth-god), then the mouth of the deceased in Spell 816 would represent the mouth of the earth. It then follows logically that the water rising in the mouth of the deceased (second line above) would represent the flood of creation, while the iron which opened the mouth would represent a primeval element bursting forth from the abyss. This iron would have opened the netherworld quite literally, and would have been washed (third line above) in the sense that it came forth amidst the flood. Furthermore, it would have been raised on high by Sokar in the sense of being lifted into the sky.

In support of this controversial interpretation, the introduction to Spell 816 speaks of the iron being broken by Anubis, while Utterance 669 of the Pyramid Texts and its derivative Spell 989 of the Coffin Texts allude to the splitting of an iron egg – the king is called 'the one who will break the egg and split the iron'.[34] These references support the view that the primeval cosmos was made of iron, which was broken and split open at the time of creation.

The iron of the sky (*bja n pet*) would therefore represent an emission

188   THE MIDNIGHT SUN

from the primeval earth, while the iron adze would utilize meteoritic iron which was terrestrial in origin. As for the shape of the adze, modelled on the northern stars, this would signify the birth of those stars from the primeval earth – their spiritualization from the limbs of Seth.

All these ideas will be discussed further in later chapters.

Creation via the Mouth

This interpretation of the opening of the mouth ritual casts new light on the role of the mouth in the Egyptian creation myths. According to the various traditions, the creator-god brought the universe into being either by spitting, speaking, coughing, or sneezing from his mouth.

The earliest example of this idea appears in the Pyramid Texts, where Atum sneezes out Shu and spits out Tefnut, while rising up in the form of the high hill and the *benben* stone.[35] Everything is thus created from the mouth of Atum.

The Coffin Texts expand upon this myth, and suggest the combination of two themes in a single image – the emission of air and the emission of semen.

The emission of air is described in Spells 75, 76, and 80, where Shu is portrayed as the air or wind which emerged from Atum's mouth. This myth would explain the origin of the atmosphere which supported the sky.

The emission of semen is described in Spells 77 and 80. Here, it is suggested that Atum masturbated his phallus to climax, but nonetheless spat the semen out of his mouth in the forms of Shu and Tefnut (see quotations in chapter three). The same idea may have been intended by the statements that Atum created Shu in a 'sneeze of the mouth' (Spells 76 and 80).

This strange combination of phallus and mouth is also preserved in the Bremner-Rhind Papyrus, where Neber-djer claims:

> I am indeed the one who masturbated with my fist, copulated with my shadow, and spewed (seed) from my mouth. I sneezed out Shu, I spat out Tefnut.[36]

The myth of Atum, Shu, and Tefnut is closely interwoven with the myth of the Eye, and it too is associated with the creator's mouth, both in ritual and myth. In the intriguing Spell 261 of the Coffin Texts, the deceased states:

> I am he whom Neber-djer made, before there came into being two things in this world [Shu and Tefnut], when he sent out his Sole Eye,

when he was alone, when something came forth from his mouth, when his millions of spirits (*kau*) were the protection of his companions who shone in his Eye.[37]

Was it the Eye that came forth from the mouth? This is indeed the origin of the Eye in the New Kingdom myth *Isis and Re*, where Re permits his secret name to go forth from his body into the body of Isis. A triumphant Isis states:

Flow out, O poison! Come forth from Re! Let the Eye of Horus come forth from the god and shine outside his mouth.[38]

The gods too originated from the creator-god's mouth (as well as from his body and limbs). This idea is first suggested in the Pyramid Texts, where the king as the creator claims: 'My lips are the two enneads, I am the great word'.[39] But it is mainly attested in later texts, which praise the creator with the formulaic words: 'The gods issued from his mouth and men from his eyes'.[40]

A second mode of creation from the mouth involved the issuance of commands or names. This idea features prominently in the Coffin Texts. In Spell 76, it is said that Atum made the names of the Infinite Ones on the day when he spoke with Nun in chaos, in darkness, and in gloom.[41] In Spell 80, Shu provides the breath of life to living creatures in accordance with 'this authority of mine which is on my lips'.[42] In Spell 261, Neberdjer is said to have taken creative utterance (*hu*) into his mouth on the day of creation when he spoke with Khepri.[43] In Spell 320, the Nile-god states: "I am the one who created what is and what is not. When I spoke, creative utterance came into being."[44] As a final example, Atum claims in Spell 335 to be 'the one who created his names, Lord of the Ennead' (the gloss in the Book of the Dead explains: 'Otherwise said, he is Re who created his names and his limbs; it means the coming into being of those gods who are in his following.').[45]

The gods, in particular, were created by divine speech. Of Amun-Re, for example, it was said 'he commands and the gods come into being'.[46]

It may be seen from these examples that creation via the mouth was a particularly strong idea in ancient Egypt, from the earliest times to the latest times. But why? According to Egyptologists, the importance of the mouth reflected the anthropomorphic view of God which was held by the Egyptians. The mouth was emphasised in particular because it allowed the creator-god to express his thoughts and wishes, and thereby provided an archetype and source of legitimacy for the magical utterances of the king and the priests. Beyond this, the mouth of the creator had no deeper significance.

But the geocentric theory of creation suggests otherwise. According to this view, the mouth of the creator signified the mouth of the old cosmos, and the opening of this mouth – its raison d'etre – signified the birth of the new cosmos. When Atum spat or sneezed the universe into being, he emitted physically from himself (the old cosmos) the primeval elements – water, matter, air, and light – which would form the new, expanded cosmos. The air of Shu thus became the atmosphere, while the water of Tefnut perhaps became the sky-ocean.

Creating via speech was a natural development of this idea, for speech was perceived as the transformation of air by the mouth.[47] Naming things into existence was a further subtle variant of the same theme.

Re and Nut

The importance of the mouth is seen also in the re-enactment of creation by the sun-god Re in his daily circuit of the earth. He too engaged in a splitting open of the earth, as we shall now see.

Each day, when Re set in the west, he entered a netherworld (*duat* or *ament*) which, in parallel with a lower sky (*nwt* or *nnwt*), stretched from the western horizon to the east. In order to be reborn fresh and strong the next morning, Re had to re-enact the creation of the cosmos by entering the netherworld and uniting with his body Osiris.

As early as the Pyramid Texts, Re's journey through the netherworld or lower sky was portrayed as his rebirth from the womb of his mother Nut.[48] This idea was elaborated during the New Kingdom, when Nut's body was made to personify the netherworld through which the sun-god would pass.[49] To this end, her mouth was placed at the western entrance to the *duat* and her thighs and vulva at the eastern exit. Re would then enter Nut's mouth in the evening, pass through her body during the hours of the night, and be reborn from her vulva the next morning. His rebirth from Nut was his emergence from the *duat*.

In the Book of Nut, Re's disc is shown entering Nut's mouth in the west, and the accompanying text indicates that she has become pregnant with him. Next, the disc is shown at her feet, having emerged from her vulva, and the text declares:

> The redness after birth... He [Re] opens in his splitting and swims in his redness... He parts the thighs of his mother Nut, and goes away to the sky.[50]

This imagery, if not the exact form of words, is echoed in the Books of the Netherworld. The image is of Re splitting open the thighs and vulva of his mother Nut in order to repeat the moment of his own creation – a

Figure 40.
THE AKHET SIGN RESEMBLES THE THIGHS OF NUT GIVING BIRTH TO THE SUN DISC.

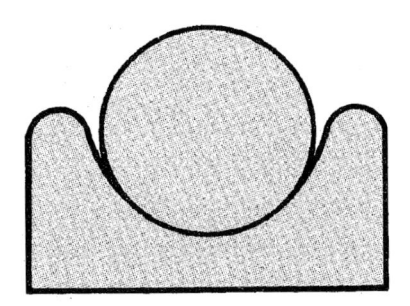

birth which marked the creation of the cosmos. Once again, then, we find that creation involves a splitting – of a mouth in the west and a vagina in the east. The significant fact is that Nut's stretched-out body represented the *duat* and *ament* – the netherworld of the earth. The splitting open of Nut's vagina thus re-enacted the splitting open of the earth at the time of creation.

The myth of Nut's womb being split open dates back to the Pyramid Texts. In Utterance 1, Nut declares proudly that her womb was split open by her eldest son Osiris,[51] while in Utterance 222 it is suggested that her womb was broken open violently at the birth of Seth.[52] Intriguingly, the Coffin Texts refer to Nut as 'she who opened the earth'.[53] This might well refer to the aforementioned birth of Osiris, but it could also refer to her own birth from the womb of Tefnut, as described in Utterances 429-432 of the Pyramid Texts.

The parallel between the opening of the mouth and the opening of the womb is striking, and there can be little doubt that these images alluded to the same mythical event – the opening of the earth.

This event could also be portrayed as a mountain splitting apart. In the Book of Gates, Re's barque enters the *duat* through the mountain of the west, which is shown divided into two parts.[54] The entire netherworld is here portrayed as a 'hidden mountain', which stretches from the west to the east. Although the splitting of the eastern mountain is not shown, it is implied by Re's emergence from that mountain. A possible illustration of the splitting eastern mountain appears in the final section of the Book of Caverns, where the sun-disc passes between 'the two mysterious caverns of *ament*' and is then shown emerging between two triangular mounds which represent the *duat* in the form of a pyramid being split apart.[55] This image is especially evocative of the rebirth of Hathor, as described in the Coffin Texts:

> The mountain is broken, the stone is split, the caverns are broken open, the eastern *akhet* is opened for Hathor. She ascends in turquoise...[56]

It also echoes the king's rebirth as described in the Pyramid Texts:

> The two mountains are split apart, the god comes into being... the two mountains are split apart, this king comes into being...[57]

Since this splitting of the mountains involves a birth – of Re, Hathor, and the king in the examples cited – it may safely be assumed that it parallels the splitting open of the womb of Nut and the splitting open of the mouth of the earth.

Furthermore, there is a parallel to the opening of doors. In the Book of Gates, Re enters the *duat* through doors in the western horizon, and exits it from doors in the eastern horizon.[58] Intriguingly, in the Am Duat, the doors of the west are described as 'the doors of Nut', the goddess being made to personify the entire *duat*. The western doors of Nut would thus appear to be synonymous with her mouth.

In summary, it seems plausible that the opening mouth, the opening vagina, the opening mountain, and the opening doors all portrayed one and the same idea – the opening up of the old cosmos for the birth of the new cosmos.

Doors of the Earth, Doors of the Sky

The idea that doors might signify the splitting open of the cosmos adds significantly to our understanding of the Egyptian funerary texts, for it is an interesting fact that all five major realms of the universe – the *nun*, the earth, the *duat*, the *akhet*, and the sky – were fitted with doors or gates, which were opened on a regular basis to facilitate the passage of the God, the gods, and the king on the eternal cosmic circuit. It has always been taken for granted that these doors existed, but it now becomes imperative to reconsider their meaning and role. Could it be that the doors belonged originally to the earth, whence they gave access directly to the sky? Were they duplicated in the eastern *akhet* in order that the sun-god and the king might re-enact the creation?

A good place to start is with the opening of the mouth of the earth. As mentioned earlier in this chapter, two spells in the Pyramid Texts refer to the mouth of the earth being split open for the king to emerge from his tomb. In both instances, this splitting coincides with Geb, the earth-god, speaking to the king. The king then ascends into the sky – not directly but via 'the eastern door of the sky'.[59] A parallel may be drawn between these two spells and three spells in which the king ascends through *the doors of Geb*, to the accompaniment of the voice of Anubis or the king. For example:

> The earth speaks. The doors of the earth-god (Aker) are opened for you, the doors of Geb are thrown open for you, you come forth at the voice of Anubis... The door of the sky at the *akhet* opens to you... [60]

In the Coffin Texts, the doors of Geb are equated with the mouth of the earth.[61] It would seem to be no coincidence that Geb was given the name 'Sharp Mouth' along with other epithets identifying him as the sole god, i.e. the creator.[62]

As with the mouth of the earth, the doors of Geb provided access to 'the door of the sky' at the eastern horizon. This door was synonymous with 'the doors of the *akhet*' – the earth-like realm which lay just below the horizon. Its doors gave access to the sky:

> Stand at the doors of the *akhet*, open the doors of the *qebhu*.[63]

> O king, stand up... go to the sky, come forth from the gate of the *akhet*.[64]

The doors of the *akhet* and the doors of the sky were one and the same set of doors, but viewed from either side of the divide – the *akhet* on the lower side and the sky on the upper side. In the Pyramid Texts, the latter perspective is the most common, the doors being called either 'the doors of the sky' (*pet*) or 'the doors of the fresh water' (*qebhu*). Both *pet* and *qebhu* signified the waters on the surface of the sky-ocean.

The majority of spells in the Pyramid Texts portray the king ascending to the sky through these doors in the eastern side of the sky. Typically, he ascends through both sets of doors simultaneously – the doors of the *pet* and the doors of the *qebhu*. For example:

> The doors of the sky (*pet*) are opened to you, the doors of the *qebhu* are thrown open for you, and you will find Re standing as he waits for you.[65]

> The doors of the sky (*pet*) are opened to you, the doors of the *qebhu* are thrown open for you, that you may travel by boat to the field of reeds.[66]

On several occasions, however, the king ascends solely through the door of *pet*. Curiously, these spells refer to a singular door rather than plural doors, and emphasise that it is an eastern door. For example:

> The eastern door of the sky (*pet*) is opened for you... Nut has laid her hands on you... She carries you for herself to the sky.[67]

What do all these doors signify? A clue is provided by the Coffin Texts, which refer to 'the noise of the flood at the eastern gate of the sky' and state that the great flood (*mehet weret*) went up to the sky from the gates of the *akhet*.[68] It is thus implied that the opening of the doors released the floodwaters, which previously had been confined in the *nun*. (Hence the *nun* too had gates.)[69] It was upon this flood, of course, that the barque of the sun-god sailed into the sky, with the king taking his seat among the gods. The passage of the barque likewise depended on the opening of the doors of the *akhet*.[70]

Might this re-enact an original flood from the cosmos that comprised the earth and the *nun*?

Significantly, the opening of the sky and its doors coincided with the opening of the earth and its doors. For example:

> The sky is opened, the earth is opened, the doors of *Sat* are opened for Horus, the doors of the lotus are thrown open for Seth.[71]

> The doors of Geb are thrown open for you... The door of the sky at the *akhet* opens to you...[72]

According to Egyptologists, these and other similar passages describe the king's *ka* breaking out of the tomb. This cannot be denied. But the fact is that the *ka* was a cosmic concept while the tomb was a microcosm of the *duat*. In splitting open the doors of his tomb, therefore, the king was re-enacting a cosmic event.

In Utterance 676, for example, we read:

> The tomb is opened for you, the doors of the coffin are drawn back for you, the doors of the sky are thrown open for you.[73]

But this is surrounded by the lines:

> You have your water, you have your flood... May you sit on your iron throne... You have shouldered the sky, you have raised up the earth... you ascend here as a star, as the morning star.[74]

It is thus evident that the king breaking out of his tomb is an allegory for a powerful cosmic evolution.

Nowhere is this more evident than in Utterance 553 of the Pyramid Texts, where the tomb takes the form of Nut:

> The doors of the sky are opened for you, the doors of the *qebhu* are thrown open for you, the doors of the tomb are opened for you, the

doors of Nut are unbolted for you.[75]

Here, the doors of Nut are the doors of the tomb, but at the same time the doors of the sky. This is most interesting, since Nut was identified with both the tomb and the sky. On the one hand, in her identities of 'Tomb' and 'Sarcophagus' she personified the *duat* – the netherworld or 'interior of the sky'. But on the other hand, in her identity as 'Sky' she personified the celestial ocean that arched over the earth upon the supports of Shu. Moreover, in her identity as 'Ladder', she provided a means for the king to ascend from the tomb to the sky.

How to explain this?

As discussed earlier, the opening of Nut's vagina and the opening of her womb signified the opening of the earth at the beginning of time. Nut is therefore to be envisaged as a mother cosmos, who gave birth to Osiris and Seth (in their spirit forms), but more importantly gave birth to herself in expanded, transcendent form, and thereby 'came into being in the sky' (see chapter six).

Nut's doors were therefore the doors of the earth and the doors of the sky, as suggested by Utterance 553. But crucially, these doors were the same doors, viewed from either side of the great divide – the earth below and the sky above. It was through these doors that the sky was created by a forcible separation from the earth.

In the light of this discussion, we should consider the possibility that the opening of the doors of the sky may refer, in some cases, to a direct ascent from the earth, as opposed to an indirect ascent from the eastern horizon.

Intriguingly, a close study of the Pyramid Texts suggests that where the doors of the sky are mentioned either separately or in parallel with the doors of the starry sky or celestial expanses they do fit the scenario of a direct ascent (i.e. there is no reference to the east side of the sky, the *akhet*, or the boarding of the barque). The following examples should be considered.

In Utterance 313, the opening of the doors of the sky is connected to a fiery *krater* of the gods, which is arguably evocative of the splitting open of the earth:

> The phallus of Babi is drawn back, the doors of the sky are opened, the king has opened the doors of the sky by means of the fire beneath the melting pot (*iknt*) of the gods.[76]

In Utterances 719 and 511, the opening of the doors of the sky coincides with an earthquake:

> The sky thunders, the earth quakes... O king, Geb has given you up and Nut has accepted you. Ascend to the sky, for the doors of the sky are opened for you, the earth is hacked up for you, and an offering is presented to you.[77]
>
> The sky thunders for me, the earth quakes for me... Those who are in charge of the divisions of the sky open the celestial doors for me, and I stand on the air (*shu*)...[78]

In Utterances 482 and 670, the opening of the doors of the sky and the celestial expanses (*pdjwt*) is marked by a great noise and commotion. In the latter spell, the king ascends directly from the *duat*:

> The doors of the sky are opened, the doors of the celestial expanses are opened. The gods in Pe are full of sorrow, and they come to Osiris-the-king at the sound of the weeping of Isis and the cry of Nephthys, at the wailing of these two spirits for this great one who has emerged from the *duat*.[79]

In Utterance 572, the opening of the doors of the sky and the starry sky (*shdu pet*) is occasioned by the assembly of the gods and an erection of a ladder:

> The gods who are (to be) in the sky are brought to you, the gods who are (to be) in the earth assemble for you. They place their hands under you, they make a ladder for you that you may ascend on it to the sky. The doors of the sky are opened for you, the doors of the starry sky are thrown open for you.[80]

There are two other references to the opening of the doors of the sky and the doors of the starry sky, but it is unfortunately not clear whether the king's ascent is direct or indirect.[81]

The doors of the sky appear separately in three further instances, all of which are ambiguous, although in Utterance 361 the lifting of the king's hand by Atum and Shu is suggestive of a direct ascent.[82]

Where the doors of the sky are combined with the doors of the *qebhu* ('the fresh water' of the sky), the ascent is usually indirect, via the east side of the sky. But even here there are spells which seem to describe a direct ascent, in which case the *qebhu* might be traced to an original flood from the earth. The pertinent spells are as follows:

> Your water is yours, your flood is yours, your efflux which issued from Osiris is yours. The doors of the sky are opened to you, the doors of Nut are opened to you, the doors of the *qebhu* are thrown open to you.[83]

> Rise up, O sleeper. The doors of the sky are opened for you, the doors of the *qebhu* are thrown open for you, that you may go forth as Wepiu.[84]
>
> The sky thunders, the earth quakes before the great one when he arises. He opens the doors of the sky, he throws open the doors of the *qebhu*. The earth is hacked up for you, and an offering is presented to you...[85]
>
> The doors of the sky are opened for you, the doors of the *qebhu* are thrown open for you, the doors of the tomb are opened for you, the doors of Nut are unbolted for you.[86]

Finally, the doors of the *qebhu* are opened separately in Utterance 724, where the king flies directly up to the sky:

> The doors of the *qebhu* which keep out the plebs are opened for the king... The king's arms are those of falcons [sic], the king's wing-feathers are those of Thoth. Geb causes the king to fly up among his brethren the gods.[87]

All these passages indicate that the fresh waters of the *qebhu* may have originated from the earth, and been lifted to the sky in the same way that Nut was lifted by Shu. The fact that the doors of the *qebhu* were placed in the east side of the sky may be explained by the need for the flood of creation to be repeated every day.

In conclusion, doors are a means of opening that which was closed, and their significance derives from the opening of the earth in the act of creation. All the doors in the cosmos are duplicates of the original set of doors in the earth (synonymous with the doors of the tomb, the doors of the *duat*, and the doors of Nut), which were opened at the beginning of time. The existence of *all* other doors in the cosmos may be explained by the duty of the gods and the king to perform eternal repetitions of this original opening in order to guarantee the eternal duration of the cosmos (*neheh* and *djet*).

As with the doors, so is the mouth a means of opening that which was closed, but here the allegory is developed to include the emission of air, sound, and bodily fluids. Air and sound signified the breath and cry of the newborn babe, while bodily fluids signified the ejaculation of the virile adult.

And as with the mouth, so are the vagina and womb means of opening that which was closed. In this allegory, the birth of the babe signified the rebirth of the cosmos.

Chapter Eight Summary

- The mummy of the king signified the body of the primeval cosmos.

- The splitting open of the mouth of the mummy re-enacted the splitting open of the primeval cosmos at the time of creation. This mythical event triggered the rebirth of the cosmos.

- The use of meteoritic iron tools to open the mouth may indicate that iron was ejected from the primeval earth.

- The creator-god usually created the universe via his mouth. His acts of spitting, speaking, coughing, and sneezing are consistent with the idea that the mouth of the primeval earth was split open.

- Splitting is seen also in Re's night-time journey through the body of Nut. The sun-god split open her mouth in the western horizon, and split open her vagina in the east. This re-enacted the splitting open of the earth at the time of creation.

- Nut's body also possessed doors, the opening of which paralleled the opening of her mouth. The opening of doors, or gates, at each stage of the king's circuit through the cosmos re-enacted the opening of the earth at the time of creation. All doors belonged originally to the earth and the primeval ocean.

- This is a first indication that the Egyptians may have possessed a rational physics of creation.

CHAPTER NINE

THE DAY OF THE STORM

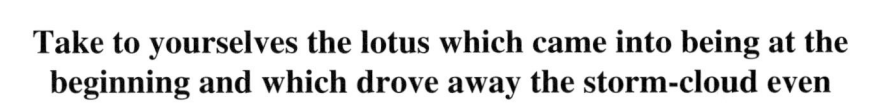

Take to yourselves the lotus which came into being at the beginning and which drove away the storm-cloud even though it knew it not.
(Address to the Primeval Gods in the ritual scene of
Offering the Lotus, Edfu Building Texts)

In the Pyramid Texts, the king does not move through a stable cosmos, but through a cosmos which is constantly coming into being. He wakes, stands, sits, bathes, travels, eats and sleeps amidst a never-ending drama of cosmic conceptions, births, initiations, and expansionary movements, all of which are designed to depict the evolving cosmos in the process of creation.

If, as I have argued, the king is re-enacting the myth of creation in his death and resurrection, then it should be possible to gain insights into the creation process from those spells and rituals which translate him to the 'other world'.

In the previous chapter, we used this principle to elucidate the ritual of opening the king's mouth. From a geocentric perspective, it would seem that this act signified a physical splitting of the old cosmos, by means of which the new cosmos was born. This interpretation is supported by the parallel myths of the creator-god being born from an egg or the womb of Nut, and by the myths of the creator bringing the universe into being by spitting, coughing, or sneezing from his mouth, or by issuing commands or pronouncing names from his mouth. It is possible that the opening of the mouth ritual was an allegory for all these ideas.

In this and the next two chapters, we are going to examine the king's ascent into the sky and ask whether it too might allegorize a physical process by which the cosmos came into being. We shall focus on three aspects of this re-enactment that are particularly suggestive: firstly, the storm in which the king ascends, secondly the iron that he encounters on his way to the sky, and thirdly his bull-like insemination of the sky. As we shall see, these three themes follow a coherent and consistent pattern of thought, and resonate strongly with several key themes in the creation myths. Piece by piece, we will reconstruct an astonishing ancient theory for the formation of the stars, the sun, and the moon.

We begin, in this chapter, with the king's ascent in a storm.

The King and the Storm

As discussed in chapter seven, the deceased king (or rather his *ka*) could make a direct ascent to the sky by rising upon the air, and this was often accomplished on the back of the storm. In the Pyramid Texts, this storm takes a number of forms.

In Utterance 258, the king ascends in a dust storm:

> The king is Osiris in a dust devil... The king is bound for the sky on the wind, on the wind![1]

In Utterance 261, the king shoots up in a flash of lightning:

> The king is one who makes the heart leap (with fright), the favourite son of Shu, long-extended, fierce of brilliance. The king is a flame moving before the wind to the end of the sky and to the end of the earth when he is thrown as a thunderbolt (*hnbu*).[2]

In Utterance 262, the king ascends upon hailstorms:

> The hailstorms (*shnyt*) of the sky have taken me, and they raise me up to Re.[3]

In Utterance 627, the king ascends in a cloud of locusts and upon a rain-cloud:

> The sky thunders, the earth quakes... The king has ascended in the body of a locust... The king has ascended on a rain-cloud...[4]

The thundering sky and quaking earth occur also in Utterance 511, where the king ascends in a hailstorm:

> The sky thunders for me, the earth quakes for me, the hailstorm (*shnyt*) is unleashed for me, and I roar like Seth.[5]

What is the significance of this great storm? To Egyptologists, the rain-clouds, hailstorm, thunder, and lightning are mundane phenomena of the everyday world. In any event, they say, no special significance should be attached to the storm because the king does not require a storm to reach the sky; he can also ascend by means of a stairway or a ladder, or fly up in the form of a bird. The storm is thus dismissed as an inconsequential idea.

But is this really the case?

If the deceased king is re-enacting the creation myth, as I have argued in chapter seven, then his ascent in a storm could represent an important aspect of that myth. The storm would in this case be no ordinary storm, but a cosmic storm of the first time.

Do the Egyptian texts bear out this theory?

The Storm of Creation

Let us consider firstly the timing of the storm. If the king is re-enacting a storm of the first time, then we ought to find some evidence of a storm in the creation myths.

The first point to make is that the king personifies Osiris and re-enacts the myth of his death and resurrection. In this regard, it is important to note that Osiris himself was resurrected amidst a storm affecting the sky and the earth. In Utterance 477, it is stated:

> The sky is in turmoil, the earth quakes. Horus comes, Thoth appears. They raise Osiris from upon his side and cause him to stand up before the two enneads.[6]

Consistent with this, the resurrection of Osiris as Horus coincides with a flash of lightning. In Spell 148 of the Coffin Texts, it is stated:

> The thunderbolt strikes, the gods are afraid, Isis awakes pregnant with the seed of her brother Osiris...[7]

This event is also alluded to in the Pyramid Texts, where Horus and Seth are conceived and born to the quaking of the earth and the trembling of the sky:

> You are born, O Horus, in your name of 'the One at whom the Earth Quakes'. You are conceived, O Seth, in this your name of 'the One at whom the Sky Trembles'.[8]

Elsewhere in the Pyramid Texts, Seth trembles beneath Osiris in the form of an earthquake.[9]

The manifestation of Osiris as Horus the sky-god was paralleled by the first appearance of Re. In the Coffin Texts, there is evidence that Re too emerged in the midst of a great storm. In Spell 326, we read:

There is tumult in the sky. "We see something new" say the primeval gods. Re shines as Horus, Lord of the Light, he has caused dread among the lords of the terrible ones... They hear the voice of Re when he shouts with a voice of great roaring.[10]

Re's appearance also caused the rain-clouds to tremble. In Spell 993, it is stated:

The skies are uncovered (?), the rain-clouds tremble... Re appears with this ennead of his, as Lord of the Light.[11]

And in a similar vein, in Spell 1029, there is a trembling of the *akhet*, the sky, and the earth, when Re ascends:

Trembling falls on the eastern *akhet* of the sky at the voice of Nut, and she clears the paths of Re... Raise yourself Re... May the great ones quake at your voice... Sky and earth fall to you, being possessed with trembling at your travelling around anew every day.[12]

The storm features also in the creation by Shu. In Spell 80 of the Coffin Texts, Shu states:

My efflux is the storm-cloud (*qrr*) of the sky; my sweat is hail-storm (*shnyt*) and half-darkness (*ikhkhu*).[13]

This statement is made in the context of Shu's appearance as air from the mouth of Atum. The implication is that the sky and the atmosphere were created amidst a storm.

A late myth, dating to the Ptolemaic period, confirms that Shu went up to the sky in a storm. According to this tale, Shu had reigned over the earth until he eventually became old, weak and blind. His followers had then revolted, and caused chaos in the palace and strife throughout the land.[14] It was around this time that Shu and his supporters left the earth and went up to the sky, leaving behind them a palace engulfed in a storm of darkness and winds:

Shu had gone up into the sky, and no-one came out of the palace for a period of nine days. And these (days) were in violence and tempest: no-one, whether god or man, could see the face of his fellow.[15]

Here, the tumult is triggered by a rebellion of the gods against an ageing creator-god. But elsewhere it is occasioned by Seth launching an assault upon Horus or Osiris.

Both Seth and Horus are lords of the storm. In the Pyramid Texts, Seth is called 'Lord of the Storm-cloud (*qrr*)', and in one instance he rages at the Eye of Horus.[16] As for Horus, he threatens to destroy Seth with the storm of his Eye, saying: "I will put flame in my Eye and it will surround you and set storm among the evildoers... and a (fiery) outburst among these primeval ones."[17] Generally, the Pyramid Texts are vague about the battle of Horus and Seth, but in later texts it is likened to a storm that engulfed both the sky and the earth (see chapter thirteen). This may reflect the earlier belief that the two gods were conceived and born to the quaking of the earth and the trembling of the sky (see earlier quote).

There has been a tendency among scholars to interpret the wars of the gods as historical conflicts between rival human groups or as allegories for solar or even stellar movements.[18] But there can be no doubt in the case of Horus and Seth that their battles allegorized the eternal struggle between order and chaos, in particular the original struggle that occurred at the beginning of time. That this is so is proven by the Pyramid Texts, which refer to a time 'when anger came into being, when noise came into being, when strife came into being, when tumult came into being, when the Eye of Horus was gouged, when the testicles of Seth were torn off'.[19] This clearly is a reference to an archetypal disorder. The storm generated by Horus and Seth was a storm of primeval times – a storm of creation.

This same principle applies to that other infamous storm-god Apep (or Apophis), who daily tried to prevent Re's barque sailing from the eastern *akhet* of the sky.[20] The 'storm of Apep' was undoubtedly a re-enactment of the storm of creation.

The texts describe this original storm as a day and night of utter chaos, when gods were annihilated, rebels repulsed, and robbers brought to justice. In the Pyramid Texts, it is 'that day of slaying the oldest ones',[21] and 'that day of decapitating the mottled snakes',[22] while in the Coffin Texts it is 'that night of slaughtering the great ones',[23] 'the day of the great slaughter',[24] 'that day when the rivals fought',[25] 'that night of making war and driving off the rebels',[26] 'that day of reckoning with the robbers in the presence of Neber-djer',[27] 'that day of smashing the heads of the mottled snakes with these throw-sticks',[28] and 'the day of putting the great hall in order and of quelling the strife of the gods'.[29]

The Genesis of the Storm

Having settled the question of the storm's timing, we may now consider the question of its nature and origins.

The extent of the storm may be judged from the facts that it covered the Two Lands (i.e. the entire world), spanned the cosmic realms (earth, *nun*, *waret*, *akhet*, and sky), and belonged to cosmic gods (such as Horus, Seth, Shu, and Re). It may therefore be described, without hesitation, as a cosmic storm.

As befitting a cosmic storm, its dynamics were those of the evolving cosmos. In Spell 80 of the Coffin Texts, the storm is the efflux and sweat of Shu, who is emitted by Atum. Its origin is therefore the centre of the cosmos. Similarly in Spell 989, the storm is traced to the womb of Nut, the mother cosmos:

> The announcers of the great storm-cloud go forth from the *akhet*, the inner compartment of her who bore the gods on the five epagomenal days (i.e. Nut).[30]

In Spell 720, Nut is said to ascend to the sky, causing the gods who are in the storm to tremble.[31] It is as if Nut gives birth to the storm and also to the gods who are in it. A passage in the Pyramid Texts describes these trembling gods as 'the violent ones who are on the storm-cloud of the sky', and ascribes their fear to a violent incident in which the ball of the Apis bull was crushed in the sky.[32]

Likewise, the battle of the gods originated in the earth, and expanded to envelop the wider cosmos. Turmoil and tumult are said to occur in the city – a microcosm of the world on the day of creation – and in, or upon, the primeval mound.[33] The tombs of the gods lie accordingly in the *duat*, the island of fire, or the island of trampling. At no time is it suggested that the battle began in the sky, although it did spread to the sky.

In his re-enactment of the storm, the king ascends to the sky from the inner *akhet*, or womb of Nut:

> The prince ascends in a great storm from the inner *akhet*... he sees the birth of the gods in the five epagomenal days.[34]

Significantly, the king *goes up* in the storm. The dust and wind takes him up; he is thrown upwards on the thunderbolt; the hailstorms raise him up to Re; the rain-cloud carries him up; the king goes up in the earthquake to the sky (see earlier quotations). It cannot be emphasised enough that we are dealing here with allegories of creation, not with everyday natural events. The Egyptian thunderbolt, for example, is not a meteorological phenomenon but a creational archetype. It cannot come down from the sky since the sky does not yet exist; it must go up from the earth since the earth is at the centre of creation. Translations such as 'thunderbolt', 'hailstorm', and 'rain-cloud' are wholly inadequate to capture the real sense of the texts. Egyptian geocentrism turns modern perceptions upside down.

Intriguingly, the storm is said to be opened, or split open. In Utterance 261 of the Pyramid Texts, the king performs 'the opening (*wpt*) of the storm' in order to ascend upon it from the east side of the sky;[35] in Spell 288 of the Coffin Texts, the deceased calls himself 'the one who opens (*wp*) the storm';[36] in Spell 631, the deceased is said to have 'split open the storm';[37] and in Spell 1112, the storm itself is urged: "Open yourself, you who are cloudy!".[38]

What does this mean? In what sense was the storm opened? Might this idea allude to the opening of the earth at the time of creation?

The texts seem to suggest that this was indeed so. In Utterance 254 of the Pyramid Texts, the storm-cloud appears in the sky at the time when the king ascends by splitting open the earth:

> Be afraid and tremble, you violent ones who are on the storm-cloud (*qrr*) of the sky! He [the king] split open the earth by means of what he knew on the day when he wished to come thence.[39]

But in Spell 622 of the Coffin Texts, this passage is reinterpreted to make the storm-cloud the subject of the splitting:

> Be afraid and tremble, you violent ones who are on the storm-cloud (*qrr*) of the sky, which he split open by means of what he knew on the day when he wished to come thence.[40]

Unless this is a copyist's error, it would appear that the scribes regarded the opening of the earth and the opening of the storm-cloud as one and the same thing.

In support of this, Utterance 511 of the Pyramid Texts, quoted earlier, suggests that the quaking of the earth coincided with the hailstorm being 'unleashed' (see earlier quote), while Spells 1069 and 1179 of the Coffin Texts suggest that the splitting of the sky coincided with the storm being 'unleashed'.[41] The verb used is *khsr*, which is usually translated 'drive away' but can also mean 'separate forcibly', as in the separation of the sky from the earth.[42] The storm might well have been separated in such a sense if the sky was in chaos at the time of its separation from the earth.

The king's ascent in the storm fits the wider pattern of his ascent to the sky. The earth quakes and the sky thunders or trembles (perhaps while it is still attached to the earth);[43] the earth is split open and hacked up;[44] the doors of the sky are opened;[45] Geb laughs, Nut shouts;[46] there is weeping, crying, and wailing;[47] the gods clap their hands and stamp their feet;[48] the king ascends in a blast of fire;[49] he roars like Seth;[50] there is terror about him;[51] he causes dread in the hearts of the gods;[52] the gods tremble in fear;[53] the stars are darkened;[54] the sky catches fire at the quaking of the earth;[55] and the king ascends amidst the winds, lightning, and hail of the storm.

This is surely a picture of a cosmos coming into being – the future sky being wrenched from the earth by means of a cosmic cataclysm, which splits open the earth and the primeval ocean.

If so, the opening or unleashing of the storm would signify the ejection of the primeval matter by means of which the old cosmos was expanded into the new. Its whirlwinds would become the air of the atmosphere, its floodwaters would become the ocean of the sky, and its flames would become the light of the stars, the sun, and the moon. Crucially, however, for this to happen, the storm would have to be brought from a state of chaos to a state of order.

Such a process is indeed described in the texts.

Clearing the Sky

The Egyptian texts portray the nascent sky in a state of chaos at the time of creation. The sky is covered with cloud;[56] the stars are darkened and stilled;[57] the gods tremble in the storm-cloud of the sky;[58] and there is war between Horus and Seth and their respective followers.

One of the primary tasks of the creator-god – and the deceased king in his re-enactment of creation – was to bring the turbulent sky to a state of order. In the Pyramid Texts, the king puts a stop to the chaos and judges the warring gods:

> I put a stop to the affair in Heliopolis [the fight of Horus and Seth], for I go forth today in the form of a living spirit, that I may break up the fight and cut off the turbulent ones.[59]
>
> I give judgement in the great flood (*mehet weret*) between the two contestants [Horus and Seth].[60]

Thus the king sets order in place of chaos and brings peace to the sky and joy to the earth:

> The sky is at peace, the earth is in joy, for they have heard that the king will set order (*maat*) in the place of chaos (*isfet*).[61]

In bringing peace to the cosmos, the king repeated the acts of Thoth, who was charged with pacifying and uniting Horus and Seth. In Spell 7 of the Coffin Texts, it is stated:

> The earth was hacked up when the rivals [Horus and Seth] fought; their feet scooped out the sacred pool in Heliopolis. Now comes Thoth adorned with his dignity... So the fighting is ended, the tumult is stopped, the fire which went forth is quenched, the anger in the presence of the tribunal of the god is calmed, and it sits to give

judgement in the presence of Geb.[62]

Elsewhere, the creator-god Shu is the one who brings order to the sky. In Spell 75 of the Coffin Texts, he states:

> I am the one who calmed the sky for himself... I am the one who pierced the height of the sky... I have extinguished the fire, I have calmed the soul of her who burns, I have quietened her who is in the midst of her rage [i.e. the Eye].[63]

Interestingly, Shu also personified the storm. In a passage cited earlier, his efflux is said to be the storm-cloud of the sky and his sweat the hailstorm and half-darkness.

A major theme in these texts is the dispersal of the storm, a task which fell to either the god or the king.

In Utterance 519 of the Pyramid Texts, the creator-god (possibly Re) drives away (*khsr*) the storm for the sake of peace – this at the time when the sky was separated from the earth.[64] Similarly in Utterance 570, Atum in his name of Re is urged to 'drive away the cloudiness of the sky at the time Horakhti shows himself' – a reference to the appearance of the sun-god of the two horizons.[65] And in Spell 1112 of the Coffin Texts, Re is said to be covered until Horus drives away the cloudiness with his fiery breath.[66]

The king repeats the action of dispersing the storm. In Utterance 311, he demands of Re:

> Take me with you, (I) the one who drives away the storm for you, who drives away the clouds for you, who breaks up the hail for you.[67]

And similarly in Spell 1099, the deceased says:

> I will drive away cloudiness so that I may see Re's beauty and display the terror of him.[68]

This dispersal of the clouds enables Re to appear – either as the sun, or as the sun, moon, and stars (depending if Re is taken to be the sun-god or the creator-god).

As a result of this forceful activity, the sky becomes clear (*zbsh*),[69] the sun shines,[70] the vision of Horus is cleared (i.e. he receives his two eyes, the sun and the moon),[71] the vision of the gods is cleared (i.e. the stars are uncovered),[72] and the paths of the sky (*wawt Nwt, wawt pet, wawt pdjwt*) are cleared (*djsr*) or opened (*wp*) for the passage of Re, the gods, and the king.[73]

Intriguingly, the opening of the ways through the sky is portrayed as a forceful action, as if to imply that the clouds formed a dense obstruction in front of the god.[74] In Spell 110 of the Book of the Dead, the deceased states: "I opened the paths of Re on the day when the sky was choked (*imt*) and stifled (*itm*)".[75] An earlier version of this spell informs us that the sky was choked and stifled 'on account of the anger of Seth at the air because of its revivifying the one who was in the egg' – an allusion to the birth of Horus.[76]

What was the nature of these clouds in the sky? Ordinary clouds these certainly were not, for they originated from the earth and came into being on the lower surface of the sky, the belly of Nut. This was a celestial sky, filled with celestial clouds at the time of creation. These clouds covered and darkened the stars, and hindered the initial passage of the creator in his barque.

Of what were these celestial clouds made? The obvious answer must be water. In the Coffin Texts, the barque of Re is said to 'sail in the cloudy sky',[77] and 'the night of the great storm' is connected specifically to the waters of creation.[78] The sky, of course, was made of water, which issued from the *nun* on 'the night of the great flood' that is mentioned in the Pyramid Texts (see chapter six). These were the waters of Nut that were uplifted by the winds of Shu. Such floodwaters would certainly have represented a formidable obstruction to the god at the time when the sky was coming into being, and it is quite plausible that their dispersal required the fiery breath of Horus.[79]

Nevertheless, there is evidence to suggest that the storm-clouds of the sky contained other material elements of the primeval earth, in addition to the floodwaters of creation. We have touched on this evidence earlier in this book, but in the next chapter we shall focus exclusively on this aspect of the Egyptian creation myth.

Chapter Nine Summary

- The king's spirit often ascended to the sky in a storm, and a storm also features in the myths of the wars of the gods. This was no ordinary storm but a storm of creation.

- The storm originated in the primeval cosmos but encompassed the sky as the sky came into being. The quaking of the earth and the trembling of the sky signified the moment when the sky was forcefully separated from the earth.

- The sun and moon appeared only after the fire had been quenched and the sky forcefully cleared. There are hints that the storm involved not only floodwaters but also material debris.

CHAPTER TEN

SPLITTING THE IRON

There is tumult in the sky... The king takes possession of the sky, he splits its iron.
(Pyramid Texts, Utterance 257)

An intriguing aspect of the Pyramid Texts is the ubiquitous presence of a substance called *bja*, which is usually translated 'iron'.[1] The deceased king (or, to be more precise, his *ka*) lifts up his bones of *bja*, splits open his egg of *bja*, sits on his throne of *bja*, splits or traverses the *bja* of the sky, comes to rest on ropes of *bja* with which the sky-barque is towed, and exits the sky through doors of *bja*.

The iron theme continues in the Coffin Texts. These texts expand on the ideas of the king splitting his egg of *bja*, splitting the *bja* of the sky, and being towed across the sky with ropes of *bja*, while introducing new ideas such as 'the enclosure wall of *bja*' which delimited the lower field of reeds, and 'the great plain of *bja*' on which the star-gods stood in the north of the sky.

What is the meaning of this? Why are the Egyptian texts littered with references to iron? According to E.A. Wallis Budge, writing in 1904, the sky comprised a flat, rectangular slab of iron, which rested upon four pillars.[2] More recently, James P. Allen has theorised that the *bja* formed a kind of basin that contained the waters of the sky.[3] One way or another, the consensus is that the iron was one of the materials of which the sky was made. This is an arresting idea, and yet it has generated very little interest in the world of Egyptology. The iron of the sky is not generally considered to be an important issue.

However, if the king's resurrection, as described in the Pyramid Texts, re-enacts the creation of the cosmos, as I have argued at length in chapter seven, then the ubiquity of the iron might signify *the physical process* by which the cosmos was made. In which case the iron of the sky would be a very important issue indeed.

In this chapter, I shall appraise this theory by examining the relevant texts in the light of our new model of geocentric and expansive creation. Might the iron of the sky have been ejected forcibly from the mouth of the earth?

The King's Bones of Iron

A good place to start is with the king's iron bones. These are mentioned in five different spells.

In Utterance 325, the king states:

> I am pure, I take to myself my iron bones, I stretch out for myself my imperishable limbs which are in the womb of my mother Nut.[4]

In all but one of the five spells, the king's iron bones are paralleled with his imperishable limbs (or in one case golden limbs), the idea being that the king has acquired the immortal body of a god.[5] The god in question is Osiris, whose bones and limbs signify the divided elements of the former cosmos.[6] In the spell quoted above, the king collects and assembles his bones, and stretches them out in the womb of Nut, in re-enactment of the gestation of Osiris.[7] It is probable that Nut is here the mother cosmos, who is about to evolve into the sky and thereby give birth to Osiris-the-king.

The king's possession of his iron bones presupposes his ascent to the sky. In Utterance 419, he is urged:

> Arise, remove your earth... You are a great one... may you provide yourself with your iron limbs. Traverse the sky to the field of reeds, make your abode in the field of offerings among the imperishable stars...[8]

This passage is interesting for the fact that the king traverses the sky to reach the celestial fields. Scholars have taken this to mean that the field of offerings lay in the northern region of the sky. But normally the field of offerings *is* the sky, in which case we might well ask: why would the king traverse the sky to reach the sky? The explanation, I believe, is that the king is here traversing the sky as it is separated from the earth, or in other words *crossing the evolving sky*.[9] This principle will prove to be crucial in due course when we examine the king's splitting of the iron of the sky.

In the above passage, the king's iron limbs are paired poetically with the imperishable stars, as if to suggest a connection. This is confirmed by Utterances 570 and 684, which state categorically that the iron limbs *are* the imperishable stars:

Do not break up the ground, O you arms of mine which lift up the sky (*Nwt*) as Shu. My bones are iron and my limbs are the imperishable stars.[10]

O Osiris, this king ascended when you ascended. His word and his *ka* are bound for the sky. The king's bones are iron and the king's limbs are the imperishable stars.[11]

This equation of the iron limbs with the stars, which is also suggested by Utterance 723,[12] supports my theory that the stars were spiritualized from the limbs of the creator-god, which signified the lands reassembled in the primeval mound (see chapters four, five, and six).

The Iron Throne

The iron throne (*khndu bjai*) is mentioned twenty times in the Pyramid Texts.[13] The king is said to sit on it, whereupon he is given offerings of meat and jars of purifying water.[14] While seated on the iron throne, the king governs, judges, and gives orders to the gods – both the gods in the *duat* ('those whose seats are hidden') and the gods in the sky (the spirits, the imperishable stars).[15] His symbols of authority are the mace and the sceptre, the latter allegedly being made of iron.[16]

The iron throne is a place from which the dead are far removed.[17] To reach it, the king must reassemble his body and rise from the tomb. This process is described in Utterances 413 and 536:

> Awake, O king, raise yourself, receive your head, gather your bones together, shake off your dust, and sit on your iron throne.[18]

> Raise yourself, loose your bonds, throw off your dust, sit on this your iron throne...[19]

The iron throne is a thing 'at which the gods marvel'.[20] It has faces which are the faces of lions, and feet which are the hooves of the Great Wild Bull.[21] To sit on this emblematic throne is to be ensured of an ascent to the sky, as numerous passages testify.[22] For example:

> You will ascend to the sky as Horus upon the *shedshed* of the sky... you being seated upon your iron throne.[23]

> Sit on this your iron throne, give commands to those whose seats are hidden. The doors of the sky are opened to you...[24]

> Sit upon your iron throne... Run your course, row over your waterway like Re on the banks of the sky.[25]

In addition, the throne is said to possess a stairway, where the gods clap their hands when the king ascends to the sky.[26]

The king's ascent in Utterance 483 is particularly intriguing. The text reads:

> The earth speaks, the gate of the earth-god is open, the doors of Geb are opened for you in your presence, and your speech goes up to Anubis... May you remove yourself to the sky upon your iron throne.[27]

At first glance, this passage seems to suggest that the iron throne is lifted from the earth to the sky. It might therefore indicate the origin of the iron of the sky. But the final line here is ambiguous; it might mean that the king's *ka* ascends to the sky while remaining seated on his throne on the earth (compare his ascent upon the *shedshed*, quoted above).

Some light is shed on this question by Utterances 673 and 676. In the first of these, the king is said to stand in the *akhet* while sitting upon the iron throne of Geb:

> O my father the king... Your porters hurry, your couriers run, they ascend to the sky and tell Re that you stand in the shrines of the *akhet* upon the void (*shu*) of the sky, and sit on the throne of your father Geb in front of the shrine upon this throne of iron at which the gods marvel.[28]

Here, the iron throne is equated with the earth (Geb) and the king sits on it (the throne is always to be sat on) while at the same time standing upon the air of the sky in the *akhet*. This is a snapshot of the creation in which the king personifies the evolving cosmos. His sitting seems to symbolise the formation of the earth (the rising of the primeval mound) while his standing seems to symbolise the creation of the sky.

This image is reinforced by Utterance 676, where the king sits on the iron throne but stands up to support the sky on his shoulders:

> Raise yourself, O king, may you sit on your iron throne... You are indeed god-like; you have shouldered the sky, you have raised up the earth.[29]

It would appear from a close study of the Pyramid Texts that the act of standing, performed by the God, the gods, and the king, indeed signified the resurrection in the sense of ascending to the sky, whereas the act of sitting down signified the resurrection in the sense of being enthroned on the risen earth. Thus the king was urged to stand up and sit down.[30]

It would seem from the foregoing discussion that the iron throne was a term for the primeval mound. This is not an identification that scholars

Figure 41.
OSIRIS ON THE THRONE, UNDER THE PROTECTION OF ISIS.
The throne symbolised the earth at the centre of the cosmos.

have yet made as far as I am aware, but the evidence for it strikes me to be undeniable. Firstly, the iron throne belonged to the earth-god Geb.[31] Secondly, it was identified with the seat of Khenti-amentiu, who was an earth-god.[32] Thirdly, it was the throne of Osiris, who was predominantly an earth-god.[33] Fourthly, it was located in Heliopolis – a microcosm of the world.[34] And fifthly, it was juxtaposed to the sky in the king's re-enactment of creation.[35]

It would therefore be reasonable to suppose that the throne was made from *bja* because this metal exemplified the earth's mineral composition and its imperishability.

The Iron Eggshell

So far, we have considered the king's iron bones and his iron throne, and it is highly likely that the two ideas are connected in that the earth (the iron throne) was created by the assembly of the creator-god's limbs (the iron bones). We turn now to a third iron theme, which provides another leg of complementary symbolism – the iron egg (*swht*).

The iron egg, or to be precise the egg with the iron shell, is mentioned just once in the Pyramid Texts, in Utterance 669. In this spell, the king's rebirth from the 'nest of Thoth' is the subject of discussion between Isis and the gods.[36] The gods say:

> You [Isis] have borne him, you have shaped him, you have ejected him, but he has no legs, he has no arms, with what can he be knit together?

Isis replies:

> This iron shall be brought for him, the *hnu*-barque shall be brought that he may be lifted up into it.

The gods then ask:

> With what shall we break his egg?

Isis replies:

> Sokar of *Pdju-sh* shall come for him, for he has fashioned his harpoon-points and has cut out his barbs... It is he who will break the egg and split the iron.[37]

Finally, the gods ask:

> With what can the king be made to fly up?

Isis replies:

> There shall be brought to you [the king] the *hnu*-barque and the *kdmu* of the *hn*-bird. You shall fly up therewith... you shall fly up and alight on account of the plumes of your father Geb.

In the midst of this conversation, the refrain is heard:

> Look, the king is born; look, the king is knit together; look, the king is in being. [Variant: look, the king has broken the egg.]

A later version of this utterance appears in the Coffin Texts as Spell 989. In response to the gods' first question, Isis speaks of a god ejaculating semen, and promises to bring the king *the iron that is in the bow of the hnu-barque*.[38] In response to the second question, Isis adds that the king's bones will be cast like a metal, as if to suggest that he (rather than Sokar) will split open the iron egg. And in response to the third question, Isis suggests that the king will fly up using the plumes of Hnu (the god of the barque?).

What is the meaning of this? Without a doubt, the egg is a term for the primeval world that gave birth to the present cosmos. Hence in Spell 223 of the Coffin Texts, the deceased states: "I am this egg which is in the Great Honker [Geb]... I am he who splits iron. I have gone round about the egg, the Lord of Tomorrow."[39] The emergence of the king from the egg would therefore signify the birth of the creator-god who created the expanded cosmos, and the splitting of the iron eggshell would represent the breaking of the boundary of the primeval world.

The use of Sokar's harpoon to split the iron is most interesting, since the harpoon (or lance, or spear) is elsewhere said to be made of iron. For example, in Spell 23 of the Book of the Dead the mouth of the deceased is split open by the iron harpoon of Shu with which he split open the mouths of the gods.[40] There may be a parallel here to the famous spear of the Falcon at Edfu, which emerged from the *nun* at the beginning of the world.[41] In any event, the opening of the mouth by Shu's iron harpoon is suggestive of the opening of the mouth of the earth (see chapter eight), and tempts one to speculate that Sokar's harpoon, which split open the iron egg, was likewise made of iron. If so, this would imply that iron was ejected from the primeval cosmos.

Such a scenario was postulated earlier in chapter eight in connection with the iron that split open the mouth of the deceased and split open the land of the west (Coffin Texts, Spell 816). By coincidence or not, it was Sokar who spiritualized that iron and uplifted it in Heliopolis, and it was reportedly 'sharp and strong'. This is usually taken as a reference to his adze, but it might equally describe his harpoon.

On the subject of sharp iron splitting open the earth, the Pyramid Texts contain an intriguing passage which seems to portray the iron throne as a sharp object:

> He [the king] has appeared upon the stone [?], upon his throne. He has sharpened the iron by means of his spirit... Be seated on your great throne... raise yourself as Min, fly up to the sky...[42]

If the iron here belongs to the throne, as seems likely, why would it be described as sharp? Might it be that the iron throne has risen up from the depths of the abyss and split open its surface? If the throne represents the primeval mound, as I concluded earlier, then such an emergence would indeed be implied by the creation myth. We thus have corroboration for the idea that iron was ejected from the egg.

Further evidence for this hypothesis comes from the role of the *hnu*-barque. In Utterance 669 above, the problem of knitting the king together is solved by bringing him iron and the *hnu*-barque; in the later version of this spell, the iron is said to be in the bow of the *hnu*-barque. The king is then placed in this barque, and it provides the means for taking him to the sky. The impression is thus given that the barque carries not only the king to the sky, but also the iron to the sky.

Everything we know about the *hnu*-barque supports this impression. Firstly, it belonged to Sokar, who was a god of the netherworld, the sky, and metalworking.[43] Secondly, it was used by Horus to lift the king into the sky in his name of Sokar.[44] And thirdly, it transported the king in the ocean of the stars, where it was apparently towed using ropes of iron (see next section).

Figure 42.
THE HNU-BARQUE OF SOKAR.

The Iron of the Sky

In the Pyramid Texts, iron is mentioned four times in relation to the sky: the king splits the iron of the sky; he traverses the iron of the sky; he comes to rest on ropes of iron with which the sky-barque is towed; and he exits the sky through doors of iron. On the face of it, these references corroborate the idea that iron was ejected from the earth into the sky (at least when viewed from a geocentric perspective). It is therefore essential that we look more closely at this theme, using the Coffin Texts, where appropriate, to build up an overall picture. As we shall now see, none of the four passages is particularly straightforward to understand.

We shall begin with the ropes of iron. In Utterance 214, the king is told:

> You shall bathe in the fresh water of the stars (*qebhu sbau*), you shall fall (*hay*) upon the iron ropes on the shoulders of Horus in his name of 'the One who is in the Hnu-barque' [i.e. Sokar].[45]

This is a difficult passage. The verb *hay* is normally translated 'descend', which would imply that the king goes down on the iron ropes in the west side of the sky. But this may not be the intention, for in the Coffin Texts the iron ropes are used to tow the sky-barque:

> These two crews of the imperishable stars and the untiring stars shall navigate you, they shall pilot you and tow you over the district of the waters with ropes of iron.[46]

Here, the ropes are not used for descending from the sky but for crossing the sky. The idea seems to be that the gods the stars are towing the boat with ropes of iron. These ropes, like the oars which are used to propel the barque of Re, would be an imaginary construct, perhaps inspired by the phenomenon of shooting stars.[47]

So, the intention in Utterance 214 may be that the king is falling on the iron ropes,[48] either in the sense of seizing them and ascending upon them (as upon a shooting star) or in the sense of coming to rest on the barque that is towed by them. In either case, the iron ropes are to be visualised as trailing across the sky, which is supported by the shoulders (or arms) of Horus.

Turning to the iron doors in the sky, these are mentioned in Utterances 469 and 584, which are virtually identical. The first of these spells reads as follows:

> I row Re to the land of the west and he establishes my seat at the head of the gods... The doors of *Ba-ka*, which is in the fresh water (*qebhu*), are opened for me, the doors of iron which are in the starry sky (*shdu*) are thrown open for me, and I go through them.[49]

Again, this is a difficult passage. The doors of iron, which are apparently synonymous with the doors of *Ba-ka*, are located 'in' the sky-ocean – in the region of *Ba-ka*. But the location of *Ba-ka* is a mystery, and so the location of its iron doors is a subject of speculation.[50]

One possibility is that doors were used to pass from the barque into the region of the northern stars. Spell 479 of the Coffin Texts refers to seven gods standing on a 'great plain of iron' in the north of the sky.[51] Might this iron plain be entered via iron doors?

Another possibility is that the iron doors were located in the west side of the sky. It may be significant that the spell duplicated in Utterances 469 and 584 is unique in its reference to Re being rowed to the land of the west (*ament*). This might explain why the iron doors appear here but nowhere else. They would be the doors through which the barque passed into the netherworld.

In support of this speculation, Utterance 469 goes on to refer to evil, which was generally associated with the netherworld, and to the presence of the *nkhkh*-stars, which belong to the lower sky in Utterance 262.[52] In addition, the determinatives used for the iron doors in Utterances 469 and 584 – the well (of water) sign in the first passage and the desert-land sign in the second passage – are both suggestive of the land of the west.⁵³

In further support of this theory, the Book of Nut describes the sun-god Re 'sailing to the limits of the *bja* of the sky', whereupon he enters Nut's mouth, or the *duat*.⁵⁴ This text confirms that the iron spanned the sky as far as the western horizon.

It therefore seems likely that the doors of iron belonged to the sky in the sense that they provided access from the sky to the netherworld in the remote west. This solution creates a puzzle in that the numerous other doors of the cosmos, such as the doors of the earth and the doors of the sky in the east, are not described as iron. Why should this be? Perhaps the explanation is that the authors of the Pyramid Texts took this fact for granted. With the exception of the doors of *Ba-ka*, the material of which the doors are made is never disclosed.

We come now to the two other passages in which iron is mentioned in relation to the sky. Once again, interpretation is difficult.

Firstly, in Utterance 257, the king splits the iron of the sky:

> There is tumult in the sky... The king takes possession of the sky, he splits its iron.⁵⁵

Secondly, in Utterance 509, the king traverses iron in his ascent to the sky:

> The sky thunders, the earth quakes... I ascend to the sky, I traverse the iron, I traverse the *hzau*-water, I demolish the ramparts of Shu, I ascend to the sky...⁵⁶

In both these passages, the word for iron (*bja*) is determined by the well (of water) sign ⌣. According to Allen, this indicates that the iron formed a basin that contained the sky-water; the king is imagined to be splitting this iron basin and traversing its waters.⁵⁷ It is taken as read by Allen and other experts that *bja* is here a term for the sky, or firmament.⁵⁸

But it may be a mistake to interpret the texts in this way. It strikes me that both passages describe a dynamic situation in which the king breaks out from the earth into the sky in re-enactment of the creation – at a time when the sky has not yet been formed. The iron which he splits – the iron basin of water – would therefore be the boundary of the primeval world. We have already encountered this boundary in the iron eggshell, and it is found too in the wall of iron which delimited the field of reeds.⁵⁹

Let's see how this works.

In the first passage above, the king would be splitting the iron in order to take possession of the sky, rather than the other way round. This iron would belong primarily to the earth, but it would also belong to the sky in the sense that the sky was originally joined to the earth. This principle has already been demonstrated in chapter eight, where the doors of the earth and the doors of the sky were found to be one and the same set of doors.

In the second passage, the king would be traversing the iron boundary of the primeval world in order to reach (or rather expand into) the sky. The fact that he traverses the iron in a nautical sense (i.e. by boat) would reflect the fact that he creates the sky with the waters of the flood (see chapter six). His demolition of the ramparts of Shu is suggestive of the breaking of the iron boundary of the primeval world, and offers support for this hypothesis.

There is a passage in Utterance 612 which offers further support for this interpretation. In it, the king is said to 'wreck the mansion' in order to sit upon his iron throne:

> Raise yourself and sit on this iron throne of yours, for your nails are what have wrecked the mansion.[60]

Here, the verb translated 'wreck' is determined with a boat sign, as if to suggest that the king damages the mansion while sailing over water. This is eerily reminiscent of Utterance 511, where the king traverses the iron and demolishes the ramparts of Shu.

In Utterance 666, the mansion appears again. This time the king hacks it open with his adzes in order to sit on his iron throne. In this spell, the mansion is called 'the mansion of *Nwt-k-nu*' – an allusion perhaps to Nut and primeval water.[61]

Interestingly, the mansion (*hwt*) is elsewhere a term for the womb of Hathor. An Egyptian text informs us that '(the child is) inside her body; inside her a mansion (*hwt*) of Horus is being prepared, hence her name is Hathor ('Mansion of Horus')'.[62] Horus is here depicted as a falcon, his mansion being akin to an egg. It is plausible that Utterance 612 (above) refers to the king as the Horus chick, clawing its way out of the mansion of the egg.

In conclusion, it is doubtful that the king split and traversed iron *while in the sky*. Rather, it seems more likely that he split and traversed iron *en route to the sky*. Accordingly, it would be wrong to suppose that the sky was a basin or firmament made of iron. The iron basin, if we may call it that, belonged to the earth, to the primeval mound. Of course, it might be that the Egyptians did imagine the sky to be a basin of iron, bearing in mind their philosophy of cosmic duality, but such a theory goes beyond what is required for our understanding of the texts. (Occam's razor demands that we should not presume two iron basins where one will do.)

This is not to deny that the sky contained iron. As we have seen, there were iron ropes in the sky and iron doors in the west at 'the limits of the *bja* of the sky', and there was a plain of iron in the north of the sky. In addition, the Coffin Texts inform us that Anubis broke the iron in the sky,[63] that the sky contained a fisherman's net whose floats and weights were made of iron,[64] and that Re 'swam in his iron' while crossing the sky.[65]

Where did this iron come from? In this chapter, we have encountered a number of clues: the king's iron bones are gestated in the womb of Nut, yet his imperishable limbs become the stars in the sky;[66] the appearance of the iron throne involves a splitting of the earth; the egg with the iron shell is split open, seemingly by an iron harpoon; the *hnu*-barque with iron in its bow sails from the earth into the sky;[67] and the king splits and traverses the iron at a time of tumult in the sky and quaking in the earth. All of this suggests that iron was ejected from the primeval world and uplifted to the sky.

This is plausible. In earlier chapters, we have seen how the primeval world burst open like a womb and ejected air and floodwaters, the latter being driven upwards by the winds to form the sky. If the boundary of this world was made of iron and was broken open, as the texts suggest, then some of this broken iron could have been uplifted by the waters of the flood and the winds of the storm. It might seem an unlikely picture to the modern mind, but it is the beliefs of the Egyptians that are the issue here.

This scenario would explain the mysterious associations between iron and water. In this chapter we have seen that the word *bja* was determined by the well sign, that the king traversed the *bja* in a nautical sense, and that ropes of *bja* were used for crossing the sky-water, while in chapter eight we saw that the *bja* of Sokar was 'washed' at the time of opening the mouth. All of this would make sense if the iron originated in the earth and was uplifted by the waters of the flood.

This theory would also explain the mysterious statement 'Anubis has broken the iron in the sky'. He would not have broken it in the sky (he was primarily a god of the netherworld), but rather at the surface of the world. But this broken iron was now in the sky, and this would be the sense in which Anubis had 'broken the iron in the sky'.

It would therefore seem that, regardless of the question of whether the sky was a flat slab of iron, or basin of iron, which must remain a matter of conjecture, the sky was almost certainly a body of water containing a scattered cloud of iron. Hence the belief that Re 'swam in his *bja*' while crossing the sky.

This brings us back to the nature of the great storm in which the king ascended to the sky. In chapter nine, we encountered the idea that the sky was somehow blocked and needed to be cleared in order for the sky-god to see and traverse his roads in the sky. In that chapter, I concluded that the storm cloud consisted of floodwaters, but previewed the possibility that it might involve something else. Now, in the light of our discussion of the iron of the sky, we may hazard an informed guess that the clouds of the storm also comprised iron and perhaps other material elements that were blasted upwards from the surface of the world. Hence the idea that the formative sky was 'choked and stifled' and 'big with gods'.[68]

The texts are not especially clear on this point. On no occasion is the storm said to contain *bja*. Nevertheless, G.A. Wainwright has argued that the thunderbolt which took the king to the sky was in fact a meteorite, the principal element of which is iron (*bja* is thought originally to have denoted meteoritic iron),[69] and it might also be argued that *shnyt* ought to be translated 'meteorite storm' rather than 'hailstorm' (particularly when used in the context of creation). In addition, it may be significant that in the myth entitled *Horus of Behdet and the Winged Disc* the enemies of Re are annihilated by Horus and his blacksmith-gods (*mesniu*), who sail in the barque of Re wielding iron harpoons and metal chains.[70] This battle, which is largely fought in the cosmic waters, allegorizes the storm of creation, and thus provides support for the theory that iron and other metals were uplifted to the sky.

Iron in the Opening of the Mouth

Our survey of iron would not be complete without considering its use in the opening of the mouth ritual. In the Pyramid Texts, this is recorded in two spells, Utterances 21 and 670, which read as follows:

> O king, I open your mouth for you with the adze of Wepwawet, I split open your mouth for you with the adze of iron (*mskhtiu m bja*) which split open the mouths of the gods... Horus has split open the mouth of this king with that wherewith he split open the mouth of his father [Osiris]... with the iron which issued from Seth, with the adze of iron which split open the mouths of the gods.[71]

> I [Horus] have given Atum to you [Osiris], I have made the two enneads for you. Your children's children together have raised you up (namely) Hapy, Duamutef, Imsety, and Qebhsenuf... Your face is washed, your tears are wiped away, your mouth is split open with their fingers of iron (*djbau m bja*)...[72]

222   THE MIDNIGHT SUN

We may now attempt a detailed interpretation of these rituals, in the light of our preceding discussion on the iron.

In the first passage, the designate king Horus performs the ritual on the mummy of his father Osiris, in re-enactment of the original resurrection of the god. He uses an adze that is modelled on the shape of the northern stars, in anticipation of the result of the ritual, i.e. the spiritualization of the gods. The significance of the adze is seen in its function as a splitting instrument. Here it splits open the mouth, but in Utterance 666 it hacks open the mansion of *Nwt-k-nu* (see earlier), while in Utterances 229 and 258 two adzes are used as cutting weapons by Horus and Seth in the city of Hermopolis.[73] The intention in all cases is that the adze splits open the mouth of the cosmos, which may be portrayed as a womb or a primeval city. The fact that it was made of iron suggests that iron forced open the mouth of the cosmos.

Ownership of the adze is credited to Wepwawet, while the iron itself is said to have issued from Seth. What does this tell us? As regards Seth, it is likely that the text refers to the meteoritic iron of which the adze was made; since the adze was modelled on the northern stars and since Seth was held to dwell in those stars, the iron of the adze would have been viewed as the metal of Seth. Nevertheless, the real significance of the iron lies in its mythical origin, which is reflected in its ownership by Wepwawet.

Wepwawet was a jackal-god, but his original form was a wolf.[74] His wolf emblem appears as one of the standards of kingship during the 1st dynasty.[75] His name meant literally 'the opener of the ways' (*Wp-wawt*), but he was also called 'the opener of the body'.[76] In the Pyramid Texts, he is said to be on high in the sky, and he opens the ways for the ascent of the king.[77] To have the face of Wepwawet was to be assured of rebirth and vision in the sky.[78] The god is also credited with dividing the waters, i.e. separating the sky from the waters of *nun*.[79] He was almost certainly a form of the creator-god.

The *shedshed* of Wepwawet may hold the key to his ownership of the adze. It is called 'the *shedshed* of the sky' and is used by Horus and the king to ascend to the sky.[80] In two spells, it arises 'in the space which separates', i.e. the void between sky and earth.[81] Although the meaning of the word *shedshed* is uncertain, it has been connected to the verb *shed*, which meant 'to extract' or 'pull up' in various senses, including that of extracting earth from the ground.[82] It is conceivable, therefore, that the *shedshed* might allegorize an extraction of materials which were destined for the sky. The appearance of the *shedshed* is not inconsistent with this interpretation. It is depicted on the front of Wepwawet's standard as a protuberance, which is sometimes covered by small dots.[83] What might this object be? Henri Frankfort suggested that it might be the placenta of the king, but he also hinted that it might be a meteorite.[84] Iron meteorites often possess pronounced regmaglypts (bowl-shaped incisions), which an artist might well illustrate by a scattering of dots. Indeed, the *shedshed* bears a striking similarity to the 'head' of Osiris in the fetish of Abydos – an object which has been identified as a meteorite or a box containing a meteorite.[85] This theory would furnish a connection to the iron of which the adze of Wepwawet was made.

Figure 43.
THE WEPWAWET STANDARD (RIGHT).
Note the shedshed protuberance at the front.

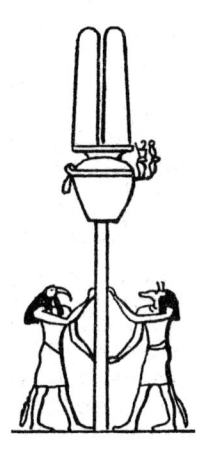

Figure 44.
THE ABYDOS FETISH (LEFT).
The head of Osiris on the pole may have signified a meteorite.

In any event, Wepwawet was the prime son who 'opened the body' of his mother and 'opened the ways' to the sky, and from this information alone we may reasonably conclude that his adze split open the womb of the earth.

Turning to the second passage, Utterance 670, there is no mention of an adze, Osiris-the-king's mouth here being opened by the 'iron fingers' of the four sons of Horus. These gods are the souls who emerged from the body of Horus, and they are re-enacting the myth of the gods creating the God, as opposed to the God creating himself (the latter is the case in Utterance 540, where the king's mouth is opened by Horus with his little finger).[86] As before, the splitting open of the mummy's mouth signifies the splitting open of the cosmos. But what is the significance of the iron fingers?

According to Ann Macy Roth, the fingers of iron describe the *netjeru*-blades which were used in the opening of the mouth ritual. These blades resembled two little fingers, and were probably modelled on the fingers of the midwife, with which she cleared the mucus from the mouth of the newborn babe.[87] But why were these 'fingers' made of iron?

Roth theorised that the *netjeru*-blades, ideally made of meteoritic iron, symbolised the northern stars, which were emblematic of the afterlife. To open the deceased's mouth with the metal of a 'fallen star' was to effect his rebirth, like a babe from the womb.

But Roth missed the bigger picture.

In Utterance 519, the king demands of Re:

> Give me these your two fingers which you gave to the Beautiful, the daughter of the great god, when the sky was separated from the earth, when the gods ascended to the sky.[88]

If Roth is correct in her theory about the two fingers of the midwife – and she is certainly persuasive – then the meaning of this passage would be that the king is seeking rebirth as a babe in the manner of the daughter of the great god – via the opening of his mouth with the two fingers of Re. But this passage states clearly that the rebirth is a re-enactment of the creation – the time 'when the sky was separated from the earth, when the gods ascended to the sky'. This supports my arguments that the mouth of the mummy signified the mouth of the cosmos, and that the birth of the child signified the rebirth of the cosmos. Moreover, the passage reminds us that the stars – on which the *netjeru*-blades were modelled – had their origin in the gods of the earth.

When seen from this perspective, it becomes clear that the iron fingers of the gods belonged originally in the earth, and were externalized for the purpose of the ritual. Fingers equipped with nails are sharp and strong – like the adze – and symbolise a means of clawing open the womb or egg of creation. That they were made of iron – like the adze and probably the harpoon of Sokar – suggests once again that iron forced open the earth at the time of creation.

It has been suggested by H.T. Velde (in the context of the Horus and Seth myth) that 'finger' might also be a euphemism for 'phallus'.[89] This is a plausible theory, not least because of the physical resemblance of the two members,[90] and may shed light on certain obscure references in the Pyramid Texts. For example: the finger of Seth is said to cause the white eye of Horus to see;[91] electrum illumines the tip of the finger of Seth;[92] the fingers of the earth-god are on the vertex of the long-horn (a bull or a snake);[93] the fingers of Atum are on the horns of the long-horn;[94] and Osiris has a diseased finger which needs to be bandaged.[95] There is also an interesting reference to the fingernail of Atum, which by extension of the euphemism might signify the head of the phallus.[96]

This adds yet another layer of symbolism to the opening of the mouth ritual. For example, where Horus opens the mouth of Osiris with his little finger, this may be interpreted as the creator-god opening the mouth of the cosmos by erecting his phallus (compare the creation myths of Atum and Neber-djer).[97] And where Horus the child has his finger in the mouth, this may be interpreted not only as an image of the creator-god creating himself, but more richly as the creator ejaculating his semen into his own mouth as a prelude to spitting it out (again compare the creation myths of Atum and Neber-djer).[98]

The myth of the creator-god opening the goddess with his two fingers is less easy to explain in this way, but might reflect the Egyptian view of the earth as a duality (*tawi*, 'the Two Lands').[99]

Figure 45.
HORUS THE CHILD WITH HIS FINGER TO HIS MOUTH.
The image suggests self-creation and the eternal circuit of the cosmos.

Addendum: Meteoritic Iron in Ancient Egypt

The Egyptian interest in iron (*bja*) is remarkable for a society that neither mined nor imported it at the time when the Pyramid Texts were inscribed inside the Old Kingdom pyramids. According to scholars, this puzzle is solved by the assumption that the Egyptians, like other ancient societies, acquired their iron from meteoritic sources, i.e. from meteorites which fortuitously fell from the sky.[100] Of the three main classes of meteorite, irons are the most commonly found.[101]

That the Egyptians used meteoritic iron is evident from archaeological finds.[102] That they knew this iron had fallen from the sky is proven by its association with the northern stars, by textual references to 'iron of the sky' (*bja n pet*), and by the description of a meteorite fall that appears in Spell 1080 of the Coffin Texts. This latter reference describes how the fallen object – the efflux of Osiris – was hidden and sealed, apparently in a granite sarcophagus:

> This is the sealed thing which is in darkness, with fire about it, which contains the efflux of Osiris, and it is put in Rostau. It has been hidden since it fell from him [Osiris], and it is what came down from him on to the desert of sand. It means that what belonged to him was put in Rostau.[103]

The Egyptians credited iron meteorites with magical powers, and smelted them to create objects for ritual use, such as sceptres, protective amulets, and tools for the opening of the mouth (the latter included the blade of the adze, the *netjeru*-blades, and the *pesesh-kef* knife).[104]

Many meteorites, however, were kept in their natural forms and placed inside temples as objects of veneration.

One of the best attested cases of meteorite worship in Egypt is the so-called *benben* stone of Heliopolis. Although it is not described explicitly as being made of *bja*, its name meant literally 'the stone that flowed out', which might well suggest an outflow of molten iron.[105] The significance of this stone, which was enshrined on a pillar in the temple of Heliopolis, will be discussed further in chapter eleven.

Another prime example is the *ka-mut.ef* cult object of Thebes, which was almost certainly a small iron meteorite.[106] Again, we will discuss this object further in the next chapter.

In addition, it is probable that meteorites were worshipped in temples at Letopolis and Abydos.[107]

This brief survey of meteorite worship may well represent the tip of an ancient iceberg, for iron meteorites have an unfortunate tendency to rust and disintegrate, and thus disappear from the archaeological record. For this reason, not to mention warfare, theft, and vandalism, our knowledge of the meteorite cult is not as good as it ideally ought to be.

Egyptologists have long been aware of the meteorite cult in Egypt, but they have generally perceived it to be an offshoot of the sun cult (in the case of the *benben* stone), or an appendage to the star cult (the meteorite being regarded as a 'fallen star'), or possibly the remnant of an archaic, primitive sky cult.[108] One way or another, scholars have taken the view that the meteorite cult is of peripheral interest to the question of ancient Egyptian religion.

These interpretations of the meteorite cult have been influenced by the modern view of meteorites. We associate them with the sky. However, as we have seen in this chapter, the ancient Egyptians believed that the iron of the meteorite had originated in the earth, whence it had been ejected into the sky. This turns our modern perspective upside down. (Though by some strange twist of fortune we still refer in the English language to 'a meteoric rise'.)

Viewed from the Egyptian, geocentric perspective, the iron meteorite becomes a remnant of creation – a sample of the iron that split open the mouth of the world – and a potent symbol of the cataclysm that marked the rebirth of the cosmos. Moreover, as we shall see in the next chapter, it signified the seed of the creator-god with which he had inseminated the womb of the sky-goddess.

Chapter Ten Summary

- Iron (*bja*) is ubiquitous in the texts which describe the king's re-enactment of creation.

- The primeval cosmos is said to have a boundary of iron. This is seen in the egg with the iron shell, the iron doors of *Ba-ka*, and the iron wall of the field of reeds.

- The iron boundary was broken when the old cosmos gave birth to the new. The king re-enacted this event when he split and traversed iron en route to the sky.

- Iron burst forth from the abyss to form the primeval mound. Hence the king sat on a throne made of iron.

- Some terrestrial iron was lifted up to the sky. There is no evidence that the sky became a basin of iron, but it is clear that it contained a cloud of iron through which Re swam and ropes of iron which were used to tow his barque.

- The stars were apparently made of iron, which was spiritualized from the limbs of the creator-god Osiris.

- Iron meteorites were worshipped in Egypt because they were regarded as the material of creation.

- The king's mouth was split open with an iron adze in the image of the northern stars in anticipation of the iron being ejected from the earth to form those stars.

CHAPTER ELEVEN

THE BULL OF THE SKY

The king is the bull of the sky... who lives on the being of every god.
(Pyramid Texts, Utterance 273)

In the Pyramid Texts, the king is often depicted as a bull (*ka*). He is 'the great bull',[1] 'the wild bull',[2] 'the enduring bull of the wild bulls',[3] 'the great wild bull',[4] 'the bull of Heliopolis',[5] 'the bull of the baboons',[6] 'the bull with radiance in his Eye',[7] 'the bull of the light',[8] and 'the bull of the sky'.[9] In keeping with this image, the king is adorned with the horns of the bull,[10] and his throne has feet which are 'the hooves of the Great Wild Bull'.[11]

In the form of a bull, the king (or rather his spiritual double, *ka*) passes through the cosmic realms. He rows from the land of the west to the field of offerings;[12] he crosses over to the green fields, to the pure places of Re;[13] he traverses the beaten path of stars (*msqt shdu*) and smites the ball in the meadow of Apis;[14] he splits open the earth and causes the gods to tremble in the storm-cloud of the sky;[15] he comes out of Heliopolis;[16] and he crosses the night sky, flashing like a spear of gold.[17]

The king is also a bull-like pillar, which is decorated with the eyes of the sun and the moon and named after the stars. In Utterance 254, he is described as:

> The one whose horn is upstanding, the eye-painted pillar, the bull of the sky.[18]

> The Pillar of the Stars... the Pillar of Kenzet, the bull of the sky.[19]

In his journey through the 'other world', the king encounters bulls at every turn. The ferryman of the winding waterway is called 'Bull of the Gods',[20] and another ferryman of the netherworld is called 'Great Bull, the Pillar of the Serpent Nome'.[21] There is also a 'Bull of Re', who seems to personify the entire netherworld. In Utterance 304, the king addresses this bull as follows:

> Hail to you, Bull of Re with your four horns: a horn of yours in the west, a horn of yours in the east, a horn of yours in the south, and a horn of yours in the north. Bend down this western horn of yours for me that I may pass.[22]

The Bull of Re confirms that the king is a 'pure westerner' who has come forth from 'the falcon city', and permits him to proceed into the field of offerings.

In addition to the Bull of Re, there is a 'Bull of the Sky', who gives his hand (sic) to the king and pulls him up to the *duat* (here the sky).[23] He too is said to bend down his horn, in this case enabling the king to go forth into the lakes of the *duat*.[24]

Finally, the Pyramid Texts describe the king eating the bull in order to effect his translation to the 'other world'. This is the theme of the famous 'Cannibal Hymn', where the bull is captured, roped, felled, slaughtered, butchered, and cooked to provide meals for the king, who in consuming them becomes bull of the sky.[25] According to Utterance 413, the king is able to repeat these meals while sitting on his throne and circulating in the sky:

> Awake, O king... sit on your iron throne, that you may eat the foreleg, devour the haunch, and partake of your rib-joints in the sky in company with the gods.[26]

What is the significance of the bull? According to my hypothesis set out in chapter seven, the king assumes the identity of the creator-god and re-enacts the creation of the cosmos. We would therefore expect the bull to be an image of the creator-god.

This is plausible, for the Pyramid Texts frequently mention bull-gods who are associated with the earth and the sky. There is a god named Bull of the Sky, who seems to personify the sky;[27] there is a god named Great Wild Bull, who is associated with Khenti-amentiu;[28] there is a god named Bull of Bulls, who is possibly Re;[29] there a god named Bull of the Two Enneads, who is possibly Re;[30] Geb is called 'Bull of the Sky (*Nwt*)';[31] Re is portrayed as the bull of the netherworld;[32] and Seth is depicted as a bull which is dismembered and eaten (see later discussion). It is believed that many of these bull-gods are of extreme antiquity.

In addition, from the earliest times, there was a cult of the Apis bull at Memphis and a cult of the Mnevis bull at Heliopolis, each animal being worshipped as a unique incarnation of the creator-god.[33]

There is no evidence linking Osiris with the bull until the Coffin Texts of the Middle Kingdom in which he receives the epithets 'Bull of the West' and 'Bull of Nedyt'.[34] At around this time too, Amun came to the fore at Thebes bearing the titles 'Bull of the Mother' and 'Bull of the Four Maidens'.[35]

Could it be that all these bull-gods were manifestations of the creator-god?

Let us put this theory to the test and see where it leads us.

Figure 46.
THE APIS BULL OF MEMPHIS.

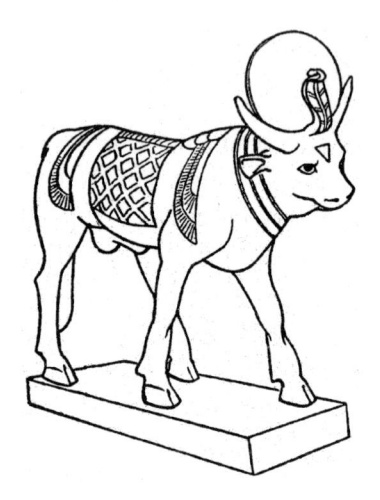

The Bull of the Gods

In Egypt, as elsewhere in the ancient world, religious rituals involved the sacrifice of bulls. To the modern eye, these sacrifices appear paradoxical, since the bull was usually venerated as a manifestation of divine power. Moreover, they appear wasteful, since the bulls were valuable economic assets. Why would an ancient society engage in such irreverent, barbaric, and expensive rituals?

The view of scholars is that the practice of making sacrificial offerings was intended to invoke the goodwill of the gods, and generate a future benefit in return. In the case of the bull, the investment was the greater to achieve the greater return. As the supreme symbol of sexual potency and rebirth, it guaranteed that the land would be fertile for the coming year, and that the crops would be bountiful. To this end, the bull was sacrificed at a propitious time, such as the spring equinox, and its blood was made to drain into the earth.[36]

But the sacrifice also involved a deep religious symbolism, pertaining to an original, archetypal sacrifice, made at the beginning of time. In *The Myth of the Eternal Return,* Mircea Eliade writes:

> A sacrifice, for example, not only exactly reproduces the initial sacrifice revealed by a god *ab origine*, at the beginning of time, it also takes place at that same primordial mythical moment; in other words, every sacrifice repeats the initial sacrifice and coincides with it. All sacrifices are performed at the same mythical instant of the beginning.[37]

This theory finds application in Egypt, for in Utterances 580 and 670 of the Pyramid Texts, the bull which is sacrificed represents Seth, the god of chaos who opposed creation. In the first of these two similar spells, Horus says:

> O my father Osiris this king, I have smitten for you him who smote you as an ox; I have killed for you him who killed you as a wild bull; I have broken for you him who broke you as a long-horn... He who stretched you out is a stretched bull; he who pierced you is a bull to be pierced; he who made you deaf is a deaf bull. I have cut off its head, I have cut off its tail, I have cut off its arms (sic), I have cut off its legs.[38]

There follows an apportionment of the bull between Kheprer, Atum, Shu, Tefnut, Geb, Nut, Isis, Nephthys, Osiris, Anubis, Khenti-irty, the four sons of Horus, and other gods, with the remainder being allocated to the gods the souls of Nekhen and the gods the souls of Pe. The bull is then eaten in order that the gods might proceed on their way to the afterlife:

> May we eat, may we eat the red ox [Seth] for the passage of the lake which Horus made for his father Osiris this king.[39]

It is quite clear from this spell that the bull sacrifice in Egypt repeated an original sacrifice in which a cosmic bull was slain and consumed for the resurrection of Osiris and the gods. This resurrection, of course, signified the death and rebirth of the cosmos itself.

This principle of original sacrifice is the key to understanding the so-called 'Cannibal Hymn' (Utterances 273 and 274) in which Osiris-the-king eats the bull and thereby becomes the bull of the sky. Significantly, in this hymn, the bull (or possibly two bulls) is equated with the totality of the primeval gods, and by eating the parts of the bull the king acquires all the powers of the gods.[40] The bull (or bulls) having been slaughtered, butchered, and cooked, it is the gods whom the king eats:

> The king is one who... lives on the gods... It is the king who eats their magic (*hekau*), who swallows their spirits (*akhu*)... He has broken the joins of the vertebrae; he has taken the hearts of the gods; he has eaten the red, he has swallowed the green; the king feeds on the lungs (*sma*) of the wise ones, and is content with living on hearts and their magic... He is satiated, their magic being inside his belly... The king has swallowed the intelligence (*sia*) of every god... Now their souls (*bau*) are in the king's belly, their spirits (*akhu*) are in the king's possession, as his soup containing the gods which is boiled from [or cooked by] their bones.[41]

As a direct result of this feast, the deceased king is reborn as the bull of the sky:

> The splendour (*shps*) of the king is in the sky, his power (*wsr*) is in the akhet... The king's male spirits (*kau*) are about him, his female spirits (*hmwst*) are under his feet, his gods are upon him... The king's neck is on his trunk. The king is the bull of the sky.[42]

What is the meaning of this? If we apply all the principles that have been explained in this book – that the creator-god personified the death and rebirth of the cosmos; that the plurality of gods signified the divided state of the old cosmos; that the deceased king became the creator-god and re-enacted the creation; and that the sacrifice of the bull repeated a cosmic sacrifice from the beginning of the world – then a clear picture emerges of *a cosmos that was portrayed as a bull*. The death and dismemberment of the bull would thus signify the old cosmos falling into a state of chaos and division; the cooking of the bull would signify the old cosmos being purified by fire and revitalised; the eating of the bull would signify the reintegration of the cosmos (in the stomach of the king, or creator-god);[43] and the king's resurrection as the bull of the sky would signify the rebirth of the cosmos – its expansion into the new cosmos.

In support of this interpretation of the 'Cannibal Hymn', the gods who symbolise the dismembered bull (or bulls) are described as originating 'with their bellies full of magic' from the island of fire (*iw nsisi*),[44] which is the centre of creation in the Hermopolite myth (see chapter three). The text thus seems to draw a parallel between the bull and the island of fire (quite appropriate in view of the cooking of the bull).

Furthermore, when the bull is being cooked for the king, the text refers to the northern stars, and alludes to their shape as the forelegs (*khpshu*) of the bull:

> It is the great ones in the north of the sky who set the fire for him, for

the cauldrons containing them [the gods], (using) the forelegs of the oldest ones.[45]

In an earlier passage, these oldest ones are said to have been killed ('on that day of slaying the oldest ones'). The quoted passage therefore seems to anticipate the spiritualization of this slain bull (or bulls), specifically in the stellar 'forelegs' that were Ursa Minor and the Plough of Ursa Major (see chapter eight). The identity of the 'oldest ones' is unclear; the name may refer to the primeval gods, or it may allude to the two great rivals Horus and Seth.

That the bull could personify the primeval cosmos is also evident from Utterance 304, where the Bull of Re is blessed with four horns, one in the west, one in the east, one in the south, and one in the north. The lowering of the western horn permits the king to enter the field of offerings (see earlier), and suggests that the bull itself *is* the field of offerings, with its horns signifying the doors into and out of this chthonian realm.[46]

The bull's horns are fitting symbols for doors since they are means of splitting open that which is closed. In Utterance 251, there is a powerful image of the king in the form of a bull, with a sharp, strong horn, passing through the *duat* towards the *akhet*:

> I am bound for this throne of mine, (even I) the pre-eminent of thrones who am behind the great god, whose head is set in place, who has assumed a sharp, strong horn as one who bears a sharp knife which cuts throats. It is the strong horn which is behind the great god that removes trouble from before the bull and causes those who are in the darkness to quake... I am not opposed in the *akhet*.[47]

This description of the bull's horn as 'sharp and strong' is echoed by that of the iron of Sokar which is 'washed, sharp and strong' in Spell 816 of the Coffin Texts. Did it split open the *duat*, just as the iron of Sokar split open the mouth and the land of the west? The 'sharp knife' analogy lends support to this hypothesis,[48] as does the quaking of the gods who are in the darkness.

It may be no coincidence that the king's rebirth as a bull is marked by the quaking and splitting of the earth.

In the inaptly named 'Cannibal Hymn', cited earlier, the appearance of the king as bull of the sky is introduced by a cataclysm in which the earth quakes:

> The sky is darkened, the stars are a-thunder, the celestial expanses (*pdjwt*) tremble, the bones of the earth-gods (*akeru*) quake.[49]

An even more vivid picture is provided by Utterance 254, where the king splits open the earth as an upright pillar, the bull of the sky with upturned horn:

> Set the rope aright, traverse the beaten path of stars, smite the ball in the meadow of Apis! Oho! Your fields are in fear, you *iad*-star before [the king] the Pillar of the Stars, for they have seen [the king] the Pillar of Kenzet, the bull of the sky, and the ox-herd is overwhelmed before him. Ho! Be afraid and tremble, you violent ones who are on the storm-cloud of the sky! He [the king] split open the earth by means of what he knew on the day when he wished to come thence – so says Wr-skat who dwells in the *duat*.[50]

This passage has traditionally been interpreted as the king splitting open the doors of his tomb. However, from a geocentric perspective, it is the primeval earth which is split open in re-enactment of the creation myth. The king's bull-like rampage then reflects the original cosmos expanding cataclysmically into the new cosmos.

This idea is also implied by the king's claim to be 'the great-faced bull which came out of Heliopolis'.[51] Since Heliopolis was a microcosm of the primeval world, the bull which came out of it is to be visualised as a newborn bull, who by means of his sharp, strong horns, breaks down the ramparts of the old cosmos.[52]

Significantly, the emergence of the bull is connected to the creation of the stars. This is implicit in the names of various bull-gods: the Bull of the Two Enneads who opens the king's path and places him at the head of the gods;[53] the Bull of the Ennead who goes forth from the *akhet*;[54] the Bull of the Hnmmt who produces seed from his phallus;[55] and the Bull of Millions who assembles the ladder for Shu.[56] The ennead and the *hnmmt* are the spiritualized gods, the stars, who were conceived to be thousands and millions.

The creation of the stars by the bull is also suggested by Utterance 254 (above), where the king is depicted as the Pillar of the Stars, but also as a bull which traverses the beaten path of stars (*msqt shdu*) and ascends to the sky, frightening the ox-herd, which is surely no specific constellation but rather the evolving stars in their entirety.[57] (The ox-herd seems to be synonymous with the gods on the storm-cloud of the sky.)

It is no surprise, from this geocentric perspective, to find that the stars of Ursa Minor and the Plough in Ursa Major symbolised the two forelegs or thighs of the bull, nor to hear that the solar 'eye' and lunar 'eye' may have been modelled on the eyes of the bull (prior to being reinvented as the eyes of the falcon).[58] The former – the forelegs or thighs – came to be associated with Seth, while the latter – the eyes – came to be associated with Horus.

The Cow of the Cosmos

Just as the bull personified the cosmos, so too did the cow. As early as the Pyramid Texts no less than four goddesses took the form of a cow, of whom three were mother to the reborn king. As the provider of milk *par excellence*, the cow was held in esteem by the Egyptians as the supreme symbol of motherhood.

The cow-goddess cited most often as the king's mother is 'the Great Wild Cow who dwells in Nekheb'.[59] She is described as 'white of headcloth, long of plumes (or hair), with pendulous breasts'.[60] She is said to conceive, bear, and suckle the king, to carry him across the waters of the abyss to the great throne which the gods made, and to lift him up into the sky.[61] Strangely, this cow-goddess also appears as a vulture, who spreads her wings and enfolds the king.[62] This vulture is Nekhbet, the goddess after whom the city of Nekheb was named and the goddess of the white crown of Upper Egypt who together with her cobra counterpart Wadjyt provided protection for the Two Lands.[63] The vulture, like the cow, was a symbol of motherhood.[64]

Curiously, the texts always speak of the Great Wild Cow in isolation – never in connection with a male partner. This was probably deliberate, since according to classical authors the Egyptians believed that there were no male vultures (the vulture being the secondary form of Nekhbet, see above).[65] The Great Wild Cow would thus be the virgin mother of the reborn king.

The second cow-goddess is Hathor. The Pyramid Texts say little about her, but she is said to support the Eye of Re on her horns,[66] and is named as mother of the reborn king in Utterance 303.[67] From the earliest times, she was depicted with the ears and horns of a cow (see figure 47), while in later times she was visualised as a cow emerging from the mountain of the west (see figure 48). Hathor was the mother of Horus the falcon-god and of Ihy the sistrum-player. In regard to the former, the texts indicate that the 'mansion of Horus', which her name embodied, signified the womb of the mother cosmos which gave birth to the sky – hence the sky too was called 'mansion of Horus'. Although her conception of Horus and Ihy is sometimes attributed to a union with a male god, it is probable that Hathor was originally the virgin mother of the world.

The third cow-goddess is Nut who is described in the Pyramid Texts as 'the long-horned one (or long-haired one), with pendulous breast'.[68] In later times, she was depicted as the cow of the sky, standing upon the

Figure 47.
HATHOR WITH THE EARS AND HORNS OF A COW.
One side of the Narmer palette. Note also the image of the king as a bull charging against a city's walls (lowermost register).

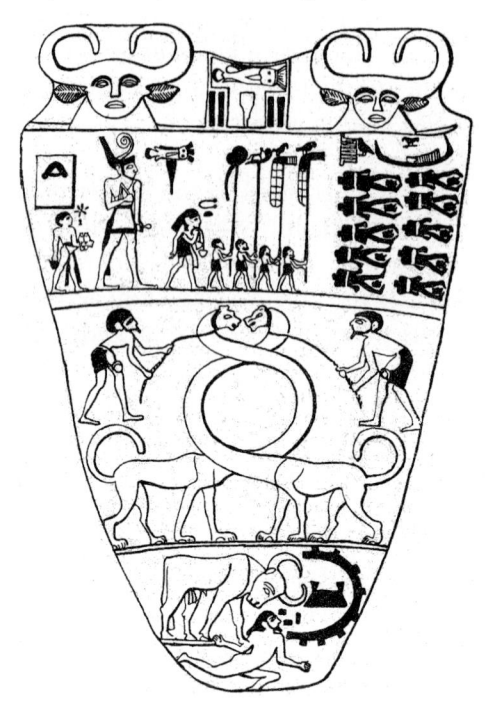

earth, supported by Shu and his air-gods (see figure 8 in chapter two). In the Book of the Heavenly Cow (late-18th dynasty), Nut is turned into the cow of the sky by Re, who ascends on her back and 'unites' with her.[69] Surprisingly, Re is not depicted in this myth as a bull, as one might expect, but as an old man, an ageing ruler, who abdicates his throne on the earth. As for Nut, the evidence discussed in earlier chapters suggests that she was originally a mother cosmos who emerged from the womb of the former cosmos to become the sky of the new.

The fourth cow-goddess in the Pyramid Texts is Mehet-weret, whose name is determined several times by the sign of a cow.[70] The texts do not provide her with the attributes of a cow, but rather depict her as the great flood of the sky, which was indeed the literal meaning of her name.

The cow-goddess could also take the form of a woman. Thus Hathor combined her cow features with a woman's face (figure 47), while in the Pyramid Texts Nut is depicted with arms that embrace the whole earth, hands that reach down to the earth, and thighs that enclose the 'island of earth'.[71]

Figure 48.
HATHOR AS A COW EMERGES FROM THE MOUNTAIN OF THE WEST.
A scene from the Book of the Dead, Spell 186.

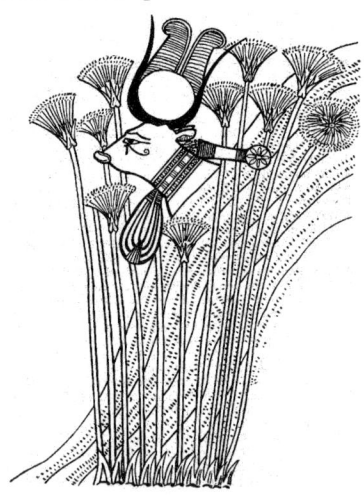

This fluid symbolism would account for the remarkable claim that the reborn king was fathered by the Great Wild Bull upon 'the great maiden who dwells in Heliopolis', who is elsewhere described as 'the pregnant woman in Heliopolis'.[72] Obviously this was an allegory, not a historical record of human sexual perversion.

Geb, the Bull of the Sky

I have argued that the cosmos was personified as a bull, who broke out of the netherworld and expanded into the sky, and there is some indication that it was separately depicted as a cow, who emerged from the womb of the old cosmos and expanded into the sky of the new. The bull may thus be regarded as a representation of the creator-god, while the cow may be regarded as a representation of the creator-goddess, the virgin mother of the world.

Occasionally, this myth was rendered dualistically as the union of the bull and the cow, their offspring the calf signifying the birth of the new cosmos and the power inherent in it.

Perhaps the oldest example of this idea is the myth of Geb and Nut. In the Pyramid Texts, Geb is called 'the Bull of Nut',[73] while Nut, as we have seen, is 'the long-horned one (or long-haired one), with pendulous breast'. Geb unites with Nut, causing the goddess in her name of 'Sky' to conceive and bear the stars, including the king as an imperishable star.[74] The reborn king, the son of Geb and Nut, is described as 'a calf of gold born of the sky'.[75] In a separate myth, Nut bears Re,[76] who in a hymn of New Kingdom times is described as a calf borne by the great flood (the cow-goddess Mehet-weret) and suckled by Nut.[77]

The union of Geb and Nut is described in rather guarded terms. In the Pyramid Texts, we have but a sole statement in which the deceased king, or perhaps Shu, states:

> I have made you [Nut] fruitful (?) by means of Geb in your name of 'Sky' (*pet*), for I have joined the entire land to you everywhere. [Variant: Geb has joined the entire land to you everywhere].[78]

This is a difficult passage, partly because the word *pnd* is of uncertain meaning, but also because the second clause is ambiguous. In what sense is the entire land joined to Nut? One possibility is that Shu has joined the earth and sky by means of his atmosphere. However, in other versions of the spell it is Geb who makes this statement. Since it is the *entire* earth that is joined to Nut, the explanation must be that the union took place in the primeval cosmos, at the time when earth and sky were one, prior to Nut's lifting into the sky.[79] Geb would therefore impregnate Nut (this seems to be the general drift of the first clause) by joining his land to her waters, whereupon she would evolve into the sky, and in due course give birth to the stars. Or to put it more simply, the sky was once united with the earth and their commingling made the future sky fruitful.

But the myth is not so straightforward, for in the Coffin Texts it is suggested that Geb married Nut *after* she had been lifted to become the sky.[80] It would therefore appear that Geb *went up to the sky* to complete his union with Nut – an idea that is corroborated in the Pyramid Texts by several appearances of the earth-god in the sky (much to the chagrin of Egyptologists, who would rather he reposed on the earth!).[81] We shall consider the significance of this idea later in this chapter.

The texts do not explain how Geb finished his business with Nut in the sky. However, we can reconstruct the myth from the king's re-enactment in the Pyramid Texts, where he is reborn as Osiris, the son of Geb and Nut.

The story begins with the king's conception in the womb of Nut, in her role as mother cosmos. In three related spells, Utterances 325, 479, and 563, we read:

> I am pure, I take to myself my iron bones, I stretch out for myself my imperishable limbs which are in the womb of my mother Nut.[82]

> O Re, make the womb of Nut pregnant with the seed of the spirit which is in her.[83]

> Pressure is in your womb, O Nut, through the seed of the god which is in you. It is I who am that seed of the god which is in you.[84]

In each of these spells, the king is then taken into the sky, as if to suggest his emergence from the womb. He is uplifted by two obscure gods Hpat and Hnny (joined on one occasion by a third god Zmnnu), who appear nowhere else in the Pyramid Texts. The role of Hpat, rather interestingly, is to press on the womb of the sky (*pet*):

> O Hpat, press on the womb of the sky with the power of the seed of the god which is in it. Behold me – I am that seed of the god which is in it. O Hpat, Hnny, Zmnnu, take me that I may dwell among you.[85]

The curious thing about these passages is that the king appears first as a seed that makes Nut conceive in the netherworld,[86] and second as a seed that makes Nut conceive in the sky. Of course, since Nut is evolving into the sky, it may be argued that there is just one conception here, which is an ongoing process.

Having understood this point, we may now consider the many diverse spells in which the king goes forth into the sky as the owner of phallus and seed, much in the manner of a young bull. In the Pyramid Texts, for example:

> I am the Great Wild Bull who went forth as Khenti-amentiu. I am the flowing fluid [i.e. semen]. I have issued from the creating of the waters...[87]

And in the Coffin Texts:

> I am this bull who is over his testicles, who went forth from Heliopolis.[88]

> I shine in the sunrise, I have come into being as the seed of the Bull of the West.[89]

> My phallus is Babi... seed is in my mouth... I am one who ejaculates when he knits together; I ejaculate as that one and this one.[90]

> I am primeval, my phallus is primeval, my seed is that of the Bull of the Hnmmt... I have travelled to Osiris and his *ka*, and he has given me... his seed that I may copulate with it... My phallus is that of Min.[91]

> I am this great soul of Osiris whom the gods commanded to copulate with him... I have remade Osiris from the efflux which was in his flesh, from the seed which issued from his phallus at the going out into the day, that he might copulate with it.[92]

The king thus enters the sky as a bull equipped with mighty phallus, and pours his seed into the womb of his own mother Nut. The sky-goddess then conceives and gives birth to the king, usually as a star. It would thus seem that the king is born twice – once from the old womb, and once in the new womb. However, this is but a continuation of the same process, as evidenced by the fact that the king splits open the womb of his mother but also splits open his place in the sky:

> (O king), may you split open your place in the sky among the stars of the sky, for you are the unique star (*sba-wati*)...[93]

This splitting open of the cosmos is at the same time a birth and an act of copulation. Seen from one perspective, the mother gives birth to her son from her vagina. But seen from another perspective, the son splits open the vagina of his mother and pours his semen into her expanding womb – the sky.

This brings us to the mystery of the *ka-mut.ef*.

Ka-mut.ef, the Bull of the Mother

After the city Thebes and its creator-god Amun rose to prominence *c.* 2000 BC, Egyptian scribes began to mention an object called *ka-mut.ef*, which was kept in the small temple of Medinet Habu (opposite the site of modern Luxor).[94] This sacred object, whose name meant literally 'bull of the mother', was associated with Amun, Min, and Horus, each of whom was revered as a god who had incarnated himself as a bull in the womb of his mother.

Amun was often given the epithet *ka-mut.ef*, and its exact meaning can be seen in the text which describes him as:

> *Ka-mut.ef* ('bull of the mother') – the one who rejoices in the cow, the husband who impregnates with the phallus.[95]

Min was a very ancient fertility-god, famed for the size of his phallus and the power of his seed. Although he was depicted as an ithyphallic man, his cult involved a white bull, to which offerings of grain were made in the annual harvest festival.[96] Min was the *ka-mut.ef* more than any other god.[97] Again, the literal meaning of the term is apparent from a dramatic text recited by the priest at the harvest festival:

> Hail to you Min, who impregnates his mother! How mysterious is that which you have done to her in the darkness.[98]

The third god associated with the *ka-mut.ef* was Horus.[99] In his case, he was said to have violently raped his mother Isis:

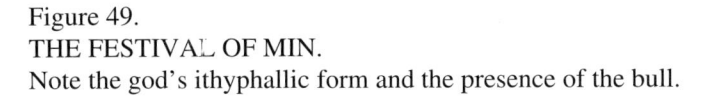

Figure 49.
THE FESTIVAL OF MIN.
Note the god's ithyphallic form and the presence of the bull.

Behold, Horus violates his mother![100]

The heart of Horus united with his mother Isis when he violated her and turned his heart toward her.[101]

Here, the erection of the phallus is substituted, to more romantic effect, by the expansion, or leaping, of the heart.[102]

What is the meaning of this? To scholars, the term *ka-mut.ef*, 'bull of the mother', signifies immortality, as witnessed in the god's mysterious ability to conceive himself in the womb of his mother.[103] This is correct in so far as it goes. However, we have seen that this is in fact an allegory for the rebirth of the cosmos – the expansion of the old cosmos into the new.

How interesting then that *ka-mut.ef* should turn out to be not only an epithet of power but also an actual object of power – the sacred relic of Amun, Min, and Horus which was worshipped in the temple at Medinet Habu.

The texts indeed refer to the *ka-mut.ef* as if it were a physical object. In the myth of *Isis and Re*, Re claims to have made the *ka-mut.ef*,[104] while in the eightieth chapter of the Great Hymn, Amun is said to have lifted it into the sky at the time of creation:

You [Amun] developed yourself into Ta-tenen, in order to cause the Primeval Ones to be born from your original primeval state. Your beauty was raised aloft as *ka-mut.ef* and you distanced yourself in the sky, as the one established in the sun...[105]

242   THE MIDNIGHT SUN

The impression given in this passage is that Amun ejected the *ka-mut.ef* object from the rising primeval earth (Ta-tenen). This fits the scenario of the iron being ejected from the earth at the time of creation, as discussed in chapter ten.

It is surely no coincidence, therefore, that studies of the cult of the *ka-mut.ef* at Thebes have concluded that it was almost certainly a small iron meteorite.[106]

These same studies have also suggested that Min – the chief god of the *ka-mut.ef* and a popular fertility-god – was a meteorite-god. According to G.A. Wainwright, Min's symbol ⇌, which resembles a double-arrow, was the sign of the thunderbolt, which in ancient times was synonymous with the meteorite.[107] The aforementioned scholar notes that this sign was used to write the name Letopolis, 'Thunderbolt City', and that an archaic form of it was used in the Pyramid Texts to describe the king being cast into the sky as a thunderbolt.[108] It would appear from this research that Min was no ordinary fertility-god, as has been supposed, but a creator-god whose erect phallus symbolised the insemination of the sky.

The *ka-mut.ef* object would therefore have signified the seed of Min – and possibly the semen of the bull.

Atum and the Benben

The bull, the phallus, and the meteorite come together again in one of Egypt's most famous creation myths, that of Atum and the *benben* stone of Heliopolis. We are now in a position to make a detailed interpretation of this story.

The myth is recorded in Utterances 527 and 600 of the Pyramid Texts, as follows:

> Atum is the one who came into being, who masturbated in Heliopolis. He took his phallus in his grasp that he might create orgasm by means of it, and so were born the twins Shu and Tefnut.[109]

> O Atum-Kheprer, you became the high hill (*qay qaa*); you rose up as the *benben* stone (*bnbn*) in the mansion of the *benu*-bird (*hwt benu*) in Heliopolis. You sneezed out Shu, you spat out Tefnut, and you set your arms about them as the embrace of *ka*, that your *ka* might be in them.[110]

The orthodox interpretation of this myth, derived in the early days of Egyptology, is that the high hill and the *benben* stone are parallel terms for the primeval mound, i.e. the risen earth. Scholars have taken it – and continue to take it – as a simple statement that Atum created the earth at the same time as he created the atmosphere and the sky – symbolised by Shu and Tefnut respectively. The masturbation of the phallus is thought to be a device for proclaiming the singularity of the creator-god. Beyond this, no deeper significance is seen.

The myth is unusual in that it relates the creation by Atum directly to a temple and a cult object, namely the mansion of the phoenix (*bnu*-bird) in Heliopolis and the *benben* stone that was enshrined therein. Neither the temple nor the stone have survived. However, it is believed that the temple contained an open courtyard in which the stone was erected upon a primitive stone pillar, while hieroglyphic references suggest that the stone itself had a conical shape. An artist's reconstruction of the temple and its *benben* stone is shown in figure 50.

What exactly was the *benben* stone? On the grounds of its high status and conical shape, several scholars have identified it as an iron meteorite (some irons acquire a conical shape while being heated as they enter the earth's atmosphere).[111] Unfortunately, the texts neither confirm nor deny that the *benben* was made of iron (*bja*), nor indeed any other substance. It is possible that the stone of historical times was a replica of an iron meteorite that rusted and fell to pieces during the pre-dynastic era.

Speculation aside, what is important is to ascertain the symbolism of the stone. Here, some Egyptologists have opined that the *benben* was a

Figure 50.
THE TEMPLE OF THE BENBEN IN HELIOPOLIS.
The drawing is a reconstruction of how the temple may have looked during the early dynastic period.

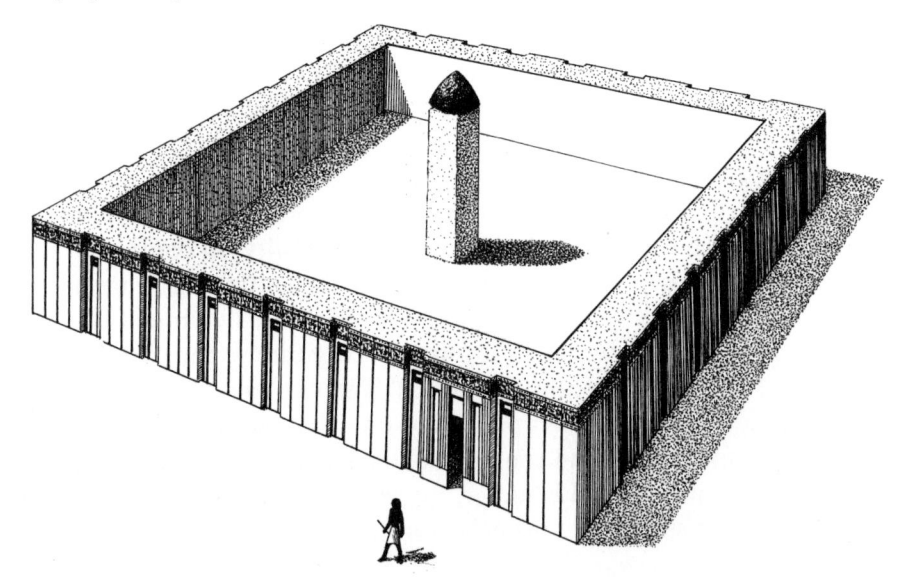

'sun-stone', in accordance with their belief that the Egyptians practised a sun cult and that the obelisk was a solar symbol (obelisks are thought to have derived from the *benben* pillar; their tips were called *benbenet* in honour of the *benben*).[112] Others meanwhile have argued that the stone symbolised the primeval mound, i.e. the earth, which the sun encircled.[113] And yet others, on the assumption that the *benben* was a meteorite, have suggested that it symbolised a 'fallen star'.[114]

All of this is to overlook the obvious phallic symbolism of the *benben* and its pillar, which Henri Frankfort highlighted in 1948:

> The pyramidion on top of the obelisk is called *bnbnt*, and the *bnbn* stone had originated as a drop of seed of Atum or of a bull (The evidence that the *benben* stone was viewed as solidified seed of Atum is conclusive...); hence it is likely that the obelisk did not serve merely as an impressive support for the stylized *benben* stone which formed its tip but that it was originally a phallic symbol at Heliopolis, the 'pillar city'.[115]

Frankfort went on to emphasise the symbolic association of the pillar and the bull.[116] There are several striking examples in the Pyramid Texts: in Utterance 254, the king is described as 'the Pillar of the Stars... the Pillar of Kenzet, the bull of the sky' and 'the eye-painted pillar, the bull of the sky';[117] in Utterance 436, the ferryman of the netherworld is called 'Great Bull, the Pillar of the Serpent Nome' (the word 'pillar' is written with an obelisk sign);[118] and in Utterance 515, the 'two obelisks of Re' include a bull's head in the writing of their name.[119] Frankfort also pointed out that a bull, Mnevis, was worshipped at Heliopolis, and that the pillar after which that city was named was portrayed with the head of a bull in the festival hall of Osorkon II (see figure 51).[120] All these associations serve to underline the phallic symbolism of the pillar, since the bull was the owner of the phallus *par excellence*.

Egyptology has been terribly slow to embrace this idea. Some writers acknowledge that the *benben* stone may have represented the 'solidified seed of Atum', but they report it only as a possibility, in contrast to the certainty expressed by Frankfort.[121] As for the theory that the pillar of the *benben* was a phallic symbol – a point on which the Pyramid Texts are suggestive, if not decisive – this is reported only rarely, and even then in the context of creation by the sun-god.[122] The vast majority of scholars simply assert that the *benben* pillar and its derivative the obelisk were symbols of sun worship, in keeping with their assumptions that Egyptian religion was a sun cult and Kheprer, Re, and Atum forms of the sun-god – a convenient if shortsighted conclusion.

Figure 51.
THE PILLAR OF HELIOPOLIS,
SURMOUNTED BY THE HEAD
OF A BULL.

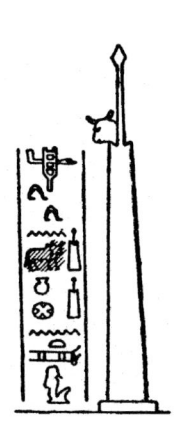

In search of an explanation for this shocking oversight, we need look no further than the sheer discomfort and embarrassment felt by scholars at the thought that the defining landmarks of this great civilisation might convey phallic imagery (for the pyramids too are linked symbolically to the *benben* and the obelisk). To write openly of this phallic symbolism would be to jeopardise the standing of ancient Egypt in the eyes of the modern world. Hence even Frankfort felt moved to relegate his insights, for the most part, to the small print footnotes at the end of his book.

That the *benben* was the semen of Atum is proved by the etymology of the words *bn* and *bnbn*, which are frequently used of sexual outflows,[123] together with an inscription in the temple of Khons at Karnak, which describes how seed flowed out from the creator-god at the beginning of time. I have inserted the original terms in brackets in order to convey the word puns that were so beloved by the Egyptians:

> Amun-Re is the god who begot (*bnn*) a place (*bu*) in the primeval ocean, when seed (*bnnt*) flowed out (*bnbn*) the first time... it flowed out (*bnbn*) under him as is usual, in its name of 'Seed' (*bnnt*).[124]

The image here might well be that of a bull, for both Amun and Re could take the form of a bull, and that animal was indeed said to be 'over' its testicles, consistent with the idea that the semen flowed out 'under' the god. Although the text is late, it provides a convincing etymology for the *benben* stone, namely 'the stone which flowed out', and confirms my hypothesis that the iron of creation flowed out from the *nun*.

What happened to this *bnbn*-seed once it had flowed out from Amun-Re? According to the inscription, it was used to create a *bu*-place in the primeval ocean – almost certainly a reference to the primeval mound that emerged from the abyss. This corroborates the idea that the mound was the iron throne (see chapter ten), and also encourages the belief that the *benben* stone symbolised the mound. But the latter is not necessarily the case, for the geocentric expansion hypothesis would suggest that the iron *continued to flow upwards* into the formative sky. Here, the name of the temple in which the inscription is found may be entered into evidence. It was Bnnt, i.e. 'Seed', a name which implies an identity between the seed of the god and the temple in its entirety.[125] Since the Egyptian temple stood *on* the primeval mound, and since its roof symbolised the sky (see chapter fifteen), it may be concluded that the *bnnt*-seed flowed (*bnbn*) all the way up from the *nun* to the surface of the sky.

The fact that the *benben* stone was set upon a tall pillar, as if to mingle with the sky, provides a clear-cut indication that the geocentric theory is correct, and that primeval materials of stone or *bja* were ejected from the earth and *nun* at the time of creation. The pillar freezes the moment of cosmic expansion in stone. We should envisage it rising up into the sky, its apex having split open the earth like the sharp horn of the young bull splitting open the womb of its mother, or the erect phallus of the young bull penetrating the vagina of its mother. It represents the phallus of the creator-god ejaculating his semen into the womb of the sky-goddess who is being simultaneously lifted by the pressure of the air. At its apex, the *benben* stone signifies the seed of creation by which the sky will be made to conceive and bear the sun, the moon, and the stars.[126] Meanwhile, the pillar's base presses down into the netherworld, subjugating the chaos-gods who threaten the creation.[127] It is the axis of the cosmos, spanning all three realms of *duat*, earth, and sky.

The High Hill

A corollary of the foregoing interpretation is that the term 'high hill' (*qay qaa*) may likewise describe the expulsion of primeval elements into the sky. This thought is suggested by the parallel between the high hill and the *benben* in Utterance 600:

> O Atum-Kheprer, you became the high hill (*qay qaa*); you rose up as the *benben* stone (*bnbn*) in the mansion of the *benu*-bird (*hwt benu*) in Heliopolis.

It has always been assumed that this high hill, *qay qaa*, was identical to the primeval mound, known variously as *khay*, *qay*, *qaa*, or *iat*, or the island of creation, *iw*, i.e. the risen earth. However, while the latter terms may be identified unequivocally with the earth (for example in the epithets of cities that were microcosms of the risen mound),[128] the exact significance of the term *qay qaa* is altogether uncertain, and there are tantalising hints in the texts that it might refer to a landform distinct from the completed earth (*ta*, Geb, *khay*, *qay*, *qaa*, *iat*, *iw*), and yet somehow related to its emergence from the abyss.[129]

Such is the elusive nature of the *qay qaa* that it is tempting to regard it as a transient phenomenon, i.e. a landmass that existed temporarily while the cosmos was in the process of creation. The repeated emphasis on its height (it was both *qay* and *qaa*) might therefore allude to it being raised above the level of the primeval mound, as with the *benben* stone per our earlier discussion. Intuitively, the completed earth has the appearance of a low, flat mound, rather than a high mound; it is high in the sense that it has been raised from the abyss, but it doesn't warrant the description 'high high'.

A possible criticism of this theory is that the primeval mound was said to have issued from Atum and Kheprer, both of whom were described as becoming high on the height. In Utterances 222 and 587 of the Pyramid Texts, we read:

> Stand upon it, this earth which issued from Atum, this spittle which issued from Kheprer.[130]

> Hail to you, Atum! Hail to you, Kheprer, self-creating! May you be high (*qay*) in this your name of 'Height' (*qaa*). May you come into being in this your name of 'Kheprer'.[131]

Unfortunately, these passages appear in separate contexts, and the second statement is ambiguous in any case. But they do raise the possibility that the high hill was a term for the earth, in which case it would not parallel the *benben* stone in Utterance 600, but complement it: Atum-Kheprer might rise initially as the high hill and then rise *further* in the form of the *benben*.

On the other hand, the Coffin Texts seem to place the high hill in the sky, or at least in the *akhet* which was the birthplace of the sky. In Spell 343, the deceased is told:

> May you join land to land at the ramp (?) of the Thinite district. You shall ascend to the top of the high hill that you may hear the weary (?) voice in the eastern gate.[132]

The meaning of this passage is elucidated in Spell 344, where the eastern gate is identified as the gate of the sky, and the voice is identified as the noise of the flood.[133] Intriguingly, this spell substitutes the high hill with 'the hill of the wind'.

Proof of this hypothesis would require a comprehensive survey of all known incidences of the term *qay qaa* and the other words for the earth-hill – a task beyond the scope of this present study. In the meantime, the plausibility of the interpretation – of the *benben* stone if not necessarily the high hill – may be established by examining the myths of the earth-god Geb.

Earlier, I mentioned that the authors of the Pyramid Texts placed Geb in the sky, and that the authors of the Coffin Texts had Geb go up to the sky to complete his conjugations with Nut. Why would the earth-god be present in the sky? One possibility, which is suggested by the body-soul duality of the creator-god, is that *the spirit* of Geb ascended to the sky. However, as tempting as this idea might be, Utterance 486 suggests that *the body* of Geb ascended to the sky:

> Hail to you, you waters which Shu brought, which the two sources lifted up, in which Geb bathed his limbs![134]

It must be emphasised that the waters in this spell do not belong to the earth, as some scholars have supposed,[135] for Shu is the god who lifts the waters and thus creates the sky. The meaning must be that the limbs of the earth-god (part but not all of his terrestrial body) are raised into the sky in the waters of the flood, in the same way that the iron bones of the king are elsewhere spiritualized to become the imperishable stars.

This is a controversial interpretation, but it does find corroboration in an address to Nun in Utterance 576:

> O Nun, raise the king's arm to the sky that he may support the earth which he has given to you.[136]

This may well be a decisive statement. Since Nun was the personification of the celestial ocean, which was extracted from the primeval waters (see chapter six), the intention here seems to be that the king has performed a parallel extraction of land from the primeval earth – land which he will now support in the sky. It is difficult to imagine any other explanation for this passage, the significance which has hitherto been overlooked.

As if this were not enough, a late myth informs us that Geb raped his mother Tefnut in the palace at Memphis at a time of great strife, shortly after Shu had ascended to the sky.[137] The violent, sexual nature of this assault is reminiscent of the rapes perpetrated by the *ka-mut.ef* gods Min and Horus upon their respective mothers, and furthermore calls to mind Geb's epithet in the Pyramid Texts – 'the Bull of Nut'. It would therefore appear that Geb indeed ascended to the sky and penetrated Tefnut and Nut with a material seed ejaculated from the earth, of similar form to the *benben* stone of Heliopolis.

This brings us neatly to the third leg of the Atum creation myth – the ejaculation of Shu and Tefnut.

Figure 52.
GEB SHOWN ITHYPHALLIC BENEATH NUT.

The Emission of Shu and Tefnut

When Atum rose up as the high hill and the *benben* stone in Heliopolis, he sneezed out Shu and spat out Tefnut; and when he masturbated his phallus to the point of orgasm in that 'Pillar City', he ejaculated Shu and Tefnut. Again, there is evidence to suggest that this ejaculation may have involved an emission of materials from the earth.

We must first address the perceived discrepancy in the origins of Shu and Tefnut. As discussed in chapter three, Atum supposedly created them by a sneeze of his mouth, and yet also by an ejaculation from his phallus (and furthermore it was alleged that Shu had been exhaled from Atum's nose). To the modern mind, these myths are baldly inconsistent. And yet to the Egyptians they represented parallel statements of mythical truth that could be blended seamlessly together, for example in the claims that Atum ejaculated semen from his mouth, and that Atum sneezed Shu from his mouth even as he masturbated with his hand.

The geocentric expansion theory enables us to square these supposedly contradictory statements. As explained in chapter eight, the mouth of the creator-god signified the mouth of the primeval cosmos, which was split open at the time of creation. This idea was rendered also by the vagina of the mother cosmos, which was likewise split open to allow the birth of the new cosmos. It is this latter allegory which gives rise to the myth of the erecting phallus.

As we have seen in this chapter, creation is initiated by a seed in the womb of the mother-goddess (e.g. Nut) which causes her to conceive and open her womb. At this point, the cosmic womb expands to the limits of the new cosmos and the seed flows outwards into it. This penetration of the vagina and raising of the seed into the expanding womb is portrayed as the creator-god erecting his phallus and ejaculating into his mother – hence the idea of *ka-mut.ef*, 'the bull of the mother'.

The phallus of Atum is a variant of this allegory, necessarily so since the priests of his cult wished to proclaim him as a sole creator-god who acted alone. He had no partner, and he certainly had no mother. Hence he masturbated his phallus. On account of this occultation of the basic story, the myth of creation via Atum's phallus has become difficult to interpret in isolation from the rest of Egyptian mythology.

Seen in this light, it is understandable that Atum's semen was sneezed and spat from his mouth, as well as ejaculated from his phallus. After all, the mouth and the phallus were but different facets of the same theory of creation, portrayed allegorically. The mouth of the earth must be opened for the phallus of the earth to ejaculate into the sky. (The mouth of Atum was perhaps borrowed from the mouth of Geb – see chapter four.) Thus were Shu and Tefnut born.

So, to the sixty-four million dollar question: what did Shu and Tefnut signify?

According to scholars, Shu represented air and Tefnut moisture, or better said *the expulsion of* air and moisture. The emission of Shu thus created the atmosphere, while the emission of Tefnut perhaps created the sky-ocean. This interpretation is plausible, and not inconsistent with the geocentric theory. If we suppose that Atum himself personified the body of the old cosmos, then it would indeed make sense that he ejaculated air and water to create the new cosmos around him. That he also expelled material elements such as the high hill and the *benben* stone is beside the point, since these elements required to be lifted into the sky by the winds of the air and the flood of the water.

But there was more to Shu than just air. In Spell 80 of the Coffin Texts, Shu states:

> My garment is the air of life, which emerged for it behind me, from the mouth of Atum, and opens the winds on my path. I am the one who made the sky light after the darkness. My skin is the pressure of the wind, which emerged behind me from the mouth of Atum. My efflux is the storm-cloud of the sky; my sweat is hail-storm and half-darkness.[138]

In this spell, the importance of Tefnut is marginalized and Shu assumes the role of sole creator-god, the manifestation of Atum. In addition to the air of the wind, he also personifies the storm of creation – a flood that may have included material elements as well as water.

Significantly, Shu is said to have originated in a cataclysm. In Spell

77, he exclaims:

> I am this soul of Shu which is the first one of the fiery blast which Atum kindled with his own hand. He created orgasm and semen fell from his mouth. He spat me out as Shu together with Tefnut.[139]

Here, the masturbatory climax of Atum is equated with a fiery cataclysm, which brings Shu and Tefnut into existence. Scholars would argue that this is a lightning bolt, and in this assumption they would probably be correct. However, as Wainwright has shown, the thunderbolt in ancient Egypt was synonymous with the meteorite, as in the example of Min and the *ka-mut.ef* cult object of Thebes. It is therefore conceivable that the fiery blast from the phallus of Atum signified an eruption of molten iron from the earth (witness the *benben* stone), and that this iron was present in the storm-cloud and 'hail-storm' of Shu.

The fiery blast is seen also in the opening of the mouth. In Utterance 319 of the Pyramid Texts, we read:

> The king is the bull with radiance in the midst of his Eye, the king's mouth is hale through the fiery blast...[140]

There is quite possibly an allusion here to the 'adze of iron' (*mskhtiu m bja*) which split open the king's mouth, as well as the mouths of Osiris and the gods. Interestingly, in later times, it was Shu who performed the latter task with his harpoon made of iron. Did Shu thus represent the iron rising out of the earth, as well as the air and the water?

A final clue to the nature of Shu is found in Utterance 222, where the king re-enacts the creation by Atum. He comes into being with Atum in the abyss, rises on high with him (but not 'high high'), and then reaches the sky via the bones of Shu:

> May you come into being with your father Atum, may you go up on high with your father Atum... Go up, open your way by means of the bones of Shu.[141]

This is the only reference to Shu's bones. What could they possibly have been? Might they be equivalent to the king's bones, which are repeatedly said to be made of iron?

In summary, the nature of Shu seems to vary from myth to myth. In the Pyramid Texts, he is portrayed as the counterpart of Tefnut – the air to her water, or the sun to her moon. Then later, in the Coffin Texts, he becomes a virtual double of Atum, a sole creator in his own right, who encompasses within himself *all* the elements of creation – air, water, and arguably materials such as iron.

Atum's emission of Shu and Tefnut is consistent in many ways with his development into the high hill and the *benben* stone. At the heart of the myth is the idea of the god coming into being by self-development – by growing high and expanding into the universe. This feat is achieved undeniably by a cataclysm – the fiery blast – and is allegorized perfectly by the phallic orgasm, representing the earthquake and the splitting of the earth, by the ejaculation of seed, representing the ejection of matter into the cosmos, by the sneezing or spitting of seed, ditto, and moreover by the expansion of the heart, which conjures up an image of Geb loving Nut. Shu and Tefnut are on high; the hill is on high; and the *benben* is raised high.

It only remains to be seen how this night of cosmic chaos gave birth to the light of cosmic order and set the stage for the creation of man.

Chapter Eleven Summary

- The bull had chthonian characteristics, but was also linked with the stars. This was because the bull personified the primeval cosmos and its evolution into the greater cosmos.
- The sacrifice of the bull commemorated the death and rebirth of the primeval cosmos. To eat the bull was to consume the magic of the gods and thus be assured of rebirth.
- The sharp, strong horns of the bull denoted its ability to split open the primeval cosmos.
- The creator-god became the 'bull of his mother' (*ka-mut.ef*) when he penetrated her womb as it expanded into the sky. Significantly, the *ka-mut.ef* denoted a physical object – an iron meteorite.
- Geb became the 'Bull of Nut' by ejecting elements of his earth into her sky.
- The *benben* of Heliopolis commemorated the ejaculation of iron into the sky. The pillar symbolised the phallus of Atum, while the stone at the apex represented the flowing semen of Atum.
- Atum's masturbation and emission of Shu was described as a 'fiery blast' – indicative of a cataclysm.
- As an image of the creator-god, the reborn king was often described as a bull. He ascended to the sky as the seed of the bull and inseminated the womb of his own mother Nut.

CHAPTER TWELVE

THE FIERY EYE

I am the fiery Eye of Horus, who went forth causing terror, Lady of Slaughter, greatly awesome.
(Coffin Texts, Spell 316)

The reader should, by now, be familiar with the idea that the two eyes – the sun and the moon – originated from the Sole Eye, the Great Goddess, the sometime companion of the Great God. But how exactly did this act of creation take place? Might the myths describe a physical process, by which the sun and moon were caused to appear? In order to take a view on this vital question, we must go to the root of it and consider the role of the Eye.

It is impossible to review the Egyptian creation myths without coming up against the problem of the Eye. Indeed, she has made an appearance in virtually every chapter of this book so far, defying the author's wish to isolate her conveniently in a chapter of her own. It has therefore been necessary to make a number of assertions about the Eye and the eyes, all of which must now be substantiated.

To begin, it may be useful to summarise the Eye's appearances in the study thus far. I shall present these in the chronological order in which I believe they belong in the creation myth, rather than the random order in which they have occurred in the writing of this book.

The story begins with 'that fear which arose on account of the Eye of Horus'. This probably refers to the occasion when Horus put flame in his Eye and set it as a 'storm among the evildoers... a (fiery) outburst among the primeval ones' (chapter nine). In a related incident, Seth gouged the Eye and carried it off, but Horus thankfully recaptured it. The Eye thus became injured and required to be healed, or knitted back together – a job that was usually assigned to Thoth. It was at this stage, arguably, that Atum sent out the Eye from the *nun* (though he was supposed to be alone there). Related myths speak of gods issuing from the root of his Eye and shining in his Eye. Other myths speak of the Eye separating from Geb's head and being uplifted to the sky, where Atum came into being with the flames of his Eye about him (chapter six). The story comes to an end with Shu pacifying the raging Eye and extinguishing her fire (chapter nine). But in a strange postscript, the Eye shed tears upon the limbs of the creator-god, and thereby caused the birth of mankind.

We have also seen that the Eye was of pivotal importance in the rituals for the resurrection of the deceased king (chapter seven). Here, the Eye symbolised the offerings – all the produce of the earth. It (or rather she) filled the deceased king, completed, purified, strengthened and protected him, opened his mouth, and endowed him with a soul. Its ointment was said to raise the king's bones, reassemble his limbs, and gather together his flesh. Having been restored thus, the king ascended to the sky and presented the Eye to Atum, in re-enactment of the uplifting performed originally by Geb, Shu, or Horus.

The Eye in Overview

The ability of the Eye to transform itself into the two eyes of the sun and the moon has, via a system of symbolic transference, persuaded scholars that the Eye *was* the sun or *was* the moon. As I shall attempt to explain, this has led to a perverted interpretation of Egyptian myths and rituals.

The Eye of Re, for example, is misidentified as the solar eye.[1] Scholars express surprise and puzzlement that this eye could act independently of its owner, the sun-god, separating itself from him to embark on distant journeys to annihilate his cosmic enemies, the forces of chaos. This Eye of Re, placed in the king's crowns in the form of Wadjyt, the fiery cobra-goddess, is supposed, erroneously, to represent the sun.

Similarly, the Eye of Horus is misidentified as the lunar eye. Scholars thus assert that the eye of the moon was lost and recovered in the battle of Horus and Seth, and that it was the moon, presented to Osiris, which effected the resurrection of the god.[2]

As for the Eye of Atum, it, like the Eye of Re, is treated as a solar eye. In the myth of Atum sending out his Eye to find Shu and Tefnut, scholars misinterpret this as a reference to the sun.[3] The fact that it is his *Sole Eye* is cast to the wind.[4]

This is all utterly wrong. The Sole Eye existed *before* the creation, and hence cannot be the sun, which appeared as a result of creation. This is proved by Spell 331 of the Coffin Texts, where the deceased as Hathor describes her origin thus:

I am that Eye of Horus, the female messenger of the Sole Lord, the like of whom shall not be seen again. I came into being before the sky was fashioned... before the earth was released...[5]

This passage goes on to refer to Hathor searching for Shu and Tefnut, the first two phenomena of Atum's creation, thus removing any doubt that the Sole Eye, here the Eye of Horus, existed before the creation of the sky.

One of the few Egyptologists to appreciate this distinction between the Eye and the eyes was R.T. Rundle Clark. In his 1959 book *Myth and Symbol in Ancient Egypt*, he stated correctly that the creator-god initially had only one Eye, that this Eye signified the Great Goddess, that it raised a storm at the beginning of time, and that it was the source of creation of the gods and mankind.[6] Clark did not manage to unravel the mystery of what the Sole Eye signified, but he was certainly on the right track, and it is a pity that his lead has not been followed by scholars since.

The Eye may or may not be 'the key to the religion', as Clark argued,[7] but it is certainly the key to understanding the two eyes, the sun and the moon. This is because the two eyes reflected the mythology of the Sole Eye, to which they owed their origin.

In the case of the sun, the 'right eye', its fiery appearance recalled the cataclysm of creation, in which the Eye was instrumental (see later). It was therefore associated with the fiery outburst which annihilated the cosmic enemies of the creator-god. But this was mere symbolism, which was never meant to suggest that the solar eye itself had attacked these enemies. Rather, it was the Sole Eye which had set fire to the evildoers (and it did not need to detach itself from the sun-god to do so, since the sun at that time did not exist).

Figure 53.
THE RIGHT EYE, THE EYE OF RE (LEFT), AND THE LEFT EYE, THE EYE OF HORUS (RIGHT).

In the case of the moon, the 'left eye', its monthly waning and waxing recalled the disappearance and reappearance of the Eye at the time of creation. It was therefore associated with the struggle of Horus and Seth, and the death and rebirth of Osiris. But this was never meant to imply that the lunar eye itself had been stolen and ravaged by Seth. Rather, it was the Sole Eye for which the rivals had fought; and it was this Sole Eye that had effected the resurrection of Osiris.

In fairness to scholars, the texts do contain profound ambiguities. The sun, for example, was called the Eye of Re, as if it were the Goddess herself, and similarly the moon was called the Eye of Horus, as if it were the Goddess herself.[8] We should not overlook the fact, however, that Re and Horus were creator-gods and sky-gods who possessed both the sun and the moon, the two eyes. The sun was thus fairly called an eye of Re, just as the moon was fairly called an eye of Horus. In the former case, the symbolism was strengthened by the fact that 'Re' was a name for the sun disc. In the latter case, the identification was less strong, and thus the Eye of Horus could also be associated with the sun.[9]

These ambiguities can make the texts difficult to interpret. However, the exact meaning – Sole Eye or subsidiary eye – can nearly always be determined from the context of the spell. Where doubt exists, it may be best to adopt the former as the default interpretation.

The Eye of the World

In the myths of creation by Atum and Neber-djer, the Eye is portrayed as an emissary of the creator-god, an agent of creation. However, when we consider the role of the Goddess in the round (Hathor and Isis were both forms of the Eye), the Eye emerges as a creator-goddess in her own right, at least an equal partner of the creator and arguably even his superior, since it was she, with her magic power, who brought his otiose body to life.

This high status is reflected in the epithets of the Eye – 'the Sole Eye', 'the Lady of All',[10] 'the Great One',[11] 'the Great of Magic',[12] 'the Opener of Roads',[13] and 'She who Opens the Ways of the God'.[14] We should not be lulled into thinking that the 'eye' was a diminutive of the 'body' of the God. To the Egyptians, it denoted a complete being, of equivalent size to her male consort.[15]

This brings us to the crucial question of what the Sole Eye signified in the Egyptian cosmos. If my hypothesis of the creator-god is correct – that he personified the primeval cosmos in its process of death and rebirth – then the creator-goddess, if this be the Eye's identity, ought to symbolise much the same thing.

Is there any evidence for this supposition?

As we have seen, the Eye was sent out from the abyss at the beginning of time, and from this we may deduce that she was present in it, in some shape or form. Nowhere is there a clear statement that the Eye equalled 'the earth and the *nun*', i.e. the totality of the primeval cosmos. However, in Utterance 587 of the Pyramid Texts the Eye is addressed in terms which are most suggestive of such an identity. This address is appended to a short spell in which Atum is urged to become 'high high' (*qay qaa*), and therefore refers to the dawn of time when the Sole Eye is about to be sent out into the wider cosmos. It begins by praising Horus for rebuilding his Eye:

> Hail to you, Eye of Horus, which he [Horus] has restored with both his hands!... You shall obey Horus. It is he who has restored you; it is he who has built you up; it is he who has set you in order, that you may do for him everything which he says to you.[16]

The allusion here is to reknitting the Eye, which had previously lain in a state of dismemberment. We will return to this point shortly.

The address then continues, in a most revealing way, by disclosing the contents of the Eye (each line is repeated twice, hence the omissions):

> You shall lift up to him [Horus] all the waters which are in you... You shall lift up to him all the trees which are in you... You shall lift up to him the bread and beer which are in you... You shall lift up to him the offerings which are in you... You shall lift up to him everything which is in you.[17]

The Eye thus contains all the produce of the earth and – most importantly – waters which must belong to the primeval ocean. It may therefore be argued that the Eye has an identity with the original cosmos, comprising the earth and the *nun*.

The next lines of the address serve to bolster this argument:

> The doors which are on you [the Eye] stand like *Iun-mut.ef*. They will not open to the westerners; they will not open to the easterners; they will not open to the northerners; they will not open to the southerners; they will not open to those (gods) who are in the middle of the earth; but they will open to Horus. It is he who made them; it is he who erected them; it is he who saved them from every ill which Seth did to them.[18]

The Eye thus had doors, which is a defining feature of a cosmic realm, as we observed in chapter eight. Since the *akhet* and the sky have not been created at this point, the doors of the Eye must correspond to the doors of the original cosmos, or otherwise said the netherworld or *duat*.

The remainder of the address is repetitive, but it is interesting to note that the Eye is identified with the 'City' of Nut, and the king reborn as Horus claims to have restored the Eye and 'built his city'.[19] Elsewhere, the king is said to have 'built the city of the god',[20] while Osiris is said to have been felled by Seth in Nedyt, 'the great city'.[21] It is probable that the term 'city', in these contexts, was a metaphor for the primeval cosmos. To rebuild the city was to rebuild the cosmos.

In the real world of Egypt, each and every major city was regarded as a microcosm of the primeval mound, or island of creation.[22] Here, too, the Eye stakes its claim for recognition. In the New Kingdom period, the city of Thebes was equated to 'the primeval mound' but also to 'the Eye of Re',[23] while its temple complex Karnak was described thus:

> I know that Karnak is the *akhet* upon earth, the illustrious primeval hill of the first time, the sacred Eye of the Lord of All.[24]

It may thus be seen that the Eye personified not only the original cosmos – the earth and the *nun* – but also the primeval mound and the *akhet* into which that cosmos developed.

An important aspect of this identification of the Eye is the tradition of its healing and reassembly, which restored it from its prior state of injury and dismemberment. This tradition echoes the myth of Osiris, and seems to be another allegory for the establishment of order out of the physical chaos of the former world.

The healing and reassembly myth appears first in the Pyramid Texts, in passages such as the following:

> I am seeking the endangered Eye of Horus (*irt Hr suit*), I am bound for the numbering of fingers.[25]

> I have come and have brought to you this reknit Eye of Horus which was in the field of strife (*sekhet chnnu*).[26]

> O king, come, don the intact Eye of Horus which is in Weaving Town.[27]

As explained earlier, this healing of the injured Eye was symbolised in the waxing and waning of the moon, and the texts sometimes anticipate the creation of the moon by having the king bring to Horus his *left eye* in a healed condition.[28]

Appropriately, it was Thoth, a creator-god who became specialised in the moon, who healed the Eye and took it to the sky. In the Coffin Texts, the deceased states:

> I am Thoth who brings justice, who healed the sacred Eye in the House of the Double Lion.[29]

> I am Thoth... I have come that I may seek out the Eye of Horus. I have brought and examined it, and I have found it complete, fully numbered, and intact.[30]

> I restored the Eye after it had been injured on that day when the rivals fought... It was Thoth who did this with his fingers.[31]

In one spell, the injury to the Eye is described as 'bleariness' (*hati*), i.e. lack of light, or failing of vision – an image which is evocative of the waning moon.[32] But the more fundamental idea was the disassembly of the Eye, even though, as with the disassembly of Osiris, the cause of this state is left unexplained.

The reassembly of the Eye marked its rebirth (again, as with Osiris), and enabled it to go forth to 'see' via its two eyes, the sun and the moon. The icon of this reborn Eye was the *wedjat*-eye, whose name meant 'the sound Eye', 'the whole Eye', or 'the restored Eye'.[33] It was used widely in Egyptian society as a magical symbol for healing, protection, strength and foresight. It also provided the system of fractions, with each part of the eye representing a certain proportion of the whole (see figure 54). In theory, these parts added to unity, but in practice they fell slightly short – a deficiency explained by the belief that Seth had consumed a small part of the Eye.[34]

All in all, the myths of the Eye are strikingly reminiscent of the myths of Osiris, whose death and rebirth, I have argued, signified a physical crisis and recovery of the former cosmos. The reknitting of the Eye, like the assembly of Osiris, would signify the unification of the divided lands of the primeval terrestrial world.

Figure 54.
THE DIVISION OF THE EYE.

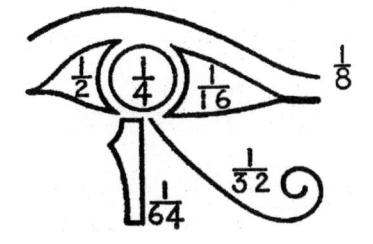

By coincidence or not, Osiris's name was written with the hieroglyphs of a throne and an eye , meaning literally 'Place of the Eye'.[35] From a creational, geocentric perspective, these signs belonged together: the throne was a metaphor for the god's seat, i.e. the risen earth; the eye signified the power of creation and rebirth immanent in the earth; and Osiris himself was the god of the death and rebirth of the earth. The name thus encapsulated the essence of Egyptian thought on the origins of life.

This interpretation also provides insights into the Eye's pivotal roles in ritual and myth. For example, the presentation of the Eye to Osiris would signify his acquisition of the powers of cosmic rebirth, while the struggle between Horus and Seth for control of the Eye would signify the danger of non-creation and the potentiality for a dark universe, devoid of light (see chapter thirteen).

We are now in a position to re-evaluate the myths of the Sole Eye and reconstruct her story from a creational, geocentric perspective.

Cataclysm in the Abyss

The most significant event in the career of the Eye was the destruction of the forces of chaos, personified by Seth and his followers. In the Pyramid Texts, Horus is made to say:

> O you hateful one, I will put flame in my Eye and it will encompass you and set storm among the doers of (evil) deeds; its (fiery) outburst (will be) among these primeval ones.[36]

There are numerous references in the Pyramid Texts to this attack upon Seth and his followers, 'the gods who make disturbance'.[37] They are said to be seized, decapitated, dismembered, and disembowelled, whereupon their hearts are presented to Osiris.[38] The Eye is mentioned only once in connection with this massacre, in the spell cited above. Elsewhere, it is Horus (perhaps using his Eye) and Thoth who annihilate the chaos-gods for Osiris.

The Eye's role in the defeat of Seth is elaborated in the Coffin Texts, where her fiery nature is emphasised. In Spell 316, she exclaims:

> I am the fiery Eye of Horus, who went forth causing terror, Lady of Slaughter, greatly awesome, who came into being in the flame of the light, to whom Re granted appearings in glory, whose children Re-Atum made enduring... My flame is behind me, the dread of me is before me, I have conquered the gods... Seth has fallen because of me... The terror of me has captured for me, the awe of me has taken

for me, there has been given to me everything in the hand of Nun.

What Re said about her: "Mighty is the fear of you, great is the dread of you, mighty is your striking-power, great is your magic in the bodies of your foes, and the hostile ones have fallen on their faces because of you. All men have been in the sleep of death because of you, and all who see you shall be afraid of you..."[39]

It is likely that the repeated references in this spell to the fear and dread of the Eye echoed the expression 'that fear which arose on account of the Eye of Horus', which is cited in the Pyramid Texts as a defining moment of the creation.[40]

Elsewhere in the Coffin Texts, the image of the fiery lady is applied to the cobra-goddess Wadjyt, who is described as 'the Great Lady of the Desert, the Lady of Flame, the Great One... who bites with her mouth... who lives on those who perish in the blast of the flame of her mouth, who rescues Re from Apep'.[41] Wadjyt was the goddess of the crown of Lower Egypt, which is described in the Pyramid Texts as 'the Fiery Serpent, the Great One, the Great of Magic', a thing which causes fear and dread.[42] By the time of the Book of the Dead, she is identified with the Eye of Re:

> I am Wadjyt, Lady of the Devouring Flame, and few approach me. *What does it mean? As for Wadjyt, Lady of the Devouring Flame, she is the Eye of Re, As for those few who approach her, it means that the confederacy of Seth are near her, because what is near her is burning.*[43]

In New Kingdom times, the Eye of Re was identified with Mut, Hathor, and Sekhmet. In a late-18th dynasty story, recorded in the Book of the Heavenly Cow, and entitled by scholars *The Destruction of Mankind,* the

Figure 55.
WADJYT AND NEKHBET, THE FIERY SERPENTS OF THE CROWNS OF LOWER AND UPPER EGYPT RESPECTIVELY.

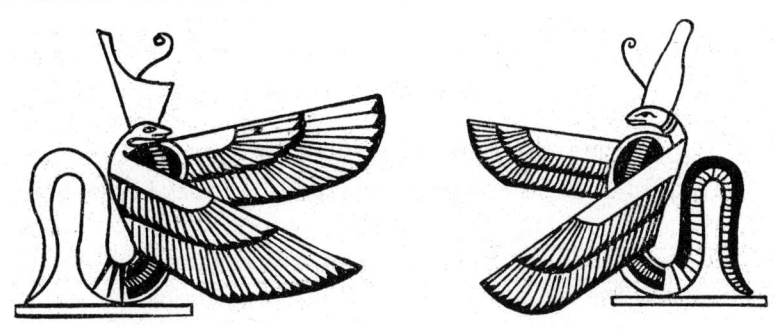

Eye in its name of Hathor is sent by Re to destroy mankind, which has risen up against him in rebellion. The Eye pursues men in the mountain lands and slaughters them mercilessly, generating a sea of blood which she then sets about drinking. But Re then creates a flood of beer in 'the meadows of the four quarters of the sky' and causes the goddess to get drunk and fall asleep. Thus the remnant of mankind is saved.[44] This story seemingly draws upon Spell 316 of the Coffin Texts, where the fiery Eye of Horus (who is also 'the companion of Re') is credited with striking down the inimical gods and casting men into 'the sleep of death'.[45]

This idea of the destruction of mankind might give the impression that the wrath of the Eye was a historical event. But this was certainly not the intent. In fact, the setting for the story is a mythical era when the sky has yet to be separated from the earth; it culminates with Re being lifted up to the sky on the back of Nut.[46] How, then, can mankind be in existence at this time? The explanation is that mankind *as we know it* did not exist then; what did exist was a mythical race of people, the inhabitants of the old world, from whom the survivors became the seeds of mankind in the new world.[47] (Hence the Greek myths of mankind being born from the womb of the earth.)[48]

All the myths of the fiery Eye are consistent with a destruction of the rebels at the beginning of time. In addition to the example just cited, the rebels are called 'the primeval ones',[49] and their rebellion is said to have occurred on 'that first day' or 'first time' (*zep tepi*).[50] The general setting of the cataclysm is the struggle between Horus and Seth which followed immediately after the death of Osiris and preceded the creation of order in the cosmos.

The ultimate test of this time line is whether or not the Eye had been sent out of *nun* at the time of its cataclysm. Where, in other words, did the cataclysm take place?

Here, scholars have been misled by the assumption that the fiery Eye represented the sun. According to their interpretation of *The Destruction of Mankind*, it was the solar eye that went forth to slaughter mankind on the mountain lands of the earth. The event is therefore dated to a post-creation epoch.

But all the evidence goes against this view. In Utterance 519 of the Pyramid Texts, the enemy-snakes are decapitated in the field of offerings – almost certainly a reference to a realm of the netherworld.[51] In Spell 284 of the Coffin Texts, the flame of Wadjyt (who later became the Eye of Re) is placed in the land of the west, the netherworld.[52] In Spell 316, the Eye of Horus claims: "The terror of me has captured for me, the awe of me has taken for me, *there has been given to me everything in the hand of Nun*", as if to suggest that her terror encompassed the primeval ocean.[53] In Spell 453, the Eye of Atum who breathes fire against Seth is called 'Mistress of the Night', as if to place her in the netherworld.[54] And in the Papyrus Salt (late-19th dynasty), Tefnut is described as 'a flame against the rebels in the earth's interior', which is self-explanatory.[55]

In a similar vein, all our sources make the netherworld the primary site of the battle of the gods and the burial place of the dead gods. In Spell 335 for example, the battlefield of the gods is defined as 'the land of the west – it was built to make the foes of the gods fight'.[56] In Spell 648, Re in his name of 'Sekhmet' has power over his foes who are in the island of fire (a microcosm of the netherworld).[57] In the Book of Gates, the mountain of the west (the netherworld) is said to contain 'the slaughter of the gods' (interestingly, this mountain is said to have slain mankind – this would be the mountain lands in which the Eye of Re destroyed mankind).[58] In *The Destruction of Mankind*, Re orders the rebels to be punished in the *duat* and 'the land of caves'.[59] And in the Edfu texts, the submerged island of creation is given the names 'island of trampling', 'island of combat', and 'fiery place of the ancestors'.[60]

These represent but a small selection of passages, drawn from a large number of sources spread over two thousand years, all of which reiterate the same idea from different perspectives. They demonstrate clearly that the Eye did not travel (for example, by detaching itself from the sun-god) in order to destroy the rebels. Rather, it released fire within the place which it itself personified, i.e. the primeval cosmos. The architect of the cataclysm was thus the Sole Eye, and the time of the cataclysm was the dawn of creation.

The Eye Flames Up

We may now examine the myths pertaining to the Eye's expansion into the greater cosmos, which are preserved in the deceased's re-enactment of creation, as described in the Pyramid Texts and Coffin Texts. As we shall see, this event too coincided with a cataclysm.

The rebirth of the Eye was initiated by its healing, or assembly, which seemingly occurred in 'the field of strife' (see earlier). The texts pick up the story when the healed Eye is delivered to the ferryman of the winding waterway, who takes it on his boat to the east side of the sky.[61] Utterance 359 informs us that Seth attacked the Eye here, in the region just beneath the eastern horizon.[62] The Eye fell, but managed to save itself by leaping up onto the wing of Thoth (who, like the ferryman, had reached the east by traversing the netherworld).[63] Thoth's task in the Pyramid Texts is to

Figure 56.
THE EYE IS SAVED AND UPLIFTED BY HORUS AND THOTH.

protect the Eye and take it to the sky (the myth of him healing it does not appear until the Coffin Texts, perhaps inspired by his role in assembling Osiris).[64] This is described in Utterance 524:

> I am Thoth who protects you [the Eye], I am not Seth who carried it off... My wing-feathers are those of Thoth. Geb causes me to fly up to the sky that I might take the Eye of Horus to him... Atum summons me to the sky, and I take the Eye of Horus to him.[65]

Thoth also takes the Eye to the sky in Utterance 478, but here his wings are supplemented by the erection of a ladder:

> The Eye of Horus gleams (?) upon the wing of Thoth on the left-hand side of the ladder of the god. O men, a serpent is bound for the sky, for I am the Eye of Horus... I take my departure as the Eye of Horus... I ascend to the sky upon the ladder of the god...[66]

In this spell, the ladder belongs to Seth, 'the Lord of the Ladder', who is said to have been begotten by Geb.[67] A direct ascent from the earth is therefore implied. Likewise, the wing of Thoth suggests a direct ascent as a bird upon the air (as opposed to an indirect ascent by boat upon the waters in the east side of the sky). The spell also goes on to state that the Eye was given to Horus in the presence of his father Geb.[68] It is thus made clear that the Eye was taken to the sky from the earth.[69]

In keeping with this geocentric principle, the Eye was also uplifted by Geb and Shu.

The uplifting by Geb is described in Utterance 689:

> Geb has raised on high the potent (?) Eye of Horus, which is on the hands of his great spirits...[70]

Elsewhere, the Eye is said to go forth from Geb's head, to manifest itself as the dual crowns of Upper and Lower Egypt.[71]

The uplifting by Shu is described in the same spell, Utterance 689:

> O Shu, supporter of Nut, raise the Eye of Horus to the sky, to the stars of the sky...[72]

Shu is also named in Spell 76 of the Coffin Texts as the one who made it possible for the Eye to provide light where there was darkness.[73]

The Shu passage quoted above is reminiscent of Utterance 434, where Shu lifts up Nut as mother to a thousand stars. Might there be a parallel here between Nut and the Eye? Elsewhere in the Pyramid Texts, the Eye is indeed identified with Nut in their shared name of 'City' (see earlier). Moreover, both Nut and the Eye are said to have children. The children of Nut (of whom Osiris is the eldest) are said to be gathered together by her in Heliopolis,[74] and by coincidence or not this happens to be the place where the injured Eye was found and reassembled.[75] As for the children of the Eye, they feature twice in the Coffin Texts as spiritualized gods:

> I [a divine falcon] am one of those gods or spirits who dwell in the light, whom Atum created from his flesh, who came into being from the root of his Eye.[76]

> I am the fiery Eye of Horus, who went forth causing terror... who came into being in the flame of the light, to whom Re granted appearances in glory, whose children Re-Atum made enduring.[77]

The meaning of this last line is that Re-Atum spiritualized the children of the Eye, i.e. made them stars. The fact that these children originated from flesh suggests that they corresponded to the dismembered limbs of the Eye (compare the origin of the gods from the creator's limbs in chapter five).

It is plausible, therefore, that the lifting of the Eye by Shu paralleled his lifting of Nut, and led to the creation of the stars. In other words, the Eye was not lifted *to* the stars in the sky; rather it was lifted *to become* the stars in the sky (see Shu passage above).

Significantly, as foreshadowed earlier, the Eye ascended amidst a fiery cataclysm. This event is not described in the Pyramid Texts (though it is probably implicit, as we shall see shortly), but it is a recurrent theme in the Coffin Texts.

In Spell 249, Thoth states:

> I have come that I may seek out the Eye of Horus; I have brought it and examined it, and I have found it complete, fully numbered and

sound. Its flame is to the sky, its breath is above and below..."[78]

In a similar vein, in Spell 946, the deceased states:

> I am the Eye of Horus, the Lady of All... I am a fire in sky and earth, and all my foes are under my flame.[79]

And in Spell 746, Atum states:

> I am Atum who came into being on the Supports of Shu, and the flames of my Eye are about me.[80]

From the first two of the above three spells, it may be deduced that the fiery cataclysm of the ascending Eye was one and the same as that which destroyed the rebels in the netherworld. The healing and assembly of the Eye, it would seem, triggered the explosion that tore apart the primeval cosmos, and effected the Eye's expansion into the greater cosmos. Hence the idea that the Eye was 'created in flame' or 'came into being in the flame of the light'.[81]

The Eye ascending in flame was symbolised by the rearing cobra, the uraeus-serpent (*iart*) . In the Pyramid Texts, the king is several times said to have gone forth as a uraeus, issuing either from Seth or from Re (in their identities as the primeval cosmos), and this event is twice linked to the Eye.

Firstly, in Utterance 478, the king exclaims:

> I am the Eye of Horus... I ascend to the sky upon the ladder of the god [Seth]. I appear as the uraeus which is on the vertex of Seth.[82]

The vertex of Seth is probably an allusion to the top of the ladder.

Secondly, in Utterance 704, it is stated:

> This king is the falcon which came forth from Re, and the uraeus which came forth from the Eye of Re.[83]

The Coffin Texts also refer to this origin of the uraeus. In Spell 313, for example, Horus states: "I created my Eye in flame... I made my Eye, a living serpent."[84]

The uraeus may be identified with the Eye of Horus and the Eye of Re, and with their respective goddesses. In the Pyramid Texts, the uraeus the Eye of Horus is named as Renenutet, the cobra-goddess. In one spell, the king says: "The flaming blast of my uraeus is that of Renenutet who is upon me."[85] It is also identified with Ikhet-the-Great.[86] In the Coffin Texts, the uraeus the Eye of Horus is named as Hathor.[87] In one spell, she is described as 'the Flaming One, Mistress of the Isles, who ascends in the flame which is on the battlements of the sky'.[88] As for the uraeus the

Eye of Re, she is identified in the Coffin Texts as the cobra-goddess Wadjyt, 'the Lady of Flame'.[89]

The uraeus the Eye of Horus has an identity with the king's crowns. In Utterances 220-21, it is equated with the red crown of Lower Egypt (the *Nt*-crown, or 'Fiery Serpent'),[90] while in Utterances 524 and 724 it is equated with the white crown of Upper Egypt .[91] In addition, it is identified with a special form of the white crown called the *wrrt*-crown, 'the great crown'.[92] The latter is also connected with the Eye of Re in the form of 'the unique star (*sba-wati*) who destroys foes'.[93]

In keeping with this symbolism, the living king's crowns were often adorned with a single cobra or, in reflection of the political union of the Two Lands, the dual forms of the vulture and the cobra, representing the tutelary goddesses Nekhbet and Wadjyt. The vulture Nekhbet sometimes took the form of a second cobra, as a result of her identification with the crown.[94]

In its identity of the dual crowns, the Eye of Horus was called Great of Magic (*weret hekau*).[95] In Utterance 592, the Eye emerges from the head of Geb to become the two crowns Great of Magic:

> The Eye has gone forth from your head (Geb) as the Upper Egyptian crown Great of Magic; the Eye has gone forth from your head (Geb) as the Lower Egyptian crown Great of Magic.[96]

These crowns also went up from Osiris's head,[97] whereupon they became the crowns of Horus,[98] sometimes equated with the two eyes of Horus – the sun and the moon. This coronation of Horus as ruler of the universe was re-enacted in the coronation of the king at Memphis. Upon wearing the crowns, the king became an incarnation of Horus, protected by the power of his Eye, the uraeus.

These Great of Magic crowns compel us to consider the isle of flames (*iw nsisi* or *iw nsrsr*), which is portrayed in the so-called Cannibal Hymn (Utterance 273) as the source of magic.[99] According to scholars, the fiery nature of this island signifies the red glow of dawn and hence the birth of the sun-god.[100] However, in the light of our discussion of the fiery origin of the Eye, not to mention 'the fiery blast' kindled by Atum's hand, this assumption requires to be re-examined. If the Coffin Texts are taken as a guide, the isle of fire should be defined as a microcosm of the primeval world, where the cataclysm of creation provided the powerful magic for the spiritualization of Osiris and the gods.[101]

It is worth mentioning at this juncture that the adze which split open the mouth and the eyes of Osiris is described in the Pyramid Texts as 'the Great of Magic Adze', as if to anticipate the emergence of the Great of

Magic Eye and eyes.[102]

Overall, the story of the Eye provides a revealing picture of cataclysm in the formation of the cosmos. The Eye's fiery destruction of the rebels in the earth and its fiery ascent (or expansion) into the sky are almost certainly aspects of one single cataclysm, which split open the mouth of the primeval world and provided the elements for the creation of the sky and the celestial bodies.

We turn now to an intriguing question: might the cataclysm of the Eye provide a physical process for the formation of the eyes, the sun and the moon?

In Search of Vision – the Eye and the Eyes

As we have just seen, the Sole Eye went up from Geb's head in the form of the two crowns Great of Magic. But this same myth was also told of the eyes, as if to suggest that their origin was connected to the emergence of the Sole Eye.

In Utterance 443, it is stated:

> O Nut, the eyes have gone forth from your head. You have carried off Horus and his Great of Magic, you have carried off Seth and his Great of Magic.[103]

And in Utterance 749, it is stated:

> O Osiris-the-king, these eyes of Horus... shall be upon you as the two crowns Great of Magic.[104]

What exactly was the relationship between the eyes and the Eye? For the most part, the texts are vague on this point. However, an important clue is furnished by Utterance 524, where the king as Thoth takes the Eye of Horus to Atum in the sky. The king demands of Re:

> Open up my road, make my seat spacious at the head of the gods, that I may take the Eye of Horus to him [Atum] and that I may cause to be reknit for him that which went forth from his head. I will cause him to see with both his intact eyes...[105]

Here, the impression is given that the Eye went forth from the primeval mound (the head of Atum) to give birth to the two eyes, in order that the creator-god might 'see'.

This is indeed a recurrent theme in the Pyramid Texts, albeit the Eye is usually mentioned alone. For example:

> O Osiris-the-king... Horus has split open your Eye for you that you may see with it.[106]

> Horus has given you your Eye that you may see with it... Horus has split open your Eye for you that you may see with it in its name of 'Opener of Roads'... it is your beloved son who has reset your eyes for you...[107]

> Horus has given you your Eye that you may see with it... Horus has split open your Eye for you that you may see with it in its name of 'She who Opens the Ways of the God'.[108]

> O Osiris-the-king, take the Eye of the living Horus that you may see with it... may your vision be cleared by means of the light... may your vision be brightened by means of the dawn (*hdj-ta*)... I put the Eye of Horus on you that you may see with it... I have split open your Eye that you may see with it.[109]

In each of these spells, the Eye is ritually split open, befitting its status as a symbol of the primeval cosmos. In the last spell, the opening of the Eye coincides with the genesis of light, the dawn of creation. The 'seeing' of the Eye would thus involve, by definition, the opening of the two eyes, the sun and the moon.

The Coffin Texts pick up this theme. In a revealing passage of Spell 316, the deceased as the Eye of Horus is told:

> Send out your soul that it may see with its eyes. Such is Horus when he has reappeared in glory and has fashioned his bodily eye.[110]

Judging from the context, the reference here to the 'bodily' eye refers either to the sun or the moon.

The Coffin Texts make an intriguing connection between the Eye and Shu and Tefnut. In regard to the creation by Atum, it is stated that he sent out his Eye in search of Shu and Tefnut, after he masturbated and spat them out of his mouth.[111] Significantly, this event is linked in Spell 76 to the creation of light. Shu states:

> I am Shu, father of the gods, in search of whom, together with my sister Tefnut, Atum sent out his Sole Eye. It was through me that it gave light to the darkness.[112]

Why would it be necessary for Atum to send out his Eye in search of Shu and Tefnut? A possible explanation for this strange claim is provided by Spell 607, where the deceased is told:

> Your right eye is the night-barque, your left eye is the day-barque, your two eyes (O Horus), which issued from Atum, are Shu and Tefnut.[113]

Thus it is suggested that Shu and Tefnut were the two eyes, the sun and the moon.[114]

This identification of Shu and Tefnut (whose duality, for the most part, is notoriously obscure) is echoed by later texts. In a hymn to Horus, for example, it is stated:

> You have your Eye, O Horus. Your right eye is as Shu, and your left eye is as Tefnut.[115]

Several other texts are suggestive in this regard. In the Pyramid Texts, Shu and Tefnut are called 'twins' – a term especially evocative of the sun and the moon,[116] while in Spell 80 of the Coffin Texts, Atum says: "I live with my twins [Shu and Tefnut]... for I am in the midst of them – both of them follow after my body."[117]

It would therefore appear that the Eye searched for and found Shu and Tefnut in the sense of going forth from the abyss and manifesting itself in the eyes of the sun and the moon. The creator-god was thus able to open his eyes and see.

This idea receives a peculiar twist in the myth of creation by Neberdjer. Instead of the Eye being sent out in search of Shu and Tefnut, Shu and Tefnut are sent out in search of it. After a period of time, they find the Eye and bring it to Atum,[118] whereupon the two eyes of the sun and the moon come into being. This version of the story circumvents the problem of the Eye being present in the *nun* (for Atum was supposed to be alone there), but ends up with the same result – the generation of the two eyes from the Eye.

The Origin of the Sun and the Moon

We have seen that the Eye ascended in flames and that it caused the birth of the two eyes, the sun and the moon, but how exactly did this process occur? How did the solar eye end up as a hot, fiery body, while the lunar eye did not?

A persistent theme from the Middle Kingdom onwards was that the original fire of the Eye was subdued. In Spell 75 of the Coffin Texts, Shu states:

> I have extinguished the fire, I have calmed the soul of her who burns, I have quietened her who is in the midst of her rage [i.e. the Eye].[119]

Similarly in Spell 325, we read:

> He [Shu] subdued the Eye when it was angry and fiery.[120]

It was also claimed that Thoth had calmed the raging Eye. In Spell 167 of the Book of the Dead, it is stated:

> Thoth brought back [or restored] the sacred Eye. He pacified the Eye after Re had sent it forth. It was raging greatly, but Thoth calmed it after it departed from the storm (*nshn*).[121]

Nowhere is it clearly explained how Shu or Thoth managed to subdue the fiery Eye. A clue, however, is provided by Spell 554 of the Coffin Texts, where Shu ascends to the sky 'with the river behind him in the flame of the light', as if he were the sole creator.[122] Shu, we should recall, was the god who uplifted the waters of Nut, and he therefore had at his disposal the means to extinguish the fire. Moreover, it is surely pertinent that the Eye itself contained primeval waters (see Utterance 587 earlier) and was thus capable of extinguishing itself.

When the fire went out, the sky would have remained in chaos for a period, prior to the emergence of the Eye as the two eyes, the sun and the moon. This, at least, seems to be the intention in the myth of creation by Neber-djer, which provides the most detailed account of the origin of the eyes. The story is obscure, perhaps deliberately so, but is recorded in two similar versions which just about make it comprehensible.

The first theme of note is the long period of chaos which followed the sending out of the Eye. Neber-djer states:

> Behold, they [Shu and Tefnut] brought to me my Eye a long time after they went forth from me.[123]

The second theme of note is Neber-djer's emergence from behind clouds in the sky:

> They [Shu and Tefnut] made my Eye weak behind them (with) their *wabu*-plants, twice, for long periods of time.[124]

In his 1912 translation of this text, E.A. Wallis Budge rendered the term '*wabu*-plants' as 'plant-like clouds'.[125] These clouds, he suggested, had covered up the Eye for long periods of time, prior to its emergence in the form of the sun and the moon. As we shall see, these 'plant-like clouds' allude to the plants that will be born in the earth when the Eye sheds its tears.

A much earlier version of the Neber-djer myth appears in Spell 335 of the Coffin Texts, which is furnished with explanatory glosses. Here, we read:

> I raised the hair from the sacred Eye at its time of wrath. *What is the sacred Eye at its time of wrath? Who raised the hair from it? It is the Eye of Re when it raged at him after he had sent it on an errand. It was Thoth who raised the hair from it.*[126]

Here, the 'errand' is the search for Shu and Tefnut, and so the rage of the Eye occurs in the sky. But what is the raising of the hair? With insight ahead of his day (1959), R.T. Rundle Clark suggested that the hair (*shen*) that covered the Eye symbolised not only the clouds which covered the sun, but also at a more profound level 'the storm (*neshen*) that the Eye raised at the beginning of the world'.[127] I find this interpretation to be convincing in view of the identical imagery (though not metaphor) that was later used in the myth of Neber-djer.

This theme of the Eye emerging from cloud-like coverings recalls the storm of creation, which was discussed in chapter nine. A crucial theme in that discussion was the dispersal of the storm, which involved driving away the cloudiness in the sky. As a result of clearing this obstruction, the roads of the sky were cleared and Horus and the gods received their vision, i.e. their eyes. That the Eye was behind this clearing of the storm is demonstrated by her epithets 'Opener of Roads' and 'She who Opens the Ways of the God'.

Returning to the Neber-djer myth, we find a unique description of the moment when the sun and moon appeared in the sky:

> After my Eye had come back to me, and found that I had made another in its place, it raged at me, and I endowed it with the splendour which I had made for the original [Eye]. I made it to occupy its place in my face, and henceforth it ruled all the limits of the earth.[128]

> I bestowed upon my Eye the uraeus of fire, when it was angry with me when another eye came and grew up in its place. Its vigorous power fell on the *wabu*-plants... and it set order among them, and it took up its place in my face and ruled all the limits of the earth.[129]

There is some ambiguity in these passages, but the intention seems to be that the Eye became jealous at the creation of the moon ('another eye in its place'), whereupon its fire was transferred to the sun, which thereafter ruled the entire earth. The fiery rage of the original Eye, which was sent out of the *nun*, is thus reproduced in the fiery rage of the solar eye, which burns with jealousy at the creation of the lunar eye.

If taken literally, this myth would indicate that the moon was created before the sun. However, there is no corroboration of this idea elsewhere, and it sounds like a clumsy aetiological myth – a folkloric explanation of how the sun came to be hot and fiery, in contrast to the moon which was cold and bright.

It is tempting to conclude from this that the Egyptians had no rational theory for the starkly different appearances of the sun and the moon, and that this phenomenon was in any case inexplicable under the assumption of geocentric creation.

Nevertheless, we should not give up the search for a more general theory of physics which might have explained the origin of the sun and the moon. After all, the 'plant-like clouds' in the Neber-djer myth do give the impression that something was physically occurring in the sky over a long period of time.

That such a theory might have existed is plausible. In this and previous chapters, I have argued that creation was by definition a physical process (rational by ancient standards) in which the primeval cosmos split open and ejected a great storm of primeval matter: wind, floodwaters, light or fire, iron (*bja*), and other materials. In that instant, the cosmos became an expanded womb, filled with the seed of primeval matter, which fertilized itself and, in the divine course of time, gave birth to the new cosmos. We read of this process in Spell 94 of the Coffin Texts, where the deceased states:

> I am this great soul of Osiris... I have remade Osiris from the efflux of his flesh, from the seed which issued from his phallus at the going out into the day that he might copulate with it.[130]

Since Osiris is the personification of the primeval cosmos, the efflux of his flesh is the seed which was ejaculated from the earth and the *nun*.

Was there a particular process by which the new cosmos developed in the womb?

A possible answer is found in the recurrent theme of the cosmos and the god being 'knit together' (*tjz* or *tjs*). In the Coffin Texts, this theme is applied to the Two Lands, the lotus, the earth-gods, Atum, the spine of Khepri, the body of Osiris, the Eye, the air-gods, the entourage of star-gods, Hathor, the dress of Hathor, and even the 'fresh water' of the sky.[131] Of particular interest are Spell 576, where the deceased is portrayed as the creator-god who 'ejaculates when he knits together', and Spell 647, where Atum 'knits seed together'.[132] Seed, in this creational sense, was a kind of building material for the cosmos.

In keeping with this theme, the eyes too were knit together. In Spell 551, there is a reference to knitting up the full eye (probably the sun) and replacing the empty eye (probably the moon).[133] This particular example of knitting can be traced back to the Pyramid Texts, where the gods knit together the face of Osiris in order that he might see with his Eye, while Thoth reknits for Atum 'that which went forth from his head', i.e. his Eye, thus causing him 'to see with both his intact eyes'.[134]

We are thus entitled to ask: with what kind of elements were the eyes knit together?

The obvious answer to this question is light in the case of the sun, and light and perhaps water in the case of the moon. But there are intriguing hints in the texts that these discs of light might also have been made of a material substance.

A tradition of Letopolis states that its chief deity Khenti-Khem (alias Khenti-irti) had 'two eyes of flame which came forth from Letopolis' but in some texts this is rephrased as 'two eyes of *ds* which came forth from Letopolis'.[135] This is a splendid example of the principle that the city was a microcosm of the world, which takes advantage of poetic licence to suggest that the eyes, as opposed to strictly speaking the Eye, originated from the earth. But what is the meaning of 'eyes of *ds*'? In an article on Letopolis, G.A. Wainwright observed that *ds* was connected with the sky, storms, the storm-god, and fire; he therefore argued that it was a thunderbolt material, similar to *bja*.[136] The official line, more cautious, is that *ds* was a hard stone substance, probably flint, which was utilized to make arrow-heads.[137] In any event, this tradition suggests that the sun and the moon were composed of a hard stone or metal.

Further evidence comes from Edfu, which was held to be the foundry (*mesnet*) in which the sun disc was made.[138] Thus in one text it is written: 'When the doors of the foundry (Edfu) are opened, the disc rises up'.[139] Edfu was the home of the blacksmith-gods (*mesniu*), who had fought for Horus armed with iron harpoons and metal chains. It is therefore implied that the sun was made of iron or a similar strong metal.

The moon too seems to have been made of a hard substance, according to the Book of the Dead, where the moon-god Thoth is described as:

Thoth, the son *anr*, who came forth from the two *anr*.[140]

Now, according to Sir Alan Gardiner's *Egyptian Grammar*, the word *anr* meant 'stone', and it is here determined by an egg hieroglyph, which suggests the translation 'stone egg'.[141] Scholars have interpreted this as a reference to the eggshell, and have thus translated the line: 'Thoth, the son of the eggshell, who came forth from the two eggshells'.[142] The stone eggshell would here refer to the primeval cosmos whence the moon-god was born. It seems to me, however, that the first *anr* refers to the moon and describes the composition of its body. A valid alternative translation would thus read: 'Thoth, the stone egg, who came forth from the two stone eggs'. This would mean that the moon emerged from the cosmic egg, the two eggs representing the old cosmos as a duality – consistent with the Egyptian view of the earth as 'the Two Lands'.[143]

There is also evidence that the stars had a mineral composition. In the Pyramid Texts, the imperishable stars are paralleled with the king's iron bones, as if to suggest that they were made of iron (see chapter ten). The fact that the northern circumpolar stars were represented by two adzes of iron provides support for this interpretation. Furthermore, in an obscure passage of the Coffin Texts, the deceased swallows magic in the form of 'iron of a star' (*bja n sbat*), which strongly suggests that stars were made of iron.[144] The same passage also identifies the magic with *saa*, possibly electrum, and *khsmt*, an unidentified metal, which may or may not have been connected with the stars.[145]

The Pyramid Texts also refer to 'the turquoise of the stars' (*mfkat n sbau*), although it is not clear whether this is a description of the stars' mineral composition or of the colour of the celestial ocean in which they sailed (elsewhere there is a field of turquoise, possibly synonymous with the field of reeds, and lakes of turquoise are said to exist in the fields of offerings).[146]

That the sun, moon, and stars were made of stone or metal is not such a strange idea. In the 5th century BC, the Greek philosopher Anaxagoras, who allegedly acquired much of his wisdom in Egypt, announced that the sun and the moon were glowing balls of metal,[147] while centuries later, in the 1st century AD, the Roman writer Pliny reported that a 'stone fallen from the sun' was worshipped at the Egyptian town of Abydos.[148] This stone was undoubtedly a meteorite.

All things considered, despite the patchiness of the evidence, there are grounds for supposing that the sun, moon, and stars were regarded by the Egyptian sages as spiritualized bodies of stone or metal, that were knitted together in the aftermath of the storm of creation.

The Fall of the Eye

While the sun and the moon were coagulating in the sky, another event took place which led to the appearance of plants, animals, and mankind on the surface of the earth. This event was known to the Egyptians as the weeping of the Eye.

The myth of the weeping Eye is first encountered in the Coffin Texts, where it is cited as the means of creating mankind. In Spell 1130, Neber-djer states:

I created the gods from my sweat, and mankind from the tears of my Eye.[149]

In later texts, this myth is amended slightly, the creator being said to give birth to the gods from his mouth and to mankind from his eyes.[150] As we shall see, this is almost certainly another example of poetic licence – it was from the Eye, rather than the eyes, that mankind was created, strictly speaking. But since the Eye had become the eyes at about the same time, it could be claimed with some justification that mankind had emerged from both the former and the latter.

So well known was this myth to the Egyptians that they felt little need to explain or elaborate it, with the exception of one late text which we shall come to in a moment. But the weeping Eye is mentioned in several other Middle Kingdom spells, which help us to reconstruct an overall picture.

In Spell 331, Hathor states:

I am that Eye of Horus... I came into being before the sky was fashioned... I seek your saliva and your spittle – they are Shu and Tefnut. I have looked and searched, and behold, I have fetched...
I have smitten everything with my hands in this my name of 'Hathor'. I have given my tears. I reduce (them) to order in my name of 'She who is over her Spittle'. I make warmth for them in this my name of 'Shezmetet'.[151]

The significance of this rather obscure passage will become apparent as we proceed. For now, the important points are that the goddess gives her tears in her time of anger ('I have smitten everything'), that the tears are equated with the spittle of Atum, and that the event coincides with the finding of Shu and Tefnut (probably the sun and the moon).

Anger is also a theme in Spells 686 and 714. In the former, a pool of water, excavated in the earth, is said to contain 'the tears of the Eye of Horus in a rage'.[152]

The reason for the anger becomes evident in Spell 711, which informs us that the tears of the Eye extinguished a fire. The deceased states:

I place maggots in the Eye of Atum, I am Re... I have come that I may repeat his tears for him, for I am Re who weeps for himself with his Sole Eye. The fire is quenched with my Eye, the ways are cooled with my tears.[153]

Commenting on this passage, Clark stated that 'the Eye must have begun to burn and God cooled it with his tears.'[154] In this interpretation, he was almost certainly correct, for other spells attest that the Eye raged in fire but was extinguished and subdued by Shu (see earlier). The fiery Eye is thus able to extinguish itself by means of its tears, the source of which are the primeval waters that have been uplifted within it.

Intriguingly, Spell 17 of the Book of the Dead suggests that the Eye wept twice. In a later version of the spell cited earlier, we read:

> I raised the hair from the sacred Eye at its time of wrath. *What does it mean? It means the right Eye of Re when it raged against him after he had sent it out. It was Thoth who lifted up the hair from it when he fetched it in good condition without its having suffered any harm. Otherwise said: It means that his Eye was sick when it wept a second time, and then Thoth spat on it.*[155]

We, in turn, must ask: what does it mean? A possible explanation is that the scribe imagined the first weeping of the Eye to be the original flood that had risen from the *nun,* and perceived the flood of tears in the sky as a second weeping. However, for this allegory to work, the flood of tears would have to be distinguished from the original flood. It would have to be more than simply an extension of that flood.

This brings us back to the creation of mankind from the tears of the Eye. For man to be created in this way, the tears would have to *fall down from the sky* into the earth, which was envisioned as the mother-womb of mankind.[156] As we shall now see, this is indeed the solution.

The missing piece of this perplexing puzzle is found in the myth of creation by Neber-djer. In part a of the myth, the god states:

> After this [the bringing of the Eye] I gathered together my limbs, and I wept over them, and that is how men and women came into being from the tears which came forth from my Eye.[157]

Here, the assembly of the limbs of Neber-djer refers to the creation of the earth, the primeval mound (see chapter four). Since the weeping of the Eye occurred in the sky – from behind the plant-like clouds where it was found by Shu and Tefnut – it must be the intention that the tears shed by the Eye fell down from the sky onto the earth, thereby fertilizing it for the creation of mankind.[158]

Plants and animals were also created by the tears of the Eye. In part a of the myth, Neber-djer states:

> When their moments fell on their *wabu*-plants, I endowed it [the solar eye?] with that which it has in it [the splendour?], and I came forth in the form of the *wabu*-plants and all the creeping things, the things that came into being from them.[159]

And in part b, Neber-djer explains:

> Plants and creeping things (came) from the god Rem through the tears that I let fall... Then I bestowed on my Eye the uraeus of fire [i.e. created the sun]... Its vigorous power fell on the *wabu*-plants... and it set order among them.[160]

These lines provide a uniquely clear and detailed explanation of an event that is largely ignored in Egyptian literature. Taken in conjunction with the preceding line, they portray beautifully the dynamics of the unfolding creation: the flood of tears falls from the Eye to fertilize the newly risen earth, while the sun appears from behind the plant-like clouds to project its beneficent rays to the ground.

Two other late myths provide broad support for this reconstruction of events. In one, Shu and Tefnut weep copious tears, which fall to the earth and engender the plants.[161] In the other, Seth plants the eyes of Horus in the ground and thereby creates the first vineyard (this is another example of poetic licence; there is no question of the eyes themselves being cast to the ground, it is rather the efflux of the Eye which falls).[162]

Although this reconstruction is based on late myths, many of the ideas are presaged in the Coffin Texts more than a thousand years earlier. In Spell 80, Atum's saliva is made to fall to the earth;[163] in Spell 325, the Eye of Re-Atum appears in the plants;[164] and in Spell 331, Hathor sets her tears in order in her name 'She who is over her Spittle', and makes them warm in her name of 'Shezmetet' (see earlier quote). The fall of the Eye is also alluded to in Spell 336, where the third portal of the netherworld is personified as a goddess who descended from the sky:

> She descends from the sky, laying down natron... the streams behind her are flames of fire. Two (streams) are fires in heat, the third is the fiery blast of the mouth of Sekhmet, the fourth is Nun...[165]

The Fall of the Sky

The fall of the Eye reflects a wider theme in Egyptian myth, which has long been neglected by scholars – the fall of the sky. By this, I do not mean to suggest that the sky fell in its entirety, but rather that elements of the sky fell at the time of its formation. By this means, the surface of the young earth was hammered out into its final form.

The myth of the fallen sky is reflected in a wide variety of ideas which appear in the texts of all periods. I shall focus here on the earliest of such references.

What is possibly the most explicit description of the fallen sky appears in Utterance 271 of the Pyramid Texts in the context of the king's re-enactment of creation. The one-line statement reads:

The two *djed*-pillars stand, though the broken rubble (?) has fallen.[166]

The significance of these *djed*-pillars is that they supported the sky after it had been lifted. They are therefore being contrasted with the something that had broken and fallen. Although the translation 'rubble' is uncertain, the general sense of the statement is reasonably clear.

Elsewhere, the texts are less explicit, if only because a god or serpent takes on the mantle of the fallen sky. But there is a clear pattern, as the following examples should demonstrate.

In the Pyramid Texts, Osiris is said to have been thrown to the earth by Seth, whereupon he acquired his name of 'Earth-attacker' (*aku-ta*).[167] This story is also reported in the Coffin Texts, which state that Osiris fell and embraced the earth in Nedyt (there is a suggestion here that he lost his teeth at the time).[168] This myth would make sense if Osiris personified the evolving cosmos, and if elements of that cosmos were cast to the sky but fell back to earth. (Incidentally, this might explain the odd references to the land being turned 'upside down'.)[169] It is otherwise difficult to explain how Osiris – a god of the netherworld – could have fallen and attacked the earth.[170]

Intriguingly, Spell 908 of the Coffin Texts suggests that Anubis, the jackal-god of the necropolis, descended from the sky in order to tend to Osiris.[171] Again, it is difficult to explain this unless Anubis personified the upheaval of the earth. The reader may recall that in Spell 816 Anubis appeared 'in the sky' as the breaker of iron – an allusion perhaps to his breaking out of the primeval earth.

Another earth-god in the sky was Geb, and there are hints that he too may have fallen back to the earth.[172] In late depictions, he is shown on the earth beneath his partner Nut in a twisted, sprawling position, as if he had fallen from her (see figure 52 in chapter eleven). Revealingly, the name Geb has an etymological connection to the verb *gbgb*, which meant 'to fall headlong'.[173]

There was also a tradition of a serpent that was ejected from the earth but then fell back down and was swallowed up by it. The serpent is said to be fiery and to have poisonous fangs which it sinks harmlessly into the dust. The following extracts from the Pyramid Texts give the flavour of this myth:

One snake is swallowed by another... O earth, swallow up what went forth from you. O monster, lie down, crawl away![174]

> Fall, O serpent which came forth from the earth! Fall, O flame which came forth from the *nun*! Fall down, crawl away![175]

> The son-of-earth snake falls with its head beneath it; the flame goes out against the earth-god; Neheb-kau [the earth-god] burns with the poison. O monster, die![176]

This falling serpent is elsewhere identified as an ennead of seven uraei, which became the seven neck vertebrae of the Bull of the Ennead, alias Neheb-kau.[177] Surprisingly, the enemy snake is not named as Seth, although in a late myth Seth is said to have entered into the earth in the form of a hissing serpent.[178]

A notable theme of the fallen sky is that it fertilized the earth and gave birth to crops and plants. In Spell 80, Shu states:

> My identity is Life... whom Atum made as the grain-god when he caused me to go down into this land, to the isle of fire, when I became Osiris the son of Geb.[179]

In this spell, Shu is the spittle of Atum, but also his hail-storm and half-darkness. Having been blasted up into the sky, he, or rather some part of his efflux, fell back to the earth and sowed the grain.

The fertilization of the earth was often associated with the sacrifice of Seth and his followers. According to a tradition at Herakleopolis (Henen-nesu), the soil was fertilized by the blood of Seth:

> When he saw what Re had done for Osiris, Seth came and cast down his face on the ground, and the blood flowed from his nose – and that is how agriculture began in Henen-nesu.[180]

This myth was re-enacted in the annual festival of 'hoeing the earth in Herakleopolis', which involved 'the hoeing of blood which came forth from Herakleopolis'.[181] In certain myths, the creator-god was said to have produced blood, as opposed to semen, from his phallus.[182]

Similarly in the tradition at Busiris (Djedu), the soil was fertilized by the blood of Seth and his followers, who were slaughtered in the form of goats.[183] Here the myth was re-enacted in the annual festival of 'the great hoeing of the earth in Busiris on that night when the earth is hoed with their blood'.[184]

Chapter Twelve Summary

- The Eye was the symbol of the Great Goddess. She personified the primeval cosmos in its process of evolution.

- The Eye expanded into the greater cosmos amidst a fiery cataclysm, which caused destruction in the netherworld and brought chaos to the sky.
- Eventually, the fire was extinguished and the storm-clouds dispersed. The Eye then manifested itself in the two eyes – the sun and the moon – which enabled the creator-god to 'see'.
- The sun and the moon (the eyes) were apparently formed by a physical process (each was 'knit together'). It would appear that they were made of stone or metal – as were the stars.
- The weeping of the Eye signified the fall of some of the elements which had been ejected from the earth – at the time when the sky was still in chaos. These elements hammered out the final shape of the earth and fertilized it, paving the way for the birth of mankind, plants, and living creatures. This process is confirmed by several other myths which allude to the fall of the sky.
- The fiery solar eye was regarded as a symbol of the fiery cataclysm of the Sole Eye, while the waning and waxing lunar eye was regarded as a symbol of the death and rebirth of the Sole Eye (i.e. its mutilation by Seth and restoration to Horus).

CHAPTER THIRTEEN

HORUS AND SETH

> You are born, O Horus, in your name of 'the One at whom the Earth Quakes'. You are conceived, O Seth, in this your name of 'the One at whom the Sky Trembles'.
> (Pyramid Texts, Utterance 215)

A major theme throughout this book has been the threat to order (*maat*) posed by chaos (*isfet*), particularly as encapsulated in the myths of Horus and Seth. It was the war and reconciliation of these two powerful rivals, in times immemorial, that provided the model for the unification of the Egyptian state, the Two Lands Upper Egypt and Lower Egypt, and it was the judgement of Geb in favour of Horus that provided the archetype for the coronation of the kings, who as incarnations of Horus for ever held in check the challenges of Seth. This was one of the oldest, most enduring, and most vital myths in ancient Egypt.

Egyptologists have long been at odds over how to interpret the cycle of myths involving Horus and Seth. To some, their wars reflect historical events in the Nile valley – a battle, or series of battles, between two rival camps.[1] To others, their contendings are allegories for celestial motions, such as the rising and setting of the sun, the sun's journey from winter solstice to summer solstice, the monthly cycle of the moon, the eclipses of the sun or the moon, or even the slow drift of the stars caused by the precession of the equinoxes.[2] And yet others see the reconciliation myth as a philosophical commentary on the inevitable presence of strife in the world and the eternal need to confront it and reconcile it.[3]

Of these three types of theory, the first is clearly absurd, the second may be applicable in isolated cases but is hardly a monolithic solution to the problem, while the third is undoubtedly on the right track, but is a little woolly. In this book, I have expanded on this third way, by arguing that the Horus and Seth myth allegorized the eternal threat to order in the cosmos, but in repetition of an original threat that was posed at the time of creation. This too might strike the reader as a little woolly.

The problem for Egyptology is that, owing to the lack of decisiveness of these theories, no consensus has ever emerged, with the result that the less acceptable interpretations continue to be repeated, sometimes with an air of caution, but at other times as a statement of fact. As recently as 2002, for example, Rosalie David lent serious credence to the historicist theory of the Horus and Seth wars, despite the fact that in 1948 no less a scholar than Henri Frankfort had rejected such thinking as 'unrealistic and sterile'.[4]

There is a pressing need, therefore, for a decisive interpretation of the Horus and Seth myth, which deals not only with the overview but also with the 'inner view' – the engine of detail that sustains the myth.

In this chapter, I shall go beyond my overview of the Horus and Seth myth to argue that the two rivals were joint creator-gods – partners in the creation – who personified the primeval cosmos in its process of rebirth and evolution. Their struggle for power over that cosmos, I will suggest, was an allegory for the *physical process* of creation, which began with a period of turmoil and chaos. As for the unification of the Two Lands, Upper Egypt and Lower Egypt, I will propose that this was a creation myth, pure and simple.

The Eye and the Testicles

The defining characteristics of the dispute between Horus and Seth, as recorded in the Pyramid Texts, are the injury to the Eye of Horus and the tearing off of the testicles of Seth. In Utterances 359, 386, and 570, we read:

> Horus has cried out because of his Eye, Seth has cried out because of his testicles.[5]

> Horus fell because of his Eye, Seth suffered because of his testicles.[6]

> The first generation for punishment... was born before anger came into being... before noise came into being... before strife came into being... before tumult came into being... before the Eye of Horus was gouged, before the testicles of Seth were torn off.[7]

What is the meaning of this? Let us consider first the Eye of Horus, and second the testicles of Seth.

The Eye of Horus is the focal point of the dispute between Horus and Seth. According to the Pyramid Texts, Seth snatched the Eye and carried it off,[8] whereupon he either placed it on his head,[9] concealed it,[10] or attempted to destroy it by raging at it, trampling it, or eating it.[11] Horus then seized the Eye back, and presented it to Osiris (his slain father) in order to effect the rebirth of his spirit (in an earlier form of the myth he would probably have presented it to his own rotting corpse, Horus of the Duat).[12] According to one version of events, Seth attacked the Eye in the east side of the sky (that is beneath the eastern horizon), however it was also suggested that he took it and wore it on his head at the battlefield in Heliopolis.[13]

The passive nature of the Eye in the Horus and Seth myth (with one or two exceptions) is unusual, and possibly indicates that it was co-opted into the story. Possession of the Eye by Horus signified the creation of light and life, whereas possession of it by Seth signified non-creation and the potentiality of a dark universe. It was poetic indeed to have the two combatants fight over a symbol that encapsulated what their battle was all about.

The gouging, concealing, and eating of the Eye were almost certainly inspired by the phenomenon of the waning and disappearing of the moon once a month. The reappearance of the moon confirmed that it had been rescued, while its waxing confirmed that its injury had been healed and its health restored. However, the moon was but a symbol of the original Sole Eye, which as discussed in chapter twelve represented the primeval cosmos. The original injury, it would seem, was the dismemberment of this Eye, which I believe signified the state of division and chaos in the cosmos. By claiming that Seth had attacked this Eye, the Egyptian myth-makers made him responsible for the lassitude of the cosmos (just as he was also blamed for the lassitude of Osiris).

Turning to the testicles of Seth, their significance is not immediately apparent from the brief references above, and there is little more to go on in the later texts. Unlike the Eye, they are not gods with an independent identity – a fact which tends to suggest that they are an original feature of the myth.

The tearing off of Seth's testicles is paralleled by the tearing off of his foreleg – an act likewise attributed to Horus.[14] Significantly, this foreleg belonged to a bull and was spiritualized in the northern circumpolar stars (see chapter eleven). Seth was indeed portrayed as a bull, whom Horus dismembered and fed to the gods,[15] and this tempts one to speculate that his testicles were those of a bull. However, the fate of the testicles in the feast of the gods is not disclosed, and there is no known myth of them being spiritualized in the sky. (There is no evidence, for example, of the testicles being identified with the sun and the moon.)

Fortunately, we can glean some insight into the significance of Seth's testicles from the Ramesseum Dramatic Papyrus of the Middle Kingdom period, in which the jubilee festival of king Senusert I is documented in a series of dramatic scenes. At the climax of this festival, the king in the role of Horus is given two sceptres which are equated with the testicles of Seth, and urged to incorporate them into his body in order to increase his power.[16] This scene sheds light on an otherwise mysterious line in the Coffin Texts, which appears to describe the very same ritual. Isis says to the deceased:

> I bring what expands the heart of Seth, I give what expands the heart of Seth, I give them to you, so seize them and join them to yourself.[17]

This line appears in conjunction with the presentation of the two eyes of Horus which are likewise said to expand the heart once they are joined to the body.[18] The expansion of the heart is undoubtedly a reference to the expansion of the primeval cosmos,[19] and it might well be intended here that Seth's testicles had the power to effect the birth of the two eyes of Horus, namely the sun and the moon.

This would make sense, for it was the ejaculation of semen by Atum which led to the creation of the cosmos, while the king, as we have seen, inseminated the sky with his seed, which in later texts was emitted from the testicles and phallus of a bull (see chapter eleven).

The position of the two testicles hanging low from the body vis-a-vis the two eyes set high in the head might well have conjured up an image of two sacs of seed in the netherworld that anticipated the creation of the sun and the moon. A statement in the Coffin Texts that Horus 'carried off' the testicles of Seth might well allude to him taking them up to the sky.[20]

In any event, it would appear likely that the testicles of Seth signified the seed of creation, and that by tearing off these balls Horus acquired the power to create.

In summary, it may be argued that both the Eye and the testicles were means of effecting the rebirth of the cosmos, personified in particular by Horus, whose two eyes were the sun and the moon. That Horus and Seth fought for ownership of these life-giving symbols provides the clearest of hints that the two contending gods personified the primeval cosmos in its earliest days of convulsion and rebirth.

Myths of Dismemberment

If Horus and Seth personified the cosmos, then we would expect to find myths of their death or dismemberment, along with myths of their rebirth or reassembly. We are not to be disappointed.

In the case of Horus, Utterance 532 of the Pyramid Texts informs us that he had a slain body, equivalent to that of Osiris, which was at risk of rotting and putrefying. It states:

> Isis comes, Nephthys comes... They have found Osiris, his brother Seth having laid him low... They prevent the smell of your corpse from becoming foul in accordance with this your name of 'Horus of Haty'. They prevent Horus of the East from putrefying; they prevent Horus Lord of Patricians from putrefying; they prevent Horus of the Duat from putrefying; they prevent Horus Lord of the Two Lands from putrefying.[21]

It is possible that Osiris took over this myth of the slain Horus some time before the composition of the Pyramid Texts, the corpse of the former thus becoming father to the soul of the latter. This would explain why the dismemberment of Horus's body is alluded to only once, in Utterance 260:

> I am Horus, my father's heir... The thrones of Geb shall revert to me, so that I may raise myself to what I have desired. My limbs which were in concealment are reunited, and I join together those who are in the *nun*.[22]

Significantly, this passage seems to suggest that the assembly of Horus's limbs gave rise to the primeval mound – 'the thrones of Geb'.

Horus's dismemberment is also recalled in the tradition of his severed hands, which were revered as cult objects in the city of Hierakonpolis (Nekhen).[23] In Spell 158 of the Coffin Texts, it is explained:

> I know the mystery of Nekhen: it is the hands of Horus of his mother's making, which were thrown into the water, when she said: "You shall be the two severed portions of Horus after you have been found."[24]

A New Kingdom text picks up on this myth to suggest that Isis severed and threw away Horus's hand, following a homosexual incident between him and Seth (to be discussed in due course).

Although Horus's dismemberment was not a major theme in Egyptian literature, it was a persistent idea, as evidenced by the fact that as late as the 1st century AD the Greek writer Plutarch wrote of 'the cutting up of Horus', which he omitted from his account of Isis and Osiris on account of its harsh and shocking nature.[25]

Turning to Seth, his bodily dismemberment is mentioned frequently in the texts. In Utterances 580 and 670 of the Pyramid Texts, he appears in the form of a wild bull, whose body is cut into pieces and fed to the gods (see chapter eleven). It has already been mentioned that his foreleg was torn off by Horus, and this also is portrayed as the limb of a bull. Other spells refer to a knife being prepared for the attacker of Osiris, although here it is unclear whether Seth is a bull or a serpent.[26]

The most vivid account of Seth's dismemberment appears in the Edfu texts, in a story entitled by scholars 'The Triumph of Horus'. In a series of dramatic scenes, Seth appears in the form of a hippopotamus which is pierced by ten harpoons, thrown by Horus and the king.[27] Afterwards, Seth's body is dismembered and his various limbs are distributed to the joyful gods. In the final scene, Seth is served up as a hippopotamus cake, which is cut up as if it were the animal itself:

> Bring in the hippopotamus in the form of a cake... I am the skilled butcher of the Majesty of Re who cuts up the hippopotamus... You are annihilated, O Seth... You are killed... felled... crushed... annihilated... cut up![28]

The dismemberment of Horus and Seth is reflected in the fact that they both had children or followers.

The children of Horus are mentioned often in the Pyramid Texts as the gods who assemble themselves to lift up Osiris (according to two spells, they gather in the place where he drowned, i.e. the *nun*).[29] It is Horus who assembles his children and presents them to Osiris. However, in one spell it is stated that the children are first united with Horus – a clue perhaps to the original form of the myth.[30] In several spells, the children are equated to the multitude of gods (*netjeru*),[31] but elsewhere they are said to be four in number – the four sons of Horus (figure 57).[32]

The children of Seth are generally described as his followers.[33] They too are assembled and presented to Osiris, possibly in one group with the children of Horus.[34] In the Pyramid Texts, they are called 'the foes', 'the evildoers', and 'the gods who make disturbance'.[35] In the Coffin Texts and Book of the Dead, they are 'the Children of Impotence' (*msu bdsht*), whom Re destroyed on 'that night of making war'.[36]

The fact that the children of Horus and Seth are assembled in a group and presented to Osiris is suggestive of a reversal of the dismemberment of their parent bodies. Indeed in Utterance 364, the assembly of the gods is paralleled with the reassembly of the limbs of Osiris.[37] This would be an allegory for the rebuilding of the cosmos, in particular the primeval mound.

In this regard, it is intriguing to note that the cosmos contained realms called the mounds of Horus and the mounds of Seth, which belonged to the earth-god Geb. In Utterance 306, Geb says:

Figure 57.
OSIRIS ACCOMPANIED BY ISIS AND THE FOUR SONS OF HORUS WHO SIGNIFY THE GODS.

> The mounds of my mound are the mounds of Horus and the mounds of Seth.[38]

These mounds might conceivably represent the assembly of the children of Horus and Seth, signifying the reconstruction of the great mound – the primeval earth.[39]

What else do we know about these mounds? In the Pyramid Texts, the revivified king is urged to turn himself about and govern the mounds of Horus and Seth;[40] having emerged from the abyss on his iron throne, and having appeared on the causeway, he circumnavigates the mounds at the head of the ennead, as if he were orbiting the earth;[41] the mounds are said to serve the king.[42]

In Utterance 665, the mounds of Horus and Seth are said to possess tombs – an allusion perhaps to the death of their children.[43] More often, the mounds are associated with living realms, in particular the field of reeds.[44] In two spells, the mounds are equated with 'the mansion of the gods who have gone to their doubles (*kau*)', which is located in the east side of the sky.[45] These gods are said to live in the mounds, and worship Re there.

These characteristics of the mounds – chthonian, yet at the same time spiritual – are suggestive of the revivification of the earth. But they are also suggestive of the rebirth of the dead gods, the children of Horus and Seth.

The idea that the gods were reborn from the mounds is corroborated in a tradition recorded some two thousand years later in the temple of Edfu. In the Building Texts, there are references to 'the sacred mounds of the Primeval Ones' (*iawt n pautiu*),[46] and these creator-gods are defined in one inscription as:

> The fathers of the fathers who came into being at the beginning, the mother of the mothers who were born since the primeval time, whose bodily forms *(djt)* were divinized in the mounds of the lands (*iawt n tawi*) .[47]

Eve Reymond, who translated these texts, provides the following useful comment on this tradition:

> We learn from our sources that the Egyptians believed in the divinization of the physical form *(djt)* of the original creators, and that their *djt*-embodiment became divine in the *iawt n tawi*, 'the sacred mounds of the earth'... perhaps the original creators were believed to undergo a metamorphosis in the island [of creation], and this, possibly, gave them what is described in our text as the *djt*-embodiment. An act of consecration of their final physical form presumably followed, and this is what is probably described in the tradition of a later date as the episode *(s)ntjr*, 'to make divine in the sacred mounds of the earth'.[48]

In the light of this tradition, it would be reasonable to surmise that the children of Horus and Seth were likewise spiritualized in the mounds of Horus and Seth.

That these mounds ultimately belonged to Geb suggests that they may have been assembled by him to form the primeval mound, or perhaps the entire earth (see later). Intriguingly, in three spells of the Pyramid Texts, the mounds of Horus and Seth are cited in connection with an assembly of the cities and districts (or nomes, *spat*) of Egypt, which is effected by Atum in the presence of Geb,[49] and in one of these spells the assembly of the districts is paralleled with an assembly of the *msmu*-lands (meaning unknown).[50] The assembly of the mounds of Horus and Seth is possibly implied.

The fact that these mounds possessed spiritualized doubles in the east side of the sky is explained by the same principle by which the primeval earth gave rise to the *akhet* in the east side of the sky, i.e. by the process of spiritualization (see chapter six).

Since Horus and Seth were said to be *in* their respective mounds,[51] it would seem that they jointly personified the primeval earth in its process of metamorphosis.

The Rivals are Reborn

If Horus and Seth personified the evolving cosmos, then there ought to be myths of their rebirth, i.e. their emergence from the primeval earth and waters, and their expansion into the greater cosmos. Moreover, these myths ought to reflect the cataclysmic aspects of creation – the splitting open of the earth and the fiery storm which engulfed the earth and the sky. Again, we are not to be disappointed.

According to a popular tradition, Horus and Seth fought each other in Heliopolis – a city which in mythological terms signified the primeval world (it was the place of the assembly of the gods and the creation by Atum). In Utterance 260, after Horus joins together his limbs in the *nun*, he boasts:

> I put a stop to the affair in Heliopolis, for I go forth today in the form of a living spirit, that I may break up the fight and cut off the turbulent ones.[52]

This myth is expanded in Spell 7 of the Coffin Texts, which provides an interesting explanation for the origin of the pool in Heliopolis:

> The earth was hacked up when the rivals [Horus and Seth] fought; their feet scooped out the sacred pool in Heliopolis. Now comes Thoth adorned with his dignity... So the fighting is ended, the tumult is stopped, the fire which went forth is quenched, the anger in the presence of the tribunal of the god is calmed, and it sits to give judgement in the presence of Geb.[53]

The timing of this incident is a little unclear, but I believe it refers to the birth of Horus and Seth from the earth. We should imagine the two gods hacking up the earth as they emerge from it, and scooping out the pool in primeval Heliopolis as they ascend into the sky (as the sky comes into being). The 'fire which went forth' would refer to the explosion which split open the primeval world, while the 'anger' in the tribunal of Geb would refer to the quaking in the heart of the earth. Thoth's appearance on the scene, as always, signifies the pacification of Horus and Seth and the promise of reconciliation and unity.[54]

A similar tradition pertained to the city of Hermopolis. The details are scant, but the Pyramid Texts refer to 'turmoil' in the city, and suggest that Horus and Seth fought each other in the city using two adzes.[55] A possible implication of this, in the light of other references to the adze, is that it was used as a cutting instrument to split open the mouth of the earth (see chapter ten, and compare the hacking up of Heliopolis above). Hermopolis was also the site of the primeval hill on which the Children of Impotence were destroyed by Re;[56] this battle, however, took place *on* the hill, and probably alluded to the chaos that was released from the earth into the sky.

A third tradition placed Horus and Seth in a castle, whose full name seems to have been 'the castle of the mace' (*h-hdj*).[57] The latter belonged to the 'great ones' (probably Horus and Seth) but was also the domain of Osiris and Thoth, and the assembly place of the gods.[58] Significantly, the castle was associated with an adze, 'the God's Castle adze', with which Horus split open the mouth and eyes of Osiris.[59] This adze possibly split open the castle, just as elsewhere the adzes of Horus hacked open 'the mansion of *Nwt-k-nu*'.[60] Needless to say, the castle would be a metaphor for the primeval cosmos.

As we would expect, the castle of Horus and Seth had a spiritualized form, which is described in Utterance 359 as 'yonder distant castle of the owners of doubles', i.e. the gods.[61] This was placed in the east side of the sky, close to 'the beaten path of stars' (*msqt shdu*), where the gods made the face of Osiris bright.[62] It was also connected geographically to the mounds of Horus and Seth.[63]

It was here in the castle of the east side of the sky that the injuries to Horus and Seth were healed. In Utterance 215, we read:

> O king... see now those who are in the castle, namely Horus and Seth. Spit on the face of Horus for him, that you may remove the injury which is on him. Pick up the testicles of Seth, that you may remove his mutilation.[64]

Both gods are thus restored by the righting of the wrongs that were done to them (in the case of Horus, one cannot help but wonder if the Eye was a cover for a more personal injury). As a result, the Eye of Horus leaps up in the east side of the sky, as do the wings of Thoth upon which the Eye will be carried to the sky.[65] It is probably with joy that Horus and Seth cry out because of (the return of) their Eye and testicles.[66]

According to Utterance 215, the healing of Horus and Seth marks their conception and birth, which notably coincides with a cataclysm. The two gods are told:

> You are born, O Horus, in your name of 'the One at whom the Earth Quakes'. You are conceived, O Seth, in this your name of 'the One at whom the Sky Trembles'.[67]

Horus, we are told, is born for Osiris, while Seth is conceived for Geb – further evidence for the geocentric hypothesis.

Seth's birth receives a separate treatment in Utterance 222, where he breaks forth violently from the womb. The king as Seth is told:

> Provide yourself with the Great of Magic, as Seth dwelling in Naqada (Nubt), Lord of Upper Egypt, nothing is lost to you... O you whom the Pregnant One [Nut] ejected, you have terminated the night, being equipped as Seth who broke forth violently...[68]

Here, the 'Great of Magic' may allude to the testicles of Seth which have been restored to him ('nothing is lost to you').[69] Thus equipped, the king finds the sexual energy to break open the womb of his mother Nut, and perhaps ejaculate his seed into the sky. In certain texts, it is suggested that Seth possessed an iron knife, which he may have used to split open the womb.[70]

This violent emergence from the womb of the cosmos is also attested in two other spells, where the king ascends to the sky with the power of Seth. In Utterances 511 and 667, we read:

> Geb laughs, Nut shouts for joy before me when I ascend to the sky. The sky thunders for me, the earth quakes for me, the hailstorm is unleashed for me, and I roar like Seth.[71]

> O king, may you ascend, your mouth being that of the Seth-animal... The sky reels at you, the earth quakes at you...[72]

At the birth of Horus and Seth, chaos engulfed the sky, and for a while the creation hung in the balance. Spell 280 of the Coffin Texts refers to the rivals as 'the two who would destroy the sky',[73] while a related myth speaks of two groups of gods entering the east of the sky, whereupon 'war broke out in the entire earth and sky'.[74] This myth finds its most explicit treatment in a late text entitled *Horus of Behdet and the Winged Disc*. According to this tale, the forces of chaos rebelled against Re in the 363rd year of his reign (the number 363 marked the birthday of Seth in the year), whereupon Re set sail in his barque with his followers, led by Horus of Behdet, to pursue and destroy the enemies. Significantly, the first battle took place in the sky, as the narrator informs us:

> And Horus of Behdet flew up into the horizon in the form of the great winged disc, for which reason he is called 'Great God, Lord of the Sky' unto this day. And when he saw the enemies in the heights of the sky, he set out to follow after them in the form of the great winged disc, and he attacked with such terrific force those who opposed him

Figure 58.
HORUS OF BEHDET, ACCOMPANIED BY ONE OF HIS BLACKSMITH-GODS, DRIVES HIS SPEAR INTO THE SETH HIPPOPOTAMUS.

that they could neither see with their eyes nor hear with their ears, and each of them slew his fellow. In a moment of time, there was not a single creature left alive.[75]

Intriguingly, Horus of Behdet was assisted in this battle by blacksmith-gods (*mesniu*), who wielded iron harpoons and metal chains. This may be significant in the light of our discussion of cataclysm and the iron of the sky (see chapter ten).

The Pyramid Texts make little of this battle allegory, focusing instead on the idea of peace and reconciliation. The king is thus portrayed with the power of the Eye, giving judgement in the sky (*mehet weret*) between the two contestants.[76]

What were the terms of this judgement?

According to the Pyramid Texts, Horus was assigned the sun and the moon to be his eyes, and the stars, the ennead, to be his followers, along with the eastern and western horizons in order that he be reborn every day. Seth, in contrast, was assigned the northern circumpolar stars (Ursa Minor and Ursa Major) and made to lift up the sky from the earth every day.[77] The cosmos was thus apportioned in favour of Horus. Whereas he had the power to orbit the Two Lands, and thereby renew the creation for ever, Seth was consigned to a supporting and relatively immobile role in the great cosmic play. In this way, the forces of chaos were harnessed to

294   THE MIDNIGHT SUN

the forces of order, and prevented from disturbing the turning wheels of cosmic time.[78]

It is probably not the case, as some scholars have suggested, that Seth was imprisoned in the netherworld. True, he is portrayed as a chthonian power who quakes beneath Osiris and lifts him up;[79] and true, he is said to bear up Osiris for ever.[80] However, these passages surely describe the original lifting of Osiris at the time of creation, which must be repeated anew each day. Viewed in this way, Seth would not bear up Osiris in a static sense, but rather in a dynamic sense of bearing him again and again for all eternity.

By the same principle, Seth's lifting of Osiris would probably involve him (Seth) emerging from the earth and supporting Osiris as the sky in the same way that Shu supported Nut. The Pyramid Texts are ambiguous on this point, since the cosmic identity of Osiris is flexible and varies from spell to spell (he may be the netherworld, the *akhet*, or a god of the sky). However, Seth is described in one spell as 'the Lord of the Ladder', and on one occasion the Eye of Horus is placed on his wing.[81] There is also evidence identifying Seth with the pillar that supported the sky. In the Ramesseum Dramatic Papyrus, Seth is identified as a sacred pillar beneath Osiris,[82] while according to G.A. Wainwright the *djed*-pillar at Busiris (Djedu) belonged originally to Seth prior to its reassignment to Osiris.[83] In addition, the Seth-animal was drawn with its ears and tail in the shape of the hieroglyph for the prop of the sky Y (figure 59).

Figure 59.
THE SETH-ANIMAL.
Note the resemblance of the ears and tail to the supports of the sky.

The Sexual Union of Horus and Seth

The foregoing is a reconstruction of the Horus and Seth myth based on the earliest sources which are by nature fragmentary. They demonstrate in overview how the myths are consistent with my hypothesis that Horus and Seth personified the evolving cosmos. However, the astute reader will realise that an author can consciously or subconsciously manipulate his raw material to suit his preconceptions. It is essential, therefore, if this interpretation is to be accepted, to seek corroboration in the narrative accounts of later periods. These sources can sometimes be untrustworthy (for example, Plutarch's 1st century *De Iside et Osiride* – a favourite of scholars). However, we are fortunate in possessing a narrative account of the Horus and Seth myth written in the Ramesside period, which clearly makes use of older mythic material. This myth, from the Chester Beatty Papyrus Number 1, has been entitled *The Contendings of Horus and Seth*.[84]

The subject of *The Contendings of Horus and Seth* is the long-running dispute between Horus and Seth for the inheritance of Osiris, namely the white crown and the kingship of Egypt. The drama is set primarily in the court of Neber-djer at Heliopolis, where he sits in judgement of the rival claims, supported by his ennead. For eighty years, Horus and Seth have appeared in the court advocating their respective claims, but despite repeated judgements in favour of Horus, no-one will take the decision to give the kingship to him. The story reads like a comedy farce, in which the council of gods dithers and prevaricates, sometimes not wanting to be bothered, at other times happy to keep the rivals in court for ever!

Eventually, the court decides to grant the kingship to Horus, but this only spurs Seth to challenge his rival to a series of further contests. In the first of these contests, Horus and Seth turn themselves into hippopotami and try to stay under water for three months. In the second, Seth removes Horus's eyes and buries them in the earth. In the third, the two gods try to inseminate one another! And in the fourth, they have a race in stone boats. Interspersed with these fantastic competitions are episodes of high comedy: the harpooning of Horus and Seth by Isis, the beheading of Isis by Seth, and the exposure of Hathor's private parts.

The third contest between Horus and Seth is of particular interest, for it involves an ejaculation of semen and results in the creation of the sun and the moon.

In the first instance, Seth attempts to inseminate Horus. He invites him to his house, saying 'come, let us pass a happy day together', and in due course lures him into the bedroom, where they lie on the bed together. During the night, Seth becomes sexually excited and inserts his phallus between the thighs of his rival. Horus, however, has been warned by Isis not to allow Seth's semen to enter his body; rather, he should catch the seed in his hand. This deception accomplished, Horus reports back to Isis, who chops off his polluted hand and throws it into the river Nile (a clue perhaps to the mystery of 'the hands of Horus' – see earlier).

Isis now hatches a cunning plan to trick Seth into swallowing Horus's semen. First, she smears the phallus of Horus with ointment, and causes the god to ejaculate into a pot. She then visits Seth's garden and pours the semen over some lettuce plants, which the god is accustomed to use as an aphrodisiac. Seth proceeds to eat the lettuce, whereupon the semen of Horus enters his body. Here, the text declares that Seth 'became with child by the seed of Horus'.[85]

Unaware of the trick that has been played, Seth informs Horus that he wishes to return to court to seek a final judgement of their case. The gods thus assemble in Heliopolis and order the rivals to make their pleas.

Seth immediately announces that he has performed upon Horus 'the deed of the victorious warrior', i.e. he has penetrated him and made his seed enter him. Upon hearing this, the ennead wretches and spits in the face of Horus.

But Horus then declares: "Not only is Seth's seed *not* in me, but *my seed is in him*! It is Seth who is disqualified (from the kingship)!".

What happens next is comical but profound. Horus requests that the gods call upon the seed itself to testify to the truth of the matter. Thoth, the god of magic, lays his hand firstly upon the arm of Horus, saying: "Come forth, O seed of Seth"; but there is no answer from the body of Horus. Thoth then lays his hand upon the arm of Seth, saying: "Come forth, O seed of Horus"; and sure enough the seed replies from within the body of Seth, saying: "Where shall I come forth?". Says Thoth: "From his ear". Says the seed: "Must I, a divine essence, come forth from his ear?". Thoth concedes the point, telling the seed: "Come forth from the vertex of his head." At this, the seed of Horus emerges from Seth's head in the form of a golden disc, i.e. the sun. Seth, furious at this ignominy, reaches up to seize the disc (*aten*), but Thoth intervenes and sets it as a crown on his own head, i.e. it becomes the moon.

This myth evidently has a cosmic dimension, and yet it has been paid scant attention by Egyptologists, many of whom have been offended by its explicit homosexual nature. In 1934, E.A. Wallis Budge labelled it 'the coarsest chapter in Egyptian literature', while in 1959 R.T. Rundle Clark described its content as 'violating every canon of modern man'.[86] The prevailing attitude at this time is best illustrated by the fact that one authoritative study included a detailed translation of the myth but omitted the homosexual encounter, which it summarised in a single sentence as 'a bawdy episode in which Seth attempts to impugn the virility of Horus, but is outwitted by Isis'.[87] Its readers missed out on the most interesting element of the story.

In fact, this myth is important because it demonstrates that Horus and Seth were not rival kings, as has often been supposed, but cosmic beings whose struggle predated the birth of the sun and the moon. Indeed, it

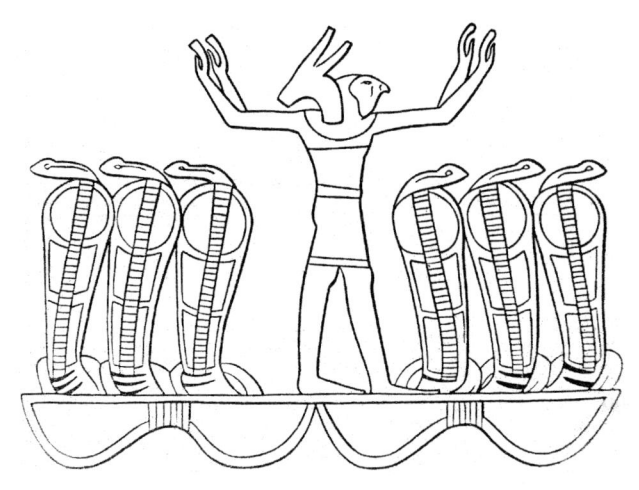

Figure 60.
HORUS AND SETH UNITED IN ONE BODY.
A scene from the tenth division of the Book of Gates.

seems to suggest, as I have hypothesised, that the two gods personified the evolving cosmos, and that their struggle was an allegory for the chaos and turmoil that preceded the act of creation. The fact that the dispute took place in Heliopolis is surely significant, but more so is the fact that the sun and the moon emerged from Seth's head.

Once we view this myth of homosexuality as an allegory for creation, its superficial coarseness disappears, and various points of contact begin to emerge with the Horus and Seth myth as it was told in the Pyramid Texts more than a thousand years earlier.

A key theme in these earlier texts is the removal of Seth's testicles by Horus – an event which is dated to the beginning of time. The meaning of this is obscure, but we later learn that the testicles were incorporated into the body of Horus, thereby giving him the power of Seth to 'expand the heart'. The story thus contains a sexual element from the beginning, which is vaguely linked to the creation of the cosmos. The *Contendings* myth seems to draw on these sources, but switches the roles of the gods, perhaps for dramatic effect, having Seth swallow Horus's semen rather than vice versa.

Even more suggestive are two ritual spells in which the finger of Seth opens the white eye of Horus. In Utterances 69 and 70 of the Pyramid Texts, the Osiris mummy is told:

> O Osiris-the-king, take the finger of Seth which causes the white eye of Horus to see – a *sma*-staff.[88]

O Osiris-the-king, take the white eye of Horus which illumines the tip of the finger of Seth – two lumps of electrum.[89]

What is the meaning of this? To take the finger of Seth first, it has been suggested by H.T. Velde that this was a euphemism for his phallus (see chapter ten). This theory finds support in the second spell above, where the finger of Seth appears to be an obelisk – a phallic symbol – with its apex coated in electrum.[90] As for the white eye of Horus, this is almost certainly a reference to the moon. Putting these interpretations together, the spells would appear to suggest that the phallus of Seth caused the birth of the moon. This, of course, is the plot of the *Contendings* myth, in a roundabout way, and would probably be reflected exactly in that myth, had its author not used poetic licence to make Horus catch the semen in his hands.[91]

A third point of contact with the Pyramid Texts is the tradition that a uraeus went forth from Seth's head. This is found firstly in Utterance 478, where the king climbs to the sky on the ladder of Seth and states: "I appear as the uraeus which is on the vertex of Seth',[92] and secondly in Utterance 570, where a uraeus is said to go forth from Seth (presumably from his head) and move incessantly.[93] The first of these spells contains a definite allusion to the moon ('the eye of Horus upon the wing of Thoth on the left-hand side of the ladder'), and suggests that these may be the earliest forms of the myth that the moon was born from the head of Seth, as it was in the *Contendings* myth.

In summary, the Ramesside myth of the homosexual union of Horus and Seth draws upon ancient sources and provides strong corroboration for my creational interpretation of their struggle.

The Unification of the Two Lands

We turn now to the role of Horus and Seth in the unification of the Two Lands – one of Egypt's oldest and most important traditions, which has hitherto eluded our study.

The myth of the unification provided political legitimacy for the king and his state apparatus, on the basis of an original act of unification of Upper Egypt and Lower Egypt which received the blessing of the gods in times immemorial. In order to assume the throne of the Two Lands, each king had to re-enact the unification, as for example in the circuiting of the walls at Memphis. Horus and Seth symbolised this unification, not because of their geographical ties to Upper and Lower Egypt, but rather because they were the archetypal rivals who had been reconciled for all eternity. These two gods were thus depicted on the king's throne, tying

Figure 61.
SETH AND HORUS TIE TOGETHER THE HERALDIC PLANTS OF UPPER AND LOWER EGYPT, SIGNIFYING THE UNION OF THE TWO LANDS.

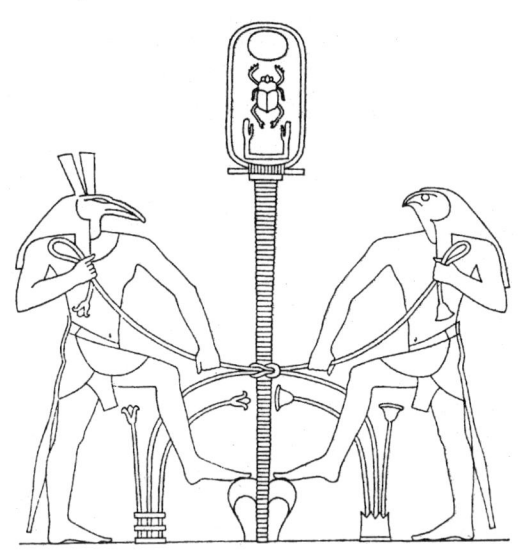

together the heraldic plants of the Two Lands (the lotus and the papyrus) around the hieroglyph *sma* (the lungs and the windpipe) – a symbol of unity (see figure 61).

In the early days of Egyptology, it was assumed that the unification of the Two Lands was a historical event in which the two regions of Upper and Lower Egypt were united by the first pharaoh Menes (*circa* 3400-3100 BC).[94] In recent decades, however, scholars have become cautious about this assumption,[95] and several have adopted Frankfort's suggestion that the unification of the Two Lands reflected a dualistic philosophy, based on the archetypes of duality enshrined in the cosmos (for example, 'sky and earth').[96] Using such an approach, one scholar, Jane Sellers, has argued that the unification recalled profound changes in the stellar skies, caused by the precession of the equinoxes.[97]

It is all too easy to impose modern predilections on ancient Egyptian traditions. It is less easy – but essential – to allow the Egyptians to speak for themselves. What do the texts say about the unification of the Two Lands?

Firstly, the texts are unequivocal on the point that the unification took place in primeval times, in the age of the gods. This idea is implicit in the Pyramid Texts, but explicit in the Coffin Texts and the later Book of the Dead. In Spell 335 of the former, the tradition is recorded with a helpful explanatory gloss, as follows:

Osiris, to you was entrusted the rulership of the gods on that day when the Two Lands were united in the presence of Neber-djer. *As for the union of the Two Lands, it means that the shroud of Osiris was ordered by his father Re.*[98]

The unification is thus dated to the time of the death and resurrection of Osiris.

Similarly in Spell 17 of the Book of the Dead, the gloss states:

As for him to whom was entrusted rulership among the gods, he is Horus the son of Isis, who was made ruler in the place of his father Osiris on that day when the Two Lands were completed. It means that land was joined to land in the tomb of Osiris.[99]

Again, the unification is dated to the time of the resurrection of Osiris in the form of his son Horus – the sky-god whose eyes were the sun and the moon.

These passages should put the lie to the long-held assumption that the unification of Egypt was a historical event. There may, or may not, have been a historical unification, but if there was, such an event would have been viewed as the re-enactment of a blueprint that dated to the time of creation.

Secondly, the texts make it clear that the Two Lands (*tawi*) signified not only Egypt but also the entire earth. This principle is made clear in the Berlin Hymn to Ptah, where Ta-tenen, the personification of the risen earth, fashions the Two Lands as his seat and is given the name 'Unifier of the Two Lands'.[100] It is also implied in the Pyramid Texts, where the Two Lands come alive upon 'the right side of Osiris',[101] and in the Coffin Texts, where Osiris is said to have 'judged the slaughterings of the Two Lands'.[102] One of the most interesting references in this regard is Spell 17 of the Book of the Dead, where a gloss describes Shu's role in forging the shape of the Two Lands:

As for the meal of faience which is in the Tjenenet-shrine, it is sky and earth. Otherwise said: It means that Shu hammered out the Two Lands in Herakleopolis. As for faience, it is the Eye of Horus. As for the Tjenenet-shrine, it is the tomb of Osiris.[103]

Here it is suggested that the Two Lands were hammered out by the fall of the sky, symbolised by the meal of faience, which in turn represented the Eye of Horus (see explanation in chapter twelve). The Two Lands here signify the entire earth.

Scholars are perfectly aware of this principle, not least because the

Greeks translated the Egyptian term for 'the Two Lands' (*tawi*) as 'the whole inhabited earth'.[104] But they have failed to explore the possibility that the entire earth was unified in a mythical sense.

As noted earlier, the unification of the Two Lands was symbolised by Horus and Seth owing to the fact that they were the archetypal rivals who had been reconciled for all eternity. This idea is captured neatly in spell 183 of the Book of the Dead, where Thoth as usual plays the role of the peacemaker:

> He [Thoth] has pacified the rivals for you [Osiris]; he has stopped the raging and the tumult for you; he has made the rivals well-disposed to you, and the Two Lands are peacefully reconciled before you. He has driven anger from their hearts for you, and they fraternize with each other.[105]

Here, the reconciliation of the Two Lands is equated to the reconciliation of Horus and Seth. This raises the fascinating possibility that Horus and Seth personified the Two Lands in the sense of two halves of the entire earth – an idea not inconsistent with the theory that has been developed throughout this chapter. The unification would thus symbolise the end of the turmoil that had existed in the earth at the beginning of the world.

But how exactly would the Two Lands have been unified? What might this mean from a geocentric perspective?

On this point, the texts are for the most part ambiguous and imprecise. The Pyramid Texts connect the unification to the emergence of primeval land from a lake;[106] the Coffin Texts connect it to the death of Osiris and a great slaughter in the earth, but also to the opening of the mouth;[107] the Book of the Dead connects it to the coronation of Horus; and the Berlin Hymn to Ptah echoes the Pyramid Texts in relating the unification to the emergence of the earth from the *nun*. It is not at all clear, therefore, what the unification of the Two Lands actually signified.

One possibility is the assembly of the primeval earth from its divided parts. This idea appears several times in the Pyramid Texts in the context of the king's re-enactment of creation. In one spell, for example, the king is informed: 'The great waters are joined together for you, the hoed lands (*mru*) are united for you and for Horus',[108] while in another he is told: 'Atum has brought the cities (of Geb) to you, he has gathered together the districts for you, he has joined together the *msmu*-lands for you'.[109] Similarly in the Coffin Texts, the deceased is urged to 'join land to land at the ramp of the Thinite district'.[110] In all these spells, the assembly of lands is a prerequisite for the ascent of the spirit into the sky.

It may be significant that Atum's assembly of the cities and districts is mentioned in connection with the mounds of Horus and the mounds of Seth. These two groups of mounds together constituted the single mound of Geb, i.e. the earth, but they were also rendered dualistically as 'the southern mounds' and 'the northern mounds',[111] and in one spell these are described as: 'the mound of Horus of the southerners' and 'the mound of Horus of the northerners'.[112]

It may also be significant that the reborn king circumnavigates these mounds, as if he were orbiting the earth. For example:

> May you circumambulate the mounds of Horus, may you circumambulate the mounds of Seth.[113]

> May you travel around your mounds of Horus, may you travel around your mounds of Seth as Min at the head of the ennead.[114]

> May you traverse the southern mounds, may you traverse the northern mounds, being seated on your iron throne.[115]

> May you occupy the mounds of Horus, may you travel around the mounds of Seth, being seated on your iron throne.[116]

This suggests the possibility of an earth divided cosmically into an upper region and a lower region – the upper being the southern mounds (alias the right side of Osiris) and the lower being the northern mounds (alias the left side of Osiris).[117]

Might these be 'the Two Lands' of the original unification?

The ultimate arbiter of this theory must be the Egyptian texts, and so it is now that we turn to the most detailed account of the unification myth, which is preserved in the text of the Shabaka Stone, otherwise known as *The Theology of Memphis*.[118]

According to this text, the unification took place during the reign of Geb, when Horus and Seth were disputing the inheritance of Geb, i.e. the earth, or Two Lands. It was Geb who made the judgement between the rivals and put an end to their quarrelling. But strangely, his resolution of the conflict was achieved in two stages.

In the first stage, Geb gave Lower Egypt to Horus and Upper Egypt to Seth. The text states:

> Thus Horus stood in one place and Seth in the other place, and they were reconciled about the Two Lands... Words spoken by Geb to Horus and Seth: "I have judged you – Lower and Upper Egypt."

But Geb then had a change of heart, and placed Horus in charge of both lands:

> It pained the heart of Geb that the portion of Horus was equal to the portion of Seth. So Geb gave his entire inheritance to Horus.

It was at this moment that the Two Lands became unified:

> Horus stood over the entire land. Thus this land was united, being proclaimed with the great name: 'Ta-tenen, the One who is South of his Wall, the Lord of Eternity'. The two Great of Magic [the crowns] grew upon his head. So it was that Horus appeared as king of Upper and Lower Egypt, who united the Two Lands in the Wall district, in the place in which the Two Lands are united.

Here, the emergence of the crowns hints at the creation of the sun and the moon (see chapter twelve). The cosmos as we know it is born.

But what is the significance of Geb's change of heart?

To begin with the first judgement, the text discloses that Horus was sent to 'the place where his father was drowned' (it is named as Pssht-tawi, 'Division of the Two Lands'), whereas Seth was sent to 'the place where he was born' (it is named as Su). To interpret this separation in geographical terms would be a grave mistake; the locations were surely intended to be mythical. The former would represent the primeval ocean, where Osiris drowned, while the latter would represent the surface of the primeval earth, whence Seth's spirit was reborn (an anachronism, since he had not yet been reborn). Horus would thus be assigned to the lower half of the primeval cosmos, or Lower Egypt, and Seth to the upper half, or Upper Egypt.[119]

The significance of this first judgement, then, is that the powers of chaos and darkness were placed over the powers of order and light. The cosmos was relieved from its state of turmoil, thanks to the separation of the rivals, but it could not expand and 'come into being'.

Turning to the second judgement, it too has a cosmic significance. By promoting Horus, the god of light, Geb set the scene for the creation of the new, expanded cosmos. Sure enough, the text refers to Ta-tenen, the risen earth, and to the appearance of the two crowns – symbols of the sun and the moon – upon the head of Horus. It was at this juncture that the Two Lands became unified.

But there is a puzzling aspect to this story: why was it necessary to disinherit Seth completely? Why was he not assigned to Lower Egypt?

The explanation, I believe, lies in the unspoken idea that Horus would emerge from the old cosmos and orbit the new. It was not sufficient that the sun, moon, and stars would rise up from his head to shed light on the upper world. It was also required that they circumnavigate the cosmos, in order to effect its rebirth each day, and thus ensure the immortality of the

Figure 62.
THE DIVISION OF THE COSMOS BY GEB, AS DESCRIBED IN THE SHABAKA STONE.

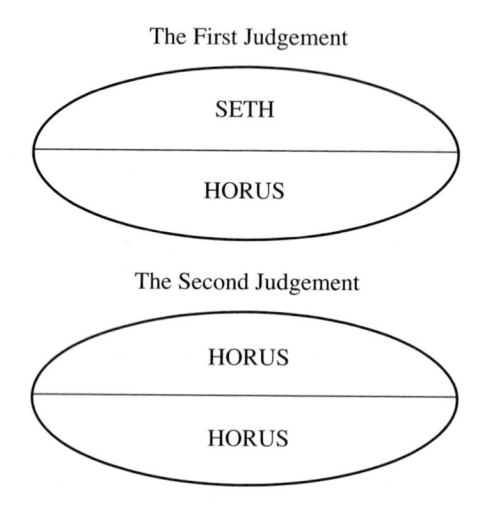

The First Judgement

SETH

HORUS

The Second Judgement

HORUS

HORUS

world. Horus thus had to have dominion over both the upper and lower parts of the earth.

Was this what was meant by the unification of the Two Lands? Was it the joining of the upper and lower parts of the earth in the sense of being able to orbit through them?

In Utterance 439 of the Pyramid Texts, the reborn king goes up to the sky to join the sun-god Re but at the same time takes possession of the Two Lands and 'the two shores' (*wdjbwi*).[120] These two shores possibly signify the two horizons, in which case it might be implied that the king unites the Two Lands by circumnavigating the shores.

The Pyramid Texts are ambiguous on this point, but they do refer to 'two banks' (*idbwi*) which are possessed by Horus and circumnavigated by the king.[121]

The significance of these two banks becomes more clear in the Coffin Texts, where they are defined as the eastern bank and the western bank. Intriguingly, the rebirth of the deceased is said to depend on the joining together of the two banks, and this is mentioned in connection with the uniting of the Two Lands. The following spells give a flavour of what is involved:

> I have brought together the two banks – the west to the east and vice versa... I will cross the sky, I will traverse the earth, I will join the river banks.[122]

Figure 63.
THE UNION OF THE TWO LANDS, A NEW INTERPRETATION.

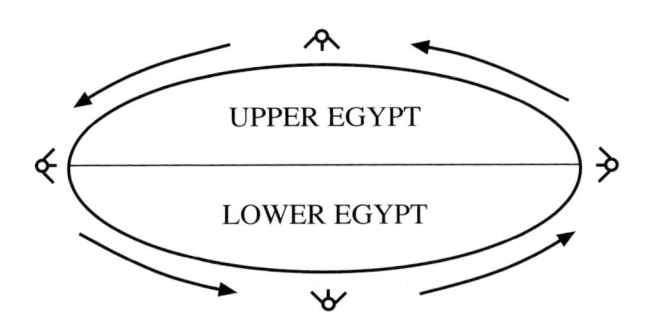

He who united the Two Lands goes forth... the banks are joined together for me.[123]

O western bank, kiss the eastern bank, bring me to land (*sma-ta*).[124]

The Two Lands are joined for my crossing; the banks are joined.[125]

I [the Nile-god] have inundated the two banks, and my soul crawls over the sky throughout the Two Lands.[126]

The hair of Isis is knotted to the hair of Nephthys... and he who reaches the *khns*-water has taken possession of the union of the Two Lands. The western bank is joined with the eastern...[127]

It is apparent from these spells that the eastern and western banks were the eastern and western horizons, and that the deceased wished to unite these banks in order to traverse the sky.[128] But the interesting thing is the connection with the Two Lands and the parallel that is drawn between the joining of the banks and the uniting of the Two Lands. Could it be that the Two Lands were united in the sense that the king was able to join together the upper and lower skies and orbit around them?

Although the texts are vague on this question, they do confirm that the king *united the two skies* by travelling around them. Firstly, in Utterance 274 of the Pyramid Texts, it is stated:

The king has travelled around the whole of the two skies complete. He has circumambulated the two banks.[129]

Secondly, in Utterance 676, Geb is urged:

Take the king's hand, let him sit on the great throne that he may join together the two *chrmt*-causeways of the sky.[130]

And thirdly, in Utterance 319, it is stated:

> The king has tied the cords of the *shmshmt*-plant; the king has united the skies.[131]

But this last spell may hold the key, for it continues:

> The king has power over the southern and northern lands and the gods who were aforetime, the king has built the city of the god...[132]

In uniting the skies, therefore, the king gained power over 'the southern and northern lands', i.e. the Two Lands of Upper and Lower Egypt. In view of the cosmic context, it is tempting to interpret these as the upper and lower parts of the earth (as with the southern and northern mounds of Horus and Seth, discussed earlier).

In support of this interpretation, Utterance 332 contains a passage in which the Two Lands (*tawi*) are paralleled to the two skies (*peti*). In his re-enactment of creation, the king states:

> I have ascended in a blast of fire, having turned myself about. The two skies come to me, the two earths (*tawi*) come to me.[133]

In view of this statement, is it too much of a leap to suppose that the king united the Two Lands at the same time as he united the two skies, and that he performed both unifications by means of his sole act of traversing the banks of the horizons?

In further support of this theory, Utterance 738 locates 'the junction of the Two Lands' at the place where the gods stand, which is evocative of the *akhet* in the east side of the sky.[134] This would make no sense from a geographical perspective, but it would fit the scenario of the Two Lands of the upper earth and lower earth being joined by the action of orbiting through the two skies.

Returning to the text of the Shabaka Stone, it is surely no coincidence that the unification was achieved by giving total dominion to Horus. He, after all, was the god who traversed the two skies, who had power in the two horizons and the two banks.[135] His first act, having received his two crowns, would have been to set the cosmos turning by uniting the two skies and orbiting the two earths. The text perhaps says this, though not in so many words, when it states succinctly that Horus 'appeared as king of Upper and Lower Egypt, and united the Two Lands in the Wall district, in the place in which the Two Lands are united'.

This place of the uniting of the Two Lands was Memphis, the capital of the Wall district, whose ancient name Ineb-hedj meant 'White Walls' or possibly 'White Fortress'. But Memphis was much more than a city in a geographical sense. It was, like all major Egyptian cities, a microcosm of the primeval cosmos: hence its name 'the divine emerging primeval island'.[136] It was upon this primeval island – the risen earth of Ta-tenen – that the Two Lands were united in Memphis.

It was here in Memphis that the first pharaoh Menes supposedly united Upper and Lower Egypt. And it was here, for more than three thousand years, that the kings were crowned in re-enactment of the coronation of Horus.

And it is here that we find another clue as to the symbolic significance of the unification of the Two Lands. It is that the coronation culminated in a double ceremony entitled 'Union of the Two Lands; Circuit of the White Walls'.[137]

One is compelled to ask, in view of the facts that Memphis, or White Walls, was a microcosm of the world and that each king was crowned as an incarnation of Horus, whether this circuiting of the walls might have referred to the orbiting of the primeval earth. Was this ritual intended to set the cosmos in motion, to set the wheels of time turning?

The same question might also be asked of the final consecration ritual that preceded the activation of a new temple. At Edfu, for example, there was a 'Festival of Entering the Temple' in which the gods of the temple were carried around the building prior to being installed therein.[138] Since the temple was a microcosm of the cosmos, this circuit too might have signified the first orbit around the earth, designed to set the two skies turning around the Two Lands.

The idea is not so far-fetched, for the sun-god's circuit of the cosmos was a fundamental idea in Egyptian religion. Moreover, in the Edfu texts the Great Primeval Mound (*khay-wr*) is described by the very suggestive epithet 'the Territory of the Circuit'.[139]

In conclusion, there is much evidence to support the view that Horus and Seth personified the Two Lands in the sense of a primeval cosmos which evolved into the cosmos as we know it. Initially they fought each other – this would signify the time of chaos in the former cosmos. Then they were separated within this cosmos, Seth being placed above Horus – this would signify a continuation of chaos: the time when Seth controlled the Eye, the head of Horus, and the ennead.[140] And finally Horus was given the entirety of the Two Lands – this would signify the expansion of the cosmos, the birth of the sun, moon, and stars, and the orbiting of those bodies around the Two Lands. (At this time, Seth would have remained in the earth bodily-wise, and his soul would have risen into the northern stars, but he would have been unable to challenge the dominion of Horus.)

Chapter Thirteen Summary

- Horus and Seth personified the primeval cosmos and the conflict within it. Hence they fought for ownership of the Eye and the testicles, each of which embodied the magic of creation.

- The mounds of Horus and Seth, which formed the mound of Geb (the earth), reflected their dismemberment, which allegorized the divided state of the former cosmos.

- Horus and Seth emerged together from the earth in a cataclysm, hence the myth of their battle in the sky. The pacification of the warring gods signified the completion of the cosmic order.

- Horus and Seth were reconciled in a way which ensured the eternal repetition of creation. Seth raised up the sky above the earth every day, while Horus as sun-god circumnavigated the cosmos.

- The Chester Beatty Papyrus confirms this interpretation with its tale of Horus impregnating Seth and causing the sun and the moon to be born from his head.

- The unification of the Two Lands was originally made effective at the time of creation. It probably signified the joining together of the two skies – the upper sky and the lower sky – which enabled Horus as sun-god to circumnavigate the Two Lands, i.e. the upper and lower parts of the earth.

- When the designate king performed the 'Circuit of the White Walls' at Memphis, he was probably re-enacting the sun-god's first orbit around the earth, which set the two skies turning around the Two Lands. This was perhaps synonymous with the unification of the Two Lands.

CHAPTER FOURTEEN

THE ONE AND THE OTHER

Amun-Re, the primordial, Supreme Being, being his own father, is described as his mother's husband... his feminine side (is) included in his own essential being, which is both male and female... all the other Egyptian gods are merely forms of these two constitutive principles, considered successively from different points of view.
(J.-F. Champollion, *Lettres*, 1828-29)

Egyptology has long been at odds over the definition of ancient Egyptian religion. On the one hand, many texts proclaim monotheistic ideas: the Great God is said to be a sole being, the first being, the supreme being, self-created, all-encompassing, the father of the gods, and the creator of all things that exist. On the other hand, certain texts seem to question the oneness or primacy of the God: he is said to have created by means of a female partner; he occasionally has a mother who gave birth to him; and in some myths he is created by his own children, the gods. In addition, the many names of the creator-god and the sheer number of other gods in Egypt (around two hundred gods or mythological beings are named in the Pyramid Texts alone) have given the impression that the religion was a polytheism.

Over the years, the shape of the monotheism versus polytheism debate has changed as new evidence has come to light. Initially, the consensus among scholars was that Egyptian religion had originally taken the form of a 'pure monotheism' which had over many centuries degenerated into a polytheism, or the outward semblance of a polytheism. According to this view, the polytheistic elements of the religion were inessential or not to be taken literally. This approach had to be abandoned toward the end of the 19th century when archaeological discoveries at Abydos and the first publication of the Pyramid Texts yielded irrefutable evidence that a wide range of gods had been worshipped since the earliest times. At this, the 'monotheists' changed tack. Some proposed that monotheism had developed alongside polytheism. Others argued that polytheism was the oldest form of Egyptian religion, but had developed into monotheism. And others still developed the idea that there had been a 'monotheism for the initiated' and a polytheism for the masses (this has been dubbed 'the neo-monotheism theory').[1]

In the 20th century, the debate became rather passé as scholars for the most part concentrated on establishing the basic facts rather than trying to interpret the religion (this is 'the positivist approach', championed by men such as Adolf Erman and Hermann Kees). The realisation dawned, however, that modern preconceptions had played a major role in shaping the initial assessment of Egyptian religion. In particular, the monotheists had found in the Egyptian texts exactly the kind of pure monotheism that accorded with their Judaeo-Christian faith. A new generation of scholars thus became sceptical of the theory of monotheism in Egypt and began to criticise its proponents or else treat the whole issue as a minefield to be steered around.

I have no particular axe to grind on this matter. However, in redefining Egyptian religion as a 'cult of creation' rather than a cult of the sun, as I have done in this book, I have established a number of principles which may well rejuvenate this age-old debate.

Firstly, my study indicates that the One God was worshipped under a variety of names which all described one and the same being – a unique creator-god. The principle here is not new.[2] But the creational framework *is* new. By placing the creator-god – as opposed to the sun-god – at the heart of Egyptian religion, the principle of 'One God, many names, many forms' is reinvigorated, as if it were a seed transplanted from barren to fertile ground. Granted, this identification of Nun, Atum, Re, Ptah, Khnum, Amun, et cetera as One God will not satisfy those scholars who require the theorised Egyptian monotheism to accord with the definition of Judaeo-Christian and Islamic monotheism, i.e. the worship of God under one name and form, to the exclusion of all other names and forms.[3] However, such an attitude is exposed for the modern conceit that it is when we allow for the implicit possibility that the multifaceted Egyptian monotheism came first and that the exclusive monotheisms of modern times derived from it, and indeed when we consider the possibility that a united civilisation of the future might well find itself honouring Yahweh, Buddha, Allah, et cetera, as parallel forms of the One God. Would our descendants be any less monotheistic than ourselves if they prayed to Allah in one city and Yahweh in another?

THE ONE AND THE OTHER 311

Secondly, this study has shown that several important deities who are generally reckoned to be evidence of polytheism in Egypt were originally forms of the creator-god or creator-goddess. In this group belong Shu, the god of the atmosphere, who is said to be 'the maker of the gods' and 'the father of the gods', Geb, the earth-god, who is described as 'the sole great god, the *ka* of all the gods', Nut, the sky-goddess, who is portrayed as a mother cosmos who evolves into the sky, and Osiris, the god of the nether regions of the earth, who personified the death and rebirth of the cosmos. Ironically, these deities have been regarded as diverse in their nature partly because the priests of Heliopolis decided to unite them and others (Tefnut, Isis, Seth and Nephthys) by means of the template of the ennead (the multitude of gods enshrined in the symbolic number nine) and subordinate them thus to another creator-god Atum – a move which if it had been repeated across the Two Lands (which it never was, since it would have become unbelievably complex) would have led eventually to a kind of monotheism more in line with the stipulations of modern-day sceptics.[4] A move in the direction of monotheism thus had the effect of suppressing the creational identities of at least four, and possibly eight, deities, while at the same time institutionalizing the picture of a universe personified by multiple beings, who became renowned more for their differences – as air, earth, sky, and netherworld – than for their innate similarities.[5] In this respect, then, a point in favour of polytheism must be struck out and re-awarded to monotheism.

Figure 64.
THE ENNEAD OF HELIOPOLIS.

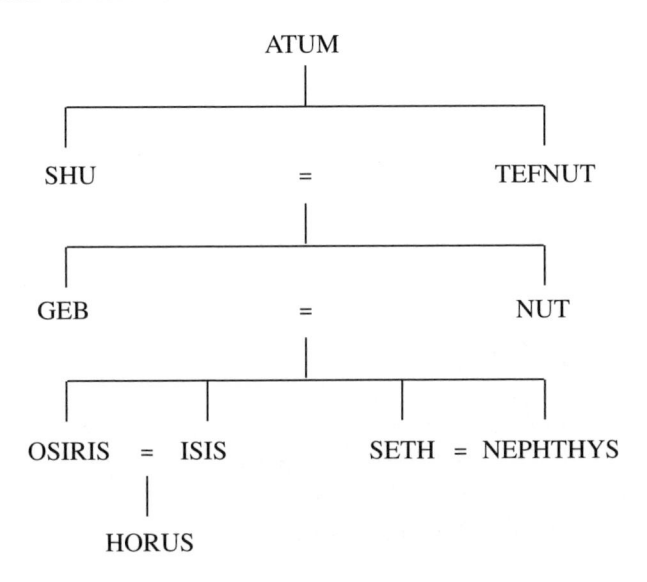

```
                    ATUM
            ┌─────────┴─────────┐
           SHU        =        TEFNUT
            ┌─────────┴─────────┐
           GEB        =         NUT
        ┌────┴────┐        ┌─────┴─────┐
    OSIRIS = ISIS         SETH = NEPHTHYS
            │
          HORUS
```

Thirdly, my study repudiates one of the most important arguments in favour of polytheism, namely the presence of 'the gods' (*netjeru*) in the literature of all periods (with the exception of the Amarna age when they were banished by Akhenaten). The existence of these gods is often cited as a 'killer' fact against the theory of monotheism in Egypt.[6] However, once we realise that the One God personified the death and rebirth of the former cosmos, and that this process entailed the dissolution, reassembly, and spiritualization of that cosmos, it becomes clear that the gods, who were assembled in the presence of God and spiritualized from his limbs to become the multitude of stars, allegorized that very process. The gods therefore had an identity with God in the beginning; they were the parts of his cosmic body which had been gathered together in order to revivify him. Hence the puzzling myth that the gods had created God, while at the same time he had created them (as the stars). There is no distinction here between the One and the many, as Erik Hornung has alleged, but rather a profound unity between the One and the many who made up the One.[7]

In these ways, the cult of creation theory bolsters significantly the case for a monotheism in Egypt, albeit one defined broadly on Egyptian terms rather than one defined narrowly on modern terms.

There remains one obstacle, however, to proclaiming a monotheism in Egypt, and that is the duality of God seen especially in the myths of the God and the Goddess. The proper question, as I see it, is not whether the religion was a monotheism or a polytheism (arguably now a redundant question) but whether it was a monotheism or a duotheism (to coin a new term). In other words, did the Egyptians worship One God – in whom the masculine and the feminine principles were united – or did they worship One God and One Goddess as two separate beings? It is to this crucial question that the remainder of this chapter is devoted.

The God and the Goddess

In numerous texts, spanning two thousand years, the Great God is held to have created himself, upon his own initiative and by his own devices, at a time when he was alone.

Atum, for example, was alone in the *nun* prior to ejaculating Shu and Tefnut; his act of masturbation was intended as proof that no other being was present.

Neber-djer, likewise, is said to have created Shu and Tefnut by an act of masturbation. As if this were not sufficient proof, he declares: "I was alone... I uttered my own name of 'Primeval Magic' (*heka*)... No other being existed to work with me in that place."[8]

Ptah Ta-tenen similarly worked alone. The Berlin Hymn proclaims: 'You assembled your own limbs, you embraced your own members, and found yourself alone... You had no father to beget you, and no mother to give birth to you. You fashioned yourself alone.'[9]

As a final example, Amun is said to have 'smelted his own egg' and 'come into being by himself'. The Great Hymn to Amun states: 'There was no other god with him who might tell of his form; there was no mother for whom his name was made, no father who begot him and said: "This is I".'[10]

But despite these protestations of independence, other texts suggest that the creator was *not* alone in the abyss – that he in fact had company in the form of his counterpart the Great Goddess, who was not only his consort but also his mother.

Atum, for example, is said to have sent his Eye out from the abyss in search of Shu and Tefnut. The impression is given that the Eye – a form of the Great Goddess – existed with him in the abyss and that she was the means by which he expanded into the new cosmos.

Shu – himself the creator in some texts – was partnered by Tefnut. A line in the Pyramid Texts refers to 'Shu and Tefnut, who made the gods, who begot the gods, and established the gods',[11] while another line states that the pure waters of the cosmos were created by 'the phallus of Shu and the vagina of Tefnut'.[12] These clues would tend to suggest that there once existed a Shu and Tefnut creation myth, in which Shu was creator and Tefnut creatress, with the gods being the offspring of their divine union.[13]

Geb in his role of creator-god was partnered by Nut. His union with the goddess – firstly in the primeval cosmos when their land and waters were joined, and secondly in the sky-ocean when Geb became her bull – resulted in the creation of the starry sky (*Nwt kha ba.s*).

Re in his role of creator-god was partnered by various goddesses. In the Pyramid Texts, there is a passing hint of a union between Re and the Eye of Re.[14] In the Coffin Texts, Re begets Ihy in the womb of Isis and then splits open her womb with his fingers that his seed might go forth into the expanding cosmos.[15] In the Book of the Heavenly Cow, Re is lifted into the sky by Nut who turns herself into a cow. And in the myth *Isis and Re*, his dying body is made to live by Isis, who uses her magic to cure him of the serpent's bite.

Osiris – the creator-god *par excellence* according to the theory set out in this book – was partnered by Isis. He is portrayed in a helpless state of lassitude until he is found and revivified by the goddess (along with her sister Nephthys). According to one version of this myth, Isis then unites

Figure 65.
ISIS AND NEPHTHYS EFFECT THE RESURRECTION OF OSIRIS-HORUS.

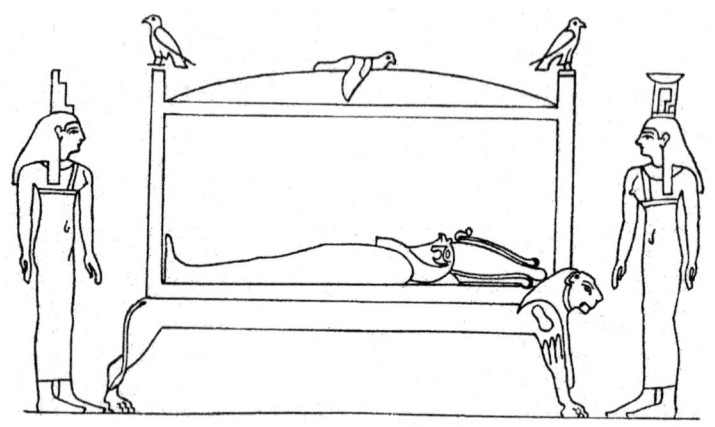

with Osiris and conceives and gives birth to Horus. The god thus requires the vagina and womb of the goddess in order to be reborn into the new cosmos. In the re-enactment of this myth, Osiris-the-king is restored to life not only by the love of Isis and Nephthys but also by the presentation of the Eye, which purifies him, protects him, and provides him with a soul.

Horus in his role of creator-god was partnered by Hathor (who was normally his mother). One of the highlights of the Egyptian calendar was the festival of Edfu in which Horus and Hathor – in the form of their cult statues – re-enacted their sacred marriage. The goddess duly conceived and, following various festivities, was taken back to Dendera, where ten months later she gave birth to the falcon-god Hor-sma-tawi, 'Horus who Unites the Two Lands'.[16] As discussed in chapter thirteen, this uniting of the Two Lands probably signified the joining of the two skies – the final phase in the creation of the cosmos.

These are the best known examples of the union of the Great God and the Great Goddess. But in addition there are many instances of the divine couple being worshipped together in cult. Thus Atum was paired with Iusaas, 'She comes, being Great';[17] Re was paired with Raet (or 'Raet of the Two Lands');[18] Ptah was paired with Sekhmet, 'the Powerful One';[19] Amun was paired with both Amaunet and Mut;[20] Khnum was paired with Satet (and later with Neit);[21] Sokar was paired with Sokaret;[22] and Anubis was paired with Anpet.[23]

The importance of the Great Goddess is thus not to be gainsaid. But what does her presence alongside the God mean for our understanding of Egyptian religion?

An Allegory for the Rebirth of the Cosmos

The essence of the hypothesis in this book is that the Great God of the Egyptians was a creator-god who personified the death and rebirth of the cosmos, and that this cosmos, which was originally in a state of darkness, division, and chaos, had given birth to a new, revitalised form of itself, characterised by light, unity and order. Contrary to the orthodox model of creation, I have argued that this rebirth involved an expansion of the old cosmos, brought about by its splitting open like a womb and ejection of material and spiritual elements which were then used to construct the atmosphere, the sky-ocean, and the celestial bodies around the hub of the old cosmos – the earth and the *nun*.

If this hypothesis is correct, then we would expect the creation myth to be rendered in monotheistic terms, for there is only one cosmos and the creation is a singular act. How, then, do we explain the presence of the Great Goddess alongside the Great God?

Generally, the role of the Goddess is less well defined than that of the creator-god. In two instances, however, her myth may be reconstructed from the textual fragments, with illuminating results.

Firstly, there is the Eye. As we saw in chapter twelve, she personified the primeval cosmos (her body had doors, contained waters and all the produce of the earth, and was reknit from a state of disassembly), but at the same time she emerged from the *nun* – amidst a fiery cataclysm – and brought light to the cosmos in the form of the two eyes – the sun and the moon. The Eye thus personified the rebirth of the cosmos.

Secondly, there is Nut. As we saw in chapter six, she was portrayed on the one hand as the primeval cosmos (for example as the daughter in the womb of her mother Tefnut), but on the other hand as the waters of the starry sky, which had been lifted up by Shu. The Pyramid Texts state that she ascended to the sky and came into being in the sky, and that the eyes issued from her head. Again, the picture is that of an evolving cosmos, personified by a goddess.

To these two examples, a third might be added, although the details are sketchy. In Hathor we have a goddess who seemingly personified the womb containing the falcon-god Horus, but who subsequently broke out of the earth ('the caverns of Hathor are broken open, she ascends in turquoise') to become 'the mansion of Horus which is in the sky', i.e. the underbelly of the sky on which the falcon-god flew (see chapter three). Arguably, Hathor too personified the primeval cosmos in the process of its evolution.

It is no great surprise to find that Nut and Hathor were both identified with the Eye. Nut was equated with the Eye as primeval cosmos in her name of 'City', while Hathor was referred to as the Eye of Re – a term which designated the Sole Eye as well as the sun. Moreover, the Eye, in turn, was equated with the goddesses Isis and Sekhmet. The principle is thus established that the Great Goddess could take many different names and forms, as could the Great God.[24]

In summary, it would seem that the God and the Goddess represented one and the same thing, namely the primeval cosmos which gave birth to the new cosmos.

It would thus make sense that these two great beings became partners in the creation. But how exactly should we understand their relationship? Why was a singular idea – the evolving cosmos – portrayed as the union of two principles, male and female?

One possibility is that the God and the Goddess were once subjects of independent creator cults, and that these cults were merged for reasons of political expediency at an early epoch in Egyptian history. In support of this idea, we do find a tradition of the Goddess as sole creator. The most obvious example is Neit – the pre-dynastic arrow-goddess of Sais – who in late times became the virgin mother of the cosmos. But it also strikes this author that Tefnut/Nut, Hathor, Isis, and Mut might originally have borne the cosmos without a male partner. A merger of God and Goddess cults would have brought Geb into the constellation of Tefnut and Nut, Horus-the-elder into the constellation of Hathor and her son Hor-sma-tawi, Osiris into the constellation of Isis and her son Horus, and Amun into the constellation of Mut and her son Khons the moon-god.

A more likely possibility (though not inconsistent with the idea of the merging of cults) is that the God and Goddess were united as a result of a philosophical view that the cosmos was an interplay of male and female principles that had ultimately derived from a unity. The original cosmos, if personified as a divine being, would thus have been a hermaphrodite or 'he-she'.

A good example of this dualistic philosophy is the myth of Geb and Nut, whose union is described in the Pyramid Texts as a joining of land to waters.[25] It is my belief that this refers to the first union of the God and the Goddess, i.e. their mingling in the original cosmos of 'the earth and the *nun*'. Significantly, the two primary components of this proto-world, primeval earth and primeval waters, are characterised as male and female principles respectively. This relationship is also maintained afterwards, when Geb evolves into the Two Lands of the earth and Nut evolves into the waters of the sky.

The logical implication of this myth is that the original cosmos was a

Figure 66.
NEIT, THE SOLE CREATOR-GODDESS OF SAIS, SHOWN HOLDING ANKH-SIGN, SCEPTRE, BOW, AND ARROWS.

'she-he' rather than a 'he-she', since by all accounts the primeval waters – the female principle – initially surrounded and contained the primordial elements of land – the male principle. The cosmos was thus conceived as a Goddess who contained within her womb-like waters a male essence, by which she would fertilize herself.

In a tradition of later periods, this place of fertilization is described as the *bnnt*. According to the Edfu texts, the Primeval Ones plunged their collective phallus into the *nun* and deposited their semen into the *bnnt* therein.[26] The *bnnt* then developed into an egg (*swht*) which floated to the surface of *nun*, hatched, and gave birth to the light. The contents of the *bnnt*, it is stated, were brought out into the light by means of 'the seed of Nun' (*mtwt n Nwn*).[27] Eve Reymond, who studied these texts, opined that the term *bnnt* meant 'embryo', but a more accurate translation would be 'ovum'.

It is highly significant that the *bnnt* also produced a cosmic outflow in the form of seed. In certain contexts, the word *bnnt* signified 'seed' in the sense of a bodily emission.[28] An inscription in the temple of Khons at Karnak describes how Amun-Re begot a place in the *nun* during the first time (*zep tepi*) when *bnnt* flowed out under him in its name of *bnnt*, i.e. 'Seed'.[29] The temple itself was even called Bnnt, as if to suggest that the seed had been ejected into the sky.[30] Another inscription in the temple of Khons refers to the place of creation as 'the *bnnt* in *nun* that fashioned the *bnnt* on the first occasion'.[31] It would thus appear that the *bnnt*-ovum produced *bnnt*-seed in the primeval ocean. Reymond's view accords with this interpretation. She writes:

> The word *bnnt*, therefore, would seem to have been used in the Egyptian cosmogony to describe a definite place within *nun* in which a specific substance was formed by a process of creation... This substance may also be called *bnnt* after the place in which it became solid matter... The *bnnt* appears here to be the essential matter in the creation of the elements.[32]

The fascinating thing about this *bnnt* is that it is primarily a female word and concept – it has the feminine ending *-t*, and it began its career as an ovum and an egg – and yet it encompasses the male principle in the form of the semen of the Primeval Ones, and it evolves into a phenomenon – the *bnnt*-seed – that is characteristically male (compare the myths of the young bull-god *ka-mut.ef* inseminating the womb of his own mother and Atum developing into the *benben* stone).[33]

It is surely beyond coincidence, therefore, that the feminine word *bnnt*, whose primary meaning was 'ovum', incorporated the male word *bnn* (or in shortened form *bn*) which signified the act of begetting offspring by means of copulation with a phallus.[34] The *bnnt* thus contained the means of its own conception, not just mythically but also hieroglyphically.

This brings us back to Nut and the myth of her union with Geb. In the Pyramid Texts, the reborn king in his identity as the son of Geb and Nut is described as 'the seed of the god' which makes the goddess conceive and causes pressure in her womb.[35] The king is then taken into the sky, as if he has emerged from Nut's womb (in another spell, he indeed splits open her womb), but continues to put pressure on the womb of the sky in his identity as 'that seed of the god which is in it'.[36] Meanwhile, Geb himself ascends to the sky to become 'the Bull of Nut'.[37] In outline, this myth is remarkably similar to that of the *bnnt*-womb which produced the *bnnt*-seed, the only real difference being that the collective phallus of the Primeval Ones is replaced by the land of Geb.

We might speculate that Nut was originally the personification of the primeval waters, these having been masculinized as Nun prior to the time of the Pyramid Texts. If so, the *bnnt*-ovum would not be a place 'in *nun*', as suggested by the Edfu texts, but rather a parallel term for the entirety of the cosmic waters.

There is a definite pattern here, which spans the space of two thousand years no less. It may be deduced that the primeval cosmos was conceived at least from the time of the Pyramid Texts as a Great Goddess who was a 'she-he' in the sense of containing within herself the male seed for her own fertilization, and that 'she' was the primeval waters while 'he' was the primeval land, both waters and land being in a state of inertness and chaos. For some mysterious reason, these primordial elements began to stir and stimulate one another, until they eventually became merged in a single fertile mass – an event allegorized by the sexual union of the God and the Goddess. We might speculate, in line with the sexual metaphor, that the waters came to life and began to flow, while the land became firm. As a result, the cosmos swelled up like a pregnant womb and then split open, ejecting light, air, water, and material into an expanded space in which the new cosmos would develop. The final phase of creation saw the light-filled primeval matter fertilize the cosmic waters a second time, the male principle thus being borne in the womb of its mother – the myth of *ka-mut.ef*. In short, the Goddess utilized the seed of the God inside her to conceive and give birth to a 'son' – the symbol of the rejuvenated and immortal cosmos.[38]

This idea of the cosmos as a hermaphrodite is attested in the texts of all periods, albeit the emphasis has been switched from 'she-he' to 'he-she' as a result of the preponderance of sole male creators as opposed to sole female creators. As regards the latter, we have but a single example in Neit of Sais, who in the late period was portrayed as a hermaphrodite – 'the father of fathers and the mother of mothers' – as well as the virgin mother of the cosmos.[39] But the list of 'he-shes', in contrast, is long and impressive.

Atum, for example, was made to declare: "I gave birth to Shu, I am the he-she (*pn tn*)".[40] Instead of simply ejaculating Shu and Tefnut from his phallus, he sneezed and spat them out from his mouth, as if his mouth were a vagina.[41] Consistent with this, Atum had union with his hand in the sense of copulation rather than masturbation,[42] and his semen (*mtwt*) is said to have 'conceived' and 'borne' for him, as if it had first been deposited in a womb.[43]

Several other creator-gods 'gave birth' as if they were a goddess. Ptah in his name of Ta-tenen 'gave birth' to the gods and all things;[44] Amun did likewise;[45] and Seth produced the sun and the moon from his head, having been made to conceive by the semen of Horus.[46]

In a similar vein, the creator was credited with laying and hatching the cosmic egg. Geb was portrayed as a mother goose, 'the Great Honker', who had laid the egg,[47] while Amun was said to have knitted his semen (*mtwt*) together with his body in order to fashion his own egg.[48]

The creator-god was thus both father and mother. Khnum was called 'the father of fathers and the mother of mothers';[49] Amun-Re was called 'the mother of gods and men';[50] Sokar was called 'father and mother';[51] Osiris was likewise called 'father and mother', and had his name written with male and female symbols;[52] and the sun-god Aten (the exclusive god of Akhenaten's monotheism) was referred to as 'father and mother'.[53]

A collective bisexuality is seen in the traditions of the creator-gods. In the Hermopolite tradition, the Ogdoad comprised four male-and-female couples: Nun and Nunet, Heh and Hehet, Kek and Keket, and Amun and Amaunet,[54] while in the Edfu texts the Primeval Ones are described as 'the fathers who fertilized, the mothers who gave birth', 'the bulls who impregnated, the cows who conceived', and 'the gods who created sexual pleasure, the goddesses who bore forth the egg that fertilized them'.[55] In reflection of this tradition, Hapi claimed to be 'the eldest of the eight Nile-gods, the Primeval Ones', and was portrayed artistically as a man with the breasts of a woman (figure 67).[56] Possibly the oldest example of this tradition appears in the Pyramid Texts where an unnamed group of gods is said to be 'the fathers and the mothers' of Geb.[57]

Figure 67.
HAPI, THE NILE-GOD, DEPICTED WITH FEMALE BREASTS.

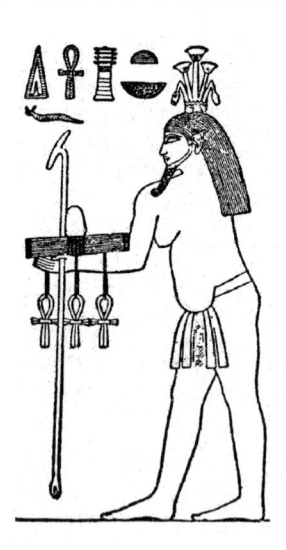

It is evident from this brief study that the hermaphroditic creator-god was a long-standing and resilient idea in Egypt, and that his bisexuality was associated particularly with the process of creation. The primacy of the male principle, however, almost certainly reflected the preponderance of sole male creators, which was a consequence of the masculinization of the religion (exemplified by the masculinization of the primeval waters as Nun). In the original scheme, the female principle had pride of place. The real meaning of 'he-she' only becomes apparent when it is inverted and read as 'she-he'.

The Divine Spark

How did the dying cosmos manage to revivify itself? A constant theme in the myths is the uniting of elements. The Ogdoad push together into a single mass; the gods gather together in assembly; the God reassembles the limbs of his body; and Geb and Nut merge their land and waters. By pulling itself together in this way, the cosmos managed to unite the male principle with the female principle, whereupon it conceived and gave birth to a rejuvenated form of itself. This process was portrayed as an act of copulation between the God and the Goddess, but it was also depicted as a coupling of male and female snakes. A line in the Pyramid Texts reads: 'The male serpent is bitten by the female serpent, and vice versa. The sky is enchanted, the earth is enchanted.'[58] This serves to remind us that we are dealing here with an esoteric allegory, not a crude tale about sex.

The process is clear enough. But less clear is the mechanism by which the process was instigated. What mysterious force brought the gods back to life and caused them to unite into a whole?

The minds of the Egyptian sages must have been greatly exercised by this question, just as modern-day philosophers and astrophysicists ponder the cause of the Big Bang (a theory which is strangely reminiscent of the Egyptian geocentric theory).[59] What theories or explanations did they come up with?

In the Ogdoad creation myth, there is a suggestion that wind was the first principle which revivified the cosmos. It was this wind which stirred up the primeval waters and the elements therein, and enabled the Ogdoad to push themselves together and form the primeval mound (see chapter three).

Wind is also a primary principle in a hymn from the New Kingdom in which Isis in the form of a bird finds the body of Osiris.[60] The goddess 'creates a wind with her wings' and thus brings to life the limbs of the god. Isis then draws seed out of Osiris's body into hers and conceives the child Horus. In this myth, however, the wind is accompanied by light and sound. Isis creates light (literally 'casts a shadow') with her feathers, and 'utters the cry of the mourning-woman'. The first cause of all things is thus a threefold phenomenon: wind, light, and sound.

In Spell 148 of the Coffin Texts, light and sound are the first principle in the form of the lightning strike, or thunderbolt. The spell begins with the intriguing line:

> The thunderbolt strikes, the gods are afraid, Isis awakes pregnant with the seed of her brother Osiris...[61]

Figure 68.
ISIS IN THE FORM OF A KITE REVIVIFIES OSIRIS, ACCOMPANIED BY NEPHTHYS AND WATCHED BY HATHOR AND HEKET.

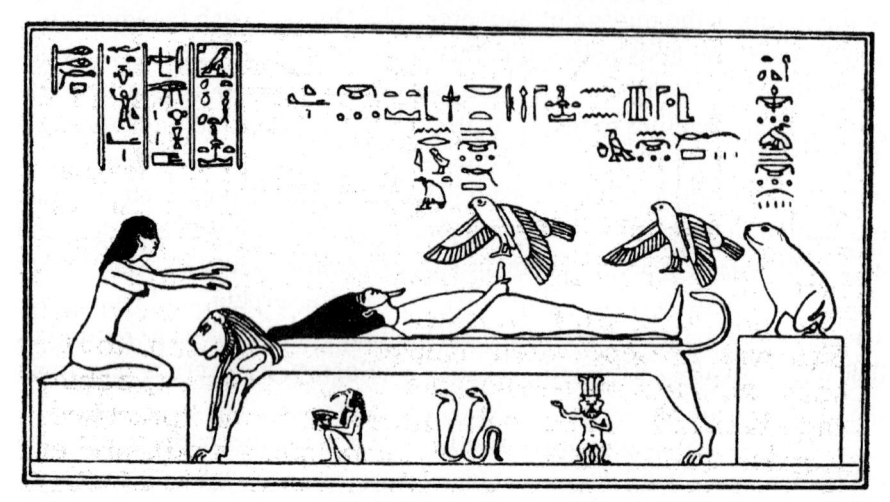

It is implied here that the thunderbolt causes Isis to conceive, but it is not at all clear where it comes from. Is it produced by Osiris or is it caused by the appearance of Isis at his side?[62] As we would expect with a first principle, the origin of the thunderbolt is left unexplained.

Elsewhere, the first principle is *heka*, which is translated 'magic', or 'words of power'. It was associated particularly with the mouth and the uttering of the names that brought things into being.

In the myth of creation by Neber-djer, the god's first act is to bring his name of 'Heka' into his own mouth, whereupon he comes into being in the forms of all things.[63] In a related spell in the Coffin Texts, *heka* is said to be the first thing which Neber-djer made, prior to sending out his Eye; it came into being when the sole god took *hu*, 'creative utterance', into his mouth, and when 'the millions of spirits' came forth from his mouth.[64] *Heka* is here called 'the father of the gods who gave life to the ennead'.[65]

In Spell 648 of the Coffin Texts, *heka* comes into being by itself, as opposed to being created by the sole god. Again it is associated with the origin of the gods – 'the millions of spirits' who came into being in his mouth.[66]

Heka was the key to the resurrection of Re in his identity as creator-god. In the myth of *Isis and Re*, the god has been laid low by a serpent's bite and his limbs are filled with pains of death. Isis then arrives with her mouth filled with the 'breath of life' and uses her magic to remove the poison from his body.[67] At this, Re's secret name issues from his body and enters hers, whereupon the Eye comes forth from his mouth. Re is thus made to live by Isis, who acquires the epithet *weret hekau*, 'Great of Magic'.

Osiris too was resurrected by the magic of Isis, but here the term used is not *heka* but *mrwt*, meaning 'love'. In the Pyramid Texts, Isis is twice said to come to her otiose partner 'rejoicing for love' of him. As a result, he ejaculates his seed into her and she becomes pregnant with Horus (Hor-Spdu).[68]

In the re-enactment of creation by the deceased king, *heka* is of pivotal importance. In the rebirth ritual, Horus presents Osiris-the-king with the Eye, one of whose names is *weret hekau*, 'Great of Magic'.[69] As a result, the two eyes, or two crowns of Upper and Lower Egypt, appear on the head of the king, who himself acquires the name 'Great of Magic'.[70] In a variation of this ritual, Isis and Nephthys place the king's heart in his body in the form of the Eye of Horus and the testicles of Seth, both of which are described as 'Great of Magic'.[71]

As the possessor of *heka*, the reborn king causes the sky to quiver and the earth to quake.[72] He ascends to the sky wearing his magic at his feet (the two eyes are said to be joined to his feet, possibly as his sandals), or wearing his magic about him as if it were a cloak.[73] In one spell, the king acquires eternal life by consuming magic in the form of the gods whose bodies are said to 'come from the island of fire with their bodies full of magic'.[74] The king thus becomes Lord of the Akhet – the god of magic who has millions of spirits in his mouth.[75]

As we might expect, *heka* was the energy of the soul (*ba*). In one spell, the king ascends to the sky saying: 'My soul has brought me, its magic has equipped me', while in another spell it is said: 'His soul is upon him, his magic is about him'.[76] *Ba* and *heka* are here virtually synonymous.

It may be seen from this brief review that *heka* was the first principle which brought all things into being. The translation 'magic' hardly does justice to the term *heka*. It was rather 'primeval magic' – the mysterious energy behind the creation – the elusive fifth element christened *physis* by the Greeks.[77] If one had to sum up Egyptian civilisation in two words, those words would be *heka* and *maat*, for it was *heka* which established *maat* at the first time and it was the ritual use of *heka* which maintained *maat* in the present time. *Heka* was the key to repeating creation because it was the force which made creation effective.

If *heka* was the first principle of creation *par excellence*, then we must recognise the Goddess herself as the first principle, for she is so often the source of the magic. Isis, as we have seen, became the goddess 'Great of Magic'.[78] She and Nephthys were 'the two sisters Great of Magic', who brought the king the trophies 'Great of Magic' from the rivals Horus and Seth.[79] And the Eye, the supreme symbol of the creator-goddess, was 'the Great of Magic' which brought about the birth of the two eyes 'Great of Magic' – the sun and the moon.

In keeping with this idea, the Goddess was frequently portrayed as the prime mover who sought and found the otiose God, came to his side, and restored him. In this genre of myth, the Goddess provides the God with a soul and causes his soul to go forth, but there is also a real sense that the Goddess *is* the soul.

The resurrection of Osiris by Isis is especially suggestive. In one myth, mentioned earlier, she flies over the earth in the form of a bird and then descends upon the corpse of her partner, whom she revivifies by means of wind from her wings (figure 68). Isis might here represent the soul of the cosmos which has descended upon its body. She would copulate with Osiris in the sense of instilling him with the energy of life.[80] The God would become ithyphallic *as a result of* the copulation.[81]

Almost as suggestive is a Theban creation myth which tells how Mut in the form of a shining serpent wound herself around Re and gave birth to him as Khons, the moon-god.[82] It is tempting to interpret Mut as the soul and Re as the body of the cosmos.

Viewed thus, the God and the Goddess would be two complementary aspects of one single being – the primeval cosmos.

The Egyptian sages would therefore be vindicated in their claims that Atum was alone even while in the presence of his Eye, that he copulated with himself, and that he brought magic (*heka*) into his own mouth; and that Ptah assembled and embraced his own limbs; and that Amun mixed his seed with his own egg. All these statements would be true because the God incorporated the Goddess within himself. She was an innate and unassailable part of his identity.

In summary, it would appear that the classical Egyptian religion was a monotheism, albeit one conceived dualistically. God was One – indeed had to be One since he personified a singular cosmos – but he was Two in cognizance of the 'male' and 'female' principles which brought about the harmony of that cosmos. A kind of Egyptian version of the Chinese Yin and Yang.

Chapter Fourteen Summary

- There were several creator-gods in Egypt, but they all represented a single being, the One Great God.

- The gods (*netjeru*) are not evidence for polytheism, since they were an integral part of God – 'the many who made up the One'.

- Egypt also had several creator-goddesses. As with the creator-god, they all represented a single being, the One Great Goddess, who was occasionally portrayed as the virgin mother of the cosmos.

- The Great God and Great Goddess were paired together, both in myth and cult. At times, she played a pivotal role in his creation.

- The chief question is whether Egyptian religion was a monotheism or a duotheism.

- The Great Goddess, like the Great God, personified the cosmos in its process of evolution. She was therefore a natural partner for him.

- God was often portrayed as a single, hermaphroditic being, a 'he-she', the 'father and mother' of all beings. But the primeval cosmos is best understood as a 'she-he', in which the feminine waters of the Goddess surrounded the masculine land of the God.

- The Goddess was particularly identified with *heka*, 'primeval magic', the first cause of creation, and in keeping with this idea she acted as the soul to the body of the God. The copulation of the Goddess and the God may have signified the first mysterious union of soul and body in the primeval cosmos.

- It is concluded that the God and the Goddess were dual aspects of a sole Supreme Being, as must indeed be the case if they personified the evolution of a sole, unique cosmos.

- Egyptian religion was therefore in essence a monotheism, albeit one defined on its own terms rather than on modern expectations of what a monotheism ought to be.

CHAPTER FIFTEEN

PYRAMIDS AND TEMPLES

O great ennead in Heliopolis, you will cause the king to endure by causing this pyramid of the king – and this his construction – to endure for eternity.
(Pyramid Texts, Utterance 601)

The visitor to Egypt is immediately struck by the monumental scale of the ancient buildings. It is encountered first and foremost at Giza in the shape of the giant pyramids and Sphinx. But it is also exemplified by the massive temples and statues of later periods which stretch from one end of the Nile valley to the other.

These extraordinary works in stone are a baffling phenomenon, which has never been adequately explained. In the case of the pyramids, which represent the greatest expenditure of time and energy, the experts cannot explain why they were built to such phenomenal heights, for they lack a coherent theory of what the pyramids symbolised. Of the many theories proposed, not one can support the evidence that stands before our eyes.

Ever since Egyptian civilisation collapsed, men have been driven to speculate about why the pyramids and temples were built. According to one popular tradition, which was handed down by Hermetic writers and Roman historians, the monuments were built in order to protect ancient wisdom from being destroyed in the Great Flood.[1] Hence their immense size and durable construction. This idea found wide support among Arab writers of the Middle Ages. According to one 14th century manuscript, the Sphinx had formerly sat on top of the Great Pyramid, but had been hurled off by the violent force of the Flood![2]

Similar theories have been advocated in modern times. According to some writers, the size of the pyramids is explained by the energy needs of the lost civilisation of Atlantis. According to others, it is explained by the requirements of extraterrestrials to have navigation beacons for their arriving spacecraft.

The cynics too have had their day, arguing that the pyramids signify an utter waste of resources. This idea was championed in 1974 by Kurt Mendelssohn, who proposed that the construction of the pyramids was a team-building exercise, designed to create a new social order. To him, it was not the pyramid that mattered but the building of the pyramid. 'The great strength and beauty of the pyramid projects', he wrote, 'lay in the complete uselessness of the final product'.[3]

The common thread in these alternative theories is that the pyramid builders must have had a material or economic motive, since no religious motive could possibly explain the scale of the construction. The theory of a sun cult has been weighed and found wanting, along with the theory of a star cult.

It is the premise of this book, however, that the Egyptian monuments can be explained by a religious motive once we recognise that Egyptian religion was not a sun cult, nor a star cult, but a 'cult of creation', that is to say a cult which celebrated the creation of the earth, sun, moon, and stars, and the origin of the gods, mankind, and all living creatures, and devoted all its available resources to ensuring that this cosmos would endure for ever.

In this chapter, we will reconsider the religious philosophy that gave birth to the pyramids and temples of Egypt, and develop a new theory of pyramid symbolism that I believe explains once and for all the efforts that were put into building them.

Figure 69.
THE PYRAMIDS OF GIZA.
An estimated 12 million tons of stone were used in the three main pyramids.

Mansions of Eternity

As explained in chapter one, the aim of the king and the Egyptian state was to preserve the cosmic order, *maat*, which had been established by the creator-god at the beginning of time. In order to achieve this aim, the king was endowed with the spirit of the creator-god and initiated into the secrets of creation. By drawing upon the magic of creation (*heka*), he was able to re-enact the events of the first time (*zep tepi*) and rejuvenate the sacred order of the cosmos.

The idea was that the king should perform eternal repetitions (*neheh*) of the creator's thoughts, words, and deeds. As long as the magic rites were repeated every day, and as long as the magic words were recited every day, the cosmos would endure for ever (*djet*). Never again would it return to the state of chaos from which it had come. It would, in effect, be made immortal.

Such was the importance of creation to the Egyptians that cities were modelled on the primeval mound – the island of earth that had emerged from the abyss (*nun*). Thus Memphis was held to be 'the divine emerging primeval island'; Hermopolis was 'the first plot of land on which Re first stood'; Abydos was 'the most ancient land'; Thebes was 'the island emerging from *nun*' and 'the mother iron of cities'; Hermonthis was 'the high ground which grew out of *nun*' and 'the egg which originated in the beginning'; Esna was 'the divine hill, the top of which emerged from *nun*'; and Elephantine was 'the city of the beginning... the joining of the land, the primeval hillock of earth, the throne of Re'.[4] By virtue of its magical association with the mound of creation, the city would be for ever firm, fertile, and peaceful. It would always be that young land which had only just emerged from the waters of creation.

The same idea was at work in temples and pyramids.

Temples designated the place of creation upon the primeval mound,[5] and were identified in many instances with the *akhet*, the 'light land' of creation.[6] At the time of its construction, the temple was brought to life by rituals that re-enacted the creation of a mythical temple which had come into being at the beginning of the world.[7] The temple thus became that mythical temple. As an inscription at the temple of Philae states: 'This temple came into being when nothing at all had yet come into being and the earth still lay in darkness and obscurity'.[8]

By virtue of its magical association with the primeval mound and the *akhet*, the temple could be made to endure for eternity. This is seen in the names given to temples: 'mansion of millions of years', and 'mansion united with eternity;[9] and to their obelisks: 'monuments of eternity'.[10]

Figure 70.
THE TEMPLE SITE OF KARNAK.

The meaning of these names is made clear in an inscription at the temple of Medinet Habu in which Ramesses III is told: 'Your mansion shall be firmly established like the sky forever',[11] while in an obelisk inscription Ramesses II is assured: 'So long as the sky exists, your monuments shall exist, and your name shall endure like the sky'.[12]

Pyramids too were places of eternity, as were the temples attached to them. The pyramid stood upon the *duat* – the birthplace of the stars – and was given the name *akhet*, while pyramid and temple together signified 'the mansion of Horus in the sky-water (*qebhu*)'.[13] In Utterances 599 and 601 of the Pyramid Texts, the assembled gods in Heliopolis are said to 'cause this pyramid of the king – and this his construction – to endure for eternity'.[14]

Temples and pyramids were made to endure for eternity by means of magic rituals, performed not only at the time of construction but also on an ongoing basis. These rituals brought the buildings into a relationship with the wider cosmos.

The focal point of the temple was the statue of the creator-god which was enshrined in the inner sanctum or 'holy of holies', alongside a model of his sacred barque. Every day, magic rituals performed by the priest in the name of the king repeated the creation and thereby brought the statue and the cosmos to life. As the sun rose at dawn, the creator-god's soul – manifest in the sun – would descend from the sky and alight upon its statue in the holy of holies.[15] Numerous texts describe the soul (*ba*) as 'uniting with', 'fraternizing with', and 'embracing' the cult image, which represented its 'body' and its 'emblem of power' (*sekhem*).[16] At the same time, the soul united with all the other divine images in the temple – both the statues of the gods and the reliefs on the walls.[17] The entire temple was thus rejuvenated each day so that it might indeed endure for millions upon millions of years.

The focal point of the pyramid was the mummy which was enshrined in the tomb chamber, 'the house of the *duat*'. Every night, the king's soul (*ba*) or spiritual double (*ka*) would descend from the sky, enter the tomb, and unite with its mummy.[18] As a result, the body was rejuvenated and caused to send out its soul and spiritual double once more, as it had done at the time of creation. The *ba* and *ka* thus ascended into the sky from the *akhet* in the east, while the *ka* rose up vertically to energize the pyramid above the tomb.[19]

Figure 71.
THE SOUL UNITES WITH THE MUMMY IN THE TOMB.
'May my soul see my corpse, may it rest on my mummy, which will never perish nor be destroyed.' (Vignette to Book of the Dead, Spell 89)

Ongoing rituals could not be performed on the mummy, since it had been sealed up in the tomb for eternity. Instead, the priests performed the magic rites on a statue which served as a substitute for the mummy. This statue, 'the *ka*-statue', was housed in the so-called 'mortuary temple' on the east side of the pyramid, and portrayed the Osiris-king standing and striding out of his tomb.[20] Every day, the priest would 'open the mouth' of this *ka*-statue in re-enactment of the first occasion when Osiris had had his mouth opened. The statue in the temple and the mummy beneath the pyramid were thus brought to life.

As a result of these magic rituals, the king's body and soul were made to endure for eternity, and so was the pyramid. As the Pyramid Texts put it:

> The king's afterlife is eternal repetition (*neheh*), his limit is eternal endurance (*djet*)... The king is this one who rises and rises, who endures and endures... His pyramid is among the living in this land for ever and eternity.[21]
>
> O Atum, set your arms about the king, about this construction, about this pyramid (of his) as the arms of a *ka*, that the king's *ka* may be in it, enduring for ever. O Atum, set your protection over this king, over this pyramid of his, over this construction of his, prevent anything evil from happening against it for ever...[22]

It is clear from this brief survey that temples and pyramids were expected and required to endure for eternity, as were the statues and mummies that were concealed within them, not to mention the reliefs and hieroglyphs that were carved and painted on the walls, pillars, and ceilings.[23] And there was no better way to achieve this end than to use the best quality stone and the monolithic method of construction. For such buildings are unlikely to perish, whether by natural disaster or by the hand of man.

The Egyptians, then, had compelling practical reasons, resulting from their religious philosophy, to build temples and pyramids in a grandiose style.

But there was another important factor at work too, which was not so much practical as symbolic.

It is a well established fact that the Egyptian temple (of the late period) symbolised the cosmos in the process of creation. Its floor signified the primeval mound which had risen from the *nun*; its columns signified the raising of the sky, and its roof signified the sky that had been separated from the earth. In the words of the *British Museum Dictionary of Ancient Egypt*:

> The temple was considered to be an architectural metaphor for the universe and for the process of the creation itself. The floor gradually rose, passing through forests of plant-form columns and roofed by images of the constellations or the body of the sky-goddess Nut, allowing the priests to ascend gradually from the outermost edge of the universe towards the sanctuary, which was a symbol of the inner core of creation, the primeval mound on which the creator-god first brought the world into being.[24]

In follows from this that temples were required to endure for eternity not only because they were the engines of cosmic renewal – the places of the rituals that sustained the cosmos – but also because they were images of the cosmos itself. This meant solid construction for practical reasons, but also monumental scale for symbolic reasons. The temple had to be huge to reflect the vastness of the cosmos.

This brings us back to the pyramids and the long-standing riddle of their meaning and symbolism. Might they too have been representations of the myth of creation?

The Pyramid Problem

There are two main types of pyramid in Egypt – step pyramids and true pyramids. The latter is the main focus of this chapter, but our study will throw light on the former type too.

True pyramids may themselves be divided into different types, though the lines of division are rather hazy. One important division is between main pyramids and satellite pyramids, the latter taking the form of 'baby' pyramids built close to the side of their 'parents'. Main pyramids too can be divided by size, between the giant pyramids – the two at Dahshur and the two at Giza – and those of a more economic size.

True pyramids vary enormously in design, having different angles of slope and different internal arrangements. In the latter respect, the norm is an entrance passage on the north side descending to an antechamber and a burial chamber. But some pyramids have multiple chambers; some have two entrance passages; and some have no means of entry and (one presumes) no internal compartments.

Another important division is between those pyramids which contain Pyramid Texts and those which don't. The earliest pyramids, including the giants of Dahshur and Giza, are devoid of inscriptions, as are most of the later pyramids. Those with the Pyramid Texts are for the most part those of the late-5th and 6th dynasties, from *c.* 2350 to 2180 BC. These include three satellite pyramids belonging to the queens of Pepi II.

The question of burial in pyramids is of particular interest. As noted in the preface, some kings built more than one pyramid for themselves, and it must therefore be the case that some main pyramids were cenotaphs rather than tombs. In addition, many small pyramids could not have been tombs, either because their internal chambers were too small, or because they had no internal chambers at all.

Again as noted in the preface, not one of the mummies recovered from Egypt's burial grounds is that of a pyramid builder (though rumour has it that such a mummy was recovered in 1881 but lost at the side of a road!). Some writers have thus argued that the pyramids never functioned as tombs for the pharaohs. But this is a difficult argument to sustain, for the names of the pyramids and the content of the Pyramid Texts prove that

Figure 72.
THE EVOLUTION FROM STEP PYRAMID TO TRUE PYRAMID.

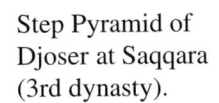

Step Pyramid of Djoser at Saqqara (3rd dynasty).

Red Pyramid of Sneferu at Dahshur (4th dynasty).

the pyramid's primary function was to despatch the king's soul to the sky and maintain it there for ever, it being implied that his body was buried in the earth below.[25]

This principle is less clear cut in the case of the earliest true pyramid builders, who were buried two centuries or more before the time of the Pyramid Texts. But all the indications are that the religion of the pyramid builders remained constant during this period.

Turning to the symbolism of the pyramid, it is appropriate to begin by examining the orthodox position.

Orthodoxy maintains that there is a lack of clear information on the symbolism of the true pyramid (this is debatable, as we shall see), but it nevertheless offers informed speculations, which are based on two main lines of evidence: firstly, the religious beliefs of the 4th dynasty pyramid builders; and secondly, the symbolism of the *benben* stone. In both cases, as we shall now see, the official interpretation of the facts is subjective and questionable.

The first key line of evidence is the prominence of the cult of Re at the time of the 4th dynasty. It was during this period that the kings added to their titulary the term *sa Re*, meaning 'son of Re' or 'the son Re',[26] while some added Re's name as a suffix to their throne names as if identifying themselves as his incarnation (witness Djedef-Re, Khaf-Re, and Menkau-Re). These developments followed the introduction of the cartouche by Sneferu, it being widely regarded as a solar symbol.[27] Egyptologists have thus concluded that a sun cult replaced an archaic stellar cult at the time of the 4th dynasty. The transition from step pyramids to true pyramids is thought to reflect this presumed change in the religion.[28]

The second key line of evidence is the *benben* stone of Heliopolis – Egypt's most famous cult object. As discussed earlier in chapter eleven, this sacred stone was mounted upon a pillar in an open courtyard in the Temple of the Benben at Heliopolis. Its significance lies in the fact that it provided the model for the apex of the obelisk and the capstone of the true pyramid, both of which were called *benbenet* (the feminine form of *benben*).[29] If we can deduce the symbolism of the *benben* stone, then we can deduce the symbolism of the pyramid itself.

Here the road forks to permit two different interpretations.

According to the first school of thought, the *benben* was a 'sun stone', the sacred symbol of the sun-god.[30] This is held to be so because: (a) the stone was worshipped in Heliopolis, literally 'Sun City'; (b) the gods of Heliopolis were sun-gods; (c) the capstone of Amenemhet III's pyramid at Dahshur refers to the sun-gods Re and the Lord of the Akhet;[31] and (d) the obelisks, derived from the *benben* on its pillar, were solar symbols, as evidenced by the fact that they were erected in honour of the sun-gods Atum, Re and Khepri.[32]

According to the second school of thought, the *benben* was a symbol of the primeval mound.[33] This is held to be so because in Utterance 600 of the Pyramid Texts the *benben* stone is raised up by Atum in parallel with the 'high hill', which is assumed to be a name for the mound.

In the light of all these facts and interpretations, scholars have reached conflicting views about the symbolism of the pyramid.

One popular view is that the pyramid symbolised the rays of the sun breaking through the clouds and descending to the earth in a pyramidal shape. One of the first Egyptologists to verbalise this idea was Alexandre Moret, who in 1926 wrote:

> These great triangles forming the sides of the pyramids seem to fall from the sky like the beams of the sun when its disc, though veiled by storm, pierces the clouds and lets down to earth a ladder of rays.[34]

This idea was later adopted by the pyramid expert I.E.S. Edwards. In his authoritative book *The Pyramids of Egypt*, Edwards asked: "What did the true pyramid form represent?", and then furnished his readers with the following answer:

> Only one answer suggests itself: the rays of the sun shining down on earth. A remarkable spectacle may sometimes be seen in the late afternoon of a cloudy winter day at Giza. When standing on the road to Saqqara and gazing westwards at the pyramid plateau, it is possible to see the sun's rays striking downwards through a gap in the clouds at about the same angle as the slope of the Great Pyramid. The impression made on the mind by the scene is that the immaterial prototype and the material replica are here ranged side by side.[35]

In recent years, this theory has been supported by other pyramid experts such as Mark Lehner and Rainer Stadelmann.[36]

Other scholars, however, following the lead of Henri Frankfort, have argued that the pyramid was but a development of the earlier mastaba tombs and step pyramids, and that all these structures symbolised the primeval mound of the creation myth.[37] This theory has been advocated most recently by Miroslav Verner and Christine El Mahdy.[38] The latter writes:

> The pyramids could not have been modelled on the shape of the rays of the sun, as the first pyramids long preceded any link with solar cults... There seems to be only one answer. The pyramid form has to be a symbolic mound, representing the place at which creation took place – the peak or pyramidion. It must represent the source of creation itself, and thus the epicentre of power enabling the rebirth or re-creation of the dead king in another world.[39]

Such is the appeal of this theory that Lehner sought to hybridize it with his vision of the pyramid as a simulacrum of sunlight. In his book *The Complete Pyramids*, he wrote:

> The pyramid is a simulacrum of both the mound of primeval earth and the weightless rays of sunlight, a union of heaven and earth that glorifies and transforms the divine king.[40]

We therefore have three theories of pyramid symbolism – but still in my opinion not the correct one.

Why are these theories incorrect?

Well, firstly there is the assumption that the pyramids were built at the time of the ascendancy of the sun cult. I would dispute this, for there is

336   THE MIDNIGHT SUN

no evidence that Re was a sun-god during the 4th dynasty. Indeed, when he first appears in the Pyramid Texts some two hundred years later he is not only a sun-god but also – and more fundamentally in my view – the god of primeval light – the creator-god become manifest in the expanded cosmos (this became apparent during our study of the creation myths in chapter three). I would therefore argue that Re was a form of the creator-god, and that his growing popularity in the 4th dynasty had nothing to do with any change in the religion. It would rather have been a case of one creator-god becoming more prominent than the others.

The second key line of evidence was the *benben* stone of Heliopolis, and here again the assumptions of orthodoxy may be questioned.

Firstly, there is the theory that the *benben* was a sacred symbol of the sun-god. The argument here is supposedly watertight, but in actual fact it leaks like a sieve. To see why this is so we must consider briefly each of the four premises listed earlier.

Premise (a) is that the *benben* was worshipped in Heliopolis, literally 'Sun City'. This is true, but unfortunately the name is Greek. In Egyptian times the city was known as Iunu, which meant 'Pillar City'. What was the significance of the pillar? While it may have had a solar symbolism in that its apex was lit up by the rays of the sun,[41] its primary symbolism was creational. This is proven by Utterances 600 and 527 of the Pyramid Texts, where Atum's rising up as the high hill and the *benben* stone is paralleled with his masturbation of his phallus.[42] It is therefore likely, as Frankfort argued in 1948, that the *benben* pillar was a phallic symbol and that the *benben* stone itself signified the solidified semen of the creator-god. Heliopolis would therefore be a city of creation.

Premise (b) is that the gods of Heliopolis were sun-gods. But this is a biased observation. The city's oldest god was Atum, who was primarily a creator-god, while Khepri signified the principle of self-creation (*kheper-djesef*). As for Re, although he was a sun-god, he is better understood as the creator made manifest in the sky. Far from being the home of just a solar cult, Heliopolis hosted a lunar cult and a stellar cult, consistent with its role as a centre of creation.[43]

Premise (c) is that the capstone of Amenemhet III's pyramid refers to the sun-gods Re and the Lord of the Akhet. This is true as far as it goes, but it doesn't go far enough. In fact, the Re-symbol on the pyramidion is surmounted by a pair of eyes, which was a cipher in Egyptian religion for the sun and the moon (see chapter six). The pattern indeed follows the creation myth, where the creator-god rose up and manifested himself in these two orbs. In addition, the inscriptions on the pyramidion refer to the stars. On the reverse face, part of the inscription reads: 'the soul of

Figure 73.
THE CAPSTONE OF THE AMENEMHET III PYRAMID AT DAHSHUR.

Amenemhet is higher than the heights of Orion',[44] while on the front face, beneath the Re-symbol, the text that supposedly refers to the sun continues in the following vein:

> The face of Amenemhet is open, he sees the Lord of the Akhet as he sails in the sky. May he [the Lord of the Akhet] cause that he [the king] rise as the Great God, Lord of Time, an indestructible star. May he be stellar among the stars.[45]

The pyramidion therefore has a stellar symbolism in addition to its solar and lunar symbolism, and to argue that it is primarily a solar icon, as Egyptologists do, is to be selective with the evidence. It does not support the argument for a solar *benben*, but it does strengthen the argument for a creational *benben* – a seed of Atum which gave birth to the sun, moon, and stars.

Premise (d) is that the obelisks, derived from the *benben* on its pillar, were solar symbols, the evidence for this being their inscriptions which honour Atum, Re and Khepri. Again, this falls into the trap of assuming that these gods were sun-gods. If they were creator-gods, as I believe, then the interpretation is profoundly altered. Against the solar theory, it is worth noting that the Egyptian word for obelisk, *tekhen*, has no known solar connotation. On the contrary, it seems to mean 'to pierce' and the inscriptions indeed refer to the obelisk 'piercing the sky'.[46] The obelisk is therefore to be understood as a 'sky-piercer' or 'sky-splitter' – an image that has nothing to do with the sun but everything to do with the creation and the idea of the pillar as phallic symbol.

Having disposed of the solar *benben* theory, we may now turn to the alternative theory that the *benben* was a symbol of the primeval mound, i.e. the earth. It is this theory which has led to the belief that the pyramid itself symbolised the primeval mound, its capstone being modelled on the *benben*.

According to this view, the mastaba tombs, the step pyramids, and the true pyramids all symbolised the mound, the mastabas having evolved into the pyramidal forms. But I find this theory to be intuitively difficult, since the mastaba has the appearance of a low, flat hill – in keeping with the Egyptian view of the earth (the Two Lands) – whereas the pyramids have the appearance of high hills.

This brings us to the crux of the issue, namely Utterance 600 of the Pyramid Texts. In this spell, Atum is said to rise up as the 'high hill' and the *benben* stone, the former being taken as a name for the mound. The *benben* thus appears to be synonymous with the mound. However, as I have argued in chapter eleven, it is possible that the high hill (*qay qaa*) was not intended to be synonymous with the *benben*, *or* that it alluded to the ejection of primeval matter from the earth into the sky – hence the repeated emphasis on height, its name signifying 'high high'. Whichever interpretation is correct, it may be argued that the *benben* signified the seed which was ejaculated from Atum's phallus or spat from his mouth, hence the next line in Utterance 600: 'You sneezed out Shu, you spat out Tefnut'.[47] In support of this argument, the obelisk inscriptions describe the obelisk's tip, the *benbenet*, as 'reaching', 'piercing', and 'mingling with' the sky, as if to suggest that the *benben* was lifted into the sky at the time of creation (as was the case with another famous cult object, the *ka-mut.ef* meteorite).[48]

The belief that the *benben* – and hence the pyramid – symbolised the primeval mound – the earth – is thus based on a misconception, and must be rejected. Instead, we should regard the *benben* and the pyramidion as reaching and inseminating the sky, with the base of the pillar or pyramid standing upon the mound, as was the case with temple architecture (see earlier).

A Stellar Pyramid?

An alternative point of view that has gained momentum in recent years is that the true pyramid had a stellar symbolism. In this regard, several lines of evidence combine to form a compelling case, which cannot be ignored

PYRAMIDS AND TEMPLES   339

in our assessment of the monument's overall significance.

Firstly, two pyramids bore names which referred explicitly to the king becoming a star. The first, admittedly a step pyramid, was called 'Horus is the Star at the Head of the Sky', whilst the second, a true pyramid, was called 'Djedefre is a Star' (*sehed*).[49] Djedefre, incidentally, was the king who introduced the supposedly solar title *sa Re*. But neither his pyramid nor the others was named in honour of the sun.

Secondly, the Pyramid Texts place a decided emphasis on the king's afterlife among the stars. *Pace* E.A. Wallis Budge and J.H. Breasted, it is my view that these texts lend greater importance to the stars than to the sun (see the review in chapter seven).[50]

Thirdly, there is evidence of stellar symbolism in the architecture of the pyramids. Although I am not entirely convinced that the 'airshafts' of the Great Pyramid were targeted at certain stars, as many Egyptologists believe,[51] it is certainly true that the pyramid's entrance passage, which was generally located in its north face, was oriented towards the northern circumpolar stars, among which the king intended to dwell for eternity.[52] It almost goes without saying that north was *not* the direction of the sun.

Finally, again on the subject of architecture, it is pertinent to note that the builders of the 5th and 6th dynasty pyramids chose to decorate the ceilings of the tomb chambers with a panoply of stars, but not with the sun.[53]

Figure 74.
PYRAMID TOMB CHAMBER, 6TH DYNASTY.
On the wall (left), the Pyramid Texts; on the ceiling (right) the stars. Both attest to the stellar significance of the true pyramid.

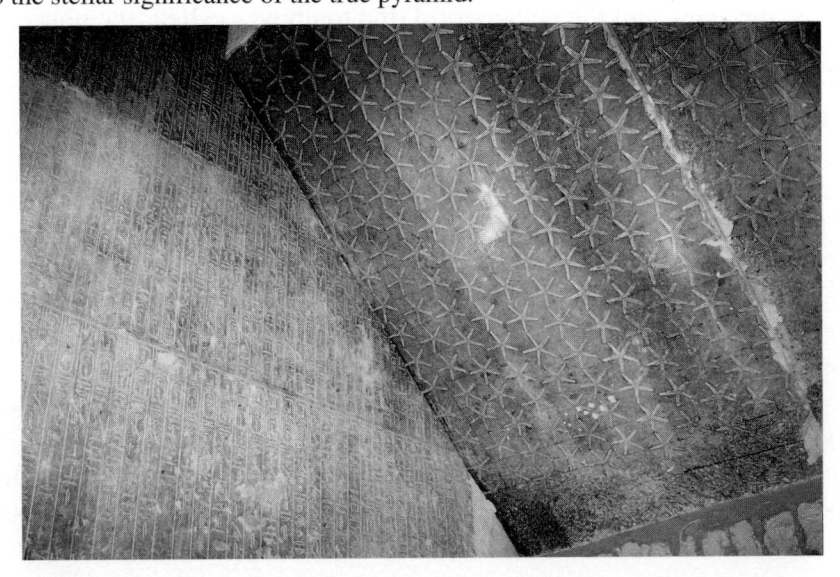

All of this makes a mockery of the solar pyramid theory, and suggests instead that the stars played the more dominant role at the time when the pyramids were built. However, while a few scholars have awoken to this idea,[54] it yet remains unclear how the pyramid's stellar attributes might translate into a theory of its shape and symbolism.

One suggestion, made by Robert Bauval, and more recently by Toby Wilkinson, is that the smooth-sided, flowing design of the pyramid may have been modelled on an 'oriented' iron meteorite, i.e. a meteorite that retains its orientation as it falls to the earth and thus acquires a conical shape.[55] Both Bauval and Wilkinson have suggested that the *benben* was such a meteorite and that the pyramidion (*benbenet*) was modelled on the meteorite, which could be described as a 'fallen star'.[56] From here, it is but one small step to identify the pyramid in its entirety as a simulacrum of a fallen star, albeit one which has been inverted in a symbolic attempt to give it rebirth in the womb of the sky.[57]

The problem with this theory is that it does not automatically follow that the meteorite would have been viewed as a star. Indeed, if we allow Egyptian mythology to be our guide, then the meteorite in the form of the *benben* had a wider significance. It was not a star per se; rather it was the semen of Atum – the seed of creation; and that creation involved not just the stars, but also the sun and the moon.

The Pyramid of Creation

It should be apparent from the foregoing discussion that the pyramid had multiple symbolisms. It was associated with the sun, but also with the moon, the stars, and the netherworld (the tomb was called 'the house of the *duat*'). To emphasise one of these symbolisms, to the exclusion of the others, is to be selective with the evidence. What is needed, if the riddle is to be solved, is a single theory of pyramid symbolism that embraces the solar, lunar, stellar, and chthonian aspects of its design. In short, there is a pressing need for a unifying framework.

In this book, I have developed exactly such a framework to reconcile the diverse strands of Egyptian religion. I have argued that the religion was not a mere sun cult, as scholars believe, but a sophisticated 'cult of creation' whose primary aim was to ensure the eternal endurance of the cosmos by perpetual repetition of the myth of creation.

A key element of my hypothesis is the reconstruction of the creation myth. For two hundred years, it has not been taken seriously by scholars, who regard it as a mishmash of superstitious and inconsistent beliefs. But my study has revealed a profound physics of creation, predicated upon the idea of the death and rebirth of the cosmos, personified by the death and rebirth of the creator-god. Crucially, this means that Osiris, the god of death and rebirth, was the creator-god *par excellence*.

Osiris was the god with whom the deceased king was identified. His mummy was held to be an image of Osiris. This means that the king's rebirth and translation to the afterlife was a re-enactment of the creation myth. His spirit went forth from the tomb just as the spirit of the creator-god had gone forth from the *duat*. He became the sun, or the moon, or a star, or all the stars, just as the creator-god had once created the sun, the moon, and the stars.

This theory is radically different from the consensus which has been adopted by Egyptologists during the past two hundred years, and it leads to a radically different interpretation of the pyramid. The theory predicts that the pyramid had a creational significance – that its shape somehow symbolised the creation of the cosmos.

Let us consider the evidence in favour of this new theory.

The first crucial piece of evidence comes from Utterance 600 of the Pyramid Texts, where the pyramid is said to be protected by the arms of the creator-god Atum. The salient passage reads as follows:

> O Atum, set your arms about the king, about this construction, about this pyramid (of his) as the arms of a *ka*, that the king's *ka* may be in it, enduring for ever.[58]

Now consider the immediately preceding line:

> O Atum-Kheprer... You sneezed out Shu, you spat out Tefnut, and you set your arms about them as the embrace of *ka*, that your *ka* might be in them.[59]

Notice the parallel here. Atum embraces the pyramid in exactly the same way as he embraces Shu and Tefnut, and he conveys his *ka* – the spirit of creation – to both. The implication of this, I believe, is that the pyramid signified the idea which Shu and Tefnut personified – and this, not to put too controversial a point on it, was the development of Atum into *the entire cosmos*.[60] The pyramid might thus be a simulacrum of the creation of the cosmos.

The second crucial piece of evidence is the capstone of the pyramid, which like the tip of the obelisk was modelled on the *benben* stone of Heliopolis. This capstone (*benbenet*) has been described as 'the complete pyramid in miniature', and as such it holds the key to the symbolism of the pyramid.[61] What did the *benben* stone signify? As discussed earlier, the *benben* was neither a symbol of the sun, nor a symbol of the primeval

342 THE MIDNIGHT SUN

Figure 75.
THE BENBEN PILLAR, THE TRUE PYRAMID, AND THE OBELISK.
All three architectural forms share a common symbolism.

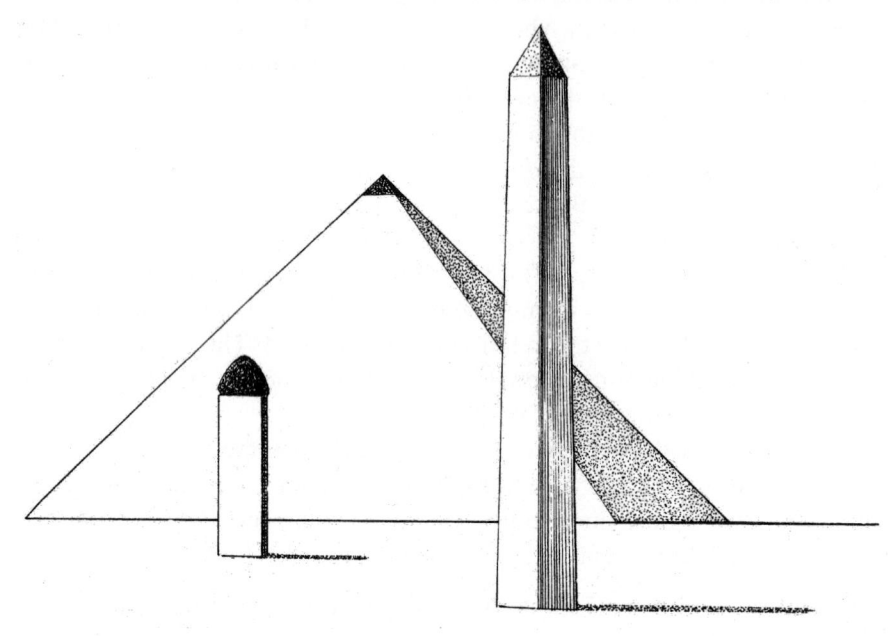

mound. Rather, it was a symbol of creation. That this was so is proven by Utterance 600 (again) which places the *benben* at the site of creation:

> O Atum-Kheprer, you became the high hill; you rose up as the *benben* stone in the mansion of the *benu*-bird in Heliopolis.[62]

Now this line occurs immediately before Atum's emission of Shu and Tefnut and his embrace of his twin children and the pyramid, and it is possible that a parallel was intended between the pyramid and the *benben* stone – and perhaps also the high hill (what is the pyramid if not a high hill?). But whether this was intended or not, the undeniable fact is that the *benben* was placed at the scene of creation – the creation of the high hill and of Shu and Tefnut.

A more precise interpretation of the *benben* can be deduced from its name and from inscriptions which describe its function on the tip of the obelisk.

The word *benben* (*bnbn*) meant 'to flow' while *bn* signified the act of begetting offspring by means of copulation with a phallus.[63] It was thus literally 'the stone which flowed out', and it is furthermore suggested by an inscription at Karnak that it 'flowed out' in the form of 'seed' in the primeval ocean.[64] On the basis of this evidence, together with Utterance

600, scholars have identified the *benben* pillar as the 'solidified seed' or 'petrified semen' of Atum.[65]

Where did the *benben* flow out to? The answer is provided by obelisk inscriptions which describe the tip (*benbenet*) as 'reaching', 'piercing', and 'mingling with' the sky. Hatshepsut, for example, dedicated one of her obelisks to Amun with the words:

> My heart directed me to make for him two obelisks of electrum, that their pyramidions might mingle with the sky...[66]

Putting all these clues together, it may be surmised that the *benben* on its pillar signified the creator-god's seed being ejaculated from the primeval ocean into the sky. It would therefore be a phallic, creational symbol – a representation perhaps of the creation myth in which Atum masturbated his phallus to a climax in Heliopolis.

According to this line of enquiry, the pyramid too would represent the seed of the creator-god rising up from the netherworld to inseminate the sky. Hence perhaps the smooth, flowing lines of its design. Once again we are drawn towards the conclusion that the pyramid was a simulacrum of the creation of the cosmos.

The third crucial piece of evidence, and the most revealing as regards the symbolism of the entire pyramid, is the pyramid's identification with Osiris and the *akhet*. Our trusted sources in this regard are the Pyramid Texts and the name of one of the 4th dynasty pyramids.

Let us consider first of all the identity of the pyramid with Osiris. In Utterance 600 (again, what a gold mine it is), Horus is beseeched:

> O Horus, this king is Osiris, this pyramid of the king is Osiris, this construction of his is Osiris; betake yourself to it; do not be far from him in his name of 'Pyramid'.[67]

What is the meaning of this? Earlier in the spell, Atum causes the king's *ka* to be in the pyramid by means of his *ka*-embrace (see passage quoted earlier). It may therefore be surmised that the pyramid is being identified with the *ka* of the reborn king, i.e. his vital spirit or spiritual double. In other words, the monument *is* the spirit of Osiris.

Egyptologists have always been cautious about this passage, since it tends to contradict their theories that the pyramid symbolised the sun or the primeval mound.[68] However, it is corroborated by the name given to the Great Pyramid, 'Akhet Khufu', since in the Pyramid Texts Osiris is given the name 'Akhet from which Re goes forth'. In Utterance 354, for example, the king is told:

> O Osiris-the-king... Live, that you may go to and fro every day. Be a spirit (*akh*) in your name of 'Akhet from which Re goes up'.[69]

In several spells, this name is associated with an embrace between Osiris and his son Horus in which the latter becomes a spirit. In Utterance 368, for example:

> O Osiris-the-king, this is Horus in your embrace, and he protects you. He has become a spirit (*akh*) through you in your name of 'Akhet from which Re goes forth'.[70]

This same embrace is probably implied in Utterance 600, quoted above, where Horus is urged to betake himself to the pyramid and be close to Osiris in his name of 'Pyramid'.

The upshot of all this is that the pyramid was conceived as an image of the *akhet* and a simulacrum of the spirit-making embrace between Osiris and Horus.

But what was the significance of the *akhet*?

Egyptologists translate *akhet* variously as 'horizon', 'light land', 'the radiant place', or 'the place of becoming *akh*'. It is believed to signify the birthplace of the sun-god and the place of his rebirth every day. The pyramid's identification with the *akhet* is thus seen as affirmation of the theory that the pyramid was a symbol of the sun.

In this book, however, we have seen that the *akhet* was much more than just the birthplace of the sun – or the birthplace of the stars, as some would interpret it.[71] It was rather the birthplace of the entire cosmos – the place where the primeval earth and waters were spiritualized to become the primeval mound, the atmosphere, the sky-ocean, the sun, the moon, and the stars.

For a deep understanding of the *akhet*, the reader is referred to chapter two, where the bare facts were set out, and chapter six, where a level of interpretation was added.

To summarise briefly, the *akhet* is described in the Pyramid Texts as a watery place, 'green with fields' and stocked with green plants. Its flood is evocative of the primeval ocean (*nun*), while its waters and fields are virtually duplicated in the other realms of the cosmos – the *duat*, the field of reeds, and the sky.

In chapter six, I suggested that the *nun*, the *duat*, the *akhet*, and the field of reeds were snapshot pictures of a dead terrestrial world in the process of being revivified. The *nun* and the *duat* seemed to signify the old cosmos, inert but pregnant with the possibilities of new life; the field of reeds seemed to signify the revived cosmos, its fertile land beginning to emerge from the floodwaters; and the *akhet* seemed to represent the final transformation in the rebirth of the cosmos – the phase in which all the primeval elements – water, air, and matter – were given their final, spiritualized forms.

The *akhet* would therefore represent the entire cosmos in its process of coming-into-being. It would be neither the old cosmos, nor the new, but that mythical place of the first time where the old *became* the new.

This creational interpretation of the *akhet* offers a unique insight into the symbolism of the pyramid. Already, we have seen the convergence of two lines of evidence, which suggest that the pyramid was a simulacrum of the creation of the cosmos. Now we have a third, which complements this picture perfectly. The pyramid, we may conclude, represented the cosmos in its process of rebirth. It was an image of the primeval world rising up from the darkness of the netherworld to give birth to a new world of light. It was a womb of cosmic seed, captured in its moment of expanding and fertilizing itself.

All the evidence is brought together in figure 76 below.

At the base of the pyramid is the risen earth, the primeval mound, which is the uppermost limit of the netherworld (*duat*).

The main body of the pyramid is the *akhet* – the 'light land', or place of spiritualization of the elements.

And the apex of the pyramid is the *benbenet* – the seed of the creator-god which flows forth from the womb of the *akhet* and inseminates itself as the womb of the sky.

Figure 76.
THE CREATIONAL SYMBOLISM OF THE TRUE PYRAMID. A NEW INTERPRETATION.

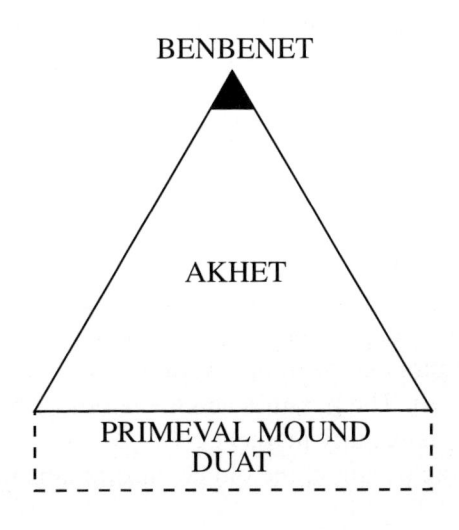

The pyramid was thus a monument to life – the afterlife of the cosmos personified by the afterlife of the king – and to cosmic order (*maat*) – the triumph of light over darkness.

The beauty of this interpretation is that it can explain all the pyramids of Egypt.

Although sometimes built in groups, conceptually each pyramid would have stood alone as a parallel statement of the Egyptian belief in the One God – in the same way that numerous temples stood as representations of the one cosmos. Big or small, main or satellite, tomb or no tomb, each pyramid would have been a monument to the creation and the miracle of life. Variations in their shapes (caused by the angle of slope) might have celebrated the diverse but complementary mathematical relationships at the heart of the cosmos. Hence the use of the sacred proportions pi and phi.

What about the step pyramid? Was it too a symbol of creation? Here, we have no option but to speculate since the texts are virtually silent on the question of its symbolism. One possibility, as discussed earlier, is that the step pyramids symbolised the primeval mound. In later periods, the earth (the *duat* of Osiris) is occasionally depicted in the shape of a step pyramid.[72] However, this might not have been true to the architect's original intention. In the Step Pyramid at Saqqara, it would appear that a structure symbolic of the primeval mound was built into the foundations of the monument.[73] It may therefore be argued that the step pyramid was the prototype of the 'high hill' or *akhet*, and that it gave way to the true pyramid not because of any change in religion or symbolism but simply because of a breakthrough in construction technology. The smooth-sided pyramid gives a better impression of the flow and the unity that were essential to the concept of creation and the creator-god.

Finally, we come to the interesting question of the relative symbolisms of the pyramid and the temple. If both symbolised the same thing – the cosmos in its process of coming-into-being – then why did the Egyptians render the idea in two distinct forms?

There are two answers to this question – a philosophical answer and a functional answer.

Firstly, there was no unique moment of creation that could be captured in stone. It was rather a fluid process involving fertilization, expansion, refertilization, and completion. Architects and artists could thus portray only one creative moment – out of several possibilities – in any one work of architecture or art. The pyramid and the temple, I believe, portray two different but complementary moments.

In the case of the pyramid, the old cosmos retains its shape as it gives birth to a new form of itself. It bears the seed (*benbenet*) for the creation of the new cosmos, but it has not yet evolved into it. The image is highly conceptualized.

In the case of the temple, the seed has been sown and the new cosmos is acquiring its final shape. The roof represents the sky and the pillars the supports of the sky. The image is less conceptualized and more 'real' in the sense that the terrestrial elements are depicted as plant-like columns being raised from the earth and the *nun* into the sky.

The pyramid thus captures the creation myth at a point in time slightly earlier than that of the temple. To the Egyptians, who relished diversity of expression, both architectural forms would have been important.

Secondly, form followed function – and the functions of pyramids and temples were subtly different.

The function of the pyramid was to revivify the mummy and despatch its soul into the wider cosmos. Accordingly, its focal point was the *duat*, the netherworld: the mummy was Osiris; the coffin was the womb of Nut in her role as mother of the cosmos; the tomb chamber was the *duat*, the birthplace of the stars; and the pyramid itself was the *akhet* emerging from the *duat*.

The function of the temple, on the other hand, was to rejuvenate the statue of the creator-god and despatch its soul into the wider cosmos. In this case, the focal point was not the netherworld but the primeval mound and the *akhet*: the raised floor of the holy of holies was the mound, while the statue shrine was the *akhet*, and the temple itself was the *akhet* and the sky rising up upon the mound.

These different emphases – one on the netherworld, the other on the risen mound – dictated precise architectural forms, invested with specific magical powers. For the mummy, the requirement was a form that would draw spirit out of the netherworld – that form was the pyramid – while for the statue, the requirement was a form that would interact with the created cosmos – that form was the temple. It is for this reason that all pyramids were built on the west bank of the Nile, as if in the process of emerging from the netherworld (the land of the west).

Chapter Fifteen Summary

- Egyptology has never been able to explain the immense size of the giant pyramids. Nor has it deciphered the religious symbolism of the true pyramid. As a result, alternative theories have proliferated.

- The true pyramid was not a symbol of the sun, nor the primeval mound, nor a star. It was a symbol of the creation – a simulacrum of the cosmos in its initial stage of coming-into-being.

- As a symbol of the cosmos, the pyramid had to be huge and precise, since the cosmos had a life span of 'millions of years'.

- Ongoing rituals performed at the pyramids caused the king's mummy – an image of the world – to live and its soul to circulate through the cosmos. It was believed that if this activity ceased the cosmos would collapse into its former state of chaos. For this reason, the mummy, the *ka*-statue, the pyramid, and its attached temple, were required to endure for eternity.

- The temple too was an image of the cosmos, but in its final stage of coming-into-being. Again, ongoing rituals were designed to keep the cosmos alive. For these reasons, the temple was built on a grandiose scale – in order that it might endure for 'millions of years'.

- The 'cult of creation' theory, presented in this book, offers a plausible explanation for the extraordinary scale of the pyramids and temples of Egypt.

CHAPTER SIXTEEN

THE TOMB OF KHUFU

Alan Alford's hypothesis of finding the real burial chamber of Khufu is laudable. It would be a triumph for Egyptology were it found.
(Christine El Mahdy, open letter, May 2003)

Foremost among the Egyptian pyramids in its size, and unique in its precision of build and highly unusual interior design, the Great Pyramid of Giza has been the subject of endless speculation on the questions of who built it and why.

According to Egyptologists, the Pyramid was built by the 4th dynasty king Khufu (or Cheops, as he was known to the Greek historians) *c.* 2550 BC to function as his tomb and resurrection vehicle. Despite the unusual internal arrangement, scholars are adamant that the building was 'a tomb and nothing but a tomb'.[1]

But many well-educated people outside Egyptology find it difficult to accept this theory. They cannot believe that a mere tomb would be built 481 feet high, or aligned to true north within 3 arc minutes (about 5% of a degree), or designed in such a way that it embodied the mathematical ratios pi and phi – to cite but a few of the Pyramid's many extraordinary features.[2] For these people, there just has to be an alternative explanation for the monument's unprecedented size and precision.

Over the centuries, dozens of different theories have been suggested. For nearly two thousand years, it was claimed that the Pyramid was the Granary of Joseph. In the 19th century, the Pyramid was regarded as a biblical prophecy in stone, or a repository of divinely-inspired weights and measures. Then, in the 20th century, came a deluge of theories: the Pyramid was interpreted as a giant water pump or power plant, a sundial or almanac, an astronomical observatory, a repository of wisdom from a lost civilisation, a temple of initiation, a navigation beacon for alien spacecraft, or an air raid shelter against meteorite impacts.

As an outsider to Egyptology myself, I have always been open-minded to new theories. However, after many years of study I have come to the view that the astonishing size and precision of the Great Pyramid can be explained by religious factors, at least when Egyptian religion is viewed as a 'cult of creation' and the pyramid as a symbol of the cosmos in the process of creation (see chapter fifteen). I might not be able to explain how the Pyramid was built, nor where the technologies came from, but I am satisfied that it was commissioned in honour of a concept – the living universe – that was held to be supremely big, divinely perfect, and, with the help of the pharaoh, capable of enduring for ever and eternity.

What, then, of the Pyramid's interior design – its bewildering array of chambers, passages, and shafts? Was the monument built as a tomb, or something more than a tomb?

Once again, I am inclined to side with the Egyptologists. However, I must hasten to add that I do not agree with them on every point. Yes, the Pyramid was built to be a tomb and resurrection device for a king, but on the purposes of its various chambers, passages, and shafts I beg to differ. In particular – and this is the focus of this chapter – I am confident that the tomb of the king was not the uppermost chamber, as Egyptologists believe, but an as yet undiscovered room concealed in the basement of the Pyramid at ground level.

It is to the discovery of this intact tomb that this book is dedicated. If I am right, and if Egyptologists have the courage to put my theory to the test, we will soon set eyes on the mummy and treasure of Egypt's most famous pyramid builder.

The Mystery of the Great Pyramid

The Great Pyramid is one of the largest buildings that the world has ever seen.[3] With a base 756 by 756 feet square and a designed height of 481 feet, the Pyramid has a volume of 91.2 million cubic feet, making it the largest pyramid in Egypt. The exact number of individual stones may never be known with certainty (since the building is anchored upon a protruding nucleus of bedrock), but a widely-used estimate suggests that two million, three hundred thousand blocks of stone were raised, while a more recent estimate revises that number upwards to nearly four million blocks.[4] With the average weight per block exceeding two tons, a total weight for the monument is indicated somewhere in the region of five to ten million tons.[5]

In accordance with general custom, the Great Pyramid was provided

Figure 77.
THE GREAT PYRAMID, VERTICAL SECTION, LOOKING WEST.

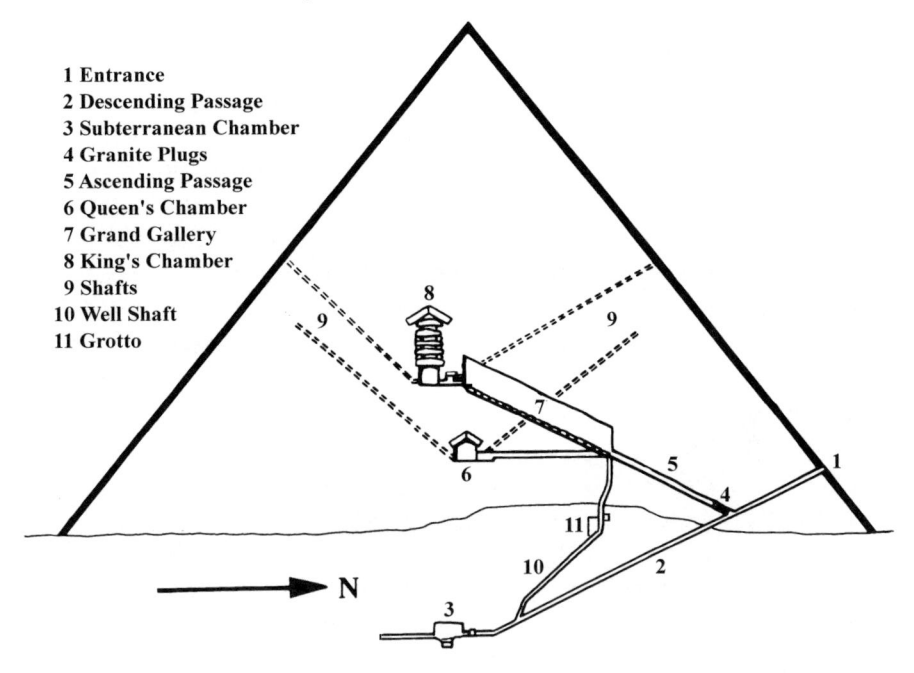

1 Entrance
2 Descending Passage
3 Subterranean Chamber
4 Granite Plugs
5 Ascending Passage
6 Queen's Chamber
7 Grand Gallery
8 King's Chamber
9 Shafts
10 Well Shaft
11 Grotto

with a northern entrance passage that sloped downward to a subterranean chamber. But, uniquely among the pyramids of Egypt, the Great Pyramid was also furnished with chambers high in its superstructure: the so-called Queen's Chamber at a height of 70 feet, the Grand Gallery at a height of 70-140 feet, and the so-called King's Chamber at a height of 140 feet, as shown diagrammatically in figure 77.

What is the meaning of this exceptional architecture?

The answer, according to Egyptologists, is revealed by the smashed granite sarcophagus in the King's Chamber (figure 78), this box being the right shape and size to have contained a human body. There being no other sarcophagi in the Pyramid, and no prima facie evidence of burial in any chamber, scholars have concluded that the King's Chamber was the king's tomb and that it was robbed in antiquity.

In 'solving' this puzzle, however, scholars have created yet another: for why would Khufu, alone among all of the pyramid building kings of Egypt, have decided to place his tomb high up in the superstructure of his pyramid?

According to one view, Khufu broke with convention in an innovative attempt to fool tomb raiders, who had already made it a national pastime to rob the graves of his ancestors. But if this were so, then why did other

Figure 78.
THE KING'S CHAMBER SARCOPHAGUS.
The broken granite box encapsulates the mystery of the Pyramid. Did it really contain the body of the king?

kings not take similar precautions?

I.E.S. Edwards advanced an alternative theory. Khufu, he suggested, decided to be buried in a granite sarcophagus, which proved too large to be introduced to the descending passageway; thus the underground tomb was abandoned. The Queen's Chamber was then built as a new tomb, at a height of 70 feet, but it too was abandoned owing to delays in delivery of the sarcophagus to the site. For this reason, the King's Chamber was built at a height of 140 feet, and it then received the sarcophagus when it was finally delivered.[6] It is an ingenious theory, but, for the majority of scholars, a step too contrived.

Other Egyptologists wondered whether the king had elevated his tomb for a religious reason, perhaps to become closer to the sun-god Re. Zahi Hawass, taking this thought to its logical limits, suggested that Khufu had sought burial in the pyramid's superstructure in order to become one with Re in the horizon (*akhet*). But this change had marked 'a religious revolution', which had 'violated the idea of *maat*'; and hence had proven short-lived.[7] Mystery solved? "No" say his colleagues, since there is no reliable evidence for a religious revolution during Khufu's reign.

There the debate has been parked, stuck in a cul-de-sac one might say, while scholars have turned to other, more pressing matters, seemingly not too concerned by the anomaly of the raised burial chamber. Khufu, it is supposed, had his reasons, which might well remain unfathomable to us. It's no big deal.

But I believe it *is* a big deal.

From the beginning to the end of Egyptian history, it was the standard practice to bury the deceased person in the earth. Every known tomb complies with this principle, and the pyramids too are consistent with it, since they are usually equipped with at least one chamber at ground level or below. On no occasion has a burial been found where the body was not in contact with the earth.

The Egyptian texts of all periods attest to this principle, asserting that the body of the god, or the king, belonged in the earth, as opposed to his soul, or spirit, which belonged in the sky. Of the various examples cited in the panel overleaf, the most important is Utterance 305 of the Pyramid Texts, which confirms that the rule was in operation at the time when the pyramids were being built. The relevant line may be rephrased succinctly as 'the body to earth, the spirit to the sky'.

Egyptology has long been aware of the Egyptian custom of placing the tomb chamber beneath the pyramid,[8] and has long been acquainted with the principle 'the body to earth, the spirit to the sky'. However, when it comes to the Great Pyramid, it has been prepared to make an exception to the rule, for the reasons outlined earlier.

This may be a fundamental mistake. In this book, I have argued that the king's death and rebirth re-enacted the myth of the death and rebirth of the cosmos, and that this myth involved a rebirth *from the earth* (and the *nun*). It was therefore imperative that the king's body be identified with that of Osiris, the god of the netherworld (*duat*), who at the time of creation had sent out his spirit *from the earth*. Under this interpretation, the mummy had to be buried in the earth beneath the pyramid, otherwise the ritual would have been devoid of its vital magic.

Everything hinges on the symbolism of the pyramid. If it symbolised the primeval mound, as some Egyptologists maintain, then a burial in its superstructure might be theoretically permissible as an exception to the general rule. But if it symbolised the sun's rays or, more plausibly, the cosmos in its process of coming-into-being, then an elevated burial would have deprived the mummy of the vital, soul-restoring contact with the earth.

In chapter fifteen, I argued that the pyramid stood upon the primeval mound and that its superstructure signified the spirit that had emerged therefrom. The evidence for this argument comprises: the pyramid name Akhet, meaning 'the place of becoming spirit' (*akh*); the identification of the pyramid with Osiris, who made a spirit of Horus in his name Akhet;

the protection of the pyramid by gods who became spirits;[9] the presence in the pyramid of the king's *ka*, his spiritual double; the hieroglyph for 'pyramid' (*mr*) which consisted of a white superstructure on a horizontal black line (the latter symbolising earth);[10] and the parallel symbolism in temples, which were built upon the primeval mound.

According to this interpretation, which I believe to be conclusive, it is simply inconceivable that Khufu or his architect would have planned a tomb at a height of 140 feet inside the Great Pyramid. Rather, the tomb had to be concealed at ground level or below, in accordance with the fundamental axiom 'the body to earth, the spirit to the sky'.

Might the Great Pyramid be an exception to this rule? After all, it was built some two centuries before the time of the Pyramid Texts on which the creational interpretation largely relies.[11]

The evidence suggests that it would *not* have been an exception.

Firstly, the Pyramid's name was 'Akhet Khufu', which suggests that it was an image of the *akhet* – a simulacrum of the evolving cosmos.[12] This is consistent with the cosmogony and cosmology of the Pyramid Texts, and indicates that the tomb does not belong in the superstructure of this particular pyramid.

Secondly, building inscriptions found in the recesses above the King's Chamber refer to the creator-god Khnum. They suggest that the Pyramid was built for a king named Khnum-khuf (for which Khufu is possibly an abbreviation) or that the pyramid itself was called Khnum-khuf, meaning

Figure 79.
THE GREAT PYRAMID.
Its name Akhet Khufu proves that it signified the realm of the spirit.

The Body to Earth, the Spirit to the Sky

O [king], you who are put under the earth and are in darkness!
(Pyramid Texts, Utterance 52)

(The king speaks:) "I come to you, O Nut, I have cast my father to the earth... my soul has brought me and its magic has equipped me."
(The sky-goddess replies:) "May you split open your place in the sky among the stars in the sky."
(Pyramid Texts, Utterance 245)

The spirit is bound for the sky, the corpse is bound for the earth.
(Pyramid Texts, Utterance 305)

(O Re) The sky belongs to your soul... and the earth belongs to your body.
(The Book Am Duat)

Let there be praise in the sky to the soul of Re, and let there be praise on earth to his body; for the sky is made young by means of his soul, and the earth is made young by means of his body.
(The Book of Gates)

The earth is for your dead body, and the sky is for your soul... O Re, whose transformations are manifold, your soul is in the sky, your body is in the earth.
(The Book of Gates)

He is the All-Lord, the beginning of that which is. His soul, they say, is that which is in the sky. It is he who is in the underworld and presides over the east [the horizon]; his soul is in the sky, his body is in the land of the west.
(Hymn to Amun)

The heavens rest upon his head, and the earth bears his feet. The sky hides his spirit, the earth hides his form, and the underworld contains his hidden mystery.
(Hymn to Amun)

[O deceased], your soul is bound for the sky, your corpse is beneath the ground.
(The Book of the Dead, Spell 169)

The sky holds your soul, the earth holds your mummy.
(The Lamentations of Isis)

356 THE MIDNIGHT SUN

'Khnum Protects'.[13] This links the monument directly to the concept of creation.

Thirdly, the Pyramid was equipped with two dismantled boats, which were buried in pits in alignment with its southern side.[14] These boats are highly evocative of certain spells in the Pyramid Texts and Coffin Texts, which refer to a boat being assembled by the gods for the voyage out of the *duat* into the sky.[15] The fact that these boats were buried in the earth suggests that the king's mummy would likewise have been buried in the earth.

And fourthly, on a more speculative note, it is possible that the Great Sphinx was carved originally as a simulacrum of the island of creation,[16] in which case the entire Giza plateau would commemorate the rebirth of the cosmos.[17]

In view of these lines of evidence, it is significant indeed that no trace of Khufu's mummy has ever been found in the King's Chamber, and that no reliable record has ever been unearthed of him having being buried in, or removed from, the Pyramid.

But the crux of the issue is this: if Khufu was not buried in the King's Chamber, then what did the broken sarcophagus contain? And if he was not buried in that room, then where was he buried?

The Mystery of the Broken Sarcophagus

Before one can embark on a quest for the 'real tomb' of Khufu, one must first provide a plausible theory for the contents of the sarcophagus. That the box did contain *something* is suggested by the removal of its lid. It would appear that the intruders smashed one of its corners, peered inside, and decided to go to the immense trouble of removing the entire lid to gain access to its contents (see figure 78).[18] So, if not a mummy, then what did the box contain?

My studies of the creation myth have led me to the conclusion that the sarcophagus contained iron meteorites. This is an original theory but not too controversial since the importance of meteoritic iron in Egypt is a well-established fact. Nevertheless, scholars are only dimly aware of the true significance of this magical metal.

As discussed in chapter ten, iron (*bja*) is ubiquitous in the Pyramid Texts. The deceased king as Osiris has his mouth split open with an adze of iron, and resurrects himself by lifting up his iron bones, splitting open his iron egg, splitting or traversing the iron of the sky, and sitting on his iron throne. The significance of this, I have suggested, is that the king was re-enacting the creation myth in which molten iron was blasted out of the earth into the sky, whereupon it formed the stars and possibly the sun and the moon.

When some of this iron fell back to earth in the form of meteorites, the Egyptian sages interpreted the flowing, twisted metal as the seed of the creator-god – the spiritualized material with which he had inseminated the sky.

It was for this reason, I believe, that iron meteorites were worshipped in ancient Egypt.

Now the problem with iron meteorites is that they begin to rust as soon as they are exposed to the earth's humid atmosphere (having previously existed in the dryness of space). In *Pyramid of Secrets*, the companion volume to this book, I suggest that the Egyptians attempted to overcome this problem by enclosing the iron inside hermetically-sealed boxes.[19] In this way, the metal was protected from the corrosive effect of the air and made to endure for eternity – effectively in a state of mummification. As absurd as this practice might sound to the modern reader, it would have been fully merited on account of the privileged status of the meteorite in Egyptian religion.

Also in *Pyramid of Secrets*, I cite possible instances where a meteorite was raised aloft upon a pillar or pole to commemorate the origin of the iron of the sky. The prime examples are the *benben* stone of Iunu, 'Pillar City', and the 'head of Osiris' which was set upon a pole and worshipped at Abydos. In the latter case, it would appear that the meteorite of the god was enclosed in a box (see figure 44 in chapter ten).[20]

It is plausible, therefore, that the sarcophagus in the King's Chamber contained iron meteorites which, unlike the body of the king, belonged in the height of the pyramid (for the same reason that the *benben* belonged at its apex). According to this theory, the King's Chamber would have been a 'chamber of creation', its twin 'airshafts' perhaps commemorating the squirting of the molten iron into the sky.[21] The fact that the builders lent this chamber such an elegant finish in granite should not surprise us, since the meteorite had at least as high a status as the king's mummy.[22] We have to learn to think as the Egyptians would.

This theory, if it be accepted, demands a complete reappraisal of the internal architecture of the Pyramid. It is possible, for example, that the upper passages and chambers were sealed off at the time of construction, in which case they would have been used initially by the king's *ka* – his spirit, or spiritual double. The Grand Gallery in particular has a spiritual feel to it, and it is conceivable that it was designed to be a simulacrum of the process of creation.[23]

Further secret passages and chambers are a distinct possibility under this hypothesis (the reader is directed to the companion volume).[24] But our primary concern here is the king's tomb. Having filled the empty coffer with the iron bones of the god, we may now search the Pyramid for the mortal bones of the king.

Where is the Real Tomb?

The Pyramid contains two rooms (that we know of) at ground level or below, which would have been suitable for a royal burial. These are the Subterranean Chamber and the Grotto.

Both these rooms would appear to be natural caves, which have been enhanced by the hand of man. Although modern archaeologists regard these caves as rough and 'unfinished', the ancient Egyptians would have held them in high esteem as symbolic of the netherworld and the womb of Nut.

We will consider each of these possible burial sites in turn.

The Subterranean Chamber

The Subterranean Chamber lies approximately 100 feet below ground level, and is entered via the Descending Passage. It is by far the largest of all known chambers in the Pyramid, measuring 46 feet east-west by 27 feet 1 inch north-south, with a maximum height of 11 feet 6 inches. It has a haphazard shape, on account of which it has been dubbed 'the chamber of chaos' (see figure 81).[25]

The only feature of interest is an eight-feet-square pit, cut in the cave's floor to an original depth of 50 to 60 feet (it is nowadays filled partly with rubble, giving it a depth of only 15 feet or so). This pit was semi-excavated by explorers during the 19th century, but nothing important was found.[26]

Might Khufu have been buried here? Although there is no evidence of a burial in this room, nor historical record of a mummy or coffin having been removed, it is possible that the tomb lies hidden at the bottom of the pit, which has been only partially explored. This would explain the great time and trouble which the builders evidently took to reach this point, 100 feet beneath the bedrock.

But there is a major problem with this idea, namely the vulnerability of the Subterranean Chamber to tomb raiders. If intruders had located the camouflaged entrance to the Pyramid and proceeded inquisitively down the Descending Passage, they would surely have discovered the tomb of the king.

It therefore seems likely that the Subterranean Chamber was designed

THE TOMB OF KHUFU 359

Figure 80.
THE GREAT PYRAMID, VERTICAL SECTION, LOOKING WEST, WITH SUBTERRANEAN FEATURES HIGHLIGHTED.

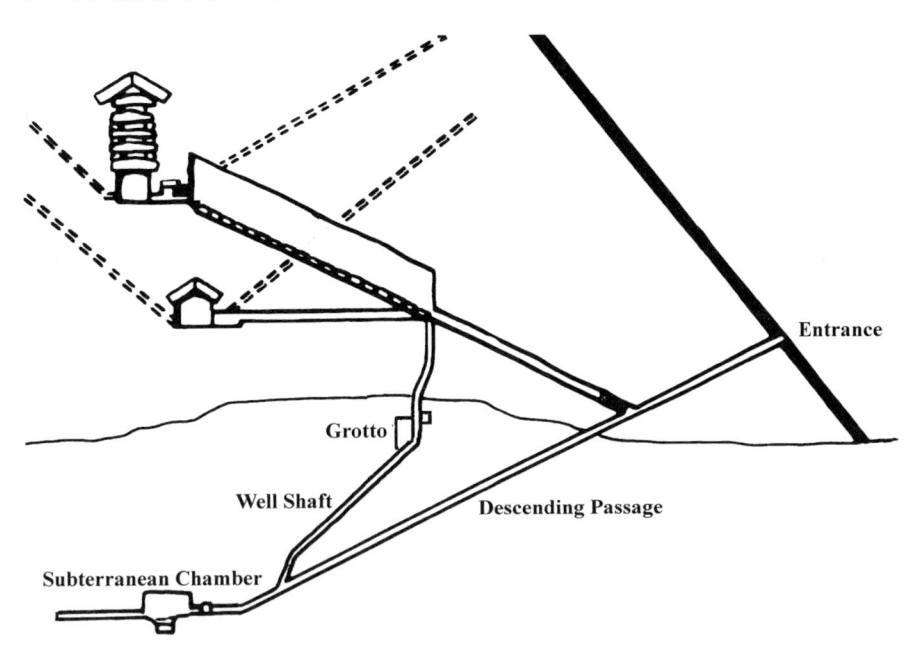

Figure 81.
THE SUBTERRANEAN CHAMBER.
Was it a decoy tomb?

to host pre-burial rituals and thereafter to serve as a decoy tomb, to throw any intruders off the scent. The latter idea is supported by the pyramid expert J.P. Lepre, who in his authoritative study *The Egyptian Pyramids* writes:

> This chamber was ideally situated to act as a ploy, to make the unsuspecting mind believe that a pharaoh had once been buried here.[27]

Let us turn, then, to the second possibility – a burial in the Grotto.

The Grotto

The Grotto lies just below the highest point of the rocky outcrop on which the Pyramid is anchored. It thus lies at ground level theoretically, although in practice it is about 15 feet above the exterior base.[28]

The Grotto is essentially a natural cave, which must have predated the building of the Pyramid. As Lepre explains, it was once an earthen oasis in the midst of the plateau bedrock:

> The Grotto of the Great Pyramid, situated just below the monument's ground level, constitutes what appears to be the hollowing-out of a once-smaller natural pocket of earth at the centre of the pyramid plateau. Unusual as it may seem, being uniquely located in the very middle of an otherwise solid rock foundation, no other explanation can be given.[29]

The Grotto may be described as a low cavern of irregular shape with its floor on three levels. The ceiling height is low, and the average person can barely stand erect at the point of maximum headroom.

The ground plan of the Grotto is shown in figure 82. The main feature here is the Well Shaft – a vertical shaft, approximately 28 inches square, which provides the entrance and exit to the room. We will discuss this shaft further in due course.

In the west side of the Grotto is the lowest floor level, in which a deep hole has been dug for a purpose unknown. In the centre of the room the floor level rises, and then it rises again. The relative floor levels and the depth of the excavation are revealed by the profile view in figure 83.

Inside the Grotto, resting on the floor near the deep hole, is a block of granite, measuring 42 by 25 by 20 inches, with a 3.5-inch hole bored through it.

The ceiling of the Grotto is low, fairly flat and highly unusual. Lepre comments:

THE TOMB OF KHUFU 361

Figure 82.
THE GROTTO, GROUND PLAN.

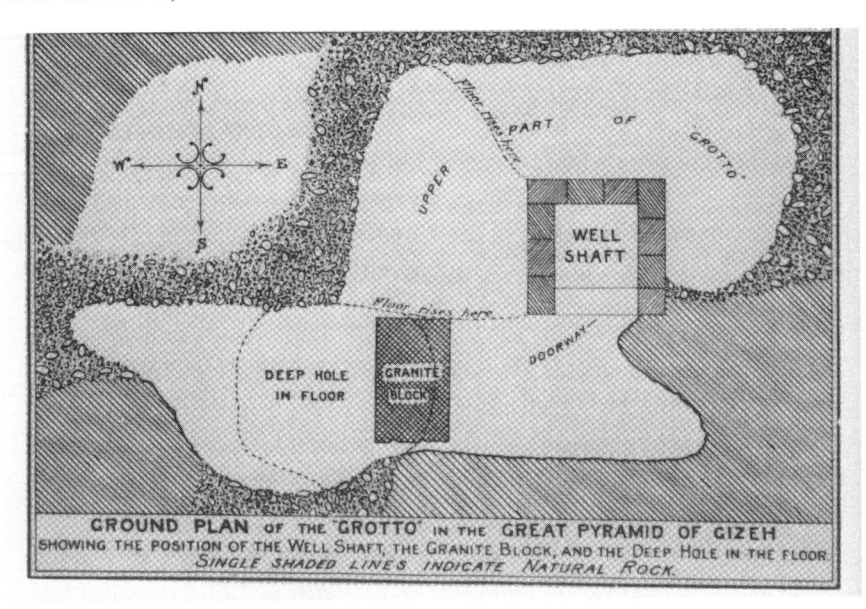

Figure 83.
THE GROTTO, VERTICAL SECTION, LOOKING NORTH.

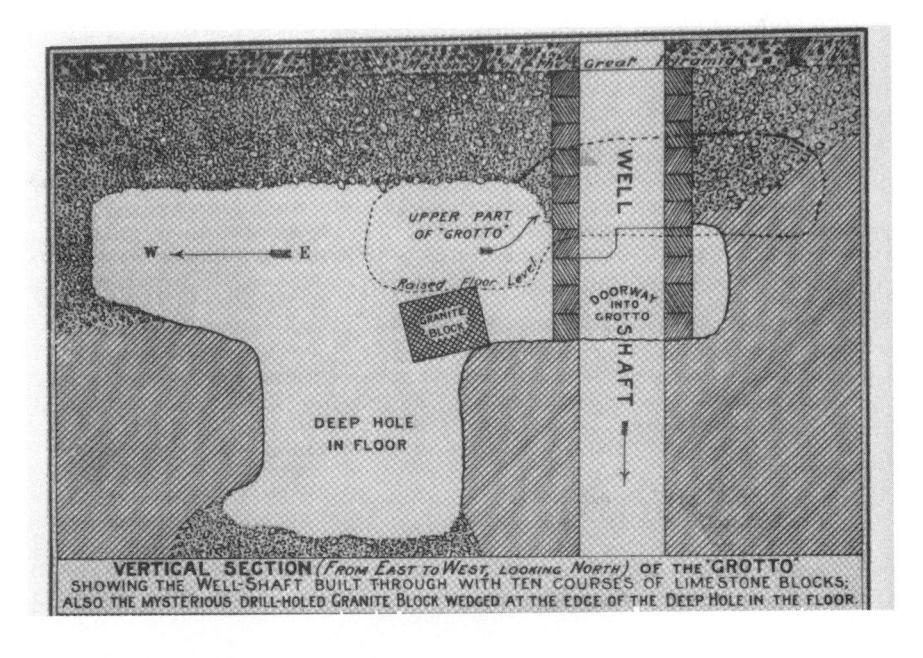

Even more curious than the presence of this earthen cavity is the fact that its ceiling is composed not of packed earth as would be expected, but of gravel packed in damp, caked sand. Whereas the earthen walls of this cavity are relatively hard to the touch, the ceiling of small stones is so loosely packed that one has only to reach up and dig in with one's fingers in order to extract whole handfuls of this material. M. Edgar collaborates this observation by stating that this ceiling 'crumbles when touched'. This is a very unusual configuration, and one which would lead us to believe that perhaps the ceiling might represent an impromptu fill-in by the builders.[30]

Lepre then noted something even more peculiar about this ceiling:

The ceiling is also unusually damp to the point where there is actually a perceptible coating – like a light frost – over the pebbles themselves. This unusual composition naturally tempts one to speculate about the existence of a nearby water source. Yet a water source – and especially one so very cool – does not seem likely in the middle of a solid rock foundation at the edge of a barren section of desert.[31]

Lepre was captivated by this strange, damp ceiling and wondered aloud about the possibility of drilling into it:

A probing of the ceiling of the Grotto would appear to be in order, but it might prove to be a hazardous venture, due to its loose condition and to the immense weight of the core of the pyramid bearing down on it from above. Oddly enough, Pliny, the Roman scholar, writing about the Great Pyramid in AD 79, makes mention of a 'water-well' being located in the monument. Could there once have been a supply of water running through this section, with the remnants of some underground reservoir still trickling in to dampen the ceiling of the Grotto?[32]

These thoughts call to mind the report by the Greek historian Herodotus (5th century BC) that Khufu had been buried in an island surrounded by water. In *Histories*, Book II, he wrote:

To make it [the causeway] took ten years – or rather to make the causeway, the works on the mound where the pyramid stands, and the underground chambers, which Cheops intended as vaults for his own use. These last were built on a sort of island, surrounded by water introduced from the Nile by a canal.[33]

Lepre must have known about this tradition, but he neglected to mention it in his book, since he supported the theory that Khufu had been buried in the King's Chamber. But he nevertheless sensed that the Grotto must have had a hitherto overlooked purpose. He wrote:

> Although seemingly insignificant when compared to the other, much more commanding, apartments of the Great Pyramid, the Grotto nevertheless had a special purpose which we are not presently familiar with.[34]

Could this special purpose have been the protection of Khufu's mummy? Might there have been a grain of truth in Herodotus's report, which he received in good faith from the priests at Giza, and which tallied with the all-important principle 'the body to earth, the spirit to the sky'?

Herodotus aside, there are good archaeological grounds for taking this hypothesis seriously. The key piece of evidence, as I shall now explain, is the Well Shaft.

The Well Shaft

The Grotto is reached via the so-called Well Shaft, which was so named by the Arabs on account of its frightening depths. As shown in figure 84, the Well Shaft begins close to the bottom of the Descending Passage and ascends in three sections as far as the Grotto and the surface bedrock on which the Pyramid was built. It then continues upwards by means of a rough tunnel (A-X) in order to provide access to the Grand Gallery (at point Z). All regular sections of the shaft measure approximately 28 by 28 inches square.

Prior to construction of the Pyramid, the Well Shaft consisted of the short section A-B, which led down to the Grotto. The cave thus predated the Pyramid, and was probably viewed as a holy place from the earliest days of Egyptian civilisation.[35]

At a later date, probably when Khufu commissioned the Pyramid, the Well Shaft was extended downwards through sections B-C, C-D, and D-E.[36] The first of these sections runs north-south for a distance of 100 feet through the bedrock, in an accurate straight line, at an angle of about 43°. The second section continues north-south for a further distance of 30 feet, but at a steeper angle of 68°. And the third section turns east-west and heads horizontally to connect with the west wall of the Descending Passage. Here, the opening in the wall was concealed by a plate of stone that could be removed and refitted like a door. Lepre writes:

> They sealed that aperture with a block of limestone which would have been indistinguishable from the other stones comprising the west wall of that corridor. Perhaps that camouflaging stone was movable and

364 THE MIDNIGHT SUN

allowed the high priests to enter and leave the shaft at will... This question may never be resolved, as the stone... has now disappeared. We know that it was there as recently as Roman times, for these people are recorded to have visited the Subterranean Chamber without ever having an inkling that the Pyramid contained chambers in its superstructure. It was removed by the Caliph al-Mamun in the ninth century AD.[37]

As a result of this Well Shaft extension (B-C-D-E), the Grotto could still be visited after the first layers of the Pyramid's masonry had been laid over its upper entrance passage A-B.

Was this the reason the Well Shaft was cut? Egyptologists, working on the dubious premise of a burial in the King's Chamber, have overlooked this possibility. To them, the shaft was first cut to provide ventilation for the workmen in the Subterranean Chamber and was afterwards extended through sections A-X, X-Y, and Y-Z to provide an escape route for the

Figure 84.
THE WELL SHAFT, WITH KEY SECTIONS LABELLED.

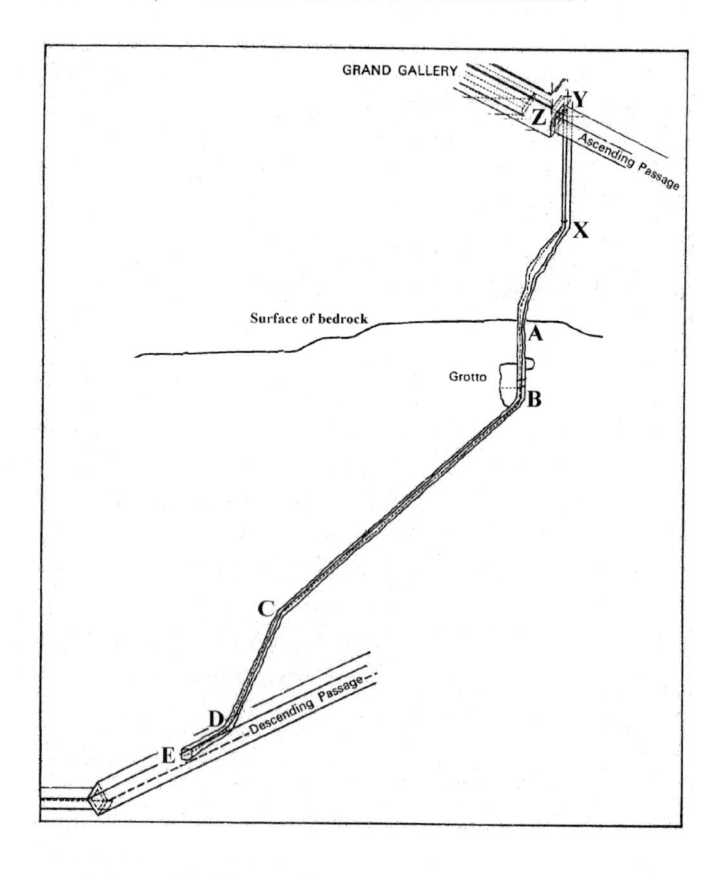

workmen who had become trapped in the Grand Gallery upon releasing the plugs into the Ascending Passage. Despite numerous criticisms that have been made of this theory, it has survived owing to the assumption about the king's burial.[38]

But what if Khufu was not buried in the King's Chamber?

I believe that the most obvious explanation of the Well Shaft has been overlooked. It was cut to retain access to the Grotto.

But why?

One possibility is that the builders sought to use the cave for ongoing rituals, perhaps at certain times of the year. But another possibility is that they required a one-off access to the Grotto for the funeral ceremony of the king.

Whilst not dismissing the first possibility, it is the second possibility that I would like to explore.

If the reader will indulge me, I would like to outline a scenario.

The Secret Burial of Khufu

The Giza plateau is devoid of its pyramids. But work is about to begin. A team of specialist workers is preparing to sink the Descending Passage of the Great Pyramid approximately 258 feet into the bedrock, where it will debouch into a subterranean chamber at a point directly under the Pyramid's central east-west axis. As they do so, however, a second team of workers has set up base on top of the rocky outcrop, about 100 feet to the south and 10 feet to the west of the first team's position. This second team, given privileged access to the holy site of the Grotto, is preparing to sink into the bedrock a shaft about 168 feet long, which, unbeknownst to the first team, will intersect with the Descending Passage some 25 feet short of the latter's terminus.

Each day, as the first team cuts the Descending Passage southwards at an angle of 26° 34', the second team slips down the vertical shaft past the Grotto, and cuts the so-called Well Shaft southwards at an angle of about 43°.

Then, one day, the architect decides (for a reason unknown to us) to shorten the Descending Passage by about 25 feet, and replace this length by *a horizontal passage* to the Subterranean Chamber. In keeping with this decision, he orders the second team to alter the angle of their passage from 43° to a much steeper 68° so that the second passage will intersect with the first passage in its sloping section, about 22 feet above the terminus, as originally planned. This change in angle is considered to be essential, since otherwise the second passage will meet the first passage in the horizontal section, where tomb robbers would be more likely to discover the secret door.

The second team extend their passage southwards at its new angle for a distance of about thirty feet. Then, having taken careful measurements of their position relative to the Descending Passage, they cut a 10-feet-long connecting passage eastwards to intersect the Descending Passage in its west wall. As they get closer and closer to the first passage, they work more and more carefully, until a reed can be poked through into the passage beyond. Then, with the utmost care, the workmen perform their most difficult and precise task: they chisel away at the rock to form a thin slab that can be removed and replaced in the wall. Having completed this task, they reinsert the secret door in the wall, ready for later use during the king's funeral.

The existence of this connecting passage and door, we may surmise, was known only to members of the second team, and to as few of them as possible. The first team, who dug the Descending Passage, would have known nothing of the secret entrance, work on their passage having been completed or suspended at the time when the final secret linkage was made.

As work begins on the Pyramid's superstructure, the priests make the final preparations for the secret funeral in the Grotto, lowering into the sacred cave any necessary ritual objects and perhaps assembling there a wooden coffin for the king. Soon afterwards, the Pyramid's masonry is laid across the entrance to the Grotto's shaft, to block off that entrance for ever. From this moment on, the Grotto becomes inaccessible, except via the Well Shaft and its secret door in the Descending Passage.

The Pyramid is completed, and the funeral of the king takes place. To outside observers, the king's mummy is conveyed into the Pyramid's main entrance, and lowered through the Descending Passage towards the Subterranean Chamber. Perhaps a burial ritual is indeed performed in that room, in order to bring the mummy to life. But a secret plan is now executed, on the orders of the late king, of which only a very few people have knowledge. Two or three of these people, we may surmise, are those who remain behind in the chamber to perform the last rites.

These trusted priests backtrack up the Descending Passage and gently prise open the secret door to the Well Shaft. With as much respect as it is possible to display in the circumstances, they remove the king's mummy from the Subterranean Chamber, carry it through the horizontal passage, and then haul it 22 feet up the Descending Passage to the secret entrance to the Well Shaft. There, having manoeuvred the mummy through the hole in the wall, the priests convey it all the way up the Well Shaft to the

Figure 85.
THE GROTTO AND WELL SHAFT, ORIGINAL DESIGN, SHOWN IMMEDIATELY AFTER COMPLETION OF THE PYRAMID.

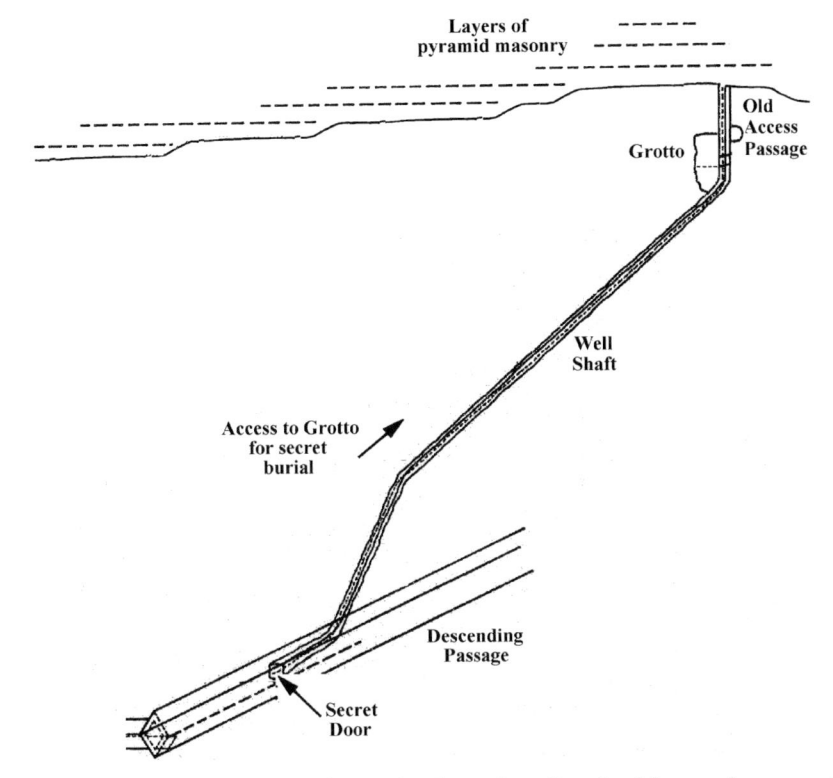

Grotto. And there they perform the last rites for the king, whose soul is forthwith translated into the Pyramid above, and to all four corners of the universe.

Now the priests make their way back down the Well Shaft and into the Descending Passage, where they refit the secret door, cementing it into place and camouflaging its joints. Having made any final arrangements in the Subterranean Chamber, which is to perform the role of a decoy tomb, they exit the Pyramid through the Descending Passage, leaving outside observers completely unaware of the cunning plan that they have executed beneath the Giza plateau.

I believe that this scenario is entirely probable, for three reasons.

Firstly, the Grotto's position amidst the stepped plateau outcrop would have corresponded to the head of the primeval mound – the risen earth of the creation myth.[39] A burial there would have been in perfect accord with the religious axiom 'the body to earth, the spirit to the sky'.

Secondly, a burial in the Grotto would have been ideal from a security point of view. The door to the Well Shaft was cunningly contrived and carefully positioned so as to make its discovery difficult (as history has shown), while the Grotto itself lay further from the Pyramid's entrance than any of the other known chambers. (It is an interesting detail that the route covers about 466 feet, not far short of the height of the Pyramid, 481 feet.)[40]

And thirdly, this theory provides far and away the best explanation of the great time and trouble which the builders took to cut the Well Shaft and provide it with a secret door.[41]

But the question remains: what happened to the king's mummy?

Where is the Body?

It must be conceded right away that the Grotto may have been discovered by tomb raiders in antiquity, in which case the mummy could have been removed and destroyed. It is likely, in my view, that intruders discovered the Well Shaft and used it to plunder the Pyramid's upper chambers long before they were 'discovered' by Caliph al-Mamun in the ninth century AD. These intruders would not have passed by the Grotto without taking a close look inside.

Ominously, a deep hole has been dug in the floor at the western end of the Grotto, apparently in ancient times (figures 82-83). With dimensions of 5 feet by 5 feet 5 inches by 5 feet 5 inches, and a maximum extension at the bottom of 6 feet 6 inches, this hole could well have accommodated the mummy of the king. The implication, of course, is that the hole was dug to exhume the mummy, which was subsequently removed from the room. Tests of the soil in the hole might be able to confirm or negate this hypothesis.

But I believe that this hole was a decoy – a last desperate attempt by the builders to persuade an intruder who managed to get this far that the tomb had already been discovered and robbed.

The real tomb would thus lie in the immediate vicinity of the Grotto.

One possibility is that the entrance to the tomb has been screened off by a false ceiling. As noted earlier, the Grotto's ceiling is highly unusual and has a frost-like veneer, as if it were close to a water source. Lepre's idea of probing this ceiling has considerable merit and might well lead to an important discovery.

In addition to examining the Grotto's ceiling, we should also check its floor and walls. Here, the best bet is the western end of the room, since it was Egyptian practice to bury the king just to the west of a pyramid's central north-south axis.[42] In this respect, it is interesting to note that the western end of the Grotto lies exactly on the Great Pyramid's north-south axis.[43] In addition to which, it is quite remarkable that the distance to the west wall from the main entrance, via the Descending Passage and the Well Shaft, is almost exactly equal to the height of the monument (481 feet). The west wall of the Grotto should therefore be probed, as should the floor in that part of the room.

But the main target of our attention should be the 10-feet-high section of the Well Shaft that runs vertically upwards from the Grotto's entrance. In contrast to the other 143 feet of the shaft, this section was lined with small limestone blocks. These blocks, arranged in ten layers, extend from the floor level of the Grotto to what used to be 'ground zero' before the Pyramid was built (see figures 83 and 85).

The question which no-one, to my knowledge, has ever asked is this: why was this section of the Well Shaft – and this section alone – given a stone cladding?

Could it be that these blocks were fitted into the shaft specifically for the purpose of concealing the entrance to Khufu's real tomb?

Might there exist a network of caves – similar to the Grotto – that has been screened off from our view?

According to my calculations, the most likely place for a hidden door would be the top three layers of stones on the southern side of the shaft (compare figure 82 to figure 83). This 'door' would provide access to a passage, which might conceivably dogleg to the west to run directly over the hole in the Grotto below. Khufu's real tomb would thus lie close to the mooted water source that affects the ceiling of the Grotto.[44]

The size of the limestone blocks in the Well Shaft (ten courses span the height of 10 feet) is such that the priests would have had no trouble in

Figure 86.
THE ENTRANCE TO THE GROTTO, SHOWING THE LOWERMOST LAYERS OF LIMESTONE CLADDING.

sealing up the entrance to the upper cave system after the burial of the king.

This hypothesis can be tested easily enough using ground-penetrating radar equipment, as has been used elsewhere in the Pyramid (but never in the Grotto or the Well Shaft). If a cavity is confirmed, as I suspect it will be, the discovery of Khufu's mummy and burial treasure would involve nothing more than the removal of a few small blocks of stone.

This book is my invitation to the authorities to think again about the religion and architecture of ancient Egypt, and put my theories to the test inside the Great Pyramid.

Already, I have the support of one Egyptologist, Christine El Mahdy, and one historian, Michael Rice, for my proposal to find the real tomb of Khufu. I now invite other Egyptologists and scholars to step forward and give this idea the backing that it needs.

I feel certain that the late J.P. Lepre would have lent his weight to this proposal, and in his honour I close my book with his closing words from *The Egyptian Pyramids* (1990):

> The reader should now be able to appreciate the fact that the pyramids have not revealed all of their many secrets. There is still an impressive amount of investigation and exploration to be done...
>
> The pharaohs who built these gigantic tombs were, by far, the greatest that ever ruled over Egypt. For the heyday of Egyptian history is synonymous with the heyday of pyramid building.
>
> And somewhere within at least one of these mighty monuments lies the mummy of at least one of these great kings. That much, at least, we can fairly well assume.
>
> King Tut is famous for being the only Egyptian pharaoh whose tomb was ever found intact, but Tut did not have a great pyramid. A greater find awaits mankind. Only future investigation will discern whether the world will ever have the opportunity to witness it.[45]

ISBN 0 9527994 2 1

You've read **The Midnight Sun**, now read the companion volume **Pyramid of Secrets**: *The Architecture of the Great Pyramid Reconsidered in the Light of Creational Mythology.*

Order through a bookshop, or buy on-line at www.eridu.co.uk

Guided Tours of Egypt

You've read the books, now see the sights!

If you would like to join one of Alan Alford's tours to Egypt – or employ him as your personal guide – please contact us via the Eridu website: www.eridu.co.uk

ACKNOWLEDGEMENTS

Sir Isaac Newton once wrote 'If I have seen further it is by standing on the shoulders of giants.' In the case of this book, those giants are all the archaeologists and scholars who have striven over the past two hundred years to reconstruct the civilisation of ancient Egypt. But some giants stand taller than others. In particular, I am indebted to Henri Frankfort for his work on the cohesiveness of Egyptian religion, Mircea Eliade for his momentous book *The Myth of the Eternal Return*, R.T. Rundle Clark for his insights into Egyptian mythology, Eve Reymond for her thorough analysis of the Edfu Building Texts, Jan Assmann for his interpretation of '*neheh* and *djet*', and J.P. Lepre for his outstanding investigations into the passages and chambers of the Great Pyramid.

On a more personal note, I would like to thank James P. Allen for sending me a spare copy of his book *Genesis in Egypt*, Michael Ricc for lending me his copy of Eve Reymond's important but out-of-print book *The Mythical Origin of the Egyptian Temple*, and for commenting on the drafts of my chapters 4, 5, 6, 7, 8, 9, 10, 11, and 12, Christine El Mahdy for supporting my proposal to explore the Grotto in the Great Pyramid, and Simon Cox for alerting me to the possibility that Sah was originally Canopus, not Orion.

Closer to home, I would like to thank my wife Sumu for her love and support during the difficult challenges of the past few years – it is now time to repay her patience and trust – and my mother and father who, by bringing me up free of religious indoctrination, made it possible for me to see a little further while standing on the shoulders of those giants...

Illustration Credits

The author owns copyright in figures 2, 3, 5, 6, 14, 29, 62, 63, 64, 69, 70, 72, 73, 74, 76, 78, 79, 81, 84, 85. In addition, the author has adapted the drawings of others as follows: 43 (after Gardiner), 77, 80 (after uncertain provenance).

Copyright in the remaining illustrations is as follows: Bauval/Cook 37, 50, 75; Bonnet 4, 34; Budge 7, 10, 12, 13, 15, 17, 18, 19, 20, 22, 23, 24, 25, 26, 27, 28, 30, 32, 33b, 35, 38, 42, 44, 46, 47, 48, 55, 56, 57, 58, 65, 66, 67, 68; Clark 16, 59; De Lubicz 49; Edgar 82, 83; Gardiner 11a, 40, 54; Naville 71; Naydler 52; Piankoff 8, 21, 60; Piankoff & Rambova 31; Roeder 41; Roth 39; Wainwright 51; Wilkinson 11b, 33a, 45, 53; Uncertain provenance 1, 9, 36, 61, 86.

The eclipse image on the front cover is copyright Fred Espenak.

NOTES

CHAPTER ONE: COSMIC TIME

1 The description of the cosmos is based on Allen, 1988 and 1989. The diagram is mine.
2 Assmann, 2001, pp. 74-80, 109-110, 120, 179, 242; Assmann, 1989, p. 59; Allen, 1988, pp. 25-27, 57.
3 Ibid.
4 Morenz, 1973, pp. 166-170, 181-82. Allen, 1988, p. 57; Clark, 1959, pp. 263-64.
5 Frankfort, *AER*, 1948, pp. 53-55, 62-64, 73; Morenz, 1973, pp. 113-17; Allen, 1988, p. 26; Hornung, 1982, p. 213; James, 1960, pp. 260-61.
6 Clark, 1959, p. 264; Morenz, 1973, pp. 167-68; Assmann, 1989, pp. 59, 62-65; Allen, 1988, p. 34.
7 Assmann, 2001, p. 3.
8 Morenz, 1973, p. 168; Frankfort et al, 1946, p. 24. Scholars do not always seem to grasp the principle that the original battle took place at the time of creation (e.g. Assmann, 2001, pp. 122-23).
9 Book of Nut (cenotaph texts of Seti I). See Allen, 1988, p. 3.
10 Papyrus Brooklyn 47.218.50, II, 10; see Assmann, 2001, p. 69.
11 Assmann, 2001, p. 4; Frankfort, *KAG*, 1948, p. 51; Allen, 1988, p. 38.
12 'The King as Priest of the Sun'. See Assmann, 1989, pp. 57-58; Assmann, 2001, pp. 3-5; Quirke, 2001, p. 20.
13 Frankfort, *KAG*, 1948, pp. 51-52, 149; Frankfort, *AER*, 1948, pp. 43, 53-57; Clark, 1959, pp. 27, 39, 263-64; Morenz, 1973, p. 168; Meeks, 1997, p. 9.
14 Clark, 1959, p. 27; Hornung, 1982, p. 214; Shafer, 1998, pp. 22-23.
15 Hornung, 1982, pp. 140-42.
16 Assmann, 2001, pp. 71-73.
17 Pyr. §1775.
18 Re was *neheh*, Osiris *djet*. See Assmann, 2001, pp. 75, 77-79, 109.

CHAPTER TWO: THE COSMOS

1 Pyr. § 480. On the mounds of Horus and Seth, see chapter thirteen.
2 Morenz, 1973, p. 43; Allen, 1988, p. 41.
3 CT, II, 28. See Lurker, 1980, p. 25.
4 On the possibility of upper and lower parts of the earth, see chapter thirteen.
5 On the significance of the Two Lands, see chapter thirteen.
6 Frankfort, *KAG*, 1948, p. 19. See Pyr. § 541; CT, II, 93.
7 Pyr. §§ 478-79, 941-42, 1474, 1522-23.
8 Pyr. § 1117.
9 Pyr. §§ 1598, 1603.
10 Pyr. §§ 135, 747, 873, 2023. They are identified with 'those who are in the tombs', § 1641.
11 Pyr. § 1641. Cf § 1878.
12 Pyr. §§ 57, 139. See also references to the Foremost of the Westerners, note 16 below.
13 Pyr. §§ 393, 658, 2202. The *akeru* belonged to the earth-god Aker, but he is not mentioned in the PT.
14 Pyr. §§ 658, 1523, 2202.
15 Pyr. §§ 478-79, 747, 799-800, 1203, 1253, 1473-74.

16 Pyr. §§ 133, 475, 1146, 1936, 1942-43, 1949, 1954-55, 1997. See also notes 17, 18, below.
17 Pyr. §§ 57, 745, 2198-99.
18 Pyr. §§ 592, 650, 759, 1886.
19 Allen, 1988, p. 4; Allen, 1989, pp. 11-12; Gardiner 1994, pp. 530, 573.
20 Pyr. § 1040.
21 Morenz, 1973, p. 177.
22 Frankfort, *AER*, 1948, p. 114.
23 Budge, 1934, pp. 173, 198, 414; Frankfort, *AER*, 1948, 114; Assmann, 2001, p. 63.
24 Pyr. §§ 237, 1778; CT, VI, 310, VII, 199.
25 Pyr. §§ 1044-45.
26 Pyr. §§ 132, 659, 728-29, 809, 1040, 1057, 1466, 1701, 2002-3, 2203-4, 2288-89.
27 Pyr. §§ 132, 551, 1078; CT, II, 7-8 ff, 24, 28; VII, 475; BD 175.
28 Pyr. §§ 1583; CT, VI, 411.
29 Pyr. § 392, a portal 'unsharp in height', i.e. flat-topped.
30 Pyr. § 268.
31 Pyr. §§ 871-72; CT, IV, 361-62.
32 Pyr. § 1174.
33 Pyr. § 1525. Cf Allen, 1989, p. 12.
34 Pyr. § 593.
35 Pyr. §§ 318-19, 871, 1166, 1486, 1679, 2147; CT, IV, 360-62.
36 Budge, 1934, p. 256. During the New Kingdom, '*pet, ta, dwat*' became the standard triple designation for the universe.
37 Book of Night, Book of Nut. See Allen, 1988, pp. 1-6. Cf Allen, 1989, pp. 20, 23-24.
38 Pyr. § 151.
39 Pyr. § 1717. Cf §§ 820-21, 1527; CT, III, 303-4.
40 Pyr. § 802. Cf Breasted, 1912, p. 144; Allen, 1989, p. 23.
41 Allen, 1989, p. 23.
42 Pyr. §§ 390-91. Cf Breasted, 1912, p. 144.
43 Pyr. §§ 1431-33. Cf §§ 803, 1717.
44 Pyr. §§ 1082-83. See also note 48 below.
45 Breasted, 1912, p. 144; Hornung, 1999, p. 6. The *duat* may also be the sky in Pyr. §§ 151, 883, 1172, which are ambiguous.
46 Book of Nut (cenotaph texts of Seti I). See Allen, 1988, pp. 1-2; Allen, 1989, pp. 24-25.
47 Pyr. § 1040.
48 CT, IV, 140. On the struggle of Horus and Seth, see chapters twelve and thirteen.
49 Allen, 1989, p. 22: 'Nut has caused her daughter the *duat* to give birth'.
50 Pyr. §§ 1527, 1973-74, 1986. Cf § 820.
51 Pyr. §§ 1207, 1301, 1734-35, 1948.
52 Budge, 1905, II, 235. In the PT, Osiris is synonymous with Horus of the Duat.
53 Pyr. §§ 782, 784-85.
54 Pyr §§ 820, 882-83, 925, 959.
55 Pyr §§ 1207, 1301. Cf § 1948.
56 Pyr § 953. See Allen, 1989, p. 21.
57 Pyr §§ 820-21, 1082-83. Cf §§ 362-63, 883.
58 Allen, 1989, p. 21. Occasionally, the determinative is a star alone, without a circle or ellipse.
59 Allen, 1989, p. 23.
60 Sethe, *Komm.*, 1935-39, I, 49; Gardiner, 1994, p. 487. 'Birthplace of the stars' is my suggestion.
61 Pyr §§ 882-83, 1677. See Allen, 1989, pp. 21-22.
62 Pyr §§ 372, 1164, 1987, 2170. Cf § 1677. Also plural form in §§ 1432-33, 1530. Cf the 'great lake' in the *nun* (§§ 871-72). Possibly the *nun* is 'the great lake' in §§ 334, 885, 1752, 1930.
63 Pyr §§ 882-83, 1987. See Allen, 1989, p. 21.
64 Pyr §§ 306, 2084-86.
65 Budge, 1905; Hornung, 1999.
66 CT, I, 347, 360.
67 Pyr. § 8. Cf § 883. See Allen, 1989, pp. 21, 23-24.
68 Pyr. §§ 1257-58, 1925. Budge, 1905; Hornung, 1999. Pyr. §§ 882-83.
69 Pyr. § 362.
70 Pyr. § 1959.
71 Pyr. § 282. Cf CT, VI, 237.
72 Pyr. §§ 272, 306, 953, 2084. Cf § 270 'those who are in darkness'.

73 CT, III, 310, 325.
74 CT, I, 347, 360.
75 Pyr. §§ 271, 290-94, 298-99. See also chapter four, note 89.
76 CT, IV, 194-98; VI, 270, 323.
77 Budge, 1905; Hornung, 1999.
78 Budge, 1905; Hornung, 1999; Budge, 1934, pp. 351-52; Allen 1988, p. 6; Allen, 1989, p. 21.
79 Lehner, 1997, p. 27; Allen, 1988, p. 6; Allen, 1989, p. 25.
80 Pyr. § 1172. Cf § 1986.
81 Pyr. § 1014.
82 Pyr. § 1986.
83 CT, III, 309; VI, 350; VII, 2. Cf 'the paths of Rostau' and 'the paths of the West'.
84 CT, VI, 91, 263.
85 A direct ascent is suggested in Pyr. §§ 257-58, 1972-74. On the indirect ascent, see note 37 above.
86 Allen, 1989, p. 17. The same sign occasionally determines the name of Nut in the PT.
87 Assmann, 1989, pp. 136-37.
88 Frankfort, *KAG*, 1948, p. 354; Allen, 1988, p. 6; Assmann, 1989, p. 136; Lehner, 1997, pp. 24, 29.
89 Frankfort et al, 1946, p. 43; Assmann, 2001, p. 65.
90 Pyr. §§ 337-41, 342, 351-53, 358-60, 926-27, 932-33, 999-1000, 1084-86, 1705-6.
91 Pyr. §§ 799, 1720.
92 Pyr. § 879.
93 Pyr. § 1583. Cf CT, IV, 38; IV, 223; VI, 80; VI, 308.
94 Pyr. § 999. See Allen, 1989, p. 17.
95 Pyr. § 202. Allen, 1989, and Assmann, 1989, see the *akhet* as a region in the sky's eastern side.
96 Pyr. § 1720. To split open the *akhet* was to split open the sky, CT, VI, 184.
97 Pyr. § 2096. Cf CT, IV, 184; VII, 324-25. See also Assmann, 2001, p. 65.
98 CT, VII, 496-97.
99 Pyr. §§ 412, 416, 341.
100 Pyr. §§ 1704, 1706.
101 Pyr. §§ 344, 353, 934, 1382, 1960.
102 Pyr. §§ 340-41.
103 Pyr. §§ 353, 928-29, 1704, 1706, 1960.
104 Pyr. § 344.
105 CT, VII, 197. Cf Pyr. §§ 1688-89.
106 CT, II, 43; IV, 75, 184 ff; BD, 17. Cf Pyr. § 395; CT, VII, 347.
107 Pyr. §§ 508-9. Cf Pyr. § 1063; CT, III, 115. Cf the banks of the sky and the winding waterway.
108 Pyr. § 2028. See Allen, 1989, p. 18.
109 On bathing, see Pyr. §§ 151, 208. On rowing, see Pyr. §§ 374, 711-12.
110 Pyr. §§ 208, 930.
111 Pyr. § 508.
112 Pyr. §§ 508-9. Cf §§ 1059-61, 1359. See Allen, 1989, p. 18.
113 Pyr. §§ 756, 2028.
114 Pyr. §§ 577-78, 1541-42, 1831.
115 Pyr. §§ 1541-42, 1863, 1992. There are a number of further references to the two shrines, where the location is not specified but the *akhet* is perhaps understood: §§ 256, 578, 732, 896-97, 1009, 1978, 1182, 1908, 2005, 2172. The two shrines may also appear as a singular shrine: §§ 938, 1262, 1993.
116 Pyr. § 757. Cf also the southern and northern shrines in Pyr. § 1297.
117 Pyr. §§ 277, 409, 1173, 2288.
118 Pyr. § 756. The king is also said to meet Re or join the barque of Re at the *akhet*.
119 CT, I, 236-37; VI, 270.
120 Pyr. §§ 4, 337, 342, 351, 358-60, 526, 926-27, 932-33, 1411, 1478. On one occasion, Horakhti and Re are combined in the form Re-Horakhti (§ 1049).
121 Pyr. §§ 374, 407, 1155, 879, 1802, 2045. On two enneads, see §§ 1201-3, 1261-62, 2170-71, 2206.
122 CT, V, 20.
123 Pyr. §§ 585, 621, 636, 1887.
124 Pyr. §§ 337, 342-44, 351-53, 358-60, 1084-87, 1102-4, 1205-6, 1687, 1704-6, 2045-46.
125 On the barque of Re, see Pyr. §§ 1345-47, 1687, 1759. On the ferryboat, see §§ 340-41, 344, 353, 360, 374, 383-87, 597-600, 658, 792, 925, 999-1000, 1091-92, 1176, 1183-94, 1201-2, 1222-23, 1254, 1381-82, 1429, 1432-33, 1738-39, 1743. On the reed-floats and the wing of Thoth, see chapter seven, note 241.
126 See note 79 above, also Pyr. §§ 1676-79.

NOTES

127 Pyr. §§ 152, 350, 409, 455, 585, 621, 636, 1046, 1261.
128 Pyr. §§ 1010, 1985. Cf § 961.
129 Pyr. §§ 372-74, 1164-65, 1987.
130 CT, IV, 220 ff.; BD, 17.
131 Ibid.
132 Ibid.
133 CT, II, 369-72.
134 CT, V, 103-5.
135 Pyr. § 374.
136 Pyr. §§ 275, 519, 822, 992-98, 1164-65, 1247, 1421-22, 1430, 1845-46; CT, II, 364-72, 388. Cf §§ 871, 920-23, 1245-46, 1366, 1719.
137 Pyr. §§ 880-81.
138 Pyr. §§ 1123-24, 1253.
139 Pyr. §§ 1247, 1421, 1430, 1704. Cf for example § 275. Cf the 'lake of waterfowl' and 'waters of geese' in CT, II, 364-65, 388.
140 Pyr. §§ 1247, 1421, 1430.
141 Pyr. §§ 289, 1165.
142 Pyr. § 1206.
143 Pyr. §§ 340, 343, 352, 374, 480, 943. Cf Pyr. § 1059; CT, VI, 267.
144 A thicket of reeds is mentioned in Pyr. § 367. It was probably understood that the gods assembled the reed-floats in order to ascend to the sky, see §§ 464, 2126.
145 Pyr. §§ 805, 1060-61.
146 Pyr. §§ 471, 564, 1059, 1065. Cf CT, VI, 267.
147 Pyr. §§ 1059, 1063, 1065-66.
148 CT, II, 369-71. The field of reeds was 'the city of Re' (CT, II, 388), hence perhaps its iron wall.
149 Budge, 1899; Budge, 1904; Budge, 1905; Budge, 1934; Edwards, 1993.
150 Pyr. § 1187. Cf § 1217.
151 Pyr. §§ 1188-89. Cf Pyr. § 1191; BD, 168.
152 Pyr. § 1216. Cf § 289.
153 Pyr. § 1216. I beg to differ with Allen, 1989, p. 6.
154 CT, III, 130-31; IV, 218-24. Cf the island of Asyut in CT, V, 10.
155 CT, II, 364-68, 388. Cf Pyr. § 916 'yonder tall, quivering sycamore in the east of the sky', and § 1433 'the two sycamores in yonder side of the sky'. Cf also Pyr. §§ 936-37 'the field of turquoise', which may be synonymous with the field of reeds.
156 Pyr. § 918.
157 Pyr. §§ 1690-91, 1010, 1985.
158 Pyr. § 1061.
159 Pyr. §§ 1092-93. Cf Pyr. §§ 1690-1700; CT, V, 209.
160 Pyr. §§ 920-23, 1245. Cf CT, V, 199-200, 209.
161 Pyr. §§ 1091, 1188, 1743.
162 Pyr. §§ 1738-39.
163 Pyr. §§ 1196-98.
164 Pyr. §§ 1193, 1736-37.
165 Pyr. § 1212.
166 CT, II, 363-72, 388.
167 BD, 145-46. See Wilkinson, 1992, p. 125.
168 On the throne, see Pyr. §§ 805, 1087. Cf 'the throne of Horus' in § 1691, 'the beautiful throne of the great god' in § 1191, and the 'stairway of the throne' in § 1295. It is possible that this throne in the field symbolised the island or mound of creation; hence it was made by the gods in §§ 1153-55.
169 Pyr. §§ 920-23, 1245-46. Cf § 26.
170 Pyr. §§ 805, 1719. Cf § 871.
171 Pyr. § 1405. Cf § 1443. See Allen, 1989, p. 13.
172 Pyr. §§ 152, 154, 156, 348, 524, 1144. In the CT and BD, the pillars of the sky are called 'the supports of Shu'.
173 Pyr. §§ 907, 1575. See discussion in chapter ten.
174 Pyr. §§ 152-58, 645, 785, 879, 1171. Cf § 369. See Allen, 1989, p. 5.
175 Mostly in early works, but occasionally in recent works, e.g. Eyre, 2002, p. 45.
176 Pyr. § 2063.
177 Pyr. §§ 1167, 1169.
178 Pyr. §§ 468, 1138. See Allen, 1989, p. 8.

378   NOTES TO PAGES 22 – 30

179 Pyr. §§ 802, 1760, 2061, 2235 (§ 802 is possibly a reference to the lower sky). *Ma-ha.f*, the ferryman of the winding waterway beneath the horizon, is named in § 383 as 'the ferryman of the sky'.
180 Pyr. §§ 128, 130, 367-68, 384-85, 464, 543, 749, 881-82, 917, 1048-49, 1165, 1167, 1171, 1250, 1777, 2122. See Allen, 1989, p. 7.
181 Allen, 1989, p. 13.
182 Allen, 1989, p. 8.
183 Ibid.
184 Pyr. §§ 525-29, 756, 873, 876, 981-85, 1025-26, 1132-37, 1291-92, 1361, 1408-11, 1480, 1927, 1943, 2238.
185 Pyr. § 138.
186 See Allen , 1989, pp. 10-11, though he misunderstands Pyr. §§ 1040, 1778.
187 Pyr. § 1778.
188 Allen, 1989, p. 11. The focus is on the depths, but it is possible that this *nun* also included the underbelly of the sky.
189 Cenotaph texts of Seti I. See Allen, 1988, pp. 1-4; Allen, 1989, pp. 10-11; Hornung, 1999, p. 114.
190 Allen, 1989, p. 12. This lower sky is compared to the womb of the sky-goddess in Pyr. § 1466.
191 Allen, 1988, p. 4; Allen, 1989, pp. 12-13: 'These indications... point to the concept of a nether sky lying inverted beneath the earth... envisaged as an ocean of water lying beneath the earth.'
192 Pyr. § 149.
193 This point is not well understood by scholars, who often assert that this field was 'in' the sky or 'part of' the sky. See, for example, Allen, 1989, p. 6, and compare his treatment of Pyr. § 749 to that taken in this chapter.
194 In addition to the five examples covered below, there are two probable references in Pyr. §§ 1200, 1249, while §§ 130, 880, 1253, 1781, 1784-85 are ambiguous.
195 Pyr. § 1066.
196 Pyr. § 2062.
197 Pyr. § 1217.
198 Pyr. §§ 1165-66.
199 Pyr. § 749.
200 Pyr. § 1180.
201 Pyr. §§ 279-80. Cf CT, VI, 231-32.
202 Pyr. §§ 525-29, 981-89, 1132-37, 1408-15.
203 Pyr. §§ 873-74.
204 Pyr. § 749.
205 Pyr. §§ 525-29, 981-89, 1132-37.
206 BD, 110.
207 Pyr. §§ 805, 1719. Cf § 871.
208 Pyr. §§ 280, 709, 2174.
209 Pyr. § 1346. See Allen, 1989, p. 13.
210 CT, III, 2-3, refers to 'the Primeval Ones of the middle sky'. CT, VII, 112, Anubis dwells in the middle sky, or 'sacred land'. CT, VII, 173, the deceased ascends to the upper sky, descends to the lower sky, and traverses the middle sky. CT, VII, 283, the deceased may descend to any sky to which he wishes to descend – in connection with the paths of Rostau which are in the limit of the sky.
211 Pyr. §§ 289, 698, 1784-85. Cf CT, IV, 26; VI, 248.
212 Pyr. §§ 1278, 1327, 1025-28. Cf § 373.
213 Pyr. § 524. But 'mansion' is also a term for the primeval cosmos – see chapter ten, note 61.
214 Pyr. § 458; it is contrasted with his throne on the earth. Cf § 1765.
215 Pyr. §§ 289-90, 508, 1059, 1065, 1131. Her name, which is often translated 'heavens' or 'celestial kine', is determined either by a water-sign or a cow-sign.
216 Allen, 1989, p. 15. See also CT, VI, 270.
217 Pyr. §§ 783, 785. See Allen, 1989, p. 5.
218 Pyr. §§ 1291, 541. Cf §§ 801, 2062. See See Allen, 1989, p. 15.
219 Pyr. § 1173.
220 Pyr. § 802 (possibly an allusion to the lower sky).
221 Pyr. § 802.
222 Pyr. §§ 383, 543. Cf CT, III, 263.
223 Pyr. § 1344. Cf § 2171.
224 Pyr. § 782. See Allen, 1989, p. 16.
225 Pyr. § 785. Cf BD, 69.
226 Pyr. § 785. Cf §§ 1048, 1285, 1303. See Allen, 1989, p. 15; Gardiner, 1994, p. 584.

227 Pyr. § 883. Cf § 820-21.
228 Pyr. §§ 1688, 1835-36. See Allen, 1989, p. 14.
229 Pyr. §§ 132, 1466. Barta has suggested that Nut was originally a feminine counterpart of Nun, the god of the abyss. Allen has suggested that her name may derive from *nwit*, 'she of the abyss', or from *nwt*, meaning 'ball' or 'oval'.
230 Pyr. §§ 347, 357. See Allen, 1989, pp. 11, 14 (note 95).
231 Pyr. §§ 698, 705, 1231, 1734, 1918-19, 2225.
232 Pyr. §§ 1688, 1835-36, 698, 705.
233 Frankfort, *KAG*, 1948, p. 145; Lurker, 1980, p. 82.
234 Pyr. §§ 387, 535, 575-76, 594-96, 635, 976, 1233, 1237-40, 1465, 1979-80. Cf CT, II, 327; III, 343-44; IV, 231-38.
235 Pyr. § 128.
236 Assmann, 2001, pp. 80-81.
237 Shaw & Nicholson, 1995, p. 151.
238 Lurker, 1980, p. 48; Frankfort, *KAG*, 1948, p. 37. The earliest allusion to this idea is Pyr §§ 1981-82.
239 On *shdu pet*, see Pyr. §§ 449, 2090-91 (abbreviated to *shdu* in §§ 727, 1474, 2001). On *qebhu sbau*, see Pyr. § 138. On *pdjt* and *pdjwt*, see Pyr. §§ 1443, 1486. See Allen, 1989, pp. 4-5, 8.
240 Pyr. § 1760.
241 Pyr. §§ 380, 998.
242 Pyr. § 1488.
243 Pyr. §§ 478, 941, 1168, 1473-74, 1490, 1523, 1834. Cf Pyr. § 462; CT, I, 241; II, 223.
244 Pyr. § 375.
245 Pyr. § 1065.
246 Pyr. § 1486.
247 Pyr. §§ 856, 1532, 1679, 2175.
248 Pyr. § 749.
249 Pyr. §§ 139, 335-36, 559, 565, 876, 1126, 1168, 1288-89, 1565, 1567, 1686, 1766, 1993, 2147, 2187, 2235. Cf CT, IV, 122; VI, 393; VII, 258. *Hnmmt* is often translated 'sun folk' or 'people of Atum'.
250 Pyr. §§ 1114-16, 458, 906, 1196-97, 1203, 1573-74, 1708. *Psdjt* (ennead) may also be rendered 'company' or 'corporation'.
251 Pyr. §§ 166, 1457, 1468-69, 1485. See Allen, 1989, pp. 12-13.
252 Pyr. §§ 207, 818, 1080, 1220.
253 Pyr. § 458.
254 Pyr. §§ 13-14; Budge, 1973, p. 122; Gardiner, 1994, p. 570. In later times, *mskhtiu* was determined by the sign of a bull's foreleg.
255 Pyr. § 405. See Eyre, 2002, p. 121.
256 Pyr. §§ 311, 315 (the two adzes here are called *nwti*). Cf § 229. See Faulkner, 1969, p. 68.
257 Pyr. §§ 13-14. See Frankfort, *KAG*, 1948, pp. 26, 71, 87, 92-95, 189, 205.
258 Pyr. § 42. But CT, VI, 25, does place Horus in the north of the sky.
259 BD, 17. See Wainwright, 1932, p. 163.
260 Pyr. § 1483. The four sons of Horus also had fingers of *bja* (§§ 1983-84), a substance which was associated in particular with the northern sky (§ 14). These gods are not to be confused with that other group of four gods, the four regional spirits made by Geb who stand at the cardinal points and support the sky (§§ 1708, 1510, 348). The latter are said to traverse Upper and Lower Egypt (§ 1510), to traverse Libya (§§ 1456-58), to stand with their staffs as wearers of the sidelock in the east (§§ 355, 360), to smear on ointment, wear red linen, and live on figs and wine (§ 1510), to announce the king's name (§§ 348, 356, 361, 1708), and to ascend from the east side of the sky (§ 1708).
261 Wainwright, 1932, p. 163.
262 Pyr. §§ 1171-72, 1439, 2172-73. Cf §§ 923, 1065, 1246, 1250-51.
263 Pyr. § 1456.
264 Pyr. §§ 132, 269, 732, 1372. See Allen, 1989, p. 14. The sun-god is said to be 'at the head of the gods'. The gods are called his 'followers' (*shmsu*).
265 BD, 89, refers to: 'you gods who are dragged in the barque of the Lord of Millions of Years, who bring the upper sky to the *duat* and who raise up the lower sky'. Cf the circlings of the *hnhnu*-barque on the ways of Khepri in CT, III, 56-57.
266 Pyr. § 2102. See Gardiner, 1994, pp. 584, 592.
267 The *akhmu-sku* form a duality with the gods of the earth to represent 'all the gods' in Pyr. § 900. They are paralleled with: 'the stars' in § 940; 'the untiring stars' in §§ 1171-72, 2173 (see also CT, I, 271); 'the stars which are in the sky' in §§ 1925-26; 'the stars who surround Re' in §§ 732-33; and 'the ennead of Heliopolis' in §§ 2225-26. Horus of the Duat is at their head in § 1301 (cf § 1948).

380   NOTES TO PAGES 30 – 44

They are the companions of Sirius and the morning star in § 1123. They row the barque of Re in § 1439. They dwell in the field of offerings as the followers of Osiris in § 749. They are guided across the field of reeds by the king in § 374. They are 'the spirits' in §§ 656, 760, 900, 1232, 1288, 1721-22, 1994-95, 2104-5. And they sail across the lower sky in §§ 1201-2, 1216, 1222-23, 1432, 1456.
268 Pyr. § 822. Budge, 1934, p. 241; Bauval & Gilbert, 1994, pp. 89, 92, 146-47, 291; Shaw & Nicholson, 1995, p. 58. By another strange coincidence, Sirius's place of heliacal rising marked the approximate place where the sun rose at the winter solstice, see R. Wells, 'Re and the Calendar' in A.J. Spalinger ed., *Revolution in Time: Studies in Ancient Egyptian Calendrics*, Van Siclen Books, San Antonio, 1994.
269 Pyr. §§ 632, 1635-36; Dramatic Texts (cenotaph of Seti I), VI, 3-6; Carlsberg I Papyrus. See Neugebauer & Parker, 1964.
270 Dramatic Texts (cenotaph of Seti I), VI, 38-43. See Neugebauer & Parker, 1964; Shaw & Nicholson, 1995, p. 192; Bauval & Gilbert, 1994, pp. 260-63.
271 Pyr. §§ 151, 723, 819-22, 1436-37, 2126.
272 Pyr. §§ 408, 959.
273 Pyr. §§ 186, 821-22, 882-83.
274 Pyr. §§ 820, 882-83, 925, 959.
275 Pyr. §§ 353, 357, 362-63, 928-30, 934-36. Budge, 1934, pp. 241-42.
276 Neugebauer & Parker, 1964, Vol I, pp. 24-25; Sellers, 1992, pp. 39-40; Bauval & Gilbert, 1994, pp. 76, 87-88.
277 Pyr. §§ 150-51. It is assumed that the text refers to events in the east side of the sky. Against this theory, the reference to Sah ahead of Sothis may be formulaic, cf §§ 723, 821-22, 1436-37, 2126.
278 Pyr. § 822.
279 Pyr. §§ 362-63. Cf §§ 347, 357. Hence Budge, 1973, p. 117, identifies this star as Jupiter. Pyr. §§ 882, 2268 possibly also imply that Sah was a single star.
280 Pyr. §§ 658, 886-87, 917, 1680. Horakhti in §§ 853-54, 2138. Cf CT, VI, 240.
281 R.E. Briggs, 1952, in appendix to S.A. Mercer, *The Pyramid Texts*; C. Muses, *Destiny and Control in Human Systems*, 1976; S. Cox, 'Canopus', private research paper, undated; P. Coppens, *The Canopus Revelation*, Frontier Publishing/Adventures Unlimited, 2004.
282 Pyr. §§ 449, 525-28, 853, 888, 981-83, 986-87, 2138.
283 Budge, 1934, p. 244; Faulkner, 1969, p. 73.
284 Pyr. §§ 341, 357, 930, 1707. Cf § 1123.
285 Pyr. §§ 632-33. Cf §§ 1635-37. See Shaw & Nicholson, 1995, p. 275.
286 Pyr. § 1207.
287 Budge, 1934, p. 244; Faulkner, 1966, pp. 153-61.
288 Pyr. § 1760.
289 Pyr. § 2061. Cf §§ 2172-73.
290 Pyr. §§ 1169-70, 1345, 1574-75, 2172-73, 1345, 2172-73, 1573-74.
291 Pyr. §§ 543, 1345, 1574-75, 2172-73.
292 Faulkner, 1966, p. 154; Davis, 1985, p. 102; Sellers, 1992, p. 97.
293 CT, IV, 111-12, 142, 145. Hapi also claims to have power in the lower *duat*, as if to suggest that he traversed the lower sky as well as the upper sky.
294 CT, IV, 147; Pyr. § 2061. See Faulkner, 1973, p. 250, note 17.
295 Budge, 1967, p. 123; Faulkner, 1985, p. 90; Bauval & Gilbert, 1994, pp. 119-24.
296 Allen, 1989, p. 7; Faulkner, 1969, p. 72.
297 Pyr. §§ 279, 334-35, 949-50. Note translation in Allen, 1989, p. 7.
298 Allen, 1989, pp. 7, 9.
299 CT, VI, 412; VII, 2. See also CT, III, 376-77; V, 45, 70; VI, 236. Note that in CT, VI, 231 *msqt shdu* has an unusual determinative – a cauldron or bowl (signs W6, W7).
300 Sethe, *Komm.*, 1935-39, II, 20; Faulkner, 1969, p. 72; Allen, 1989, pp. 7, 9.

CHAPTER THREE: THE CREATION

1 Breasted, 1912, p. 46.
2 See discussion in chapter fourteen.
3 Frankfort et al, 1946, p. 19; Frankfort, *AER*, 1948, pp. viii-ix, 1-2, 16-20; Frankfort, *KAG*, 1948, p. 378 note 10. See also Morenz, 1973, p. 20; Assmann, 1989, p. 57.
4 Allen, 1988, pp. 62-63.
5 Allen, 1988, pp. 7, 9, 14-18, 24-25, 56-58. See discussion in chapter six.
6 Edwards, 1947, p. 6; Frankfort, *KAG*, 1948, p. 381 note 27; Clark, 1959, pp. 37-39; Shaw &

Nicholson, 1995, p. 124; Quirke, 2001.
7   Frankfort et al, 1946, p. 53; Allen, 1988, pp. 9-10; Hornung, 1982, p. 66; Assmann, 2001, pp. 119-20.
8   CT, III, 27; VI, 131, 341. See Budge, 1912, pp. xvii, 216; Budge, 1934, pp. 102, 141; Allen, 1988, p. 9; Hornung, 1982, pp. 169, 234.
9   Pyr. §§ 1248-49.
10 Pyr. §§ 1652-53 (trans. Faulkner/Allen/Alford). Alternatively, 'you became high as the hill' or 'high on the hill'. Cf § 1587.
11 Frankfort, *KAG*, 1948, p. 381 note 27.
12 Frankfort et al, 1946, p. 54; Frankfort, *KAG*, 1948, p. 182; Morenz, 1973, pp. 269-70; Shaw & Nicholson, 1995, p. 270; Quirke, 2001, p. 32.
13 Clark, 1959, p. 45; Lurker, 1980, p. 42; Allen, 1988, pp. 9, 26; Assmann, 2001, p. 78.
14 CT, VI, 220; Thoth's Litany for Horus, Metternich Stele, 142-50 (see Budge, 1912, p. 177; Budge, 1934, p. 419). See Lurker, 1980, pp. 100-2, 112, 119. The sun and the moon are perhaps envisaged also in CT, II, 32. Shu appears to be the sun-god in CT, IV, 178.
15 Allen, 1988, p. 10.
16 Pyr. § 1587.
17 Allen, 1988, 10-11, 29; Assmann, 2001, p. 120.
18 Assmann, 2001, p. 120.
19 CT, II, 39.
20 CT, II, 7-8. See Allen , 1988, p. 18. This is the place where Shu fathered the Infinite Ones, CT, II, 6, 11-17, 28.
21 CT, II, 33-35 (trans. Faulkner/Allen/Alford). See Allen, 1988, pp. 22-23.
22 CT, IV, 184-92; BD, 17 (trans. Faulkner/Allen). See Allen, 1988, pp. 31-33.
23 CT, IV, 218-27; BD, 17.
24 CT, II, 20; V, 289; BD, 38a. Cf CT, II, 25; BD, 3.
25 CT, I, 314-405; II, 1-43.
26 CT, II, 5, 21. See also CT, VI, 154.
27 CT, II, 6.
28 CT, II, 6, 31. See Allen, 1988, p. 20.
29 CT, II, 6 (variant). See Faulkner, 1973, p. 79 note 19.
30 CT, I, 314-20 (trans. Faulkner/Allen).
31 CT, II, 31-32. See Allen, 1988, p. 22. Cf Shu's origin from the nose of Atum in CT, II, 35-36, 39-40, and from the mouth of Atum in CT, II, 29-30.
32 Pyr. §§ 299, 784-85, 1101, 1443, 1454, 2091.
33 CT, II, 372 (trans. Allen/Alford). See Faulkner, 1973, p. 76 note 33; Allen, 1988, p. 16.
34 CT, II, 4 (trans. Allen). See Allen, 1988, p. 18.
35 CT, II, 29-30 (trans. Faulkner/Allen/Alford). See Allen, 1988, p. 22.
36 CT, II, 2-3 (trans. Faulkner/Allen/Alford). See Allen, 1988, p. 18. Cf CT, I, 332-36.
37 CT, II, 19 (trans. Faulkner). Cf Allen, 1988, p. 21. Cf CT, II, 39, where it is Atum who separated Geb and Nut.
38 CT, I, 318. See Faulkner, 1973, p. 75 note 3; Allen, 1988, p. 15.
39 CT, II, 2-3 (trans. Faulkner/Allen/Alford). See Allen, 1988, p. 18. Cf CT, II, 34.
40 CT, II, 25 (trans. Faulkner/Clark/Alford). See Clark, 1959, p. 85.
41 CT, II, 28-29 (trans. Faulkner/Allen/Alford). See Allen, 1988, p. 21. Cf CT, VI, 154.
42 CT, II, 2.
43 CT, II, 19-20. See Faulkner, 1973, p. 81 note 6.
44 The *ḥḥ*-gods are sometimes rendered 'the chaos-gods', e.g. Faulkner, 1973-78.
45 CT, II, 7-8, 19, 22-24, 28.
46 CT, II, 23-24. Cf CT, II, 7, 19-20, 22.
47 CT, II, 8-10.
48 CT, II, 1-2, 8-10.
49 The *ḥḥ*-gods are raised by Nun in CT, II, 20; allotted to Geb and Nut by Shu in CT, II, 28; spat out by Shu in CT, II, 22 (variant); in charge of the limbs of the sky in CT, II, 1 (see Allen, 1988, p. 19).
50 CT, II, 28. See Allen, 1988, p. 21. Cf CT, II, 20-21, the realm of the *ḥḥ*-gods spans 'the length of the sky' and 'the breadth of the earth'.
51 CT, VI, 341. Atum is also described in CT, V, 211 as 'Lord of Kheperu', which provides another connection to the myth of creation by Neber-djer. See Allen, 1988, pp. 9, 29.
52 Budge, 1912, pp. xvii, 216; Budge, 1934, pp. 102, 141; Faulkner, 1973, p. 144; Allen, 1988, p. 9; Hornung, 1982, pp. 169, 234.
53 Allen, 1988, pp. 27-28.

54 Pyr. §§ 1248-49, 1652-53; CT, II, 5, 33; IV, 174, 240-42.
55 Bremner-Rhind Pap., part a, 3-25 (trans. Budge/Faulkner/Allen/Alford). See Budge, 1904, I, pp. 308-11; Budge, 1912, pp. 2-5; Pritchard, 1969, p. 6; Allen, 1988, p. 28.
56 Bremner-Rhind Pap., part a, 31-32.
57 Bremner-Rhind Pap., part a, 33 ff. Cf CT, II, 33. This subject is discussed further in chapter twelve.
58 Bremner-Rhind Pap., part a, 35 ff. Again, see chapter twelve.
59 On the creation of Re by ancestor-gods, see chapter four, note 4.
60 CT, VI, 270.
61 Ibid.
62 BD, 15. See Meeks, 1997, p. 111.
63 Book of the Heavenly Cow. See Budge, 1912, pp. xxix, 27; Allen, 1988, p. 19; Gardiner, 1994, p. 555. This is consistent with the field of offerings being the entire sky and the field of reeds a region in the sky (see chapter two).
64 Pleyte & Rossi, 1876; Budge, 1904, I, pp. 372-87; Budge, 1912, pp. 43-55.
65 Budge, 1904, I, pp. 385-86; Budge, 1912, pp. 52-55.
66 See discussion of eyes in chapter six.
67 Pyr. § 1635.
68 Pyr. § 632.
69 Budge, 1934, p. 202; Clark, 1959, pp. 105-6; Assmann, 2001, pp. 145-46.
70 CT, II, 223-26.
71 CT, II, 209-10. See discussion in chapter fourteen.
72 See chapters twelve and thirteen.
73 Gardiner, 1994, pp. 183, 568, written with signs Y5 and F35 (pp. 534, 465). Memphis was also called Ineb-hedj, meaning 'White Walls' or perhaps 'White Fortress'.
74 Allen, 1988, p. 41. Ptah is mentioned only briefly in the PT in §§ 560, 566, 1482.
75 Allen, 1988, p. 41. Cf CT, VI, 267. Ptah supposedly invented the opening of the mouth ritual.
76 Shabaka Stone, 12-15; CT, VI, 268, 339. The Memphis region was known as 'White Wall' and 'the Wall district'. See Allen, 1988, pp. 39-40. 'South' of the wall might mean 'above' it.
77 Great Harris Papyrus. See Morenz, 1973, p. 182.
78 Morenz, 1973, p. 43; Allen, 1988, p. 41. See also Hornung, 1982, pp. 80, 88.
79 Berlin Hymn to Ptah (trans. Budge/Wolf/Allen/Alford). See Budge, 1934, p. 259; Frankfort, *KAG*, 1948, p. 181; Allen, 1988, p. 40.
80 Morenz, 1973, pp. 92, 160; Lurker, 1980, p. 97; Allen, 1988, p. 41.
81 Shabaka Stone, 53-58. The concept of creative thought and utterance is found in the texts of the Middle Kingdom, notably CT, VI, 268. See Allen, 1988, pp. 39-42.
82 Shabaka Stone, 58-61 (trans. Junker/Allen/Alford). See Pritchard, 1969, p. 5; Allen, 1988, p. 44.
83 Abu was known also as 'the City of the Beginning'; see Budge, 1912, pp. 124-25. The city's name was written with the signs for elephant and foreign land. The Greeks named it Elephantine after their word for elephant, *elephas*. On Khnum, see James, 1960, p. 207; Shaw & Nicholson, 1995, p. 151.
84 Budge, 1904, II, p. 50; Faulkner, 1969, p. 91, 324; Gardiner, 1994, p. 587.
85 CT, IV, 133, 136, 143; Legend of Khnum, see Budge, 1912, pp. 120-25.
86 Legend of Khnum. See Budge, 1912, p. 133; Budge, 1934, p. 257.
87 Pyr. §§ 445, 1227-28, 1585-86.
88 James, 1960, p. 207; Reymond, 1969, p. 61; Morenz, 1973, p. 161; Meeks, 1997, p. 197.
89 Budge, 1899, p. 99; Budge, 1904, II, pp. 50-52; Budge, 1934, pp. 173, 256; Morenz, 1973, p. 174.
90 Shaw & Nicholson, 1995, pp. 31-32, 286-88. The *was*-sceptre was associated with winds and the supports of the sky, and its top was made in the shape of the head of the sacred animal of Seth; see Wainwright, 1932, pp. 165, 171.
91 Allen, 1988, p. 48; Hart, 1990, pp. 22-25; David, 2002, p. 184.
92 Pyr. §§ 446, 1541.
93 Great Hymn to Amun, 80 (trans. Allen/Alford). See Allen, 1988, p. 50.
94 Great Hymn to Amun, 90 (trans. Allen/Alford). See Allen, 1988, p. 51.
95 Hart, 1990, p. 24.
96 Allen, 1988, p. 94 note 19.
97 Great Hymn to Amun, 100 (trans. Gardiner/Erman-Blackman/Allen/Alford). See Frankfort, *KAG*, 1948, p. 161; Pritchard, 1969, p. 368; Allen, 1988, p. 52.
98 Great Hymn to Amun, 40. See Allen, 1988, pp. 49, 94; Budge, 1934, p. 17; Frankfort, *KAG*, 1948, p. 170; Hart, 1990, p. 24; Watterson, 1984, p. 141.
99 Great Hymn to Amun, 200 (trans. Erman-Blackman/Allen/Alford). See Pritchard, 1969, p. 368; Allen, 1988, p. 52.

100 On the union of Re with the body of Osiris, see chapter four.
101 Elsewhere, the Hermopolitans are the enemies of the creator-god; see BD, 17, cited earlier. In Great Hymn to Amun, 90, they are equated to the toes of Amun's body.
102 Watterson, 1984, pp. xxii, 88-89; Reymond, 1969, pp. 51, 287.
103 Reymond, 1969, pp. 13, 55, 96, 108-9. Cf Allen, 1989, pp. 5-6.
104 Reymond, 1969, pp. 13, 109, 119.
105 Ibid., pp. 13, 109.
106 Ibid., pp. 13, 55, 109. Cf Watterson, 1984, p. 91.
107 Reymond, 1969, pp. 14-15, 30-31, 121. The reeds are relics of a destroyed world, the island of trampling, *iw titi,* to be discussed in chapter four.
108 Ibid., pp. 14-15.
109 Ibid., pp. 15, 30-31.
110 Ibid., pp. 7, 14-15.
111 Ibid., pp. 26, 158.
112 Ibid., pp. 15, 17, 173.
113 Ibid., pp. 24-27, 55, 161, 172.
114 Ibid., pp. 17-18, 137, 153, 161, 172.
115 Ibid., pp. 18-19, 25, 154.
116 Ibid., pp. 16, 27-28, 69-70, 136, 180, 187. On the sailing gods motif, cf CT, VII, 462.
117 Notably the traditions of the Primeval Ones (synonymous with the Ogdoad), the isle of flames, and the lotus in the pool. Reymond, 1969, p. 70. The expression *wba iwau* meant literally 'ring opener'.
118 Reymond, 1969, p. 63. Cf Naydler, 1996, p. 53.
119 Reymond, 1969, pp. 76-77.
120 Ibid., p. 66. Cf the Greek myths of floating islands.
121 Ibid., pp. 68, 73.
122 Ibid., pp. 68, 70-71. The name may also be rendered 'isle of fire' or 'isle of two flames'. In the Edfu tradition, it is the emerged form of the island of the egg, which has risen from the depths of *nun*.
123 Ibid., p. 61.
124 Ibid., pp. 67-68.
125 Ibid., p. 68.
126 Ibid., pp. 76-77.
127 Ibid.
128 Ibid., pp. 77, 90. See quote in chapter thirteen. Light thus issued from their physical forms, p. 68.
129 Ibid., p. 77.
130 Ibid., pp. 82-83.
131 Ibid., pp. 70-71, 82.
132 Ibid., p. 78.
133 Ibid., pp. 76-77.
134 Morenz, 1973, p. 43; Hart, 1990, p. 20. In the PT, Hermopolis is called Unu. It is also the cult centre of Thoth, who in one tradition was the leader of the Ogdoad (the eight were his souls). But Thoth does not have a prominent role in the creation myth.
135 *Hh* here means the flood, not infinity. See Hart, 1990, p. 20.
136 The names signified the chaos that preceded creation: see Frankfort et al, 1946, pp. 10, 52; Frankfort, *KAG*, 1948, pp. 28, 155. Amun and Amaunet may have been a late addition: see Hornung, 1982, p. 84. There was also a tradition of five gods at Hermopolis: see Budge, 1934, p. 154.
137 Shaw & Nicholson, 1995, p. 210. Frogs symbolised fertility, creation, and regeneration (pp. 103-4, 123), also perhaps the emergence from water to land.
138 Sethe, 1929, § 151. See Morenz, 1973, p. 176; Hart, 1990, p. 24.
139 Sethe, 1929, §§ 123, 151, 263. See Morenz, 1973, p. 176.
140 Sethe, 1929, § 96. See Morenz, 1973, p. 176.
141 Frankfort, *KAG*, 1948, p. 151; Morenz, 1973, p. 176.
142 Sethe, 1929, §§ 100, 160. See Budge, 1934, p. 155; Morenz, 1973, pp. 176, 178; Hart, 1990, p. 21.
143 Reymond, 1969, p. 106.
144 Ibid., p. 70.
145 Watterson, 1984, p. 123.
146 Budge, 1934, pp. 228-29; James, 1960, pp. 82-83; Reymond, 1969, pp. 78-79.
147 Morenz, 1973, p. 23; Watterson, 1984, p. 113; Shaw & Nicholson, 1995, p. 119. Cf Pyr. §§ 1027-28, 1278, 1327.
148 Frankfort, *KAG*, 1948, p. 172; Lurker, 1980, p. 55; Shaw & Nicholson, 1995, p. 119.
149 CT, VI, 48-49.

150 CT, VI, 63-64.
151 Meeks, 1997, p. 179.
152 Meeks, 1997, pp. 182-84; Watterson, 1984, pp. 123, 126-28.
153 Shaw & Nicholson, 1995, pp. 119, 169.
154 CT, IV, 181, 182.
155 Frankfort, *KAG*, 1948, p. 356 note 19.
156 CT, II, 210-26 (= Spell 148, cited earlier in this chapter).
157 Shaw & Nicholson, 1995, p. 119; Meeks, 1997, p. 164.
158 James, 1960, p. 83.
159 Watterson, 1984, p. 181; Gardiner, 1994, pp. 447 (sign A47), 588. Her emblem was two arrows crossed over a shield.
160 Morenz, 1973, p. 23; Hornung, 1982, p. 280 (from *nrt*). Alternatively, her name may derive from *nt*, 'water', or *ntt*, 'to weave'; see Budge, 1904, I, p. 451; Budge, 1934, pp. 57-59; James, 1960, p. 84.
161 Budge, 1904, I, p. 454; James, 1960, p. 84. Cf the role of Nut.
162 Lurker, 1980, p. 85.
163 Chester Beatty I Papyrus. See Clark, 1959, p. 198.
164 Budge, 1904, I, p. 463; Schulz & Seidel, 1998, p. 440.
165 Ibid., also James, 1960, pp. 84-85.
166 Ibid., also Lurker, 1980, pp. 33, 85.
167 Budge, 1904, I, pp. 457-62; Budge, 1934, pp. 24, 59, 139; James, 1960, p. 84; Watterson, 1984, p. 179.
168 Watterson, 1984, p. 179.
169 Reymond, 1969, pp. 83-84, 92, 173-74.
170 BD, 17.
171 CT, IV, 62: 'I am Re who issued from the *nun* in this my name of Khepri'.

CHAPTER FOUR: POWER IN THE EARTH

1 Quirke, 2001, p. 23. Cf p. 31.
2 CT, III, 372.
3 Assmann, 2001, p. 91.
4 Temple of Medamud. See Reymond, 1969, p. 51. The temple is said to be the mound (*iat*), the place (*bu*) where Re arrived. The explanation follows that Re came to that place while invoking the ancestors, and they then renewed that place in which they created him. Cf Book of the Heavenly Cow, where Re addresses the gods as 'you gods of ancient time, my ancestors' (Budge, 1912, p. 17).
5 Breasted, 1912, pp. 10, 13, 76, 112, 161, 316; Budge, 1934, p. 238; Frankfort, *KAG*, 1948, p. 66; Lehner, 1997, p. 34; Allen, 1988, pp. 10-12, 31; Quirke, 2001, pp. 25, 32.
6 Budge, 1925, p. 5; Wainwright, 1938, pp. 106-7; Frankfort, *KAG*, 1948, p. 381 note 27.
7 Pyr. § 600; Wainwright, 1938, p. 97; Frankfort, *KAG*, 1948, p. 381 note 27; Betro, 1996, pp. 200-1.
8 Clark, 1959, pp. 39-40; Sellers, 1992, p. 89.
9 Clark, 1959, p. 39.
10 Turin Papyrus, *Isis and Re*. See Pleyte & Rossi, 1876; Budge, 1904, I, p. 384; Budge, 1912, pp. 52-53; Assmann, 2001, p. 107. The three names of Re appear first in Pyr. § 1695.
11 Pyr. § 1778; CT, VI, 310; VII, 199.
12 Scholars do appreciate that Kheprer was a chthonian creator. See Frankfort, *AER*, 1948, pp. 19, 145 (quoted at the beginning of this chapter), and Allen, 1988, p. 10 ('the newborn sun "born from the earth" like a scarab beetle').
13 The Two Lands signified the entire cosmos. On the significance of unification, see chapter thirteen.
14 Pyr. §§ 138, 1967-68; CT, VI, 15; VII, 198. Sokar lent his name to the necropolis of Saqqara. See Allen, 1988, pp. 41, 71 note 138.
15 Great Harris Papyrus, as quoted in chapter three (Morenz, 1973, p. 182).
16 Berlin Papyrus 13603. See Reymond, 1969, p. 57.
17 Frankfort, *KAG*, 1948, p. 203.
18 E.A.E. Reymond, *The Mythical Origin of the Egyptian Temple*, Manchester University Press, 1969.
19 Reymond, 1969, p. 6: 'It is largely an unknown and untranslated group of texts that forms the centre of this study.' and p. 43: 'nowhere are there texts that, in their length and richness, can compare with the Edfu records, which hitherto have been unknown and have not consequently been utilized in previous studies.'
20 This point is indisputable as regards the late era in which the Edfu temple was built.
21 Reymond, 1969, pp. 36-42.

NOTES 385

22. On the battle vs the snake, see Reymond, 1969, pp. 34-36, 252.
23. This is 'the island of the egg', alias 'the island of trampling'. See Reymond, 1969, pp. 66, 69, 72, 93.
24. The perch is said to be made of reed. It may be surmised that the shelter and temples were constructed likewise.
25. Reymond, 1969, pp. 63-65. Ir-ta is identified with Ta-tenen, both in these texts and other late sources.
26. Ibid., p. 110 identifies Mesenti as an earth-god.
27. Ibid., p. 110 states that the Pn-god *may* have been an earth-god. He was also a falcon-god (p. 131).
28. Ibid., pp. 110, 297.
29. Ibid., p. 115.
30. Ibid., pp. 110-11, 114. It means the place where the soul originated and whence it emerged.
31. Ibid., pp. 94, 111-12, 115.
32. Ibid., pp. 110, 279, 296.
33. Ibid., pp. 285, 294, 296.
34. Ibid., pp. 294, 297-98. Cf p. 296: 'The temple was believed to be the direct outcome of the earth'.
35. Ibid., pp. 292, 297.
36. Watterson, 1984, p. 167. Cf Reymond, 1969, p. 279: 'The temple of Wetjeset-Netjer is, in a sense, the resurrection of the home of the *Ka* – the *Ka* who was an earth-god.'
37. Reymond, 1969, p. 46.
38. Reymond, 1969, p. 275: 'Perhaps the Edfu accounts reveal in greater detail the theory of which a slight hint only has been preserved in the texts of the Shabaka Stone.'
39. Pyr. § 199.
40. This will be a recurrent theme in subsequent chapters. As we shall see, the ennead was born in Heliopolis; the gods were assembled in Heliopolis; the Eye was found and reassembled in Heliopolis; Horus and Seth fought in Heliopolis; their dispute was adjudged by the court of Neber-djer in Heliopolis; and a great bull came forth from Heliopolis.
41. CT, IV, 60. Cf BD, 79.
42. CT IV, 187, 220-27; V, 289.
43. Pyr. §§ 1615-18. Cf § 1646.
44. Pyr. §§ 1645-48.
45. Pyr. §§ 840, 843. Cf § 1277 where the pyramid and temple are 'a boon which Geb and Atum grant'.
46. Pyr. § 301.
47. Pyr. §§ 479-80.
48. Pyr. §§ 942-43.
49. Pyr. §§ 961, 992-94, 1475.
50. CT, II, 2-3. Cf II, 34.
51. CT, II, 35.
52. But this ennead was an artificial construction. See Frankfort, *KAG*, 1948, p. 182, and discussion of its members in chapter fourteen.
53. Frankfort, *KAG*, 1948, pp. 181-82 writes 'The same veneration of the powers in the earth which proclaims Ptah the first cause addresses itself sometimes to Geb... it is possible that at some time and place he was worshipped as the creator.'
54. Pyr. §§ 1617, 1623. Cf Atum as *ka* of Shu and Tefnut in § 1653.
55. Pyr. §§ 1617-18.
56. Pyr. §§ 255, 1465, 1618-26, 1645-46, 1835, 1868-69, 1919-20, 2103, 2142, 2226.
57. Pyr. § 316. The significance of this epithet is discussed in chapter eleven.
58. Pyr. §§ 2087-88. The spirits (*kau*) of Geb may correspond to his children (§ 1018).
59. Pyr. § 1624. Cf §§ 1816, 1832. We are dealing here with the origin of two eyes, see § 2279. This myth is discussed in depth in chapter twelve.
60. Pyr. §§ 2268, 1210. The four gods are probably the four regional spirits, who were fashioned by Geb (§ 1510). On these gods, see chapter two, note 260.
61. Pyr. §§ 1142-43.
62. Pyr. § 1033.
63. Pyr. §§ 1297 (cf §§ 576-77, 649-50), 577 (Isis and Nephthys), 583-84, 590, 634-35, 640-41 (Horus), 639 (Thoth).
64. Pyr. §§ 578, 1032-35, 1619, 1728, 1812, 1922, 2229.
65. Pyr. §§ 398-99, 483-84, 957, 1219, 1327, 1538, 1689, 1814-16, 2236. Note: Geb may award his heritage to Horus via Osiris, since Horus is Osiris reborn. Osiris reigns through Horus.
66. Pyr. §§ 102, 258, 794, 1013, 1353, 1810-12.
67. Pyr. § 1986.
68. Budge, 1934, pp. 91, 134, 149-50; Clark, 1959, pp. 56, 213; Watterson, 1984, p. 36. Cf BD, 54-59.

This idea was inspired by the fact that the word for goose was *gb*.
69 Frankfort, *KAG*, 1948, p. 181; Lurker, 1980, p. 54.
70 Reymond, 1969, pp. 106-7. Cf p. 114.
71 Ibid., p. 107. On p. 109 Reymond writes: 'The primeval water might have submerged the island as a consequence of a fight, and the island become the tomb of the original divine inhabitants; thus the *hbbt*-water became the *waret*-water.'
72 Ibid.
73 Ibid. 'The exact nature of this fight is difficult to explain.'
74 Ibid., pp. 15, 110, 114. The texts make it clear that the *duat n ba* predated the creation of the world.
75 Ibid., p. 110: 'Since we can quote evidence that Osiris was believed to have been pre-eminent (there)... it is evident that there is a clear allusion to a burial place, which was possibly, it may be suggested, that of the earth-god.'
76 Ibid., pp. 16, 136.
77 Ibid., pp. 114-15. On the sages as dead gods, see pp. 16-17, 81, 93-95, 109-10.
78 Ibid., pp. 110-11.
79 Ibid., pp. 14, 30-31. As noted in chapter three, the reed seems to be planted in a field of reeds that still remains submerged beneath the surface of the *waret*.
80 Ibid., pp. 14, 111, 121-22. The willow tree is likewise portrayed as a relic of a former world, pp. 26, 158, 160.
81 Ibid., pp. 21, 30, 89, 117. The restoration of the *djed*-pillar echoes Pyr. §§ 389-90.
82 Ibid., p. 122. See also pp. 111, 122-23.
83 Ibid., pp. 108-11. On p. 111, Reymond writes: 'Words such as *waret* and *akht*, 'relic', and *dwat n ba* suggest that closely connected with the island of creation there was a place that had obvious funerary associations, a place which was conceived as the burial place of a deity who died, whose soul had flown to the sky and whose material form remained in the same place: this *Ka* who dwelt among the reeds of the island.'
84 Ibid., pp. 22, 112-13, 148: 'this mansion might have been found destroyed... There was perhaps a storm in which the first sacred domain, represented by the Mansion of Isden, was thought to have perished.' The earth-god who enters is 'the God of the Temple'; he is connected to Ta-tenen (as is Ir-ta) and is probably the earth-god who becomes incarnate in the temple, see pp. 294-95. On the Mansion of Isden, see pp. 22, 99, 101.
85 Ibid., pp. 22-23, 30, 99, 149-50. Reymond translates *djt-wtt* as 'the member of progenitor'.
86 This theme is ubiquitous in the Pyramid Texts.
87 Nowhere in the PT is Osiris said to be dismembered by Seth. See Frankfort, *KAG*, 1948, p. 201; Hornung, 1999, p. 6.
88 Frankfort, *KAG*, 1948, p. 201.
89 Osiris is thrown down or laid low by Seth in Pyr. §§ 958, 972, 1256, 1500. Seth and his followers are mutilated in §§ 42, 81, 84, 962-63, 1286-87, 1337, 1339, 1543-50.
90 CT, VII, 99.
91 Pyr. §§ 24-25, 616, 766-67, 1297.
92 Pyr. § 616.
93 Pyr. § 1297.
94 Pyr. §§ 24-25, 616, 619-20, 766-67.
95 Pyr. §§ 788, 848, 868, 1291, 1360-61, 2007, 2031-32.
96 Pyr. §§ 1360-61. Cf CT, VII, 34.
97 CT, I, 307.
98 CT, VI, 306.
99 CT, I, 306-7.
100 Shabaka Stone, 62-63 (trans. Junker). See Pritchard, 1969, p. 5.
101 Pyr. §§ 721, 819, 1008, 1033, 1799-1800.
102 Pyr. §§ 958, 972, 1007, 1033, 1256, 1500.
103 Pyr. § 1362. Cf § 908, and see Wainwright, 1932, p. 162.
104 The role of Horus as saviour of his father is examined in chapter seven.
105 Pyr. §§ 1033, 1297.
106 Pyr. §§ 623 (with Nephthys), 828-29, 835-36, 1036-37, 1629-30.
107 Pyr. §§ 3, 308, 577, 584, 610, 616 (Nephthys only), 628-32, 872, 1004-8, 1255-58, 1280-83, 1425-26, 1630-35, 1786 (Nephthys only), 1951, 1973, 1981, 2144-45, 2192-93. Cf § 164.
108 On the turning of the body from left side to right side, see chapter seven. On the opening of the mouth, see chapters seven and eight. On the opening of the eyes, see chapters seven and twelve. On the mystical union, see chapter fourteen.

109 Budge, 1899; Budge, 1904; Budge, 1911; Budge, 1934; Breasted, 1912, p. 78; Frankfort, *KAG*, 1948, pp. 207, 212; Clark, 1959, pp. 103, 180; A.H. Gardiner, *JEA* 46 (1960), p. 104; Bauval, 1999, p. 58; David, 2002, pp. 156, 160, 409.
110 Breasted, 1912, pp. 8, 18-21, 23, 145-46; Budge, 1912, p. 137; Budge, 1934, p. 183; Frankfort, *KAG*, 1948, pp. 185-95; Frankfort, *AER*, p. 105; Clark, 1959, pp. 100, 118, 161, 174; James, 1960, pp. 137-38; Wilson, 1997, pp. 13, 21; Assmann, 2001, pp. 129-30; David, 2002, pp. 11, 157, 159.
111 Budge, 1934, pp. 44, 183, 192, 209, 279, 288; Clark, p. 159; Sellers, 1992, p. 135.
112 Budge, 1934, pp. 45, 138-39, 183, 192, 209; Frankfort, *KAG*, 1948, pp. 195-96, 211; James, 1960, p. 208; Lurker, 1980, pp. 46, 82, 93; Sellers, 1992, p. 135; David, 2002, p. 159.
113 Budge, 1934, pp. 44, 183, 279; Frankfort, *KAG*, 1948, pp. 195-96; Bauval, 1989 (reprinted in Bauval, 1999, pp. 356-65); Sellers, 1992, pp. 19, 39-40, 131. Osiris was associated particularly with Orion.
114 Plutarch, *De Iside et Osiride*, § 42 (see Budge, 1912, pp. 245-46); Budge, 1934, pp. 182-83; Lurker, 1980, pp. 46, 82, 93; Sellers, 1992, pp. 22, 135.
115 Budge, 1934, p. 183.
116 Frankfort, *KAG*, 1948, p. 201; Lurker, 1980, p. 93.
117 The PT refute Osiris's human parentage. See chapter seven, notes 75, 76, 77.
118 On Memphis, see Shabaka Stone. On Nedyt, see Pyr. §§ 260, 721, 754, 819, 1008-9, 1256, 1500, 2108-9, 2188. On Ghsty, see §§ 972-73, 1033, 1487, 1799-1800. On Andjet, see CT, IV, 331 (cf Pyr. §§ 182, 614). There are also hints that Osiris died in other towns, such as Heliopolis, Abydos, Djedu, and Rostau. Each signified the 'great city', i.e. the world. In the same way, Horus was born in Chemmis, which was synonymous with the netherworld, see §§ 1703, 2190.
119 Pyr. § 1886. Cf §§ 1598, 1603.
120 On Geb, see Pyr. §§ 258, 793-94, 1013, 1353, 1810-12, 1986. On Anubis, see Pyr. §§ 796-98, 1015, 1336, 1523, 1996, 2150, 2178. Anubis is named in §§ 745, 2198-99 as 'Foremost of the Westerners', i.e. the ruler of the netherworld. He is also connected with 'the sacred land' and 'the god's booth'.
121 Pyr. §§ 1008-9, 1951, 2144-45, 1360-61.
122 CT, VI, 306.
123 Pyr. §§ 628-29, 1630-32. In § 629 he is also 'circular and round as the circle which surrounds the *Hau-nbwt*' (cf § 847 where *Hau-nbwt* has the sky-sign as its determinative).
124 Pyr. § 848; CT, I, 307. The floodwaters become the heritage of Horus the living king, § 22.
125 Shabaka Stone, 63. The bringing to land motif is found also in the CT ferry-boat spells, e.g. II, 163: 'I have found the ferry-boat which was lost in its flood-waters and I have brought it to land.'
126 See notes 66 and 67 above.
127 Pyr. §§ 585, 621, 636, 1887. Cf §§ 645-46.
128 On Osiris Lord of the Duat, see chapter two, notes 67, 68, 78. On the *akhet* as the offspring of the *duat*, see discussion in chapter six.
129 Pyr. §§ 464-65.
130 Pyr §§ 820, 882-83, 925, 959.
131 Pyr §§ 1454, 2051-52. Cf §§ 749, 2244-45.
132 Pyr §§ 1816, 1981-82, 2279. Cf CT, VI, 384.
133 Pyr § 1528. Cf § 1156.
134 Pyr §§ 1002-3, 1047, 1747-48, 1878-79, 1938, 2182-83.
135 Plutarch, *De Iside et Osiride*, § 32 (see Budge, 1912, p. 239). Cf Pyr. §§ 1193-94. 1528.
136 See especially Budge, 1899, pp. 59-60; Budge, 1911, I, pp. 312-15; Budge, 1934, pp. 287-88.
137 Budge, 1934, pp. 184-90; Wainwright, 1938, pp. 20, 98; Frankfort, *KAG*, 1948, pp. 198-207; Clark, 1959, pp. 97-98, 131; Watterson, 1984, pp. 54-56, 170-71; Shaw & Nicholson, 1995, pp. 213-14, 230, 273-74; Betro, 1996, p. 73; Meeks, 1997, pp. 164-66.
138 Pyr. §§ 592, 614, 620, 650, 759, 1256-58, 1712, 1824, 1826-27, 1925, 1996-97, 2240.
139 Breasted, 1912, pp. 8-9, 40, 140, 142, 150, 158, 160, 163; James, 1960, p. 169; Assmann, 2001, p. 124.
140 Breasted, 1912, pp. xvi, 73, 78-79, 103, 139-40, 142, 148-50, 154, 156, 158, 250-51, 275-77.
141 Reymond, 1969, pp. 110, 114, 117.
142 Pyr. § 616.
143 Reymond, 1969, pp. 7, 28-29, 31, 34-36, 38-39, 41-42, 233-34, 283, 308-9.
144 The temple was certainly a model of the cosmos in the late period, but the evidence is less clear for the temples of the Old Kingdom.
145 CT, II, 2-3. Cf II, 34.
146 CT, II, 33-35 (trans. Faulkner/Allen/Alford). See Allen, 1988, pp. 22-23.
147 Berlin Hymn to Ptah (trans. Budge/Wolf/Allen/Alford). See Budge, 1934, p. 259; Frankfort, *KAG*, 1948, p. 181; Allen, 1988, p. 40.

148 Ibid.
149 Assmann, 2001, p. 25.
150 Pyr. §§ 23, 260, 721, 735, 741, 875, 1006, 1501, 1901, 1915, 1927, 2224.
151 BD, 183. See trans. in Clark, 1959, p. 174.
152 Allen, 1988, pp. 33-34; Assmann, 2001, pp. 77-80, 109.
153 CT, IV, 192-93, 201-3. Cf BD, 17. See Allen, 1988, pp. 33-34.
154 Pyr. §§ 585, 621, 636, 1887. Cf §§ 645-46.
155 Pyr. §§ 1505-9. Re and Osiris also share the *wrrt*-crown in §§ 2018-21.
156 Pyr. § 285. Cf CT, VI, 237.
157 CT, VII, 19. Cf CT, VII, 255 where Re counts his bones and collects his limbs together.
158 CT, IV, 276-83. Cf CT, VII, 360-62, where the souls of Re and Osiris are synonymous.
159 BD, 17.
160 See Hornung, 1999.
161 Budge, 1905, III, p. 106; Hart, 1990, pp. 52, 58-61.
162 The scenes are reminiscent of hell, see Hornung, 2001, p. 73. Hence the title of Budge, 1905.
163 James, 1960, p. 177.
164 See notes 139-140 above.
165 Osiris is thus viewed as 'the sun-god of night', whose death and rebirth reflected the solar cycle. See Meeks, 1997, pp. 85, 152.
166 Hornung, 1999, p. xvii.
167 Hornung, 1999, p. xviii; Assmann, 1989, pp. 152-55.
168 Frankfort, *AER*, 1948, p. 107. Cf Frankfort, *KAG*, 1948, p. 375 note 14; David, 2002, p. 95.
169 Assmann, 2001, pp. 77-79, 109.
170 Ibid., pp. 109, 120.
171 Book of Nut (cenotaph texts of Seti I). See Allen, 1988, pp. 2-3.
172 Clark, 1959, pp. 36, 40, 47, 264; Morenz, 1973, p. 171; Hornung, 1982, pp. 161-62, 181; Meeks, 1997, p. 162; Assmann, 2001, p. 122; David, 2002, p. 84.
173 Frankfort et al, 1946, p. 24; Morenz, 1973, pp. 167-68; Assmann, 2001, p. 104, 122.
174 Frankfort, *KAG*, 1948, p. 156; Meeks, 1997, pp. 158-59; Hornung, 1999, p. 41.
175 Budge, 1905, I, pp. 65, 93, 144, 257-59, 277; II, pp. 16, 38, 254, 285-86, 291; Hornung, 1999, pp. 37-38, 41, 59-60, 62, 64-65, 79, 85-90, 97-103. See figure 23 in chapter five.
176 Budge, 1905, I, pp. 1, 14, 19, 138, 224, 246, 257-59; II, pp. 91, 103, 111, 118, 120, 130, 222-23, 238, 260, 280, 285; Hornung, 1999, pp. 34-37, 40, 64-65, 85-87.
177 Budge, 1905, II, pp. 82, 91, 120, 262, 282, 304-5; Hornung, 1999, p. 57.
178 Budge, 1905, I, pp. 154-59, II, pp. 87, 262-66, 273-77, 287-88, 291; Hornung, 1999, pp. 39, 101-2.
179 Allen, 1988, pp. 33-34 comes close to the truth: 'Osiris, the principle of potential new life... the sun [Re], the manifest realisation of that potential. The two together embody the cycle of life – a cycle that began at the creation and continues in daily life.'

CHAPTER FIVE: GOD AND THE GODS

1 CT, IV, 62-63 (trans. Faulkner/Alford).
2 Morenz, 1973, p. 172; Allen, 1988, pp. 36, 48, 50; Quirke, 2001, p. 26.
3 Pyr. §§ 1248-49, 1587, 1652-53. Cf CT, II, 32-33. See Assmann, 2001, p. 120.
4 Pyr. § 199.
5 Bremner-Rhind Pap., part a, 30-31. Cf part b. See Budge, 1904, I, pp. 311-12; Budge, 1912, pp. 4-5; Allen, 1988, pp. 28-29.
6 Bremner-Rhind Pap., part b (trans. Budge/Alford). See Budge, 1899, p. 24; Budge, 1904, I, p. 314; Budge, 1912, pp. 6-7; Budge, 1934, pp. 144, 435; Allen, 1988, p. 29.
7 Berlin Hymn to Ptah. See quote in chapter four.
8 Berlin Hymn to Ptah. See Morenz, 1973, p. 161. Cf Hymn to Amun in Pritchard, 1969, p. 367.
9 Berlin Hymn to Ptah. See Budge, 1934, p. 259.
10 CT, II, 1, 7-8, 19-21, 23-24, 27-28.
11 Papyrus Nesi-Khensu. See Budge, 1899, p. 105. Cf Great Hymn to Amun, 80.
12 Great Hymn to Amun, 80 (trans. Allen/Alford). See Allen, 1988, p. 50.
13 The prime example is Ptah in *The Theology of Memphis*. See Frankfort, *AER*, 1948, pp. 23-29. Allen, 1988, pp. 48, 53-55, 62 sees transcendence in Amun. For a sceptical view of the transcendent God in Egypt, see Hornung, 1982, pp. 190-96.
14 Notably in the case of Amun. See Allen, 1988, pp. 48, 53-55, 61-62.
15 Allen, 1988, pp. 61-62.

NOTES 389

16 The Ogdoad, or Primeval Ones, created Re and the Great Lotus (see chapter three); frog-goddesses bore Re (CT, III, 372); ancestor-gods created Re (see chapter four, note 4); Geb has fathers and mothers (Pyr. § 1619). Atum was begotten by the *akhet*-gods (CT, II, 36); and the king as primeval god is fashioned by the gods in the *akhet* (Pyr. § 344).
17 Pyr. §§ 1257-58. Cf § 19, 55, 831, 1925, 2275. Cf § 1355 (the tomb of Horus). There is also a correlation between the spiritual aspects of Osiris and Horus of the Duat in that both are at the head of the imperishable stars, see §§ 749, 1301.
18 Pyr. §§ 605-6.
19 CT, IV, 64. Cf BD, 85.
20 CT, VI, 44. Cf VI, 74: 'I am that corpse for which Atum wept, which Anubis buried.'
21 CT, IV, 73-76.
22 CT, VI, 267.
23 CT, VI, 152.
24 CT, I, 314-20.
25 CT, II, 1, 7, 19. Cf CT, II, 23-24, 28.
26 CT, VII, 19.
27 CT, I, 303-5. Cf Pyr. §§ 1257-58.
28 CT, II, 327-28.
29 Great Hymn to Amun, 40.
30 Great Hymn to Amun, 80.
31 Great Hymn to Amun, 200.
32 Budge, 1905, I, pp. 65, 70, 77, 98; II, pp. 16, 25, 196, 200, 244, 251, 257-58; Lehner, 1997, pp. 28-29.
33 Budge, 1905, I, p. 144; Hornung, 1999, pp. 33-41, 85-90.
34 Hornung, 1999, pp. 95-103.
35 Ibid., p. 99.
36 On *The Destruction of Mankind*, see Budge, 1904, I, pp. 388-99; Budge, 1912, pp. 14-41; Budge, 1934, pp. 463-67; Clark, 1959, pp. 181-85; Hart, 1990, pp. 47-49. On *Isis and Re*, see Budge, 1904, I, pp. 372-87; Budge, 1912, pp. 42-55; Hart, 1990, pp. 44-45.
37 Hornung, 1982, p. 154; Hart, 1990, p. 47; Hornung, 2001, pp. 16-17.
38 Budge, 1904, I, p. 388; Budge, 1912, pp. 14-15.
39 Budge, 1904, I, pp. 398-99; Budge, 1912, pp. 23-25.
40 Budge, 1904, I, p. 376; Budge, 1912, p. 45.
41 Budge, 1904, I, pp. 377-79; Budge, 1912, pp. 47-49.
42 See discussion of *ka* in chapter seven.
43 CT, I, 314-18.
44 See chapter four, notes 139 and 140.
45 Pyr. §§ 316, 655-56, 783, 1039; CT, VI, 185. See Allen, 1989, pp. 3-4.
46 CT, IV, 189. See Faulkner, 1973, p. 266 note 5.
47 CT, II, 158.
48 Pyr. §§ 852, 1145, 1444-48, 1583, 1987, 2032. In the Book of Gates, Horus calls Osiris 'the great one who begot me in the *duat*'. Re also claims to be 'a great one, the son of a great one' (*Re and Isis*).
49 Geb is father to the spirit of Horus in §§ 466, 973-74. Cf §§ 301, 316-17.
50 Assmann, 2001, p. 91.
51 Hornung, 1982, pp. 221-23; Allen, 1988, p. 8; Hart, 1990, p. 13; Hornung, 1999, p. 33.
52 The exception is the ennead of Heliopolis, which has obviously been contrived to make certain named gods subordinate to Atum.
53 All these modes of creating the gods are mentioned in the creation by Ptah Ta-tenen in *The Theology of Memphis*. On speech, see also chapter eight, notes 39-41, 45. On birth, see also chapter fourteen, notes 40, 44-45.
54 Geb is *ka* of all the gods in Pyr. § 1623 and Osiris likewise in § 1609.
55 Reymond, 1969; Assmann, 2001, pp. 37-38.
56 Pyr. §§ 478-79, 1473-75. Cf §§ 941-42, 1253, 1522-23.
57 Pyr. §§ 135, 747, 873, 2023. They are identified with 'those who are in the tombs', § 1641.
58 Pyr. § 447. Cf § 2065.
59 Pyr. § 446. See Allen, 1988, pp. 49, 72 note 161.
60 CT, II, 34. Cf IV, 75. See Allen, 1988, p. 23; Meeks, 1997, p. 14; Assmann, 2001, pp. 179-80.
61 CT, V. 166. Cf CT, II, 34-35.
62 Bremner-Rhind Pap., part a, 10 (trans. Allen/Alford). See Allen, 1988, p. 28.
63 CT, II, 6-8, 28. Cf CT, IV, 178.
64 BD, 17. Cf CT, IV, 184-190.

NOTES TO PAGES 104 – 123

65 Shabaka Stone, 58-61. See Pritchard, 1969, p. 5; Allen, 1988, p. 44.
66 Great Harris Papyrus. See Morenz, 1973, p. 182.
67 Great Hymn to Amun, 80. See Budge, 1934, pp. 17-18; Allen, 1988, p. 50.
68 Reymond, 1969, p. 77.
69 Pyr. § 1623; Frankfort, *KAG*, 1948, p. 181.
70 Pyr. §§ 353, 934, 1383, 1705-6.
71 Pyr. §§ 1208-9. Cf CT, IV, 36-37.
72 Pyr. § 1114. Cf §§ 459, 549-50, 799-800, 2231, 2247.
73 Pyr. §§ 784-85 (trans. Faulkner/Budge/Clark/Alford). See Budge, 1911, I, pp. 151-52; Clark, 1959, p. 49.
74 Great Hymn to Amun, 90 (trans. Allen). See Allen, 1988, p. 51.
75 Hornung, 1982, p. 228; Allen, 1989, p. 3.
76 Pyr. §§ 327, 598, 719, 824, 829, 907, 948, 975, 1165-66, 1216, 1574.
77 Meeks, 1997, p. 25. Cf Budge, 1934, p. 419.
78 Reymond, 1969, pp. 21-22.
79 Ibid., pp. 76-78: 'they created themselves, issued from themselves – the progenitors who begot themselves'.
80 Ibid., pp. 67, 76-77: it was 'the great ennead, who caused the gods to be, who gave birth to the Primeval Ones'.
81 Ibid., pp. 77. See also pp. 68, 73, 90.
82 Cf Pyr. § 480. See discussion of earth-mounds in chapter thirteen.
83 Reymond, 1969, p. 112.
84 Meeks, 1997, p. 180. Cf pp. 103-4. See also Reymond, 1969, p. 267; Morenz, 1973, p. 25.
85 Meeks, 1997, p. 180.
86 Ibid.
87 Ibid.
88 Pyr. §§ 141, 255, 1563.
89 CT, IV, 102.
90 CT, II, 1 (trans. Faulkner/Allen/Alford). See Allen, 1988, p. 18.
91 CT, II, 19 (trans. Faulkner/Allen).
92 CT, II, 23-24 (trans. Faulkner/Allen).
93 CT, IV, 74-76 (trans. Faulkner/Alford). Cf BD, 78.
94 BD, 17 (trans. Faulkner/Alford). Cf Budge, 1899, p. 90; Frankfort et al, 1946, p. 53.
95 Budge, 1904, I, pp. 377-79; Budge, 1912, pp. 46-49.
96 Budge, 1905, I, pp. 16, 18.
97 Budge, 1905, I, pp. 165, 214; II, p. 84.
98 CT, II, 1.
99 On the dismemberment of Horus, see chapter thirteen.
100 On the dismemberment of Seth, see chapter thirteen.
101 On the dismemberment of the Eye, see chapter twelve.
102 CT, VI, 333.
103 Pyr. §§ 1647-48.
104 Pyr. §§ 1616-18.
105 Pyr. §§ 615, 619-20, 647, 1831.
106 Pyr. §§ 613, 641.
107 Pyr. §§ 613, 641.
108 Pyr. §§ 577-78, 645, 1830-31. The gods knit together his face for him, §§ 642-43.
109 Pyr. § 613.
110 Pyr. § 1633. Osiris is united with the gods in Heliopolis per § 1744.
111 Pyr. §§ 619-20, 641-43, 645-47.
112 Pyr. § 647.
113 Pyr. § 2101.
114 Pyr. § 1333.
115 Pyr. §§ 24-25, 766-67. Cf §§ 615-16.
116 Pyr. §§ 619-20, 637, 643, 1333-34, 1823. Cf § 1824.
117 Pyr. §§ 645-47.
118 Pyr. § 1824.
119 Pyr. §§ 2101-2.
120 Pyr. §§ 590-91, 1824, 1830. Cf §§ 576-78, 634.
121 Pyr. §§ 478-79, 941-42, 1473-74.

122 Pyr. §§ 478-79, 941-42.
123 Pyr. §§ 478-79, 1473-74. Cf §§ 941-42, 1253. Cf also the stairway raised by the souls of Heliopolis in § 1090, and the ladder raised by the various groups of gods in CT, II, 7-12.
124 Pyr. §§ 318-19. Cf § 1486.
125 CT, VI, 186-87. Cf CT, II, 25: Shu was in the *nun* when the earth-gods had not yet been knit together.

CHAPTER SIX: RAISING THE SKY

1 Pyr. § 1778; CT, VI, 310; VII, 199.
2 Pyr. §§ 299, 1039, 1101, 1443, 1454, 2091; CT, II, 2, 5, 19-22, 35.
3 Pyr. §§ 784-85.
4 Pyr. §§ 1208-9. Cf CT, II, 93, IV, 36-37.
5 Hornung, 1982, p. 171. It was also the case, as we shall see, that water was separated from water.
6 Allen, 1988, p. 58.
7 The Shu texts comprise CT Spells 75-81 (I, 314 to II, 44).
8 Allen, 1988, pp. 7, 56-57. Cf pp. 19-20, 25, 30, 58.
9 Email communication, 18th September 2003. Cf Allen, 1988, pp. 4, 7, 17, 56-57.
10 Allen, 1988, p. 31. Cf pp. 10-12.
11 Ibid.
12 Ibid., p. 16.
13 Allen, 1989, p. 13. See Pyr. § 1405. Cf § 1443.
14 Pyr. § 1652. Cf Allen, 1988, pp. 13-14.
15 Pyr. §§ 1208-9.
16 CT, II, 2, 35. Cf Allen, 1988, pp. 18, 23.
17 CT, II, 34. Cf Allen, 1988, p. 22.
18 CT, IV, 63 (Re), 63-64 (Nun). Cf BD, 85.
19 CT, IV, 178.
20 Allen, 1989, p. 3 (Pyr. §§ 1208-9).
21 In the Shu texts, Atum and Shu use a ladder to escape from the abyss, while Shu ascends on a ladder to the sky having delegated its supports to the Infinite Ones. Pyr. §§ 1585-86 refer to a ladder which Khnum made which is used for ascending to the sky.
22 Edfu texts, see Reymond, 1969, and summary in chapter three. See also solar hymn quoted in Assmann, 2001, p. 91.
23 It should be noted, however, that Allen sees the original *nun* as infinite.
24 CT, IV, 184. See Faulkner, 1973, pp. 262, 266 note 5.
25 BD, 17.
26 Morenz, 1973, p. 177.
27 Budge, 1912, p. 133.
28 BD, 85. Cf CT, IV, 62-64. The creation of darkness would relate to the *nun*, the *duat*, and the depths of the celestial ocean.
29 CT, VI, 343-44 (trans. Faulkner/Allen/Alford). See Allen, 1988, pp. 13-14. Owing to the constraints of his model, Allen fails to realise that there is a separation of waters from waters here.
30 See chapter two, note 23.
31 CT, V, 289. Cf Clark, 1959, p. 181.
32 BD, 38a. Cf BD, 3. Consistent with this, the Shu texts describe how Atum created the sky, ascended to it, and floated upon it (or possibly became it); he is said to go to rest upon 'the great flood of Atum', the waters for which were assembled by Geb.
33 Pyr. § 782 (trans. Faulkner/Alford).
34 Pyr. § 1020.
35 Pyr. §§ 784-85 (trans. Faulkner/Budge/Alford). See Budge, 1911, I, pp. 151-52.
36 CT, II, 2-3. Cf CT, II, 19. According to CT, II, 39, it was Atum who separated Geb and Nut.
37 Pyr. § 779.
38 Pyr. § 780.
39 Pyr. § 781.
40 Budge, 1905, II, pp. 57-59.
41 We see here a possible explanation for the duality of goddesses in Egyptian mythology, e.g. Isis and Nephthys.
42 Pyr. § 638.
43 Pyr. §§ 1082-83. See Allen, 1989, p. 22. This is very suggestive of Nut giving birth to the sky.
44 Pyr. § 2057.

45 Pyr. § 1688.
46 Pyr. § 1. Cf the birth of Seth in § 205.
47 Allen, 1988, pp. 5-6.
48 Budge, 1905, I, p. 19.
49 Budge, 1905, II, p. 38.
50 Hornung, 1999, p. 27. On the idea of the sky in the middle of the earth, see chapter two, note 210.
51 Nut is called 'the mysterious one' in the Books of the Netherworld. See Hornung, 1999, pp. 88, 98.
52 Pyr. §§ 777-79, 825, 827-28, 834-35, 838, 842-43.
53 Pyr. §§ 623, 828, 835, 1037.
54 Pyr. §§ 829, 836, 2178.
55 Pyr. § 838.
56 Pyr. §§ 208, 616, 1300.
57 Pyr. §§ 1, 623, 626, 1145, 1428, 1703, 1833, 1835, 2057.
58 Pyr. §§ 623, 781, 1145.
59 Pyr. §§ 275, 519, 756, 1090, 1247, 1430, 1757-58, 2034-35, 2107, 2171.
60 Pyr. §§ 2053-54, 2171-72.
61 Pyr. §§ 1417, 2107.
62 Pyr. §§ 883, 2172. She also bears him en route to the sky, §§ 530-31, 990, 1416-17 (see discussion in chapter eleven). The *pet*-sky likewise conceives and gives birth to him, see §§ 820-21, 1443, 1527.
63 Pyr. § 782.
64 Pyr. § 1835.
65 Pyr. § 783.
66 Pyr. § 785.
67 Pyr. § 616 (trans. Faulkner/Assmann). See Assmann, 2001, p. 85. Cf §§ 1361-62. The term *hrt* can also signify 'tomb' as well as sky; see § 1264 and Faulkner, 1969, p. 202 note 2.
68 Pyr. § 941.
69 It is explained as rebirth symbolism. Nut is the king's mother and must therefore be brought down to the tomb. A cosmographic explanation is wanting. See Frankfort, *KAG*, 1948, pp. 175-76.
70 In Pyr. § 1936, the king states: "I have come to you, you whose seats are hidden, seeking you for the sky. He is secret: I cannot find him in the sky's resting place, in the earth's resting place." (trans. Faulkner/Allen). See Allen, 1989, p. 25.
71 Allen, 1989, p. 16.
72 CT, V, 166 (Atum in his name of Neber-djer). Cf CT, II, 7-8, 34-35.
73 CT, II, 5. See Allen, 1988, p. 18.
74 CT, II, 10, 14-15, 23-25, 28.
75 CT, II, 6-8, 24, 28.
76 The *nun* and the flood are also synonymous in Pyr. § 551.
77 BD, 175. See Allen, 1988, p. 14.
78 Pyr. § 508.
79 CT, VII, 462-63.
80 Pyr. §§ 1065-66. Cf Re in § 1173.
81 CT, II, 25.
82 Pyr. §§ 266. Cf CT, VII, 184; BD, 174. 'Great One' is a designation of Nut in §§ 782, 1020, 1145.
83 Pyr. § 499.
84 Pyr. §§ 721, 735, 741, 819, 2018, 2188, 2224.
85 CT, II, 25. Cf CT, II, 20.
86 CT, II, 2.
87 Pyr. § 1039. This passage is discussed further in chapter eleven.
88 CT, II, 29.
89 CT, III, 35.
90 CT, VI, 154.
91 CT, IV, 368.
92 CT, II, 120.
93 CT, VII, 347. On the meaning of the name Neheb-kau, see CT, II, 52-53; Frankfort, *KAG*, 1948, p. 104; Allen, 1988, p. 90.
94 Gardiner, 1994, p. 487. This sign is used as a determinative for individual stars and groups of stars.
95 Pyr. § 138. See Allen, 1989, p. 8.
96 Allen, 1989, pp. 4, 7. On the significance of *msqt shdu*, see discussion in chapter two.
97 Pyr. §§ 332, 909, 1574-75, 2005. On the meaning 'aged ones', see Budge, 1911, I, p. 131; Faulkner, 1969, pp. 110, 237.

98 On Sopdet and Netjer-dwau, see chapter two.
99 Pyr. §§ 251, 877, 1048, 1384, 1899, 1920, 1945, 2226-27. On the significance of the 'unique star' or 'lone star', see chapter twelve, note 93.
100 Pyr. §§ 882, 1038. In CT, IV, 357, 'great star' is a textual variant for 'lone star', and seemingly relates to Venus as evening star and morning star.
101 Pyr. § 280; CT, VI, 141, 330, 341.
102 Pyr. § 458 associates *mskhtiu* with 'the two enneads'. The term possibly signified two adzes – see discussion in chapter two. Hence my suggestion that it might have originally designated the northern circumpolar stars in their entirety.
103 On Sah as Orion/Canopus, see discussion in chapter two.
104 Pyr. §§ 207, 818, 1080, 1220. See chapter two, note 267.
105 Pyr. § 1760.
106 Pyr. §§ 380, 998.
107 Pyr. § 1216 (the passage places these gods beneath the horizon, pending their birth).
108 Pyr. § 1457. Cf §§ 166, 1468-69, 1485.
109 CT, I, 241.
110 Pyr. §§ 1583-84.
111 The day-barque and night-barque are like realms of the cosmos, see Pyr. §§ 485, 1194.
112 Allen, 1988, p. 8.
113 Shabaka Stone, 56 (trans. Junker). See Pritchard, 1969, p. 5.
114 Pyr. § 1116. See Allen, p. 3.
115 Gardiner, 1994, p. 486.
116 CT, IV, 190. Cf Pyr. §§ 1834-35.
117 Pyr. §§ 177-78. See Hornung, 1982, p. 223.
118 Pyr. §§ 1044 (*nun*), 1045 (*duat*), 1092-93 (field of reeds), 1196-98 (field of offerings), 1201-3, 1261-62, 2170-71, 2206 (*akhet*).
119 Pyr. §§ 906, 1573-74.
120 Pyr. § 458. Cf § 405. See discussion of *mskhtiu* in chapter two. The two enneads of the northern sky were possibly seen as superior to the regular stars, see §§ 1689-90.
121 Pyr. §§ 656, 759-60, 900, 1220. Cf §§ 1288, 1567, 1721-22, 1994-95, 2104.
122 Pyr. §§ 656, 899, 1232, 1994-95, 2104. Cf §§ 57, 481, 579, 800, 833, 1506-9, 1725, 2096, 2103-4.
123 Pyr. §§ 460, 531, 1262, 1305, 1689-90. The souls of Heliopolis were also earth-gods or *akhet*-gods, § 1090.
124 Pyr. §§ 478, 942. The souls of Pe and Nekhen were also earth-gods or *akhet*-gods, § 1253.
125 Pyr. § 904.
126 Pyr. §§ 621, 723, 1559, 1730, 1921, 2120-21, 2228.
127 Pyr. §§ 1725, 1899, 1914, 2096, 2103-4.
128 Pyr. § 785 (trans. Faulkner/Clark/Alford). See Clark, 1959, p. 49.
129 Pyr. §§ 1208-9.
130 Great Harris Papyrus. See Morenz, 1973, p. 182.
131 Shabaka Stone, 58, (trans. Junker/Allen/Alford). See Pritchard, 1969, p. 5; Allen, 1988, p. 44.
132 Great Hymn to Amun, 80 (trans. Allen/Alford). See Allen, 1988, p. 50.
133 Reymond, 1969, p. 77. Cf p. 90. See quotation in chapter five.
134 Pyr. § 2268. Cf § 2266; CT, II, 144, 146.
135 Pyr. § 1623; Frankfort, *KAG*, 1948, p. 181.
136 Pyr. §§ 13-14.
137 Pyr. §§ 1298-1301, 1340, 1984-86; CT, I, 265; III, 312-13, 316, 325-26; BD, 23.
138 Budge, 1905, II, p. 106. Cf Hornung, 1999, pp. 59-60, 64.
139 Pyr. §§ 353, 928, 933, 1383, 1705-6.
140 CT, IV, 184 ff; BD, 17. Cf Horus in CT, II, 223.
141 Pyr. §§ 496-97. See Allen, 1989, p. 5.
142 Pyr. § 368. Cf solar hymn in Assmann, 2001, p. 65.
143 Pyr. §§ 480, 598, 916, 948. Cf the mounds of the earth from which the Primeval Ones were spiritualized. See further discussion in chapter thirteen.
144 Pyr. §§ 585, 621, 636, 1887. Cf § 645.
145 Pyr. § 621.
146 Pyr. § 1986.
147 Allen, 1989, p. 17. This oval-shaped sign was also used on occasion to determine the name Nut and the word *djet* 'eternal endurance'.
148 The *duat* too was a watery place with green fields (see chapter two). Interestingly, the path to the field

NOTES TO PAGES 135 – 150

of reeds and the east side of the sky is called 'power of the earth' in CT, V, 105.
149 Hence the primeval mound is never said to be 'in' the *akhet*. The primeval mound and the *akhet* are the same cosmic realm, seen from two different perspectives.
150 Pyr. §§ 559, 565, 1065-66. The *hnmmt*, 'beings of light' are sky-gods, i.e. stars (see chapter two).
151 Pyr. § 1131. On the ascent to the sky, cf §§ 525-33.
152 CT, VI, 270 (trans. Faulkner/Alford). The ennead follows the god up to the sky, cf CT, IV, 181.
153 CT, VII, 462. Cf the Edfu myth of the Shebtiu.
154 Pyr. §§ 1209-10. The building of a cosmic boat is also ascribed to Khnum in §§ 445, 1227-28.
155 CT, V, 75-160; VI, 3-45; BD, 99. See also Assmann, 2001, pp. 93-94.
156 Pyr. § 2206.
157 Budge, 1905, II, pp. 103, 106-7. Cf Hornung, 1999, pp. 59-60.
158 Pyr. §§ 138, 620-21, 1824, 1826-27, 1933, 1968-70; CT, I, 178; III, 258; VI, 309; VII, 198.
159 CT, II, 175-76, 261-64; III, 56; V, 262, 290-91; VI, 66; VII, 245.
160 Pyr. § 1185.
161 CT, IV, 62, 184 ff; Books of the Netherworld (see Budge, 1905; Hornung, 1999); Book of the Heavenly Cow (see Budge, 1912, p. 17). See also Budge, 1934, pp. 138, 153; Frankfort, *AER*, 1948, p. 114; Lurker, 1980, p. 105; Meeks, 1997, p. 30.
162 On the lotus and the egg, see chapter three.
163 CT, III, 372.
164 On the myth of Re and the Primeval Ones, see chapter three.
165 Pyr. § 1688.
166 Assmann, 2001, p. 91.
167 Reymond, 1969, pp. 67-68, 70-71, 76-77, 80-81, 290.
168 Ibid., p. 51.
169 CT, IV, 184 ff. Book of the Heavenly Cow (see Budge, 1912, pp. 24-27).
170 CT, VI, 270.
171 Frankfort, *KAG*, 1948, pp. 145, 169.
172 Frankfort, *KAG*, 1948, p. 169; Meeks, 1997, p. 67. This myth is discussed further in chapter eleven.
173 Lurker, 1980, pp. 82-83, 85.
174 CT, I, 27-31.
175 Chester Beatty I Papyrus. See Budge, 1934, p. 453; Clark, 1959, p. 206; Watterson, 1984, p. 182.
176 S. Sauneron, *Esna*, Vol. 5, Cairo, 1962, p. 266; Meeks, 1997, p. 78.
177 Pyr. § 709.
178 Book of the Heavenly Cow. See Budge, 1912, pp. 31-34. Cf CT, IV, 380.
179 Frankfort, *KAG*, 1948, p. 180. On the significance of this myth, see chapter fourteen.
180 Egyptologists generally fail to consider this distinction and assume that every reference to Re means 'Re the sun' as opposed to 'Re the creator'. This generates a solar bias which undermines our understanding of the creation myth and the religion.
181 James, 1960, pp. 205-6; Meeks, 1997, pp. 100-1.
182 Wainwright, 1932, pp. 164, 170.
183 Ibid., p. 170. Cf CT, VII, 20: 'I am Horus, who issued from Isis, whom Nut bore within the secret places of the house of Geb. I am born blind.'
184 Lurker, 1980, p. 48; Frankfort, *KAG*, 1948, p. 37.
185 Budge, 1934, p. 259.
186 Morenz, 1973, p. 141.
187 Further examples of the right eye and left eye are quoted in chapter twelve.
188 Pyr. §§ 1981-82. Cf §§ 2279, 2285.
189 Gardiner, 1994, pp. 489, 584, 606. See also Frankfort, *KAG*, 1948, pp. 57, 148, 150-51; Frankfort, *AER*, 1948, pp. 53, 56.
190 Pyr. § 823 (trans. Faulkner/Alford). See also chapter thirteen, note 20.
191 Gardiner, 1994, pp. 125, 492, 614.
192 Pyr. § 2279. Cf §§ 1624-25, 1816, 2036-37.
193 Pyr. §§ 1624-25. The Eye also goes forth as the two crowns from the head of Osiris in § 1816.
194 Budge, 1934, p. 163. Cf §§ 1098-99. The head seems to signify the primeval land.
195 BD, 82. See also Meeks, 1997, p. 27.
196 Pyr. §§ 1588-1606.
197 Pyr. § 1722.
198 CT, IV, 109.
199 CT, VI, 221.
200 CT, VII, 20. See note 183 above.

201 Budge, 1904, I, pp. 385-86; Budge, 1912, pp. 52-55.
202 CT, IV, 106-7.
203 CT, II, 5; VI, 375.
204 Papyrus Boulaq 17. See Pritchard, 1969, p. 367.

CHAPTER SEVEN: KING OF CREATION

1 Kings lists of later times inserted Atum or Re before Osiris.
2 *Per-aa* meant literally 'great house'. This signified more than an institution of government. It evoked the expanse of the cosmos (cf the mansion of Horus).
3 On Menes, see Frankfort, *KAG*, 1948, pp. 15, 17-18, 22-25, 89-90.
4 Frankfort, *KAG*, 1948, p. 45; Morenz, 1973, p. 37; Hornung, 1982, pp. 138-39.
5 'The King as Priest of the Sun' (trans. Assmann). See Assmann, 1989, pp. 57-59; Assmann, 2001, pp. 3-5.
6 In fact, Osiris is not attested until the 5th dynasty. My references to 'Osiris-Menes' and 'Osiris-Aha' are illustrative only, but reflect the Egyptian view of their own kingship history. It is possible that the original duality was Horus-Sokar (Pyr. §§ 620, 1824) or Khenti-amentiu-Horus (Pyr. §§ 592, 650).
7 A king was called 'son of Isis' as early as the 1st dynasty. See Frankfort, AER, 1948, p. 7; Morenz, 1973, p. 34. His identity as son of Osiris is not attested until much later, in the PT.
8 Quirke, 1990. The cartouche signified a sacred space, namely the cosmos which the sun orbited.
9 Hornung, 1982, p. 192. Cf Frankfort, *KAG*, 1948, p. 355 note 7.
10 Frankfort et al, 1946, p. 75.
11 Hornung, 1982, p. 142: 'Even for the Egyptians this divinity of the king was a problem...'
12 Nebre; Djedefre; Khafre; Menkaure; Sahure; Neferirkare; Niuserre; Djedkare; Merire; Merenre; Neferkare.
13 Hornung, 1982, p. 139.
14 Hornung, 1982, pp. 139-40; Morenz, 1973, p. 41.
15 Hornung, 1982, p. 234.
16 Morenz, 1973, p. 114.
17 Frankfort, *KAG*, 1948, p. 181; Wainwright, 1938, pp. 16-17, 86.
18 Frankfort et al, 1946, p. 65: 'the king *was* each of them... the king *was* each of these gods or goddesses.'
19 Wainwright, 1938, pp. 16-17, 86.
20 Frankfort, *KAG*, 1948, p. 173. Cf Morenz, 1973, p. 97.
21 Frankfort, *KAG*, 1948, pp. 172, 181. Pritchard, 1969, p. 4 (Shabaka Stone, 6).
22 Thutmose (var. Thothmes) meant 'begotten of Thoth'. Cf Ramesses 'begotten of Re'.
23 Morenz, 1973, pp. 34-35, 61.
24 Frankfort, *AER*, 1948, p. 43; James, 1960, p. 108.
25 Meeks, 1997, p. 189.
26 Frankfort, *AER*, 1948, pp. 50-56; Hornung, 1982, pp. 138-39, 142, 209; Morenz, 1973, p. 168; El Mahdy, 2003, pp. 64-65.
27 It was natural and almost inevitable that the Horus sky-god became the Horus sun-god. See James, 1960, pp. 70-71, 201, 301.
28 Quirke, 2001, pp. 17-18.
29 CT, IV, 179, 181. Cf Pyr. §§ 990, 1508. Cf Frankfort et al, 1946, pp. 74-75.
30 By classical religion, I exclude the Amarna religion in which 'son of the sun' might have assumed some philosophical meaning.
31 CT, II, 158: 'I am Re, father of Re'. CT, VII, 19.
32 Pyr. §§ 886-87, 952, 1316-18, 1492-95, 1508.
33 Pyr. § 160. Cf § 213.
34 Pyr. § 285.
35 Pyr. §§ 1091-92, 2047, 2206.
36 Re appears in a triad with Atum and Kheprer (Pyr. § 1695). Atum and Kheprer are associated with the creation from the earth and the abyss (§§ 888, 1248, 1587, 1652, 2206) whereas Re is associated more with the visible sky. The king is thus urged to stand on the earth which issued from Atum and Kheprer and to be seen by Re (§ 199). The name Re-Atum (§§ 152-58, 1686, 1694) seems to designate the sun, i.e. the emerged form of Atum (cf CT, IV, 184 ff).
37 Allen, 1988, p. 6; Allen, 1989, p. 25; Lehner, 1997, p. 27.
38 Budge, 1925, pp. 309, 313-14.
39 The accession took place at the earliest opportunity. The coronation was delayed until a favourable

396 NOTES TO PAGES 150 – 165

    date in the calendar.
40 Sellers, 1992, p. 302. Cf J.H. Breasted, *Ancient Records of Egypt*, II, pp. 142-43.
41 Frankfort, *KAG*, 1948, pp. 102-3. See also pp. 104, 110.
42 Ramesseum Dramatic Papyrus (accession mystery play of Senusert I). See Frankfort, *KAG*, 1948, chapter 11.
43 On the significance of these rituals, see chapter thirteen.
44 Frankfort, *KAG*, 1948, pp. 57, 148, 150-51; Frankfort, *AER*, 1948, pp. 53, 56; Quirke, 1990, p. 11.
45 Lurker, 1980, pp. 11, 30.
46 Hornung, 1982, p. 141; Quirke, 2001, p. 19.
47 Frankfort, *AER*, 1948, p. 55.
48 Restoration Stele. See Morenz, 1973, pp. 114, 168; James, 1960, pp. 206, 261; Pritchard, 1969, p. 251.
49 Frankfort, *KAG*, 1948, pp. 21-22, 129, 360 note 15, 377 note 9; Schulz & Seidel, 1998, p. 420. It is significant too that the deceased king is reborn as Horus and Seth in §§ 143-44, 518, 798.
50 Frankfort, *KAG*, 1948, p. 51; Hornung, 1982, p. 139; Allen, 1988, p. 38; Assmann, 2001, p. 4.
51 Frankfort et al, 1946, p. 76. Cf Quirke, 2001, p. 20.
52 On these daily rituals, see Shafer, 1991, pp. 22-23.
53 Shafer, 1991, p. 13.
54 One of the king's main duties was to make offerings to the gods; he is often described as 'Lord of Making Offerings'. See Assmann, 1989, p. 58; Quirke, 2001, p. 20; Assmann, 2001, pp. 3-5.
55 Pyr. §§ 962-70. On offerings by the son at the tomb of the father, see §§ 655-57, 760-61, 1748.
56 The pyramids of Unas, Teti, Pepi I, Merenre and Pepi II, plus the pyramids of three queens of Pepi II (Wedjebten, Neit, and Iput). The PT are also found in the 8th dynasty pyramid of Ibi at Saqqara.
57 Lehner, 1997, p. 31. Cf Breasted, 1912, p. 93. The number of utterances comes from Faulkner's edition of the PT.
58 Siliotti, 1997, p. 13.
59 Quirke, 2001, p. 129.
60 Edwards, 1947, pp. 14-16, 176-78; James, 1960, p. 173; Allen, 1989, pp. 1-3, 25; Hornung, 1999, pp. 5-6; Verner, 2002, p. 41.
61 Edwards, 1947, p. 176.
62 Breasted, 1912, pp. 90-91. Cf Frankfort, *AER*, 1948, p. v.
63 Breasted, 1912, p. 136. Cf p. 278.
64 Budge, 1934, pp. 322, 338, 340.
65 See chapter four, notes 139 and 140.
66 Breasted, 1912, pp. 101-2; Budge, 1934, pp. 337-38, 340, 345.
67 See Sellers, 1992, pp. 8-9, 70, quoting the concerns of Alexandre Piankoff.
68 Frankfort, *AER*, 1948, p. v. Breasted's book was dedicated to Adolf Erman.
69 Ibid., pp. v-vi.
70 Ibid., pp. 91, 99, 107, 120-21.
71 Meeks, 1997, pp. 3-4. Kate Spence has suggested the need to view the solar and stellar aspects of the PT as a unified scheme.
72 Edwards, 1993 edition, pp. 15-16; Lehner, 1997, p. 32; David, 2002, pp. 93-96; Eyre, 2002, pp. 5-6; Verner, 2002, p. 41.
73 J.B. Sellers, *The Death of Gods in Ancient Egypt*, Penguin Books, London, 1992.
74 R. Bauval & A. Gilbert, *The Orion Mystery*, William Heinemann, London, 1994.
75 Pyr. §§ 659, 728-29, 809-10, 2002-3, 2203-4.
76 Pyr. § 132. Cf §§ 1057, 1701.
77 Pyr. § 1040. Cf § 1466.
78 Pyr. § 809.
79 Pyr. § 1466. Cf §§ 2288-89: 'The king was conceived in the nose, the king was born in the nostril.'
80 Edwards, 1947, pp. 14-15; Clark, 1959, pp. 122-23; James, 1960, p. 170; Lehner, 1997, p. 23.
81 Pyr. §§ 167, 193, 1090, 1297, 1368, 1419, 2051, 2092-94. Cf § 992 (re-enactment of Atum's ascent).
82 Pyr. §§ 135, 147, 992, 1298-99.
83 Pyr. § 603.
84 Pyr. §§ 895, 1645-46.
85 Pyr. §§ 272-74, 1582-83, 1686-95. Cf CT, VI, 342.
86 Pyr. §§ 5, 198, 304, 316, 346, 353, 362, 493, 503, 518, 659, 741, 795-804, 874, 881, 928-29, 1086, 1114, 1301, 1719, 1730-35, 1948, 2032, 2047.
87 Pyr. §§ 1948, 1993.
88 Pyr. §§ 1233-40, 1725, 1900, 1914.

89   Pyr. §§ 1010, 1979, 2032. Cf §§ 769, 2262.
90   Pyr. §§ 727, 1277, 1725, 1899, 1907, 1914, 1927.
91   Pyr. § 1378.
92   Pyr. § 266.
93   Pyr. §§ 445, 620, 1429, 1824, 1826-27, 2240.
94   Pyr. § 516.
95   Pyr. §§ 1019, 1094, 1152.
96   Pyr. §§ 486, 1146, 1477.
97   Pyr. § 1146.
98   Pyr. §§ 976-77, 1147, 1460.
99   Pyr. §§ 698, 705, 1231, 1918-19, 2225.
100 Pyr. §§ 251, 877, 1048, 1384, 1899, 1920, 2226-27.
101 Pyr. § 1724.
102 Pyr. §§ 769, 1303-15.
103 Pyr. §§ 140, 167, 211, 605, 992, 1466.
104 Pyr. §§ 199-200, 390, 727, 886-87, 1492-95.
105 Pyr. §§ 152, 154, 156, 158, 160.
106 Pyr. §§ 324, 593.
107 Pyr. §§ 507, 510.
108 The king is 'the bodily son' or 'son of the body', see Pyr. §§ 1 (Geb), 160 (R-Atum), 213 (Atum).
109 Pyr. § 1483.
110 Pyr. §§ 1510-11.
111 Pyr. § 1041. 'Born in Heliopolis' means 'born in the primeval cosmos'.
112 On the *ka*, see Budge, 1934, pp. 328-30; Edwards, 1947, pp. 17-18; Frankfort, *KAG*, 1948, chapter five; Clark, 1959, pp. 231-34; Lurker, 1980, pp. 73-74; Shaw & Nicholson, 1995, p. 146.
113 Pyr. §§ 1652-53. The body of Atum may be implied; if we suppose that the *ka* emerged from Atum's body, then we may also visualise it here as his 'double'. On the *ka* as the vital force of creation, see Shafer, 1997, p. 132; David, 2002, p. 117. According to CT, I, 377; III, 383-84, Atum's *ka* comprised 'millions of ka' – the gods – who were united by Shu.
114 Pyr. §§ 17, 826, 832, 948, 975, 1165-66, 1327.
115 Pyr. §§ 815, 1275-76, 1431, 2051, 2061, 2252.
116 Pyr. §§ 826-29, 832-36, 1328, 2051.
117 Pyr. § 149.
118 Pyr. § 563.
119 Pyr. § 894.
120 Pyr. §§ 338, 907-8.
121 Pyr. §§ 789-90, 1357.
122 Pyr. § 456.
123 Pyr. §§ 929-30.
124 Pyr. §§ 839, 841, 2203.
125 Pyr. § 372.
126 Pyr. § 2028.
127 Pyr. §§ 815, 1275-76, 1431, 2051, 2061, 2252.
128 Possible examples of the *ka* as the mummified body are Pyr. §§ 149, 338, 354, 361, 372, 563, 703-4, 894, 908, 929-30, 1277-78, 1327, 1357, 1673, 1822, 1832.
129 Pyr. §§ 1255-57. Cf §§ 1280-83.
130 Pyr. §§ 1683-85.
131 Pyr. §§ 1406-7. Cf § 1609: 'O king (Osiris), you are the *ka* of all the gods'. Cf § 464: 'The gods set down reed-floats for Osiris when he ascended to the sky'. Cf CT, II, 211, where Osiris is called 'the father of the gods'.
132 Pyr. §§ 1002-3, 1047, 1747-48, 1878-79, 1938-39, 2182-83.
133 Pyr. §§ 734, 774. Cf § 868: 'O king, your cool water is the great flood which issued from you.'
134 Pyr. §§ 788, 2007-8, 2031-32.
135 Pyr. § 1883. Cf §§ 707, 734, 1873.
136 Pyr. §§ 24-25. Cf §§ 22-23. Elsewhere, the king is given 'water which issued from Elephantine' (§§ 864, 1908) or 'this first cold water of yours which came from Chemmis (§§ 1877-78).
137 Pyr. §§ 1180-81.
138 Pyr. §§ 745-46. Cf § 773.
139 Pyr. §§ 19-117, 1588-92. See Breasted, 1912, pp. 78-79.
140 Pyr. §§ 858-59. Cf §§ 654-55, 1226, 2006.

141 Pyr. §§ 42, 81, 84, 1544-50.
142 Pyr. § 37.
143 Pyr. § 55. Cf §§ 33, 283, 1681-82.
144 Pyr. §§ 114, 192, 614, 1800, 1858.
145 Pyr. § 308.
146 Pyr. §§ 113, 320-21, 1801-2, 2075.
147 Pyr. §§ 139, 578-79, 2075. Cf § 192.
148 Pyr. §§ 55, 99, 1807-8.
149 Pyr. §§ 9, 102, 583 (Geb), 583-84 (Horus).
150 Pyr. §§ 69-71. Cf §§ 22-23, 1315.
151 Pyr. § 11.
152 Pyr. § 13. According to § 2220, the adze was used on both the mouth and the eyes.
153 Pyr. §§ 610, 643, 1806, 1807-9, 2280-81.
154 Pyr. § 22.
155 Pyr. §§ 36, 39, 63, 93.
156 Pyr. § 1801.
157 Pyr. § 1340. Cf §§ 640-44.
158 Pyr. § 1340.
159 Pyr. §§ 837-38, 843.
160 Pyr. §§ 2106-7.
161 Pyr. § 199. Here the king is imagined as standing upon the primeval mound, just as the creator had done at the beginning of time; the passage is followed by spells which call for the ascension of the king's soul into the sky. Cf §§ 990-91.
162 Pyr. §§ 280, 283. Cf CT, VI, 232.
163 Pyr. §§ 1022-23. Similarly, the turning of Osiris-the-king onto his right side signifies the emergence of the primeval mound, see §§ 1194, 1528-29. Cf § 2013: 'You are indeed god-like; you have shouldered the sky, you have raised up the earth.' Cf also CT, IV, 362, where the deceased joins land to land at the Thinite District (a microcosm of the primeval mound).
164 Pyr. §§ 585, 621, 636, 1887. Cf §§ 645-46.
165 Pyr. §§ 1149-51 (trans. Faulkner/Alford).
166 Pyr. § 540. Cf § 539.
167 Pyr. §§ 1757-58. Cf § 208 'Go up... by means of the bones of Shu', and § 1353 'You are raised aloft on the hands of Shu and Tefnut.'
168 Pyr. §§ 891-92. Cf §§ 1771-73, 2178-79.
169 Pyr. § 1770.
170 Pyr. §§ 2042-43. Cf §§ 1777-84, 1948, 1970-71, 2247.
171 Pyr. §§ 308-9.
172 Pyr. § 336. Cf §§ 1149-51, 1961. See further discussion of the storm in chapter nine.
173 Pyr. §§ 1774, 1777, 2054.
174 Pyr. §§ 1107-8. Cf §§ 751, 1680. There is no mention in this spell (or other similar spells) of the east side of the sky, and it should be recalled that the light of Re emerged primarily from the primeval cosmos, i.e. from the earth and the *nun*.
175 Pyr. §§ 365-66. A stairway also features in §§ 1090, 1717, 1749, 1941.
176 Pyr. §§ 472, 2078-80. There were different types of rigid ladder, §§ 995-96. The ladder was said to have been made by Re (§ 390), by Khnum (§§ 1585-86), by Horus and Re (§ 472), by the children of Horus (§ 2079), or by the gods (§§ 1253, 1474).
177 Pyr. §§ 1431-33, 1763-67, 2078-82.
178 Pyr. § 542. The intention seems to be that the gods of the earth will grasp the king's hand and be lifted to the sky.
179 Pyr. §§ 1473-75. I have inserted the bracketed terms to bring out the meaning as I see it. Cf §§ 478-79, 941-43, 1253. The gods are *in* the earth, not *on* the earth, see Hornung, 1982, p. 228.
180 Pyr. §§ 478-79.
181 Pyr. § 941.
182 Pyr. § 388 (trans. Faulkner/Alford). The context suggests 'irrigated' rather than 'inundated'.
183 Pyr. §§ 2063-64. Again, I have inserted the bracketed terms to bring out the meaning as I see it.
184 Pyr. § 2067. Cf § 1023 where Shu presses down the earth with his feet.
185 CT, II, 120; IV, 368.
186 Pyr. § 688 (trans. Faulkner/Alford). Cf §§ 667, 694. The translation of *sk* as 'drowned' is my suggestion, based partly on § 1162.
187 Pyr. § 130. Cf § 1082: 'The sky is pregnant of wine'.

NOTES

188 Pyr. § 128.
189 Pyr. §§ 1687-89. Cf §§ 710-12, 922-23, 1246, 1250-51, 2172-73.
190 Pyr. §§ 703-5. Cf § 698. The ninth spell in which the king is identified with Re is § 2126. A possible tenth is § 1582.
191 Pyr. § 1231.
192 Pyr. §§ 2051-52.
193 Pyr. §§ 2244-45. Cf CT, VI, 108-9.
194 Pyr. § 1516.
195 Pyr. § 1144.
196 Pyr. § 347. 'This star' is possibly the morning star, Netjer-dwau.
197 Pyr. § 537.
198 Pyr. § 1455.
199 Pyr. §§ 1583-84.
200 Pyr. § 940.
201 Pyr. § 1925.
202 Pyr. § 732. Cf § 1372.
203 Pyr. § 2005.
204 In addition to those cited above, see Pyr. §§ 263, 749, 802, 1253, 1469-70, 1720, 1845-46, 1925, 2090-91.
205 Pyr. § 906.
206 Pyr. §§ 1171-72. Cf § 889: 'I row Re when traversing the sky (as) a star of gold... a spear of gold belonging to him who traverses the sky.' A star is implied in the many instances where the king takes his seat as a rower in the barque, see §§ 367-68, 461, 1143, 1250-51, 1439-42, 1573-75, 1764-65, 2045-46, 2122-25.
207 Pyr. § 1080.
208 Pyr. § 818.
209 Pyr. § 1220.
210 Pyr. §§ 380, 998, 1761.
211 Pyr. §§ 408, 820, 882-83, 925, 959. Sah was also identified with Horus, see chapter two, note 275.
212 Pyr. §§ 632-33, 1635-37.
213 Pyr. §§ 357, 935-36, 1707. Cf § 1123, 1207-8. The dawn-light can also be regarded as feminine, see § 341 (daughter of Sopdet), 1082-83 (daughter of Nut), and can itself give birth, see § 820-21.
214 Hence Osiris in his name 'Dweller in Sah' is said to have 'a season in the sky and a season in the earth', Pyr. § 186.
215 Hence in Pyr. § 1886 Isis states: 'O Osiris the King, I am Isis. I have come into the middle of this earth – into the place where you are. I have come and have laid hold of you.'
216 The heliacal rising of Sah took place against a blood red sky that was symbolic of rebirth from the womb, and was apparently celebrated by the consumption of red wine, Sah being 'the Lord of Wine in the *Wag*-festival'. See Pyr. §§ 820-21, 1082-83.
217 Hence in Pyr. § 1207 the morning star is called 'Horus of the Duat... whom the sky bore', the son Horus being born from the union of his parents in the *duat*.
218 Pyr. §§ 341, 357, 363, 935, 1123-24, 1707.
219 Pyr. § 723.
220 Pyr. § 2116.
221 Pyr. §§ 805, 1719 (Sah is mentioned in § 803).
222 Pyr. §§ 871, 1366, 1719-20, 2014. Cf § 1295 (Venus as the evening star?).
223 Pyr. §§ 1719-20.
224 Pyr. § 1366. Cf § 2014.
225 Pyr. §§ 150-51. Cf §§ 186, 882-83.
226 Pyr. §§ 820-22.
227 Pyr. § 2180.
228 Pyr. §§ 882-83. The great star is masculine, so cannot be Sirius/Sopdet. There is an allusion here to the seventy days of invisibility in the *duat*.
229 Pyr. § 723.
230 Pyr. § 458.
231 Pyr. §§ 479-80. Cf §§ 162, 305, 622-23, 961, 1010.
232 Pyr. § 943. Cf §§ 135, 961, 1475.
233 Pyr. §§ 4-5. Cf §§ 202, 307, 919.
234 Pyr. §§ 941-42. Cf § 620.
235 Pyr. §§ 1574, 2126, 2179-80.

236 Pyr. §§ 149, 207, 306, 821-22, 867, 910, 1044-45, 1055-56, 1249, 1275, 1679.
237 Pyr. §§ 150, 209-10, 932-33, 1171-72, 1479.
238 Pyr. §§ 332, 882-83, 1466-69, 1456-58.
239 Pyr. § 1677. Cf § 658.
240 Pyr. §§ 340-41, 343-44, 352-53, 359-60, 594-601, 1102-6, 1139, 1382, 1541, 1704, 1736-37.
241 On the reed-floats, see Pyr. §§ 337, 342, 351, 358, 926-27, 932-33, 999-1000, 1084-86, 1103-4, 1206, 1705-6. On the wing of Thoth, see §§ 387, 594-96, 1176, 1376-77, 1429.
242 Pyr. § 888. Cf §§ 608, 919.
243 Pyr. §§ 1835-36. Cf §§ 450, 698, 1469-70.
244 Pyr. § 406. Cf § 854.
245 Pyr. § 1455. Cf §§ 362-63, 733.
246 Pyr. §§ 352-53. Cf § 343-44, 1704.
247 Pyr. §§ 1205-6. Cf § 1183.
248 For the horizon ascent by reed-float, see Pyr. §§ 208-9, 455, 1179-80 (it is perhaps also implied by the crossing to the horizon on the reed-floats of the sky, §§ 337, 342, 351, 358, 926-27, 999-1000, 1084-86, 1103-4, 1206, 1705-6). For the horizon ascent by barque, see §§ 368, 374, 496, 710-12, 920-23, 1245-46, 1687-88, 1708-9, 2045-46.
249 Pyr. §§ 275, 289, 519, 918, 1247, 1421, 1430.
250 Pyr. §§ 920-23, 1245. Cf § 26.
251 Pyr. §§ 519, 1247.
252 Pyr. § 275. Cf §§ 519, 1247, 1430.
253 Pyr. §§ 1123-24. Cf §§ 1206, 1216, 1253.
254 Pyr. § 1187.
255 Pyr. §§ 1188-89.
256 Reymond, 1969, p. 124 observed the connection between the creation myth and the field of reeds.
257 Pyr. §§ 289 (pool, or lake), 1165 (lotus). The field of reeds would therefore be synonymous with the isle of flames.
258 On the role of Re in the field of the sky, see Pyr. §§ 120-22, 310, 706-9.
259 Pyr. §§ 873-74.
260 Pyr. § 128. Cf §§ 553, 803, 1217-20, 1722.
261 Pyr. §§ 1217-20.
262 Pyr. §§ 120-22, 717. Or three meals, one in the sky and two in the earth, § 1072.
263 Pyr. §§ 564, 789-90, 1357.
264 Pyr. §§ 1059-60, 1063, 1064, 1065-66, 1215, 1784-85. This transitory paradise is only vaguely described in the PT, but it was later embellished to become a permanent dwelling place for the blessed dead.
265 Pyr. §§ 412, 414 (trans. Faulkner/Eyre). See Eyre, 2002, pp. 10, 134-35; Allen, 1989, p. 2.
266 Pyr. §§ 1653-54. Cf §§ 1649, 1660-61.

CHAPTER EIGHT: OPENING THE MOUTH

1 Pyr. §§ 63, 106, 618.
2 Pyr. §§ 11-12, 13, 179, 589, 644, 1330, 2220 (Horus), 1983-84 (four sons).
3 Pyr. § 1331. Cf §§ 11, 644.
4 On alternative means of opening the mouth, see Pyr. §§ 26, 1329; CT, III, 299; VII, 137.
5 These two constellations have a similar shape, each resembling an adze or a bull's foreleg.
6 Pyr. §§ 13-14.
7 Pyr. §§ 1747-48.
8 Pyr. § 2220.
9 Pyr. § 39. Cf §§ 63, 93, 106.
10 Pyr. § 42. It is not clear whether both stellar forelegs belonged to Seth, but CT, IV, 29 refers to 'the two adzes of Seth'. The thigh was the fleshy part of the foreleg, comprising four of the seven stars.
11 On *mskhtiu*, see discussion in chapter two. The term was originally determined by the sign of an adze (Pyr. § 458), but later by the sign of the bull's foreleg, see Gardiner, 1994, p. 570.
12 Gardiner, 1994, p. 570.
13 Pyr. § 12.
14 Pyr. § 42.
15 Pyr. § 14. Cf CT, IV, 29; VI, 108.
16 Pyr. §§ 13-14, 1330; CT, III, 180-82.
17 Pyr. §§ 13-14 (by the adze of Wepwawet, as well as the adze of iron of Seth); CT, III, 278, 299.

18 Wainwright, 1932; Roth, 1993, pp. 69-72; Bauval & Gilbert, 1994, pp. 200-6 (the meteorite is here deemed to be 'the material representation of the sky gods... the star gods'); Bauval, 1999, pp. 78-79.
19 Pyr. §§ 11, 644, 1299.
20 See chapter six, note 137.
21 Pyr. §§ 277, 1343, 2169-70; CT, I, 11; VI, 95.
22 Pyr. §§ 1394-95.
23 Pyr. § 1343.
24 Pyr. §§ 2169-70.
25 CT, I, 11. Cf CT, I, 280; IV, 143; VI, 95.
26 CT, II, 261-64. Cf CT, II, 175-76.
27 Pyr. §§ 281-82.
28 Pyr. §§ 2063-64. Cf CT, IV, 16; VI, 63-64.
29 Pyr. § 2234.
30 Pyr. §§ 817, 978, 1138, 1395, 2234.
31 CT, VI, 91, 263; VII, 433, 435, 447, 484 (cf II, 113); VII, 15.
32 See Faulkner, 1969, p. 65 note 17.
33 CT, VII, 15. Cf Pyr. §§ 13-14, 63; CT, VI, 257.
34 CT, VII, 15; Pyr. §§ 1967-69; CT, VII, 198. See quotations in chapter ten.
35 Pyr. §§ 1652-53.
36 Bremner-Rhind Pap., part a, 22-25 (trans. Budge/Faulkner/Allen/Alford). See Budge, 1904, I, pp. 310-11; Budge, 1912, pp. 4-5; Pritchard, 1969, p. 6; Allen, 1988, p. 28. Cf CT, III, 334-35; VI, 191.
37 CT, III, 383-84. See Allen, 1988, p. 37. Cf Bremner-Rhind Pap., part a, 6: 'Many were the beings which came forth from my mouth'. Cf also CT, VI, 270.
38 Budge, 1904, I, p. 386; Budge, 1912, pp. 54-55. The splitting open of Re's mouth may account for the injury to his mouth in the dispute with the serpent over the division of Heliopolis, see CT, II, 276.
39 Pyr. § 1100.
40 Budge, 1899, p. 106; Reymond, 1969, p. 82; Pritchard, 1969, p. 366; Assmann, 2001, p. 95;
41 CT, II, 7-8. Cf CT, II, 23-25.
42 CT, II, 43.
43 CT, III, 384. See Allen, 1988, pp. 37-38.
44 CT, IV, 145. This is one of several spells where the Nile-god claims to be the creator.
45 CT, IV, 190; BD, 17. See Frankfort et al, 1946, p. 53; Allen, 1988, pp. 31, 36-37.
46 Hymn to Amun-Re. See Pritchard, 1969, p. 366; Assmann, 2001, pp. 195-96.
47 Assmann, 1989, p. 63; Assmann, 2001, p. 197.
48 Pyr. § 1688.
49 Books of the Netherworld; Book of Nut; Book of the Night. See Hornung, 1999.
50 Book of Nut (cenotaph texts of Seti I). See Allen, 1988, pp. 2-3, 6.
51 Pyr. § 1. He was at the same time the son of the body of Geb, § 1.
52 Pyr. § 205. Cf Plutarch, *De Iside et Osiride*, § 12 (see Budge, 1912, p. 217).
53 CT, VI, 3. Hence perhaps the late myth of her head being split open, see Meeks, 1997, p. 27.
54 Budge, 1905, II, p. 80.
55 Hornung, 1999, p. 90; Lehner, 1997, pp. 28-29; Meeks, 1997, p. 162.
56 CT, VI, 63-64. In this spell, the creation of the starry sky is described poetically as the weaving of the dress of Hathor.
57 Pyr. §§ 2063-64.
58 Budge, 1905, II, pp. 86-91, 304-5.
59 Pyr. §§ 1343, 2169-70.
60 Pyr. § 796. Cf §§ 1014-15, 1713.
61 CT, II, 176.
62 Pyr. §§ 1616-26. See discussion of Geb in chapter four. Generally in the PT, Geb is the epitome of the creator-god with magical speech.
63 Pyr. § 255. CT, III, 361 refers to Horus ascending from 'the lips of the *akhet*' as if it were opening like a mouth.
64 Pyr. §§ 2095-96. Cf § 496.
65 Pyr. §§ 756-57.
66 Pyr. § 873. For other ascents through both sets of doors, see §§ 525-29, 876-77, 981-85, 1025-26, 1132-37, 1408-11, 1480.
67 Pyr. §§ 2170-71. Cf §§ 1343-44 ('the eastern door of the sky'), 1720 ('the door of the sky at the *akhet*').
68 CT, IV, 368; II, 120.

69 Pyr. §§ 392, 1583.
70 Pyr. § 496.
71 Pyr. § 518.
72 Pyr. § 1713. Cf §§ 796-99.
73 Pyr. § 2009. Cf § 572.
74 Pyr. §§ 2007, 2012-14.
75 Pyr. §§ 1361-62. Cf §§ 616, 1291.
76 Pyr. §§ 502-3 (trans. Faulkner/Alford). Cf CT, II, 10: 'O Lord of Flame guarding the doors of the *nun*' (Variant: 'doors of the sky'). Cf CT, IV, 33: 'A flame has gone up from the *akhet*'. On *iknt*, cf CT, VI, 296-97.
77 Pyr. § 2234.
78 Pyr. §§ 1149-51.
79 Pyr. §§ 1972-74 (trans. Faulkner/Alford). Cf § 1004.
80 Pyr. §§ 1472-75.
81 Pyr. §§ 727, 2001. Cf §§ 658-59.
82 Pyr. §§ 604, 2232, 2252.
83 Pyr. §§ 1291-92. *Qebhu* here is determined by a sky sign.
84 Pyr. § 1927.
85 Pyr. § 2238.
86 Pyr. § 1361.
87 Pyr. §§ 2246-47.

CHAPTER NINE: THE DAY OF THE STORM

1 Pyr. §§ 308-9.
2 Pyr. §§ 324-26 (trans. Faulkner/Alford). Cf CT, IV, 40.
3 Pyr. § 336.
4 Pyr. §§ 1771-72, 1774, 1777. An ascent as a locust features also in § 892.
5 Pyr. §§ 1149-51.
6 Pyr. § 956. Cf § 2238.
7 CT, II, 209-10.
8 Pyr. § 143.
9 Pyr. §§ 581-82. Cf § 1150 (Seth roars when the king ascends). The theme of Seth in the earth beneath Osiris is discussed further in chapter thirteen.
10 CT, IV, 158-60. A variant reads: 'There is tumult in the northern sky' (i.e. the lower sky?).
11 CT, VII, 205 (trans. Faulkner/Alford).
12 CT, VII, 252. Cf BD, 133.
13 CT, II, 30-31 (trans. Faulkner/Alford). See also Allen, 1988, p. 22; Assmann, 2001, p. 178.
14 *Legend of Shu and Geb*. See Budge, 1934, p. 441.
15 Budge, 1934, p. 441; Wainwright, 1938, p. 80.
16 Pyr. §§ 261, 1407.
17 Pyr. §§ 298-99.
18 See chapter thirteen, notes 1 and 2.
19 Pyr. § 1463.
20 CT, II, 38; V, 244-47; VII, 377, 403, 517; BD, 39.
21 Pyr. § 399.
22 Pyr. §§ 1211-12.
23 CT, II, 163.
24 CT, III, 264.
25 CT, IV, 234.
26 CT, IV, 283-84. Cf CT, IV, 335.
27 CT, IV, 300.
28 CT, VI, 316.
29 CT, VI, 328.
30 CT, VII, 197. Cf Pyr. § 1961.
31 CT, VI, 348.
32 Pyr. §§ 279-81. Cf CT, VI, 231-32, 236-37. Might this allude to one of the Apis bull's testicles?
33 Pyr. §§ 229, 318; CT, II, 276; BD, 17; *Horus of Behdet and the Winged Disc* (Budge, 1912, p. 73); *Legend of Shu and Geb* (see earlier quote).
34 Pyr. § 1961. Cf CT, VI, 308.

NOTES 403

35 Pyr. §§ 324-26. See Faulkner, 1973, p. 216 note 9.
36 CT, IV, 40 (P. Gard. III). See Faulkner, 1973, p. 216 note 9. Hence the name Wepwawet (*Wp-wawt*) 'the Opener of the Ways'.
37 CT, VI, 253-54. See Faulkner, 1977, p. 215 note 12.
38 CT, VII, 441.
39 Pyr. §§ 281-82.
40 CT, VI, 237.
41 Pyr. §§ 1149-51; CT, VII, 332, 517.
42 On *khsr*, see Gardiner, 1994, pp. 586, 611. It is similar in meaning to *djsr*, see Faulkner, 1977, p. 103 note 7; Gardiner, 1994, p. 604; Allen, 1989, p. 10. *Djsr* meant 'to separate' in the sense of 'lifting up', see Faulkner, 1978, p. 140 note 1. Hence CT, I, 223: 'The sky is separated (*djsr*), the *akhet*-dwellers rejoice when Re rises from the double gates.' The two terms are paralleled in CT, V, 388-89: 'He has separated (*djsr*) the sky, he has joined the land together, he has separated (*khsr*) Nut.' A separation from the earth is implied.
43 Pyr. §§ 549, 924, 956, 1110, 1120, 1149-50, 1366, 1771-72, 1933, 1935-36, 2063, 2109-10, 2234, 2238.
44 Pyr. §§ 281 (split open), 817, 978, 1138, 1395, 2234 (hacked up).
45 The opening of the doors of the sky coincides with the earthquake in §§ 1149-51, 2234, 2238.
46 Pyr. §§ 1149-50. Cf the speaking of the earth in §§ 796, 1014, 1713, 2169.
47 Pyr. §§ 1004-5, 1366, 1711, 1973, 2013-14.
48 Pyr. §§ 1004-5, 1366, 2014. Cf §§ 1120-21 'the two domains of the god roar'.
49 Pyr. § 541. Cf §§ 324, 502-3, 2063.
50 Pyr. §§ 1149-51. See earlier quotation.
51 Pyr. §§ 477, 941, 1472. Or terror at his feet, § 993.
52 Pyr. § 724. Cf §§ 324, 900.
53 Pyr. §§ 257, 281, 1110-11.
54 Pyr. §§ 393, 1149-51.
55 Pyr. § 2063.
56 Pyr. § 393.
57 Pyr. §§ 393, 1151-52. Cf CT, VII, 418: 'Do not let cloudiness come into being among the *hnmmt* [stars] on the day of separating (*djsr*) the god.'
58 Pyr. § 281. Cf CT, VI, 237, 348.
59 Pyr. §§ 318-19. Cf § 1769; CT, IV, 159-60: 'N has come that he may stop the tumult'.
60 Pyr. §§ 289-90. The king also judges the gods or the rivals (Horus and Seth) in §§ 399, 712-13, 732, 770, 797, 1127, 1749-50, 1761, 1963, 2005, 2267. This may imply an identity with Geb or Thoth.
61 Pyr. §§ 1775-76. Cf § 1936.
62 CT, I, 19-21.
63 CT, I, 320, 376-80. On the fiery Eye, see chapter twelve.
64 Pyr. § 1207.
65 Pyr. § 1449 (trans. Faulkner/Alford).
66 CT, VII, 441.
67 Pyr. § 500. This in connection with Re's appearance as 'the Great Flood which came forth from the Great One'.
68 CT, VII, 408.
69 Pyr. § 458.
70 Pyr. § 1948.
71 Pyr. §§ 555, 1807, 2249; CT, VII, 1, 205, 228, 373-74, 426. Cf § 1443: 'the face of the sky is washed'. Cf CT, IV, 238: 'I raised the hair from the *wedjat*-Eye'.
72 Pyr. § 373.
73 Pyr. §§ 57, 208, 468, 503, 541, 801-2, 822, 921, 1010, 1090, 1215, 1237, 1757-58, 1933, 1943, 2062, 2251; CT, II, 150; IV, 161-62, 341-42; VII, 252.
74 Two CT spells are introduced by the declared aim 'To open what was blocked' (CT, IV, 152-53).
75 BD, 110. Cf CT, V, 337: 'that day of choking and stifling the sky'.
76 CT, V, 337.
77 CT, IV, 125, 144.
78 CT, IV, 392-99; V, 10-11; VII, 72. Cf BD, 57.
79 The clouds and the great flood are connected in Pyr. §§ 499-500.

CHAPTER TEN: SPLITTING THE IRON

1. The general consensus is that *bja* was iron – specifically meteoritic iron – though some scholars have argued that it may have been a name for copper. For this minority view, see A. Nibbi, *JARCE* 14 (1977), p. 59; C. Lalouette, *BIFAO* 79, p. 67.
2. Budge, 1904, I, pp. 156-57, 167, 491; II, p. 241.
3. Allen, 1988, pp. 2, 76; Allen, 1989, p. 9.
4. Pyr. §§ 530-31.
5. Pyr. §§ 530-31, 1454, 2051-52, 2244 (golden limbs). The exception is § 749 where the iron bones are not mentioned but the iron limbs are mentioned in conjunction with the imperishable stars. See also CT, VI, 108-9: 'Raise yourself upon your iron bones and golden flesh, for this body of yours belongs to a god... May your flesh be born to life, may your life be the life of the stars...'
6. Cf Pyr. § 393: 'The bones of the earth-gods (*akeru*) tremble.'
7. Cf Pyr. § 1.
8. Pyr. § 749.
9. Cf Pyr. § 749 to §§ 1165-66. It may be no coincidence that both these spells refer to iron.
10. Pyr. § 1454. Cf the first line of this spell, § 1443.
11. Pyr. §§ 2051-52.
12. Pyr. § 2244. See quotation in chapter seven.
13. Pyr. §§ 736, 770, 800-1, 865, 873, 1016, 1124-25, 1166, 1293, 1301, 1364, 1562, 1721, 1735, 1927, 1934, 1992-93, 1996, 2012, 2091.
14. Pyr. §§ 736, 865 (meat), 1293-94, 1364-66, 2012 (water – from the castle or canal of the god).
15. Pyr. §§ 770, 865, 873, 1125-27, 1166-67, 1562, 1721, 1934, 1996.
16. Pyr. §§ 1166, 1562. Cf § 1915.
17. Pyr. § 1927.
18. Pyr. § 736.
19. Pyr. § 1293. Cf §§ 1364, 1735, 2012.
20. Pyr. §§ 1992-93.
21. Pyr. §§ 1124-25.
22. In addition to the three passages cited here, see Pyr. §§ 865-67, 1293-96, 1364, 1562-67, 1719-23, 1735, 1933-36.
23. Pyr. §§ 800-1. Cf § 1015.
24. Pyr. § 873.
25. Pyr. §§ 1166-67.
26. Pyr. §§ 1293-96.
27. Pyr. § 1016.
28. Pyr. §§ 1992-93.
29. Pyr. §§ 2012-13.
30. Pyr. §§ 895, 1067, 1068. Cf § 1563 where the king orders the gods to stand up and sit down.
31. Pyr. §§ 1992-93. The iron throne is probably identical with 'the great throne of Geb' in § 2015.
32. Pyr. §§ 1996-97.
33. The king is, of course, Osiris when he sits on the throne. The throne of Osiris is paralleled with the iron throne in Pyr. §§ 1298, 1301. Cf the iron throne of Horus in § 2091.
34. Pyr. §§ 770, 1721. The iron throne may therefore be identical with 'the great throne' in Heliopolis in § 895.
35. The location of the throne is vague, as if it were blindingly obvious to the authors and editors of the PT, but it is always a place that precedes the sky as the king moves through the cosmos, for example at the border of the field of offerings in Pyr. §§ 1123-24.
36. For the following quotations, see Pyr. §§ 1966-71.
37. This passage is restored with the help of CT, VII, 198.
38. For this and the following, see CT, VII, 198-99.
39. CT, III, 208-10.
40. BD, 23. Cf Pyr. §§ 13-14; BD, 108.
41. On the Edfu spear, see Reymond, 1969, pp. 23, 26, 94-95, 218; Reymond, *JEA* 48 (1962), pp. 81-88; *JEA* 49 (1963), pp. 140-46; *JEA* 50 (1964), pp. 133-38; *JEA* 51 (1965), pp. 144-48; Meeks, 1997, p. 194. Cf CT, II, 93: 'the sounding-pole (?) which went forth from the *nun*'.
42. Pyr. §§ 1945-48. Cf CT, IV, 54: 'a fair falcon of gold upon his pointed stone (*bnwt*)'. Cf CT, VII, 366: 'the *bnwt* of Rostau'. Cf CT, IV, 100: 'that plateau of the stone of brightness' (perhaps an allusion to the tip of an obelisk?). The association of the sharp iron with Min is interesting; he was a partner in the *ka-mut.ef* meteorite of Thebes.

43 Budge, 1934, pp. 19-20, 269; Watterson, 1984, p. 171; Betro, 1996, p. 82; Allen, 1988, pp. 41, 71 note 135. Both Horus and Geb had a stake in the *hnu*-barque, the former in Pyr. §§ 138, 620-21, the latter in CT, III, 258. Sokar was the god of Rostau, famous for its 'mysteries'.
44 Pyr. §§ 619-21. Cf § 1970 quoted earlier.
45 Pyr. § 138 (trans. Faulkner/Budge/Alford). See Budge, 1911, I, p. 105.
46 CT, I, 271.
47 Wainwright, 1932, pp. 168-69.
48 For 'fall' as a meaning of *hay*, see Gardiner, 1994, pp. 579, 612. For 'falling' in the sense of 'coming to rest', see Pyr. §§ 1541, 1760.
49 Pyr. §§ 906-7. Cf §§ 1573-75.
50 Faulkner, 1969, p. 158 notes that *Ba-ka* is 'an unknown region of the sky' (citing Sethe, *Komm.* iv, 182).
51 CT, VI, 38-39. Cf 'the great plain' in CT, V, 399, 'the great celestial plain' in CT, VI, 24, 'the very great plain to the south of the *akhet* of the sky' in CT, VI, 80, 'the great northern plain' in CT, VI, 196, and 'the plain of the pure place of the sky' in CT, VII, 89. The deceased is said to reach 'land in the northern sky', CT, VI, 196. The great plain of iron on which the gods stand is compared to a fisherman's boat in these spells. The gods cast down a net, whose floats and weights are made of iron, to catch fish which apparently are swimming in the sky. See note 64 below.
52 Pyr. §§ 909, 332.
53 Allen, 1989, p. 9.
54 Book of Nut (cenotaph texts of Seti I). See Allen, 1988, pp. 2, 76 note 10.
55 Pyr. § 305. Cf CT, IV, 158-62. Cf Pyr. § 251: 'May you split open your place in the sky among the stars of the sky'.
56 Pyr. §§ 1120-22. Cf CT, IV, 63; BD, 85.
57 Allen, 1989, p. 9.
58 Faulkner, 1969, pp. 67, 184 describes the *bja* as 'the visible canopy of the sky' and 'the firmament'.
59 BD, 109, 149. These passages refer to the field of reeds below the horizon.
60 Pyr. § 1735. This passage probably refers to the goddess Mafdet who dwelt in the Mansion of Life. Other spells refer to her fingers and claws, and she is said to strike and scratch, see §§ 440, 442, 677-78, 685-86.
61 Pyr. §§ 1926-27. *Nwt-k-nu* was an inimical god of the netherworld, see §§ 851, 1639, 1905, 2231, 2291. Cf the Mansion of Life of Mafdet (note 60 above), the Mansion of the Prince in Heliopolis (§ 957), the lower mansion of Nut (§ 2), 'the Lady of the Mansion' (Nephthys), and 'the Lord of the Mansion, the bull of the cavern' (§ 444).
62 Frankfort, *KAG*, 1948, p. 356 note 19.
63 CT, VII, 15.
64 CT, VI, 24, 27, 35, 38, 44. The floats and weights are said to be in the sky on the hands of Re.
65 CT, IV, 294. See Allen, 1988, p. 76.
66 It is possible that the iron bones formed the ladder to the sky. Cf the bones of Shu which are a means of ascent to the sky in Pyr. § 208, and the stellar ladder in § 1763.
67 There is perhaps a connection between the *hnu*-barque of Sokar and the *hnhnu*-barque of Khepri, Atum, and Re, which opened the mouth of the earth.
68 CT, V, 337; BD, 110; Meeks, 1997, p. 78.
69 Wainwright, 1932, pp. 160, 165.
70 *Horus of Behdet and the Winged Disc*. See Budge, 1912, pp. xli, 61, 63, 65, 67, 73, 79, 83, 85.
71 Pyr. §§ 13-14.
72 Pyr. §§ 1982-84. The expression 'children's children' must mean the spiritual offspring of the God's physical offspring, i.e. the spirits, the gods.
73 Pyr. §§ 229, 311. See Faulkner, 1969, p. 68 note 8.
74 Watterson, 1984, p. 64.
75 Frankfort, *KAG*, 1948, pp. 71, 85, 87, 92-93; Betro, 1996, p. 78.
76 Frankfort, *KAG*, 1948, pp. 71, 92.
77 Pyr. §§ 953, 1011, 1090, 1374, 1638. See also note 80 below.
78 Pyr. §§ 769, 1304, 2262.
79 Pyr. §§ 2031-32. Cf §§ 539-40.
80 Pyr. §§ 539, 540, 800, 1036.
81 Pyr. §§ 539, 540.
82 Ritner, 1989, p. 109; Gardiner, 1994, p. 594.
83 Frankfort, *KAG*, 1948, pp. 92, 364-65.
84 Frankfort, *KAG*, 1948, pp. 364-65 (citing Sethe, *Komm.*, III, 11-12).

85   Wilkinson, 1992, pp. 132, 168-69; Budge, 1911, I, pp. 212-14; Budge, 1912, p. 230; Budge, 1934, pp. 107, 273; Lurker, 1980, p. 94; Alford, 2003, pp. 184-85, 195-97.
86   Pyr. § 1330. On the gods creating the God, see explanation in chapter five.
87   Roth, 1993, pp. 63-69.
88   Pyr. § 1208. Cf CT, IV, 181.
89   Velde, 1967, pp. 49-53.
90   Compare the hieroglyphic signs D50 and D52 in Gardiner, 1994, p. 456. The phallus is like the finger turned horizontally and furnished with testicles.
91   Pyr. § 48. The white eye of Horus is probably the moon.
92   Pyr. § 48.
93   Pyr. § 504.
94   Pyr. § 1302.
95   Pyr. § 1203. Cf the injury to his thigh, connected with the phallus in CT, VII, 182.
96   Pyr. § 229: 'This here is the fingernail of Atum which is (pressed) down on the spine of Neheb-kau, and which stilled the turmoil in Hermopolis'. This is possibly a reference to an obelisk, the fingernail of Atum being the tip and the spine of Neheb-kau being the shaft. The erection of the shaft would symbolise the triumph of order over chaos. Its base would subjugate the rebels in the netherworld.
97   Pyr. § 1330.
98   Pyr. § 664.
99   A multitude of 'fingers' would also be permissible, signifying the gods who made up the ennead.
100 Wainwright, 1932, p. 3; M. Eliade, *A History of Religious Ideas*, University of Chicago Press, 1978, p. 52; B. Scheel, *Egyptian Metalworking and Tools*, Shire Egyptology, Aylesbury, 1989, p. 17; Roth, 1993, pp. 69, 72.
101 The three classes of meteorite are: stony, iron, and stony-iron. Irons best survive the passage through the atmosphere and are the easiest to spot on the ground.
102 Roth, 1993, p. 69. Meteoritic iron (actually an alloy of iron-nickel) can be distinguished from terrestrial iron by scientific analysis.
103 CT, VII, 352-53. The 'fire about it' may be a reference to a granite box (granite being an igneous rock, hence its use in obelisks). This would explain why the object was sealed and in darkness. I have argued elsewhere that the Egyptians stored meteorites in sealed boxes to shut out the corrosive effect of the air (Alford, 2003, chapter five).
104 Budge, 1925, pp. 326-27; Shaw & Nicholson, 1995, p. 211; Roth, 1992, 1993.
105 *Bnbn* meant 'to flow' especially in a sexual sense. On the basis of its conical shape, some scholars have identified the *benben* stone outright as a meteorite, see chapter eleven, note 111.
106 Wainwright, 1931, 1932, 1935.
107 Alford, 2003, pp. 170-71.
108 See chapter eight, note 18.

CHAPTER ELEVEN: THE BULL OF THE SKY

1   Pyr. §§ 121, 1359.
2   Pyr. § 486.
3   Pyr. §§ 481, 1477.
4   Pyr. §§ 625, 1146.
5   Pyr. §§ 486, 716. Cf CT, III, 124; VII, 225, 347.
6   Pyr. § 516.
7   Pyr. § 513.
8   Pyr. § 889.
9   Pyr. §§ 280, 283, 293, 397.
10   Pyr. §§ 252, 513, 625.
11   Pyr. §§ 1124-25.
12   Pyr. §§ 282-84.
13   Pyr. § 1359.
14   Pyr. §§ 279-80.
15   Pyr. §§ 281-82.
16   Pyr. § 486. Cf CT, III, 124.
17   Pyr. § 889.
18   Pyr. § 283. Cf CT, I, 151; III, 325 . Note the deliberate phallic imagery here.
19   Pyr. § 280. Cf CT, VI, 232. On Kenzet, see §§ 121, 126, 920, 1141, 1207, 1245, 1541. According to Frankfort, *KAG*, 1948, p. 170, Kenzet was the land of the dead.

20 Pyr. § 925. On this ferryman *Ma-ha.f*, see §§ 383, 597-99, 1222, 1227, 1769.
21 Pyr. § 792.
22 Pyr. § 470.
23 Pyr. §§ 803, 1717. Cf § 547 where the king ascends by grasping *the tail* of the sun-god.
24 Pyr. §§ 1432-33. The lakes of the *duat* represent the sky here (see chapter two).
25 Pyr. §§ 393-414. Cf §§ 1026-27. On the Cannibal Hymn, see Eyre, 2002.
26 Pyr. § 736. Cf §§ 1544-50.
27 Pyr. § 332. Cf §§ 803, 1717, 1432-33. This god is named *Gaswti* in § 2080.
28 Pyr. § 1146. His hooves are the feet of the king's iron throne.
29 Pyr. § 547. Cf §§ 285, 470, 547 (was Re originally the creator-god in the form of a bull?).
30 Pyr. § 2249. Cf § 2105.
31 Pyr. § 316. Cf CT, VI, 185.
32 Pyr. § 470.
33 Shaw & Nicholson, 1995, pp. 35-36, 189.
34 CT, III, 307-12. Cf Osiris as Andjeti the bull of vultures, CT, V, 374, 385.
35 Wainwright, 1934, 1963; Frankfort, *KAG*, 1948, pp. 169, 180.
36 On the subject of bull sacrifice, see Rice, 1998, chapter 4.
37 Eliade, 1954, p. 35. See also Eliade, *A History of Religious Ideas*, op. cit., p. 229.
38 Pyr. §§ 1544-45. Cf §§ 1976-78.
39 Pyr. § 1550.
40 Eyre, 2002, pp. 85, 121, 134.
41 Pyr. §§ 400, 403, 409-11 (trans. Faulkner/Eyre/Alford). See Eyre, 2002, pp. 8-10, 86, 118-19, 132-34.
42 Pyr. §§ 395-97 (trans. Faulkner/Alford).
43 The king is indeed described as 'assembling his spirits' in § 398. Cf CT, III, 383; VI, 270.
44 Pyr. § 397.
45 Pyr. § 405 (trans. Faulkner/Eyre/Alford). See Eyre, 2002, pp. 8-9, 119-21. Cf 'the cooking-pot of Horus' in § 245.
46 In support of this idea, the Book of Gates shows the barque of the earth with two bulls' heads, see Budge, 1905, II, pp. 103-7.
47 Pyr. §§ 270-71.
48 Cf the sharp knife which came forth from Seth, §§ 1906, 1927, 1999 (presumably an iron knife).
49 Pyr. § 393 (trans. Faulkner/Alford).
50 Pyr. §§ 279-82. The 'upturned horn' is mentioned in § 283. Cf CT, VI, 231-32, 236-37.
51 Pyr. § 486.
52 The king is a newborn bull, see CT, VII, 225, 249, 347.
53 Pyr. § 2249. Cf § 2105. In the CT, the *nu*-serpent Neheb-kau is Bull of the Enneads, see II, II, 53-54.
54 CT, III, 169. Cf CT, V, 386.
55 CT, VII, 182.
56 CT, II, 13.
57 Pyr. §§ 279-80. Cf CT, III, 388: 'the bulls of the sky' (*kau nw pt*). Faulkner, 1969, p. 63, supposes the ox-herd to be 'a star or constellation'.
58 Lurker, 1980, p. 49.
59 Pyr. §§ 729, 2003. Cf §§ 388-89, 1370-71, 1566-67.
60 Pyr. §§ 729, 1566-67, 2003, 2203-5.
61 Pyr. §§ 388-89, 729, 1153, 1370-71, 1566-67, 2003.
62 Pyr. §§ 1370-71, 2203-4. Cf §§ 568-69.
63 Lurker, 1980, pp. 85-86; Shaw & Nicholson, 1995, p. 201.
64 Hence the name of the vulture-goddess Mut (*mwt*), meaning 'mother'. See Betro, 1996, p. 103.
65 Betro, 1996, p. 103.
66 Pyr. § 705.
67 Pyr. § 466.
68 Pyr. § 1344. Cf § 2171.
69 Budge, 1912, pp. 25-27.
70 Allen, 1989, p. 16.
71 Pyr. §§ 258, 459-60, 519, 782, 1036, 1049, 1090, 1189, 1247, 1300, 1430, 2034-35.
72 Pyr. §§ 809-19, 728, 2002; CT, VII, 225.
73 Pyr. § 316.
74 Pyr. §§ 782-85.
75 Pyr. §§ 1029-30. His parents are said to be Geb and Nut.
76 Pyr. § 1688; CT, VI, 270. Cf § 990.

77 Frankfort, *KAG*, 1948, p. 169.
78 Pyr. § 783.
79 Clark, 1959, pp. 49-50 interprets it this way. The 'entire land' is mentioned also in Pyr. § 782, where it clearly represents the entire earth in opposition to the sky.
80 CT, II, 34. See Allen, 1988, pp. 22, 25.
81 Pyr. §§ 316, 655-56, 783, 1039; Allen, 1989, pp. 3-4. Similarly, in CT, VI, 270 the *akeru* earth-gods appear in the sky.
82 Pyr. §§ 530-31.
83 Pyr. § 990. The king is asking Re to ensure Nut becomes pregnant with the seed which he – the king – has provided,
84 Pyr. §§ 1416-17. Cf §§ 1505, 1508: 'The king is your seed (*mtwt*) O Osiris... the king is your seed (*mtwt*) O Re.'
85 Pyr. § 532.
86 Cf Pyr. § 1469: 'The king's mother was pregnant with him in the lower sky... before the sky existed, before the earth existed.'
87 Pyr. § 1146.
88 CT, III, 124.
89 CT, IV, 130-31.
90 CT, VI, 191. Cf the phallus of Babi which opens the doors of the sky in Pyr. § 502.
91 CT, VII, 182.
92 CT, II, 67-68. Cf CT, II, 75-81.
93 Pyr. § 251. Cf § 1.
94 Wainwright, 1931, 1932, 1935; Lurker, 1980, p. 74.
95 Frankfort, *KAG*, 1948, p. 180. Cf Budge, 1904, I, p. 464. On Amun as the *ka-mut.ef*, see also the hymn to Amun-Re in Pritchard, 1969, p. 365.
96 Frankfort, *KAG*, 1948, pp. 188-89.
97 Wainwright, 1931, 1932, 1935; Frankfort, *KAG*, 1948, pp. 45, 188.
98 Frankfort, *KAG*, 1948, p. 188.
99 Wainwright, 1931, 1932, 1935. There was a close relationship between Horus and Min, both being treated as the son of Osiris, see Frankfort, *KAG*, 1948, p. 189.
100 Frankfort, *KAG*, 1948, p. 179. See also Meeks, 1997, p. 67.
101 Frankfort, *KAG*, 1948, p. 189.
102 The heart is an important motif in the creation myth. The expansion of the heart seems to allegorize the physical union of the expanding earth and sky – the marriage of Geb and Nut.
103 Frankfort, *KAG*, 1948, pp. 177, 180, 388 note 96.
104 Budge, 1912, pp. 50-51.
105 Great Hymn to Amun, 80 (trans. Allen/Alford). See Allen, 1988, p. 50.
106 Wainwright, 1931, 1932, 1935. Unfortunately, the relic has not survived the passage of time.
107 Wainwright, 1932, pp. 159-62, 165. This symbol originated in the pre-dynastic period, see Shaw & Nicholson, 1995, p. 187.
108 Wainwright, 1932, p. 165; Pyr. §§ 324-25.
109 Pyr. §§ 1248-49.
110 Pyr. §§ 1652-53 (trans. Faulkner/Allen/Alford).
111 E.A. Wallis Budge in 1926, Jean-Philippe Lauer in 1978, Robert Bauval in 1989 and 1994, and Toby Wilkinson in 2001. On the conical shape of the *benben* stone, see: Edwards, 1947, pp. 6, 282; Frankfort, *KAG*, 1948, p. 153; Bauval & Gilbert, 1994, p. 200.
112 See discussion and notes in chapter fifteen.
113 See chapter fifteen, note 33.
114 Bauval, 1989. See reprint in Bauval, 1999, pp. 358-64.
115 Frankfort, *KAG*, 1948, p. 381 note 27.
116 Ibid., pp. 169, 381.
117 Pyr. §§ 280, 283. Cf CT, VI, 232, 236.
118 Pyr. § 792. See Frankfort, *KAG*, 1948, p. 381 note 27.
119 Pyr. § 1178. See Frankfort, *KAG*, 1948, p. 381 note 27.
120 Frankfort, *KAG*, 1948, p. 381 note 27. See also Wainwright, 1938, pp. 106-7.
121 Hart, 1990, p. 11; Frankfort, *KAG*, 1948, pp. 153, 381.
122 Quirke, 2001, pp. 134-35, 141. Betro, 1996, p. 201 strikes an unusually positive note.
123 R.O. Faulkner, *A Concise Dictionary of Middle Egyptian*, 82; A. Erman & H. Grapow, *Worterbuch*, I, pp. 456 ff; J. Baines, *Orientalia*, 39 (1970), pp. 389-95.
124 Frankfort, *KAG*, 1948, pp. 153, 380 note 26 (citing Sethe, *Amun*, p. 118).

125 Frankfort, *KAG*, 1948, p. 380 note 26.
126 Bauval comes close to this idea in his 1989 article (see Bauval, 1999, p. 358), but this is not just about the creation of a single star.
127 This idea is inspired by Pyr. § 229. See chapter ten, note 96, above.
128 Karnak was called 'the noble mound of the first time', while Thebes was called 'the mound (*qay*) placed in *nun* at the beginning'. See further reference to this idea in chapter fifteen.
129 Reymond, 1969, p. 49: 'At Karnak mention is made of a land which emerged from *nun* before the high hill, and which was the birth-place of the earth-maker, and it is said there that the high hill was created before the *pay*-land emerged, and before sky, earth, and underworld had come into existence.'
130 Pyr. § 199. Cf § 990.
131 Pyr. § 1587.
132 CT, IV, 364.
133 CT, IV, 368.
134 Pyr. § 1039.
135 Faulkner, 1969, p. 173 (he titles the spell 'an address to the Nile').
136 Pyr. § 1517.
137 *Legend of Shu and Geb*. See Budge, 1934, pp. 440-41; Frankfort, *KAG*, 1948, p. 388 note 96; Watterson, 1984, p. 36; Meeks, 1997, p. 67. Geb is said to have loved his mother; his heart yearned for her.
138 CT, II, 29-30.
139 CT, II, 18. Cf CT, II, 31; III, 334-35.
140 Pyr. § 513. One of the leitmotifs of Egyptian myths in the Middle Kingdom and New Kingdom periods is the fiery blast on the mouths of the gods. See, for example, CT, II, 225.
141 Pyr. §§ 207-8.

CHAPTER TWELVE: THE FIERY EYE

1 Hornung, 1982, pp. 154, 282; Shaw & Nicholson, 1995, p. 95.
2 Morenz, 1973, p. 83; Lurker, 1980, p. 67.
3 Allen, 1988, p. 20.
4 CT, II, 5; III, 383.
5 CT, IV, 173-74. Or literally 'the Eye who shall not be repeated'.
6 Clark, 1959, pp. 47, 95, 218, 220, 226. But he mistakes the fire as solar, p. 222.
7 Clark, 1959, p. 227: 'the Eye is the key to the religion'.
8 Wilkinson, 1992, p. 43.
9 Frankfort, *KAG*, 1948, p. 131; Lurker, 1980, p. 67; Meeks, 1997, p. 14.
10 CT, IV, 86.
11 Pyr. §§ 194, 295, 509, 1305; CT, V, 323. Cf the epithet of Nut in §§ 782, 1020, 2052-53.
12 Pyr. §§ 194-95, 1795.
13 Pyr. § 643.
14 Pyr. § 1806.
15 Meeks, 1997, pp. 58-59.
16 Pyr. §§ 1588-90.
17 Pyr. §§ 1590-92.
18 Pyr. §§ 1593-94.
19 Pyr. §§ 1595-97, 1605. The Eye and Nut are also identified indirectly in CT, IV, 244-50 and BD, 17, where the celestial cow Mehet-weret is an alter ego of Nut.
20 Pyr. § 514.
21 Pyr. §§ 2108-9. For the attack by Seth in Nedyt, see chapter four, note 118.
22 Alford, 2003, p. 14. The idea of the primeval city is also discussed in chapter fifteen of this book.
23 Pritchard, 1969, p. 8; Assmann, 2001, pp. 24-25.
24 Habachi, 1984, p. 66; Assmann, 2001, p. 24.
25 Pyr. § 601.
26 Pyr. § 1227. 'You' is the ferryman.
27 Pyr. § 1642. Cf CT, VI, 221.
28 Pyr. §§ 451-52.
29 CT, II, 327. On the House of the Double Lion, see CT, V, 290-91; VII, 217.
30 CT, III, 343.
31 CT, IV, 231-38.
32 CT, VII, 373-79, 426. Cf Clark, 1959, p. 225.

33 Wilkinson, 1992, p. 43; Gardiner, 1994, p. 197.
34 Pyr. § 61.
35 Lurker, 1980, pp. 48, 92; Gardiner, 1994, pp. 500, 562.
36 Pyr. §§ 298-99.
37 Pyr. § 392.
38 Pyr. §§ 82, 83, 575-59, 587-90, 634-35, 643, 653, 1212, 1286.
39 CT, IV, 98-99, 101, 105, 107-8. Cf CT, III, 300; V, 323, 325-26.
40 Pyr. § 1040. Alternatively, it may have been fear about the fate of the Eye in the midst of the struggle between Seth and Horus (cf § 1463).
41 CT, IV, 34.
42 Pyr. §§ 194-97.
43 BD, 17.
44 Budge, 1912, pp. xxiii-xxvii, 15-23.
45 CT, IV, 99. The Eye is also said to preside over 'what is red', i.e. blood, CT, IV, 108.
46 Hart, 1990, p. 47: 'The scene is set in... a remote mythological past'.
47 Cf CT, I, 366-68, where Shu says: "My soul impregnates the people who are in the isle of fire".
48 See A.F. Alford, *The Atlantis Secret*, Eridu Books, 2001.
49 Pyr. § 299. See earlier quotation from Utterance 255.
50 Meeks, 1997, pp. 26-27.
51 Pyr. § 1212.
52 CT, IV, 34.
53 CT, IV, 107-8.
54 CT, V, 323. Cf CT, V, 325-26.
55 Meeks, 1997, p. 174.
56 CT, IV, 194-200. Cf CT, II, 84; BD, 17.
57 CT, VI, 270.
58 Budge, 1905, II, p. 82.
59 Budge, 1912, pp. 33-35.
60 Reymond, 1969, pp. 12-13, 55, 107, 118.
61 Pyr. §§ 599-601, 1227.
62 Pyr. §§ 594-96. Cf §§ 600-1; CT, V, 73, 75-77.
63 Pyr. §§ 594-96. On the wings of Thoth, see §§ 387, 1176, 1254, 1429.
64 Pyr. §§ 639, 830. Thoth was possibly also an assembler of 'the great throne', §§ 1153-54.
65 Pyr. §§ 1233, 1235-36, 1238. Cf §§ 2247-48.
66 Pyr. §§ 976-79.
67 Pyr. §§ 971-75.
68 Pyr. §§ 977-78.
69 Cf CT, IV, 135; VI, 221.
70 Pyr. §§ 2087-88.
71 Pyr. §§ 1624-25. The Eye also goes forth from the head of Osiris (§§ 1816, 1819-21, 1832) and Atum (§§ 1239-40).
72 Pyr. § 2091.
73 CT, II, 5. Cf CT, VI, 375. See Allen, 1988, p. 18.
74 Pyr. § 823. Heliopolis is the place of the assembly of the gods, §§ 1647-48, 1744. This myth may have been corrupted by the invention of the ennead of Heliopolis, which made Nut the mother of five renowned gods, of whom Osiris was the eldest (§§ 825, 1608). But there are hints that Nut's children were originally the cohorts of Horus and Seth, see Pyr. § 823, BD, 175.
75 Pyr. §§ 318, 1242, 2250; BD, 125.
76 CT, IV, 75.
77 CT, IV, 98.
78 CT, III, 343-44. See Clark, 1959, pp. 224-25.
79 CT, VII, 162.
80 CT, VI, 375.
81 CT, IV, 91, 98.
82 Pyr. §§ 976, 979-80. Cf §§ 1459, 2047-48.
83 Pyr. § 2206. Cf §§ 1092, 1568, 2047.
84 CT, IV, 91.
85 Pyr. § 302. Cf §§ 451-54, 1755, 1794.
86 Pyr. §§ 194-98. Cf § 1147.
87 CT, IV, 172-73.

88 CT, IV, 46.
89 CT, IV, 34. See quotation earlier in this chapter.
90 Pyr. §§ 194-98. Cf §§ 295, 1147.
91 Pyr. §§ 1234, 2246-47.
92 Pyr. §§ 634, 844-45, 2074-76. See Gardiner, 1994, pp. 504, 561.
93 Pyr. §§ 1920, 2226-27. The identification of the 'unique star' or 'lone star' has long been a puzzle. As the Eye of Re, it may be connected with the sun, but in CT, VI, 350-51 it is identified with the morning star, i.e. Venus. I believe the solution to this puzzle lies in viewing the unique star not as an astronomical body, but as the creator-goddess. She would then become manifest in all the celestial bodies, especially those with a feminine character.
94 Lurker, 1980, pp. 85-86.
95 Pyr. §§ 194-98, 1795, 1832, 2285.
96 Pyr. §§ 1624-25.
97 Pyr. §§ 1813-16, 1819-21, 1832.
98 Shabaka Stone, 12-15. See Pritchard, 1969, pp. 4-5.
99 Pyr. § 397. See Eyre, 2002, p. 82.
100 Frankfort, *KAG*, 1948, p. 154; Pritchard, 1969, p. 9; Lurker, 1980, p. 50; Eyre, 2002, p. 81.
101 CT, I, 117-18, 137-41, 148-50, 161, 166, 174-77; II, 129; III, 321, 327-28; IV, 88, 91, 113, 378; V, 74, 351; VI, 272, 295; VII, 237. See comment by Eyre, 2002, p. 82.
102 Pyr. §§ 2220-21.
103 Pyr. § 823. Similarly, in a New Kingdom ritual hymn, Re is given 'your two eyes, your two sisters who have emerged from your head, so that you might live', see Quirke, 2001, p. 60.
104 Pyr. § 2279. Cf § 2037.
105 Pyr. §§ 1239-40: 'both his intact eyes, by means of which he will make his foes pass away'.
106 Pyr. § 610. Cf §§ 2276, 2280-81.
107 Pyr. §§ 641-43.
108 Pyr. §§ 1805-6.
109 Pyr. §§ 1807-9.
110 CT, IV, 102-3. Cf CT, IV, 98, 106.
111 CT, II, 5, 33. Cf CT, IV, 241.
112 CT, II, 5 (trans. Allen/Alford). See Allen, 1988, p. 19. Cf CT, II, 30.
113 CT, VI, 220 (the roles of the eyes are here switched; the right eye is usually the day-barque, the sun, and the left eye the night-barque, the moon). The eyes are also identified with the two barques in Pyr. §§ 1981-82, 1315 (cf §§ 69-71); CT, VI, 384.
114 This is an established identification, see Lurker, 1980, pp. 100-2, 112, 119.
115 Budge, 1912, p. 177; Budge, 1934, p. 419.
116 Pyr. § 1249.
117 CT, II, 32.
118 Bremner-Rhind Papyrus. See Budge, 1904, I, pp. 311, 317; Budge, 1912, pp. 4-5, 10-11. Atum has by now expanded himself into the sky, cf CT, VI, 375. This myth was embellished in later times, it being suggested that the Eye had wandered off into a remote region of the earth and needed to be 'brought back'.
119 CT, I, 378-80. The context shows that this fire was in the sky. This spell was surely known to the authors of the Neber-djer myth.
120 CT, V, 155. Cf Clark, 1959, p. 76.
121 BD, 167 (trans. Faulkner/Budge/Alford). See Budge, 1925, p. 317.
122 CT, VI, 154.
123 Bremner-Rhind Papyrus, part b. See Budge, 1904, I, p. 317; Budge, 1912, p. 11. Similarly in part a, Neber-djer states: "My Eye was weary behind them [Shu and Tefnut] because they departed from me for long periods of time." See Budge, 1904, I, p. 311; Budge, 1912, p. 5.
124 Bremner-Rhind Papyrus, part b. See Budge, 1904, I, p. 319; Budge, 1912, p. 11.
125 Budge, 1912, pp. 7, 11.
126 CT, IV, 238-43. Cf BD, 17. On the raging Eye, see also CT, V, 155.
127 Clark, 1959, pp. 225-26. There is a pun here between *neshen*, 'storm', and *shen*, 'hair'.
128 Bremner-Rhind Papyrus, part a. See Budge, 1904, I, p. 312; Budge, 1912, pp. 5-7.
129 Bremner-Rhind Papyrus, part b. See Budge, 1904, I, pp. 319-20; Budge, 1912, pp. 11-13.
130 CT, II, 68, 71-72. Cf CT, II, 78-79.
131 CT, I, 393; II, 2, 24-25, 34, 218; III, 364; IV, 137-38, 183; VI, 53-54, 63-64, 151, 221, 270.
132 CT, VI, 191; VI, 267.
133 CT, VI, 151. This may be an allusion to the fact that the solar eye remains full whereas the lunar eye

disappears completely once a month.
134 Pyr. §§ 610, 642-43, 1805-6, 1239-40. Cf Pyr. §§ 1227, 1642.
135 BD, 125; Wainwright, 1932, pp. 164-65. Cf Edfu texts, E. VI, 16, 6-9, see Reymond, 1969, p. 83.
136 Wainwright, 1932, p. 165.
137 Ibid.
138 Budge, 1904, I, p. 476.
139 Ibid.
140 BD, 134. See Budge, 1934, p. 157.
141 Gardiner, p. 554; Budge, 1934, p. 157. The egg determinative is sign H8.
142 Faulkner, 1985, p. 123. See also Morenz, 1973, p. 325 notes 90, 96.
143 There may also be an allusion to Horus and Seth who together personified the primeval earth (see chapter thirteen). There are hints of a lost myth in which the moon originated from Seth's two testicles.
144 CT, VI, 294.
145 Faulkner 1977, p. 239 note 17.
146 Pyr. §§ 567, 569. On the field of turquoise, see §§ 936-37. On the lakes of turquoise, see §§ 1784-85. Hathor is said to 'ascend in turquoise', CT, VI, 64. An overlooked theme in the texts is the ascent of the deity adorned with minerals such as lapis lazuli, gold, and electrum, see CT, IV, 46; V, 385-86.
147 See R. Temple, *The Crystal Sun*, Century, London, 2000, pp. 287-88; A.F. Alford, *The Atlantis Secret*, Eridu Books, 2001, pp. 36, 41-43. The sun is also said to be made of metal in the legend of Tantalus, per the scholiast on Pindar; see R. Graves, *The Greek Myths*, p. 391.
148 Pliny, *Natural History*, II.
149 CT, VII, 465. Cf CT, II, 33; VI, 344.
150 See chapter eight, note 40, above.
151 CT, IV, 175. See Faulkner, 1973, p. 256 note 12. Cf CT, II, 32.
152 CT, VI, 316 (its lotus-leaves are said to be a hailstorm!). Cf CT, VI, 344.
153 CT, VI, 342.
154 Clark, 1959, p. 96.
155 BD, 17. Saliva was believed to have healing powers, hence Thoth spat on the Eye.
156 CT, II, 33. Cf CT, I, 366-67. See Clark, 1959, p. 46.
157 Bremner-Rhind Papyrus, part a. See Budge, 1904, pp. 311-12; Budge, 1912, pp. 4-5. Cf part b: 'My Eye cried, and mankind came into being.'
158 This explains the Edfu myth where the builder-gods 'raised the seed for gods and man'. The gods came into being directly, but man came into being after the seed had fallen back to the earth.
159 Bremner-Rhind Papyrus, part a. See Budge, 1904, pp. 312-13; Budge, 1912, pp. 6-7. 'Their moments' probably refers to Shu and Tefnut.
160 Bremner-Rhind Papyrus, part b. See Budge, 1904, pp. 319-20; Budge, 1912, pp. 11-13.
161 Budge, 1934, p. 148.
162 Meeks, 1997, pp. 75-76; Eyre, 2002, pp. 87-88.
163 CT, II, 31-32, though cf different translation in Allen, 1988, p. 22.
164 CT, V, 154.
165 CT, IV, 329.
166 Pyr. § 389.
167 Pyr. §§ 957-59. Cf CT, VII, 37.
168 CT, V, 133.
169 CT, IV, 352: 'ferry across the sky when the sacred land is turned upside down'.
170 An alternative interpretation might be suggested by the Mesopotamian creation myth, which places the creator-god in the sky at the beginning and has him disintegrate and fall to the earth (I have deemed this 'the exploded planet' myth). But I now take the view that the Egyptian and Mesopotamian (and Greek) creation myths were quite distinct
171 CT, VII, 112. Cf CT, VII, 15.
172 CT, VII, 30: 'I am Geb who entered into the earth'.
173 Gardiner, 1994, p. 598.
174 Pyr. §§ 225-26.
175 Pyr. § 237. Cf §§ 442-43, 673-75.
176 Pyr. §§ 2254-55. Cf §§ 241, 247. The invocation is directed at the inimical snake, not at Neheb-kau.
177 Pyr. §§ 511-12. Cf CT, II, 51-54.
178 *Horus of Behdet and the Winged Disc*. See Budge, 1912, p. 76.
179 CT, II, 40-41 (trans. Faulkner/Allen). See Allen, 1988, p. 23. Cf CT, II, 100, 108.
180 Clark, 1959, p. 137.

181 Wainwright, 1938, pp. 29-30.
182 CT, VI, 144; BD, 17; Meeks, 1997, p. 21.
183 Wainwright, 1938, pp. 29, 31; Lurker, 1980, p. 64. Plutarch reported a similar tradition, that the vine originated from soil which had been fertilized by the bodies of the gods, see Budge, 1912, p. 206.
184 Wainwright, 1938, pp. 29-30.

CHAPTER THIRTEEN: HORUS AND SETH

1 Budge, 1904; Budge, 1911; Budge, 1912; S.B. Mercer, *Horus, Royal God of Egypt*, 1942; James, 1960, pp. 72, 204; Watterson, 1984, p. 83; David, 2002, pp. 156, 160.
2 Breasted, 1912, pp. 28, 31; Lurker, 1980, p. 82; Sellers, 1992; Schulz & Seidel, 1998, pp. 311, 514.
3 Frankfort, *KAG*, 1948, p. 22; Hornung, 1982, p. 217.
4 David, 2002, pp. 156, 160; Frankfort, *KAG*, 1948, pp. 21-22, 356 note 20. Frankfort argued that the historicist theory barred a proper understanding of the important fact that the struggle between Horus and Seth was an allegory for strife in the universe.
5 Pyr. § 594.
6 Pyr. § 679. Cf § 51. This is elaborated in CT, IV, 234: Horus carried off the testicles and Seth inflicted a wound on the face of Horus.
7 Pyr. § 1463. Cf § 60.
8 Pyr. §§ 40 (+15), 1233.
9 Pyr. § 1242.
10 Pyr. § 2282.
11 Pyr. §§ 40 (+11), 40 (+13), 60, 61, 88, 1407, 2250.
12 Pyr. §§ 36, 39, 40, 578-79, 591, 1859.
13 Pyr. §§ 1242-43. That Seth wore the Eye on his head is probably a figure of speech, not to be taken literally as a sign of the expansion of the cosmos. For the attack by Seth in the east side of the sky, see chapter twelve, notes 62, 63.
14 Pyr. § 42.
15 Pyr. §§ 1544-50.
16 Frankfort, *KAG*, 1948, pp. 129-30.
17 CT, VII, 61.
18 CT, VII, 61-62. Cf Pyr. §§ 40 (+10), 69-71.
19 The heart of the creator-god is often mentioned in the texts. Atum begot the ennead by spreading his heart wide (Pyr. §§ 1655-56); Atum created Shu in his heart (CT, I, 344); Geb lifted up Atum's heart (CT, II, 35); the heart of Isis was lifted by the seed of Osiris (CT, II, 210); Ta-tenen made the sky by means of his heart (Great Harris Papyrus); Amun made the sky and earth by means of his heart (hymn to Amun); Re's heart came forth from his body at the same time as the Eye and the eyes (*Isis and Re*); Horus turned his heart towards his mother Isis and united his heart with her when he violated her; and the Ogdoad made light through the radiance of their hearts.
20 CT, IV, 234. There are references in Pyr. § 823 and CT, VI, 118-19 to 'Horus and his Great of Magic' and 'Seth and his Great of Magic'. These may well allude to the eyes and the testicles. They are connected to the heart of the deceased in CT, VI, 118-19 and are seemingly carried off to the sky by Nut in Pyr. § 823.
21 Pyr. §§ 1255-58. Cf CT, I, 303-5.
22 Pyr. § 316.
23 Meeks, 1997, p. 75.
24 CT, II, 349. Cf BD, 113. The hands of Horus are briefly mentioned in the PT at § 2239.
25 Plutarch, *De Iside et Osiride*, § 20 (see Budge, 1912, p. 229).
26 Pyr. §§ 1337, 1339.
27 Hart, 1990, pp. 37-38; Sellers, 1992, pp. 66-67; Meeks, 1997, p. 23. A similar scene occurs in *Horus of Behdet and the Winged Disc*; the spearing of Seth is said to commemorate the time when there was a storm in the District (the primeval mound), see Budge, 1912, p. 73.
28 See Sellers, 1992, pp. 66-67.
29 Pyr. §§ 24, 637, 766-67, 1823.
30 Pyr. § 647.
31 Pyr. §§ 24, 613, 615, 619, 766-67, 1824.
32 Pyr. §§ 1092, 1228, 1339-40, 1828-29, 1983, 2078-79, 2101-2.
33 Pyr. §§ 575, 588.
34 Pyr. §§ 575, 579, 590-91, 1632-33. Cf §§ 647, 1824, 1830-31.
35 Pyr. §§ 16, 298-99, 392, 614, 653, 758-59, 1614, 1920, 1979, 2072-73, 2227.

36 CT, IV, 289-90; BD, 17.
37 Pyr. § 617.
38 Pyr. § 480. Faulkner, 1969, p. 95 note 2. It is Geb who assigns the mounds, §§ 943, 961, 994, 1475.
39 The 'great mound' is mentioned in Pyr. § 574. The 'ready fighter' (Horus) is in it.
40 Pyr. §§ 218, 222. Or see the mounds, § 1904.
41 Pyr. §§ 1735, 1928, 2099, 2233. Cf the southern and northern mounds, §§ 1364, 2011.
42 Pyr. § 135.
43 Pyr. § 1904. See Budge, 1911, I, pp. 98-99.
44 Pyr. §§ 480, 487, 943, 961, 994, 1475.
45 Pyr. §§ 598, 948. Cf §§ 915-17.
46 Reymond, 1969, pp. 9, 28, 266-67, 305, index.
47 Ibid., p. 77.
48 Ibid., p. 90.
49 Pyr. §§ 961, 993-94, 1475.
50 Pyr. §§ 993-94.
51 Pyr. § 487.
52 Pyr. §§ 318-19.
53 CT, I, 19-21. The feet are an important theme in the ascension of the god. The eyes of Horus are joined to the king's feet (Pyr. §§ 69-71, 477, 941, 1472-73), the earth quakes at his feet (§ 2110), and his foot is said to press down on the earth (§§ 990, 2067).
54 On the peace-making role of Thoth, see Pyr. §§ 1465, 1962-63; BD, 183.
55 Pyr. §§ 229, 311, 315.
56 BD, 17.
57 Pyr. §§ 141-42.
58 Pyr. §§ 334-35, 949-50 (the Great Ones), 1900 (Thoth and Osiris), 1914 (assembly place of the gods). Osiris is probably the 'Great One of the castle of the mace' in § 1725 and 'the god' of 'the castle' in §§ 1293, 1908, 2237.
59 Pyr. § 2220.
60 Pyr. §§ 1926-27.
61 Pyr. § 598.
62 Pyr. §§ 947-50, 1659. On *msqt shdu*, see chapter two.
63 Pyr. § 598. Cf § 948.
64 Pyr. §§ 141-42.
65 Pyr. §§ 946-47, 594; CT, V, 73.
66 Cf the crying out in Pyr. § 594 to the restoration of the Eye and testicles in Pyr. §§ 141-42, 946-47; CT, V, 73, 75-76, 120.
67 Pyr. § 143. To be born for Horus and conceived for Seth meant to have power in the body, § 211.
68 Pyr. §§ 204-5.
69 See note 20 above.
70 Pyr. §§ 1906, 1927. Cf CT, VII, 99.
71 Pyr. §§ 1149-51.
72 Pyr. §§ 1935-36. Faulkner prefers to render *r*, 'mouth', as 'face'.
73 CT, IV, 29.
74 CT, IV, 290; BD, 17. The Edfu texts also refer to a battle taking place in the sky, in this case between the Falcon and the *sbti*-snake. See Reymond, 1969, p. 35.
75 Budge, 1912, p. 59. Horus is here described as a being of light who came forth from the *akhet* (p. 93).
76 Pyr. § 290. Cf § 1775.
77 On Seth and the northern stars, see Pyr. §§ 14, 42, 2157-58; CT, VI, 196; Budge, 1904, II, pp. 249-50; Meeks, 1997, p. 118. On Seth and lifting the sky, see notes 79 and 80 below.
78 Seth was in later times promoted to the barque, but his powers were restrained, see BD, 175.
79 Pyr. §§ 581-82, 588-89, 626-28, 649, 1258, 1627-28, 1699, 1855, 1993.
80 Pyr. §§ 1258, 1699, 1993.
81 Pyr. §§ 971-75, 1742.
82 Sellers, 1992, p. 314.
83 Wainwright, 1938, p. 29.
84 A.H. Gardiner, *The Library of A. Chester Beatty, Description of a Hieratic Papyrus* etc, London, 1931. For a summary of contents, see Budge, 1934, pp. 444-57; Clark, 1959, pp. 195-208; Pritchard, 1969, pp. 14-17; Watterson, 1984, pp. 86, 106-8; Hart, 1990, pp. 34-37.
85 Budge, 1934, p. 453.
86 Budge, 1934, p. 452; Clark, 1959, p. 205.

87 Pritchard, 1969, p. 15.
88 Pyr. § 48.
89 Pyr. § 48.
90 The tips of obelisks were often sheathed in electrum. See Habachi, 1984, pp. 57-59, 62-63, 66, 70-71, 165.
91 Were the hands used to tear off the testicles from Seth? In BD, 113 it is written: 'I know the mystery of Nekhen, it is the hands of Horus and what is in them.' Perhaps what is in them is the testicles.
92 Pyr. § 980.
93 Pyr. § 1459.
94 This theory still persists, but it is nowadays viewed as a long historical process, see Schulz & Seidel, 1998, p. 520.
95 Hoffman, 1979, p. 289; Quirke, 1990, p. 10; Quirke, 2001, p. 83; Schulz & Seidel, 1998, p. 26; Assmann, 2001, pp. 135, 139.
96 Frankfort, *KAG*, 1948, pp. 15-23, 349 note 6, 351 note 19.
97 Sellers, 1992, pp. 99, 104, 116, 159, 227. Her theory in turn inspired Robert Bauval in his books co-authored with Adrian Gilbert and Graham Hancock respectively.
98 CT, II, 317-18.
99 BD, 17 (trans. Faulkner/Budge/Alford). See Budge, 1904, II, p. 59.
100 See quotation in chapter four.
101 Pyr. § 1194.
102 CT, II, 211.
103 BD, 17.
104 Frankfort, *KAG*, 1948, p. 19; Assmann, 2001, p. 37. See chapter two, note 6.
105 BD, 183.
106 Pyr. §§ 388-89.
107 On the unification of the Two Lands and the opening of the mouth, see CT, VI, 333.
108 Pyr. § 1728.
109 Pyr. § 993. Cf §§ 961, 1475. The cities and districts of Geb do not belong to the real world but to the time and place of creation. They are equivalent to the towns and settlements in §§ 1676-79, which lie in the eastern horizon or perhaps in the sky. This was the terrestrial paradise in which the blessed dead sought to dwell in the afterlife.
110 CT, IV, 362.
111 Pyr. §§ 1364, 2011.
112 Pyr. § 1295.
113 Pyr. § 1735. Cf § 2099.
114 Pyr. § 1928. Cf § 2233.
115 Pyr. § 1364. Cf § 2011.
116 Pyr. § 770.
117 Pyr. §§ 1002-3, 1047, 1194, 1528, 1747-48, 1878-79, 1938, 2182-83. The Egyptians oriented themselves to the south. South was up, and north was down.
118 For the following translations, see Pritchard, 1969, pp. 4-5.
119 Upper Egypt and Lower Egypt are occasionally cited in a way that is suggestive of this interpretation. See Pyr. §§ 854, 959, 1510-11.
120 Pyr. § 812.
121 Pyr. §§ 1436, 406. These 'two banks' are possibly not the same as the 'banks' of the winding waterway, which apparently spanned the sky from horizon to horizon.
122 CT, III, 30-33.
123 CT, III, 39.
124 CT, III, 44-45. Cf CT, VI, 160.
125 CT, III, 46.
126 CT, IV, 145.
127 CT, VI, 162.
128 Note that elsewhere the uniting of the banks can signify the negation of creation, Pyr. § 279; CT, VI, 231. But that is clearly not the intention here.
129 Pyr. § 406 (trans. Faulkner/Eyre). See Eyre, 2002, pp. 9, 123. Cf CT, VI, 180.
130 Pyr. § 2015. Cf § 1367. See Faulkner, 1969, p. 214 note 14 and p. 290 note 11.
131 Pyr. § 514.
132 Pyr. § 514.
133 Pyr. § 541.
134 Pyr. § 2268.

135 Pyr. §§ 4, 1436.
136 Frankfort, *KAG*, 1948, p. 380 note 21.
137 Ibid., pp. 23, 104, 106.
138 Reymond, 1969, pp. 40-41.
139 Ibid., pp. 18-19, 25, 154.
140 Pyr. §§ 1242, 2157-58. CT, IV, 140; VI, 261.

CHAPTER FOURTEEN: THE ONE AND THE OTHER

1 For a thorough discussion of the historical debate, see Hornung, 1982.
2 See, for example, Budge, 1911, I, pp. 354, 358-60; James, 1960, p. 301.
3 Hornung, 1982, pp. 53, 185-86 is guilty of this attitude.
4 Atum originally counted as one of the nine, see Pyr. § 1655. Horus son of Isis was later added as a tenth member of the group.
5 Scholars have been completely fooled by the ennead of Heliopolis. Although some have recognised it as a corruption (Frankfort, *KAG*, 1948, p. 182), others have tried to read it as if it were a genuine theogony providing a succession to royal office for Horus, see Morenz, 1973, p. 162; Assmann, 2001, pp. 119-22. The problem is that there is no myth by which Shu and Tefnut gave birth to Geb and Nut.
6 Budge, 1911, I, p. 358; Hornung, 1982, pp. 53-54.
7 Hornung, 1982.
8 Budge, 1904, pp. 315-16; Budge, 1912, p. 9.
9 Budge, 1934, p. 259; Allen, 1988, p. 40.
10 Great Hymn to Amun, 100.
11 Pyr. § 447.
12 Pyr. § 2065. It has been suggested that Tefnut might have signified the moisture of the vagina, see Naydler, 1996, p. 42.
13 Shu is called 'father of the gods' in CT, II, 5; VI, 154. Tefnut bore the ennead in CT, II, 22. Cf Heftnut the mother of the gods in Pyr. § 1419.
14 Pyr. § 2206.
15 CT, IV, 179, 181.
16 Watterson, 1984, pp. 126-28; Meeks, 1997, pp. 178-83.
17 Or 'She who Grows as She Comes'. See CT, VI, 247; Clark, 1959, p. 43; Lurker, 1980, pp. 31, 57; Hornung, 1982, p. 278; Quirke, 2001, p. 31.
18 Hornung, 1982, pp. 84, 218.
19 Ibid., pp. 63, 218.
20 Hornung, 1982, p. 84; Shaw & Nicholson, 1995, pp. 31-32, 193.
21 Lurker, 1980, p. 33; Shaw & Nicholson, 1995, pp. 35, 151, 252-53.
22 Hornung, 1982, pp. 85, 218.
23 Ibid., pp. 85, 218.
24 Clark, 1959, p. 266 comments astutely: 'All the major goddesses are really forms of the one Great Goddess.'
25 Pyr. § 783.
26 Reymond, 1969, p. 63. Consistent with this act, the Primeval Ones were called 'the males without female among them' (p. 78). But they were also portrayed as both male and female.
27 Reymond, 1969, p. 64. The seed of Nun is here equated with the lotus.
28 Budge, *A Hieroglyphic Vocabulary to the Book of the Dead*, 1911, p. 134.
29 Frankfort, *KAG*, 1948, pp. 153, 380 note 26. See quotation in chapter eleven.
30 Frankfort, *KAG*, 1948, p. 380 note 26.
31 Reymond, 1969, p. 64.
32 Ibid., pp. 64-65.
33 In this regard, it should be noted that the pyramidion has the feminine name *bnbnt*.
34 R.O. Faulkner, *A Concise Dictionary of Middle Egyptian*, 82; A. Erman & H. Grapow, *Worterbuch*, I, pp. 456 ff; J. Baines, *Orientalia*, 39 (1970), pp. 389-95.
35 Pyr. §§ 1416-17.
36 Pyr. § 532.
37 Pyr. § 316.
38 There is a notable emphasis on the idea of a son, but occasionally there are allusions to a daughter cosmos, e.g. the myth of Tefnut giving birth to Nut and the myth of Nut giving birth to her daughter the *duat*.

NOTES   417

39 Budge, 1904, I, pp. 457-63. The Greeks called Neit a 'he-she', see Morenz, 1973, p. 26.
40 CT, II, 161. Cf Clark, 1959, pp. 41, 80. Atum also gave birth to the gods, CT, IV, 60.
41 See treatment of Shu and Tefnut in chapter three.
42 Pyr. § 1248; Bremner-Rhind Pap. See Budge, 1904, I, pp. 310, 318; Lurker, 1980, p. 31. Atum's hand thus became his consort in Heliopolis.
43 CT, III, 334-35. Cf Bremner-Rhind Pap.
44 Frankfort, *KAG*, 1948, p. 353 note 7; Pritchard, 1969, p. 5; Allen, 1988, pp. 43-44. The Greeks called Ptah a 'he-she', see Morenz, 1973, p. 26; Lurker, 1980, p. 33.
45 Great Hymn to Amun, 40, 90, 600. Also in Papyrus Nesi-Khensu.
46 Budge, 1934, p. 453. See chapter thirteen.
47 Budge, 1934, p. 149.
48 Great Hymn to Amun, 40.
49 Budge, 1899, p. 99; Budge, 1904, II, p. 51; Budge, 1934, p. 256.
50 Breasted, 1912, pp. 316, 318; Budge, 1934, p. 10; Pritchard, 1969, p. 368.
51 Morenz, 1973, p. 26.
52 Breasted, 1912, p. 348. The name Osiris was written with a throne and an eye.
53 Breasted, 1912, p. 330; Hornung, 1982, p. 171.
54 Hornung, 1982, p. 221. See the treatment of the Ogdoad in chapter three.
55 Reymond, 1969, pp. 76-77.
56 Budge, 1934, p. 101; Lurker, 1980, pp. 16, 33.
57 Pyr. § 1617. Cf § 1018.
58 Pyr. § 233. Cf the serpent bite in the myth *Isis and Re*.
59 The Big Bang is as much a myth as the Egyptian geocentric creation. For the lowdown on this, and continuing updates, see www.metaresearch.org.
60 Hymn to Osiris, see quote in chapter three. Cf Pyr. §§ 1255-56, 1280.
61 CT, II, 209-10.
62 The Goddess was usually the prime mover, and was particularly associated with fire.
63 Budge, 1904, I, p. 315; Budge, 1934, pp. 32-33, 117; Allen, 1988, p. 30. Ptah is also called 'Magic' in the Berlin Hymn, see Allen, 1988, pp. 39-40.
64 CT, III, 382-89. See Allen, 1988, pp. 36-38.
65 CT, III, 385. See Allen, 1988, pp. 37-38.
66 CT, VI, 270.
67 Budge, 1904, I, p. 380; Budge, 1912, p. 49.
68 Pyr. §§ 632, 1635. Cf §§ 645-47 where Osiris unites with the children of Horus who have loved him.
69 Pyr. § 1795.
70 Pyr. §§ 1825, 2279.
71 CT, VI, 118-19. Cf Pyr. § 823.
72 Pyr. §§ 924-25.
73 Pyr. §§ 477, 941, 993, 1472-73. Cf §§ 69-71.
74 Pyr. §§ 397, 411. Cf § 1318.
75 Pyr. §§ 395, 409; CT, VI, 270.
76 Pyr. §§ 250, 992-93.
77 On the importance of *heka*, see Hornung, 1982, pp. 208-10; Quirke, 2001, pp. 36, 46; David, 2002, p. 284.
78 *Isis and Re*. See Budge, 1904, I, p. 385; Budge, 1912, pp. 54-55.
79 CT, VI, 118-19, 384. Cf Pyr. § 1981 'the two great and mighty sisters'.
80 The idea of the soul copulating with the body is seen also in the myth of Re uniting with the body of Osiris. See CT, II, 67, 70-71, 77, 79; BD, 17; Books of the Netherworld.
81 A second copulation occurs when Osiris sends out seed from his phallus into the expanding cosmos, see CT, II, 68, 71-72, 78-81.
82 Frankfort, *KAG*, 1948, p. 180. See quotation in chapter six.

CHAPTER FIFTEEN: PYRAMIDS AND TEMPLES

1 See Alford, 2003, pp. 229-31.
2 Hornung, 2001, p. 157.
3 K. Mendelssohn, *The Riddle of the Pyramids*, Thames & Hudson, 1974, pp. 77, 153, 196, 199. A similar theory was aired by Cornelius de Pauw in 1773.
4 On Memphis, see Frankfort, *KAG*, 1948, p. 380. On Hermopolis, see BD, 17; Budge, 1934, p. 153. On Abydos (the Thinite district), see Frankfort, *KAG*, 1948, p. 25; Clark, 1959, p. 132. On Thebes,

see Frankfort, *KAG*, 1948, p. 380; Morenz, 1973, p. 43; Lurker, 1980, pp. 39, 96; Assmann, 2001, p. 25. On Hermonthis, see Frankfort, *KAG*, 1948, p. 380; Reymond, 1969, p. 86. On Esna, see Lurker, 1980, p. 39. On Elephantine, see Budge, 1912, p. 125. Similar traditions existed for Heliopolis, Herakleopolis and Medinet Habu.
5   Frankfort et al, 1946, pp. 21-22; Reymond, 1969, pp. 48-50; Pritchard, 1969, p. 8; Schulz & Seidel, 1998, p. 183; Assmann, 2001, pp. 38-39.
6   Lurker, 1980, p. 65; Shafer, 1997, pp. 8, 96, 98, 100; Assmann, 2001, pp. 36-37, 42.
7   Reymond, 1969.
8   Frankfort et al, 1946, p. 21; Frankfort, *KAG*, 1948, p. 152; Reymond, 1969, p. 43.
9   Shafer, 1997, pp. 29, 75, 88-89, 99, 102, 107-8, 110, 115; Schulz & Seidel, 1998, p. 191; Quirke, 2001, pp. 100-2.
10 Habachi, 1984, p. 155.
11 Shafer, 1997, p. 109.
12 Habachi, 1984, p. 155.
13 Lehner, 1997, pp. 27, 29, 33, 108. Pyr. § 1278.
14 Pyr. §§ 1650, 1660-61. Cf §§ 1653-56.
15 Assmann, 2001, pp. 41-43. The holy of holies symbolised the primeval mound and the *akhet*.
16 Assmann, 2001, p. 43. This mystical union may have recurred during the night in respect of the stars, hence the descent of Osiris with his gods, see Morenz, 1973, pp. 151-52; Assmann, p. 42.
17 Morenz, 1973, p. 152; Assmann, 2001, pp. 42-45.
18 Assmann, 2001, pp. 43-44.
19 Pyr. § 1653.
20 The modern designation 'mortuary temple' is a misnomer. This building was a house of life for the reborn king. It probably signified the *duat* as an extension of the tomb or an interstitial realm between the earth and sky (as would later be described in the Books of the Netherworld).
21 Pyr. §§ 412, 414.
22 Pyr. §§ 1653-54. The opening of the mouth of the *ka*-statue each day caused the *ka* of the deceased king to rise up and fill the pyramid, in the same way that the *ka* of the chthonian creator-god was made to rise up and fill the temple.
23 On the permanence of reliefs and hieroglyphs, see Quirke, 2001, pp. 21-22. The sacred proportions of art were crucial to their cosmic symbolism.
24 Shaw & Nicholson, 1995, pp. 285-86. See also Alford, 2003, p. 23.
25 A notable theme in the pyramid names is the endurance of the king's soul , see Lehner, 1997, p. 24.
26 On the meaning of *sa Re*, see chapter seven. The title is first attested for Djedefre, the successor to Khufu.
27 Quirke, 2001, pp. 122-23, 127. The cartouche actually symbolised the circuit of the cosmos (see Lurker, 1980, p. 38; Shaw & Nicholson, 1995, p. 62.). It was solar in the sense of the sun repeating the creation.
28 Edwards, 1947, p. 284.
29 Breasted, 1912, pp. 15, 70-72; Quirke, 2001, p. 115. The feminine nature of the pyramidal *benben* is interesting in the light of our discussion of the *bnnt* in chapter fourteen.
30 Breasted, 1912, pp. 15, 72; Budge, 1925, pp. 452, 455; Lehner, 1997, p. 35; Quirke, 2001, p. 115.
31 Breasted, 1912, p. 73; Lehner, 1997, p. 34.
32 Breasted, 1912, pp. 15, 70-71; Budge, 1925, p. 452; Frankfort, *KAG*, 1948, p. 154; Lurker, 1980, pp. 90-91; Shaw & Nicholson, 1995, p. 208; Schulz & Seidel, 1998, p. 517.
33 Frankfort et al, 1946, p. 22; Frankfort, *KAG*, 1948, p. 153; Lurker, 1980, p. 96; Hart, 1990, p. 11; Schulz & Seidel, 1998, pp. 512, 517; Quirke, 2001, p. 115.
34 A. Moret, *Le Nil et la Civilisation Egyptienne*, 1926, p. 203, cited by I.E.S. Edwards, 1993, p. 282.
35 I.E.S. Edwards, 1993, p. 282.
36 Hart, 1990, p. 93; Lehner, 1997, pp. 6, 35, 105; El Mahdy, 2003, p. 158; Siliotti, 1997, pp. 13-14, 156; Quirke, 2001, p. 115.
37 Frankfort et al, 1946, p. 22; Frankfort, *KAG*, 1948, p. 153; Frankfort, *AER*, 1948, p. 156. This view was criticised by Edwards, 1947 (revised ed. 1993), pp. 279 ff, though he agreed that the mastaba did signify the primeval mound, p. 279.
38 Verner, 2002, pp. 28, 45; El Mahdy, 2003, pp. 157-58, 165. See also Hart, 1990, p. 87.
39 El Mahdy, 2003, p. 165.
40 Lehner, 1997, p. 35. Cf pp. 74, 235, 240. Several of Lehner's comments refer vaguely to the idea of creational symbolism, see pp. 9, 29, 35,
41 Breasted, 1912, p. 72; Habachi, 1984, pp. 5, 34, 63, 70-71, 110; Quirke, 2001, pp. 137-38.
42 Pyr. §§ 1248-49, 1652-53. In both spells Atum creates Shu and Tefnut.

43 Clark, 1959, pp. 39-40; Sellers, 1992, p. 89.
44 Bauval & Gilbert, 1994, pp. 88, 106; Bauval, 1989 (see Bauval, 1999, pp. 361-62); Quirke, 2001, p. 116.
45 Bauval, 1989 (see Bauval, 1999, pp. 361-62); Quirke, 2001, p. 25.
46 Faulkner, 1978, p. 50 note 27 (CT, VII, 96); Gardiner, 1994, p. 600; Habachi, 1984, pp. xiii, 70.
47 Pyr. §§ 1652-53. Cf §§ 1248-49.
48 Habachi, 1984, pp. xiii, 66, 70, 95, 182.
49 Lehner, 1997, p. 17; Quirke, 2001, p. 116.
50 Budge and Breasted both played down the stellar aspects of the Pyramid Texts, regarding them as a hangover and intrusion from a more ancient and primitive sky cult.
51 Edwards, 1947, pp. 284-85; Hart, 1991, p. 93; Lehner, 1997, pp. 112-13; Quirke, 2001, pp. 115-16. My scepticism is shared by Rudolf Gantenbrink. Our doubts are prompted by the various bends in the shafts and the builder's obsession with making them exit on the Pyramid's central north-south axis.
52 Edwards, 1947, p. 284; Lurker, 1980, pp. 92, 98; Lehner, 1997, p. 29; Schulz & Seidel, 1998, p. 57.
53 Lepre, 1990, p. 156, observes that the stars on the tomb ceilings were 'symbolic of the pharaoh's association with the astral [after-] life.'
54 Quirke, 2001, pp. 115-17.
55 Bauval & Gilbert, 1994, includes some excellent photographs of oriented iron meteorites.
56 Bauval, 1989 (see Bauval, 1999, pp. 356-65); Wilkinson expressed his ideas to a Bloomsbury archaeological summer school at University College London in 2001; see 'Pyramids seen as Stairways to Heaven', in *The Guardian*, London, 14th May 2001. On the conical shape of the *benben* stone, see chapter eleven, note 111.
57 Bauval, 1989 (see Bauval, 1999, p. 358).
58 Pyr. § 1653.
59 Pyr. §§ 1652-53.
60 One could be more controversial by arguing that Shu and Tefnut were the sun and the moon. The idea would then be that the pyramid represented the elements that would become the sun and the moon.
61 Lehner, 1997, p. 34.
62 Pyr. § 1652.
63 Some scholars claim that *benben* derived from *weben*, 'to rise'. This seems somewhat fanciful.
64 Frankfort, *KAG*, 1948, pp. 153, 380 note 26 (citing Sethe, *Amun*, p. 118).
65 Frankfort, *KAG*, 1948, pp. 153, 380-81 notes 26 & 27; Hart, 1990, p. 11.
66 Habachi, 1984, p. 66.
67 Pyr. §§ 1657-58. Note that the king himself is identified with the pyramid (Lehner, 1997, p. 34).
68 Breasted, 1912, pp. 73 note 3, 158.
69 Pyr. § 621. Cf §§ 585, 636, 645-46, 1887.
70 Pyr. § 636 (trans. Faulkner/Allen). See Allen, 1989, p. 19. Cf §§ 585, 1887.
71 Quirke, 2001, pp. 25, 117 (solar); Bauval & Gilbert, 1994, pp. 279-80 (stellar).
72 See Clark, 1959, p. 171.
73 Edwards, 1947, pp. 37, 280.

CHAPTER SIXTEEN: THE TOMB OF KHUFU

1 Budge, 1925, p. 406.
2 On the precision of the Great Pyramid, see Alford, 2003, pp. 41-45.
3 It ranks among man-made structures such as the Great Wall of China and the largest pyramid in Mexico. It was not rivalled in the modern era until the construction of Boulder Dam.
4 A.P. Sakovich, 'Counting the Stones', in *KMT*, 13:3 (Fall 2002), pp. 53-57. It is impossible to make an exact calculation, not least because the Pyramid is built around a nucleus of protruding bedrock.
5 M. Lehner, 1997, pp. 108-9, 206, cites an average weight per block of 2.5 tons, but p. 225 suggests that this figure requires further study (he hints at a downward adjustment).
6 Edwards, 1947 (revised ed. 1993), pp. xxii, 287, 291.
7 Z. Hawass in update to W.M.F. Petrie, *The Pyramids and Temples of Gizeh*, Histories & Mysteries of Man Ltd, London, 1990, pp. 99-100.
8 Lepre, 1990, p. 20; Lehner, 1997, p. 18; Edwards, 1947, p. 288; Breasted, 1912, pp. 72, 77, 80.
9 Pyr. § 1650.
10 Lehner, 1997, p. 34; Verner, 2002, p. 460.
11 Some scholars are cautious about applying the Pyramid Texts to periods prior to their time of origin in the late-5th dynasty. See, for example, Eyre, 2002, pp. 3, 17-19.
12 Lehner, 1997, pp. 17, 24, 108.

13 Shaw & Nicholson, 1995, p. 152; Lehner, 1997, p. 108. The second interpretation is mine.
14 Lehner, 1997, pp. 118-19.
15 Pyr. §§ 1209-10; CT, V, 73 ff; VI, 3 ff; BD, 99.
16 This theory is prompted by the image of the human-headed island on the Narmer palette. The head and body of the Sphinx have since been recarved.
17 In an inscription of later date, Giza is called 'the splendid place of the first time'.
18 I am indebted to Lepre for this insight. See Lepre, 1990, pp. 280-82.
19 Alford, 2003, pp. 185-94, 204.
20 Ibid., pp. 194-96, 204. On the head of Osiris, see Budge, 1911, I, pp. 54-56, 212-14; Budge, 1912, p. 230; Budge, 1934, pp. 107, 273; Lurker, 1980, p. 94.
21 Alford, 2003, pp. 200-4, 265.
22 Ibid., pp. 199, 203-4.
23 Ibid., pp. 111, 292, 297, 303, 311, 358, 379-80, 414; Lepre, 1990, pp. 79, 81.
24 Alford, 2003, pp. 313-69.
25 Stadelmann regards the chamber as symbolic of the underworld, see Lehner, 1997, p. 114.
26 In the 19th century, Vyse and Perring had the pit excavated to a depth of about 38 feet.
27 Lepre, 1990, p. 279.
28 The rocky outcrop rises about 22-25 feet above the Pyramid's exterior base, whilst the Grotto is buried about 10 feet deep in the outcrop.
29 Lepre, 1990, p. 117.
30 Ibid.
31 Ibid.
32 Ibid., pp. 117-18.
33 Herodotus, *The Histories*, Book II, 124.
34 Lepre, 1990, p. 118.
35 See P. Jordan, *Riddles of the Sphinx*, Sutton Publishing, 1998, p. 77.
36 The Well Shaft was cut from the top downwards, see Lepre, 1990, p. 117.
37 Lepre, 1990, p. 117. See also Petrie, op. cit., pp. 89, 92.
38 Alford, 2003, pp. 142-47. The most fatal objection to this theory is that the digging of the shaft would have provided a back door route to the supposed tomb. There is simply no way that the king would have authorised this.
39 I.E.S. Edwards, in a private letter to Robert Bauval in 1993, wrote: 'I believe it [the outcrop of rock underneath the Great Pyramid] represented the primeval mound on which life first appeared.'
40 The route comprises 323 feet of the Descending Passage and a 143 feet segment of the Well Shaft.
41 For an explanation of sections A-X, X-Y, and Y-Z, see Alford, 2003, pp. 144-46, 154-55, 284-88.
42 Lepre, 1990, p. 271.
43 On this axis too lies the sarcophagus in the King's Chamber.
44 The thought occurs that if there is a second grotto then its shape might have inspired the otherwise-inexplicable pattern of the Subterranean Chamber. In other words, the latter may have been modelled upon the former.
45 Lepre, 1990, pp. 287-88.

ABBREVIATIONS

Pyr. (or PT) = Pyramid Texts
CT = Coffin Texts
BD = Book of the Dead

Unless otherwise stated, Pyramid Texts translations are from Faulkner, 1969, Coffin Texts translations from Faulkner, 1973-78, and Book of the Dead translations from Faulkner, 1985.

BIBLIOGRAPHY

Alford, A.F., *Pyramid of Secrets*, Eridu Books, 2003.
Allen, J.P., *Genesis in Egypt: The Philosophy of Ancient Egyptian Creation Accounts*, YES 2, New Haven, Connecticut, 1988.
—— 'The Cosmology of the Pyramid Texts', in Simpson, W.K., ed., *Religion and Philosophy in Ancient Egypt*, YES 3, New Haven, Connecticut, 1989.
Assmann, J., *The Search for God in Ancient Egypt*, Cornell University Press, Ithaca & London, 2001 (first published in German, 1984).
—— 'State and Religion in the New Kingdom', in Simpson, W.K., ed., *Religion and Philosophy in Ancient Egypt*, YES 3, New Haven, Connecticut, 1989.
—— 'Death and Initiation in the Funerary Religion of Ancient Egypt', in Simpson, W.K., ed., *Religion and Philosophy in Ancient Egypt*, YES 3, New Haven, Connecticut, 1989.
Bauval, R., 'Investigation on the Origin of the Benben Stone: Was it an Iron Meteorite?', in *DE* 14 (1989), pp. 5-17.
—— *Secret Chamber*, Century, London, 1999.
Bauval, R. & Gilbert. A., *The Orion Mystery*, William Heinemann, London, 1994.
Betro, M.C., *Hieroglyphics: The Writings of Ancient Egypt*, Abbeville Press, New York, 1996.
Blackman, A.M., 'The rite of opening the mouth in ancient Egypt and Babylonia', in *JEA* 10 (1924), pp. 47-59.
Breasted, J.H., *Development of Religion and Thought in Ancient Egypt*, Charles Scribner, 1912 (reprinted by University of Pennsylvania Press, 1972).
Budge, E.A. Wallis, *Egyptian Religion*, 1899 (reprinted by Arkana, 1987).
—— *The Gods of the Egyptians*, 2 vols, Methuen & Co, London, 1904 (reprinted by Dover Publications, 1969).
—— *The Egyptian Heaven and Hell*, 3 vols, Kegan Paul, Trench, Trubner & Co Ltd, London, 1905 (reprinted by Dover Publications, 1996).
—— *Osiris and the Egyptian Resurrection*, 2 vols, Medici Society, 1911 (reprinted by Dover Publications, 1973).
—— *Legends of the Egyptian Gods*, Kegan Paul, Trench, Trubner & Co Ltd, London, 1912 (reprinted by Dover Publications, 1994).
—— *The Mummy*, 2nd edition, 1925 (reprinted by Dover Publications, 1989).
—— *From Fetish to God in Ancient Egypt*, Oxford University Press, 1934.
Clark, R.T. Rundle, *Myth and Symbol in Ancient Egypt*, Thames and Hudson, 1959.
David, R., *Religion and Magic in Ancient Egypt*, Penguin Books, 2002.
Davis, V.L., 'Identifying Ancient Egyptian Constellations', in *Archaeoastronomy* 9 (1985).
Edwards, I.E.S., *The Pyramids of Egypt*, Penguin Books, London, 1947 (revised edition, 1993).
Eliade, M., *The Myth of the Eternal Return*, Princeton University Press, 1954 (first published in French, 1949).
—— *The Sacred and the Profane*, Harcourt Brace Jovanovich, London, 1959.
El Mahdy, C., *The Pyramid Builder: Cheops, the Man Behind the Great Pyramid*, Headline, London, 2003.
Eyre, C., *The Cannibal Hymn*, Liverpool University Press, 2002.

Faulkner, R.O., *The Ancient Egyptian Pyramid Texts*, Oxford University Press, 1969.
—— *The Ancient Egyptian Coffin Texts*, 3 vols, Aris & Phillips, Warminster, 1973, 1977, 1978.
—— *The Ancient Egyptian Book of the Dead*, British Museum Publications, 1985.
—— 'The King and the Star-Religion in the Pyramid Texts', in *JNES 25* (1966), pp. 153-61.
Frankfort, H. et al, *The Intellectual Adventure of Ancient Man*, University of Chicago Press, Chicago & London, 1946.
Frankfort, H., *Kingship and the Gods*, University of Chicago Press, Chicago & London, 1948 (reprinted 1978).
—— *Ancient Egyptian Religion: An Interpretation*, Columbia University Press, New York, 1948 (reprinted by Dover Publications, 2000).
Gardiner, A., *Egyptian Grammar*, Third Edition Revised, Griffith Institute, Ashmolean Museum, Oxford, 1994.
Griffiths, J.G., *The Conflict of Horus and Seth from Egyptian and Classical Sources*, Liverpool University Press, Liverpool, 1960.
Habachi, L., *The Obelisks of Egypt – Skyscrapers of the Past*, The American University in Cairo Press, Cairo, 1984.
Hart, G., *Egyptian Myths*, British Museum Press, London, 1990.
—— *Pharaohs and Pyramids*, The Herbert Press, London, 1991.
Hoffman, M.A., *Egypt Before The Pharaohs*, 1979 (reprinted by Barnes & Noble, 1993).
Hornung, E., *Conceptions of God in Ancient Egypt: the One and the Many*, Cornell University Press, Ithaca, New York, 1982 (first published in German, 1971).
—— *The Ancient Egyptian Books of the Afterlife*, Cornell University Press, 1999.
—— *The Secret Lore of Egypt*, Cornell University Press, 2001 (first published in German, 1999).
James, E.O., *The Ancient Gods*, Weidenfeld & Nicolson Ltd, 1960 (reprinted by Phoenix, Orion Books, 1999).
Lehner, M., *The Complete Pyramids*, Thames and Hudson, London, 1997.
Le Page Renouf, P., *Lectures on the Origin and Growth of Religion as Illustrated by the Religion of Ancient Egypt*, London, 1880, 4th edition, 1897.
Lepre, J.P., *The Egyptian Pyramids*, McFarland & Co, Jefferson, 1990.
Lurker, M., *The Gods and Symbols of Ancient Egypt, An Illustrated Dictionary*, Thames and Hudson, 1980 (first published in German, 1974).
Massey, G., *Ancient Egypt: The Light of the World*, 2 vols, T. Fisher Unwin, London, 1907.
Meeks, D. & Favard-Meeks, C., *Daily Life of the Egyptian Gods*, John Murray, 1997 (first published in French, 1993).
Morenz, S., *Egyptian Religion*, Cornell University Press, Ithaca, New York, 1973 (first published in German, 1960).
Naydler, J., *Temple of the Cosmos*, Inner Traditions, Rochester, Vermont, 1996.
Neugebauer, O. & Parker, R., *Egyptian Astronomical Texts*, Vols 1-3, Brown University Press, Providence, 1960-69.
Pleyte, W. & Rossi, F., *Papyrus de Turin*, Leiden, 1876.
Pritchard, J.B. ed., *Ancient Near Eastern Texts Relating to the Old Testament*, Third Edition with Supplement, Princeton University Press, 1969.
Quirke, S., *Who were the Pharaohs?*, British Museum Press, London, 1990.
—— *The Cult of Ra*, Thames and Hudson, London, 2001.
Reymond E.A.E., 'Worship of the Ancestor Gods at Edfu', in *CdE* 38 (1963), pp. 49-70.
—— 'A Late Edfu Theory on the Nature of God', in *CdE* 40 (1965), pp. 61-71.
—— *The Mythical Origin of the Egyptian Temple*, Manchester University Press, 1969.
Rice, M., *Egypt's Making*, Guild/Routledge, London, 1990.
—— *The Power of the Bull*, Routledge, London & New York, 1998.
Ritner, R.K., 'Horus on the Crocodiles: A Juncture of Religion and Magic in Late Dynastic Egypt', in Simpson, W.K., ed., *Religion and Philosophy in Ancient Egypt*, YES 3, New Haven, Connecticut, 1989.
Roth, A.M., 'The Pss-kf and the "Opening of the Mouth" Ceremony: A Ritual of Birth and Rebirth', in *JEA* 78 (1992), pp. 113-47.
—— 'Fingers, Stars and the "Opening of the Mouth": The Nature and Function of *Ntrwj*-blades' in *JEA* 79 (1993), pp. 57-80.
Sandman-Holmberg, M., *The God Ptah*, Lund, 1946.

BIBLIOGRAPHY 423

Sauneron, S., & Yoyotte, J., 'La Naissance du monde selon l'Egypte ancienne', in *Sources orientales, I: La Naissance du monde*, Paris, 1959, pp. 17-91.
Schulz, R., & Seidel, M., eds., *Egypt: The World of the Pharaohs*, Konemann, 1998.
Sellers, J.B., *The Death of Gods in Ancient Egypt*, Penguin Books, London, 1992.
Sethe, K., *Amun und die acht Urgotter von Hermopolis*, APAW, 1929: 4, Berlin, 1929.
Shafer, B.E., ed., *Temples of Ancient Egypt*, Cornell University Press, 1997 (I.B. Tauris edition, 1998).
—— Religion in Ancient Egypt: Gods, Myths and Personal Practice, New York and London, 1991.
Shaw, I. & Nicholson P, *British Museum Dictionary of Ancient Egypt*, British Museum Press, London, 1995.
Siliotti, A., *The Pyramids*, Weidenfeld & Nicolson, London, 1997.
Simpson, W.K., *The Literature of Ancient Egypt*, Yale University Press, New Haven, 1973.
Tompkins, P., *Secrets of the Great Pyramid*, Harper & Row, New York, 1971.
—— *The Magic of Obelisks*, Harper & Row, New York, 1981.
Velde, H.T., *Seth: God of Confusion*, E.J. Brill, London, 1967.
Verner, M., *The Pyramids: Their Archaeology and History*, Atlantic Books, London, 2002 (first published in Czech, 1997).
Wainwright, G.A., *The Sky Religion in Egypt*, University Press, Cambridge, 1938 (Greenwood Press edition, 1971).
—— 'Iron in Egypt', in *JEA* 18 (1932), pp. 3-15.
—— 'Letopolis', in *JEA* 18 (1932), pp. 159-72.
—— 'Some Aspects of Amun', in *JEA* 20 (1934), pp. 139-53.
—— 'The Origins of Storm-Gods in Egypt', in *JEA* 49 (1963), pp. 13-20.
—— 'The Origins of Amun', in *JEA* 49 (1963), pp. 21-23.
—— 'A Pair of Constellations' in *Studies for F. Ll. Griffith*, 1932.
—— 'Amun's Meteorite and Omphali', in *ZAS* (1935).
—— 'Orion and the Great Star', in *JEA* 21 (1936).
—— 'Some Celestial Associations of Min', in *JEA* 21 (1935), pp. 152-70.
—— 'The Emblem of Min', in *JEA* 17 (1931), pp. 185-95.
Watterson, B., *Gods of Ancient Egypt*, Batsford, 1984 (reprinted by Sutton Publishing, 1996).
—— *The House of Horus at Edfu: Ritual in an Ancient Egyptian Temple*, Stroud, Tempus, 1998.
Wilkinson, R.H., *Reading Egyptian Art*, Thames and Hudson, London, 1992.
Wilkinson, T., *Genesis of the Pharaohs*, Thames and Hudson, 2003.
Wilson, H., *People of the Pharaohs*, Michael O'Mara, London, 1997.

GREAT PYRAMID

For a complete reading list on the Great Pyramid, see the Bibliography in the companion volume to this book.

ABBREVIATIONS

APAW Abhandlungen der Preussischen Akademie der Wissenschaften, Phil.-hist. Klasse (Berlin).
BIFAO Bulletin de l'Institut Francais d'Archeologie Orientale (Cairo).
CdE Chronique d'Egypte (Brussels).
DE, Discussions in Egyptology (Oxford).
JARCE Journal of the American Research Center in Egypt (Boston).
JEA Journal of Egyptian Archaeology (London).
JNES Journal of Near Eastern Studies (Chicago)
YES = Yale Egyptological Studies (New Haven, Connecticut).
ZAS Zeitschrift fur Agyptische Sprache und Altertumskunde (Berlin).

INDEX

Aa (Shebtiu-god) 56
Abydos 92, 117, 223, 226, 275, 309, 328 (see also Fetish of; Thinite district)
Adzes 29, 130, 132, 166-67, 181-84, 187-88, 215, 219, 221-24, 226-27, 251, 267, 275, 290-91 (see also God's Castle adze; Iron)
Aha 143
Aker 9, 93, 193, 374
Akeru 10, 44, 233, 404, 408
Akh (spirit) 15, 17, 27, 74, 79-80, 82, 88, 92, 98, 103, 108, 112, 123-24, 128-30, 133-34, 153-54, 160, 168, 175, 178, 180, 196, 206, 211, 215, 232, 238, 265, 290, 301, 322, 344
Akhenaten 312, 320
Akhet 8, 12, 14-19, 22, 40-41, 46, 49, 61, 63, 73, 82, 89-90, 92, 104-5, 125-28, 133-36, 141, 153, 159-61, 168, 172, 175-80, 191-95, 202-4, 212, 232-34, 247, 258, 263, 289, 293, 304-6, 328-30, 343-47 (see also Inner akhet; Lord of the Akhet)
Allah 310
Allegorical astronomy 174
Allen, J.P. 35-36, 68, 114-17, 120-23, 126, 138, 209, 218, 372
Al-Mamun 364
Amarna age 312
Amaunet 53, 60, 314, 320
Amenemhet II 145
Amenemhet III 144, 151, 334, 336-37 (see also Pyramidion)
Amenhotep II 144, 150
Ament (land of the west) 10, 13-14, 62, 89, 99, 123-24, 138, 170, 176, 186-87, 190-91, 215, 217, 228, 230, 233, 262-63
Amun
- creator-god 53-55, 66, 87, 96, 99, 104-5, 119-20, 131, 140, 240-42, 313, 324, 355
- body and soul of 355
- transcendent and immanent 97, 355
- as a bull 230
- god of the ka-mut.ef (bull of his mother) 240-42

- paired with Amaunet and Mut 314, 316
- a he-she 319
- obelisk inscription 343
- member of Ogdoad 60, 320
Amun-Re 141, 189, 245, 309, 319
Anaxagoras 275
Andjet 81
Andjeti 84, 407
Aner (stone) 274-75
Animals, creation of 45-46, 62, 275, 277-78, 281
Animism 157
Ankh 162, 317
Anpet 314
Anubis 10, 14, 79, 81, 163, 182, 187, 193, 212, 220, 231, 279, 314, 387
Apep 3-4, 14, 41, 90, 203, 261
Apis bull 204, 229, 230, 402 (see also Meadow of Apis)
Apuleius, Lucius 91
Arrows 62, 150, 316-17
Assembly of cities and districts 73, 170, 289, 301
Assembly of the gods 44, 60, 73, 78, 95, 103, 105-13, 136, 163-64, 170, 172, 176, 185, 196, 231-32, 265, 287, 291, 296, 312, 321, 329
Assembly of land 247, 259, 289, 301, 403
Assembly of waters 301
Assmann, Jan 39, 92, 94, 372
Aswan 52
Aten 144, 150, 296, 319-20
Atlantis, lost civilisation of 326
Atum
- created Shu and Tefnut 38, 41-43, 96, 188, 242, 249-52, 276, 278, 280
- created the gods 189
- sent out his Eye 39-40, 253, 269-70
- came into being in the sky with his Eye 141, 264, 266
- became Re 40-41, 64, 207
- Lord of All, Lord to the Limit 38

INDEX   425

- signified non-being and completion 38, 55
- a chthonian power 72-75
- emerged from earth 72-73, 136, 185
- emerged from nun 39-41, 73, 86, 121, 126
- ascended from field of reeds 19
- emerged from akhet 16, 18, 41, 73, 108, 134
- traversed nun and duat to reach field of reeds and akhet 41
- ascended from lower waters to upper waters 41, 44, 121
- knitted seed together 273
- assembled the cities and districts of Geb 73, 170, 289, 301
- earth issued from 72, 96, 167, 247
- eyes issued from 270
- Eye went forth from his head? 268, 274
- body of 108-9, 270
- flood of 44, 126-27
- identified with celestial ocean 41-42, 44, 119, 121, 126-27, 391
- identified with setting sun 46, 67-68, 92, 98
- fingers and fingernail of 224, 406
- paired in cult with Iusaas 314
- a he-she 319, 324
- children of 107, 110, 123
- gods assembled for 95, 110
- obelisks dedicated to 334, 337
- pharaoh identified with 145-46
- father of the reborn king 158, 176, 180, 251
- protector of the reborn king and his pyramid 180, 331, 341
- see also Atum-Kheprer; Eye of Atum; Heliopolis; Limbs; Re-Atum
Atum-Kheprer
- became the high hill and the benben stone 38-39, 116, 188, 242, 246-47, 249, 252, 257, 336, 338, 342
- created Shu and Tefnut and gave them his ka 38, 43, 161, 188, 242, 249, 338, 341
- see also Benben stone
Ausars 96

Ba (soul) 26-27, 33, 41-44, 46, 63, 71, 73, 76, 80, 88-89, 93-99, 101-3, 105-7, 111-13, 120, 123-24, 127-28, 130, 133, 141, 146-48, 150, 155, 158, 165-67, 174-75, 180-82, 184, 207, 232, 254, 269-70, 273, 314, 323-24, 329-30, 333, 336-37, 347-48
Babi 160, 195, 239, 408
Baboons 228
Ba-ka 22, 217-18, 227
Banks 16, 19, 22, 32, 81, 126, 134, 211, 304-5, 415
Barque, model in temple shrine 329
Barque of the earth 132-33, 136, 185, 407
Barque of Khepri 122, 136, 185
Barque of Osiris 117

Barque of Re 14, 17, 21, 25, 27, 30, 32, 89-91, 93, 100, 122, 129, 132, 135-36, 159, 172-73, 177, 191, 194, 203, 208, 217, 292
Barque of the Two Enneads 30, 32
Bastet 145
Bathing/cleansing 13, 16, 19, 21, 23-24, 124, 139, 152-53, 161, 163, 170, 177, 221
Battles of the gods
- battlefield of the gods 263
- slaughterings of the Two Lands 300-1
- battle in the netherworld 14, 263
- battle in the island of trampling 76, 263
- battle on the hill in Hermopolis 41, 287, 291
- battle in the sky 292-93, 414
- that day, that night 203, 233, 283
- Horus versus Seth and his followers - see Horus of Behdet; Horus rival of Seth; Seth
- Re versus the serpent 3-4, 14, 41, 70, 90, 203, 261, 401
- re-enacted in the netherworld every night 92-93
Battlements of the sky 266
Bauval, Robert 157, 340, 415
Bee 123
Beetle - see Scarab
Benben Stone of Heliopolis
- manifestation of Atum 38, 43, 116, 188, 226, 242, 246, 249-50, 318, 334, 338, 342
- semen of Atum theory 244, 252, 341-43
- bnbn etymology 245, 342
- meteorite theory 226, 243-44, 251-52, 340
- primeval mound theory 242, 244-46, 334, 338, 341-42
- solar theory 243-44, 334, 336, 341
- stellar theory 244
- phallic symbol 244-45, 248, 252, 336-38, 343
- creational symbol 246, 248, 251-52, 337-38, 342-43
- see also Temple of the Benben
Benbenet (pyramidion) 244, 334, 338, 341, 345, 347
Benu-bird 38, 42, 242-43, 246, 342
Berlin Hymn to Ptah (Papyrus 3048) 50-51, 69, 86, 300-1, 313
Berlin Papyrus 13603 69
Big Bang 321
Big Dipper - see Plough
Bja - see Iron
Blacksmith-gods 221, 274, 293
Blood 62, 280, 410
Bnnt
- seed 245-46, 317-18
- ovum 57-59, 317-18
Bnwt (stone) 404
Body-soul duality - see Copulation; Gods; Great God; Osiris; King, Deceased and reborn; Re

Bones
- of the gods 232-33
- of iron - see Iron
- of Shu 251
Book of Caverns 89, 99, 191
Book of the Dead 20, 182, 237, 330
Book of the Earth 89, 99
Book of Gates 89, 111, 122, 132-33, 191, 263
Book of the Heavenly Cow 47, 100, 137, 236, 261-62, 313
Book of the Hidden Chamber (Am Duat) 89, 99, 123-24, 192
Books of the Netherworld 9, 13-14, 17, 30, 88-90, 93, 99, 123-24, 132, 148, 190-92
Book of Nut 4, 23, 92, 123, 190, 218
Breasted, James H. 35, 155-57, 339, 419
Bremner-Rhind Papyrus 44, 104, 188
British Museum Papyrus 10059
Buddha 310
Budge, E.A. Wallis 156-57, 209, 271, 296, 339, 419
Builder-gods 412
Bull
- of Min 240-41
- Re as 407
- Bull of Re 228-29
- Seth as 229, 231, 284, 286-87
- Eye of 228, 251
- eyes of 234
- foreleg of 29, 167, 182-83, 229, 232-34, 284, 287
- sacrifice of 229-32, 252
- chthonian symbol 132, 228-29, 233, 405
- linked symbolically with pillar 168, 228, 234, 244-46
- king re-enacted creation as a bull 168, 228-29, 232-34, 236, 244, 251-52
- deceased re-enacted creation as a bull 62
- bull as creator-god and personification of creation myth 58, 229-30, 232-33, 237, 240-42, 252, 320
- see also Apis bull; Calf; Eating the bull; Great Bull; Great Wild Bull; Heliopolis; Horns; Mnevis bull; Testicles; Thighs; Stars, circumpolar
Bull of Bulls 229
Bull of the Ennead 234, 280
Bull of the Gods 228
Bull of the Hnmmt 234, 239
Bull of Millions 234
Bull of Nedyt 230
Bull of Re 228-29, 233
Bull of the Sky
- name of god 229
- epithet of Geb 73, 229, 237, 248, 313, 318
- epithet of king 168, 228-29, 232-34, 239-40, 244

Bull of the Two Enneads 229, 234
Bull of the West 230, 239
Busiris (Djedu) 88, 280, 294

Calf 138, 237-38
Cannibal Hymn 229, 231-33, 267
Canopus 31-32, 129, 174, 372
Cartouche 144, 334, 395, 418
Castle of the mace 33, 291, 414
Cat - see Bastet
Cauldron 29, 233
Causeways of the sky 288, 305
Caverns 11, 52, 61, 89, 106, 191-92, 263, 315, 405 (see also Book of Caverns)
Celestial ocean - see Nun
Champollion, J.-F. 309
Chaos - see Isfet
Chemmis 397
Cheops - see Khufu
Chester Beatty Papyrus 295-96, 308
Children of Impotence 40-41, 287, 291
Circuit of the Walls ritual 150, 298, 308
Cities of Geb 73, 170, 289, 301, 415
City as primeval mound 246, 258, 328
City metaphor 21, 72, 81, 87, 140, 185, 204, 213, 229, 234, 236, 258, 274, 284, 290-91, 306-7, 316, 377, 387
City of Nut 258, 265, 316
Clark, R.T. Rundle 67, 255, 272, 276, 296, 372
Clearing the sky 176, 202, 206-8, 221, 272, 281
Clouds (cosmic phenomenon)
- rain-clouds 169, 200, 202, 204, 206-8
- storm-clouds 185-86, 199, 202, 204-8, 221, 228, 234, 250-51, 281
- plant-like clouds 271-73, 277
Cobra 235, 254, 261, 266-67
Coffin - see Nut
Coffin Texts 9
Contendings of Horus and Seth 295-98
Copernicus, Nicolaus 7
Copulation, soul with body 88, 188, 239, 321, 324-25, 417
Copulation with the sky 239, 273
Cosmos
- described 1-2, 7-8, 10, 114, 119
- system of maintenance 2-6, 102, 151-53, 178-80, 328, 348
Cows 25-26, 58, 61, 235-36, 240, 320 (see also Great Wild Cow; Hathor; Mehet-weret; Nut)
Cox, Simon 372
Creation myth
- review of myths 34-65
- re-enacted in nature iii, 2
- re-enacted by stars 2
- re-enacted by sun - see Sun
- re-enacted by king - see King

INDEX   427

- new interpretation summarised iii, 64-68, 94-97, 113, 117-18, 141, 180-81, 198-200, 208-10, 227, 252, 280-81, 283, 308, 315, 319, 324-25, 340-41, 346
Creator-god defined 36-37, 64-65, 116, 118, 146, 232, 315 (see also Great God)
Creator-goddess - see Great Goddess
Crowns of Upper and Lower Egypt 73, 140, 142, 150, 261, 265, 267-68, 303, 323
Cult of creation defined iii, 65, 327, 340

Dahshur i-iii, 332-34
David, Rosalie 283
Day-barque 82, 129, 134, 136, 139, 185, 270, 393
Death and rebirth
- in nature iii
- in the sky iii, 30, 32
- of the sun 4, 76, 90, 93-94
- of the cosmos 71, 76-85, 93-97, 134-35, 146, 153, 158-59, 177, 180, 231-32, 315, 321-25, 341, 344
Decapitation 21, 231, 262, 295
Dendera 61-62, 314
Desert 261
Destruction of Mankind 100, 261-63
Diodorus Siculus 83
Dismemberment - see Limbs
Djeba-perch 56, 70, 76
Djedefre 334, 339
Djed-pillar 51, 71, 76, 162, 279, 294
Djedu - see Busiris
Djer 143
Djet - see Neheh
Djsr (verb) 207, 403
Djt-embodiment 57-58, 60, 289
Doors
- of the nun 11, 192, 198, 402
- of the earth/Geb 14, 89, 192-94, 198, 212, 218-19
- of the coffin and tomb 194-95, 197
- of the duat 14, 18, 33, 89, 123-24, 192, 197-98, 218
- of the akhet 15, 22, 126-27, 136, 152, 171, 175, 192-94, 247
- of Ba-ka 22, 217-18, 227
- of the sky and qebhu 22-24, 127, 135, 152, 168, 171, 175, 178, 185-86, 192-97, 205, 211, 218-19, 247, 402
- of the starry sky 195-96
- of the celestial expanses 195-96
- of Nut (sky) 25, 192, 195-98
- of Nut (duat) 124
- of the Eye 257, 315
- of the lotus 194
- creational interpretation 192, 197
Dress of Hathor 61, 273, 401

Ds (flint or iron) 274
Duat
- archaic name for sky 12
- a region of the sky 12, 229
- netherworld, birthplace of the sky 8, 10-14, 17, 25, 32, 50, 53, 71, 74, 76, 82, 89-93, 115, 117, 122-26, 132-35, 153, 159, 161, 174-76, 178-80, 186, 190-91, 196, 204, 218, 228-29, 233, 258, 263, 329-30, 340-41, 344, 346-47
Duotheism 312, 325

Earth (ta) 9-12, 36, 65, 68, 72, 96, 134, 145, 167, 171, 176, 225, 246-47, 255, 278, 281 (see also Aker; Geb; Geocentrism; Mound(s); Primeval mound; Ta-tenen)
Earth-hill (kha n ta) 170
Earth quaked at ascents of gods/king 168, 171, 175, 186, 195-97, 200-1, 204-5, 208, 218, 220, 233, 252, 282, 290-92, 294, 323 (see also Geb, voice of; Nut, voice of)
Earth split open 186-87, 191-92, 198, 205-6, 215, 220, 223, 228, 233-34, 249, 252 (see also Mountain)
Earth hacked up 186, 196-97, 205-6, 290 (see also Hoeing the earth ritual)
Earth lifted to the sky 248 (see also Geb)
Eating the bull 229, 231-32, 252
Eating the gods 228, 231-32, 252, 261, 323
Eclipses of sun and moon 28, 157, 282
Edfu 55-60, 69, 75, 106, 178, 274, 314
Edfu Building Texts 55, 69, 75, 104, 131, 199, 287, 289, 317
Edwards, I.E.S. 335, 352, 420
Efflux (material)
- of Osiris 226
- of Shu 202, 250, 280
Egg of creation 42-43, 46, 49, 54-55, 57-60, 62-64, 75, 99, 106, 120, 136, 187, 208, 213-15, 219-20, 224, 227, 274-75, 313, 317-20, 324, 328 (see also Island of the egg)
Egyptology
- Judaeo-Christian and Western bias ii-iii, 20, 34-35, 65, 83, 157, 309-10
- theory of Egyptian religion ii-iii, v, 36-37, 64, 67, 84, 146, 156, 244, 309-10
- view of creation myth vi, 34-36, 64-67, 69, 92-93, 114-18, 146, 149, 189, 340
- view of Atum and Kheprer 67, 115, 244, 334, 336
- view of Re 64, 66-67, 84, 90, 115, 144, 146, 149, 156, 244
- view of Osiris 80-81, 83-84, 90, 93, 144, 156, 343
- view of the gods 105, 108, 312
- view of battles of the gods 203, 282-83
- view of meteorite cult 226

- theories of the benben stone 242-44, 334
- theory of obelisks 334
- theories of pyramids ii-iii, v, 333-35, 343-44
- theory of Great Pyramid v, 351-53
- view of kingship 144-49
- view of unification of the Two Lands 299-300
- view of opening the mouth 183-84
- view of Pyramid Texts 155-57, 339
- view of Books of the Netherworld 90
- view of king breaking out of the earth 186, 194, 234
- view of the storm 200-1
- view of the akhet 344
- view of the island of fire 267
Electrum 224, 275, 298, 343
Elephantine 52, 328, 382, 397
Eliade, Mircea 231, 372
El Mahdy, Christine 335, 349, 370, 372
Elysian fields 20, 400, 415
Enigmatic Book of the Netherworld 89-90
Ennead 10, 28, 39-42, 45-46, 73, 97, 103-11, 129-30, 136, 160, 202, 234, 280, 288, 293, 295-96, 302, 307, 311, 322, 326 (see also Bull of; Great ennead; Two enneads)
End of time 126, 150, 155, 260, 348
Epagomenal days 204
Erman, Adolf 157, 310
Esna 63, 328
Evil 79, 163, 180, 203, 217, 287
Expansion of the heart 252, 285, 408, 413 (see also Heart)
Extraterrestrial visitation theory 326-27
Eye of Atum
- sent out by Atum 39-40, 253, 256-57
- sent out by Atum to find Shu and Tefnut 44-45, 254-55, 269-70, 276, 313
- lifted by Shu 141, 269
- surrounded Atum with fire in the sky 141, 266
- fiery rage pacified by Shu 207, 254, 270-71
- fire quenched by Re's tears 276-77
- gods came into being from it 108, 254
- breathed fire against Seth 263
- maggots in 276
- misidentified as the sun 254-56
Eye of Horus
- attacked by Seth but rescued by Horus 28, 49, 152, 165-66, 183, 202-3, 253, 259-60, 263-64, 283-84
- dismembered but reassembled 109, 253, 257-59, 263, 265, 273, 284, 315
- rebuilt by Horus 257-58
- restored by Thoth 258-59, 271
- contained waters and all the produce of the earth (the offerings) 140, 152, 165-67, 182-83, 254, 257, 271, 277, 300, 315
- possessed doors 257, 315
- lifted by Horus 141

- lifted by Thoth 28, 263-64, 268, 291
- lifted by Seth 294
- lifted to the sky to Atum 254, 264-66, 268
- issued from the earth 140-41
- issued from the head of Geb 73, 140, 267
- emerged from the mouth of Re 141, 189, 323
- created in fire 266
- created fire in sky and earth 266
- became a fiery uraeus 266
- epithet City of Nut 140, 258
- epithet Great of Magic 267, 324
- epithets Opener of Roads and She who Opens the Ways of the God 166, 269
- children of 260, 265
- fear of 253, 260-63
- fiery destroyer of gods 253, 255, 260-62, 265-66
- injury and healing reflected in phases of the moon 28, 281, 284
- tears of 276
- identified with Hathor 266
- misidentified as the moon 254-56
- presented to Osiris-the-king, split open his mouth, revivified him 164-67, 181-83, 254, 260, 284, 314
- split open that Osiris-the-king might see 166, 269
- Osiris-the-king reborn as 160, 266
- protected the pharaoh 267
- in the duat 14
Eye of Neber-djer
- sent out by Neber-djer 188-89, 256, 322
- brought to Neber-djer by Shu and Tefnut 45, 270-71, 277
- fiery wrath 272
- wept on his limbs and caused birth of mankind, animals and plants 45, 254, 275-76, 278, 281
Eye of Re
- fiery wrath 272, 277
- destroyer of gods 254-55, 261-63, 267
- gave birth to an uraeus 266
- fire quenched by its tears 276-77
- pacified by Thoth 271, 277
- Thoth raised the hair from it 272, 277
- supported on the horns of Hathor 172, 235
- union with Re? 313
- identified with Wadjyt, Lady of Flame 261, 267
- identified with Hathor 100, 261-62, 316
- identified with Sekhmet 261, 263
- identified with Mut 261
- identified with the lone star 267
- fiery rage manifested in the sun 277-78, 281
- generated the moon too 172
- misidentified as the sun 27, 254-56
- Osiris-the-king reborn as 160, 172

- name of Thebes 258
Eye of Re-Atum 271, 278
Eye of the bull 228, 251
Eyes
- designated the sun and the moon 28, 45-47, 49, 56, 58, 82, 102, 138-41, 207, 228, 234, 267-74, 281, 285, 336, 411
- identified with Shu and Tefnut 270, 411
- created by the Eye 49, 73-74, 140-41, 165-67, 253-55, 265-76, 315, 323-24
- lifted by Thoth 141
- appeared in the head of Osiris 82, 139-40, 268
- issued from the head of Nut 139-40, 268
- issued as crowns from the head of Osiris 267
- originated from the earth 58, 140-41, 274
- originated in fire 274
- planted in the earth 278, 295
- gave birth to mankind 276
- epithet Great of Magic 324, 413
- guided Osiris-the-king to the sky 166, 170, 323
- see also Khenti-irti

Faience 300
Falcon 25, 47-49, 55-56, 61-62, 70-71, 75-76, 98, 102, 139, 143, 147, 169, 197, 219, 229, 234-35, 265-66, 315
Fall of the sky 277-81, 300
Far-strider 31
Feathers 21, 48, 214, 235, 264, 321
Feet
- of Horus and Seth 290
- of reborn king 166, 168-70, 175, 177, 323, 414
Ferryboat/ferryman 11, 17, 19-21, 176, 228, 244, 263, 387
Fetish of Abydos 223
Fetishism 157
Field of the ka 161
Field of Kheprer 21
Field of life 24
Field of offerings
- below the horizon 17, 19-22, 24, 126, 159-60, 176-78, 228-29, 233, 262
- name of the sky 23-25, 47, 105, 160, 178-79, 210, 275
Field of reeds
- below the horizon 17-22, 24, 126, 135, 159-60, 170, 175-78, 209, 218, 288, 344
- region of the sky 24-25, 47, 160, 178-79, 193, 210, 275
- in Edfu creation myth 56, 76
Field of strife 258, 263
Field of turquoise 275
Fields of khakha 24
Fields of Re in Iasu 24-25
Fiery place of the ancestors 263

Fingers 221, 223-25, 258-59, 297-98, 313
Fire
- fiery blast of Atum 43, 252, 267
- fiery blast at opening of the mouth 251
- fiery breath of Horus 207-8
- at ascent of gods/king 195, 205-6, 290, 306, 402
- in the sky 141, 171, 186, 200, 205-7, 266
- see also Island of fire; Eye of Atum; Eye of Horus; Eye of Re
First cause 321-25
First time - see Zep tepi
Flood
- of nun 11, 36, 39, 43-44, 46, 48, 52, 86, 104, 120-21, 126-27, 136, 141, 164, 177, 194, 197-98, 206, 219-20, 248, 277
- of fields 19-21, 32, 56, 126, 135, 176-77
- of akhet 127-28, 135-36, 171, 194, 247, 344
- of sky 126, 135-37, 208, 236
- of Nut 25
- of Osiris 78, 81-82, 164, 170-71, 187, 194, 196
- see also Mehet-weret; Night of the great flood; Re, epithet Great Flood
Flood, The Great 326
Followers of Horus 21, 177, 293
Followers of Osiris 24, 28
Followers of Re 28, 40, 45, 100, 105
Followers of Shu 202
Foreleg - see Bull; Seth; Stars, circumpolar
Foundry of the sun-disc at Edfu 274
Four sons of Horus - see Horus
Fractions, system of 259
Frankfort, Henri 35, 66, 69, 78, 92, 156-57, 223, 244-45, 283, 299, 335-36, 372
Frogs 60, 66, 137, 383 (see also Heket)

Gardiner, Alan 274
Geb
- earth-god 9, 14, 42, 44, 49, 73-74, 115, 121-22, 132, 134, 140-41, 168, 176, 185-86, 192-93, 196-97, 207, 212-13, 238, 247-49, 264, 286-90, 292, 302, 316
- creator-god 73-75, 104, 110, 140, 193, 214, 311, 313, 316, 321
- son of Shu and Tefnut 73
- father of Osiris 102, 147, 238
- father of Horus 102, 147
- sole great god and ka of all the gods 73, 132
- assembled the gods for Osiris 111
- found, assembled and revivified Osiris 74, 78-79, 81-82, 163
- assembled Atum 39-40, 73, 109-10
- knit together the Two Lands for Atum 43, 73, 85
- gathered together the flood for Atum 43, 73, 127

- lifted the heart of Atum 39, 73, 86
- laid the cosmic egg as goose 54, 74-75
- lifted the Eye 254, 264
- Eye went forth from his head 73, 140, 254, 265, 267-68
- gods issued from his head 74
- fertilized Nut in the earth 125, 237-38, 313, 316-19, 321
- went up to the sky 101, 238, 248, 252, 279
- married Nut in the sky 39, 237-38, 248, 252, 313, 318
- Bull of Nut 73, 248
- raped Tefnut 248
- spirits of 73, 112
- four regional spirits of 160, 177, 264, 379
- mouth of 193, 250
- voice of 73, 205, 292
- gods the fathers and mothers of 320
- corpse of 93, 99

Geocentrism iii, 7, 33, 68-94, 117-18, 122, 126, 128, 133-35, 138, 141, 157, 159-60, 181, 185-87, 189, 199, 204, 210, 216, 226-27, 234, 246, 249-50, 260, 264, 273, 292, 301, 315, 321

Ghsty 81

Giza
- plateau and environs i
- pyramids iii, 326-27, 332, 335
- splendid place of the first time 420
- see also Great Pyramid

Goats 280

Gods
- of nun 11, 39, 86, 104, 112, 126, 129-30, 286-87
- of earth and duat 10, 13-14, 44, 103, 105, 111, 113, 123, 129-30, 133, 170, 176, 196, 211, 224, 246, 257, 263, 273
- of field of reeds 19-21, 130
- of akhet 15-19, 103-4, 129-30, 291, 306, 403
- of storm-cloud 185-86, 204-6, 228, 234
- of sky 10, 23-24, 28-30, 49, 103-5, 111, 113, 126, 129-31, 141, 170, 172-73, 176, 179, 196-97, 207, 209, 211, 217, 221, 229, 234, 265, 273
- of lower sky 29-30, 129
- of atmosphere - see Infinite Ones
- body-soul duality 103-113, 131-32, 265
- dead gods 14, 21, 103, 105-7, 113, 133, 204, 263
- living gods, souls and spirits 107, 111, 113, 120, 129-32, 136, 170, 174, 179, 189, 231
- as birds and fishes 21, 106, 129
- mouths opened by iron adze 132, 166, 182-84, 215, 221-22
- created the God and brought him out of nun 35, 63, 97, 103, 108, 110, 113, 223, 309, 312, 320

- made a field 20, 179
- made a great throne 235
- built the boat of Horus 136
- ascended to the sky 46, 74, 104-6, 114, 116, 130-31, 135-37, 141, 161, 224
- rowed or towed the sun-god's barque 17, 30, 89-90, 93, 103, 129, 132-33, 172-73, 217
- knit together the face of Osiris-the-king 274
- children of creator ii, 31, 41, 47, 50, 75, 103-4, 106-10, 119, 127, 131-32, 137, 287
- identified with limbs of creator 41, 45, 109-13, 164, 172, 189, 312
- origin of the gods 16, 40, 45, 50-51, 53-54, 61-64, 69, 72-74, 76, 97-98, 103-6, 108-10, 119, 130-35, 141, 176, 189, 222, 241, 254-55, 276, 288-89, 312-13, 322
- see also Assembly of the gods; Ennead; Followers; Hnmmt; Ogdoad; Primeval Ones

God's Castle adze 182, 291

Gold 61, 138, 172, 210, 228, 237, 399, 404

Goose 169, 319 (see also Great Honker)

Granite 226

Great Bear - see Ursa

Great Bull, Pillar of the Serpent Nome 228, 244

Great ennead 326

Great God
- of many names ii, 103, 309-10, 324
- personified evolution of cosmos iv, 65, 95, 97, 105, 133, 146, 232, 256, 312, 315-16, 325, 340-41
- body-soul duality 41-42, 44, 47-50, 53, 71, 80, 82, 89, 93-102, 105, 107, 112-13, 119-20, 124, 143, 146-48, 158, 160-61, 180, 184, 248, 355 (see also Copulation)
- transcendent and immanent ii, 97
- totality of all the gods ii, 107-13, 164, 232, 312, 324-25
- created by the gods 35, 63, 97, 103, 108, 110, 113, 223, 309, 312, 320 (see also Assembly of the gods)
- sole creator 35, 40, 45, 50, 54, 60, 63-64, 72, 104, 108, 120, 242-43, 250, 312-13, 324
- assisted by Goddess 35, 39, 45, 47-49, 60-61, 63, 256, 309, 312-16, 318-19, 325 (see also Copulation)
- paired with Goddess in cult 53, 314, 325
- a he-she ii, 53, 63, 175, 260, 309, 316-20, 325
- see also Amun; Atum; Khnum; Neber-djer; Osiris; Ptah; Ta-tenen

Great Goddess
- of many names 316, 325
- symbolised by the Eye 28, 253, 255-56, 276, 280, 324
- sole creatress 35, 61, 63, 235, 237, 316, 319
- assisted the God 35, 40, 60-61, 63, 256
- personified evolution of cosmos 185, 256-81,

284, 315-16, 318, 325
- as first principle/soul 323-25
- Goddess and God a single being 315-25
- see also Eye; Hathor; Isis; Neit; Nut
Great Harris Papyrus 50-51, 69
Great Honker 54, 74, 214, 319
Great Hymn to Amun 53-55, 99, 241
Great Lotus 57-58, 60, 71, 106
Great of Magic 73, 139-40, 182, 256, 261, 267-68, 292, 303, 323, 413
Great Primeval Mound 56, 307
Great Pyramid
- design of ii, 349-52, 356-70
- theories of 349-53
- named Akhet Khufu 343, 352, 354
- built in honour of Khnum 354-56
- airshafts, theories of 339, 357
- dismantled boats buried alongside 356
- sarcophagus in upper chamber may have enshrined meteoritic iron 356-57
- secret passages and chambers 357-58
- new theory on Khufu's tomb i, v-vi, 353-70
Great Wild Bull 158, 160, 211, 228-29, 237, 239
Great Wild Cow 158, 235
Greek myths 262, 383
Greek mysteries 90-91

Hailstones/hailstorms (cosmic phenomenon) 168-69, 200, 202, 204-5, 207, 221, 250-51, 280, 292
Hair
- of Eye 272, 277
- of Isis and Nephthys 305
Hapi 33, 52, 189, 305, 320, 380
Harpoon 214-15, 220-21, 224, 251, 274, 287, 293, 295
Hathor
- creator-goddess 61-62, 315
- depicted as a cow 61, 235
- mother of Horus the Falcon 25, 62, 235, 314-15
- mother of Ihy 235
- ascended to the sky 61, 191-92, 315
- alter ego of Isis 62
- identified with Eye 100, 254-56, 261-62, 266, 276, 278, 315-16
- horns of 172, 235
- exposure of 295
- dress of 61, 273
- mother of the pharaoh 145, 235
Hatshepsut 343
Hau-nbwt 387
Hawass, Zahi 352
Hawk 69
Hbbt (primeval waters) 56, 70
Head metaphor 73-74, 82, 138-40, 223, 254,

265, 267-68, 274, 295-87, 307, 315, 319, 357
Heart 39, 45, 49-51, 69, 73, 79, 86, 120, 123-24, 138, 164, 167, 171, 179, 200, 205, 232, 241, 252, 260, 285, 297, 301, 323, 343, 409 (see also Expansion of the heart)
Heftnut 416
Heh and Hehet 60, 320
Heka - see Magic
Heka (god) 93
Heket 48, 79
Heliopolis
- ancient name Iunu, 'Pillar City' 38, 67, 244-45, 336
- hosted solar, lunar, and stellar cults 67, 334, 336
- hosted cult of Mnevis bull 229, 244
- site of creation by Atum and Atum-Kheprer 38-39, 43, 69, 72, 96, 242, 246, 249, 342-43
- place of Neber-djer's court 295-96
- home to Atum's body 98
- home of the great ennead 326
- home of the great maiden 237
- bull came forth from 228, 234, 239
- assembly place of the gods 73, 95, 110, 265, 329 (see also Souls of Heliopolis)
- birthplace of the gods 160
- place where Sokar raised iron 187, 215
- place where Horus fought Seth and hacked up the earth 206, 284, 290
- place where the Eye was found and assembled 265, 284
- place where Re united with his corpse Osiris 55, 88
- battle over its division 401
- microcosm of the primeval world 72, 81, 86, 213, 234, 290
- see also Benben stone; Temple of the Benben
Henen-nesu 280
Herakleopolis 280, 300
Hermonthis 328
Hermopolis 29, 40-41, 55, 57, 60, 137, 178, 222, 232, 290-91, 320, 328
Herodotus 362-63
Heron 169
Heter-her 56
Hierakonpolis (Nekhen) 286
Hieroglyphics 155, 179, 330-31
High hill 38-39, 43, 58, 116, 188, 242, 246-50, 252, 257, 334, 336, 338, 342, 346, 409
Hippopotamus 287, 293, 295
Hmwst (female spirits) 232
Hnhnu-barque 136-37, 185, 405
Hnmmt (star-gods) 28, 135, 234 (see also Bull of Hnmmt)
Hnny 239
Hnu 214

Hnu-barque 136, 214-16, 220, 405
Hoed lands 301
Hoeing the earth ritual 280
Horakhti 17-18, 24, 27, 31, 147, 176, 207
Horizon - see Akhet
Horns
- of bull 224, 228-29, 233-34
- of cow 235-36
- symbol of doors 233
Hornung, Erik 124, 312
Horus of the Akhet 15
Horus of Behdet 221, 274, 292-93
Horus of the Duat 12-13, 32, 84, 98-99, 109, 136, 176, 284, 286
Horus of the East 286
Horus of Edfu 55-56, 61-62, 147, 314, 316
Horus as father
- children of Horus 78, 110-11, 164, 287-89
- four sons of Horus 29, 111-12, 160, 166, 181, 221, 223, 231, 287-88
Horus of the field of reeds 19, 21, 24, 177
Horus of Hierakonpolis (mystery of the hands of Horus) 286, 295, 298, 413, 415
Horus of the hnu-barque 136, 216
Horus of Letopolis 139
Horus Lord of Patricians 286
Horus partner of Sopdet 31
Horus Lord of the Two Lands 286
Horus who Unites the Two Lands 62, 314, 316
Horus rival of Seth
- fought him in Hermopolis 29, 222, 290-91
- fought him in Heliopolis 206, 284, 290
- fought him in the sky 206, 292-93
- smote Seth and his followers 29, 49, 79, 142, 202-3, 208, 253, 260
- rescued the Eye from Seth 49, 152, 165-66, 182, 253, 259-60, 283-84, 291
- his Great of Magic 139, 268, 413
- lifted the Eye 141, 254
- contests with Seth 295
- sexual union with Seth 286, 294-98, 308, 319
- depicted as one body with Seth 297
- dwelt with Seth in castle 291
- born in fiery earthquake with Seth 201, 282, 290-91, 308
- ascended with Seth into the sky 194
- reconciled with Seth in the Two Lands 293-94, 298-308
- together with Seth lifted Osiris-the-king into the sky 12
- allegory for geocentric creation 282-308
- see also Mounds of Horus and Seth
Horus upon the shedshed 211, 222
Horus the sky-god 28, 47, 49, 144, 147, 202, 256, 285, 293, 300, 395
Horus son of Atum 178
Horus son of Hathor 25, 61-62, 235, 314-15

Horus son of Isis
- fathered by Osiris 48-49, 80, 82, 147, 201, 316
- born in the duat 13, 32
- assembled the gods for Osiris 110-11, 164, 287
- assembled and revivified Osiris 74, 79, 102, 163, 166, 181-82, 201, 221-23, 225, 269, 291
- inherited the Two Lands 49, 74
- provided model for kingship 4, 47, 147, 149-51
- god of the ka-mut.ef, bull of his mother 240-41, 248
- identified with morning star 32, 174-75
- see also Horus rival of Seth; Horus-Spdu; King, Reigning
Horus-Spdu 32, 323
Horus the sun-god 135, 147, 308, 395
House of the Double Lion 259
Hpat 239
Hrt (name of sky) 22, 25, 119, 125, 392
Hu (creative utterance) 4, 95, 151, 189, 322
Hunefer (scribe) 182

Iad-star 128, 234
Ihy 62, 235, 313
Ikhet-the-Great 266
Ikhkhu-stars 47
Imperishable stars 13, 21, 24, 28-30, 32, 82, 107, 111, 124, 129, 170, 172-74, 176-77, 179, 210-11, 217, 220, 248, 275
Incense smoke 169
Ineb-hedj (White Walls) 306, 382
Infinite Ones 25-26, 44, 47, 96, 98, 108, 126, 189, 236, 273, 381
Inner akhet 204
Ir-akht 71
Iron
- smelted from meteorites 225-26
- mentioned frequently in Pyramid Texts and Coffin Texts 209
- adze 132, 166, 181-83, 187-88, 198, 221-24, 227, 251, 275
- bones of god-king 172, 209-11, 220, 238, 248, 251, 275, 405
- doors 22, 209, 216-18, 220, 227
- eggshell 187, 209, 213-15, 218, 220, 227
- fingers 221, 223-24
- floats and weights 220, 405
- harpoon of Shu 215, 220, 224, 251
- harpoons and chains of blacksmith-gods 221, 274, 293
- knife 292
- plain in northern sky 209, 217, 220
- ropes 209, 216-17, 220, 227
- sceptre 211

- throne 194, 209, 211-13, 215, 219, 227, 229, 245, 288, 302
- wall of field of reeds 20, 209, 218, 227
- of Sokar 69
- in hnu-barque 214, 220
- in the sky 184, 187, 218-20, 225, 227, 293
- material of stars 132, 210-11, 220, 227, 275, 281
- traversed and split by the king en route to the sky 209, 216, 218-20, 227
- washed, sharp and strong 187, 215, 220, 233
- spiritualized 187, 215
- emission theory (geocentric creation) 187-88, 198, 210, 215-16, 220-22, 224, 226-27, 242, 245-46, 249-52, 268, 273, 315, 338
- see also Meteorites and meteoritic iron

Ir-ta 71, 76
Isfet 3-5, 143-46, 149, 151, 206, 282
Isis
- mother of Horus 47-49, 143, 145, 147, 201, 316, 321-22
- partner of Osiris 32, 48-49, 316, 321-22
- alter ego of Hathor 62, 256, 313
- identified with Eye 256, 316
- identified with Sopdet/Sirius 30-32, 174-75
- Great of Magic 322-23
- revivified Re 100, 189, 313, 322-23
- impregnated by Re 148, 313
- found Osiris in the earth 48, 81, 321, 399
- with Nephthys assembled and revivified Osiris 74, 78-79, 81-82, 139, 163, 196, 286, 313-14, 321-24
- raped by Horus 241
- decapitation of 295
- hair of 305
- breast and milk of 164

Isis and Re creation myth 47, 100, 141, 189, 241, 313, 322-23
Island of combat 263
Island of creation 9, 20-21, 36, 57-59, 63, 65, 70, 75-77, 82, 116, 178, 246, 258, 289, 307, 328
Island of earth 20, 177, 236
Island of the egg 57-59, 106
Island of fire/flames 14, 57-60, 63, 99, 127, 204, 232, 263, 267, 280, 323, 410
Island of trampling 75-76, 204, 263
Iunu - see Heliopolis
Iusaas 314

Jackal 62, 222, 279
James, E.O. 62
Jesus Christ, similarity to Osiris myth 83
Joining the river banks 304-5

Ka
- of Atum 38-39, 96, 180, 242, 341

- of Ptah 71
- of Osiris 239
- of the earth 71, 93
- in Edfu creation myth 71
- of Osiris-the-king 158, 161-62, 167, 171-72, 179-80, 184, 200, 209, 211-12, 228, 232, 330-31, 341, 343
- embodied in the pharaoh 147, 150
- embodied in the temple 151
- name of the Primeval Ones 104
- ka of all the gods (epithet) 73, 103, 108, 311, 397
- going to one's ka 24, 101, 105, 288
- the gods have ka 51
- millions of ka 46, 136, 189
- bestowed by Neheb-kau 128

Ka-embrace 38, 180, 242, 331, 341, 343
Ka-statue 152, 330, 348, 418
Ka-mut.ef (bull of the mother)
- cult object 54, 240-42, 252, 338
- created by Amun 53, 96
- identified as meteorite 226
- gods of - see Amun; Horus; Min
- name of Amun 230
- king acts as 240, 252, 318
- explanation of inseminating the mother 246, 249-50, 252, 318-19

Karnak 138, 245, 258, 329, 342, 409
Kees, Hermann 310
Kek and Keket 60, 320
Kemet 10
Kenzet - see Pillar of
Khafre ii, 334
Khem - see Letopolis
Khenti-amentiu 10, 84, 124, 213, 229, 239, 395
Khenti-irti 138, 231
Khenti-Khem 274
Kheper-djesef (self-creating) 39-40, 42, 46, 52-53, 55, 64, 96, 101, 105, 113, 119-20, 147, 160, 163, 181, 223, 225, 247, 252, 309, 312-13, 336
Kheprer/Khepri
- creator-god 21, 39, 44-45, 64, 66, 68, 72, 93, 96, 99, 116, 124, 136, 167, 169, 176, 185, 189, 247, 273, 336, 384
- identified with rising sun 67-68, 92

Khnum
- creator-god 11, 52-53, 66, 96, 120
- paired with Satet and Neit 314
- a he-she 319
- pharaoh identified with 145-46

Khnum-khuf 354-56
Khons 28, 137-38, 245, 316, 324
Khsr (verb) 205, 207, 403
Khufu
- builder of Great Pyramid i-ii, v, 349
- body never found 356

- tomb intact beneath Great Pyramid i, v-vi, 350-70
- see also Khnum-khuf

Kingship
- mythical origins of 142-43, 180, 282, 295-96, 299-303, 306-8
- an Osiris-Horus unit 143, 147, 149-50, 152-53, 180
- creational theory of 143-54

King, Reigning
- coronation 2, 4, 6, 150, 180, 267, 282, 307, 395-96
- embodiment of creator-god iv, 4, 6, 142-43, 150-52, 180, 267, 282, 307, 328
- maintained the cosmos by re-enacting creation iii-iv, 3-4, 37, 47, 151-53, 180, 328-29, 396

King, Deceased and reborn
- identified with Osiris iv, 5, 77, 84, 93, 110, 124-25, 143, 149, 152-54, 158, 160, 163, 172, 180-81, 184, 186, 200-1, 210-11, 232, 330, 341, 343
- identified with all the gods 164, 172
- personified creator-god and re-enacted creation iv, 5, 11, 13, 16-17, 93, 105, 124, 133, 154, 158-81, 185-86, 192-201, 204-25, 228-29, 231-34, 236, 238-40, 251-52, 258, 264, 266, 268, 279, 288, 292-93, 301-2, 304-6, 314, 318, 323, 337, 341
- created the sky-ocean 170-71, 180
- became the sun-god 156, 171-72, 180
- became the moon 171-72, 180
- became a star 129, 150, 153, 156, 160, 173-77, 240, 337, 339
- became all the stars 172-73, 180
- circulated through the cosmos iv, 5-6, 20, 153-55, 158-59, 161-62, 176-80, 331, 348
- soul united with body in tomb iv, 153-55, 161-62, 179, 330

Kite 163
Knife 233, 292, 407
Knitting theme 39-40, 43-46, 50, 85-87, 96, 104, 108, 214-15, 239, 258, 268, 273-74, 281, 319

Ladders 12, 44, 52, 103, 111, 116, 125, 169-70, 196, 200, 234, 264, 266, 294, 298, 391, 398, 405
Lakes 11-13, 16, 18-19, 21, 161, 171, 177, 229, 231, 275, 301, 375
Legend of Shu and Geb 202
Lehner, Mark 154, 335
Leiden Papyrus 35, 53-55, 99, 104, 131, 241
Lepre, J.P. 360, 362-64, 368, 370, 372
Letopolis 138-40, 226, 242, 274
Lettuce plants 296
Light, creation of 40, 42, 47, 54, 57-60, 63-64, 97, 104, 127, 139, 250, 265, 269, 317, 321
Lightning - see Thunderbolt

Limbs
- of Atum and Neber-djer 39-41, 45, 85-86, 94, 96, 109-10, 189, 254, 277
- of the Eye 265
- of Geb 248
- of Horus 286
- of Osiris 49, 79, 82, 85-87, 94, 124, 139, 149, 163-64, 167, 172, 176, 210, 227, 287, 321
- of Ptah Ta-tenen 50, 85-86, 94, 109, 313, 324
- of Re 47, 100, 109, 189, 322
- of Seth 183, 188
- of the sky 44, 108, 168, 196

Lions 211, 225, 259 (see also House of the Double Lion; Sekhmet)
Locust 169, 200
Lone star 128, 160, 240, 267, 393, 411
Lord of the Akhet 16-17, 27, 46, 136, 323, 334, 337
Lord of All 38, 44, 145, 258
Lord of the Ennead 40, 109, 129, 189
Lord of Eternity 303
Lord of Kheperu 381
Lord of the Ladder - see Seth
Lord of the Light 202
Lord to the Limit 38
Lord of Time 337
Lord of the Wing 71
Lotus-flower 19, 39-40, 57-60, 86, 112, 116, 178, 194, 199, 273
Lotus-plant of Upper Egypt 299
Love 48, 79, 111, 114, 121, 176, 181, 269, 314, 323
Lower Egypt 111, 302-8

Maat 1-6, 28, 49, 65, 143, 151-52, 154, 206, 282, 323, 328, 346
Mace 211
Mafdet 405
Maggots 276
Magic (heka)
- first cause iii, 34, 46-47, 56, 87, 232, 261, 267-68, 308, 312-13, 322-25
- in rituals 4, 6, 151, 275, 323, 328-29
- in king's re-enactment of creation 170, 177, 323, 355
Ma-ha.f 378, 407
Maiden(s) 230, 237
Mankind, creation of 45-46, 50, 53, 62-63, 189, 254-55, 262, 275-77, 281
Mankind, destruction of 100, 261-63
Mansion
- of the gods 288
- of Horus (name of Hathor) 25, 61-62, 219, 235
- of Horus in the sky 25, 235, 315, 329

- of Isden 76
- of Nwt-k-nu 219, 222, 291, 405
- of Life 405
Mastaba tombs 335, 338, 418
Masturbation as mechanism of creation 35, 38, 42-45, 103, 188, 242-43, 249-52, 269, 285, 312, 319, 336, 343
Maxims of Ptahhotep 1
Meadow of Apis 24, 228, 234
Meadows of the sky 262
Medamud inscriptions 66, 137
Medinet Habu 240-41
Mehet-weret (goddess) 25, 119, 138, 236, 238
Mehet-weret (great flood, name of sky) 16, 19, 23, 28, 44, 73, 119, 126-28, 135-36, 194, 206, 236, 293
Memphis 50, 68-69, 72, 75, 81, 142, 150, 229, 248, 267, 298, 306-7, 328
Mendelssohn, Kurt 327
Menes 142, 299, 307
Menkaure 2, 334
Merenptah 144
Mesenti 71
Mesniu - see Blacksmith-gods
Mesopotamian creation myth 412
Meteorites and meteoritic iron
- characteristics 225-26, 243, 340, 357, 406
- used in sacred tools and rituals 184, 188, 221-25
- buried in tombs 225
- fall recorded in Coffin Texts 225-26
- oriented shape an inspiration for the true pyramid? 243, 340
- viewed as sky cult 184, 226
- viewed as sun cult 226
- viewed as star cult 184, 222, 225-26
- shedshed link? 223
- head of Osiris 223, 357
- benben stone 226, 243, 340, 357
- ka-mut.ef object 226, 242, 252, 338
- thunderbolt symbol 242
- Letopolis and Abydos 226, 275
- creational significance 188, 222-27, 243-46, 340, 357
- kept in boxes 357
- raised on pillars/poles 357
- see also Benben Stone; Great Pyramid; Iron; Ka-mut.ef
Midnight sun 5, 8, 14, 89-91, 93-94, 124
Milk 164, 234
Milky way - see Msqt shdu; Winding waterway
Min
- god of the ka-mut.ef 240, 242, 251
- raped his mother 138, 240, 248
- festival of 241
- double-arrow symbol 242
- king and deceased went forth as 160, 215, 239, 302
Mnevis bull 229, 244
Monotheism ii-iii, 35, 97, 103, 309-12, 320, 324-25
Montju 160
Moon
- myths of origin 38, 45, 47, 58, 137-41, 253, 270-73, 281, 295-98, 303, 308
- made of stone 274-75, 281
- as left eye, white eye, and empty eye of Horus 139, 172, 224, 255-56, 258, 270, 272-73, 297-98
- geocentric theory of 137-41, 253-81, 308
- see also Eclipses
Moon-god - see Khons; Thoth
Moret, Alexandre 334
Morning star 13, 21, 24, 30-32, 128, 173-75, 177-78, 194, 399
Mortuary temple and rituals iv, 152-55, 180, 326, 329-31, 341, 347-48, 418
Mound of Geb 9, 134, 287-88, 302, 308 (see also Primeval mound)
Mounds
- of Horus and Seth 9, 134, 170, 176, 287-89, 291, 302, 306, 308
- of the Primeval Ones 289
- of the Two Lands 58, 106, 132, 289
Mountain
- of the West (the netherworld) 191, 235, 237, 263
- split apart 61, 186, 191-92
Mountains, creation of 46, 53
Mouth
- in creation myth 35, 42-43, 45-47, 54, 104, 136, 141, 184, 189-90, 198, 239, 249, 319, 322-23, 401
- of the earth 136, 185-87, 192-93, 215, 249-50
- see also Nut's mouth; Opening of the mouth; Speech as mechanism of creation
Mskhtiu 29, 129, 132, 183, 393
Msqt shdu (milky way) 24, 32-33, 128, 228, 234, 291
Mummies and mummification iv, 5, 14, 31, 93-94, 101, 149, 152, 154, 161, 163-64, 167-68, 170, 179-82, 186-87, 198, 222-24, 330-31, 341, 348
Mut 138, 261, 314, 316, 324

Nails 219, 224
Naqada 292
Narmer palette 236, 420
Neber-djer 38, 44-45, 55, 96, 104, 126, 145, 188-89, 203, 225, 271-73, 275-78, 295, 300, 312, 322
Nedyt 81, 163, 230, 258, 279
Nefertem 160
Neheb-kau 128, 160, 280, 406-7, 412

436 THE MIDNIGHT SUN

Neheh and djet 2-4, 6, 30, 50, 67, 77, 88, 92-93, 142-43, 153-54, 158, 179-80, 197, 328, 331, 340, 372, 374
Neit 61-63, 138, 160, 314, 316-17, 319, 384, 417
Nekhbet 235, 261, 267
Nekheb 158, 235
Nekhen - see Hierakonpolis
Nephthys
- Great of Magic 323
- rebuilt Osiris in her name of Seshat 85
- with Isis found, mourned, assembled and revivified Osiris 74, 78-79, 81-82, 139, 163, 196, 286, 313-14
- hair of 305
Netherworld - see Ament; Duat
Netjer (the God) 103, 110, 150
Netjeru (the gods) 97, 103, 110, 129, 312, 324
Netjeru-blades 223-24, 226
Netjer-dwau 31, 128, 174-75, 177 (see also Morning star)
Netjer-khert 10
Newton, Isaac 372
Night-barque 26, 82, 129, 134, 136, 139, 176, 185, 270, 393
Night of the great flood 127
Night of the great storm 208
Nile river iii, 2, 11, 30-33, 46, 52, 68, 80, 121, 142, 151, 160, 295 (see also Hapi)
Nkhkh-stars 128, 173, 217
Noise - see Sound of creation
Nun, lower (primeval ocean/abyss) 9-12, 23, 36, 39-40, 44-46, 50, 52, 54-60, 62-65, 68, 73, 82, 86, 93, 95, 97, 103-4, 108, 112, 116-17, 119-22, 124, 126-27, 131, 133, 135-36, 140-41, 146, 158, 194, 203, 215, 222, 245-46, 248, 253, 257, 262, 270, 280, 301, 303, 312-13, 315-18, 321, 328, 331, 342-43, 347
Nun, upper (celestial ocean) 11, 23, 44, 46, 95, 97, 108, 115-17, 119-21, 248, 275
Nun (god) 10, 25, 39, 41, 60, 86, 93, 95, 98-99, 101-2, 104, 116, 119-22, 126, 137, 147, 189, 248, 261, 263, 278, 317-18, 320
Nunet 60, 66, 104, 320
Nurse canal 19, 176
Nut
- goddess of starry sky 25-27, 105, 114-16, 121, 124-26, 130-31, 195, 211, 316
- goddess of lower sky or duat 14, 26-27, 92, 123-24, 190-92, 195
- goddess of inner akhet 16, 204
- creator-goddess, mother of the cosmos 121-26, 140-41, 195, 210, 236-39, 311, 315-16
- daughter of Tefnut 123, 126, 191, 316
- lifted by Shu 39, 42, 44, 47, 74, 86, 121-22, 126, 137, 208, 262
- depicted as a cow 25-26, 47, 137, 235-36, 313
- depicted as a woman 25-27, 74
- identified with the Eye 265, 315-16
- gave birth to Re 46, 123, 136-38, 238
- bore Re every day 26-27, 124, 190-91, 198
- suckled Re in the sky 238
- gave birth to Osiris 123-24, 191
- gave birth to Seth 191, 292
- gave birth to the five gods 16, 204
- gave birth through the duat 12-13, 123
- eyes went forth from her head 139-40, 268, 315
- fertilized by Geb's earth 125, 237-38, 313, 316-19, 321
- inseminated by Geb in the sky 39, 73, 237-38, 248, 252, 313, 318
- argument with Geb 140, 401
- opener of the earth 191
- children of 265, 410
- doors of - see Doors
- mouth of 26, 123, 190-92, 198, 218
- thighs of 20, 123-24, 177, 190-91, 236
- vagina of 26, 123-24, 190-92, 198
- voice of 202, 205, 292
- reassembled and revivified Osiris-the-king 124, 163-64
- gestated the iron bones and seed of the Osiris-king 210, 238, 318
- conducted Osiris-king in the akhet 16, 124
- took Osiris-king to the sky 124, 177, 186, 194, 196, 318
- gave duat and akhet to Osiris-king 176
- bore the Osiris-king every day 125, 176
- her name of Ladder 125, 170, 195
- her names of Coffin/Sarcophagus and Tomb 125, 149, 195, 347

Obelisk
- derived from benben 334, 337, 341
- tip called benbenet 244, 334, 338, 341
- pierced, split and mingled with the sky 337-38, 343
- monument of eternity 328-29
- finger of Seth 298
- solar symbol theory 244, 334, 337
- phallic symbol theory 244, 338, 406
- see also Two obelisks of Re
Offerings
- in temples 4, 152, 396
- at tombs 153, 183
- at pyramids 164-67, 170, 186, 196-97
- key to eternal life 89
- created by Hathor 62
- symbolised by the Eye 152, 165-67, 182-83, 254, 257, 300
- location of in 'other world' 19-21, 23-24, 178-79, 211, 229
Ogdoad 55, 60, 110, 112, 320-21, 383, 413

INDEX 437

Opening of the eyes of Osiris-the-king 80, 164, 166-67, 185, 291
Opening of the Eye of Osiris-the-king 185, 269
Opening of the mouth
- of Osiris 80, 166, 183, 221
- of the gods 132, 166, 182-83, 215, 221
- of the deceased's mummy 153, 164, 166, 181-84, 186-87, 221-26
- of statues 181, 329-30
- creational interpretation 184-99, 221-25, 233, 251, 268, 273, 291
- see also Adzes; Eye; Meteorites and meteoritic iron
Order - see Maat
Orion 31-32, 129, 174, 337
Osiris
- bodily death of 30-31, 48, 78-80, 83-84, 98-100, 111, 163-64, 174, 258, 287, 300-1, 303
- body turned from left side to right side 79, 83, 164, 182, 300, 302, 306
- partner of Isis 32, 48-49, 316, 321-22
- assembly and revivification of 74, 78-83, 87, 100, 110-12, 125, 139, 163, 166-67, 201, 221-22, 225, 231, 254, 286, 300, 313-14, 321-24
- mouth opened by iron adze 166, 183, 221-22, 330
- face knit together by the gods 274
- bandaged finger of 224
- body-soul duality of 17, 80, 82, 101-2, 112, 124, 134, 143, 147, 160, 164, 166, 168, 174-75, 184, 286
- son of Geb 74, 79-80, 82, 102, 124, 134, 147, 158, 160, 280, 311, 318
- son of Nut 79-80, 123-25, 149, 158, 160, 191, 311, 318
- born from earth and the duat 12, 80, 82, 134, 196
- father of Horus 13, 32, 47-49, 80, 82, 101-2, 134, 147, 164, 174-75, 201, 316
- embrace with Horus 134, 164, 343-44
- identified with Sah 31, 82, 174
- identified with Khenti-amentiu 10, 124
- epithets Bull of the West and Bull of Nedyt 230
- accreted cults of other dying-and-rising gods 84, 124, 163
- in nun 11
- lord of the duat 13, 76, 111, 386
- personified duat 14, 17, 82, 122
- traversed the duat 175
- lord of the field of reeds 21
- personified akhet 17, 21, 80, 82, 88, 134, 343-44
- eyes appeared in his head 139
- ascended to sky 24, 82
- fell back to earth 226, 279
- body was power source for rebirth of the sun-god Re 5-6, 14, 17, 77, 87-90, 92, 99, 190
- creator-god theory iv, 55, 80-95, 109, 127, 143, 147-49, 153-54, 158, 160, 165, 180, 184, 186, 227, 232, 259-60, 273, 279, 294, 311, 313-14, 316, 319, 341
- first king of Egypt 1, 142, 262, 300-1
- crowns went up from his head 267
- model for death and rebirth of the king iv, 5-6, 77, 84, 93, 110, 124-25, 143, 149, 152-54, 158, 160, 163, 172, 180-81, 184, 186, 200-1, 210-11, 232, 330, 341, 343
- see also Egyptology, view of Osiris; Head of Osiris
Osorkon II 244
Ouroboros 128, 225
Ox-herd (name for stars) 234, 407

Palace 4, 69, 202, 248
Papyrus-plant of Lower Egypt 299
Papyrus Salt 263
Pat-land 177
Pay-lands 56, 409
Pautt (primeval matter) 36, 96
Pdjt/pdjwt (celestial expanses) 28, 196, 233
Pepi II 5, 332
Per-aa 395
Per duat (name of tomb chamber) 14, 149, 330
Pesesh-kef knife 226
Pet (sky) 22-23, 25, 28, 116, 119, 125
Phallus 32, 35, 38, 43-45, 48, 67, 96, 188, 195, 224-25, 234, 239-46, 249-52, 273, 280, 285, 295, 298, 313, 317-19, 336, 338, 342-43, 408, 417
Philae 328 (see also Temple of Philae)
Phoenix - see Benu-bird
Pi/phi 346, 349, 418
Piercing 207, 231 (see also Obelisk)
Pillar of Heliopolis 67, 245 (see also Benben Stone; Heliopolis; Temple of the Benben)
Pillar of Kenzet 168, 228, 234, 244, 406
Pillar of the Stars 168, 228, 234, 244
Pillars of the sky 22, 25, 53, 173, 209, 294
Pillar symbolism 67, 116, 168, 228, 244-46, 252, 298, 336
Placenta of king 223
Plants, creation of 45, 275, 277-78, 281
Platform of the jzkn 134
Pliny 275, 362
Plough, The 29, 129, 181, 183, 233-34
Plutarch 83, 286, 295
Pn-god 71, 76, 85
Polytheism 35, 97, 309-12, 324
Pools 19, 56-60, 116, 177-78, 206, 276, 290
Precession of the equinoxes 157, 282, 299
Priests/priesthoods 4, 151, 155, 163-65, 179, 181, 187, 311, 329

Primeval mound 9, 21, 36, 40-41, 45, 50-51, 53-56, 60, 63-66, 69-75, 82, 85-87, 94, 96, 104, 106, 109-10, 112, 115-17, 126, 131, 137, 140, 150, 168, 170, 178, 181, 204, 211-12, 215, 219, 242, 245-47, 258, 268, 277, 286-89, 291, 301, 321, 328, 331, 334-35, 338, 346-47, 367 (see also Temple; True pyramid)
Primeval ocean - see Nun
Primeval One 55, 57, 71, 120
Primeval Ones 49, 53-54, 57-60, 95-96, 103-4, 106, 120, 131-32, 199, 241, 289, 317-18, 320, 390, 416
Psdjt (ennead) 28
Pssht-tawi 303
Ptah
- creation by 50-51, 66, 69, 72, 96, 129, 131, 139, 152, 300, 313, 319, 324, 382
- paired with Sekhmet 314
- a he-she 319, 417
- see also Ta-tenen
Ptah-Sokar 69
Ptah-Sokar-Osiris 69
Pyramids - see Step pyramid; True pyramid
Pyramidion (benbenet)
- linked to benben 244, 338, 341
- of Amenemhet III 334, 336-37
- solar theory 334, 336-37
- primeval mound theory 335
- stellar and lunar symbolism 336-37
- creational symbolism 337, 341-42
- see also Benben stone; Obelisk; True Pyramid
Pyramid Texts
- generally ii, 9, 154-55, 179-80, 209, 309-10, 331-32, 396, 419
- orthodox view of 155-157, 339
- re-enactment of creation theory 157-80

Qebhu (name of sky) 23, 28, 46, 82, 119, 128, 166, 171, 193, 196-97, 216-17, 273, 329
Quirke, Stephen 7, 66

Raet 314
Ram 52, 89
Ramesses II 144-45, 152, 329
Ramesses III 329
Ramesseum Dramatic Papyrus 285, 294
Rape of the mother-goddess - see Geb; Horus; Min
Re
- bodily crisis of 100, 141, 322
- body-soul duality 101, 147-48, 355
- son of the Great God 40-41, 66, 116, 137, 147, 207
- borne by Mut as Khons 138, 324
- borne by Nut 46, 66, 92, 123, 136-37, 172, 238
- borne by Neit 63
- borne by frog-goddesses 66, 137
- created by the Ogdoad or Primeval Ones and emerged from lotus/pool in the island of fire 55, 58-60, 66, 106, 110, 112, 116-17, 137
- revivified by Isis 47, 100, 141, 189, 241, 313, 322-23
- born from an egg in nun 75, 137
- emerged from the nun as Khepri 95, 384
- bathed in the field of reeds and went forth thence to the sky 19-21, 177
- lord of the akhet 16-18, 24, 172, 178, 193, 212, 228, 288
- emerged from the akhet 16, 40-41, 63
- went forth from Osiris-the-Akhet 17, 82, 88, 134, 148, 343-44
- lifted into the sky by Nut and united with her 47, 100, 137, 236, 262, 313
- epithet Great Flood 127, 148
- field(s) of in the sky 23-25, 178-79
- creator-god 40, 46-47, 66, 95-96, 100, 105-7, 109, 138, 141, 189, 207-8, 291-92, 313, 322-24, 328, 336
- god of light 40-41, 46, 58, 60, 64-65, 148, 169, 202, 207, 256, 336, 395
- paired with Raet and possibly the Eye of Re 313-14
- impregnated Isis 148
- sun-god 3-6, 28, 30, 38, 46, 50, 65, 68, 87-88, 92-94, 109, 123-24, 129, 134, 169, 171-72, 178-79, 190, 202, 207-8, 211, 218
- borne every day by Neit 62-63
- borne every day by Nut 26, 92, 124, 172
- terror at his ascent 207
- nightly journey through the duat 5, 8, 13-14, 17, 27, 88-93, 99, 109, 123-24, 133, 190-92
- nightly journey through the body of Nut 14, 123-24, 190-92, 198
- united in duat with his body Osiris 5, 14, 55, 87-90, 92-94, 99
- wept for his corpse in Heliopolis 88, 98
- in the earth in his fetters 88
- mouth injured in battle for Heliopolis 401
- Bull of 228-29, 233
- two fingers of 224
- uraeus etc went forth from 148, 266
- made ladder for Osiris-the-king 12
- made Nut pregnant by Osiris-the-king 238, 408
- Osiris-the-king reborn as 158, 160, 171-72, 176-77, 211
- see also Barque of Re; Egyptology, view of Re; Eye of Re; Isis and Re
Re-Atum 148, 160, 260, 265
Re-Horakhti 376
Red crown 267
Reed-floats 15, 17, 19, 21-22, 176-78

INDEX 439

Reed island 56, 70, 75-77, 84, 178 (see also Field of reeds)
Rem 278
Renenutet 266
Reymond, Eve 69-72, 75-77, 84-85, 289, 317-18, 372
Rice, Michael 370, 372
Rituals - see Circuit of the Walls; Hoeing the earth; Kingship; Magic; Mortuary temple; Temple; True Pyramid
River of Shu 127, 271
Rostau 160, 226, 405
Roth, Ann Macy 223-24

Sacrifice - see Bull; Goats
Sages (djajsu) 76
Sah 12-13, 26, 30-31, 82, 129, 174-75, 177 (see also Canopus; Orion)
Sais 62, 316, 319
Saliva/spittle
- of Atum = Shu and Tefnut 276
- of Kheprer, becomes earth 72, 167, 247
- of Re, used to make serpent 100
Saqqara 154, 157, 346, 384
Sarcophagus - see Nut
Sa Re (title of king) 143-48, 334, 339
Satellite pyramids 332, 346
Satet 314
Sba (word for star) 28, 128, 130, 216, 240
Sba-wati - see Lone star
Sba-wr (great star) 128, 175
Scarab beetle 39, 66, 68, 81, 116, 169 (see also Kheprer; Kheper-djesef)
Sceptres
- of sky 22
- of king 211, 285
Secret name of Re 47, 100, 189, 322
Seed/semen 32, 43, 45, 48-49, 55, 62-63, 72-73, 99, 188, 201, 214, 225, 227, 234, 238-42, 244-46, 248-52, 273, 280, 285, 292, 295-97, 313, 317-24, 336-38, 342-43, 345, 347, 412, 417
Sekhmet 145, 261, 263, 278, 314, 316
Sellers, Jane 157, 299
Senusert I 145, 285
Serekh 49, 143
Serpents 45-47, 60, 70, 100, 108, 136, 138, 203, 224, 228, 235, 254, 261-62, 264, 266-67, 279-80, 287, 313, 321-22, 324, 401, 414 (see also Apep; Cobra; Ouroboros; Uraeus)
Seshat 85
Seth
- god of chaos 3, 5, 12, 28, 41, 49, 282-83, 292, 297, 307-8
- attacked the Eye 28, 49, 152, 165-66, 183, 202-3, 253, 259-60, 263-64, 283-84, 413
- attacked Osiris 78-79, 83, 142, 163, 231, 258, 286
- anger at the birth of Horus 208
- vanquished by Horus 49, 79, 142, 202-3, 208, 253, 260
- vanquished by the children of Horus 111
- vanquished by the Eye 202-3, 253, 260-61, 263
- vanquished by Geb 74
- driven off by Thoth 28, 260
- sun and moon born from his head 138, 295-87, 319
- uraeus went forth from 266, 298
- planted the eyes of Horus in the earth 278, 295
- reconciled with Horus in the Two Lands 293-94, 298-308
- born in fiery earthquake with Horus 201, 282, 290-91, 308
- born violently from womb of Nut 191
- begotten by Geb 264, 292
- Lord of the Ladder 264, 294
- pillar of the sky 294
- forced to lift up Osiris 49, 201, 293-94
- dwelt in the northern stars 29, 222, 234, 293, 307
- entered earth as a hissing serpent 280
- children and followers of 111, 203, 253, 260, 287-89
- testicles of, Great of Magic, torn off by Horus 49, 139, 203, 268, 283-85, 291-92, 297, 323-24, 413, 415
- foreleg of, torn off by Horus 29, 49, 183, 284, 287
- finger of 224, 297-98
- body dismembered as a bull or hippopotamus 109, 229, 231, 284, 286-87
- sacrificed as a goat 280
- blood of 280
- roaring of 168, 200, 205, 292
- animal of 292, 294
- iron adze of 29, 132, 182-83, 221-22
- opened the mouth of Osiris-the-king 172
- birthday of 292
- see also Horus rival of Seth
Shabaka Stone 50-51, 69, 302-8 (see also Theology of Memphis)
Shd (word for star) 28, 32-33, 128, 217, 339
Shebtiu-gods 56, 76
Shedshed 169, 211-12, 222-23
Shetit 99
Shezmetet 276, 278
Shmshmt-plant 306
Shooting stars 217
Shores 126, 304
Shrine (of temple) 151-52, 329, 347, 418
Shrines of the akhet and the sky 16, 212

Shu
- created by Atum or Atum-Kheprer 38, 43, 64, 96, 161, 188, 242, 249-52, 276, 312, 319, 338, 341-42
- created by Neber-djer 45, 188, 312
- created by Amun 54
- creator-god 41-44, 96, 101, 104, 108, 250-51, 311, 313
- co-creator of the gods with Tefnut 104, 313
- co-creator of the waters with Tefnut 313
- co-creator of the plants with Tefnut 278
- possessed breath of life 189
- ascended to sky from field of reeds 19
- ascended to sky at head of great flood 44, 127
- ascended on ladder 44, 234
- ascended in storm 202, 207, 248, 250-51, 280
- calmed the sky and the Eye 207, 270-71, 277
- lifted up Atum 44, 116, 141
- lifted up waters 127, 141, 248, 271
- lifted up Eye 141, 254, 264-65
- lifted up Nut and supported the sky 22, 25-27, 38, 42, 47, 50, 64, 74, 83, 114-17, 121, 141, 171, 208, 211, 236, 265, 271, 315
- god of air or wind 22, 38, 42, 44, 64, 83, 115-17, 120-21, 169, 188-90, 202, 208, 236, 243, 250-51
- sun-god 38-39, 115, 251, 270, 276
- feet pressed down on the earth 42, 168, 171
- hammered out Two Lands 300
- fertilized the earth 280
- opened the mouths of Osiris and the gods 251
- lifted Osiris-the-king into the sky 177
- in nun 44, 126
- in duat 14
- in field of reeds and field of offerings 19, 21
- in akhet 16
- river of 127, 271
- ramparts of 218-19
- bones of 251
- body of 98, 101, 108
- corpse of 93, 98-99
Sia 4, 93, 145, 151, 232
Sirius 30-32, 128, 174-75, 380
Sistrum 62, 235
Sky (sky-ocean)
- upper 22-27, 135
- lower 11, 22-23, 25-27, 29-30, 62-63, 115, 133, 135, 176, 190, 217, 378, 408
- inner/middle 25, 123-24, 195, 378
- starry 23-24, 26, 28, 47, 128, 160, 195-96, 228, 313
- separated from earth and nun 11, 23, 36, 42, 65, 68, 70, 74, 82-83, 97, 104, 114-18, 120-23, 130-31, 136, 141, 170, 195, 198, 205-8, 210, 219, 222, 224, 248, 403
- split open by Osiris-the-king 240
- geocentric theory of origin 119-28

- choked and stifled at time of creation 208, 221
- paths cleared in the sky 176, 202, 206-8, 221, 272, 281
Sma-staff 297
Sma-symbol (union) 299
Snakes - see Serpents
Sneezing as mechanism of creation - see Atum; Atum-Kheprer; Neber-djer
Sneferu i-iii, 334
Sobek 160
Sobek-Re 139
Sokar 69, 84, 93, 136, 160, 163, 187, 214-16, 220, 233, 314, 319, 395
Sokaret 314
Sopdet 30-32, 128, 174-77 (see also Sirius)
Sothis 30, 174 (see also Sirius; Sopdet)
Soul - see Ba; Body-soul duality
Souls
- of Heliopolis 130, 393
- of Nekhen 111, 130, 170, 231, 393
- of Pe 111, 130, 136, 170, 196, 231, 393
Sound of creation
- laughter of Geb 168, 205, 292
- shouting of Nut 168, 205, 292
- shouting and roaring of Re 202
- roaring of Seth 168, 200, 205, 292
- clapping of hands and stamping of feet by the gods 205, 212
- wailing of Isis and Nephthys 79, 163, 196, 205, 321
- when noise came into being 283
- see also Battle of the Gods; Earth quaked
Spear of the Falcon at Edfu 215
Speech as mechanism of creation 35, 40, 44, 51, 63, 100, 103, 108-9, 172, 184, 188-90, 198-99, 211, 322-23, 401
Spence, Kate 396
Sphinx of Giza 326, 356
Spitting as mechanism of creation - see Atum; Atum-Kheprer; Neber-djer; Re
Stadelmann, Rainer 335
Staffs 29
Stairways 169-70, 185, 200, 212
Standard of the god 116
Standards of kingship 222
Stars
- words for 28, 128-29
- imperishable 30, 129
- disappeared into duat and akhet 12, 31
- myths of origin 26, 47, 105, 130
- birthplace in duat 12-13
- were dark and stilled during first stage of creation 206-7
- described as gods 28-30, 105-7, 113, 128-37, 141, 173, 179, 234
- described as souls and spirits 130, 174, 179

- geocentric theory of 130-37, 141
- made of iron 132, 210-11, 220, 227, 275, 281
- deceased king became a star or all the stars 129, 150, 153, 156, 160, 172-77, 180, 240, 337, 339
- see also Allegorical astronomy; Gods; Imperishable stars; Untiring stars; Morning star; Mskhtiu; Sah; Sopdet; Stars, circumpolar; Ursa

Stars, circumpolar
- imperishable 30, 129
- described as gods and spirits 129, 173-74, 179
- named mskhtiu 29
- seen as two adzes or a bull's forelegs 29, 130, 132, 181-84, 188, 222, 224, 227, 232-34, 275, 284
- stood on a plain of iron 209
- abode of Seth 293, 307
- deceased king became a circumpolar star 173-74
- pyramid entrance passage aligned to 339

Statue of the god 4, 151, 181, 329-31, 347
Statues of the king 326 (see also Ka-statue)
Step pyramids i, 332-35, 338-39, 346
Storm
- of the Eye 202-3, 253, 255, 260-61, 271-72
- of Apep 203
- of Nut 204
- of Re 201-2
- of Seth 202, 413
- of Shu 202, 204, 207, 250-51
- storm-cloud of the sky 185-86, 202, 205, 228, 234, 250
- driven away or cleared 199, 207-8, 221, 281, 290, 301
- in king's re-enactment of creation 169, 185-86, 200-8, 221
- see also Night of the great storm; Sky choked and stifled; Thunderbolt; Thundering of sky

Su (birthplace of Seth) 303
Sun
- death and rebirth re-enacted the death and rebirth of the cosmos 4, 46, 50, 63, 76, 90, 93-94
- myths of origin 38, 45, 47, 53-54, 58, 63, 137-41, 295-96, 303
- made of iron 274-75, 281
- as right eye, full eye, and fiery eye of Horus 139, 255, 270, 272-73, 277
- as eye of Re 27, 172, 255-56
- geocentric theory of 137-41, 253-81, 308
- sunrise symbolism 4, 159
- see also Eclipses; Egyptology, theory of Egyptian religion

Sun-god
- maintained the cosmic order 3-6, 27, 37, 46, 50, 87-88

- relationship with creator-god 37, 65
- see also Lord of the Akhet; Re; Horakhti

Supports of Shu 40, 141, 195, 266
Swallow (bird) 21, 129, 169
Swallowing
- the gods 106
- the sun and the stars 26, 123, 190, 198, 218
- the flood 128
- the serpent of the earth 279
- see also Eating the gods

Sweat 202, 204, 207, 276
Swht (egg) 46, 49, 57-59, 213, 317
Sycamore trees 21, 377

Ta - see earth
Ta-djesert 10
Ta-meri 10
Ta-netjer 15
Ta-tenen
- creator-god, personification of risen earth 9, 50-51, 53-55, 63, 66, 69, 71-72, 74, 86, 96, 102, 104, 109, 115, 129, 131, 137, 139, 145, 147, 241-42, 300, 303, 307, 313, 319
- father of Re 66, 137, 147
- children of 137

Tears - see Eye
Teeth of Osiris 279
Tefnut
- created by Atum or Atum-Kheprer 38, 43, 96, 161, 188, 242, 249, 251-52, 276, 312, 319, 338, 341-42
- created by Neber-djer 45, 188, 312
- created by Amun 54
- co-creator of the gods with Shu 313
- co-creator of the waters with Shu 313
- co-creator of the plants with Shu 278
- mother of Nut 123, 191, 315-16
- goddess of moon 38-39, 251, 270, 276
- supported the lower sky 22, 115
- personified moisture 38, 64, 190, 243, 250-51, 313, 416
- fiery aspect 263
- raped by Geb 248
- presided over field of reeds and field of offerings with Shu 21
- corpse of 93, 99
- see also Eye

Tekhen (word for obelisk) 337
Temple
- image of the cosmos 4, 69-72, 77, 94, 151, 246, 331, 346-48, 387
- built upon primeval mound 63, 70, 72, 246, 328, 338
- offspring of the earth 69-72, 151
- home of creator and the gods 103, 307
- mansion of eternity 328-32, 348
- identified with akhet 328, 347

- mythical history 69-72, 75, 77, 85, 328
- reliefs and hieroglyphs 330-31
- commissioning ritual 307, 329
- rituals re-enacted creation 3-5, 142, 150-52, 329-31, 347-48
- see also Barque; Mortuary temple; Shrine; True pyramid

Temple of the Benben 38, 67, 226, 242-43, 246, 334, 342
Temple at Edfu 55-57, 61-62, 69-72, 85, 307
Temple of Eternity 95
Temple of Khons 245-46
Temple at Medinet Habu 240, 329
Temple at Philae 328
Temple of Ptah 71
Temples of the sun-god 70
Testicles
- of bull 239, 245, 402
- of Seth 49, 139, 203, 268, 283-85, 291-92, 297, 323-24, 413
Thebes 53, 87, 226, 230, 240-42, 258, 324, 328, 409
Theology of Memphis 35, 50-51, 69, 78, 104, 131, 302-8
Thighs
- of Hathor 62
- of Nut 20, 123-24, 177, 190-91, 236
- of bull, seen in circumpolar stars 29, 183, 234
Thinite district 247, 301
Thoth
- moon-god, saviour of the Eye 28, 138, 171, 179, 253, 259, 263-65, 271, 274-75, 277, 296
- god of writing, measurement and time 28, 151
- peacemaker of the gods 206, 271, 290, 301
- drove off Seth 28, 260
- creator-god 138, 258-59, 383
- birth of 137-38
- assembled and revivified Osiris 74, 79, 87, 201, 264
- lifted the Eye 259, 264, 268
- lifted the eyes 141
- pacified the raging Eye 271-72, 277
- corpse of, identified with Osiris 98-99
- nest of 213
- wing(s) of 17, 21, 28, 176, 197, 263-64, 291
- fingers of 259
- father of pharaoh 145
- Osiris-the-king reborn as 160
Throne
- of Osiris 111-12
- of Re 328
- of king in 'other world' 16, 21, 53, 73, 172, 377, 404 (see also Iron throne)
Thrones of Geb 112, 286, 305
Throw-stick 79, 203
Thunderbolt 49, 200-1, 204-5, 242, 251, 274, 321
Thundering of sky - see Earth quaked
Thutmose III 150
Tjenet-shrine 300
Tomb/earth symbolism - see True pyramid
Triumph of Horus (Edfu texts) 287
True pyramid
- history of i-iii
- names of 332, 339, 343, 354
- entrance passage 332
- variations in design 332, 346
- inscribed with Pyramid Texts ii, 9, 154-55, 179-80, 332
- referred to in Pyramid Texts 179-80, 326, 329-31, 341, 343
- as royal resurrection device 333, 347
- as cenotaph i-ii, 332, 346
- as tomb (body buried beneath in duat) iv-v, 149, 329-30, 332-33, 340, 347, 353, 355
- tomb is microcosm of the cosmos 168, 194 (see also Per duat)
- stars on ceiling of tomb chamber 329, 339
- identified with akhet 329, 343-44, 347, 354
- identified with Osiris 343-44
- solar symbol theory ii-iii, v, 334-35, 343-44, 347
- stellar symbol theory ii, 337-40, 347
- primeval mound theory ii, 335, 338, 343, 347
- giant size unexplained 326-27, 347
- built for eternity iv, 180, 329-31, 348
- creational symbol theory iv-v, 338, 340-48, 353-54, 419
- see also Mortuary temple; Pyramidion; Satellite pyramids
Turin Papyrus 1993 100
Turquoise 21, 61, 192, 275, 315
Tutankhamun i, 151, 167, 370
Two enneads 17, 21, 28-29, 130, 173, 189, 201, 221, 229, 234 (see also Barque of; Bull of)
Two Lands
- name of Egypt and the entire earth 9-10, 33, 50-51, 64, 74, 85-86, 120, 142, 145, 150-51, 203, 225, 235, 275, 286, 293, 300-1, 306, 314, 316
- hammered out by Shu 300
- unification of 51, 62, 68, 86, 142, 150, 267, 273, 282, 298-308, 314
Two obelisks of Re 244
Two skies 22, 27, 30, 33, 176, 305-6
Two lower skies 25

Underworld - see Ament; Duat
Unification
- of Two Lands - see Two Lands
- of two skies 305-6, 314
Unique star - see Lone Star
Untiring stars 28, 30, 129, 173, 217

Upper Egypt 29, 111, 302-8
Upside-downness 279
Upuaut - see Wepwawet
Uraeus 266-67, 272, 278, 280, 298
Ursa Major and Ursa Minor 29, 129, 181, 183, 233-34, 293 (see also Plough)

Velde, H.T. 224, 298
Verner, Miroslav 335
Venus 32, 128, 174 (see also Morning star)
Vineyard - see Wine
Virgin mother 63, 235-36, 316, 325
Vulture 235, 267

Wa (Shebtiu-god) 56
Wadjyt 235, 254, 261-62, 267
Wag-festival 399
Wainwright, G.A. 221, 242, 251, 274, 294
Wall
- district of Memphis 303, 306
- name of Osiris 82
- in name of Ptah Ta-tenen 50, 303
Walls - see Circuit of the White Walls
Waret 56, 70, 76, 203, 386
War of the gods - see Battle of the gods
Was-sceptre 53, 382
Wedjat-eye 259, 272
Well 123, 126, 217-18, 220
Wepiu 160, 197
Wepwawet 29, 132, 160, 166, 181, 207, 221-23, 403 (see also Shedshed)
Wetjeset-Netjer 56
White crown 49, 235, 267, 295
White eye of Horus 224, 297-98
Wilkinson, Toby 340
Willow tree 56
Wind 48, 60, 97, 169, 188, 200, 202, 205, 208, 220, 247, 250, 321, 324
Winding waterway
- in fields of lower sky 19, 25, 32, 160, 176, 228, 263
- in upper sky 17, 22, 32-33, 160
- identified as milky way 32-33, 160
Wine/vineyard 12, 171, 179, 278, 398-99, 413
Wing(s)
- of Kheprer 169
- of Seth 294
- of Thoth 17, 21, 28, 176, 197, 263-64, 291
- of Isis 48, 321, 324
Winged disc 221, 292
Wolf 222
Womb
- of Nut 123, 238-39
- of Tefnut 123, 126, 191
- of sky 239
Wrrt-crown 267
Wr-skat 14, 234

Yahweh 310
Yin and Yang 324

Zep tepi (first time) 2-3, 11, 46, 50, 54, 58, 60, 63, 92, 94, 100, 106, 120, 146, 151, 262, 289, 299, 317, 328, 330
Zmnnu 239
Zuntju 160